About Island Press

Since 1984, the nonprofit organization Island Press has been stimulating, shaping, and communicating ideas that are essential for solving environmental problems worldwide. With more than 800 titles in print and some 40 new releases each year, we are the nation's leading publisher on environmental issues. We identify innovative thinkers and emerging trends in the environmental field. We work with world-renowned experts and authors to develop cross-disciplinary solutions to environmental challenges.

Island Press designs and executes educational campaigns in conjunction with our authors to communicate their critical messages in print, in person, and online using the latest technologies, innovative programs, and the media. Our goal is to reach targeted audiences—scientists, policymakers, environmental advocates, urban planners, the media, and concerned citizens—with information that can be used to create the framework for long-term ecological health and human well-being.

Island Press gratefully acknowledges major support of our work by The Agua Fund, The Andrew W. Mellon Foundation, Betsy & Jesse Fink Foundation, The Bobolink Foundation, The Curtis and Edith Munson Foundation, Forrest C. and Frances H. Lattner Foundation, G.O. Forward Fund of the Saint Paul Foundation, Gordon and Betty Moore Foundation, The JPB Foundation, The Kresge Foundation, The Margaret A. Cargill Foundation, New Mexico Water Initiative, a project of Hanuman Foundation, The Overbrook Foundation, The S.D. Bechtel, Jr. Foundation, The Summit Charitable Foundation, Inc., V. Kann Rasmussen Foundation, The Wallace Alexander Gerbode Foundation, and other generous supporters.

The opinions expressed in this book are those of the author(s) and do not necessarily reflect the views of our supporters.

The Ecological Design and Planning Reader

The Ecological Design and Planning Reader

Edited by Forster O. Ndubisi

ISLANDPRESS

WASHINGTON | COVELO | LONDON

Library of Congress Cataloging-in-Publication Data

The ecological design and planning reader / edited by Forster O. Ndubisi.
     pages cm
   Includes bibliographical references and index.
    ISBN 978-1-61091-490-1 (hardback) — ISBN 1-61091-490-2 (cloth) — ISBN 978-1-61091-489-5 (paper)
1. Urbanization—Environmental aspects. 2. City planning—Environmental aspects. 3. Land use—Environmental aspects. 4. Land use—Planning. 5. Nature—Effect of human beings on. 6. Human ecology.
I. Ndubisi, Forster, 1955– editor of compilation.
   HT241.E368 2014
   304.2′091732—dc23
                                                                                              2014013858

Printed on recycled, acid-free paper

Manufactured in the United States of America
10 9 8 7 6 5 4 3 2 1

Keywords: Adaptation, biodiversity, bioregionalism, ecological design, ecological urbanism, ecosystem approach, environmental conservation, land ethic, land suitability, landscape, landscape ecology, nature, regionalism, resilience, Smart Growth, urban sustainability

For my parents,
    the late Dr. Bennett E. Ndubisi and Lady Mary Ndubisi
My in-laws,
    the late Mr. William and Mrs. Mary Martin
and
    My wife *June* and daughter *Danielle*.

Contents

Part Two: Ethical Foundations

Part Three: Substantive Theory

Part Four: Procedural Theory

Part Five: Methods and Processes

Part Six: Dimensions of Practice

Note from the Publisher

This volume is a collection of previously published writings on ecological design and planning chosen by Forster Ndubisi and his advisors with input from professors in the field. Professor Ndubisi has written a new introduction to frame the collection, new introductions to each section that explain the importance of the writings, as well as a conclusion that lays a foundation for future thinking and practices.

We have chosen to set the papers, which range from journal articles to book chapters, in a consistent format and typeface but have otherwise retained the style and idiosyncrasies of the originals. The figures have been reproduced for quality purposes and renumbered for ease of use.

The author has chosen to excerpt some of the selections rather than reprint them in their entirety, and the footnotes and endnotes have been removed to allow more space for the essays. Publishing information for each paper can be found in the Copyright Information section in the back matter.

Preface

In one volume, *The Ecological Design and Planning Reader* assembles and synthesizes selected seminal published scholarly works in ecological design and planning from the past 150 years. Existing information on the growing field of ecological design and planning is unfocused, fragmented, and scattered across numerous articles, books, and other publications. This collection of readings provides students, scholars, researchers, and practitioners with a condensed history, key theoretical and methodological innovations, and exemplary practices in ecological design and planning during this period, as well as a critical synthesis on its continuing evolution.

This book has two complementary objectives: educational and scholarly. The educational objective is to provide a teaching resource for upper-division undergraduates and graduate students in design, planning, and allied disciplines such as architecture, environmental sciences, geography, and forestry. The volume offers insights into key themes that shape the theory and practice of ecological design and planning—the evolution, theory, methods, and exemplary past and contemporary practice. By offering a critical analysis and synthesis of the continued advancement of these theories, methods, and practices, the volume examines future issues to be addressed by scholars and researchers.

Public awareness of the undesirable effects of human actions on the landscape has grown rapidly since the mid-twentieth century. There has been increased legislation worldwide in the areas of environmental protection and resource management, as well as accelerated advances in scientific knowledge and technology for balancing human use with ecological concerns. The roots of ecological problems have been widely debated and solutions have been offered. Yet ecological problems continue to intensify at all spatial scales—global, national, regional, local, and site. We are constantly reminded of climate change and urban sprawl as we see the effects in the fragmentation of landscapes, soil erosion, disruption of hydrologic processes, degradation of water quality, destruction of unique animal and plant habitats, the reduction of biological diversity, and the loss of prime agricultural lands.

Ecological planning is one promising direction for balancing human use with environmental concerns. It is the application of the knowledge of ecological relationships in decision making about the sustained use of the landscape, while also accommodating human needs. A related term, *ecological design*, relies on this knowledge to create objects and spaces with skill and artistry across the landscape mosaic. The two concepts are closely intertwined. Ecological planning is not a new idea, but the level of ecological awareness required in balancing human actions with ecological concerns has increased over the past five decades, at least in North America and Europe, and arguably in many parts of the world, including Asia and South America. The prominent landscape architect and planner Ian McHarg provided an inspiring synthesis of ecological planning in his seminal book, *Design With Nature* (1969). Yet ecological planning still remains an unfinished, evolving field and an uncharted territory for rigorous scholarly work.

Over the past twenty-four years, I have taught courses in ecological design and planning at the undergraduate and graduate levels. I have engaged my students on its various facets. There is considerable information on different dimensions of this topic, but it is scattered across numerous journals and reports. The key books on ecological planning focus on a specific aspect—for example, theories of applied human ecology or landscape ecology, or on methods, or on specific themes, such as the resiliency of ecological systems in urban design and landscape planning. The breadth of the subject matter in ecological planning is very diverse.

This book provides a road map to guide the reader through the diverse terrain, illuminating important contributions in the field of ecological design and planning. The readings focus on published scholarly articles from peer-reviewed journals, books, book chapters, and monographs, as well as published professional reports. As a result, the substantive information in a significant majority of the readings has already been validated by peers and leaders in the field of ecological design and planning. The time span of selected readings begins in the mid-1800s, especially those dealing with the historical context. Some important writings by visionary thinkers such as Ralph Waldo Emerson, George Perkins Marsh, and Frederick Law Olmsted occurred during this period. The 1930s through the early 1960s laid the foundation for contemporary developments in ecological design and planning. Parallel developments in ecological science occurred during the same period, notably in 1935 when English botanist Sir Arthur Tansley coined the term "ecosystem" to describe the biological and physical features of the environment considered in its entirety.

The specific articles in each part of the book were chosen largely through a survey of thirty prominent leaders in the field of ecological planning and design. Each was asked to nominate key readings/articles on the history, theory, method, and practice of ecological design. I ultimately selected those included here with guidance from the book's advisory committee of leaders in the field. To the best of my knowledge, no other book exists that compiles classic, authoritative, and contemporary writings in one volume on the history, evolution, theory, methods, and exemplary practice of ecological design and planning.

The information presented in this book will be useful for students, teachers, planners, designers, researchers, and the general public who are interested in balancing ecological concerns with human use of the landscape. Students and teachers in landscape architecture, and by extension, allied disciplines such as urban and regional planning, geography, rangeland science, forestry, and soil science, will find it an important text in landscape and environmental land use assessment, design, and planning courses. Practitioners in the private and public sectors will use this book as a reference tool for understanding the theory, methods, and exemplary practice in analyzing landscapes, as well as for making informed decisions on how and when to use them.

Land developers, interested citizens, and conservation groups will find the book a useful source of information for understanding how landscape architects and planners prescribe options for the design, planning, and management of landscape change. Because ecological design and planning is still an unfinished, evolving field, researchers will have the opportunity to address the issues raised in the book, and as a result, contribute in advancing the much needed theory and methods of ecological design and planning.

Acknowledgments

I am indebted to many people who made significant contributions to the development of this book. I thank my former and current research assistants for their invaluable efforts, especially Kent Milson and Jaekyung Lee. Travis Witt assisted in editorial reviews of the entire document. Yuan Ren participated in redrawing most of the illustrations. My former student worker Sheridan Brooks deserves credit for translating the original essays into Word files. Tsung-Pei (Eric) Cheng, my former doctoral student, deserves special mention for his impeccable support during the earlier phases of the development of the manuscript.

I benefited extensively from the insightful reviews and criticisms of Frederick R. Steiner, Dean, College of Architecture, University of Texas; Laura Musacchio at the University of Minnesota; and my colleagues in the Department of Landscape Architecture and Urban Planning at Texas A&M (TAMU): Ming Han Li, June Martin, Walt Peacock, and Shannon Van Zandt. My former colleague Dr. Michael Murphy deserves special credit for his critical insights. He reviewed many versions of the entire manuscript.

I owe particular thanks to Trisha Gottschalk, and especially Thena Morris, for their invaluable contribution in getting this manuscript into form. Thena ensured that I got all the permissions we needed for the essays and artwork. Debby Bernal also deserves credit for her support and assistance. Many of my friends and current colleagues—far more that I can name here— provided help and advice at various stages in the preparation of this manuscript: Jon Rodiek, George Rogers, and Chanam Lee.

I thank Dr. Jorge Vanegas, Dean of the College of Architecture as well as Chris Novosad and his team in the College of Architecture business office, for providing monetary support and processing the financial transactions that enabled me to obtain the necessary permissions for the essays in this document in a timely manner. I also express my gratitude to Heather Boyer, my editor, for her persistent support and encouragement and for reviewing the drafts of this manuscript. I appreciate the efforts of the Island Press team, especially Rebecca Bright for her insights and review of the artwork in the manuscript.

Lastly, I thank my family, especially my brothers and sisters Chinedu, Bennett, Uju, Ngozi, and Chioma for their encouragement and support; my daughter Danielle for her patience and thoughtful insights, and my wife June for her inspiration and review of earlier drafts of this manuscript.

Introduction

Concerted efforts to balance human use with ecological concerns sustainably in the twenty-first century continue to be necessary. In the eighteenth and nineteenth centuries, visionary giants like George Catlin, Ralph Waldo Emerson, George Perkins Marsh, Frederick Law Olmsted, and Ebenezer Howard alerted us to the negative impacts of human actions on the landscape. Today, almost two hundred years later, human impacts are greater and more complex, making solutions increasingly difficult to achieve. Landscapes serve as life support systems for people and other organisms but continue to gradually degrade, even as promising solutions are offered. An urgent need, thus, exists to continue to search for ways to effectively balance human use with ecological concerns.

The landscape is the geographical template in which human activities take place. It lies at the interface between natural and cultural processes. It implies the totality of the natural and cultural features on, over, and in the land.[1] Put simply, the landscape "is that portion of land that the eye can comprehend in a single view, including all its natural and cultural characteristics."[2] As such, "landscapes are dynamic entities defined by their interactive parts and integrative whole."[3] Landscapes change over time as humans mold natural processes, sometimes in harmony with the processes, and at other times, altering them. When altered in adverse ways, ecological problems arise and are expressed in different ways at varied spatial and temporal scales—global, national, regional, local, and site.

In the last few decades, the type, scope, magnitude, and complexity of ecological issues and problems have expanded and intensified in response to changing demographic, social, economic, and technological forces. These forces are the key drivers of change in the landscape.[4] We are currently witnessing rapid population growth worldwide. For instance, the world population grew more than tenfold, from 22 million in 1900, to about 2.9 billion in 1999.[5] In 2012, 7.2 billion people inhabited the earth. The United Nations (UN) estimates that this population will reach 8.2 billion in 2030, and 9.2 billion in 2050, of which more than 70 percent will reside in metropolitan areas.[6]

Increased population growth in metropolitan areas has intensified pressures on landscapes to accommodate our daily needs for food, work, shelter, and recreation. Variability in the nature and intensity of these needs across communities and regions is directly related to consumption patterns and practices, resulting in varying levels of demand on the natural, social, and economic resources required to satisfy these needs. These demands are translated directly onto the landscape, altering it either positively or, more often, negatively (figure 0-1).

The term *nature* is used widely throughout this book, thus clarification is essential. Nature is a very complex social construct. The concept of nature has a long history with diverse interpretations.[7] Nature is sometimes used synonymously with the term *environment* or *landscape*. Nature is commonly thought of as a part of the physical world other than humanity and its constructions. The *natural* usually implies phenomena occurring without human involvement. Yet, it is difficult to find an environment that is not impacted by humans, either directly or indirectly. As a result, discussions about nature must embrace humanity. Neil Everton asserted: "Once we accept, through the study of Nature, that all life is organically related, organically the same through the linkage of evolution, then humanity is literally a part of Nature. Not figuratively, not poetically, but literally an object like other natural objects."[8]

I concur with Everton and many others that nature is a social construct that reveals how people interpret their interactions with the natural world. As such, it should embrace humanity. But nature embraces humanity at different levels of intensity. These intensities span from nature as the natural, wild, and undisturbed environment with little human influence, to nature as the fully humanized world. I use the term nature to imply the "natural" as well as those aspects of people's interactions with the environment that are "harmonious" rather than "destructive."[9]

Figure 0-1 Flooding in Calgary, Canada (Photograph from Wikimedia Commons, accessed March 10, 2014).

Effects of Landscape Change

One type of land use conversion—sprawl—results from the haphazard distribution of land uses and infrastructure, often on greenfields beyond the urban center. It has been linked to dramatic consumption of resources, expensive infrastructure expansion, declining quality of life, and intense financial burdens to communities. Sprawl degrades the environment, accelerates the conversion of large amounts of agriculturally productive soils into urban uses, and may cause visual pollution.[10] Between 2005 and 2007, about 4.1 million acres (1.7 million ha.) of agricultural lands were converted into urban uses in the United States.[11] This trend continues.

The need to accommodate metropolitan growth has led to the fragmentation or division of land into smaller parcels, which in turn, leads to land conversions and changes in land use type and intensity. The development of metropolitan areas influences ecological conditions through alterations in the physical condition of the landscape mosaic.[12] The term *mosaic* emphasizes that landscapes are spatially heterogeneous geographical units characterized by diverse interacting ecosystems in which human actions occur. Landscape fragmentation isolates, degrades, and homogenizes habitats;[13] which in turn, affects biogeochemical cycling and leads to the erosion of biodiversity.[14] Alterations to the landscape may also modify the operation of hydrological systems, and tend to create soils with high concentrations of heavy and inorganic materials. The modifications may also decrease soil permeability and overflow, increasing pollution runoff. In short, the development of metropolitan landscapes disrupts ecological function—the flow of energy, minerals, and species across the landscape. Sprawl exacerbates the negative ecological effects of urban development. Land use alterations are further linked to rapidly changing climate regimes and urban heat island effects, intensified by the growing concentrations of energy consumption for transportation, industry, and domestic use.

Population and economic growth in metropolitan areas in the United States have had positive effects such as increased wealth, economic prosperity, and job creation for many people.[15] The economic prosperity, however, has not been distributed equitably. For instance, central cities lost population from the 1950s to the 1980s as a result of the suburbanization of jobs and income, rapid mechanization of agriculture, and the search for a better quality of life by the city's prosperous residents.[16] Consequently, the population of central cities became poorer. Neighborhoods that were once socially and economically viable have witnessed substantial social dislocation. Fortunately, inner cities have grown modestly since the 1980s.[17] This trend has become a catalyst for reinvestment in inner-city areas, creating a demand for the rehabilitation and restoration of derelict urban landscapes.[18] Contemporary social, demographic, and economic changes have further shaped the character of urban and rural landscapes. Accelerated advances in communications, transportation, and information technology coupled with globalization have intensified decentralization by increasing the capacity for social interaction at a distance, especially when social and economic forces favor it.[19] The interactions among these demographic, social, and technological forces are dynamic, and some of the effects are not yet understood.

Interventions

Ecological planning and design provides a promising way to balance human actions and ecological concerns. Put simply, it is a way of managing change in the landscape so that human actions are more in tune with natural processes.[20] It is a form of intervention that enables us to anticipate the nature and dynamics of landscape change and to plan effectively how to manage both desirable and undesirable effects. *Ecology* deals with the "reciprocal relationship of all living things to each other (including humans) and to their biological and physical environments."[21] Of all the natural and social sciences, ecology arguably provides the best understanding of the relationships between our physical and social worlds. The essence of ecology is, therefore, to know and understand reality in terms of relationships. This in turn is the rationale, among many, for its use in design and planning.

Ecological planning is the application of the knowledge of the relationships in decision making about how to achieve the sustained use of the landscape, while also accommodating human needs. A related term, *ecological design*, relies on this knowledge to create objects and spaces with skill and artistry across the landscape mosaic.[22] Ecological design and ecological planning are closely intertwined. The objects and spaces created through design, in turn, are employed in facilitating decision making at multiple spatial and temporal scales to create and sustain places. It is difficult to find any decision related to the organization of the physical environments that does not contain an ecological aspect at some level. The development of modern ecology as both a theoretical and an applied science, however, has dramatically heightened interest in employing ecological ideas in a systemic way in design and planning. Although the level of ecological awareness in balancing human actions with ecological concerns has increased over the past five decades, ecological design and planning is not new.

When visionary thinkers such as Thoreau, Marsh, Olmsted, Howard, and Geddes alerted us to human abuses of the landscape, many of them offered solutions as well (see part 1, essay 1). George Perkins Marsh (1801–1882) put forth a persuasive argument that efforts by people to transform the landscape should be accompanied by a sense of social responsibility and he proposed an approach for restoring degraded landscapes (see part 1, essay 2). David Lowenthal, the noted scholar on George Perkins Marsh, provided additional authoritative perspectives on the significance of Marsh's contributions (part 1, essay 3). Although Frederick Law Olmsted Sr.'s (1822–1903) work is not included in the essays in part 1, it is noteworthy that he made significant contributions to the evolution of ecological design and planning by advocating an understanding of the landscape from ecological and aesthetic perspectives. He was successful in translating his ideas into practice, as evidenced by in the numerous landscapes he designed, such as Central Park and Prospect Park in New York, and the plan for the Yosemite Valley Park in California.

Ebenezer Howard (1850–1928), the English proponent of the garden city concept, advocated new communities that fused the beneficial quality-of-life attributes of cities with the naturalness of the countryside (see part 1, essay 4). Like Olmsted, he implemented his ideas in the development of the new towns of Letchworth (1904) and Welwyne (1917) in England. Patrick Geddes (1854–1932), the Scottish botanist and planner, proposed a regional survey method grounded on "folk-work-place" attributes (see part 1, essay 5). Benton Mac-Kaye (1879–1975) articulated the conceptual linkages between regional planning and ecology in an authoritative fashion (see part 1, essay 6). The solutions proposed by these visionaries have been modified, refined, and expanded by others to adapt to the twentieth- and twenty-first-century social, economic, political, and technological realities. Notable contributions include the works of Lorien Eisley, Jens Jenson, Benton MacKaye, Lewis Mumford, Rachael Carson, Ian McHarg, Philip Lewis, Eugene Odum, Carl Steinitz, Richard Forman, and Frederick Steiner (see part 1, essays 6 and 7).

Since the 1960s, legislation in the areas of environmental protection and resource management has increased dramatically worldwide, and at varied spatial scales. These legislations and policies address a wide spectrum of ecological concerns, from natural resource and habitat conservation, to the protection of clean air and water quality, to the reduction of landscape fragmentation, and collectively, to the prevention and correction of the degradation of landscape resources. Examples of federal legislation include the National Environmental Policy Act (1970), as amended in 1975 and 1982; Clean Water Act (1972), as amended in 1977 and 1987; and the National Endangered Species Act (1973), as amended in 1978, 1979, and 1982). Many states and communities have ordinances in place to balance human use with ecological concerns as well.

Increased interest in ecological design and planning has resulted in a proliferation of theoretical concepts and methodological innovations for understanding and evaluating landscapes to ensure a better "fit" between human actions and ecological systems. This has manifested in movements or sub disciplines such as eco-design, green design and architecture, green infrastructure, low-impact development, sustainable development, smart growth, sustainable regionalism, ecological urbanism, and landscape urbanism. Although we now have an impressive array of approaches for balancing ecological concerns with human actions, it is important to understand the foundational ideas and approaches to understanding and solving the ecological degradation of the landscape. The historical and contemporary approaches are brought together in this book.

Map of the Book

In this book, I bring together classic and important contemporary published works on the history, theory, methods, and practice of ecological design and planning. In the new material, I provide a critical analysis and synthesis of the key issues and discuss the similarities and differences of complementary approaches, with the intent to find a common base of understanding. The readings include seminal contributions from landscape architecture, planning, geography, ecology, environmental science, and green architecture.

This book contains an introduction, seven parts, and a conclusion looking at future thinking and practice. The parts are historical precedents, ethical foundations, substantive theory, procedural theory, methods and processes, dimensions of practice, and emerging frameworks. In part 1, "Historical Precedents," I introduce key writings on the history of ecological planning with the acknowledgment that ecological problems remain evident at all spatial scales, despite promising interventions. Planners and designers are beginning to acknowledge the significance of ecology as a guiding principle in decision making about the optimal uses of the landscape.

In part 2, "Ethical Foundations," I examine the ethical foundations for ecological design and planning, emphasizing contributions from Ian McHarg, Aldo Leopold, Rachel Carson, Timothy Beatley, and Baird Callicot. A consistent theme in the readings is that people are intricately interdependent with their biological and physical environments. A disturbance in one part of the system affects the behavior of other parts, suggesting specific ethical positions on how we ought to behave toward the land. I conclude that various ethical positions co-exist today and that establishing priorities in reconciling them will become increasingly important.

In part 3, "Substantive Theory," I point out that a feature of the continued development of ecological design and planning is the emergence of methodological directives for translating ecological ideas into practice. I draw a distinction between substantive and procedural theories—the former deals with content theory while the latter emphasizes the processes for balancing human uses with ecological concerns.

Part 4, "Procedural Theory," highlights the contributions of many designers, planners, and ecologists, including Ian McHarg, John Tillman Lyle, and Richard Forman. A consistent theme found in the readings is a search for optimal uses of the landscape, with each author offering ideas about how this may best be achieved, thereby contributing to the richness and diversity of approaches. I conclude that each of the readings has something to offer for the continued advancement of the theoretical-methodological base in ecological design and planning.

In part 5, "Methods and Processes," I review selected ecological design and planning methods to illustrate the diversity of approaches. Each method strives to ascertain the fitness of a tract of land for a particular use, but does so in varied and complementary ways. The suitability method associated with Ian McHarg, for instance, was widely cited by the other authors, especially for its novelty in pulling together an ethical framework, working theories, and ideas for putting theory into practice. I conclude that no single approach can address every ecological problem. Rather, designers and planners should draw upon the strengths of each approach and ignore their less desirable aspects.

I examine case studies of exemplary practice in part 6, "Dimensions of Practice." Each of these represents a wide spectrum of global ecological design and planning practices. They span from those that originate from the research environment, such as professor Carl Steiner's San Pedro River Basin study in the United States; to others that stem from private practice, for instance, the Design Workshop's Aguas Claras mining reclamation and satellite community scheme in Brazil. The type of ecological problems addressed range from new community and restoration schemes, to biodiversity and resource conservation proposals at spatial scales from national to local, from many parts of the world, including Africa, China, South America, and the United States. The studies reveal, to varying degrees, a skillful blending of aesthetic form, functional utility, and ecological health and process in the proposed design and planning solutions. I conclude that each case study makes a unique contribution to the continued development of ecological design and planning practice.

In part 7, "Emerging Frameworks," the essays reflect that the world is becoming increasingly urban and that the problems associated with this are becoming progressively complex. Because urban landscapes are complex, heterogeneous, and interacting ecological systems, comprehending them and proposing sustainable solutions to their problems necessitate an interdisciplinary and holistic perspective. Each author offered solutions or provided insights for ways to understand or even resolve these concerns. Ethical framework, resilience, adaptation, regeneration, sustainability, ecosystem services, regional thinking, evidence-based solutions, aesthetic appreciation of landscapes, and collaboration, are the major themes embedded in the solutions. These will continue to be important as we seek to effectively balance human use with ecological concerns (figure 0-2).

In the conclusion, I provide a critical analysis and synthesis of the themes covered in the essays to illuminate issues that scholars and researchers need to address in the continued advancement of the theory, methods, and future practice of ecological design and planning. I argue that new ideas on how to effectively balance human use with ecological concerns are necessary due to the increasing diversity, magnitude, timing, and complexity of ecological problems arising from changing societal forces.

I offer principles built upon the rich foundations laid by others. At the core of the principles is the quest for *creating and maintaining adaptive regenerative places that are beautiful.* I explore supportive principles for creating such places.

Future solutions will embrace the creation of places that move beyond the promise of sustainability, to those that are beautiful, adaptable to change, and yet conserve, repair, restore, and regenerate the flow of energy, materials, and

Figure 0-2 Conserved natural corridors through the city serve as ecological networks in Cape Town, South Africa (Photograph by author).

species across the landscape mosaic. I conclude that new research and knowledge that has been drawn from reflective practice will be needed, and will enrich our understanding and make us more effective in creating and maintaining viable adaptive and regenerative places.

Notes

1. Aldo Leopold, "The Land Ethic," in *A Sand County Almanac, and Sketches Here and There* (New York: Oxford University Press, 1949); Forster Ndubisi, *Ecological Planning: A Historical and Comparative Synthesis* (Baltimore: Johns Hopkins University Press, 2002), 4.
2. Frederick Steiner, "Landscape," in *Human Ecology: Following Nature's Lead* (Washington, DC: Island Press, 2002), 77.
3. Ibid., 86.
4. Frederick Steiner, *Design for A Vulnerable Planet* (Austin, Texas: University of Texas Press, 2011): Landscape Architecture Foundation [LAF], 2000.
5. Mariana Alberti, "The Effects of Urban Patterns on Ecosystem Function," *International Regional Science Review* 28, no. 2 (2005): 168.
6. The United Nations, accessed September 10, 2013, and January 25, 2014. http://www.un.org. Demographic change and dynamics in the United States follows a similar trend. Between 1960 and 2010, the population of the United States grew from 179.3 million to 308.7 million,

representing a 72.2 percent increase. It is estimated that by the year 2050, the population of the United States will be approximately 410 million, and 86 percent of this growth will be located in metropolitan areas.

7. Neil Everton, "The Fragile Division," in *The Social Creation of Nature* (Baltimore: Johns Hopkins University Press, 1992), 93. Two distinct viewpoints about people's relations to nature emerged that are still evident today. The first is that nature has an order, a pattern that humans have to understand, conserve, and manage with wisdom. The other is that nature is a resource to be used by people for their exclusive use (Worster 1979). Different people, in different ways, and for different reasons have aligned themselves on either side of the duality. Those who subscribe to the first viewpoint believe that nature has an order that has an intrinsic value, that is, a value that exists independent of humans, that needs to be nurtured and preserved. On the contrary, adherents of the second viewpoint look to nature as a storehouse of resources to be organized and used by people. The scientific historian Donald Worster commented on the ramifications of this duality for understanding the history of ecology. "In any case, one might cast the history of ecology as a struggle between rival views of the relationship between humans and nature: one view devoted to the discovery of intrinsic value and its preservation, the other to the creation of an instrumentalized world and it exploration." In David Worster, *Nature's Economy: The Roots of Ecology* (San Francisco, CA: Sierra Club Books, 1979), xi.

8. Everton, "The Fragile Division," 93.

9. Anne W. Spirn, "The Authority of Nature: Conflict, Confusion, and Renewal in Design, Planning, and Ecology," in *Ecology and Design: A Framework for Learning*, Kristina Hill and Bart Johnson (eds.), (Washington, DC: Island Press, 2001), 32. Landscape architect Anne Whiston Spirn's views on this topic are equally instructive. She pointed out that "Nature is mirror of and for culture. Ideas about nature reveal as much or more about human society as they do about non-human processes and features." Yet, people's interactions with the environment may be harmonious or destructive.

10. Forster Ndubisi, "Sustainable Regionalism Evolutionary Framework and Prospects for Managing Metropolitan Landscapes," *Landscape Journal* 27, no. 1 (2008): 51–68.

11. American Farmland Trust, accessed February 16, 2011. http://www.farmland.org/resources; Steiner, *Design for A Vulnerable Planet.*

12. Alberti, "The Effects of Urban Patterns on Ecosystem Function."

13. Ndubisi, "Sustainable Regionalism Evolutionary Framework and Prospects"; Alberti, "The Effects of Urban Patterns on Ecosystem Function"; Mark McDonnell et al., "Ecosystem Processes Along an Urban-to-Rural Gradient," *Urban Ecosystems* 1, no. 1 (1997): 21–36.

14. Bruce Wilcox and Dennis D. Murphy, "Conservation Strategy: The Effects of Fragmentation on Extinction," *The American Naturalist* 125, no. 6 (1985): 879.

15. Ndubisi, "Sustainable Regionalism Evolutionary Framework and Prospects," 51.

16. John M. Levy, *Contemporary Urban Planning* (Englewood Cliffs, NJ: Prentice Hall, 1988).

17. U.S Bureau of the Census, 2010.

18. The resurgence of population into the inner city has some costs. For instance, it is creating inequality in urban areas. Those who have more access to resources and power benefit substantially from inner-city investments, while the underprivileged and economically challenged miss out on the emerging opportunities; for instance, see http://www.theatlantic cities.com/jobs-and-economy/2014/02/why-income-inquality-so-much-worse-atlanta -omaha/8451/.

19. Levy, *Contemporary Urban Planning.*

20. Ndubisi, *Ecological Planning: A Historical and Comparative Synthesis.*

21. Frederick Steiner. *The Living Landscape: An Ecological Approach to Landscape Planning* (Washington, DC: Island Press, 2008), 4.

22. Frederick Steiner, *Human Ecology: Following Nature's Lead*; Ndubisi, *Ecological Planning: A Historical and Comparative Synthesis.*

Part One
Historical Precedents

Introduction to Part One

In the early nineteenth century, many visionary thinkers espoused various ideas about how humans and other organisms relate to nature, thus establishing the rudimentary foundations of contemporary ecological planning and design.[1] Knowledge of these relationships has been used by the general public and professionals in a variety of fields as a means of justifying the decisions they make about the use of the landscape, such as allocating natural resources for the exclusive use of humans; as a mandate for moral action; as an aesthetic norm for beauty; and as a reliable source of scientific evidence to guide future uses.[2] These various ways of employing the knowledge of these relationships are intertwined. I will attempt to unfold them as I sketch the history of ecological planning.

Early urban civilizations, especially those of classical Greece and Mesopotamia, viewed nature as a wild beast to be tamed. For instance, the prominent Greek philosopher Aristotle (384–322 B.C.) and the early Stoics claimed that nature was a resource for the exclusive use of humans.[3] In contrast, another noted Greek philosopher Plato (422–347 B.C.), who was a mentor to Aristotle, lamented the loss of the verdant hills and forests within the fertile Mediterranean basin surrounding Athens that occurred during that era as a result of deforestation for shipbuilding and fuel. He cautioned:

> To command nature, we must first obey her.[4]

Even during that era, twenty-five centuries ago, Plato understood the significance of the interdependent relationships between people and nature, which essentially is ecology as we know it today. He urged us to seek understanding of the intrinsic and intimate dimensions of these relationships—the essence of the place—and to employ the resultant knowledge in making decisions about the alternative futures of landscapes. Plato's insights are timeless.

Fourteenth-century Italian artists depicted through their paintings that the landscape's intrinsic and aesthetic values could be appreciated for pleasure. This was contrary to earlier medieval beliefs about hidden fears associated with unknown nature.[5] Many English landscape gardeners and painters portrayed landscapes as being both productive agriculturally and yet beautiful to behold. This sort of English landscape has become idealized as a beautiful landscape and has formed the image that has inspired much of Western landscape design.[6]

Appreciation of the beauty of the natural environment was also clearly evident in the writings of nineteenth-century visionary thinkers in the United States, such as Catlin, Emerson, Thoreau, and Muir. These visionaries alerted us to the fact that the beauty of a landscape is a function of its natural character, a thinking that is widely prevalent today. The more natural, the more beautiful! Indeed, some contemporary architects, designers, and planners employ naturalistic themes in many ways as an authority to justify the incorporation of nature or ecological ideas and insights into the design and planning decisions they make.

Transition from Agrarian to Industrial Economy

The coming of the industrial economy in the United States and Europe brought about major shifts in population dynamics, growth, and migration. From the late 1800s through the early 1920s, employment in industry grew slowly initially but increased rapidly after the 1870s. By 1850, the U.S. population was 23.19 million, representing a 337 percent increase from 1800. The accelerating population growth, especially evident after the Civil War, coincided with a massive migration of population from rural areas to cities. By 1920, the U.S. population was 106 million, a 357 percent increase over the 1850 census. For the first time, the U.S. population residing in urban areas, at 51 percent, surpassed those living in rural areas at 49 percent. This period coincided with the westward expansion of the American frontier.

Increased population growth and dispersal intensified pressures on urban landscapes to accommodate people's needs for food, work, shelter, and health. Unfortunately, many urban areas did not have adequate human and physical infrastructure or resources to accommodate the new growth. Urban sprawl and blight became the order of the day, causing prime agricultural lands and resources to be converted haphazardly into urban uses. Agriculture as a source of employment lost its local market and declined as an occupation. Rural areas became severely impoverished. The degradation of forest resources, decreased water quality, and soil erosion were rampant.

Cultural, artistic, and intellectual movements emerged as reactions against the erosion of traditional values, the fragmentation of the closely knit social structures of agricultural communities, and the destruction of valued resources in rural landscapes. It was within this sociocultural, economic, and political context that many visionary thinkers emerged and expressed their concerns about the deteriorating quality of life in both urban and rural areas. They romanticized the richness, beauty, and moral order the natural landscape provided. Through their works, including philosophical statements, paintings, poetry, and designed works, thinkers such as Emerson, Thoreau, Marsh, and Olmsted put forth powerful arguments about the felt need to preserve and conserve the natural landscape (figure 1-1).

The readings in part 1 of this book illuminate key ideas and important contributions in the evolution of ecological planning. It is not feasible to include readings from all these visionary thinkers in the historical account presented here. As a result, the readings may best be viewed as an outline map, offering an overview of the historical foundations. I invite the reader to explore the notes at the end of each reading, which provide references for more detailed readings on the subject.

Readings

Except for the essay from David Lowenthal, the first five of the six essays in the section are classics on the historic foundations of ecological planning and environmental thinking, presented here in a historical sequence. The last one is an important work on the subject that summarizes key themes in the history and explores the future of ecological planning. In the first reading, "Higher Laws," originally published in *Walden; or, Life in the Woods* (Boston: Ticknor and Fields, 1854),[7] eighteenth-century visionary thinker, poet, and philosopher Henry David Thoreau documented his experiences over a two-year period (1845–1847) in a cabin near Concord, Massachusetts. He argued forcefully that active experiential engagement was a superior way of knowing, and in particular, of understanding nature and achieving true *humanity*. The book is regarded as an American classic that "explores natural simplicity, harmony, and beauty as models of just social and cultural conditions."[8]

George Perkins Marsh's 1864 timeless masterpiece *Man and Nature; or, Physical Geography as Modified by Human Action* is the next reading.[9] In

Figure 1-1 Frederick Law
Olmsted Sr. (Photo from http://
blog.chicagodetours.com/2013/02
/riversides-story-as-the
-first-planned-suburb).

the introductory chapter, he examines how human actions can dramatically destroy the landscape and advocates the possibility of restoration as a solution. No person before Marsh was more effective in arguing that culture was an integral part of, and not distinct from, nature. As a result, he laid the foundational ideas about what would eventually become the conservation movement that began in the early 1900s. Excerpts of the original chapter appear, as it is too extensive to be included in its entirety. To better appreciate the richness of his contributions and better understand the importance of their originality, I also include the "New Introduction" to the 2003 edition, written by David Lowenthal, a distinguished historical geographer and the world's leading scholar on George Perkins Marsh.[10]

The next reading is "The Town-County Magnet" in Ebenezer Howard's influential and visionary book *To-morrow: A Peaceful Path to Reform* (1898), republished four years later, in 1902, as *Garden Cities of To-morrow*.[11] Howard (1850–1928) was an English proponent of the garden city concept. His book laid out a powerful vision for how to best accommodate urban growth by combining the essences of urban and country life in a harmonious, interdependent way. The impact of Howard's contribution was immense. Lewis Mumford (1895–1990), a philosopher, social historian, and cultural critic, noted in 1944 that "*Garden Cities of To-morrow* has done more than any other single book to guide the modern town planning movement and to alter its objectives."[12] He contended that the originality of Howard's contribution was in his "character synthesis . . . of the interrelationship of urban functions within the community and the integration of urban and rural patterns, for the vitalizing of urban life on one hand and the intellectual and social improvement of rural life on the other."[13] In short, Howard examined rural and urban improvement as a unified problem.

Scottish botanist and urban planner Patrick Geddes's work follows. Geddes is credited with providing the intellectual basis for a regional survey approach. His article "The Study of Cities" from his seminal book *Cities in Evolution: An Introduction to the Town Planning Movement and to the Study of Civics* (1915) is presented here. In the article, Geddes introduced a "method of civic study and research, a mode of practice, and application."[14] His approach was founded on science but grounded in empirical observations of a place to illuminate the relations among culture, work, and environment ("folk-work-place"). Revealing these connections implies an understanding of the ecological relationships among the folk-work-place attributes, even though he did not explicitly use the term ecology.

Geddes encouraged the use of civic surveys, which included documenting and visualizing the regional landscape. He urged citizens to study the resources of the region "with utmost realism, and then seek to preserve the good and abate the evil with the utmost realism."[15] Geddes's approach may be summed as an artistic yet technical reading of the existing conditions in regions.[16] Today, Geddes's folk-work-place attributes are remarkably similar to ideas embedded in the widely known concept of sustainability.

Next is a classic from regional planner Benton MacKaye. He was a champion of primeval landscapes and father of the Appalachian Trail, a 2,000-mile wilderness hiking trail through the Appalachian Mountains. His condensed article, "Regional Planning and Ecology," provides the much-needed conceptual linkages among regions, planning, and ecology in a succinct and persuasive narrative.[17] He argued that the sprawling expansion of metropolitan areas, and especially the outward flow of population, resulted in the degradation of valued natural resources—"its material resources, its energy resources, and its psychological resources."[18] He believed that conservation, or the sustained use of natural resources, was crucial in finding solutions to the sprawling expansion of the metropolis. MacKaye explicitly linked regional planning to ecology, and more specifically to human ecology.

The last article is "Ecological Planning: Retrospect and Prospect," written by Frederick Steiner, Gerald Young, and Ervin Zube, which appeared in *Landscape Journal* in 1988.[19] It provides a condensed account of the historical foundations of ecological planning until the mid-1980s, identifies the major themes from both theory and practice, and evaluates the continued evolution of the field. It is the only article in the book so far that synthesizes key national and state legislation and policy formulated to balance human use with environmental concerns.

Although not included in the readings because of space constraints, two articles on history are worthy of mention. The first is Harvard professor emeritus Carl Steinitz's survey of the history of influential ideas in landscape planning, published in 2008.[20] The other is "Ecological Planning in a Historical Perspective," published in 2002, which is a succinct summary of the historical developments in ecological planning from the early to mid-1800s to the late 1990s. In fact, it expands upon numerous ideas from the previous article, updating them to the early 2000s.[21] I also review contemporary forces influencing the continued advancement of the field. I end the article by asserting that ecological planning, or at least its theoretical dimension, has advanced rapidly in North America. Yet it still remains an unfinished, evolving field and an uncharted territory for rigorous scholarly work.

Notes

1. Forster Ndubisi, *Ecological Planning: A Historical and Comparative Synthesis* (Baltimore, MD: Johns Hopkins University Press, 2002), 35.
2. Anne Whiston Spirn, "The Authority of Nature: Conflict, Confusion, and Renewal in Design, Planning, and Ecology," in *Ecology and Design: A Framework for Learning*, Kristina Hill and Bart Johnson (eds.), (Washington, DC: Island Press, 2001), 21–49.
3. Derek Wall, *Green History: A Reader in Environmental Literature, Philosophy and Politics* (London: Routledge, 1994).
4. Alexander Pope quoted in Frederick Steiner, *The Living Landscape: An Ecological Approach to Landscape Planning*, 2nd ed. (New York: McGraw-Hill, 1999), 187; also in Benton MacKaye, "Regional Planning and Ecology," *Ecological Monographs* 10 (1940), 340.
5. Aesthetic means "appreciative of the beautiful" (*Merriam-Webster Dictionary*). Aesthetic experiences "deal with the subjective thoughts, feelings, and emotions expressed by an individual during the course of an experience." Richard Chenoweth and Paul Gobster, "The Nature and Ecology of Aesthetic Experiences in the Landscape," *Landscape Journal* 9, no. 1 (1990), 1–8. Aesthetic experiences are an important aspect of people-landscape interactions.
6. Carl Steinitz, "Landscape Planning: A History of Influential Ideas," *Journal of Landscape Architecture* 3, no. 1 (2008), 74.
7. Henry David Thoreau, "Higher Laws," in *Walden; or, Life in the Woods* (Boston: Ticknor and Fields, 1854).
8. "Henry David Thoreau," http://en.wikipedia.org/wiki/Henry_David_Thoreau, accessed March 1, 2013.
9. George Perkins Marsh, *Man and Nature; or, Physical Geography as Modified by Human Action* (New York: Charles Scribner, 1864).
10. David Lowenthal, "New Introduction," in *Man and Nature*, by George Perkins Marsh. David Lowenthal (ed.), (Seattle, WA: University of Washington Press, 2003).
11. Ebenezer Howard, *Garden Cities of To-morrow (Being the Third Edition of "To-morrow: A Peaceful Path to Real Reform")* (London: S. Sonnenschein & Company, Limited, 1902).

12. Lewis Mumford, "The Garden City Idea and Modern Planning," in *Garden Cities of To-morrow,* reprinted in 1944 (Great Britain: Faber and Faber Ltd.), 29.
13. Ibid., 35.
14. Patrick Geddes, *Cities in Evolution: An Introduction to the Town Planning Movement and to the Study of Civics* (London: Williams & Norgate, 1915), 320.
15. Philip Boardman, *The Worlds of Patrick Geddes: Biologist, Town Planner, Re-educator, Peace Warrior* (London: Routledge & Kegan Paul, 1978), 14.
16. Emily Talen, *New Urbanism and American Planning: The Conflict of Cultures* (London: Routledge, 2005).
17. Benton MacKaye, "Regional Planning and Ecology," *Ecological Monographs* 10, no. 3 (1940), 349–53.
18. David Startzell, "Foreword," in *The New Exploration: A Philosophy of Regional Planning,* by Benton MacKaye (Urbana, IL: University of Illinois Press, 1990).
19. Frederick Steiner, Gerald Young, and Ervin Zube, "Ecological Planning: Retrospect and Prospect," *Landscape Journal* 7, no. 1 (1988), 31–39.
20. Steinitz, "Landscape Planning: A History of Influential Ideas," 74.
21. Ndubisi, "Ecological Planning in a Historical Perspective," in *Ecological Planning: A Historical and Comparative Synthesis* (Baltimore, MD: Johns Hopkins University Press, 2002), 9–33.

Higher Laws
Walden (1854)

Henry David Thoreau

As I came home through the woods with my string of fish, trailing my pole, it being now quite dark, I caught a glimpse of a woodchuck stealing across my path, and felt a strange thrill of savage delight, and was strongly tempted to seize and devour him raw; not that I was hungry then, except for that wildness which he represented. Once or twice, however, while I lived at the pond, I found myself ranging the woods, like a half-starved hound, with a strange abandonment, seeking some kind of venison which I might devour, and no morsel could have been too savage for me. The wildest scenes had become unaccountably familiar. I found in myself, and still find, an instinct toward a higher, or, as it is named, spiritual life, as do most men, and another toward a primitive rank and savage one, and I reverence them both. I love the wild not less than the good. The wildness and adventure that are in fishing still recommended it to me. I like sometimes to take rank hold on life and spend my day more as the animals do. Perhaps I have owed to this employment and to hunting, when quite young, my closest acquaintance with Nature. They early introduce us to and detain us in scenery with which otherwise, at that age, we should have little acquaintance. Fishermen, hunters, woodchoppers, and others, spending their lives in the fields and woods, in a peculiar sense a part of Nature themselves, are often in a more favorable mood for observing her, in the intervals of their pursuits, than philosophers or poets even, who approach her with expectation. She is not afraid to exhibit herself to them. The traveller on the prairie is naturally a hunter, on the head waters of the Missouri and Columbia a trapper, and at the Falls of St. Mary a fisherman. He who is only a traveller learns things at second-hand and by the halves, and is poor authority. We are most interested when science reports what those men already know practically or instinctively, for that alone is a true *humanity*, or account of human experience.

. . . Almost every New England boy among my contemporaries shouldered a fowling piece between the ages of ten and fourteen; and his hunting and fishing grounds were not limited like the preserves of an English nobleman, but were more boundless even than those of a savage. No wonder, then, that he did not oftener stay to play on the common. But already a change is taking place, owing, not to an increased humanity, but to an increased scarcity of game, for perhaps the hunter is the greatest friend of the animals hunted, not excepting the Humane Society.

. . . There is a period in the history of the individual, as of the race, when the hunters are the "best men," as the Algonquins called them. We cannot but pity the boy who has never fired a gun; he is no more humane, while his education has been sadly neglected. This was my answer with respect to those youths who were bent on this pursuit, trusting that they would soon outgrow it. No humane being, past the thoughtless age of boyhood, will wantonly murder any creature, which holds its life by the same tenure that he does. The hare in its extremity cries like a child. I warn you, mothers, that my sympathies do not always make the usual phil-*anthropic* distinctions.

Such is oftenest the young man's introduction to the forest, and the most original part of himself. He goes thither at first as a hunter and fisher, until at last, if he has the seeds of a better life in him, he distinguishes his proper objects, as a poet or naturalist it may be, and leaves the gun and fish-pole behind. The mass of men are still and always young in this respect. In some countries a hunting parson is no uncommon sight. Such a one might make a good shepherd's dog, but is far from being the Good Shepherd. . . .

I have found repeatedly, of late years, that I cannot fish without falling a little in self-respect. I have tried it again and again. I have skill at it, and, like many of my fellows, a certain instinct for it, which revives from time to time, but always when I have done I feel that it would have been better if I had not fished. I think that I do not mistake. It is a faint intimation, yet so are the first streaks of morning. There is unquestionably this instinct in me which belongs to the lower orders of creation; yet with every year I am less a fisherman, though without more humanity or even wisdom; at present I am no fisherman at all. But I see that if I were to live in a wilderness I should again be tempted to become a fisher and hunter in earnest. Beside, there is something essentially unclean about this diet and all flesh, and I began to see where housework commences, and whence the endeavor, which costs so much, to wear a tidy and respectable appearance each day, to keep the house sweet and free from all ill odors and sights. Having been my own butcher and scullion and cook, as well as the gentleman for whom the dishes were served up, I can speak from an unusually complete experience. The practical objection to animal food in my case was its uncleanness; and, besides, when I had caught and cleaned and cooked and eaten my fish, they seemed not to have fed me essentially. It was insignificant and unnecessary, and cost more than it came to. A little bread or a few potatoes would have done as well, with less trouble and filth. Like many of my contemporaries, I had rarely for many years used animal food, or tea, or coffee, &; not so much because of any ill effects which I had traced to them, as because they were not agreeable to my imagination. The repugnance to animal food is not the effect of experience, but is an instinct. It appeared more beautiful to live low and fare hard in many respects; and though I never did so, I went far enough to please my imagination. I believe that every man who has ever been earnest to preserve his higher or poetic faculties in the best condition has been particularly inclined to abstain from animal food, and from much food of any kind.

. . . Is it not a reproach that man is a carniverous animal? True, he can and does live, in a great measure, by preying on other animals; but this is a miserable way,—as any one who will go to snaring rabbits, or slaughtering lambs, may learn,—and he will be regarded as a benefactor of his race who shall teach man to confine himself to a more innocent and wholesome diet. Whatever my own practice may be, I have no doubt that it is a part of the destiny of the human race, in its gradual improvement, to leave off eating animals, as surely as the savage tribes have left off eating each other when they came in contact with the more civilized.

If one listens to the faintest but constant suggestions of his genius, which are certainly true, he sees not to what extremes, or even insanity, it may lead him; and yet that way, as he grows more resolute and faithful, his road lies. The faintest assured objection which one healthy man feels will at length prevail over the arguments and customs of mankind. No man ever followed his genius till it misled him. Though the result were bodily weakness, yet perhaps no one can say that the consequences were to be regretted, for these were a life in conformity to higher principles. If the day and the night are such that you greet them with joy, and life emits a fragrance like flowers and sweet-scented herbs, is more elastic, more starry, more immortal,—that is your success. All nature is your congratulation, and you have cause momentarily to bless yourself. The greatest gains and values are farthest from being appreciated. We easily come to doubt if they exist. We soon forget them. They are the highest reality. Perhaps the facts most astounding and most real are never communicated by man to man. The true harvest of daily life is somewhat as intangible and indescribable as the tints of morning or evening. It is a little star-dust caught, a segment of the rainbow which I have clutched. . . .

Our whole life is startlingly moral. There is never an instant's truce between virtue and vice. Goodness is the only investment that never fails. In the music of the harp which trembles round the world it is the insisting on this which thrills us. The harp is the travelling patterer for the Universe's Insurance Company, recommending its laws, and our little goodness is all the assessment that we pay. Though the youth at last grows indifferent, the laws of the universe are not indifferent, but are forever on the side of the most sensitive. Listen to every zephyr for some reproof, for it is surely there, and he is unfortunate who does not hear it. We cannot touch a string or move a stop but the charming moral transfixes us. Many an irksome noise, go a long way off, is heard as music, a proud sweet satire on the meanness of our lives.

. . . Yet the spirit can for the time pervade and control every member and function of the body, and transmute what in form is the grossest sensuality into purity and devotion. The generative energy, which, when we are loose, dissipates and makes us unclean, when we are continent invigorates and inspires us. Chastity is the flowering of man; and what are called Genius, Heroism, Holiness, and the like, are but various fruits which succeed it. Man flows at once to God when the channel of purity is open. By turns our purity inspires and our impurity casts us down. He is blessed who is assured that the animal is dying out in him day by day, and the divine being established. Perhaps there is none but has cause for shame on account of the inferior and brutish nature to which he is allied. I fear that we are such gods or demigods only as fauns and satyrs, the divine allied to beasts, the creatures of appetite, and that, to some extent, our very life is our disgrace. . . .

Every man is the builder of a temple, called his body, to the god he worships, after a style purely his own, nor can he get off by hammering marble instead. We are all sculptors and painters, and our material is our own flesh and blood and bones. Any nobleness begins at once to refine a man's features, any meanness or sensuality to imbrute them.

John Farmer sat at his door one September evening, after a hard day's work, his mind still running on his labor more or less. Having bathed he sat down to recreate his intellectual man. It was a rather cool evening, and some of his neighbors were apprehending a frost. He had not attended to the train of his thoughts long when he heard someone playing on a flute, and that sound harmonized with his mood. Still he thought of his work; but the burden of his thought was, that though this kept running in his head, and he found himself planning and contriving it against his will, yet it concerned him very little. It was no more than the scurf of his skin, which was constantly shuffled off. But the notes of the flute came home to his ears out of a different sphere from that he worked in, and suggested work for certain faculties which slumbered in him. They gently did away with the street, and the village, and the state in which he lived. A voice said to him,—Why do you stay here and live this mean moiling life, when a glorious existence is possible for you? Those same stars twinkle over other fields than these.—But how to come out of this condition and actually migrate thither? All that he could think of was to practise some new austerity, to let his mind descend into his body and redeem it, and treat himself with ever increasing respect.

References

Cady, Lyman V. "Thoreau's Quotations from the Confucian Books in *Walden.*" *American Literature* 33, no. 1 (1961): 20–32.

Chaucer, Geoffrey. *The Canterbury Tales.* Macmillan, 1954.

Kirby, William, and William Spence. *An Introduction to Entomology.* Longman, Green, Longman & Roberts, 1860.

Introduction (excerpts)

Man and Nature; or, Physical Geography as Modified by Human Action (1864)

George Perkins Marsh

Preface

The object of this present volume is: to indicate the character and, approximately, the extent of the changes produced by human action in the physical conditions of the globe we inhabit; to point out the dangers of imprudence and the necessity of caution in all operations which, on a large scale, interfere with the spontaneous arrangements of the organic or the inorganic world; to suggest the possibility and the importance of restoration of disturbed harmonies and the material improvement of waste and exhausted regions; and, incidentally, to illustrate the doctrine, that man is, in both kind and degree, a power of a higher order than any of the other forms of animated life, which, like him, are nourished at the table of bounteous nature.

In the rudest stages of life, man depends upon spontaneous animal and vegetable growth for food and clothing, and his consumption of such products consequently diminishes the numerical abundance of the species which serve his uses. At more advanced periods, he protects and propagates certain esculent vegetables and certain fowls and quadrupeds, and, at the same time, wars upon rival organisms which prey upon these objects of his care or obstruct the increase of their numbers. Hence the action of man upon the organic world tends to subvert the original balance of its species, and while it reduces the numbers of some of them, or even extirpates them altogether, it multiplies other forms of animal and vegetable life. . . .

Introduction

Physical Decay of the Territory of the Roman Empire, and of other parts of the Old World

If we compare the present physical condition of the countries [the Roman Empire] of which I am speaking, with the descriptions that ancient historians and geographers have given of their fertility and general capability of ministering to human uses, we shall find that more than one half of their whole extent—including the provinces most celebrated for the profusion and variety of their spontaneous and their cultivated products, and for the wealth and social advancement of their inhabitants—is either deserted by civilized man and surrendered to hopeless desolation, or at least greatly reduced in both productiveness and population. Vast forests have disappeared from mountain spurs and ridges; the vegetable earth accumulated beneath the trees by the decay of leaves and fallen trunks, the soil of the alpine pastures which skirted and indented the woods, and the mould of the upland fields, are washed away; meadows, once fertilized by irrigation, are waste and unproductive, because the cisterns and reservoirs that supplied the ancient canals are broken, or the springs that fed them dried up; rivers famous in history and song have shrunk to humble brooklets; the willows that ornamented and protected the banks of the lesser watercourses are gone, and the rivulets have ceased to exist as perennial currents, because the little water that finds its way into their old channels is evaporated by the droughts of summer, or absorbed by the parched earth, before it reaches the lowlands; the beds of the brooks have widened into broad expanses of pebbles and gravel, over which, though in the hot season passed dryshod, in winter sealike torrents thunder; the entrances of navigable streams are obstructed by sandbars, and harbors, once marts of an extensive commerce, are shoaled by the deposits of the rivers at whose mouths they lie; the elevation of the beds of estuaries, and the consequently diminished velocity of the streams which flow into them, have converted thousands of leagues of shallow sea and fertile lowland into unproductive and miasmatic morasses. . . .

It appears, then, that the fairest and fruitfulest provinces of the Roman Empire, precisely that portion of terrestrial surface, in short, which, about the commencement of the Christian era, was endowed with the greatest superiority of soil, climate, and position, which had been carried to the highest pitch of physical improvement, and which thus combined the natural and artificial conditions best fitting it for the habitation and enjoyment of a dense and highly refined and cultivated population, is now completely exhausted of its fertility or so diminished in productiveness, as, with the exception of a few favored oases that have escaped the general ruin, to be no longer capable of affording sustenance to civilized man. If to this realm of desolation we add the now wasted and solitary soils of Persia and the remoter East, that once fed their millions with milk and honey, we shall see that a territory larger than all Europe, the abundance of which sustained in bygone centuries a population scarcely inferior to that of the whole Christian world at the present day, has been entirely withdrawn from human use, or, at best, is thinly inhabited by tribes too few in numbers, too poor in superfluous products, and too little advanced in culture and the social arts, to contribute anything to the general moral or material interests of the great commonwealth of man.

Causes of this Decay

The decay of these once flourishing countries is partly due, no doubt, to that class of geological causes, whose action we can neither resist nor guide, and partly also to the direct violence of hostile human force; but it is, in a far greater proportion, either the result of man's ignorant disregard of the laws of nature, or an incidental consequence of war, and of civil and ecclesiastical tyranny and misrule. Next to ignorance of these laws, the primitive source, the *causa causarum*, of the acts and neglects which have blasted with sterility and physical decrepitude the noblest half of the empire of the Caesars, is, first, the brutal and exhausting despotism which Rome herself exercised over her conquered kingdoms, and even over her Italian territory; then, the host of temporal and spiritual tyrannies which she left as her dying curse to all her wide dominion, and which, in some form of violence or of fraud, still brood over almost every soil subdued by the Roman legions. Man cannot struggle at once against crushing oppression and the destructive forces of inorganic nature. When both are combined against him, he succumbs after a shorter or a longer struggle, and the fields he has won from the primeval wood relapse into their original state of wild and luxuriant, but unprofitable forest growth, or fall into that dry and barren wilderness. . . .

Reaction of Man on Nature

But, as we have seen, man has reacted upon organized and inorganic nature, and thereby modified, if not determined, the material structure of his earthly home. The measure of that reaction manifestly constitutes a very important element in the appreciation of the relations between mind and matter, as well as in the discussion of many purely physical problems. But though the subject has been incidentally touched upon by many geographers, and treated with much fulness [sic] of detail in regard to certain limited fields of human effort, and to certain specific effects of human action, it has not, as a whole, so far as I know, been made matter of special observation, or of historical research by any scientific inquirer. Indeed, until the influence of physical geography upon human life was recognized as a distinct branch of philosophical investigation, there was no motive for the pursuit of such speculations; and it was desirable to inquire whether we have or can become the architects of our own abiding place, only when it was known how the mode of our physical, moral, and intellectual being is affected by the character of the home which Providence has appointed, and we have fashioned, for our material habitation. . . .

Importance and Possibility of Physical Restoration

Many circumstances conspire to invest with great interest the questions: how far man can permanently modify and ameliorate those physical conditions of terrestrial surface and climate on which his material welfare depends; how far he can compensate, arrest, or retard the deterioration which many of his agricultural and industrial processes tend to produce; and how far he can restore fertility and salubrity to soils which his follies or his crimes have made barren or pestilential. Among these circumstances, the most prominent, perhaps, is the necessity of providing new homes for a European population which is increasing more rapidly than its means of subsistence, new physical comforts for classes of the people that have now become too much enlightened and have imbibed too much culture to submit to a longer deprivation of a share in the material enjoyments which the privileged ranks have hitherto monopolized. . . .

Stability of Nature

Nature, left undisturbed, so fashions her territory as to give it almost unchanging permanence of form, outline, and proportion, except when shattered by geologic convulsions; and in these comparatively rare cases of derangement, she sets herself at once to repair the superficial damage, and to restore, as nearly as practicable, the former aspect of her dominion. In new countries, the natural inclination of the ground, the self-formed slopes and levels, are generally such as best secure the stability of the soil. They have been graded and lowered or elevated by frost and chemical forces and gravitation and the flow of water and vegetable deposit and the action of the winds, until, by a general compensation of conflicting forces, a condition of equilibrium has been reached which, without the action of man, would remain, with little fluctuation, for countless ages.

We need not go back to reach a period when, in all that portion of the North American continent which has been occupied by British colonization, the geographical elements very nearly balanced and compensated each other. At the commencement of the seventeenth century, the soil, with insignificant exceptions, was covered with forests; and whenever the Indian, in consequence of war or the exhaustion of the beasts of the chase, abandoned the narrow fields he had planted and the woods he had burned over, they speedily returned, by a succession of herbaceous, arborescent, and arboreal growths, to their original state. Even a single generation sufficed to restore them almost to their primitive luxuriance of forest vegetation. The unbroken forests had attained to their maximum density and strength of the growth, and, as the older trees decayed and fell, they were succeeded by new shoots or seedlings, so that from century to century no perceptible change seems to have occurred in the wood, except the slow, spontaneous succession of crops. The succession involved no interruption of growth, and but little break in the "boundless contiguity of shade;" for, in the husbandry of nature, there are no fallows. Trees fall singly, not by square roods, and the tall pine is hardly prostrate, before the light and heat, admitted to the ground by the removal of the dense crown of foliage which had shut them out, stimulate the germination of the seeds of broad-leaved trees that had lain, waiting this kindly influence, perhaps for centuries. Two natural causes, destructive in character, were, indeed, in operation in the primitive American forests, though, in the Northern colonies, at least, there were sufficient compensations; for we do not discover that any considerable permanent change was produced for them. I refer to the action of beavers and of fallen trees in producing bogs, and of smaller animals, insects, and birds, in destroying the woods. Bogs are less numerous and extensive in the Northern States of the American union, but the natural inclination of the surface favors drainage; but they are more frequent, and cover more ground, in the Southern States, for the opposite reason. They generally originate in the checking of watercourses by the falling of timber, or of earth and rocks, across their channels. If the impediment thus created is sufficient to retain a permanent accumulation of water behind it, the trees whose roots are overflowed soon perish, and then by their fall increase the obstruction, and of course, occasion a still wider spread of the stagnating stream. This process goes on until the water finds a new outlet, at a higher level, not liable to similar interruption. The fallen trees not completely covered by water are soon overgrown with mosses; aquatic and semi-aquatic plants propagate themselves, and spread until they more or less completely fill up the space occupied by the water, and the surface is gradually converted from a pond to a quaking morass. The morass is slowly solidified by vegetable production and deposit, they very often restored to the forest condition by the growth of black ashes, cedars, or, in southern latitudes, cypresses, and other trees suited to such a soil, and thus the interrupted harmony of nature is at least reestablished. . . .

Restoration of Disturbed Harmonies

In reclaiming and reoccupying lands laid waste by human improvidence or malice, and abandoned by man, or occupied only by a nomade [sic] or thinly scattered population, the task of the pioneer settler is of a very different character. He is to become a coworker with nature in the reconstruction of the damaged fabric which the negligence or the wantonness of former lodgers has rendered untenantable. He must aid her in reclothing the mountain slopes with forests and vegetable mould, thereby restoring the fountains which she provided to water them; in checking the devastating fury of torrents, and bringing back the surface drainage to its primitive narrow channels; and in drying deadly morasses by opening the natural sluices which have been choked up, and cutting new canals for drawing off their stagnant waters. He must thus, on the one hand, create new reservoirs, and, on the other, remove mischievous accumulations of moisture, thereby equalizing and regulating the sources of atmospheric humidity and of flowing water, both which are so essential to all vegetable growth, and, of course, to human and lower animal life. . . .

Forms and Formations most liable to Physical Degradation

The character and extent of the evils under consideration depend very much on climate and the natural forms and constitution of surface. If the precipitation, whether great or small in amount, be equally distributed through the seasons, so that there are neither torrential rains nor parching droughts, and if, further, the general inclination of ground be moderate, so that the superficial waters are carried off without destructive rapidity of flow, and without sudden accumulation in the channels of natural drainage, there is little danger of the degradation of the soil in consequence of the removal of forest or other vegetable covering, and the natural face of the earth may be considered as substantially permanent. These conditions are well exemplified in Ireland, in a great part of England, in extensive districts in Germany and France, and, fortunately, in an immense proportion of the valley of the Mississippi and the basin of the great American lakes, as well as in many parts of the continents of South America and of Africa.

Destructive changes are most frequent in countries of irregular and mountainous surface, and in climates where the precipitation is confined chiefly to a single season, and where the year is divided into a wet and a dry period, as is the case throughout a great part of the Ottoman empire, and, more or less strictly, the whole Mediterranean basin. It is partly, though by no means entirely, owing to topographical and climatic causes that the blight, which has smitten the fairest and most fertile provinces of Imperial Rome, has spared Britannia, Germania, Pannonia, and Moesia, the comparatively inhospitable homes of barbarous races, who, in the days of the Caesars, were too little advanced in civilized life to possess either the power or the will to wage that war against the order of nature which seems, hitherto, an almost inseparable condition precedent of high social culture, and of great progress in fine and mechanical art.

In mountainous countries, on the other hand, various causes combine to expose the soil to constant dangers. The rain and snow usually fall in greater quantity, and with much inequality of distribution; the snow on the summits accumulates for many months in succession, and then is not unfrequently almost wholly dissolved in a single thaw, so that the entire precipitation of months is in a few hours hurried down the flanks of the mountains, and through the ravines that furrow them; the natural inclination of the surface promotes the swiftness of the gathering currents of diluvial rain and of melting snow, which soon acquire an almost irresistible force, and power of removal and transportation; the soil itself is less compact and tenacious than that of the plains, and if the sheltering forest has been destroyed, it is confined by few of the threads and ligaments by which nature had bound it together, and attached it to the rocky groundwork. Hence every considerable shower lays bare its roods of rock, and the torrents sent down by the thaws of the spring, and by occasional heavy discharges of the summer and autumnal rains, are seas of mud and rolling stones that sometimes lay waste, and bury beneath them acres, and even miles, of pasture and field and vineyard.

Physical Decay of New Countries

I have remarked that the effects of human action on the forms of the earth's surface could not always be distinguished from those resulting from geological causes, and there is also much uncertainty in respect to the precise influence of the clearing and cultivating of the ground, and of other rural operations, upon climate. It is disputed whether either the mean or the extremes of temperature, the periods of the seasons, or the amount or distribution of precipitation and of evaporation, in any country whose annals are known, have undergone any change during the historical period. It is, indeed, impossible to doubt that many of the operations off the pioneer settler tend to produce great modifications in atmospheric humidity, temperature, and electricity; but we are at present unable to determine how far one set the effects is neutralized by another, or compensated by unknown agencies. This question scientific research is inadequate to solve, for want of the necessary data; but well conducted observation, in regions now first brought under the occupation of man, combined with such historical evidence as still exists, may be expected at no distant period to throw much light on this subject. . . .

The geological, hydrological, and topographical surveys, which almost every general and even local government of the civilized world is carrying on, are making yet more important contributions to our stock of geographical and general physical knowledge, and, within a comparatively short space, there will be an accumulation of well established constant and historical facts, from which we can safely reason upon all the relations of the action and reaction between man and external nature.

But we are, even now, breaking up the floor and wainscoting and doors and window frames of our dwelling, for fuel to warm our bodies and seethe our pottage, and the world cannot afford to wait till the slow and sure progress of exact science has taught it a better economy. Many practical lessons have been learned by the common observation of unschooled men; and the teaching of simple experience, on topics where natural philosophy has scarcely yet spoken, are not to be despised.

In these humble pages, which do not in the least aspire to rank among scientific expositions of the laws of nature, I shall attempt to give the most important practical conclusions suggested by the history of man's efforts to replenish the earth and subdue it; and I shall aim to support those conclusions by such facts and illustrations only, as address themselves to the understanding of every intelligent reader, and as are to be found recorded in works capable of profitable perusal, or at least consultation, by persons who have not enjoyed a special scientific training.

New Introduction by David Lowenthal (2003)

Man and Nature (1864)

George Perkins Marsh

Others taught that "the earth made man"; *Man and Nature* would show that "man in fact made the earth." Men fell trees, clear the land, till the soil, dam rivers. Was nature the same afterward? Did streams flow as before? Were plants, fish, birds, animals unchanged? Assuredly not.

Anyone who wields an ax knows its likely impact, but no one before George Perkins Marsh had gauged the cumulative effects of all axes—let alone chainsaws. After Marsh's 1864 book, the conclusion was clear. Humans depend upon soil, water, plants, and animals. But exploiting them deranges and may devastate the whole supporting fabric of nature. To forestall such damage we need to learn how nature works and how we affect it. And we must then act in concert to retrieve a more viable world.

Over millennia of reshaping the earth, humans had immeasurably enriched but at the same time ominously impoverished nature and imperiled their own future. The threat was now dire and imminent. "For fuel to warm our bodies and seethe our pottage," Marsh warned, "we are, even now, breaking up the floor and wainscoting and doors and window frames of our dwelling." Wanton destruction and profligate waste were fast depleting the world, and "another era of equal human crime and human improvidence . . . would reduce it to such a condition of impoverished productiveness, of shattered surface, of climatic excess, as to threaten the depravation, barbarism, and perhaps even extinction of the species." *Man and Nature* was written to expose the menace, to explain its causes, and to prescribe antidotes. The human capacity to wreck must instead be used to replenish nature.

In linking culture with nature, science with history, Marsh's *Man and Nature* was the most influential text of its time next to Darwin's *On the Origin of Species*, published just five years earlier. With Darwin, Marsh put paid to traditional faith in a designed nature and preordained harmony between humanity and the rest of creation. Many before Marsh had noted various specific facets of environmental change; none had seen or traced the effects of human impact as an interrelated whole. Moreover, any such influence had been assumed largely benign; damage was thought trivial or short-lived. None recognized that wanted and unwanted effects were everywhere entwined. Marsh was the first to recognize that man's environmental impacts were not only enormous and fearsome, but even cataclysmic and irreversible.

Published at the peak of Western resource optimism, *Man and Nature* refuted the myth of limitless plenty and spelled out needs for conservation. Few before Marsh had worried about the effects of clearing and tilling land, damming and channeling streams. Afterward, his ecological insights and warnings became virtual gospel. In Lewis Mumford's phrase, *Man and Nature* was "the fountain-head of the conservation movement." The sweep of its data, the clarity of its synthesis, and the force of its conclusions soon made it an international classic. Marsh had "triumphantly" investigated a subject "so abstruse, so vast, and so complex," it was said at his death, that "he had no rival." For geography he achieved "what Adam Smith did for Political Economy, what Buffon did for Natural History and what Wheaton and Grotius did for International Law," a synthesis of all available knowledge. "One of the most useful and suggestive works ever published," wrote a reviewer of the book's second (1874) edition, retitled *The Earth as Modified by Human Action*, it had "come with the force of a revelation."

Indeed, its revelatory impact largely coincided with the new edition. In 1864 few had thought resources seriously at risk, recalled Princeton's James McCosh. "Our woods: were they not exhaustless? What need had we to bring lands under irrigation when the unsurveyed public domain amounted to fifteen million acres, . . . all of the same exuberant fertility with the prairies of Illinois and Iowa?" A decade later the outlook was much more somber. Railroad building had stripped the east of trees; the west was proving ever more barren, infertile, forbidding. Marsh's book urged contrition for Americans' "restless disturbance of the equilibrium of nature" and resolute zeal to save what was left from waste and abuse. To be sure, naive confidence in unlimited plenty only gradually gave way to anxiety about stewarding resources. But *Man and*

Nature was, as Wallace Stegner put it, "the rudest kick in the face that American initiative, optimism and carelessness had yet received."

The first and foremost effect was on forestry. *Man and Nature* aroused Americans "to our destructive treatment of the forests, and the necessity of adopting a different course." The book inspired every leading American forester; scores of them sought Marsh's support. His widely excerpted warnings sparked scientists' successful 1873 petition for a national forestry commission. A federal forest reserve system emerged in 1891, watershed protection in the Reclamation Act of 1902, a national resource-conservation program by 1911. The U.S. Forest Service, the Sierra Club, at length even timber companies came to accept the sustained-yield premises set by *Man and Nature.* Termed "epoch-making" by forestry chief Gifford Pinchot, it was again reprinted for Theodore Roosevelt's 1908 White House conservation conference. Countless later celebrants echo interior secretary Stewart Udall's tribute to *Man and Nature* as "the beginning of land wisdom in this country."

Beyond America, Marsh's precepts were also early espoused. The French geographer Élisée Reclus's *La Terre* (1868) owed much to *Man and Nature.* Italian foresters and engineers found Marsh's advice invaluable in framing national forest acts of 1877 and 1888. *Man and Nature* inspired British officials seeking to curb deforestation in India, Burma, and the Himalayas, was cited as gospel to halt the "barbarous improvidence" of tree felling in New Zealand, and spurred early conservation reform in Australia, South Africa, and Japan.

Floods and soil erosion during the Dust Bowl and other 1930s disasters rekindled *Man and Nature*'s salience for the American environment The Scottish planner Patrick Geddes alerted Lewis Mumford to Marsh's work; together with the geographer Carl Sauer, Mumford led a score of scholars to reassess "Man's Role in Changing the Face of the Earth" at a 1955 conference dedicated to Marsh's memory. My 1965 Harvard reprint of *Man and Nature* helped quicken the Earth Day crusade launched in 1970 by devotees of Rachel Carson and Aldo Leopold. Marsh's family home in Woodstock, Vermont, in 1967 became a National Historic landmark, in 1998 the site of a new National Historical Park. The express mission of the Marsh-Billings-Rockefeller park is to impart the history and lessons of national conservation. In thus honoring the begetter of American environmental awareness, the park service also signals the nation's commitment to the renewal of his cause.

Both what we know and what we fear about the environment have vastly amplified since Marsh's day; anxiety about human impact extends to realms and terrors undreamed of by him. Updating *Man and Nature* yet again, a 1987 symposium stressed the augmented pace of change by replacing Marsh's "Earth as Modified" with "Earth as *Transformed* by Human Action." Yet Marsh's appraisal of forest cover and erosion remains largely valid, his cautions about watershed control still cogent, his call for stewardship ever more pertinent. *Man and Nature* persists in steady demand, each new crisis rekindling its relevance. It is worth reading not only for having taught lessons crucial in its day, but for teaching them still so well. Though much more is now known, Marsh's exposé of the global damage humans have done and may yet do remains peerlessly graphic.

At first glance, Marsh seems an unlikely pioneer of conservation. He was a small-town lawyer and legislator, a long-serving diplomat, a linguistically gifted savant. Esteemed as a philologist, a historian, and a litterateur, he was a self-styled dummy in science. Hailed today as "the last person to be individually omniscient in environmental matters," Marsh held himself a mere dabbler in natural history—a quirky sideline to his many-faceted career. Even his publisher discounted his scientific nous; on receiving the manuscript for *Man and Nature* he urged Marsh to abandon it for a textbook "in the department of English languages and literature of which you are the acknowledged head." Not until half a century after Marsh's death was *Man and Nature* accepted as his magnum opus.

How did he accomplish such a work? He read insatiably in twenty languages. He traveled widely in lands where human impact was strikingly apparent. He was in easy touch with scholars and statesmen the world over. He remembered almost all he read, saw, and heard. Blessed with an intuitive grasp of natural and historical processes, he incessantly checked conjecture against facts. A Renaissance inclusiveness was his ideal, then still just about attainable. He joked that he would put into *Man and Nature* all that he knew and had not yet told, and name the book "Legion"; the jest comes close to truth. Seeing the world whole, he sensed how all its components meshed. No detailed expert study of a single aspect of them could have shown that. Marsh was a self-proclaimed amateur. Both conviction and modesty led him to insist that *Man and Nature*" makes no scientific pretensions and will have no value for scientific men"; he only hoped that "it may interest some people who are willing to look upon nature with unlearned eyes." That remains its great value.

Who was this polymath? Born in 1801 in Woodstock, Vermont, "on the edge of an interminable forest," in Marsh's own words, he saw most of it cut down for timber, fuel, and potash. His childhood scene was in swift transition from frontier to settlement, from woods to fields and pastures. Jolting along ridge-top roads in a two-wheeled chaise, young Marsh's father, Woodstock's leading lawyer and a painstaking taskmaster, pointed out "the general configuration of the surface, the direction of the different ranges of hills; told me how the water gathered on them and ran down their sides. . . . He stopped his horse on the top of a steep hill, bade me notice how the water there flowed in different directions, and told me that such a point was called a *watershed*. "Marsh never forgot those landforms or the physical forces that shaped them. And as a boy, when eye ailments for several years left him unable to read, he nurtured a love of nature that inspired him all his life, from the wild woodlands of his Vermont childhood to then well-tended groves of Vallombrosa in Italy, where he died in 1882.

Marsh's desultory schooling ended with graduation from Dartmouth, not far northeast of Woodstock. Litigation against the state of New Hampshire— the landmark Dartmouth College case—disrupted his instruction in classics and the "common-sense" moral philosophy then in vogue. He mastered Germanic and Romance languages and literature on his own. Marsh next briefly taught Greek and Latin at nearby Norwich military academy; recurrent eye trouble put a welcome end to this unrewarding stint. He passed the bar examination by being read to at home, and in 1825 crossed the Green Mountains to Burlington, on Lake Champlain. His legal, business, and political career in Vermont's "Queen City" dragged on for thirty-five years; it left him virtually bankrupt when, in 1861, he crossed the Atlantic as America's newly appointed envoy to Italy.

Marsh proved ill-suited to the law. High-minded, abstruse, aloof, hyper-critical, he quit active legal practice in 1842. Nor did he succeed in business. Yet Marsh engaged in every local enterprise: he bred sheep, ran a woolen mill, built roads and bridges, sold lumber, speculated in land, chartered a bank, mined a marble quarry. Widespread economic depression at the time impoverished many Vermonters. But Marsh's failures stemmed also from his own unworldliness. He was a gullible entrepreneur, an inept promoter, and an execrable judge of business partners. His family life also came to grief. In 1833 his wife of five years and their elder son died; his newborn surviving son was a chronic disappointment. Marsh's second wife soon became a lifelong partial invalid, but theirs proved a happy and productive partnership. . . .

Marsh's political career began as badly as his commercial. In promoting his law partner's failed bid for Congress in 1832, Marsh was censored by the local press as "high-toned" and "aristocratic." Aversion to popular causes—Anti-Masonry, debtors' relief, French settler distress in Quebec—ended his brief tenure in Vermont's Legislative Council. But Burlington business links made him a Whig party nominee for Congress in 1843. A doughty campaigner and stump speaker, Marsh won this and the next three biennial elections. In the House of Representatives, Marsh backed woolen tariffs vital to Vermont and opposed the extension of slavery, the Mexican War, and expansionist Manifest Destiny. Disgusted by the hurly-burly of sectional politics, he was more at home among Washington's scientists and foreign diplomats.

Marsh played a crucial role in shaping the Smithsonian Institution, newly created by the gift of an English donor. The Vermonter failed to make it the seat of a great national library that would secure American progress in "higher knowledge" and end "slavish deference" to England. But he championed the Smithsonian's publications, its exploring expeditions, its worldwide collecting endeavors, and its pioneering surveys of weather, geology, and American prehistory. And Marsh's devoted protégé Spencer Baird became the Smithsonian's second and most influential head.

Northern studies and Smithsonian efforts led Marsh to advocate a radically new American social history, one of ordinary men and women, wholly unlike the conventional annals of wars and kings. He believed that a democratic people needed a history not of their rulers but of themselves: they should study "the fortunes of the mass, their opinions, their characters, . . . their ruling hopes and fears, their arts and industry and commerce; we must see them in their daily occupations in the field, the workshop, and the market." Museums of everyday tools and domestic artifacts would help teach Americans, now too impatient of tradition, too restless, too mobile, to be more mindful of their own hearths and heritage. Such insights, long pre-dating the outdoor museums and the populist social history of the twentieth century, also pervade *Man and Nature*.

Appointed American envoy to Turkey in 1849—a reward for Marsh's vigorous electioneering on behalf of President Zachary Taylor—he gained vivid intimacy with Old World nature and history. In Constantinople he aided Kossuth and other 1848 revolutionaries fleeing Austrian reprisal, shielded Protestant missions from Islamic and Greek Orthodox animus, arbitrated thorny extraterritorial disputes, and penned cogent dispatches on the plight of the Ottoman Empire, now on the verge of the Crimean War. Touring Egypt, Palestine, central Europe, and Italy, he collected flora and fauna for the Smithsonian. And he took note, from atop his camel, of environmental damage in arid lands anciently laid waste. Marsh's book *The Camel* (1856) persuaded the American government to import these "ships of the desert" into the Southwest as aids to army transport.

Back home in 1854, Marsh faced financial ruin. His woolen mill had failed; Burlington business partners had betrayed and cheated him; the Vermont Central Railroad had stolen his land and squandered his investment; Catholic and other enemies long blocked expected congressional recompense for his judicial and other special tasks abroad. Marsh turned down offers in law and in journalism, rejected a Vermont senate seat and governorship, and, with keenest regret, declined a Harvard chair in history, because none of these promised to pay enough to clear his debts. Glass instrument-making, marble quarrying, and circuit lecturing all profited nothing. The English language and literature courses he taught at Columbia in 1856 and at Boston's Lowell Institute in 1860, trenchant analyses of the merits and faults of Noah Webster's and Joseph Worcester's rival dictionaries, and scholarly texts on word origins, drawing on sources from Arabic and Catalan to Flemish and Anglo-Saxon, earned Marsh much renown but little money. . . .

Marsh's scholarly renown, along with his services to the Republican party (backed by former Whig anti-slavery Vermonters), led President Lincoln to appoint him envoy to the newly united kingdom of Italy. He served as ambassador in Turin, then in Florence, and finally in Rome from 1861 until his death in 1882—a twenty-one-year term unmatched by any American diplomat before or since.

His two final decades in Italy were Marsh's most fulfilling and productive. He penned a thousand cogent dispatches on Civil War concerns (efforts to enlist Garibaldi in the Union army and to blockade Southern privateers), Italian nation-building and European power politics, trade and immigration issues, boundary disputes, and "suits of fools" from ever more numerous and demanding tourists. He wrote scores of essays and three books, among them *Man and Nature*—to which Marsh devoted so much time that he felt obliged to explain to Secretary of State W. H. Seward that he had written it for a patriotic purpose: "to show the evils resulting from too much clearing and cultivation, and often so-called improvements in . . . the United States." . . .

Environmental issues Marsh addressed in *Man and Nature* continued to absorb him for the rest of his life. In 1874 he arbitrated a long disputed Italo-Swiss boundary athwart Alpine land northwest of Locarno. Documentary data forced Marsh to back Italy's territorial claim against his own firm conviction that a summit-line border would best serve watershed protection in both countries. Marsh's closely argued decision became a landmark of international boundary-making. Still more pivotal was his 1875 irrigation report for the U.S. Commissioner of Agriculture. American developers were eager to exploit arid Western lands by diverting water from streams and aquifers. Marsh warned that their grandiose schemes were fraught with risk; excessive irrigation in the Nile Valley and the Po Plain had wrought both physical damage (saline soils, diminished stream flow, reduced fertility) and social misery (land engrossment by wealthy at the expense of peasant cultivators).

Modes of forest management preoccupied Marsh more than ever in his last years. During his final summer, at Vallombrosa, the ancient monastic site of Italy's forestry school near Florence, he noted improvements in both native and exotic plantations. Letters to Charles Sprague Sargent, director of Harvard's new Arnold Arboretum, reiterated Marsh's view that primeval forests were less useful than woodlands enriched by silviculture. His "conviction of the vital importance to the future of our race of a wiser economy . . . in the use of Nature's gifts," remarked his publisher for the posthumous edition of *Man and Nature*, animated Marsh "to the last day of his earthly life."

In 1847, seventeen years before *Man and Nature*, Marsh voiced one of its cardinal tenets: wholesale forest clearance depleted soils, impaired drainage, and, in general, deranged the state of nature. Calamitous in the Old World, deforestation's erosive damage was already evident in Vermont. Denuding hillsides, damming streams, and overgrazing had unleashed changes "too striking to have escaped the attention of any observing person," Marsh told a local farm audience. "Every middle-aged man who revisits his birth-place after a few years of absence, looks upon another landscape than that which formed the theatre of his youthful toils and pleasures."

Nowhere had forests been razed and soils washed away faster than on Marsh's natal Green Mountains. And when Vermonters turned from wheat to wool, close-browsing merino sheep augmented the devastation. If many deplored such losses, few heeded their lessons. Early Vermont pioneers deserved praise for subduing the wild, filling "with light and life, the dark and silent recesses of our aboriginal forests." But trees were no longer the encumbrance they had been to Marsh's forebears. Too much land had been cleared; downpours scoured barren slopes, springs dried up, drought and floods alternated. Rain and snow-melt once absorbed by trees and undergrowth now "flow swiftly over the smooth ground . . . fill every ravine with a torrent, and convert every river into an ocean. The suddenness and violence of our freshets will soon convert the valleys of many of our streams from smiling meadows into broad wastes of shingle and gravel and pebbles, deserts in summer, and seas in autumn and spring." To curb excessive runoff, some Europeans had begun to conserve forest cover by logging only mature trees at stated intervals. Americans should do likewise, for their children's sake if not for their own. "Enlightened self-interest," Marsh then hoped, should suffice "to introduce the reforms, check the abuses, and preserve us from an increase of the evils."

A year later Marsh sent a draft forest research program to the Harvard botanist Asa Gray, with a note on how his own interest had arisen: "I spent my early life almost literally in the woods; a large portion of the territory of Vermont was, within my recollection, covered with the natural forest; and having been personally engaged . . . in clearing lands, and manufacturing, and dealing in lumber, I have had occasion both to observe and to feel the effects resulting from an injudicious system of managing woodlands." Such, in brief, was the genesis of *Man and Nature*.

Five years around the Mediterranean as envoy to Turkey magnified Marsh's environmental awareness. His previous comparisons came from wide reading; what he saw on the ground now vivified the contrasts. The age and magnitude of Old World human impact were awesome: "the meadows leveled and the hills rounded, not as [in America] by the action of mere natural forces, but by the assiduous husbandry of hundreds of generations." Just as evident were marks of degradation. The same agencies of destruction—extirpating forests and wild life, overgrazing, exhaustive agriculture—had presaged the collapse of every ancient empire. Long ago fertile and populous, the sterile Sahara, the sinkholed Karst, the malarial Roman Campagna, the rock-strewn ravines of Provence and Dauphiné were now desolate testaments to greed and improvidence. These Old World disasters informed Marsh's warnings back home.

Ecological cautions underpinned Marsh's 1857 fisheries report. Vermont's once plentiful salmon, shad, and trout were now "almost as extinct" as forest game. Some causes, like the rapacious gutting of fish stocks in the spawning season, were willful; others—changes in river regimes induced by tree felling, sawmilling, and dam building—were unintended, often unnoted until too late. The unforeseen results of civilizing progress had upset the whole fabric of organic and inorganic nature. Marsh's fisheries essay, over a century later judged "one of the most influential, prophetic and thoughtful studies ever written on the subject," was a prelude in miniature to *Man and Nature*.

Old World tactics for stemming forest depletion next came under Marsh's reforming scrutiny. In the seventeenth century heavy consumption of trees for shipbuilding and fuel had led France to limit felling. Torrents and landslides triggered by alpine deforestation caused much alarm, and widespread forest destruction after the French Revolution magnified abuses; rivers in spate abraded fertile valleys or buried them under silt. Fire, logging, and overgrazing in alpine France ravaged millions of arable acres below. In the 1840s French engineers showed that forest cover was essential to protect soils and moderate stream flow in mountain terrain. Trees intercepted rainfall and stored snow, slowing the pace of melting. Organic debris on forest floors absorbed ten times its weight in water, further reducing runoff and erosion. To equalize stream flow, conserve soil, and protect croplands below, tree cover above was vital; mountain grazing should be prohibited. Controlling drainage became a moral crusade enacted into national law; by the time of *Man and Nature*, France had begun to quell torrential damage. Facing analogous timber shortages and flood losses, German and Italian foresters likewise urged state control. Throughout Alpine Europe Marsh noted concurrence with the concerns about erosion he voiced in America.

Both the need for reform and its likely agency struck Marsh with redoubled force on his return to Italy in 1861. Alpine devastation fortified his augury that ruin might be imminent in the New World, too. Along the upper Durance and other branches of the Rhone, Marsh witnessed havoc that presaged similar disaster in Vermont and confirmed his view of its causes. Rash exploitation, notably excessive tree felling and overgrazing, accelerated normal erosive processes; sods were carried off faster than they were rebuilt, denuded pastures were gullied, stream channels deepened, dams and harbors silted up. Against such evils rural communities, often indigent and isolated, were helpless. Physical degradation eroded human will as well, portending the common doom of land and people—perhaps even the extinction of humanity.

What the Old World had suffered, Marsh warned, might soon be the fate of the New. Yet novel European remedies also held promise. Tuscany's reclaimed Maremma swamp and Val di Chiana impressed Marsh as "remarkable triumphs of humanity over physical nature, [where] a soil once used, abused, exhausted, and at last abandoned, had been reoccupied" and again made fruitful. Marsh drew other hopeful examples from Europe. But his key credos—zeal for reform, faith in its success—were archetypally American. "The work of geographical regeneration" seemed to him far likelier among progressive and dynamic Yankee yeomen than in Europe's long-ravaged lands and among her pauperized, dispirited peasantries.

Marsh began *Man and Nature* three times: in March 1860 in Burlington, Vermont (suspended for political and other chores); in April 1862 in Turin, Italy (postponed by diplomatic toil and Alpine travel); finally in November 1862 in the Genoese Riviera hamlet of Pegli, his retreat for the winter. *Man and Nature* was half completed by March 1863 when Marsh moved to a turreted castello in Piòbesi, a village on the Po plain southwest of Turin. His study looked out on a terrace facing the snow-covered Alps to the west and north. Rising early, Marsh wrote steadily all morning, putting down his pen briefly to watch starlings sweep around the tower. These months were the least intruded on, the best for work in Marsh's life. The first nightingale sang on April 27; two days later Marsh finished his first draft. But as fast as he wrote new sources piled up; he grew so despondent his wife feared a "libricide." From cool spring Piòbesi passed to scalding summer; flies were everywhere—on Marsh's eyelids, his inkstand, the very point of his pen. Yet early July saw the final revision. But edited proofs languished for months at the publisher's, their author losing patience and interest. By the time the book came out in May 1864, Marsh thought its prospects so bleak that he donated his copyright to charity (Vermont relatives bought it back for him).

Man and Nature's structure is straightforward. The preface states Marsh's three aims: to show how humanity has affected the face of the earth, often for the worse; to suggest means of environmental reform and conservation; to confirm mankind's unique potency. The first chapter links the decay of ancient Rome to deforestation, erosion, imperial tyranny, and land abandonment. Marsh documents how avarice, ignorance, and neglect have similarly laid waste much of the world. Technological progress has since aggravated the mischief: the plow razes more than the hoe, the saw more than the ax. To repair these ravages and restore a fruitful environment calls for exhaustive appraisals of human impact the world over. But damage meanwhile so escalates that immediate reform is essential; "the world cannot afford to wait until the slow and sure progress of exact science has taught it a better economy." Marsh hence seeks practical lessons in the history of efforts to subdue and replenish the earth.

The next four chapters survey human impacts, both intended and inadvertent, on various realms of nature: plants and animals; woods and grasslands; seas and lakes and rivers; sand dunes and deserts. For each realm Marsh assesses the injuries without scanting the gains. And for each he reviews remedies—afforestation, draining and irrigation, dikes and dams, biological controls, public oversight and ownership.

For the harm done—extreme fluctuations of runoff and stream flow, eroded soils and landslides, depleted flora and fauna—Marsh blames the wholesale felling of trees most of all. Many fondly hoped tree-planting would bring rain and ameliorate drought; on this point Marsh thinks the evidence "vague and contradictory." But on rain that does fall, forest influence is beyond doubt: by absorbing precipitation and shielding the ground beneath, trees conserve moisture and reduce runoff. Some severely deforested lands have been too eroded to sustain new tree growth for centuries to come, but elsewhere planting and woodland care might soon restore fertility.

The final chapter peruses the likely environmental effects, for good and ill, of large-scale impending projects like the Suez and Panama canals. Marsh goes on to speculate on remoter prospects for harnessing natural forces to reforest mountains, to water deserts, even to deflect or curtail earthquakes and volcanic eruptions. In a prescient concluding passage, he surmises that human power enhanced by technology may alter the very structure, orbit, and destiny of the earth.

Man and Nature is a stylistic mélange, at once pedantic and lively, solemn and witty, turgid and incisive, objective and impassioned. A casual glance dismays: one sees long sentences, endless paragraphs, Latinate words, contorted phrases, exorbitant punctuation. Yet many passages are direct, vivid, and evocative. The apt metaphor, the scathing censure, the barbed moral, the distilled summation—at such devices Marsh excelled. They infuse this book with life.

Its subject matter is protean: extracts from French engineers on stream abrasion and German foresters on tree growth; vignettes from Marsh's childhood and travels; résumés from classical authors; snippets from news stories and private letters; etymologies, census data, snatches of poems and plays. So wildly are these juxtaposed that *Man and Nature* seems less a finished work than one about to be born. For all its basis in history, the book has an up-to-the-minute vitality; half of Marsh's notes refer to things penned less than five years past.

Yet this helter-skelter air is just what makes it engrossing and convincing. The lengthy quotes, the familiar asides, the partisan diatribes, the confessions of doubt, the pleas for further study are marks of an intensely personal book. They guide the captivated reader through a thorny terrain along the author's own paths of discovery.

Such charms festoon many of Marsh's footnotes. Almost every page has some pungent aside on the pitfalls of statistics, the perils of nicotine, papal iniquity, corporate corruption. Their bulk—as great as the text—makes the notes formidable. But to skip them is to miss this volume's scope and flavor. Here is an epitaph for migratory birds deranged by Vermont village lights; here a clue, from progressively thicker and less-burnt brickwork, to growing fuel scarcity and deforestation in imperial Rome; here a harangue, provoked by grain storage hazards in Egypt, on the "want of foresight in Oriental life." To the notes Marsh consigns most of his recollections, raptures, and crochets. He does not hesitate to digress. He admits a long aside on "cooking" railway surveys "is not exactly relevant to my subject; but it is hard to 'get the floor' in the world's great debating society"; a speaker "must make the most of his opportunity." Marsh certainly did.

"Man the Disturber of Nature's Harmonies" was the title Marsh first proposed for the book. His publisher demurred. "Does not man act in harmony with nature? And with her laws? Is he not a part of nature?" "No," rejoined Marsh, "nothing is further from my belief, that man is a 'part of nature' or that his action is controlled by the laws of nature; in fact a leading object of the book is to enforce the opposite opinion, and to illustrate the fact that man . . . is a free moral agent working independently of nature."

Nature left to itself, in Marsh's view, remained in stable harmony, at least within the brief time-frame of human history. Beyond longer-term geological convulsions, natural change was small in scope, cyclical, or self-correcting.

Reacting to any injurious event, nature tended to revert to its previous state of approximate balance, moderating climatic extremes and promoting conditions favorable to organic diversity.

Marsh's vision of a self-regulating approach toward natural equilibrium became the ecological paradigm of the early twentieth century; it continues to pervade popular conceptions of nature among the general public, including most environmental activists, to this day. Professionals, however, long ago jettisoned the equilibrium model. Gone are yesteryear's balanced equilibria and enduring climaxes, stabilities deranged only by geologically rare events or by human intervention. In their place is a turbulent and chaotic nature buffeted by episodic uncertainties and erratic disturbances. The balanced harmonies of past ecological theory are now seen as at best circumscribed and evanescent, punctuated by disruptive and unpredictable fluctuations over the whole of earth history.

Marsh himself did not suppose nature had ever been wholly stable, only that the dynamics of its organic and inorganic components tended toward stability in the short term. He observed that plants continuously alter their milieus, often making them more conducive to other species than to their own. "Every generation of trees leaves the soil in a different state," he noted of forest succession; "every tree that springs up in a group of trees of another species than its own, grows under different influences of light and shade and atmosphere from its predecessors." Alertness to the flux of change within the ramified network of dead and living matter is a major strength of *Man and Nature*. Yet his tableau of a more or less self-regulating nature, then crucial to his reform message, is today far less credible.

Marsh's second and more radical insight concerned man's role in nature. The then general belief was that humans had been blessed with God-given power to subdue all other creatures and a mission to fructify the earth. Their impact on nature was thought ipso facto benign or else negligible. Men improved their earthly home in accordance with divine intent, and the bounty that followed forest clearing, swamp draining, and cultivation attested divine approval. Adverse side-effects were easily dismissed, especially in America. Soils eroded or exhausted were simply vacated for new lands farther west; forests logged and burned seemed trifling by comparison with the wealth of timber beyond the horizon. Meanwhile nature left alone would heal itself.

But this recuperative scenario accorded less and less with witnessed facts. Exploiting the New World did not redress the balance of the Old; it exposed that balance as a wishful fiction. Long-settled European landscapes were now apt to be more slowly modified, but a single lifetime saw vast American tracts cleared, cultivated—and despoiled. The fundamental tenet of *Man and Nature* was that nature did *not* heal itself; land once exploited and then abandoned seldom regained its previous plenitude but remained for ages, if not forever, depleted. The ultimate consequence of human impact was the need for perpetual human care. Just as man was a force above nature, so Marsh saw conquered nature permanently dependent on rational aid.

The harm done by human impact did not preclude dominion over nature: to the contrary, it mandated more intensive governance. Marsh lauded science for advancing the conquest of nature. He rebuked those who felt progress soul-destroying and who mourned human intrusion. Nature was not sacred; man must rebel against its limits, subjugate it, impose order; for "wherever he fails to make himself her master, he can but be her slave." As Marsh wrote in an 1860 essay, science had "already virtually doubled the span of human life by multiplying our powers and abridging" the time needed for gaining a livelihood. Ongoing mastery of the forces of inorganic nature would achieve the "more or less complete emancipation of man from slavery to his own necessities."

Greed was only partly to blame for the harm humanity had done; most damage was unintended, often unseen. Men did not mean to derange nature; they were oblivious to doing so. The old belief that all was for the best in a divinely ordered cosmos had long blinded them to the ruin they wrought. But myopia was not incurable. Awareness could prompt reform: the powers humans deployed to break nature might also mend it. Once understood, processes that revivified the environment could be protected and emulated by man as a co-worker with nature.

Though political and social progress seemed to Marsh more dubious as he aged, he never abandoned faith in scientific advance. For all his dire portents, a pragmatic optimism pervades *Man and Nature*. It is a diatribe, but not a jeremiad; Marsh believed that humans could learn to manage the environment for their own sake and for nature's good. To "the great question" with which it concludes, "whether man is of nature or above her," Marsh never doubted the answer.

How could a self-schooled nineteenth-century Vermonter, immersed in the day-to-day turmoil of a new nation's manifold enterprises, fashion this sweeping panoply of environmental destiny? Largely *because* Marsh spread his net so wide. Young America had other multifaceted men of affairs, other polymath scholars; but none so well combined these two distinct penchants as did Marsh. Omniscient learning leavened with commonplace experience infuses *Man and Nature*. Marsh was no aloof bookworm; he lived enmeshed in worldly affairs. More than any of his erudite contemporaries he was realistic, pragmatic, down-to-earth. Enforced intimacy with mundane enterprise patterned his tastes, tested his ideas against reality, and gave him a relish for hard facts, a zest for homely details. These traits forged *Man and Nature* and annealed its authority.

They were also supremely American traits, as Marsh himself stressed. New World pioneers with no precursors to turn to had to master every calling themselves. Hence "every man is a dabbler in every knowledge," Marsh put it. "Every man is a divine, a statesman, a physician, and a lawyer to himself." That portrayal fits its author, whose omnicompetence was legendary. "If you live much longer," wrote a friend "you will be obliged to invent trades, for you will have exhausted the present category." Marsh epitomized his own American scholar: "not a recluse devoted to quiet literary research, but one who lives and acts in the busy whirl of the great world, shares the anxieties and the hazards of commerce, the toils and the rivalries of the learned professions, or the fierce strife of contending political factions, or who is engaged perhaps in some industrial pursuit, and is oftener stunned with the clang of the forge and the hum of machinery, than refreshed by the voice of the Muses."

The making of *Man and Nature* embodied all these metiers and every strand of Marsh's life: the early near-blindness that led him to cherish and study nature; Transcendental faith that stressed free will and human agency; environmental lessons made manifest in barren and degraded Old World lands; language skills that bonded him with like-minded Europeans; his love of tool-making; alertness to the homely artifacts along with the luminous texts of the past; righteous outrage at corporate greed; patriotic ardor for national stewardship.

Marsh's insights were honed on habits of transatlantic contrast then common. Americans were given to lauding their New World as superior to the Old—more enterprising, free, egalitarian, progressive, hopeful. Foreign observers like Alexis de Tocqueville and Charles Lyell fortified their self-admiration. Wide reading and direct scrutiny on both continents uniquely equipped Marsh to amplify and rectify such comparisons. Unusually, he took note not just of the cultural peaks of arts and letters, but of prosaic, workaday matters like those he himself met as farmer, carpenter, mechanic, road builder, logger, quarryman. "Wherever I go," Marsh declared, "I find the mudpiles better worth study than the superstructure of the social edifice." Such "earthy taste" stirred him to note myriad mundane aspects of human impact in *Man and Nature*. Like Marsh's eclectic breadth, his down-to-earth pragmatism was distinctively American.

So was his concern with the future. For all the novelty of Marsh's insights, his overriding credos—belief in progress and faith in reform were highly American. And they were bound up with commitment to the future. *Man and Nature* takes it for granted that the welfare of generations to come matters more than immediate gain. For our offspring, if not for ourselves, we need a sounder husbandry. But to steward the future Americans must learn to care for the past. Marsh chided his countrymen for a restless mobility that severed them from home, from forebears, and from tradition. In landscape as in language, rapid change was risky; "the future is more uncertain than the past." Marsh likened cultural to environmental stability: "Like the ultimately beneficial rains of heaven, social changes produce their best effect when neither very hastily precipitated, nor very frequently repeated."

Marsh preached no panacea. Nor did he profess despair, though glumly convinced that selfishness prevailed among most men. For all his misanthropy Marsh was more concerned with mankind than with the cosmos. It was not for nature's sake that he would save it from human folly, but for humanity's. Nature was indifferent; only mankind, however benighted, had conscious will and moral purpose. Humanism suffused his career and drove his commitments.

Man and Nature inaugurated a modem way of viewing the fabric of landscape, of seeing how people use and abuse the earth they inhabit. Until Marsh, mankind was widely assumed to be one thing, nature another—the former destined to master and exploit the latter. Marsh pioneered in showing how human agencies acted in and reacted on the whole web of soil and water, plants and animals. Most such actions were unintended and their effects unpredictable, because nature was too ramified to fully fathom, human impacts too obscured or long persisting to adequately assess.

Marsh did more than account for such interactions. He crafted a compelling depiction of the damage wrought and added an impassioned plea to arrest loss and restore the fabric of nature. He urged physical controls to maximize resources, political controls to minimize private and corporate avarice— avarice that extorted instant profits at the cost of long-term social needs. Four generations on, Marsh's fusion of ecological insight with social reform is still convincing.

Most crucially, Marsh showed that human actions had momentous unforeseeable consequences. Technology might repair previous damage, but science could never keep abreast of the ongoing repercussions of continuing human action. The interweaving of myriad perdurable deeds made their cumulative impact impossible to gauge. This led Marsh to deductions both fabulously sanguine and hugely depressing. The energy of winds and waves, solar heat and electricity might be harnessed to reclad the globe's denuded mountains, to temper extremes of drought and flood. Yet technology also spawned ever more ruinous machines of exploitation, more ruthless weapons of annihilation. Human manipulations beat against natural limits that were far narrower than most realized; a globe grown too hot or too cold, too wet or too dry, too abruptly altered in any terrestrial rhythm, would forfeit the quasi-equilibria that had brought into being and sustained the health of animate life and landscape.

Why reissue *Man and Nature*? What environmental relevance has a nineteenth-century diplomat-linguist's views today? Why bother with what one modern admirer terms this "doctrinaire, maudlin, cant, overripe, moralistic cough drop of a book"? Marsh's concerns are now superseded by other conservation issues, demanding new solutions to still graver dilemmas. To be sure, those Marsh tackled—deforestation, soil erosion, desertification—are still with us, his insights on their causes still germane, his remedies still apropos. But these are not the menaces now uppermost. Impact fears today focus more on mass extinctions, global warming, chemical pollutants, nuclear contaminants. No one in Marsh's day was aware of any of these problems. Indeed, most of them did not then exist.

Many today echo Marsh's environmental fears and salute his pioneering efforts to comprehend and overcome them. But we confront them in an altogether different spirit. The problems we face, our faith in resolving them, our views of nature, humanity, culture, progress, ecology, and history—all have utterly changed since *Man and Nature* first appeared in 1864, even since I introduced its 1965 reissue. It is not only the threats that are new, but also our notions of what and whom to blame, how to reverse present damage and cope with future risks, and whether or not we are likely to succeed.

The Enlightenment state of mind that infused *Man and Nature* runs counter to most conventional wisdom today. We cannot recapture the technological optimism and spiritual faith that inspired Marsh. But it is worth recalling three of his underlying premises: that human agency is uniquely self-conscious; that our terrestrial impact is unavoidable and bound to go on magnifying; that its gravest ecological risks are perforce unpredictable.

Compared with the hidden and long-incubating dangers we now confront, those detailed in *Man and Nature* were for the most part visible to the naked eye and swiftly apparent. Whereas much of the damage Marsh gauged seemed easily repaired at small expense, the remedies now needed to restore a sustainable globe dismay us as dauntingly difficult and economically crippling. Marsh's plea for more, not less, control over nature repels many of today's friends of the earth; few share his confidence in rational collective action or in a suitably managed world.

Even more than Marsh, we now condemn our saga of environmental impingement as malign, if not catastrophic. In revulsion against humanity's wreckage of habitats, some idealize nature devoid of human fault and yearn for an uncontaminated world. It is an idle aspiration. We may amend our influence, but we can neither halt it nor curtail its intensity. The effects of our impress will be ever greater—and graver.

To relinquish dominion over nature, in Marsh's view, would mean regression to amoral misery ruled by hunger, fear, and superstition. Short of total global collapse, such a relapse was unimaginable. Every human act alters nature; every technical advance augments the potential for harm. The resultant damage might be countered, not by ceasing to alter nature but by taking greater care in doing so. Growing human might called not for abating, but intensifying, global manipulation. We inherit a world indelibly marked by being both managed and mismanaged; it is up to us to manage it better.

Yet even effecting the best intentions cannot ensure a sound environment. As Marsh emphasizes time and again, most human impact is unintended. "Vast as is the . . . magnitude and importance [of] intentional changes," they are "insignificant in comparison with the contingent and unsought results which have flowed from them." As impacts proliferate, their unsought, unwanted, perhaps lethal consequences remain never fully foreseen, let alone preventable.

This insight has even greater relevance in our time, when "the secondary, distant, and surprising effects of which Marsh spoke have become commonplace." We are ever more alert to environmental evils that are invisible and unexpected. We no longer suppose natural history predictable, because we now know that most of nature is neither uniform nor regular, let alone in equilibrium. But we have not yet learned to accept, much less how to live with, the humbling ecological uncertainty that informs *Man and Nature*—nature's "baffling complexity, its inherent unpredictability, its daily turbulence."

Most salient for today's world is *Man and Nature*'s social morality. Resource husbandry, Marsh had come reluctantly to realize, could not rely on enlightened self-interest. Collective stewardship crucial to environmental health required rescinding "the sacred right of every man to do what he will with his own" property. Yet every man's stake in the land—a stake that transcended immediate pecuniary value—demanded an active role in managing and conserving. Proud of being an amateur, Marsh preached the civic necessity of informed public participation. Environmental expertise alone was impotent. As amateur citizens, all of us need to care enough for our environment to become capable of shaping and ready to promote the reforms essential to its sustenance.

The Town-Country Magnet

Garden Cities of To-morrow (1898)

Ebenezer Howard

... Religious and political questions too often divide us into hostile camps; and so, in the very realms where calm, dispassionate thought and pure emotions are the essentials of all advance towards right beliefs and sound principles of action, the din of battle and the struggles of contending hosts are more forcibly suggested to the onlooker than the really sincere love of truth and love of country which, one may yet be sure, animate nearly all breasts.

There is, however, a question in regard to which one can scarcely find any difference of opinion. It is wellnigh universally agreed by men of all parties, not only in England, but all over Europe and America and our colonies, that it is deeply to be deplored that the people should continue to stream into the already over-crowded cities, and should thus further deplete the country districts.

Lord Rosebery, speaking some years ago as Chairman of the London County Council, dwelt with very special emphasis on this point:

> There is no thought of pride associated in my mind with the idea of London. I am always haunted by the awfulness of London: by the great appalling fact of these millions cast down, as it would appear by hazard, on the banks of this noble stream, working each in their own groove and their own cell, without regard or knowledge of each other, without heeding each other, without having the slightest idea how the other lives—the heedless casualty of unnumbered thousands of men. Sixty years ago a great Englishman, Cobbett, called it

a wen. If it was a wen then, what is it now? A tumour, an elephantiasis sucking into its gorged system half the life and the blood and the bone of the rural districts. (March 1891.)

Sir John Gorst points out the evil, and suggests the remedy:

> If they wanted a permanent remedy of the evil they must remove the cause; they must back the tide, and stop the migration of the people into the towns, and get the people back to the land. The interest and the safety of the towns themselves were involved in the solution of the problem. (*Daily Chronicle*, 6th November 1891).

. . . The Press, Liberal, Radical, and Conservative, views this grave symptom of the time with the same alarm. The *St. James's Gazette*, on 6th June 1892, remarks:

> How best to provide the proper antidote against the greatest danger of modern existence is a question of no mean significance.

. . . All, then, are agreed on the pressing nature of this problem, all are bent on its solution, and though it would doubtless be quite Utopian to expect a similar agreement as to the value of any remedy that may be proposed, it is at least of immense importance that, on a subject thus universally regarded as of supreme importance, we have such a consensus of opinion at the outset. This will be the more remarkable and the more hopeful sign when it is shown, as I believe will be conclusively shown in this work, that the answer to this, one of the most pressing questions of the day, makes of comparatively easy solution many other problems which have hitherto taxed the ingenuity of the greatest thinkers and reformers of our time. Yes, the key to the problem how to restore the people to the land—that beautiful land of ours, with its canopy of sky, the air that blows upon it, the sun that warms it, the rain and dew that moisten it—the very embodiment of Divine love for man—is indeed a *Master Key*, for it is the key to a portal through which, even when scarce ajar, will be seen to pour a flood of light on the problems of intemperance, of excessive toil, of restless anxiety, of grinding poverty—the true limits of Governmental interference, ay, and even the relations of man to the Supreme Power.

It may perhaps be thought that the first step to be taken towards the solution of this question—how to restore the people to the land—would involve a careful consideration of the very numerous causes which have hitherto led to their aggregation in large cities. Were this the case, a very prolonged enquiry would be necessary at the outset. Fortunately, alike for writer and for reader, such an analysis is not, however, here requisite, and for a very simple reason, which may be stated thus: Whatever may have been the causes which have operated in the past, and are operating now, to draw the people into the cities, those causes may all be summed up as 'attractions'; and it is obvious, therefore, that no remedy can possibly be effective which will not present to the people, or at least to considerable portions of them, greater 'attractions' than our cities now possess, so that the force of the old 'attractions' shall be overcome by the force of new 'attractions' which are to be created. Each city may be regarded as a magnet, each person as a needle; and, so viewed, it is at once seen that nothing short of the discovery of a method for constructing magnets of yet greater power than our cities possess can be effective for redistributing the population in a spontaneous and healthy manner.

So presented, the problem may appear at first sight to be difficult, if not impossible, of solution. 'What', some may be disposed to ask, 'can possibly be done to make the country more attractive to a workaday people than the town—to make wages, or at least the standard of physical comfort, higher in the country than in the town; to secure in the country equal possibilities of social intercourse, and to make the prospects of advancement for the average man or woman equal, not to say superior, to those enjoyed in our large cities?' The issue one constantly finds presented in a form very similar to that. The subject is treated continually in the public press, and in all forms of discussion, as though men, or at least working men, had not now, and never could have, any choice or alternative, but either, on the one hand, to stifle their love for human society—at least in wider relations than can be found in a straggling village—or, on the other hand, to forgo almost entirely all the keen and pure delights of the country. The question is universally considered as though it were now, and for ever must remain, quite impossible for working people to live in the country and yet be engaged in pursuits other than agricultural; as though crowded, unhealthy cities were the last word of economic science; and as if our present form of industry, in which sharp lines divide agricultural from industrial pursuits, were necessarily an enduring one. This fallacy is the very common one of ignoring altogether the possibility of alternatives other than those presented to the mind. There are in reality not only, as is so constantly assumed, two alternatives—town life and country life—but a third alternative, in which all the advantages of the most energetic and active town life, with all the beauty and delight of the country, may be secured in perfect combination; and the certainty of being able to live this life will be the magnet which will produce the effect for which we are all striving—the spontaneous movement of the people from our crowded cities to the bosom of our kindly mother earth, at once the source of life, of happiness, of wealth, and of power. The town and the country may, therefore, be regarded as two magnets, each striving to draw the people to itself—a rivalry which a new form of life, partaking of the nature of both, comes to take part in. This may be illustrated by a diagram of 'The Three Magnets', in which the chief advantages of the Town and of the Country are set forth with their corresponding drawbacks, while the advantages of the Town-Country are seen to be free from the disadvantages of either.

The Town magnet, it will be seen, offers, as compared with the Country magnet, the advantages of high wages, opportunities for employment, tempting prospects of advancement, but these are largely counterbalanced by high rents and prices. Its social opportunities and its places of amusement are very alluring, but excessive hours of toil, distance from work, and the 'isolation of crowds' tend greatly to reduce the value of these good things. The well-lit streets are a great attraction, especially in winter, but the sunlight is being more and more shut out, while the air is so vitiated that the fine public buildings, like the sparrows, rapidly become covered with soot, and the very statues are in despair. Palatial edifices and fearful slums are the strange, complementary features of modern cities.

The Country magnet declares herself to be the source of all beauty and wealth; but the Town magnet mockingly reminds her that she is very dull for lack of society, and very sparing of her gifts for lack of capital. There are in the country beautiful vistas, lordly parks, violet-scented woods, fresh air, sounds of rippling water; but too often one sees those threatening words, 'Trespassers will be prosecuted'. Rents, if estimated by the acre, are certainly low, but such low rents are the natural fruit of low wages rather than a cause of substantial comfort; while long hours and lack of amusements forbid the bright sunshine and the pure air to gladden the hearts of the people. The one industry, agriculture, suffers frequently from excessive rainfalls; but this wondrous harvest of the clouds is seldom properly ingathered, so that, in times of drought, there is frequently, even for drinking purposes, a most insufficient supply. Even the natural healthfulness of the country is largely lost for lack of proper drainage and other sanitary conditions, while, in parts almost deserted by the people, the few who remain are yet frequently huddled together as if in rivalry with the slums of our cities.

But neither the Town magnet nor the Country magnet represents the full plan and purpose of nature. Human society and the beauty of nature are meant to be enjoyed together. The two magnets must be made one. As man and woman by their varied gifts and faculties supplement each other, so should town and country. The town is the symbol of society—of mutual help and friendly co-operation, of fatherhood, motherhood, brotherhood, sisterhood, of wide relations between man and man—of broad, expanding sympathies—of science, art, culture, religion. And the country! The country is the symbol of

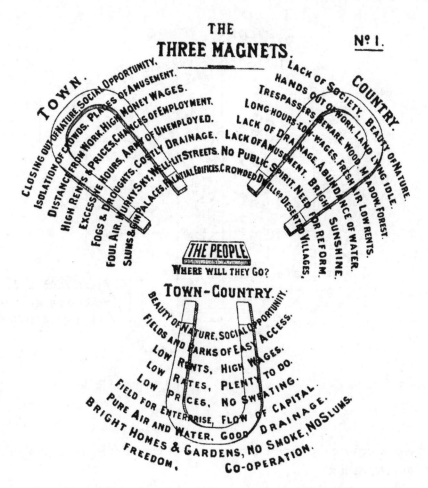

Figure 1-2 Ebenezer Howard's depiction of "The Three Magnets" (Howard, 1898, Public domain).

God's love and care for man. All that we are and all that we have comes from it. Our bodies are formed of it; to it they return. We are fed by it, clothed by it, and by it are we warmed and sheltered. On its bosom we rest. Its beauty is the inspiration of art, of music, of poetry. Its forces propel all the wheels of industry. It is the source of all health, all wealth, all knowledge. But its fullness of joy and wisdom has not revealed itself to man. Nor can it ever, so long as this unholy, unnatural separation of society and nature endures. Town and country *must be married,* and out of this joyous union will spring a new hope, a new life, a new civilization. It is the purpose of this work to show how a first step can be taken in this direction by the construction of a Town-country magnet; and I hope to convince the reader that this is practicable, here and now, and that on

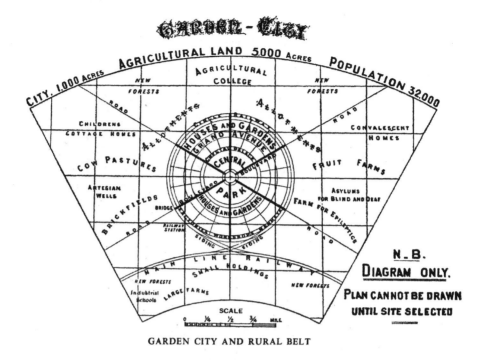

GARDEN CITY AND RURAL BELT

Figure 1-3 Howard's garden city proposal (Howard, 1898, Public domain).

principles which are the very soundest, whether viewed from the ethical or the economic standpoint.

I will undertake, then, to show how in 'Town-country' equal, nay better, opportunities of social intercourse may be enjoyed than are enjoyed in any crowded city, while yet the beauties of nature may encompass and enfold each dweller therein; how higher wages are compatible with reduced rents and rates; how abundant opportunities for employment and bright prospects of advancement may be secured for all; how capital may be attracted and wealth created; how the most admirable sanitary conditions may be ensured; how beautiful homes and gardens may be seen on every hand; how the bounds of freedom may be widened, and yet all the best results of concert and co-operation gathered in by a happy people.

The construction of such a magnet, could it be effected, followed, as it would be, by the construction of many more, would certainly afford a solution of the burning question set before us by Sir John Gorst, 'how to back the tide of migration of the people into the towns, and to get them back upon the land.' . . .

References

Abercrombie, Patrick. *Greater London Plan, 1944*. London: H.M. Stationery Office, 1945.
Purdom, Charles Benjamin. *The Garden City: A Study in the Development of a Modern Town*. London: JM Dent & Sons, 1913.

The Study of Cities

Cities in Evolution: An Introduction to the Town Planning Movement and to the Study of Civics (1915)

Patrick Geddes

We have seen that many, and in all countries, are awakening to deal with the practical tasks of citizenship. Indeed, never, since the golden times of classic or mediaeval cities, has there been so much interest, so much goodwill as now. Hence the question returns, and more and more frequently, how best can we set about the study of cities? How organise speedily in each, in all, and therefore here and there among ourselves to begin with, a common understanding as to the methods required to make observations orderly, comparisons fruitful and generalisations safe? It is time for sociologists—that is for all who care for the advance of science into the social world—to be bringing order into these growing inquiries, these limitless fields of knowledge.

The writer has no finally formulated answer, since his own inquiries are far from concluded; and, since no bureaucrat, he has not a cut-and-dried method to impose meanwhile: nor can he cite this from others: he may best describe his own experience. The problem of city study has occupied his mind for thirty years and more: indeed his personal life, as above all things a wandering student, has been largely determined and spent in restless and renewed endeavours towards searching for the secrets of the evolution of cities, towards making out ways of approach towards their discovery. And his interests and experiences are doubtless those of many.

The nature lover's revolt from city life, even though in youth strengthened and reinforced by the protest of the romantics and the moralists, of the painters and the poets, may be sooner or later overpowered by the attractions, both cultural and practical, which city life exerts. Studies of economics and statistics, of history and social philosophy in many schools, though each fascinating for a season, come to be felt inadequate. An escape from libraries and lecture-rooms, a return to direct observation is needed; and thus the historic culture-cities—classic, mediaeval, renaissance—with all their treasures of the past—museums, galleries, buildings and monuments—come to renew their claim to dominate attention, and to supply the norms of civic thought.

Again the view-points of contemporary science renew their promise—now doctrines of energetics, or theories of evolution, at times the advance of psychology, the struggle towards vital education, the renewal of ethics—each in its turn may seem the safest clue with which to penetrate the city's labyrinth. Geographer and historian, economist and aesthete, politician and philosopher have all to be utilised as guides in tum; and from each of these approaches one learns much, yet never sufficient; so that at times the optimist, but often also the pessimist, has seemed entitled to prevail.

Again, as the need of co-ordination, of all these and more constantly makes itself felt, the magnificent prosynthetic sketch of Comte's sociology or the evolutionary effort of Spencer reasserts its central importance, and with these also the historic Utopias. But all such are too abstract constructions, and have as yet been lacking in concrete applications, either to the interpretation or to the improvement of cities; they are deficient in appreciation of their complex activities. Hence the fascination of those transient but all the more magnificent museums of contemporary industry which we call International and Local Exhibitions, centring round those of Paris on 1878, '89 and 1900, with their rich presentments of the material and artistic productivity of their present, alike on its Paleotechnic and Neotechnic levels, and in well-nigh all substages and phases of these.

As we return from these, at one time the roaring forges of industrial activity of Europe and America must seem world-central, beyond even the metropolitan cities which dominate and exploit them. Yet at another time the evolutionary secret seems nearer through the return to nature; and we seek the synoptic vision of geography with Reclus, or of the elemental occupations with Le Play and Demolins, with their sympathetic study of simple peoples, and of the dawn of industry and society with the anthropologists.

And thus we return once more, by way of family unit and family budget, to modern life; and even to its statistical treatments, to Booth and Rowntree for poverty, to Galton and the eugenists, and so on. In such ways and more, ideas accumulate, yet the difficulties of dealing with them also; for to leave out any aspect or element of the community's life must so far lay us open to that reproach of crudely simplified theorising, for which we blame the political economist.

One of the best ways in which a man can work towards this clearing up of his own ideas is through the endeavour of communicating them to others: in fact to this the professoriate largely owe and acknowledge such productivity as they possess. Well-nigh every writer will testify to a similar experience: and the inquirer into sociology and civics may most courageously of all take part in the propaganda for these studies.

Another of the questions—one lying at the very outset of our social studies, and constantly reappearing—is this; what is to be our relation to practical life? The looker-on sees most of the game; a wise detachment must be practised; our observations cannot be too comprehensive or too many-sided. Our meditations too must be prolonged and impartial; and how all this if not serene?

Hence Comte's "cerebral hygiene," or Mr. Spencer's long and stoutly maintained defence of his hermitage against the outer world, his abstention from social responsibilities and activities, even those faced by other philosophers.

Yet there is another side to all this: we learn by living; and as the naturalist, beside his detached observations, and even to aid these, cannot too fully identify himself with the life and activities of his fellow-men in the simple natural environments he wishes to investigate, so it may be for the student of societies. From this point of view, "when in Rome let us do as the Romans do"; let us be at home as far as may be in the characteristic life and activity, the social and cultural movements, of the city which is our home, even for the time being—if we would understand its record or its spirit, its qualities and defects, its place in civilisation.

Still more must we take our share in the life and work of the community if we would make this estimate an active one; that is, if we would discern the possibilities of place, of work, of people, of actual groupings and institutions or of needed ones, and thus leave the place in some degree the better of our life in it; the richer, not the poorer, for our presence. Our activity may in some measure interrupt our observing and philosophising; indeed must often do so; yet with no small compensations in the long run. For here is that experimental social science which the theoretic political economists were wont to proclaim impossible; but which is none the less on parallel lines and of kindred experimental value to the practice which illuminates theory, criticising it or advancing it, in many simpler fields of action—say, engineering or medicine for choice. It is with civics and sociology as with these. The greatest historians, both ancient and modern, have been those who took their part in affairs. Indeed with all sciences, as with the most ideal quests, the sample principle holds good; we must live the life if we would know the doctrine. Scientific detachment is but one mood, though an often needed one; our quest cannot be attained without participation in the active life of citizenship.

In each occupation and profession there is a freemasonry, which rapidly and hospitably assimilates the reasonably sympathetic newcomer. Here is the advantage of the man of the world, of the artist and art-lover, of the scholar, the specialist of every kind; and, above all of the citizen, who is alive to the many-sidedness of the social world, and who is willing to help and to work with his fellows.

Moreover, though the woof of each city's life be unique, and this it may be increasingly with each throw of the shuttle, the main warp of life is broadly similar from city to city. The family types, the fundamental occupations and their levels may thus be more readily understood than are subtler resultants. Yet in practice this is seldom the case, because the educated classes everywhere tend to be specialised away from the life and labour of the people. Yet these make up the bulk of the citizens; even their emergent rulers are often but people of a larger growth, for better and for worse. Hence a new demand upon the student of cities, to have shared the environment and conditions of the people, as far as may be their labour also; to have sympathised with their difficulties and their pleasures, and not merely with those of the cultured or the governing classes.

Here the endeavour of the University Settlements has gone far beyond the "slumming" now happily out of fashion, but the civic student and worker needs fuller experiences than these commonly supply. Of the value of the settlement alike to its workers, and to the individuals and organisations they influence much might be said, and on grounds philanthropic and educational, social and political; but to increase its civic value and influence a certain advance is needed in its point of view, analogous to that made by the medical student when he passes from his dispensary experience of individual patients to that of the public health department.

In all these various ways, the writer's ideas on the study of cities have been slowly clearing up, throughout many years of civic inquiries and endeavours. These have been largely centred at Edinburgh (as for an aggregate of reasons one of the most instructive of the world's cities, alike for survey and for experimental action), also at the great manufacturing town and seaport of Dundee, with studies and duties in London and in Dublin, and especial sympathies and ties in Paris, and in other continental cities and also American ones—and from among all these interests and occupations a method of civic study and research, a mode of practice and application, have gradually been emerging.

Each of these is imperfect, embryonic even, yet a brief indication may be at least suggestive to other students of cities. The general principle is the synoptic one, of seeking as far as may be to recognise and utilise all points of view—and so to be preparing for the Encyclopaedia Civica of the future. For this must include at once the scientific and, as far as may be, the artistic presentment of the city's life: it must base upon these an interpretation of the city's course of evolution in the present: it must increasingly forecast its future possibilities; and thus it may arouse and educate citizenship, by organising endeavours towards realising some of these worthy ends.

Largely in this way, yet also from the complemental side of nature studies and geography, there have been arising for many years past the beginnings of a Civic Observatory and Laboratory in our Edinburgh Outlook Tower. A tall old building, high upon the ridge of Old Edinburgh, it overlooks the city and even great part of its region; and of the educative value of this synoptic vision every visitor has thus a fresh experience. Hence, for at least two generations before its present use, it has been the resort of tourists; and its camera obscura, which harmonises the striking landscape, near and far, and this with no small element of the characteristic qualities of modern painting, has therefore been retained; alike for its own sake and as an evidence of what is so often missed by scientific and philosophic minds, that the synthetic vision to which they aspire may be reached more simply from the aesthetic and the emotional side, and thus be visual and concrete. In short, here as elsewhere, children may see more than the wise. For there can be no nature study, no geography worth the name apart from the love and the beauty of Nature, so it is with the study of the City.

Next, a storey below this high Outlook of the artist, and its associated open-air gallery for his scientific brother the geographer, both at once civic and regional in rare completeness, there comes—upon the main platform of the level roof, and in the open air—the "Prospect" of the special sciences.

Here, on occasion, is set forth the analysis of the outlook in its various aspects—astronomic and topographical, geological and meteorological, botanical and zoological, anthropological and archeologic, historical and economic, and so on. Each science is thus indicated, in its simple yet specialised problem. This or that element of the whole environment is isolated, by the logical artifice of science, from the totality of our experience. The special examination of it, thus rendered possible, results in what we call a "science," and this with a certainty which increasingly admits of prevision and of action. Yet this science, this body of verifiable and workable truths, is a vast and wholesale suppression of other (and it may be more important) truths, until its reintegration with the results of other studies, into the geographic and social whole, the regional and civic unity before us.

Here in brief, then, is our philosophy of civics, and our claim for civics in philosophy. Thus upon our prospect, the child often starts his scientific studies, the boy-scout his expedition. Yet to this the expert must return, to discuss the relation and applications of his own science with the philosopher as citizen and the citizen as philosopher.

The storey below this prospect is devoted to the City. Its relief-model maps, geological and other, are here shown in relation to its aspects and beauty

Figure 1-4
Outlook Tower,
Edinburgh
(Geddes, 1915,
Public domain).

expressed in paintings, drawings, photographs, etc.; while within this setting there has been gradually prepared a Survey of Edinburgh, from its prehistoric origins, and throughout its different phases, up to the photographic survey of the present day. In this way the many standpoints usually divided among specialists are here being brought together, and with educative result to all concerned.

The next lower storey is allotted to Scotland, with its towns and cities. The next to Greater Britain, indeed at times to some representation of the whole English-speaking world, the United States no less than Canada, etc., the language being here taken as a more sociological and social unity than can be even the bond of Empire.

The next storey is allotted to European (or rather Occidental) civilisation, with a general introduction to historical studies and their interpretation,

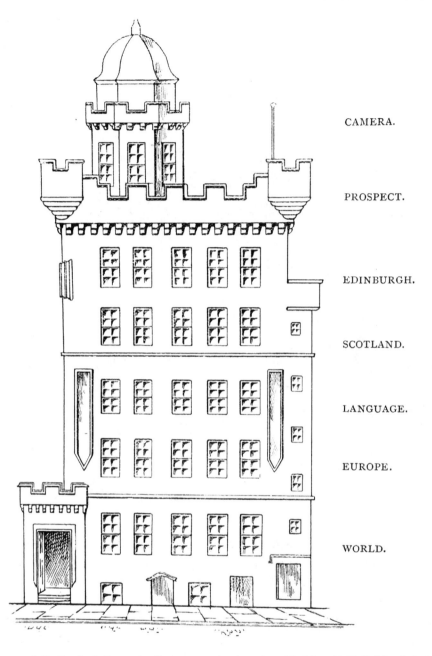

CAMERA.

PROSPECT.

EDINBURGH.

SCOTLAND.

LANGUAGE.

EUROPE.

WORLD.

Figure 1-5 Outlook Tower in diagrammatic elevation (Geddes, 1915, Public domain).

and also with the work of a Current Events Club, with its voluminous press-cuttings on many subjects, largely international and general; and furthermore to the comparison of Occidental cities.

Finally the ground-floor is allocated to the Oriental civilisations, and to the general study of Man, departments naturally as yet least developed.

The general principle—the primacy of the civic and social outlook, intensified into local details with all the scientific outlooks of a complete survey; yet in contact with the larger world, and this successively in enlarging social zones, from that of the prospect outwards—will now be sufficiently clear; and of course be seen as applicable to any city. It may be experimented with in any city, in anyone's study, even begun upon the successive shelves of a book-case, or, still better in the co-operative activity of a Current Events Club; and this again, if possible, along with a Regional and Civic Survey Committee. On any and every scale, personal or collective, it will be found to reward a trial.

What now of practical applications? Returning for the present purpose to the top storey, the City's storey alone, though the main presentment is that of a survey, an exhibition of facts past and present, a Civic Business-room adjoins this. Here has been for many years in progress the main practical civic work of this Tower—its various endeavours towards city betterment. Largely the improvement of those slums, already referred to as the disgrace and difficulty of Old Edinburgh; a work of housing, of repair or renewal, of increase of open spaces and when possible of gardening them; of preservation of historic buildings, of establishment of halls of collegiate residence with associated dwellings and so on.

Each piece of work has been undertaken as circumstances and means allowed; yet all as part of a comprehensive scheme of long standing, and which at an increasing rate of progress may still be long of accomplishment. Briefly stated, it is that of the preservation and renaiscence of historic Edinburgh, from the standpoints both of town and gown; that is, at once as City and as University, and each at their best. This demands the renewal—and within this historic area especially, dilapidated and deteriorated though it at present be—of that intimate combination of popular culture and of higher education, and of that solidarity of civic and national spirit, with openness and hospitality to the larger world—English, Colonial, American, Continental—which are among the best traditions of Edinburgh, indeed of Scotland, with her historic universities and schools.

But all this, it may be said, is too academic, too much the mere record of a wandering student, and of his changing outlooks and view-points, his personal experiments and endeavours. What of other than university cities? How are civic surveys and endeavours to be applied more generally? . . .

Regional Planning and Ecology

Ecological Monographs (1940)

Benton MacKaye

This title implies a discussion of the relation of regional planning to ecology, and of the problems going with such relation.

Discussion of the relation itself would seem to be a fairly simple matter; it amounts apparently to a few clarifying definitions. What is *ecology*, and what is *regional planning*? But these are big questions in themselves. They are questions not of fact nor principle but of mutual understanding. Toward this a start can be made through the dictionary and the encyclopedia.

Ecology is defined as the relation of organisms to their environment. Human ecology, then, would be the relation of human organisms to their environment. And from this it would seem to follow that human ecology, when *applied* to the actual needs and welfare of human organisms, is the search for the *optimum* relation to environment.

Environment is "the sum of the agencies and influences which affect an organism from without; (extrinsic conditioning as opposed to intrinsic)."

Regional planning is best defined by splitting the term in two. What is *planning*?—and what is *region*? These terms for the purposes at hand, are still in the making. They involve not merely what the dictionary states but what it is that planners really mean.

The term *planning* appears to cover two basic ideas: (1) contriving and (2) recording. Which does the planner have in mind?

Let us take the case of the civil engineer in "planning" an efficient railroad grade across a mountain range. His first job is to record or map the topography, and thus to visualize the environment in question. Somewhere in this there exists already some particular line across the mountain range, which marks a grade more efficient than any other line across said range. The engineer proceeds to *find* that line already fixed by nature; he does *not contrive* or invent some line to suit his fancy. Thus the engineer visualizes the potential railroad grade there already within the actual terrain.

From this case we should say that planning is *discovery* and not invention. It is a new type of exploration. Its essence is visualization—a charting of the potential now existing in the actual.

And what is the thing that is planned? Is it an *area* or a *line* merely, or is it something else? It is something else. The engineer plans for something more than a line across the mountain; he plans for *movement* of freight and passengers. And so with planning generally: the final thing planned is not mere area or land, but movement or activity.

This truism gives a clue to what the planner means by *region*. It is something more than area, it is an area or seat of movement; it is what the dictionary calls a *sphere* ("a circuit or range of action or influence").

A good example of a "sphere" is the "range of action" of water within a single river system. Take the Ohio River system. The flow of water at Cairo is influenced by that at Pittsburgh and in the Allegheny headwaters; it is influenced by the flow from the entire Ohio River watershed. If we would plan the flow of a river the object of our planning would be the watershed; this would be the "region" to be planned; *not* as an *area of land* but as a *range of water flow*.

Another example of sphere or region is the range of action or flow of some *commodity* (such as milk) with respect to some city such as Columbus. This city (and every other) is the center of a "milkshed" bounded by a "divide" nearly as definite as that of water drainage. Milksheds (and "commodity-sheds" generally) differ from watersheds in that they overlap. But each one is a sphere of unit flow or movement, and hence a "region" in the planner's sense.

A third example is the range of flow of *population* with respect to the city of Columbus. This city (and every other) is the eye of centrifugal flow as well as centripetal. A tendency exists of population movement from center to outskirts—what is called the "backflow" into the suburbs and beyond along the radiating highways. Here again we have a series of overlapping spheres or regions.

These three examples illustrate the respective ranges (or regions) for the three kinds of movement (or flow) with which the regional planner is concerned: they are (1) water flow; (2) commodity flow; and (3) population flow.

We are now prepared to suggest a definition of *regional planning*. But let us first turn to an encyclopedia:

> Regional Planning, a term used by community planners, engineers, and geographers to describe a comprehensive ordering of the natural resources of a community, its material equipment and its population for the purpose of laying a sound physical basis for the "good life".... Regional planning involves the development of cities and countrysides, of industries and natural resources, as part of the regional whole.
> —Encyclopaedia Britannica, 14th Edition, 1929.

Being the co-author with Mr. Lewis Mumford of this definition of the Britannica article, I feel at liberty to interpret it. The elements contained follow:

1. "A comprehensive ordering." This refers to a visualization of nature's permanent comprehensive "ordering" as distinguished from the interim makeshift orderings of man. In this we would apply the thought of Plato—"To command nature we must first obey her."
2. An ordering of "development"—a development of "natural resources," of "material equipment," of "population," of "cities and countrysides," of "industries." Such development implies movement, activity, flow—comprised in the three flows mentioned of water, of commodities, and of population.
3. "A regional whole"—which implies an integral or unit sphere of activity, or range of flow.
4. The purpose of the "good life" (or optimum human living—what Congress calls the "general welfare," Jefferson's "pursuit of happiness").

We may now restate the Britannica definition in more specific terms:

> *Regional planning* is a comprehensive ordering or visualization of the possible or potential movement, activity, or flow (from sources onward) of waters, commodities, or population, within a defined area or sphere, for the purpose of laying therein the physical basis for the "good life" or optimum human living.

The relation to ecology of general planning as here defined is, as stated, a simple matter indeed. Regional planning is ecology. It is *human ecology*; its concern is the relation of the human organism to its environment. The region is the unit of environment. Planning is the charting of activity therein affecting the good of the human organism; its object is the application or putting into practice of the optimum relation between the human and the region. Regional planning in short is applied human ecology.

So much for definitions—the attempt to understand the key words that we use (ecology, region, planning). So much to make sure that we know indeed "what we are talking about." . . . And now what of it? Of what earthly use (or human use) is human ecology? Answer—none at all except as it is applied. Here then our subject really begins. How to apply our definitions and the tenets they imply? How to adapt environment to folks, and folks to environment? How to do it for the purpose of optimum living for the folks?

Let us cite one illustration. Take a particular environment such as the region or sphere of water flow in the Ohio River system. How to adapt this sphere (this particular environment) to the inhabitants thereof? This is a problem in charting water flow. And *vice versa*: how to adapt inhabitants to habitat? This is a problem in charting population flow.

Here is a mutual charting—of region to man, and of man to region. There is nothing new about this mutual regional planning—it is as old as man himself. Yet we are just beginning to tackle it in a comprehensive would-be-scientific manner.

What are the elements of this mutual—this twin—this complemental—problem? These elements focus largely in the river flood plain. How should this plain be divided between river and man? What is the natural zone of water flow—high water as well as low? What is the legitimate zone of human occupancy—whether for work or general living? What portions of the flood plain belong respectively to river—and to man?

The river's portion, within limits, can be modified by man. He can restrict the river in one place by expanding it elsewhere. He can narrow the river's precinct in the flood plain downstream by storing the river's water on the flood plain upstream. Thereby he widens man's domain downstream by restricting it upstream. He pays his money and he takes his choice.

What should this choice be? What is the proper balance of man's flood plain domain as between upstream and downstream? How much flooding is warranted of rural valleys on the Ohio River tributaries to prevent flooding of urban centers on the main Ohio River? Not but what the Ohio flood plain between cities can be used for farming and various purposes, even though occasionally flooded. The precise question at hand concerns the main stream *cities* only. It is the problem of balancing rural areas on the tributaries with urban areas on the main stream.

This is a problem of distributing people as well as distributing water. What should these mutual distributions be? This depends on the ultimate objective. If the purpose is to maintain the commercial *status quo*, estimated in values of present vested property interests, then we arrive at one kind of answer. This would be the answer of the commercialist. If the purpose is to attain regional habitability, estimated in values of ultimate optimum human living, then we arrive at another kind of answer. This would be the answer of the human ecologist.

Various projects are under way (including those of the United States Government) for charting and controlling the flow and distribution of waters within the sphere or region of the Ohio River watershed. These projects automatically affect the flow and distribution, within this sphere and region, of the folks themselves or population.

These projects combine in varying degree the objectives of the commercialist with those of the human ecologist. The appraisal of these projects from the latter's standpoint would serve a very useful function. In this the final test, of course, would be the effect on optimum human living of the respective projects.

This test is readily broken down into a series of subtests. These would include the effects on healthful population densities, on the proper proportion of urban to rural population, on employment opportunities, on educational and recreational facilities, on the proper balance of urban, rural and primitive settings.

Herein we have a very practical and immediate job for the human ecologist (or regional planner) in case he should desire to undertake it. It would serve as a useful check on the engineer, the forester, and the other land-use specialists. It would indeed complement their efforts. Such an appraisal would make a working problem in "applied human ecology" as we have defined it.

The problem described is perhaps the most pointed and timely illustration that can be cited of the subject of this paper. Hence its use to show by example what the present writer has in mind by his definition of regional planning and its relation to the broader field of human and total ecology.

References

Adams, Charles C. "The Relation of General Ecology to Human Ecology." *Ecology* 16, no. 3 (1935): 316–35.

———. "The Relation of the Natural Resources to Regional and County Planning." *NY State Mus. Bul.* 310 (1937): 121–41.

Alihan, Milla. *Social Ecology: A Critical Analysis.* New York, 1938.

Bews, J. W. *Human Ecology.* London, Eng., 1935.

Geddes, Patrick, and Victor Branford. *The Making of the Future. The Coming Polity. A Study in Reconstruction.* London, Eng., 1917.

Lynd, Robert S. *Knowledge for What? The Place of Social Science in American Culture.* NJ: Princeton, 1939.

MacKaye, Benton. *The New Exploration: A Philosophy of Regional Planning.* Champaign, IL: University of Illinois Press, 1928.

Mead, Margaret, and F. Mackenzie. "Planned Society: Yesterday, Today, Tomorrow." Edited by F. Mackenzie, *Discussion* 257 (1937): 3.

Mukerjee, Radhakamal. *Regional Sociology*. The Century Co., 1926.

Mumford, Lewis. "Regional Survey for Citizenship." *New York Bul.* 1143 (1938): 37–47.

Odum, Howard Washington, and Harry Estill Moore. *American Regionalism: Cultural-Historical Approach to National Integration*. H. Holt, 1938.

———. *Southern Regions of the United States*. Agathon Press, 1969.

Stein, Clarence S., and Henry Wright. "Report of the Commission of Housing and Regional Planning to Governor Alfred E. Smith." May 7, 1926. Albany, 82.

Thomson, John Arthur, and Patrick Geddes. *Life: Outlines of General Biology*. Vol. 2. Williams & Norgate Limited, 1931.

Van Kleeck, Mary, and Mary L. Fleddérus. "On Economic Planning." *Covici, Friede* (1935): 23–27.

Vance, Rupert Bayless. *Human Geography of the South: A Study in Regional Resources and Human Adequacy*. Russell & Russell, 1932.

Wells, Herbert George, Julian S. Huxley, and George Philip Wells. *The Science of Life*. New York, 1934.

Whitbeck, Ray Hughes, and Olive Jackman Thomas. *The Geographic Factor: Its Role in Life and Civilization*. Kennikat Press, 1932.

Ecological Planning: Retrospect and Prospect
Landscape Journal (1988)

Frederick Steiner, Gerald Young, and
Ervin Zube

Planning, because it is an applied field, is marked by two kinds of history: its development through literature and its development in practice. This review will emphasize the development of ecological planning literature, but examples from practice will be provided where particularly relevant—especially those that emerge from or are related to the classical writings and/or are of landmark significance. Literature and practice do overlap of course, but they do not necessarily coincide; many suggestions in the literature never reach practice and many practitioners do not publish their work. The existence of an impressive literature on ecological planning does not mean ecology is emphasized to an equal measure in practice.

Historical Foundations of Ecological Planning
On the Shoulders of Giants
Ecological planning, like most fields, owes a large debt to a small handful of visionary thinkers. Three giants who span the late nineteenth and early twentieth centuries deserve special mention: George Perkins Marsh, John Wesley Powell, and Patrick Geddes. *Man and Nature; or, Physical Geography as Modified by Human Action* (Marsh, 1864) was the first comprehensive work on the need for the coordinated planning of human action—the first major call for the need to design with nature rather than against the environment. Marsh (1864,

pp. 28 and 136) was appalled by the impacts of human actions on the environment in the Mediterranean region and wrote his book as a holistic, international perspective on "the importance and possibility of physical restoration" and the need to use nature to "mitigate extremes." He discussed in detail the Dutch reclamation schemes (in a historical perspective) and the need for rational human/environmental planning for a wide variety of problems in a range of settings.

John Wesley Powell (1879, p. viii), in his *Report on the Lands of the Arid Region of the United States*, suggested that "the redemption of these lands will require extensive and comprehensive plans," plans including consideration of "the character of the lands themselves," as well as the engineering problems and the necessary legislative action since "here, individual farmers, being poor men, cannot undertake the task." As Kraenzel (1955, p. 292) has noted, Powell's report to the U.S. Congress "stressed the need for new land and water use policies, an adapted land-settlement pattern, and an adapted institutional organization and way of living that was intimately suited to the conditions of the arid and semi-arid lands."

Scottish botanist and land planner Patrick Geddes (1979, p. 138) more explicitly and more strongly emphasized the complexities and the comprehensiveness of the ties between human action and environment: "the types of people, their kinds of styles of work, their whole environment, all become represented in the mind of the community, and these react upon the individuals, their activities, their place itself." Geddes (1968, p. 351) suggested the use of regional surveys to understand these relationships; these were surveys to be based on information from the natural sciences, on "soil and geology, climate, rainfall, winds, etc." His goal was to bring nature into urban areas or in his words, to "let civic designers give rustics access to the city, as well as townsmen access to nature, that way lies the regional ideal" (Kitchen, 1975, p. 332). He went on to claim that "some day men will enter through this portal into paradise regained" (Kitchen, 1975, p. 332; also see Boyer, 1983, pp. 72–73).

Fin de Siecle Influences

The emigration of ecological ideas from biology into planning coincided with the early use of similar ideas in other fields, among them several of the social sciences, as well as some applied fields, especially landscape architecture (Young, 1983). The "Chicago School" so prominent in the history of ecology is also conspicuous in the linkages between biological ecology and the development of ecological ideas in landscape architecture and planning.

Because of these parallels and linkages, Zube's (1986a) comments on ecological influences in landscape architecture are also appropriate for planning.

He suggests that the development of ecological thinking in these fields had its genesis in three turn-of-the-century developments. First was recognition of the aesthetic and functional values of native plant materials and of the need to protect unique and significant natural landscapes. The primary linkage here was between Chicago landscape architect Jens Jensen and University of Chicago ecologist Henry Cowles. Both were participants in a small group of influential Chicagoans who espoused the causes of conservation in the face of spreading urbanization.

The second development occurring around the turn of this century was the planning of park and open space systems for a number of cities in the Midwest and Northeast. These systems were frequently planned around hydrological characteristics and provided for the protection of natural processes as well as recreational opportunities and visual amenities. Notable examples of such systems include Olmsted and Vaux's plans for the Back Bay Fens and Muddy River in Boston in 1878, H.W.S. Cleveland's plan for the park systems of Minneapolis and St. Paul in 1888, Charles Eliot's comprehensive plan for Boston in 1893, and Jens Jensen's proposal for South Chicago in the 1920s.

The third development was the invention of the overlay technique for analyzing natural and cultural resources information. Warren Manning appears to be the originator of this technique which served as a primary mode of analysis until the development of more sophisticated and powerful computer-based approaches. The earliest evidence of Manning's use of this technique is found in his 1913 plan for the Town of Billerica, Massachusetts. Such innovations by landscape architects involved the use of ecological information in the planning and design of human communities.

The garden city movement also was a turn-of-the-century innovation that should be included with the three mentioned by Zube in 1986. The movement was exemplified in Ebenezer Howard's (1902) *Garden Cities of To-morrow*, a book that proposed to control and direct growth by deliberate planning. Each garden city was to be an ecologically self-sufficient unit containing both residences and places of work (within walking distance of each other) and surrounded by a permanent agricultural belt. Any further growth was to be accommodated by new garden cities rather than by expansion of those already in existence.

The Regional Planning Association: MacKaye and Mumford

The Regional Planning Association of America, organized in 1923, was influenced by Geddes and the English garden cities movement. Its members included Benton MacKaye, Lewis Mumford, Clarence Stein, Henry Wright, Catherine

Bauer, and others. MacKaye and Mumford especially espoused an ecological perspective.

Benton MacKaye (1940, p. 351) explicitly linked regional planning to ecology. He defined regional planning as "a comprehensive ordering or visualization of the possible or potential movement, activity or flow (from sources onward) of water, commodities or population, within a defined area or sphere, for the purpose of laying therein the physical basis for the 'good life' or optimum human living." According to MacKaye (1940, p. 350) it was first necessary in planning to grasp "a visualization of nature's permanent comprehensive 'ordering' as distinguished from the interim makeshift orderings of man." MacKaye quoted Plato to emphasize this thought: "To command nature we must first obey her." MacKaye found the purpose of the "good life" or optimum human living incorporated in what the U.S. Congress has called the "general welfare" and what Thomas Jefferson called the "pursuit of happiness." MacKaye concluded that "regional planning is ecology," especially human ecology and provided the following definition:

> Human ecology: its concern is the relation of the human organism to its environment. The region is the unit of environment. Planning is the charting of activity therein affecting the good of the human organism, its object is the application or putting into practice of the optimum relation between the human and the region. Regional planning in short is applied human ecology (MacKaye, 1940, p. 351).

In book after book after book and seemingly innumerable articles, Mumford has voiced what Goist (1972, p. 390) described as the conviction that if humans "do not work toward a world in which the realization of human potential is at least a possibility, they will continue by unconscious choices to bring about an environment divested of life." Ecological planners follow Mumford by working toward conscious choices and environments integrated with human life. For Goist (1972, p. 390), it is Mumford's "holistic or historicist method of understanding our total cultural and physical environment that gives his work its vitality." And, in addition, Mumford (1931, p. 78) joined MacKaye at an early date in mandating that working toward such integration is the task of "human ecology . . . a dynamic interpretation of basic social and economic relationships."

Recent Statements on Ecological Planning

Numerous voices have been raised in recent decades of the twentieth century to advocate an ecological approach to planning. Certainly Mumford and MacKaye should be counted as should other Americans of diverse backgrounds.

One of the most prominent of these was the wildlife biologist and forester Aldo Leopold. Among the best known of his many publications on land use is an early article widely lauded for its extension of human ethics to the land and natural world. More than anything else, however, that particular article is a wise and considered argument for an ecological approach to land-use planning: "ecological reactions [and] conditions circumscribe, delimit, and warp all enterprises, both economic and cultural, that pertain to land" (Leopold, 1933, p. 637). He argued for use of ecological concepts that would allow a "universal symbiosis with land, economic and esthetic, public and private," and asserted strongly that "interactions between man and land are too important to be left to chance," but should be planned and managed with great care (Leopold, 1933, p. 637). Planners, to the degree they utilize ecological concepts, are well placed for the realistic attainment of such goals, to diminish the obstacles to good land use, and to integrate ecological considerations with economic ones. Leopold's words, in such classics as *Sand County Almanac* or *Round River*, were aimed at planners and all of those people who would influence the shaping of the human environment: conservation, good management, and adequate planning mean working toward "a state of harmony between man and land. By land is meant all of the things on, over, or in the earth" (Leopold, 1953, p. 145).

The prolific Odum family has been a significant source of concepts and theory for ecological planning. Howard W. Odum, a sociologist, was a proponent of regionalism and regional planning (cf., H. W. Odum, 1951) and helped to establish the Department of City and Regional Planning at the University of North Carolina (Kantor, 1973). His sons, Howard T. and Eugene, are both well-known biological ecologists who advocate the use of their science in public policy and planning. Howard T. has been involved in modeling energy systems (H. T. Odum, 1971) and has influenced energy management while Eugene Odum (1953) summarized his view of the relationship of ecology to human societies as follows:

> The study of general ecology can contribute to the social sciences through the connecting link of human ecology by emphasizing the natural processes which insure that the rate of flow of materials, food, etc., needed by mankind will be cyclic and adequate. . . . However, we must go beyond the principles of general ecology because human society has several very important characteristics which make the human population unit quantitatively, if not qualitatively, different from all other populations. In the first place, man's flexibility in behavior and his ability to control his surroundings are greater than those of other organisms. In the second place, man develops culture which, except to a very rudimentary extent, is not a factor in any other species. . . . In so doing,

however, it is equally important not to lose sight of man's essential natural environment, which along with his cultural environment determines his ecology (E. Odum, 1953, p. 344).

Beginning in the 1960s and continuing to the present, ecological planning literature has been marked by three significant changes: 1) the literature on ecological planning has proliferated and its sources have become more broadly based, with more and more planners (and scholars from other disciplines) calling for the increased use of ecology in planning; 2) the movement, if it can be called that, has become more explicit, uses language that is more explicitly ecological and more clearly mandates that planning be ecological; and 3) more of the literature is now oriented toward planning as applied human ecology rather than just incorporating bio-ecology concepts into land-use or landscape planning.

Many of the early articles and books on what is now called ecological planning predated the emergence of ecology as a distinct discipline (Marsh, Powell, and Geddes, for instance) and even later works often did not use explicit ecological language. Mumford, for example, seldom used the term "ecology," though many now consider him to be one of the first and greatest of modern ecologists, especially as an urban ecologist or ecological planner. Other giants have emerged from the shadows of Marsh, Powell, and Geddes as ecology has attained new significance in planning. Note the status and influence of, among others, Glikson (1956, 1971; Mumford, 1972), Hills (Hills, 1961; Belknap et al., 1967), and McHarg (see Steinitz, 1970; McHarg, 1978).

Only in recent decades has the literature proliferated, the base broadened, and the language of ecology and planning merged so that the integration of concepts and theory and applications between the two fields is more easily achieved (Young et al., 1983). Cain (1968) and Holling and Goldberg (1971) provide illustrations of statements by bio-ecologists and Giliomee (1977), Travis (1977), and Steiner and Brooks (1981) offer examples of statements by planners. The interdisciplinary journal *Biological Conservation* has been prominent in this ongoing merger (Tubbs and Blackwood, 1971; Dearden, 1978). The trend toward a final synthesis in planning as applied human ecology will be discussed in a later section of this article.

Major Themes and Issues

A number of themes and issues have emerged as ecological planning has developed in the United States and western Europe; many of these ideas were espoused by early members of the Regional Planning Association of America and used on a broad scale during President Franklin D. Roosevelt's New Deal administration. Among these themes and issues are a search for the optimum unit in ecological planning; attempts to clarify the interface between town and country as environments where people can reside; a search for more specificity in the conservation movement, especially towards saving the life-giving soil; a formal acceptance, through legislation, of the multiple-use concept as a management and planning tool; the incorporation of the ideas of sustained yield and carrying capacity into public planning; the acceleration of the movement toward holistic planning; and the recognition of the need to design "with" nature rather than against it.

Unit and Region: The Tennessee Valley Authority

The Tennessee Valley Authority (T.V.A.) stands as one of the most successful examples of planning at a more holistic regional scale, either in the United States or internationally. President Franklin Roosevelt's 1933 message urging approval of the bill authorizing the T.V.A. described it as "national planning" that "should be charged with the broadest duty of planning for the proper use, conservation, and development of the natural resources of the Tennessee River drainage basin and its adjoining territory" (Lilienthal, 1944, p. 52). Roosevelt went on to note that "many hard lessons have taught us the human waste that results from lack of planning" and declared that it is "time to extend planning to a wider field" (Lilienthal, 1944, p. 53). Under this New Deal legislation, a broad plan was proposed for the river basin, an area that covered almost 39,000 square miles in parts of seven states. A semi-independent authority was created to promote the economic and social wellbeing of the people of the entire region. It was a region where rich timber and petroleum resources had been ruthlessly exploited, leaving a derelict landscape and an economically depressed people; this population ranked among the poorest in the United States at the height of the Great Depression. The T.V.A. advocated and continues to stress cooperation among levels of government and the provision of multiple benefits for citizens. To date, the T.V.A. provides the best model for Eugene Odum's (1971) ideal of the use of river basins as the optimum unit for ecological planning.

The 1933 act recognized the potential of water as a basic resource that could be used to revitalize the region. The authority was conceived as having multiple purposes and was granted three broad, basic powers: the control of flooding, the development of navigation, and the production of hydroelectric power. The multiple-use plan was extended beyond the three basic purposes to include reforestation, soil conservation, outdoor recreation, new community building, the retirement of marginal farmland, and the manufacture of fertilizer.

Toward Better Environments: The Town and Country Interface

The idea of a better interface between town and country, in the form of Greenbelt New Towns, to make a more holistic, regional approach to the problem of urban squalor, again was given impetus by those involved in the Regional Planning Association. In this case, the influence came initially from the architects Clarence Stein and Henry Wright. Other influences included Howard's British garden cities proposal, popularized in America by members of the Regional Planning Association, and also the ideas of Patrick Geddes. In addition to a regional approach to overcome urban squalor, the objectives included the provision of employment and housing at a reasonable cost. A solution offered was the establishment of new communities buffered by gardens or green space.

The person most responsible for the Greenbelt New Towns was the New Deal economist Rexford Guy Tugwell who received his education from the University of Pennsylvania and taught at Columbia University and the University of Chicago. As an undersecretary in the Department of Agriculture, Tugwell proposed the Resettlement Administration which developed a comprehensive approach to alleviate the socio-economic problems of rural regions. In less than two years (1935 and 1936) Tugwell's agency planned and constructed three new communities and planned a fourth (Myhra, 1974).

The three new communities that were built include Greenbelt, Maryland, Greenhills, Ohio, and Greendale, Wisconsin (a fourth, Greenbrook, New Jersey, was planned but never built). Tugwell's ideas for these new communities diverged from those of the Regional Planning Association in his unbiased acceptance of the automobile as an element to be affirmatively considered in the planning process. The design of the new communities consisted of low rise, single and multifamily housing units of traditional design, clustered commercial and public facilities, a surrounding greenbelt, and a road network linking the communities to their metropolitan region. Each town had its own interdisciplinary design team consisting of landscape architects, planners, engineers, and architects. Through time, these communities have proved quite popular with their residents and remain an outstanding example of new town planning in America (Miller, 1981).

Soil and Other "Conservations"

It could be claimed that conservation, in all its manifestations, is ecological planning, because it is always an attempt to reestablish a sustainable balance between human demand and the ultimately limited bounty of the earth. To be effective, ecological planning and conservation must both, in some way or another, be applied human ecology. The emergence of concern for soil conservation during the New Deal era is an example. Largely through the efforts of H. H. Bennett, the son of a North Carolina farmer, the Soil Erosion Service was organized in 1933. During the 1930s drought struck the Great Plains and the Dust Bowl resulted. In a dramatic display of the serious consequences of erosion, wind deposited dust landed on the steps of the Capitol Building in Washington, D.C. Bennett (1939) claimed the task of "safeguarding the land" to be the biggest job ever undertaken in human affairs.

In 1935, the Soil Conservation Service (S.C.S.) was established as a permanent agency under the Soil Conservation Act. In the early days of the S.C.S., a multidisciplinary team made up of soil scientists, geologists, engineers, and biologists prepared demonstration conservation plans. This approach is quite similar to the ecological planning advocated by McHarg (1969). As the demand for plans increased the team approach was not practical because of the costs involved. Specialists, known as soil conservationists, now receive multidisciplinary training to develop the many skills necessary for conservation planning. After an eighteen-month apprenticeship with S.C.S., these conservationists respond to requests from land users for technical assistance.

A unique part of the operations of the S.C.S. is the use of a system of locally elected conservation district boards responsible for soil and water conservation policy in almost every county of the United States. These districts receive technical assistance locally from professional conservationists who assist individual land users to prepare conservation plans. Currently, conservation districts have been organized in areas that encompass over 97 percent of the agricultural land in the United States.

Multiple Use and Sustained Yield

After auspicious beginnings during the New Deal era, ecological planning languished in the post–World War II period and needed the environmental movement of the 1960s to kindle a renaissance. An exception to this was the passage of the Multiple Use–Sustained Yield Act of 1960, which mandated the U.S. Forest Service to recognize 1) the diversity and ecosystemic characteristics of lands in the National Forest system, and 2) the need to regulate the resource yields of these lands in a way that could be sustained. The public forests of the United States had become producer systems for American lumber (on timbered lands) and livestock (on range lands) interests. The Multiple Use–Sustained Yield Act mandated long-range planning in a holistic way and that was cognizant of the nature of the land and environment and of the variety of human uses of those lands.

In 1976, a similar act (the Federal Land Policy and Management Act) established the same mandate for lands managed by the U.S. Bureau of Land

Management. Furthermore, this act called for use of a systematic, interdisciplinary approach to achieve integrated consideration of biological, physical, economic, and other sciences, and to protect areas of critical environmental concern.

Two acts, the Forest and Rangeland Renewable Resources Act of 1974 and the National Forest Management Act of 1976, called for plans and practices to protect soils, slopes, watersheds, watercourses, and fish habitat. These laws were initiated and passed in response to public objections about clear-cutting practices on national forests. As a result of this legislation, the U.S. Forest Service has established a system for land and resource management planning that directs each regional forester to develop a regional plan. Development of the plan must follow a specific process that includes: establishment of planning criteria; inventory of data and collection of information; analysis of the forest's management situation; formulation of alternatives; evaluation of the alternatives; selection of an alternative; implementation of the plan; and the ongoing monitoring and evaluation of the plan. An interdisciplinary team approach is used to develop these plans; the team is charged with the task of integrating ecological information into the planning process. By whatever label it receives, this is a congressionally mandated, agency-centered application of the McHargian method of ecological planning.

Holistic, Comprehensive Planning

The T.V.A., regional new towns, and multiple use planning—mandated in scope for at least a ranger district or a national forest unit—are all examples of progress toward the ecological ideal of holistic planning. The environmental movement of the 1960s did kindle a resurgence of interest in environmental management and better planning—i.e., ecological planning—though some of the legislation did precede this rise in consciousness. Part of the resurgence was a spate of environmental legislation that did call, explicitly or implicitly, for ecological approaches in planning. The National Environmental Policy Act (N.E.P.A.) of 1969 set the stage for much of the legislation that followed. That same year, McHarg's (1969) *Design With Nature* established an ecological framework for program and project implementation. The requirements of N.E.P.A. forced federal officials to consider the environmental consequences of agency projects *before acting* and called for interdisciplinary analytical approaches to environmental management and planning. The act required all agencies of the federal government to "initiate and utilize ecological information in the planning and development of resource-oriented projects" (N.E.P.A., Sec. 102, 2, h). Other recent examples that grew out of this increasing awareness and work such as McHarg's include the Coastal Zone Management Act of 1972; the California Coastal Commission: the Land Conservation and Development Commission (L.C.D.C.), which, initiated by the Oregon Legislature in 1973, mandated state-wide planning; and state coordination of planning for the New Jersey Pinelands.

The Coastal Zone Management Act of 1972 called for consideration of environmental, economic, and aesthetic values in the development of management plans. The act also provided for the protection of significant estuaries. A number of participating states adopted resource inventory and suitability analysis techniques similar to those advocated by McHarg.

The California Coastal Commission was established by a citizen initiative, also in 1972. The commission is responsible for coastal policy and regulation. Under its aegis extensive ecological inventories have been conducted of the state's shoreline with the inventories then used in the commission's regulatory functions. The commission is also involved in agricultural land protection efforts. Under state statute it may "acquire fee title, development rights, easements, and other interests in land located in the coastal zone in order to prevent loss of agricultural land to other uses" (Little, 1984, p. 134).

The state legislature in Oregon created the Land Conservation and Development Commission to establish planning goals with which every city and county plan, zoning ordinance, and subdivision regulation in the state must comply. Nineteen state-wide planning goals established policy for citizen involvement; the protection of agricultural, forest and natural resource lands; the protection against or elimination of natural hazards; the creation of adequate housing; the monitoring of urban growth; and the management of critical coastal zones (Eber, 1984). State law requires that localities conduct extensive inventories for each of these goals.

The Oregon effort has been generally recognized as a success. The program enjoys wide public support, as is evidenced by the overwhelming vote by the citizens of Oregon opposing four attempts to repeal the law. According to De-Grove (1984, p. 290), "Oregon's growth-management law has come through a 'trial by fire' and seems destined to gain strength as the state moves through the 1980s."

Design with Nature

The method outlined in *Design with Nature* and the case studies McHarg (1969) presented on such topics as coastal zone management, metropolitan open space, farmlands protection, highway alignment, and other issues helped to frame planning issues for the next two decades. That frame depended on a kind of ecological determinism, but one that did mandate consideration of nature in place and examination of the totality in that place, a comprehensive or holistic approach. Among the ecological success stories that can be traced to these issues are the New Jersey Pinelands Commission and the Woodlands New Community (as well as the California Coastal Commission and Oregon's Land Conservation and Development Commission already discussed).

The New Jersey Pinelands is a million-acre (405,000 hectares) area with unique landscape qualities in the midst of the most densely populated region of the United States. The plan for the area derives from the designation by the U.S. Congress, in 1978, of the Pinelands as a national reserve, and the passage, in 1979, of the Pinelands Protection Act by the New Jersey Legislature. To comply with these laws, the Pinelands Planning Commission was established by New Jersey Governor Brendan T. Byrne. This commission is responsible for coordinating the planning efforts of local, state and national governments (Pinelands Commission, 1980).

The Comprehensive Management Plan developed for the region by this commission includes such techniques and strategies as a natural resource assessment; an assessment of scenic, aesthetic, cultural, open space, and outdoor recreational resources; a land-use capability map; a comprehensive statement of land-use and management policies; a financial analysis; a program to ensure local government and public participation in the planning process; and a program to put the plan into effect (Pinelands Commission, 1980). The Pinelands plan has been successful in managing growth in the region. However, the effort has been controversial. Berger and Sinton (1984) have been especially critical of the insensitivity of planners to local values. They note that "some areas are overly regulated, while others become the dumping grounds for future development. There is a sense that the plan does not fit the place" (Berger and Sinton, 1984, p. 22). The Pinelands process is an evolving one, however, and is capable of overcoming its initial shortcomings.

The Woodlands, a new community located in Texas, was planned and designed by McHarg and his colleagues (in the consulting firm Wallace, McHarg, Roberts, and Todd; now Wallace, Roberts and Todd). The planning of the Woodlands is noteworthy for its success and for the utilization of an interdisciplinary planning and design team. An ecological inventory and land-use suitability analysis was completed by a team of planners, landscape architects, ecologists, and geologists. These studies were then used in conjunction with market research to develop a master plan and siting criteria for the new town. The Woodlands has been an economic and environmental success and has become a desirable place for people to live (Spirn, 1984).

The Needed Synthesis: Planning as Applied Human Ecology

To the degree that planning is concerned with the interrelationships of an organism to its environment, it is ecological. Because the organism of primary concern is human, planning is human ecology. To redefine ecological planning then, it is application of ecological concepts, an ecological approach, to the ordering of the human environment. Planning is, in its ultimate expression, *applied human ecology* as MacKaye, Mumford, and Eugene Odum all suggested. Since organism/environment concerns are central to planning, it is unfortunate, and sometimes disastrous, when planners lack training in ecology or do not think in ecological terms. Ecological synthesis is essential to the fundamental purposes of planning.

To this point, this article has traced the progress of planning toward the acceptance of ecological concerns and concepts as central to the field—and there has been progress. At the turn of the century, there were a few giants in the field. Today, there still are giants, though perhaps of lesser stature, and dozens of planners are writing about ecological planning and probably many more practitioners are actually putting ecological ideas into operation.

The trends and patterns from this century of work should be more than evident just from the discussion in this paper: ecological planning is 1) concerned with the character of land and environment and of the natural inhabitants thereon; 2) at its best is holistic, expressed, for example, in its application in a comprehensive way at the regional level; 3) indicates awareness of the need to integrate human activities with place and environment; 4) is interdisciplinary, recognizing that no single discipline is capable of comprehending or ordering all the elements of person-place complexities; and 5) in its final expression or ordering is applied human ecology.

None of this is perfected nor can planners expect it ever to be. But the effort is there and it is quickening as evidenced by the hundred years of progress and the dramatically increased attention to ecological planning that has emerged in the literature of the last three decades or so. Planning as applied human ecology is receiving much of this attention—in the literature, in the curricula of several graduate schools or departments of planning, and in practice.

The conviction that planning must be, at least to some degree, applied human ecology was certainly present in Geddes' writing and in the garden city movement (which was designing communities, in place, for human beings). McHarg (1981), influenced by Geddes, has recently summarized his approach as "human ecological planning." Most calls for planning as applied human ecology have come from McHarg, his former students, or individuals influenced by McHarg's work and writings (cf., Berger, 1978; Rose, 1979; Jackson and Steiner,

1985; Young et al., 1983). McHarg's approach has had the strongest influence on the modern shift to planning, first as ecological planning and then as applied human ecology (Young, 1974).

Human ecological planning has emerged during the past three decades from the work of McHarg and his colleagues in the Department of Landscape Architecture and Regional Planning at the University of Pennsylvania (cf., McHarg, 1966, 1969, 1981; Giliomee, 1977; Steiner and Brooks, 1981; Johnson, 1982; Koh, 1982; University of Pennsylvania, 1985; Zube, 1986). The main setting for ecological planning instruction at Pennsylvania has been the studio. The studio was largely abandoned in American planning education during the 1960s, but was retained at Pennsylvania in regional planning, as well as in city planning and urban design. As Lang (1983, p. 128) notes, the studio/workshop format involves "learning by doing" and should not only be retained but emphasized in an applied field like planning.

One approach to human ecological planning has evolved from a one semester graduate studio offered at Pennsylvania. This is the only course taken during the introductory semester and is required for both landscape architecture and regional planning students; it requires a full-time commitment. The course is arranged in a series of topical modules including climatology, geology, geomorphology, hydrology, soils, plant ecology, wildlife ecology, human ecology, aerial photography, computation, graphics, and suitability analysis. This course provides a common core of knowledge, albeit introductory, for students from diverse disciplines. The challenge is to provide an adequate common educational foundation in critical content areas for all students in the area of specialization (Zube, 1986b).

The course is also a direct expression of the need for multidisciplinary involvement in human ecological planning. The school catalogue lists nine instructors representing various natural and social sciences, planning professionals, and specialists in inventory and analysis methods. Topics introduced in this modular course are reinforced in subsequent studio and field courses.

Ecology and anthropology are cornerstones of the curriculum. Students are required to have field ecology experience, as well as classroom instruction in the science. They are also required to develop skills in social methods for design and planning. The integration of bio-physical and socio-cultural inventory and analysis is emphasized throughout the curriculum and particularly in the subsequent studio courses. Problems offered in the studios vary from having equal emphasis on ecological and social issues to either one being emphasized over the other (Zube, 1986b). The curriculum at Pennsylvania is similar to that at many other institutions with environmental planning programs. What is different at Pennsylvania, however, is that McHarg has advanced well beyond his theoretical-methodological conceptualization of 1969 and has responded to criticisms raised at that time (Krieger and Litton, 1971). He has developed a theory of human ecological planning that is central to the curriculum and its content. McHarg has summarized this theory as:

> All systems aspire to survival and success. This state can be described as syntropic-fitness-health. Its antithesis is entropic-misfitness-morbidity. To achieve the first state requires systems to find the fittest environment, adapt it and themselves. Fitness of an environment for a system is defined as that requiring the minimum work of adaptation. Fitness and fitting are indications of health and the process of fitting is health giving. The quest for fitness is entitled adaptation. Of all the instrumentalities available to man for successful adaptation, cultural adaptation in general and planning in particular, appear to be the most efficious for maintaining and enhancing human health and well-being (McHarg, 1981, pp. 112–113).

Planning as the real-world application of the principles of human ecology has been successful if erratic. Concepts and theory in the literature are becoming more sophisticated and are achieving a more satisfactory interdisciplinary synthesis. Education in human ecological planning is spreading in influence, especially as graduates from the Department of Landscape Architecture and Regional Planning of the University of Pennsylvania become more prominent. Certainly the consciousness of planners to the intricacies and complexities of satisfactorily fitting humans into and with a variety of physical and built environments has been raised (at least for those who involve themselves with the professional literature in the field and for those who have graduated from Pennsylvania or come under the influence of those who have).

But the classroom and the journal or book are not the field. There, in the field, demonstrated successes have been fewer. There are examples of partial successes, such as the T.V.A., the Woodlands, and others briefly described in these pages—mostly at the state or federal level. But, it is difficult to assess how much good human ecological planning takes place at those levels where planners traditionally work, namely in established cities and in the counties in the United States. Other countries have been somewhat more successful, but even in places like western Europe the record is uneven and erratic. Numerous questions remain in concept, in theory, and in practice.

Prospectus: On Ecological Fitting

The central questions for ecological planners can be summarized as Orians (1980, p. 79) did for biological ecology: "Ecology shares with all sciences the difficult problems associated with moving from micro-analysis to macro-analysis of complex systems." The same challenge noted by Orians, that of building "conceptual bridges between micro- and macro-ecology" is shared by planners: it is one thing to claim that human ecological planning must be holistic and quite another thing to be successful in fitting innumerable elements into a complex whole. Many problems are incorporated into this one large problem: the relationships between individual and community, between neighborhood and city, between city and region, and between humans and environment. These are questions of integration, of fitness.

Planners seldom work at the level of the individual, but their ordering of the human environment may ultimately determine how successfully individuals are accommodated into that environment. Accommodating the variety of individuals and then fitting the plan to the place seems to be the challenge and the promise of human ecological planning. Planners must "consult the genius of the place" as Alexander Pope advised in the 18th century, but in the process they must follow McHarg's lead in moving from determinism to human ecological planning. Fit depends on human adaptation of and to place: planning is a means for achieving such a fit.

Humans have changed very little, biologically, over the past ten thousand or so years. But, through changes in culture and technology, they have spread to almost every place on earth, whether marvelous or miserable. Humans are profound examples of Dan Janzen's (1985, p. 310) suggestion that "a species does not have to evolve in a habitat in order to participate in the interactions in that habitat. Widespread species are not adapted to their habitats, they just are." Rather than plan, in too many places we plunk down and "just are." As Leopold (1933) so aptly put it:

> We inherit the earth, but ... we also rebuild the earth,—without plan, without knowledge of its properties, and without understanding of the increasingly coarse and powerful tools which science has placed at our disposal. We are remodeling the Alhambra with a steam shovel (Leopold, 1933, p. 637)

Our unplanned, uncoordinated, and extensive alterations of the land are done in reference only to ourselves, without reference to others even of our own kind, and certainly too often without consideration of other kinds or the environments in which they live. Such callousness and indifference can result in a habitat that is unfit for ourselves, as Marsh, Powell, Mumford, Leopold, and so many others have warned, as well as one that is unfit for other humans and other species.

Though over-emphasized in the United States, individual fitness is an appropriate ecological goal, an ongoing struggle for every human in every culture and environment on earth. But, that goal alone is incomplete, uncoordinated, short term, and narrowly based: out of context, it is probably unachievable. Individual fitness must be viewed in the larger perspective of fitness of the part with the whole, of the whole and the part, with the understanding that individuals exist in the context of other individuals, other groups, other species, and the environment: no part can function separate from the whole. Recognizing, and acting upon, the need to reconnect and integrate—to plan ecologically—is a challenge in the daily lives of all people everywhere. It is the challenge for planners working toward a future that is secure by achieving a sustainable fit between humans and environment.

References

Belknap, R. K., and J. Furato. *Three Approaches to Environmental Resource Analysis*. Washington, DC: The Conservation Foundation, 1967.

Bennett, Hugh Hammond. *Soil Conservation*. New York: McGraw-Hill, 1939.

Berger, Jonathan, and John W. Sinton. *Water, Earth, and Fire*. Baltimore, MD: The Johns Hopkins University Press, 1984.

Berger, Jonathan. "Toward an Applied Human Ecology for Landscape Architecture and Regional Planning." *Human Ecology* 6, no. 2 (1978): 179–99.

Boyer, Christine M. *Dreaming the Rational City*. Cambridge, MA: MIT Press, 1983.

Cain, Stanley A. "The Importance of Ecological Studies as a Basis for Land-Use Planning." *Biological Conservation* 1, no. 1 (1968): 33–36.

Dearden, Philip. "The Ecological Component in Land Use Planning: A Conceptual Framework." *Biological Conservation* 14, no. 3 (1978): 167–79.

DeGrove, John Melvin. *Land, Growth & Politics*. Chicago: The Planners Press, 1984.

Eber, Ronald. "Oregon's Agricultural Land Protection Program." In *Protecting Farmlands*, edited by Frederick Steiner and John Theilacker, 161–71. Westport, CT: AVI Publishing Company, 1984.

Geddes, Patrick. *Cities in Evolution*. New York: Howard Fertig, 1968.

———. "Civics as Applied Sociology." In *The Ideal City*, edited by Helen E. Meller. Leicester, England: Leicester University Press, 1979.

Giliomee, J. H. "Ecological Planning: Method and Evaluation." *Landscape Planning* 4 (1977): 185–91.

Glikson, Artur. "Notes on Landscape Planning and Ecology." In *Proceedings and Papers, Sixth Technical Meeting of the International Union for the Conservation of Nature and Natural Resources*. Edinburgh, Scotland: Food and Agriculture Organization, 1956.

———. *The Ecological Basis of Planning*. Edited by Lewis Mumford. The Hague, Netherlands: Martinus Nijhoff, 1971.

Goist, Park Dixon. "Seeing Things Whole: A Consideration of Lewis Mumford." *Journal of the American Institute of Planners* 38, no. 6 (1972): 379–91.

Hills, G. Angus. *The Ecological Basis for Land-use Planning*. Ottawa, Canada: Ontario Department of Lands and Forests, Research Branch, 1961.

Holling, Crawford S., and Michael Arthur Goldberg. "Ecology and Planning." *Journal of the American Institute of Planners* 37, no. 4 (1971): 221–30.

Howard, Ebenezer. *Garden Cities of Tomorrow*. London: S. Sonnenschein & Company, Limited, 1902.

Jackson, Joanne Barnes, and Frederick Steiner. "Human Ecology for Land-use Planning." *Urban Ecology* 9, no. 2 (1985): 177–94.

Jenzen, Daniel H. "Dan Janzen's Thoughts from The Tropics 1: On Ecological Fitting." *Oikos* 45, no. 3 (1985): 308–10.

Johnson, Arthur H., ed. "Human Ecological Planning." *Landscape Planning* 8, no. 2 (1982): 105–234.

Kantor, Harvey A. "Howard W. Odum: The Implications of Folk, Planning, and Regionalism." *American Journal of Sociology* 79, no. 2 (1973): 278–95.

Kitchen, Paddy. *A Most Unsettling Person: The Life and Ideas of Patrick Geddes, Founding Father of City Planning and Environmentalism.* New York: Saturday Review Press, 1975.

Koh, Jusuck. "Ecological Design: A Post-Modern Design Paradigm of Holistic Philosophy and Evolutionary Ethic." *Landscape Journal* 1, no. 2 (1982): 76–84.

Kraenzel, Carl Frederick. *The Great Plains in Transition.* Norman, OK: University of Oklahoma Press, 1955.

Krieger, Martin, and Burton Litton. "Design with Nature by Ian McHarg" (book review). *Journal of the American Institute of Planners* 37, no. 1 (1971): 50–52.

Lang, Jon. "Teaching Planning to City Planning Students: An Argument for the Studio/Workshop Approach." *Journal of Planning Education and Research* 2, no. 2 (1983): 122–29.

Leopold, Aldo. "The Conservation Ethic." *Journal of Forestry* 31, no. 6 (1933): 634–43.

———. *Round River: From the Journals of Aldo Leopold.* Edited by Luna B. Leopold. Illustrated by Charles W. Schwartz. New York: Oxford University Press, 1953.

Lilienthal, David Eli. *TVA: Democracy on the March.* Westport, CT: Greenwood Press, 1944.

Little, Charles E. "Farmland Conservancies: A Middleground Approach." In *Protecting Farmlands,* 131–45. Westport, CT: AVI Publishing, 1984.

MacKaye, Benton. "Regional Planning and Ecology." *Ecological Monographs* 10, no. 3 (1940): 349–53.

Marsh, George Perkins. *Man and Nature: Physical Geography as Modified by Human Action.* New York: Charles Scribner, 1865.

McHarg, Ian L. "Ecological Planning: The Planner as Catalyst." In *Planning Theory: A Search for Future Directions.* New Brunswick, NJ: Rutgers University, 1978.

———. "Human Ecological Planning at Pennsylvania." *Landscape Planning* 8, no. 2 (1981): 109–120.

———. "Ecological Determinism" In *Future Environments of North America,* edited by Fraser Darling and John Milton. Garden City, NY: The Natural History Press, 1966.

McHarg, Ian L., and Lewis Mumford. *Design with Nature.* New York: American Museum of Natural History, 1969.

Miller, Zane L. *Suburb: Neighborhood and Community in Forest Park, Ohio, 1935–1976.* Knoxville: University of Tennessee Press, 1981.

Mumford, Lewis. "Artur Glikson: The Planner as Ecologist." *Journal of the American Institute of Planners* 38, no. 1 (1972): 3–10.

———. *The Brown Decades.* New York: Harcourt, Brace and Company, 1931.

Myhra, David. "Rexford Guy Tugwell: Initiator of America's Greenbelt New Towns, 1935–1936." *Journal of the American Institute of Planners* 40, no. 3 (1974): 176–87.

Odum, Eugene. *Fundamentals of Ecology.* Philadelphia, PA: W.B. Saunders Company, 1971.

Odum, Howard T. *Environment, Power, and Society.* New York: Wiley-Interscience, 1971.

Odum, Howard W. "The Promise of Regionalism." In *Regionalism in America,* edited by Merrill Jensen. Madison, WI: University of Wisconsin Press, 1965.

Orians, Gordon H. "Micro and Macro in Ecological Theory." *BioScience* 30, no. 2 (1980): 79.

Pinelands Commission. *New Jersey Pinelands Comprehensive Management Plan.* New Jersey Pinelands Commission, New Lisbon, NJ: The Commission, 1980.

Powell, John W. *Report on the Lands of the Arid Region of the United States.* With Maps. Vol. 3. Washington, DC: Government Printing Office, 1879.

Rose, Dan, Frederick Steiner, and Joanne Jackson. "An Applied Human Ecological Approach to Regional Planning." *Landscape Planning* 5, no. 4 (1979): 241–61.

Spirn, Anne W. *The Granite Garden: Urban Nature and Human Design*. New York: Basic Books, 1984.

Steiner, Frederick, and Kenneth Brooks. "Ecological Planning: A Review." *Environmental Management* 5, no. 6 (1981): 495–505.

Steinitz, Carl. *A Comparative Study of Resource Analysis Methods*. Cambridge, MA: Research Office, Department of Landscape Architecture, Graduate School of Design, Harvard University, 1970.

Travis, Anthony S. "Planning as Applied Ecology: The Management of Alternative Futures." *Town Planning Review* 48, no. 1 (1977): 5–16.

Tubbs, C. R., and J. W. Blackwood. "Ecological Evaluation of Land for Planning Purposes." *Biological Conservation* 3, no. 3 (1971): 169–72.

University of Pennsylvania. *Landscape Architecture and Regional Planning 501 Course Primer*. Philadelphia: Department of Landscape Architecture and Regional Planning, University of Pennsylvania, 1985.

Young, Gerald L. "Human Ecology as an Interdisciplinary Concept: A Critical Inquiry." *Advances in Ecological Research* 8 (1974): 1–105.

Young, Gerald L., ed. *Origins of Human Ecology*. Vol. 12. Stroudsburg, PA: Hutchinson Ross Pub. Co., 1983.

Young, Gerald, Frederick Steiner, Kenneth Brooks, and Kenneth Struckmeyer. "Determining the Regional Context for Landscape Planning." *Landscape Planning* 10, no. 4 (1983): 269–96.

Zube, Ervin H. "Landscape Planning Education in America: Retrospect and Prospect." *Landscape Planning* 13 (1986): 367–78.

———. "The Advance of Ecology." *Landscape Architecture* 76, no. 2 (1986): 58–67.

Part Two
Ethical Foundations

Introduction to Part Two

The harmony and conflict in interactions people have with the landscape is a reflection of their changing values, moral rules of conduct, ethical positions, and attitudes toward the land. The primary themes examined in the five essays in this section are ways in which people relate to the landscape, the ethical positions they hold, their obligations in subscribing to these positions, and the ways in which these positions and obligations should guide their response to pervasive ecological concerns.

In the first reading, "Man and the Environment," published in *The Urban Condition* (1963, 1998),[1] noted landscape architect and planner Ian McHarg provides an insightful historical synthesis of mankind's relations with the environment, illuminating the duality that exists in these relations. McHarg concluded the article by making a powerful case for the recognition and adoption of an "Ecological View." This is characterized by an intricate interdependency between man and nature, in which the survival of man depends on the continued existence of other organisms in our biophysical world. He argued persuasively that if man subscribes to an interdependent view in his relations with nature, then "he will have learned that when he destroys, he also destroys himself; that when he creates, he also adds to himself."[2] Interdependence, therefore, is the basis for survival.

In "The Land Ethic," by the forester and wildlife biologist Aldo Leopold, published in his highly influential book A *Sand County Almanac*, in 1949,[3] he laid the foundation for the ethical basis of people's relation to the land—the land ethic. He rejected the American utilitarian approach to resource conservation based solely on economic self-interest. He contended that it "is hopelessly lopsided. It tends to ignore, and thus eventually to eliminate, many elements of the land community that lack economic value, but they are (as far as we know) essential to its healthy functioning."[4] He further asserted that this type of conservation "defines no right or wrong, assigns no obligation, calls for no sacrifice, implies no change in the current philosophy of values."[5] Leopold argued that there are right and wrong ways of behaving toward the land that go beyond mere exchanges and privileges to include moral responsibilities and obligations. He concluded, "A thing is right when it tends to preserve the *integrity, stability, and beauty* of the biotic community. It is wrong when it tends otherwise."[6]

Next, American biologist Rachael Carson's (1907–1964) astonishing essay "Obligation to Endure," in the 1962 classic *Silent Spring*,[7] alerted us to the far-reaching detrimental effects of pesticides on ecosystems. Supported by substantial data, she demonstrated that these effects spread beyond the target pest and damage broad ecosystems within which humans live. She alerted the world that the trend regarding human abuse of the landscape was unsustainable. Carson further contended that the general public must decide whether it wished to continue along this destructive pathway, but only after obtaining all of the relevant facts. She concluded the chapter by reminding us of the words of Jean Rostand, "The obligation to endure gives us the right to know."[8]

Carson was the force of reason in asserting that we have ethical responsibilities and moral obligations to protect the environment. The first publication of her book in 1962 is widely acknowledged as the beginning of the American environmental movement, which ultimately led to the passage of the first major environmental legislation in the United States. The National Environmental Policy Act of November 1969 was signed into law by President Richard Nixon on January 1, 1970.

The article by planner Timothy Beatley, "Ethical Duties to the Environment," in *Ethical Land Use: Principles of Policy and Planning* (1994),[9] explores the value of natural areas in human life and investigates the viability of adopting a non-anthropocentric land-use ethic by extending the moral community to embrace other life forms. He contended in an uncompromising fashion that we [people] have undeniable ethical obligations to protect natural areas, and that nature, including sentient (organisms that feel pain) and non-sentient life forms have an inherent value that deserves protection. He concluded that the ethical obligations we hold have substantial ramifications for how we balance human use with ecological concerns.

The last reading by environmental philosopher J. Baird Callicott, "Whither Conservation Ethics?," in *Beyond the Land Ethic: More Essays in Environmental Philosophy* (1999),[10] provides a summation of the American conservation ethic as a context for his enlightening exploration of the moral standard for conservation in the future. Callicott is the leading authority on the scholarly works and contributions of Aldo Leopold. Callicott alerted us that as we encounter deepening environmental challenges, we should be reminded that Aldo Leopold was emphatic in his view of conservation, that we should "ensure the continued functioning of natural processes and the integrity of natural systems. For it is upon these, ultimately, that human resources and human well-being depend."[11] In closing, he argued that economic interests will continue to be pervasive as we seek to sustainably balance human use with ecological concerns.

One consistent theme among the nineteenth-century visionary thinkers (Catlin, Emerson, Thoreau, and Marsh) and the authors of the readings presented here (Ian McHarg, Aldo Leopold, Rachel Carson, Timothy Beatley, and J. Baird Callicott) is an unequivocal consensus that people are intricately interdependent on their biological and physical environments. Disturbance in one component of the system affects the rest. This interdependence suggests specific ethical positions related to how we ought to behave toward the land. There are variations, even within similar positions. It is our responsibility to make explicit the differences in our ethical positions when they occur. Variations of these coexist today and will probably continue to do so in the future. Establishing priorities in reconciling competing positions will become increasingly important. The priorities we set hold substantial implications on how to sustainably balance human use and ecological concerns.

In *The Future of Life* (2002), the prominent biologist, bio-sociologist, and writer Edward O. Wilson summarized three potential types of ethical choices and inalienable rights to which people subscribe.[12] These are (1) *anthropocentrism*, in which the intrinsic rights of humanity are primary; (2) *pathocentrism*, in which intrinsic rights are extended to sentient organisms that have feelings; and (3) *biocentrism*, in which intrinsic rights are extended to all organisms. Wilson acknowledged that these rights and choices often conflict in the real world and offered a solution. When it is a matter of life and death, the priority in resolving these conflicts should occur in the following sequence: humanity, intelligent animals, and other life forms. Wilson's ideas, along with similar ideas proposed by others, reflect the type of purposeful thinking essential to balancing human needs with environmental concerns.

Lastly, human impacts may lead to serious environmental degradation despite our "best" efforts to prevent it. Discussions and actions on how best to restore degraded landscapes will continue to be important in the future. Many, including Timothy Beatley, have recommended ethical directions essential to restoring degraded landscapes. For a survey of the full spectrum of approaches in the field of environmental ethics by a renowned environmental ethicist and philosopher, see *A New Environmental Ethics: The Next Millennium for Life on Earth*, by Rolstom Holmes III.[13]

Notes

1. Ian McHarg, "Man and the Environment," in *The Urban Condition*, Leonard Dahl and John Powell (eds.), (New York: Basic Books, 1963), 44–58. McHarg, Ian L., *To Heal the Earth*, F. Steiner (ed.), (Washington, DC: Island Press, 1998), 10–23.
2. Ibid., 13.
3. Aldo Leopold, "The Land Ethic," in *A Sand County Almanac, and Sketches Here and There* (New York: Oxford University Press, 1949).
4. Aldo Leopold, "The Land Ethic," 179.
5. Ibid., 173.
6. Ibid., 189.
7. Rachel Carson, "The Obligation to Endure," in *Silent Spring* (Boston: Houghton Mifflin, 1962).
8. Ibid., 13.
9. Timothy Beatley, *Ethical Land Use: Principles of Policy and Planning* (Baltimore: Johns Hopkins University Press, 1994).
10. J. Baird Callicott, "Whither Conservation Ethics?" in *Beyond the Land Ethic: More Essays in Environmental Philosophy* (Albany: State University of New York Press, 1999).
11. Ibid., 326.
12. E. O. Wilson, *The Future of Life* (New York: Vintage Books, 2002).
13. Rolstom Holmes III, *A New Environmental Ethics: The Next Millennium for Life on Earth* (New York: Routledge, 2012).

Man and the Environment
The Urban Condition (1963)

Ian McHarg, with introduction by
Frederick Steiner

Ian McHarg considered the writing of this paper, published in The Urban
Condition *edited by Leonard Duhl, as "a threshold in my professional life
and . . . the first summation of my perception and intentions." It began
when McHarg was invited by Duhl to join his Committee on Environmental Variables and Mental Health. Duhl, a medical doctor, was director
of research for the National Institute of Mental Health. He selected the
members of the committee, which included Herbert Gans, J. B. Jackson, and
Melvin Webber.*

*For McHarg, the paper represented a "tremendous leap in scale." He
changed his focus from small-scale urban concerns to a larger regional
vision. He wrote "Man and Environment" at the time when he was organizing his* The House We Live In *television program for CBS. The influence
of the guests from that program is evident in this paper. Not only did the
scale of McHarg's concerns change, but also the nature of his audience.
Prior to 1962, his lectures outside of Penn had been limited to state associations of garden clubs, where he agreed to devote half his speech to
garden design history if he could spend the other half speaking about the
environment. This paper is a "coming out," where the half garden designer
is shed for the complete environmentalist. It was, according to McHarg,*

"my most embracing address on the subject of the environment to that point." (McHarg and Steiner, 1998, p. 10)

The nature and scale of this enquiry can be simply introduced through an image conceived by Loren Eiseley. Man, far out in space, looks back to the distant earth, a celestial orb, blue-green oceans, green of verdant land, a celestial fruit. Examination discloses blemishes on the fruit, dispersed circles from which extend dynamic tentacles. The man concludes that these cankers are the works of man and asks, "Is man but a planetary disease?"

There are at least two conceptions within this image. Perhaps the most important is the view of a unity of life covering the earth, land and oceans, interacting as a single superorganism, the biosphere. A direct analogy can be found in man, composed of billion upon billion of cells, but all of these operating as a single organism. From this the full relevance of the second conception emerges, the possibility that man is but a dispersed disease in the world-life body.

The conception of all life interacting as a single superorganism is as novel as is the conception of man as a planetary disease. The suggestion of man the destroyer, or rather brain the destroyer, is salutary to society which has traditionally abstracted brain from body, man from nature, and vaunted the rational process. This, too, is a recent view. Yet the problems are only of yesterday. Pre-atomic man was an inconsequential geological, biological, and ecological force; his major power was the threat of power. Now, in an instant, post-atomic man is the agent of evolutionary regression, a species now empowered to destroy all life.

In the history of human development, man has long been puny in the face of overwhelmingly powerful nature. His religions, philosophies, ethics, and acts have tended to reflect a slave mentality, alternately submissive or arrogant toward nature. Judaism, Christianity, Humanism tend to assert outrageously the separateness and dominance of man over nature, while animism and nature worship tend to assert total submission to an arbitrary nature. These attitudes are not urgent when human societies lack the power to make any serious impact on environment. These same attitudes become of first importance when man holds the power to cause evolutionary regressions of unimaginable effect or even to destroy all life.

Modern man is confronted with the awful problem of comprehending the role of man in nature. He must immediately find a *modus vivendi*, he must seek beyond for his role in nature, a role of unlimited potential yet governed by laws which he shares with all physical and organic systems. The primacy of man today is based more upon his power to destroy than to create. He is like an aboriginal, confronted with the necessity of operating a vast and complex machine, whose only tool is a hammer. Can modern man aspire to the role of agent in creation, creative participant in a total, unitary, evolving environment? If the pre-atomic past is dominated by the refinement of concern for man's acts towards man, the inauguration of the atomic age increases the dimension of this ancient concern and now adds the new and urgent necessity of understanding and resolving the interdependence of man and nature.

While the atomic threat overwhelms all other considerations, this is by no means the only specter. The population implosion may well be as cataclysmic as the nuclear explosion. Should both of these threats be averted there remain the lesser processes of destruction which have gathered momentum since the nineteenth century. In this period we have seen the despoliation of continental resources accumulated over aeons of geological time, primeval forests destroyed, ancient resources of soil mined and sped to the sea, marching deserts, great deposits of fossil fuel dissipated into the atmosphere. In the country, man has ravaged nature; in the city, nature has been erased and man assaults man with insalubrity, ugliness, and disorder. In short, man has evolved and proliferated by exploiting historic accumulations of inert and organic resources, historic climaxes of plants and animals. His products are reserved for himself, his mark on the environment is most often despoliation and wreckage.

The Duality of Man and Nature

Conceptions of man and nature range between two wide extremes. The first, central to the Western tradition, is man-oriented. The cosmos is but a pyramid erected to support man on its pinnacle, reality exists only because man can observe it, indeed God is made in the image of man. The opposing view, identified with the Orient, postulates a unitary and all-encompassing nature within which man exists, man in nature.

These opposing views are the central duality, man and nature, West and East, white and black, brains and testicles, Classicism and Romanticism, orthodoxy and transnaturalism in Judaism, St. Thomas and St. Francis, Calvin and Luther, anthropomorphism and naturalism. The Western tradition vaunts the individual and the man-brain, and denigrates nature, animal, non-brain. In the Orient nature is omnipotent, revered, and man is but an aspect of nature. It would be as unwise to deny the affirmative aspects of either view as to diminish their negative effects. Yet today this duality demands urgent attention. The adequacy of the Western view of man and nature deserves to be questioned. Further, one must ask if these two views are mutually exclusive.

The opposition of these attitudes is itself testimony to an underlying unity, the unity of opposites. Do our defining skin and nerve ends divide us from environment or unite us to it? Is the perfectibility of man self-realizable? Is the earth a storeroom awaiting plunder? Is the cosmos a pyramid erected to support man?

The inheritors of the Judaic-Christian-Humanist tradition have received their injunction from Genesis, a man-oriented universe, man exclusively made in the image of God, given dominion over all life and non-life, enjoined to subdue the earth. The naturalist tradition in the West has no comparable identifiable text. It may be described as holding that the cosmos is unitary, that all systems are subject to common physical laws yet having unlimited potential; that in this world man is simply an inhabitant, free to develop his own potential. This view questions anthropocentrism and anthropomorphism; it does not diminish either man's uniqueness or his potential, only his claims to primacy and exclusive divinity. This view assumes that the precursor of man, plant and animal, his co-tenant contemporaries, share a cosmic role and potential.

From its origin in Judaism, extension in Classicism, reinforcement in Christianity, inflation in the Renaissance, and absorption into the nineteenth and twentieth centuries, the anthropomorphic-anthropocentric view has become the tacit view of man versus nature.

Evolution of Power

The primate precursors of man, like their contemporary descendants, support neither a notably constructive, nor a notably destructive role in their ecological community. The primates live within a complex community which has continued to exist; no deleterious changes can be attributed to the primate nor does his existence appear to be essential for the support of his niche and habitat. When the primates abandoned instinct for reason and man emerged, new patterns of behavior emerged and new techniques were developed. Man acquired powers which increased his negative and destructive effect upon environment, but which left unchanged the possibility of a creative role in the environment. Aboriginal peoples survive today: Australian aborigines, Dravidians and Birbory in India, South African Bushmen, Veda in Ceylon, Ainu in Japan, Indians of Tierra del Fuego; none of these play a significantly destructive role in the environment. Hunters, primitive farmers, fishermen—their ecological role has changed little from that of the primate. Yet from aboriginal people there developed several new techniques which gave man a significantly destructive role within his environment. The prime destructive human tool was fire. The consequences of fire, originated by man, upon the ecology of the world cannot be measured, but there is reason to believe that its significance was very great indeed.

Perhaps the next most important device was that of animal husbandry, the domestication of grazing animals. These sheep, goats, and cattle, have been very significant agents historically in modifying the ecology in large areas of the world. This modification is uniformly deleterious to the original environment. Deforestation is perhaps the third human system which has made considerable impact upon the physical environment. Whether involuntary, that is, as an unconscious product of fire, or as a consequence of goat and sheep herding, or as an economic policy, this process of razing forests has wrought great changes upon climate and microclimate, flora and fauna. However, the regenerative powers of nature are great; and while fire, domestic animals, and deforestation have denuded great areas of world surface, this retrogression can often be minimized or reversed by the natural processes of regeneration. Perhaps the next consequential act of man in modifying the natural environment was large-scale agriculture. We know that in many areas of the world agriculture can be sustained for many centuries without depletion of the soil. Man can create a new ecology in which he is the prime agent, in which the original ecological community has been changed, but which is nevertheless self-perpetuating. This condition is the exception. More typically agriculture has been, and is today, an extractive process in which the soil is mined and left depleted. Many areas of the world, once productive, are no longer capable of producing crops. Extractive agriculture has been historically a retrogressive process sustained by man.

The next important agent for modifying the physical environment is the human settlement: hamlet, village, town, city. It is hard to believe that any of the pre-classical, medieval, Renaissance, or even eighteenth-century cities were able to achieve a transformation of the physical environment comparable to the agents mentioned before—fire, animal husbandry, deforestation, or extensive agriculture. But with the emergence of the nineteenth-century industrial city, there arose an agent certainly of comparable consequence, perhaps even of greater consequence, even more destructive of the physical environment and the balances of ecological communities in which man exists, than any of the prior human processes.

The large modern metropolis may be thirty miles in diameter. Much, if not all, of the land which it covers is sterilized. The micro-organisms in the soil no longer exist; the original animal inhabitants have largely been banished. Only a few members of the plant kingdom represent the original members of the initial ecology. The rivers are foul; the atmosphere is polluted; the original configuration of the land is only rarely in evidence; climate and microclimate have retrogressed so that the external microclimate is more violent than was the case before the establishment of the city. Atmospheric pollution may be so severe as to account for 4,000 deaths in a single week of intense "fog," as was the case in London. Floods alternate with drought. Hydrocarbons, lead, carcinogenic agents, carbon dioxide, carbon monoxide concentrations, deteriorating conditions of atmospheric electricity—all of these represent retrogressive processes introduced and supported by man. The epidemiologist speaks of neuroses, lung cancer, heart and renal disease, ulcers, the stress diseases, as the badges of urban conditions. There has also arisen the specter of the effects of density and social pressure upon the incidence of disease and upon reproduction. The modern city contains other life-inhibiting aspects whose effects are present but which are difficult to measure: disorder, squalor, ugliness, noise.

In its effect upon the atmosphere, soil as a living process, the water cycle, climate and micro-climate, the modern city represents a transformation of the original physical environment certainly greater over the area of the city than the changes achieved by earlier man through fire, animal husbandry, deforestation, and extensive agriculture.

Indeed, one can certainly say that the city is at least an ecological regression, although as a human institution it may represent a triumph. Whatever triumphs there are to be seen in the modern city as an institution, it is only with great difficulty that one can see any vestige of triumph in the modern city as a physical environment. One might ask of the modern city that it be humane; that is, capable of supporting human organisms. This might well be a minimum requirement. In order for this term to be fully appropriate—that is, that the city be compassionate and elevating—it should not only be able to support physiological man, but also should give meaning and expression to man as an individual and as a member of an urban society. I contend that far from meeting the full requirements of this criterion, the modern city inhibits life, that it inhibits man as an organism, man as a social being, man as a spiritual being, and that it does not even offer adequate minimum conditions for physiological man; that indeed the modern city offers the least humane physical environment known to history.

Assuredly, the last and most awful agent held by man to modify the physical environment is atomic power. Here we find post-atomic man able to cause evolutionary regressions of unimaginable effect and even able to destroy all life. In this, man holds the ultimate destructive weapon; with this, he can become the agent of destruction in the ecological community, of all communities, of all life. For any ecological community to survive, no single member can support a destructive role. Man's role historically has been destructive; today or tomorrow it can be totally, and for all life existent, irrevocably destructive.

Now, wild nature, save a few exceptions, is not a satisfactory physical environment. Where primitive peoples exist in a wild nature little adapted by man, their susceptibility to disease, life expectancy, vulnerability to climatic vagaries, and to the phenomena of drought and starvation is hardly ideal. Yet the certainty that man must adapt nature and himself does not diminish his dependence upon natural, non-human processes. These two observations set limits upon conceptions of man and nature. Man must adapt through both biological and cultural innovation but these adaptations occur within a context of natural, non-human processes. It is not inevitable that adapting nature to support human congregations must of necessity diminish the quality of the physical environment.

Creation of a physical environment by organisms as individuals and as communities is not exclusively a human skill. The chambered nautilus, the beehive, and the coral formation are all efforts by organisms to take inert materials and dispose them to create a physical environment. In these examples the environments created are complementary to the organisms. They are constructed with great economy of means; they are expressive; they have, in human eyes, great beauty; and they have survived periods of evolutionary time vastly longer than the human span. Can we hope that man will be able to change the physical environment to create a new ecology in which he is primary agent, but which will be a self-perpetuating and not a retrogressive process? We hope that man will be able at least to equal the chambered nautilus, the bee, and the coral—that he will be able to build a physical environment indispensable to life, constructed with economy of means, having lucid expression, and containing great beauty. When man learns this single lesson he will be enabled to create by natural process an environment appropriate for survival—the minimum requirement of a humane environment. When this view is believed, the artist will make it vivid and manifest. Medieval faith, interpreted by artists, made the Gothic cathedral ring with holiness. Here again we confront the paradox of man in nature and man transcendent. The vernacular architecture and urbanism of earlier societies and primitive cultures today, the Italian hill town, medieval village, the Dogon community, express the first view, a human correspondence to the nautilus, the bee, and the coral. Yet this excludes the Parthenon, Hagia Sofia, Beauvais, statements which speak of the uniqueness of man and his aspirations. Neither of these postures is complete, the vernacular speaks too little of the consciousness of man, yet the shrillness of transcendence asks for the muting of other, older voices.

Perhaps when the achievements of the past century are appraised, there will be advanced as the most impressive accomplishment of this period the great extension of social justice. . . . The modern city wears the badges which distinguish it as a product of the nineteenth and twentieth centuries. Polluted rivers, polluted atmosphere, squalid industry, vulgarity of commerce, diners, hot dog stands, second-hand car lots, gas stations, sagging wire and billboards, the whole anarchy united by ugliness—at best neutral, at worst offensive and insalubrious. The product of a century's concern for social justice, a century with unequaled wealth and technology, is the least humane physical environment known to history. It is a problem of major importance to understand why the nineteenth and twentieth centuries have failed in the creation of a physical environment; why the physical environment has not been, and is not now, considered as a significant aspect of wealth and social justice.

Renaissance and Eighteenth Century

If we consider all the views in our Western heritage having an anti-environmental content, we find they represent a very impressive list. The first of these is the anthropomorphic view that man exclusively is made in the image of God (widely interpreted to mean that God is made in the image of man). The second assumption is that man has absolute dominion over all life and nonlife. The third assumption is that man is licensed to subdue the earth. To this we add the medieval Christian concept of other-worldliness, within which life on earth is only a probation for the life hereafter, so that only the acts of man to man are of consequence to his own soul. To this we add the view of the Reformation that beauty is a vanity; and the Celtic, and perhaps Calvinistic, view that the only beauty is natural beauty, that any intent to create beauty by man is an assumption of God's role, is a vanity, and is sacrilegious. The total of these views represents one which can only destroy and which cannot possibly create. The degree to which there has been retention of great natural beauty, creation of beauty and order, recognition of aspects of natural order, and particularly recognition of these aspects of order as a manifestation of God, would seem to exist independently of the Judaic-Christian view. They may be animist and animitist residues that have originated from many different sources; but it would appear, whether or not they are espoused by Christian and Jew, that they do not have their origins in Judaism or Christianity. It would also appear that they do not have their origins in classical or humanist thought, or even in eighteenth-century rationalist views.

These two opposed views of man's role in the natural world are reflected in two concepts of nature and the imposition of man's idea of order upon nature. The first of these is the Renaissance view most vividly manifest in the gardens of the French Renaissance and the projects of André le Nôtre for Louis XIV. The second is the eighteenth-century English picturesque tradition. The gardens of the Renaissance clearly show the imprint of humanist thought. A rigid symmetrical pattern is imposed relentlessly upon a reluctant landscape. . . .

If the Renaissance sought to imprint upon nature a human order, the eighteenth-century English tradition sought to idealize wild nature, in order to provide a sense of the sublime. The form of estates in the eighteenth century was of an idealized nature, replacing the symmetrical patterns of the Renaissance.

The form of ideal nature had been garnered from the landscape painting of Nicolas Poussin and Salvator Rosa; developed through the senses of the poets and writers, such as Alexander Pope, Abraham Cowley, James Thomson, Joseph Addison, Thomas Gray, the third earl of Shaftesbury, and the Orientalist William Temple—a eulogy of the *campagna* from the painters; a eulogy of the natural countryside and its order from the writers; and from Temple, the occult balance discovered in the Orient. However, the essential distinction between the concept of the Renaissance, with its patterning of the landscape, and that of eighteenth-century England was the sense that the order of nature itself existed and represented a prime determinant, a prime discipline for man in his efforts to modify nature. The search in the eighteenth century was for creation of a natural environment which would evoke a sense of the sublime. The impulse of design in the Renaissance was to demonstrate man's power over nature; man's power to order nature; man's power to make nature in his human image. With so inadequate an understanding of the process of man relating to nature, his designs could not be self-perpetuating. Where the basis for design was only the creation of a superficial order, inevitably the consequence was decoration, decay, sterility, and demise. Within the concepts of eighteenth-century England, in contrast, the motivating idea was to idealize the laws of nature. The interdependence of micro-organisms—plants, insects, and animals, the association of particular ecological groupings with particular areas and particular climates—this was the underlying discipline within which the aristocrat-landscape architect worked. The aim was to create an idealized nature which spoke to man of the tranquility, contemplation, and calm which nature brought, which spoke of nature as the arena of sublime and religious experience, essentially speaking to man of God. This represents, I believe, one of the most healthy manifestations of the Western attitude toward nature. To this eighteenth-century attitude one must add a succession of men who are aberrants in the Western tradition, but whose views represent an extension of the eighteenth-century view—among them, Wordsworth and Coleridge, Thoreau and Emerson, Jonathan Edwards, Jonathan Marsh, Gerald Manley Hopkins, and many more. . . .

The Ecological View

It remains for the biologist and ecologist to point out the interdependence which characterizes all relationships, organic and inorganic, in nature. It is the ecologist who points out that an ecological community is only able to survive as a result of interdependent activity between all of the species which constitute the community. To the basic environment (geology, climate) is added an extraordinary complexity of inert materials, their reactions, and the interaction of the organic members of the community with climate, inert materials, and other organisms. The characteristic of life is interdependence of all of the elements of the community upon each other. Each one of these is a source of stimulus; each performs work; each is part of a pattern, a system, a working cycle; each one is to some lesser or greater degree a participant and contributor in a thermodynamic system, This interdependence common to nature—common to all systems—is in my own view the final refutation of man's assumption of independence. It appears impossible to separate man from this system. It would appear that there is a system, the order of which we partly observe. Where we observe it, we see interdependence, not independence, as a key. This interdependence is in absolute opposition to Western man's presumption of transcendence, his presumption of independence, and, of course, his presumption of superiority, dominion, and license to subdue the earth.

A tirade on the theme of dependence is necessary only to a society which views man as independent. Truly there is in nature no independence. Energy is the basis for all life; further, no organism has, does, or will live without an environment. All systems are depletive. There can be no enduring system occupied by a single organism. The minimum, in a laboratory experiment, requires the presence of at least two complementary organisms. These conceptions of independence and anthropocentrism are baseless.

The view of organisms and environment widely held by natural scientists is that of interdependence—symbiosis. Paul Sears of Yale University has written:

> Any species survives by virtue of its niche, the opportunity afforded it by environment. But in occupying this niche, it also assumes a role in relation to its surroundings. For further survival it is necessary that its role at least be not a disruptive one. Thus, one generally finds in nature that each component of a highly organized community serves a constructive, or, at any rate, a stabilizing role. The habitat furnishes the niche, and if any species breaks up the habitat, the niche goes with it. . . . That is, to persist they [ecological communities] must be able to utilize radiant energy not merely to perform work, but to maintain the working system in reasonably good order. This requires the presence of organisms adjusted to the habitat and to each other, so organized as to make the fullest use of the influent radiation and to conserve for use and re-use the materials which the system requires. The degree to which a living community meets these conditions is therefore a test of its efficiency and stability (Sears 1956).

Man, too, must meet this test. Sears states:

Man is clearly the beneficiary of a very special environment which has been a great while in the making. This environment is more than a mere inert stockroom. It is an active system, a pattern and a process as well. Its value can be threatened by disruption no less than by depletion.

The natural scientist states that no species can exist without an environment, no species can exist in an environment of its exclusive creations, no species can survive, save as a non-disruptive member of an ecological community. Every member must adjust to other members of the community and to the environment in order to survive. Man is not excluded from this test.

Man must learn this prime ecological lesson of interdependence. He must see himself linked as a living organism to all living and all preceding life. This sense may impel him to understand his interdependence with the microorganisms of the soil, the diatoms in the sea, the whooping crane, the grizzly bear, sand, rocks, grass, trees, sun, rain, moon, and stars. When man learns this he will have learned that when he destroys he also destroys himself; that when he creates, he also adds to himself. When man learns the single lesson of interdependence he may be enabled to create by natural process an environment appropriate for survival. This is a fundamental precondition for the emergence of man's role as a constructive and creative agent in the evolutionary process. Yet this view of interdependence as a basis for survival, this view of man as a participant species in an ecological community and environment, is quite contrary to the Western view.

I have reminded the reader that the creation of a physical environment by organisms, as individuals and as communities, is not exclusively a human skill; it is shared with the bee, the coral, and the chambered nautilus, which take inert materials and dispose them to create a physical environment, complementary to—indeed, indispensable to—the organism.

When man abandoned instinct for rational thought, he abandoned the powers that permitted him to emulate such organisms; if rationality alone sufficed, man should at least be able to equal these humble organisms. But thereby hangs a parable:

> The nuclear cataclysm is over. The earth is covered with gray dust. In the vast silence no life exists, save for a little colony of algae hidden deep in a leaden cleft long inured to radiation. The algae perceive their isolation; they reflect upon the strivings of all life, so recently ended, and on the strenuous task of evolution to be begun anew. Out of their reflection could emerge a firm conclusion: "Next time, no brains."

References

Sears, Paul B. "The Process of Environmental Change by Man." In *Man's Role in Changing the Face of the Earth*. Edited by W. L. Thomas, Jr. Chicago: University of Chicago Press, 1956.

The Land Ethic

A Sand County Almanac, and Sketches Here and There (1949)

Aldo Leopold

When god-like Odysseus returned from the wars in Troy, he hanged all on one rope a dozen slave-girls of his household whom he suspected of misbehavior during his absence.

This hanging involved no question of propriety. The girls were property. The disposal of property was then, as now, a matter of expediency, not of right and wrong.

Concepts of right and wrong were not lacking from Odysseus' Greece: witness the fidelity of his wife through the long years before at last his black-prowed galleys clove the wine-dark seas for home. The ethical structure of that day covered wives, but had not yet been extended to human chattels. During the three thousand years which have since elapsed, ethical criteria have been extended to many fields of conduct, with corresponding shrinkages in those judged by expediency only.

The Ethical Sequence

This extension of ethics, so far studied only by philosophers, is actually a process in ecological evolution. Its sequences may be described in ecological as well as in philosophical terms. An ethic, ecologically, is a limitation on freedom of action in the struggle for existence. An ethic, philosophically, is a differentiation of social from anti-social conduct. These are two definitions of one thing. The thing has its origin in the tendency of interdependent individuals or groups to evolve modes of cooperation. The ecologist calls these symbioses. Politics and economics are advanced symbioses in which the original free-for-all competition has been replaced, in part, by co-operative mechanisms with an ethical content.

The complexity of co-operative mechanisms has increased with population density, and with the efficiency of tools. It was simpler, for example, to define the anti-social uses of sticks and stones in the days of the mastodons than of bullets and billboards in the age of motors.

The first ethics dealt with the relation between individuals; the Mosaic Decalogue is an example. Later accretions dealt with the relation between the individual and society. The Golden Rule tries to integrate the individual to society; democracy to integrate social organization to the individual,

There is as yet no ethic dealing with man's relation to land and to the animals and plants which grow upon it. Land, like Odysseus' slave-girls, is still property. The land-relation is still strictly economic, entailing privileges but not obligations.

The extension of ethics to this third element in human environment is, if I read the evidence correctly, an evolutionary possibility and an ecological necessity. It is the third step in a sequence. The first two have already been taken. Individual thinkers since the days of Ezekiel and Isaiah have asserted that the despoliation of land is not only inexpedient but wrong. Society, however, has not yet affirmed their belief. I regard the present conservation movement as the embryo of such an affirmation.

An ethic may be regarded as a mode of guidance for meeting ecological situations so new or intricate, or involving such deferred reactions, that the path of social expediency is not discernible to the average individual. Animal instincts are modes of guidance for the individual in meeting such situations. Ethics are possibly a kind of community instinct in-the-making.

The Community Concept

All ethics so far evolved rest upon a single premise: that the individual is a member of a community of interdependent parts. His instincts prompt him to compete for his place in that community, but his ethics prompt him also to co-operate (perhaps in order that there may be a place to compete for).

The land ethic simply enlarges the boundaries of the community to include soils, waters, plants, and animals, or collectively: the land.

This sounds simple: do we not already sing our love for and obligation to the land of the free and the home of the brave? Yes, but just what and whom do we love? Certainly not the soil, which we are sending helter-skelter downriver. Certainly not the waters, which we assume have no function except to turn turbines, float barges, and carry off sewage. Certainly not the plants, of which we exterminate whole communities without batting an eye. Certainly not the animals, of which we have already extirpated many of the largest and most beautiful species. A land ethic of course cannot prevent the alteration, management, and use of these "resources," but it does affirm their right to continued existence, and, at least in spots, their continued existence in a natural state.

In short, a land ethic changes the role of *Homo sapiens* from conqueror of the land-community to plain member and citizen of it. It implies respect for his fellow-members, and also respect for the community as such.

In human history, we have learned (I hope) that the conqueror role is eventually self-defeating. Why? Because it is implicit in such a role that the conqueror knows, *ex cathedra*, just what makes the community clock tick, and just what and who is valuable, and what and who is worthless, in community life. It always turns out that he knows neither, and this is why his conquests eventually defeat themselves.

In the biotic community, a parallel situation exists. Abraham knew exactly what the land was for: it was to drip milk and honey into Abraham's mouth. At the present moment, the assurance with which we regard this assumption is inverse to the degree of our education.

The ordinary citizen today assumes that science knows what makes the community clock tick; the scientist is equally sure that he does not. He knows that the biotic mechanism is so complex that its workings may never be fully understood.

That man is, in fact, only a member of a biotic team is shown by an ecological interpretation of history. Many historical events, hitherto explained solely in terms of human enterprise, were actually biotic interactions between people and land. The characteristics of the land determined the facts quite as potently as the characteristics of the men who lived on it.

Consider, for example, the settlement of the Mississippi valley. In the years following the Revolution, three groups were contending for its control: the native Indian, the French and English traders, and the American settlers. Historians wonder what would have happened if the English at Detroit had thrown a little more weight into the Indian side of those tipsy scales which decided the outcome of the colonial migration into the cane-lands of Kentucky. It is time now to ponder the fact that the cane-lands, when subjected to the particular mixture of forces represented by the cow, plow, fire, and axe of the pioneer, became bluegrass. What if the plant succession inherent in this dark and bloody ground had, under the impact of these forces, given us some worthless sedge, shrub, or weed: Would Boone and Kenton have held out? Would there have been any overflow into Ohio, Indiana, Illinois, and Missouri? Any Louisiana Purchase? Any transcontinental union of new states? Any Civil War?

Kentucky was one sentence in the drama of history. We are commonly told what the human actors in this drama tried to do, but we are seldom told that their success, or the lack of it, hung in large degree on the reaction of particular soils to the impact of the particular forces exerted by their occupancy. In the case of Kentucky, we do not even know where the bluegrass came from—whether it is a native species, or a stowaway from Europe.

Contrast the cane-lands with what hindsight tells us about the Southwest, where the pioneers were equally brave, resourceful, and persevering. The impact of occupancy here brought no bluegrass, or other plant fitted to withstand the bumps and buffetings of hard use. This region, when grazed by livestock, reverted through a series of more and more worthless grasses, shrubs, and weeds to a condition of unstable equilibrium. Each recession of plant types bred erosion; each increment to erosion bred a further recession of plants. The result today is a progressive and mutual deterioration, not only of plants and soils, but of the animal community subsisting thereon. The early settlers did not expect this: on the ciénegas of New Mexico some even cut ditches to hasten it. So subtle has been its progress that few residents of the region are aware of it. It is quite invisible to the tourist who finds this wrecked landscape colorful and charming (as indeed it is, but it bears scant resemblance to what it was in 1848).

This same landscape was "developed" once before, but with quite different results. The Pueblo Indians settled the Southwest in pre-Columbian times, but they happened *not* to be equipped with range livestock. Their civilization expired, but not because their land expired.

In India, regions devoid of any sod-forming grass have been settled, apparently without wrecking the land, by the simple expedient of carrying the grass to the cow, rather than vice versa. (Was this the result of some deep wisdom, or was it just good luck? I do not know.)

In short, the plant succession steered the course of history; the pioneer simply demonstrated, for good or ill, what successions inhered in the land. Is history taught in this spirit? It will be, once the concept of land as a community really penetrates our intellectual life.

The Ecological Conscience

Conservation is a state of harmony between men and land. Despite nearly a century of propaganda, conservation still proceeds at a snail's pace; progress still consists largely of letterhead pieties and convention oratory. On the back forty we still slip two steps backward for each forward stride.

The usual answer to this dilemma is "more conservation education." No one will debate this, but is it certain that only the *volume* of education needs stepping up? Is something lacking in the *content* as well?

It is difficult to give a fair summary of its content in brief form, but, as I understand it, the content is substantially this: obey the law, vote right, join some organizations, and practice what conservation is profitable on your own land; the government will do the rest.

Is not this formula too easy to accomplish anything worth-while? It defines no right or wrong, assigns no obligation, calls for no sacrifice, implies no change in the current philosophy of values. In respect of land-use, it urges only enlightened self-interest. Just how far will such education take us? An example will perhaps yield a partial answer.

By 1930 it had become clear to all except the ecologically blind that southwestern Wisconsin's topsoil was slipping seaward. In 1933 the farmers were told that if they would adopt certain remedial practices for five years, the public would donate CCC labor to install them, plus the necessary machinery and materials. The offer was widely accepted, but the practices were widely forgotten when the five-year contract period was up. The farmers continued only those practices that yielded an immediate and visible economic gain for themselves.

This led to the idea that maybe farmers would learn more quickly if they themselves wrote the rules. Accordingly the Wisconsin Legislature m 1937 passed the Soil Conservation District Law. This said to farmers, in effect: *We, the public, will furnish you free technical service and loan you specialized machinery, if you will write your own rules for land-use. Each county may write its own rules, and these will have the force of law.* Nearly all the counties promptly organized to accept the proffered help, but after a decade of operation, *no county has yet written a single rule.* There has been visible progress in such practices as strip-cropping, pasture renovation, and soil liming, but none in fencing woodlots against grazing, and none in excluding plow and cow from steep slopes. The farmers in short, have selected those remedial practices which were profitable anyhow, and ignored those which were profitable to the community, but not clearly profitable to themselves.

When one asks why no rules have been written, one is told that the community is not yet ready to support them; education must precede rules. But the education actually in progress makes no mention of obligations to land over and above those dictated by self-interest. The net result is that we have more education but less soil, fewer healthy woods, and as many floods as in 1937.

The puzzling aspect of such situations is that the existence of obligations over and above self-interest is taken for granted in such rural community enterprises as the betterment of roads, schools, churches, and baseball teams.

Their existence is not taken for granted, nor as yet seriously discussed, in bettering the behavior of the water that falls on the land, or in the preserving of the beauty or diversity of the farm landscape. Land-use ethics are still governed wholly by economic self-interest, just as social ethics were a century ago.

To sum up: we asked the farmer to do what he conveniently could to save his soil, and he has done just that, and only that. The farmer who clears the woods off a 75 per cent slope, turns his cows into the clearing, and dumps its rainfall, rocks, and soil into the community creek, is still (if otherwise decent) a respected member of society. If he puts lime on his fields and plants his crops on contour, he is still entitled to all the privileges and emoluments of his Soil Conservation District. The District is a beautiful piece of social machinery, but it is coughing along on two cylinders because we have been too timid, and too anxious for quick success, to tell the farmer the true magnitude of his obligations. Obligations have no meaning without conscience, and the problem we face is the extension of the social conscience from people to land.

No important change in ethics was ever accomplished without an internal change in our intellectual emphasis, loyalties, affections, and convictions. The proof that conservation has not yet touched these foundations of conduct lies in the fact that philosophy and religion have not yet heard of it. In our attempt to make conservation easy, we have made it trivial.

Substitutes for a Land Ethic

When the logic of history hungers for bread and we hand out a stone, we are at pains to explain how much the stone resembles bread. I now describe some of the stones which serve in lieu of a land ethic.

One basic weakness in a conservation system based wholly on economic motives is that most members of the land community have no economic value. Wildflowers and songbirds are examples. Of the 22,000 higher plants and animals native to Wisconsin, it is doubtful whether more than 5 per cent can be sold, fed, eaten, or otherwise put to economic use. Yet these creatures are members of the biotic community, and if (as I believe) its stability depends on its integrity, they are entitled to continuance.

When one of these non-economic categories is threatened, and if we happen to love it, we invent subterfuges to give it economic importance. At the beginning of the century songbirds were supposed to be disappearing. Ornithologists jumped to the rescue with some distinctly shaky evidence to the effect that insects would eat us up if birds failed to control them. The evidence had to be economic in order to be valid.

It is painful to read these circumlocutions today. We have no land ethic yet, but we have at least drawn nearer the point of admitting that birds should continue as a matter of biotic right, regardless of the presence or absence of economic advantage to us.

A parallel situation exists in respect of predatory mammals, raptorial birds, and fish-eating birds. Time was when biologists somewhat overworked the evidence that these creatures preserve the health of game by killing weaklings, or that they control rodents for the farmer, or that they prey only on "worthless" species. Here again, the evidence had to be economic in order to be valid. It is only in recent years that we hear the more honest argument that predators are members of the community, and that no special interest has the right to exterminate them for the sake of a benefit, real or fancied, to itself. Unfortunately this enlightened view is still in the talk stage. In the field the extermination of predators goes merrily on: witness the impending erasure of the timber wolf by fiat of Congress, the Conservation Bureaus, and many state legislatures.

Some species of trees have been "read out of the party" by economics-minded foresters because they grow too slowly, or have too low a sale value to pay as timber crops: white cedar, tamarack, cypress, beech, and hemlock are examples. In Europe, where forestry is ecologically more advanced, the noncommercial tree species are recognized as members of the native forest community, to be preserved as such, within reason. Moreover some (like beech) have been found to have a valuable function in building up soil fertility. The interdependence of the forest and its constituent tree species, ground flora, and fauna is taken for granted.

Lack of economic value is sometimes a character not only of species or groups, but of entire biotic communities: marshes, bogs, dunes, and "deserts" are examples. Our formula in such cases is to relegate their conservation to government as refuges, monuments, or parks. The difficulty is that these communities are usually interspersed with more valuable private lands; the government cannot possibly own or control such scattered parcels. The net effect is that we have relegated some of them to ultimate extinction over large areas. If the private owner were ecologically minded, he would be proud to be the custodian of a reasonable proportion of such areas, which add diversity and beauty to his farm and to his community.

In some instances, the assumed lack of profit in these "waste" areas has proved to be wrong, but only after most of them had been done away with. The present scramble to reflood muskrat marshes is a case in point.

There is a clear tendency in American conservation to relegate to government all necessary jobs that private landowners fail to perform. Government ownership, operation, subsidy, or regulation is now widely prevalent in forestry, range management, soil and watershed management, park and wilderness conservation, fisheries management, and migratory bird management, with more to come. Most of this growth in governmental conservation is proper and logical, some of it is inevitable. That I imply no disapproval of it is implicit in the fact that I have spent most of my life working for it. Nevertheless the question arises: What is the ultimate magnitude of the enterprise? Will the tax base carry its eventual ramifications? At what point will governmental conservation, like the mastodon, become handicapped by its own dimensions? The answer, if there is any, seems to be in a land ethic, or some other force which assigns more obligation to the private landowner.

Industrial landowners and users, especially lumbermen and stockmen, are inclined to wail long and loudly about the extension of government ownership and regulation to land, but (with notable exceptions) they show little disposition to develop the only visible alternative: the voluntary practice of conservation on their own lands.

When the private landowner is asked to perform some unprofitable act for the good of the community, he today assents only with outstretched palm. If the act costs him cash this is fair and proper, but when it costs only forethought, open-mindedness, or time, the issue is at least debatable. The overwhelming growth of land-use subsidies in recent years must be ascribed, in large part, to the government's own agencies for conservation education: the land bureaus, the agricultural colleges, and the extension services. As far as I can detect, no ethical obligation toward land is taught in these institutions.

To sum up: a system of conservation based solely on economic self-interest is hopelessly lopsided. It tends to ignore, and thus eventually to eliminate, many elements in the land community that lack commercial value, but that are (as far as we know) essential to its healthy functioning. It assumes, falsely, I think, that the economic parts of the biotic clock will function without the uneconomic parts. It tends to relegate to government many functions eventually too large, too complex, or too widely dispersed to be performed by government.

An ethical obligation on the part of the private owner is the only visible remedy for these situations.

The Land Pyramid

An ethic to supplement and guide the economic relation to land presupposes the existence of some mental image of land as a biotic mechanism. We can be ethical only in relation to something we can see, feel, understand, love, or otherwise have faith in.

The image commonly employed in conservation education is "the balance of nature." For reasons too lengthy to detail here, this figure of speech fails to describe accurately what little we know about the land mechanism. A much truer image is the one employed in ecology: the biotic pyramid. I shall first sketch the pyramid as a symbol of land, and later develop some of its implications in terms of land-use.

Plants absorb energy from the sun. This energy flows through a circuit called the biota, which may be represented by a pyramid consisting of layers. The bottom layer is the soil. A plant layer rests on the soil, an insect layer on the plants, a bird and rodent layer on the insects, and so on up through various animal groups to the apex layer, which consists of the larger carnivores.

The species of a layer are alike not in where they came from, or in what they look like, but rather in what they eat. Each successive layer depends on those below it for food and often for other services, and each in turn furnishes food and services to those above. Proceeding upward, each successive layer decreases in numerical abundance. Thus, for every carnivore there are hundreds of his prey, thousands of their prey, millions of insects, uncountable plants. The pyramidal form of the system reflects this numerical progression from apex to base. Man shares an intermediate layer with the bears, raccoons, and squirrels which eat both meat and vegetables.

The lines of dependency for food and other services are called food chains. Thus soil-oak-deer-Indian is a chain that has now been largely converted to soil-corn-cow-farmer. Each species, including ourselves, is a link in many chains. The deer eats a hundred plants other than oak, and the cow a hundred plants other than corn. Both, then, are links in a hundred chains. The pyramid is a tangle of chains so complex as to seem disorderly, yet the stability of the system proves it to be a highly organized structure. Its functioning depends on the co-operation and competition of its diverse parts.

In the beginning, the pyramid of life was low and squat; the food chains short and simple. Evolution has added layer after layer, link after link. Man is one of thousands of accretions to the height and complexity of the pyramid. Science has given us many doubts, but it has given us at least one certainty: the trend of evolution is to elaborate and diversify the biota.

Land, then, is not merely soil; it is a fountain of energy flowing through a circuit of soils, plants, and animals. Food chains are the living channels which conduct energy upward; death and decay return it to the soil. The circuit is not closed; some energy is dissipated in decay, some is added by absorption from the air, some is stored in soils, peats, and long-lived forests; but it is a sustained circuit, like a slowly augmented revolving fund of life. There is always a net loss by downhill wash, but this is normally small and offset by the decay of rocks. It is deposited in the ocean and, in the course of geological time, raised to form new lands and new pyramids.

The velocity and character of the upward flow of energy depend on the complex structure of the plant and animal community, much as the upward flow of sap in a tree depends on its complex cellular organization. Without this complexity, normal circulation would presumably not occur. Structure means the characteristic numbers, as well as the characteristic kinds and functions, of the component species. This interdependence between the complex structure of the land and its smooth functioning as an energy unit is one of its basic attributes.

When a change occurs in one part of the circuit, many other parts must adjust themselves to it. Change does not necessarily obstruct or divert the flow of energy; evolution is a long series of self-induced changes, the net result of which has been to elaborate the flow mechanism and to lengthen the circuit. Evolutionary changes, however, are usually slow and local. Man's invention of tools has enabled him to make changes of unprecedented violence, rapidity, and scope.

One change is m the composition of floras and faunas. The larger predators are lopped off the apex of the pyramid; food chains, for the first time in history, become shorter rather than longer. Domesticated species from other lands are substituted for wild ones, and wild ones are moved to new habitats. In this world-wide pooling of faunas and floras, some species get out of bounds as pests and diseases, others are extinguished. Such effects are seldom intended or foreseen; they represent unpredicted and often untraceable readjustments in the structure. Agricultural science is largely a race between the emergence of new pests and the emergence of new techniques for their control.

Another change touches the flow of energy through plants and animals and its return to the soil. Fertility is the ability of soil to receive, store, and release energy. Agriculture, by overdrafts on the soil, or by too radical a substitution of domestic for native species in the superstructure, may derange the channels of flow or deplete storage. Soils depleted of their storage, or of the organic matter which anchors it, wash away faster than they form. This is erosion.

Waters, like soil, are part of the energy circuit. Industry, by polluting waters or obstructing them with dams, may exclude the plants and animals necessary to keep energy in circulation.

Transportation brings about another basic change: the plants or animals grown in one region are now consumed and returned to the soil in another. Transportation taps the energy stored in rocks, and in the air, and uses it elsewhere; thus we fertilize the garden with nitrogen gleaned by the guano birds from the fishes of seas on the other side of the Equator. Thus the formerly localized and self-contained circuits are pooled on a world-wide scale.

The process of altering the pyramid for human occupation releases stored energy, and this often gives rise, during the pioneering period, to a deceptive exuberance of plant and animal life, both wild and tame. These releases of biotic capital tend to becloud or postpone the penalties of violence.

This thumbnail sketch of land as an energy circuit conveys three basic ideas:

(1) That land is not merely soil.
(2) That the native plants and animals kept the energy circuit open; others may or may not.
(3) That man-made changes are of a different order than evolutionary changes, and have effects more comprehensive than is intended or foreseen.

These ideas, collectively, raise two basic issues: Can the land adjust itself to the new order? Can the desired alterations be accomplished with less violence?

Biotas seem to differ in their capacity to sustain violent conversion. Western Europe, for example, carries a far different pyramid than Caesar found there. Some large animals are lost; swampy forests have become meadows or plow-land; many new plants and animals are introduced, some of which escape as pests; the remaining natives are greatly changed in distribution and abundance. Yet the soil is still there and, with the help of imported nutrients, still fertile; the waters flow normally; the new structure seems to function and to persist. There is no visible stoppage or derangement of the circuit.

Western Europe, then, has a resistant biota. Its inner processes are tough, elastic, resistant to strain. No matter how violent the alterations, the pyramid, so far, has developed some new *modus vivendi* which preserves its habitability for man, and for most of the other natives.

Japan seems to present another instance of radical conversion without disorganization.

Most other civilized regions, and some as yet barely touched by civilization, display various stages of disorganization, varying from initial symptoms to advanced wastage. In Asia Minor and North Africa diagnosis is confused by climatic changes, which may have been either the cause or the effect of advanced wastage. In the United States the degree of disorganization varies locally; it is worst in the Southwest, the Ozarks, and parts of the South, and least in New England and the Northwest. Better land-uses may still arrest it in the less advanced regions. In parts of Mexico, South America, South Africa, and Australia a violent and accelerating wastage is in progress, but I cannot assess the prospects.

This almost world-wide display of disorganization in the land seems to be similar to disease in an animal, except that it never culminates in complete disorganization or death. The land recovers, but at some reduced level of complexity, and with a reduced carrying capacity for people, plants, and animals. Many biotas currently regarded as "lands of opportunity" are in fact already subsisting on exploitative agriculture, i.e. they have already exceeded their sustained carrying capacity. Most of South America is overpopulated in this sense.

In arid regions we attempt to offset the process of wastage by reclamation, but it is only too evident that the prospective longevity of reclamation projects is often short. In our own West, the best of them may not last a century.

The combined evidence of history and ecology seems to support one general deduction: the less violent the manmade changes, the greater the probability of successful readjustment in the pyramid. Violence, in turn, varies with human population density; a dense population requires a more violent conversion. In this respect, North America has a better chance for permanence than Europe, if she can contrive to limit her density.

This deduction runs counter to our current philosophy, which assumes that because a small increase in density enriched human life, that an indefinite increase will enrich it indefinitely. Ecology knows of no density relationship that holds for indefinitely wide limits. All gains from density are subject to a law of diminishing returns.

Whatever may be the equation for men and land, it is improbable that we as yet know all its terms. Recent discoveries in mineral and vitamin nutrition reveal unsuspected dependencies in the up-circuit: incredibly minute quantities of certain substances determine the value of soils to plants, of plants to animals. What of the down-circuit: What of the vanishing species, the preservation of which we now regard as an esthetic luxury? They helped build the soil; in what unsuspected ways may they be essential to its maintenance? Professor Weaver proposes that we use prairie flowers to reflocculate the wasting soils of the dust bowl; who knows for what purpose cranes and condors, otters and grizzlies may some day be used?

Land Health and the A-B Cleavage

A land ethic, then, reflects the existence of an ecological conscience, and this in turn reflects a conviction of individual responsibility for the health of the land. Health is the capacity of the land for self-renewal. Conservation is our effort to understand and preserve this capacity.

Conservationists are notorious for their dissensions. Superficially these seem to add up to mere confusion, but a more careful scrutiny reveals a single plane of cleavage common to many specialized fields. In each field one group (A) regards the land as soil, and its function as commodity-production; another group (B) regards the land as a biota, and its function as something broader. How much broader is admittedly in a state of doubt and confusion. . . .

In all of these cleavages, we see repeated the same basic paradoxes: man the conqueror *versus* man the biotic citizen; science the sharpener of his sword *versus* science the searchlight on his universe; land the slave and servant *versus* land the collective organism. Robinson's injunction to Tristram may well be applied, at this juncture, to *Homo sapiens* as a species in geological time:

> Whether you will or not
> You are a King, Tristram, for you are one
> Of the time-tested few that leave the world,
> When they are gone, not the same place it was.
> Mark what you leave.

The Outlook

It is inconceivable to me that an ethical relation to land can exist without love, respect, and admiration for land, and a high regard for its value. By value, I of course mean something far broader than mere economic value; I mean value in the philosophical sense.

Perhaps the most serious obstacle impeding the evolution of a land ethic is the fact that our educational and economic system is headed away from, rather than toward, an intense consciousness of land. Your true modern is separated from the land by many middlemen, and by innumerable physical gadgets. He has no vital relation to it; to him it is the space between cities on which crops grow. Turn him loose for a day on the land, and if the spot does not happen to be a golf links or a scenic area, he is bored stiff. If crops could be raised by hydroponics instead of farming, it would suit him very well. Synthetic substitutes for wood, leather, wool, and other natural land products suit him better than the originals. In short, land is something he has "outgrown."

Almost equally serious as an obstacle to a land ethic is the attitude of the farmer for whom the land is still an adversary, or a taskmaster that keeps him in slavery. Theoretically, the mechanization of farming ought to cut the farmer's chains, but whether it really does is debatable.

One of the requisites for an ecological comprehension of land is an understanding of ecology, and this is by no means co-extensive with "education"; in fact, much higher education seems deliberately to avoid ecological concepts. An understanding of ecology does not necessarily originate in courses bearing ecological labels; it is quite as likely to be labeled geography, botany, agronomy, history, or economics. This is as it should be, but whatever the label, ecological training is scarce.

The case for a land ethic would appear hopeless but for the minority which is in obvious revolt against these "modern" trends.

The "key-log" which must be moved to release the evolutionary process for an ethic is simply this: quit thinking about decent land-use as solely an economic problem. Examine each question in terms of what is ethically and esthetically right, as well as what is economically expedient. A thing is right when it tends to preserve the integrity, stability, and beauty of the biotic community. It is wrong when it tends otherwise.

It of course goes without saying that economic feasibility limits the tether of what can or cannot be done for land. It always has and it always will. The fallacy the economic determinists have tied around our collective neck, and which we now need to cast off, is the belief that economics determines *all* land-use. This is simply not true. An innumerable host of actions and attitudes, comprising perhaps the bulk of all land relations, is determined by the land-users' tastes and predilections, rather than by his purse. The bulk of all land relations hinges on investments of time, forethought, skill, and faith rather than on investments of cash. As a land-user thinketh, so is he.

I have purposely presented the land ethic as a product of social evolution because nothing so important as an ethic is ever "written." Only the most superficial student of history supposes that Moses "wrote" the Decalogue; it evolved in the minds of a thinking community, and Moses wrote a tentative summary of it for a "seminar." I say tentative because evolution never stops.

The evolution of a land ethic is an intellectual as well as emotional process. Conservation is paved with good intentions which prove to be futile, or even dangerous, because they are devoid of critical understanding either of the land, or of economic land-use. I think it is a truism that as the ethical frontier advances from the individual to the community, its intellectual content increases.

The mechanism of operation is the same for any ethic: social approbation for right actions: social disapproval for wrong actions.

By and large, our present problem is one of attitudes and implements. We are remodeling the Alhambra with a steam-shovel, and we are proud of our yardage. We shall hardly relinquish the shovel, which after all has many good points, but we are in need of gentler and more objective criteria for its successful use.

The Obligation to Endure
Silent Spring (1962)

Rachel Carson

1. A Fable for Tomorrow

There was once a town in the heart of America where all life seemed to live in harmony with its surroundings. The town lay in the midst of a checkerboard of prosperous farms, with fields of grain and hillsides of orchards where, in spring, white clouds of bloom drifted above the green fields. In autumn, oak and maple and birch set up a blaze of color that flamed and flickered across a backdrop of pines. Then foxes barked in the hills and deer silently crossed the fields, half hidden in the mists of the fall mornings.

Along the roads, laurel, viburnum and alder, great ferns and wildflowers delighted the traveler's eye through much of the year. Even in winter the roadsides were places of beauty, where countless birds came to feed on the berries and on the seed heads of the dried weeds rising above the snow. The countryside was, in fact, famous for the abundance and variety of its bird life, and when the flood of migrants was pouring through in spring and fall people traveled from great distances to observe them. Others came to fish the streams, which flowed clear and cold out of the hills and contained shady pools where trout lay. So it had been from the days many years ago when the first settlers raised their houses, sank their wells, and built their barns.

Then a strange blight crept over the area and everything began to change. Some evil spell had settled on the community: mysterious maladies swept the flocks of chickens; the cattle and sheep sickened and died. Everywhere was a

Figure 2-1 A Fable for Tomorrow (Carson, 1962).

shadow of death. The farmers spoke of much illness among their families. In the town the doctors had become more and more puzzled by new kinds of sickness appearing among their patients. There had been several sudden and unexplained deaths, not only among adults but even among children, who would be stricken suddenly while at play and die within a few hours.

There was a strange stillness. The birds, for example—where had they gone? Many people spoke of them, puzzled and disturbed. The feeding stations in the backyards were deserted. The few birds seen anywhere were moribund; they trembled violently and could not fly. It was a spring without voices. On the mornings that had once throbbed with the dawn chorus of robins, catbirds, doves, jays, wrens, and scores of other bird voices there was now no sound; only silence lay over the fields and woods and marsh.

On the farms the hens brooded, but no chicks hatched. The farmers complained that they were unable to raise any pigs—the litters were small and the young survived only a few days. The apple trees were coming into bloom but no bees droned among the blossoms, so there was no pollination and there would be no fruit.

The roadsides, once so attractive, were now lined with browned and withered vegetation as though swept by fire. These, too, were silent, deserted by all living things. Even the streams were now lifeless. Anglers no longer visited them, for all the fish had died.

In the gutters under the eaves and between the shingles of the roofs, a white granular powder still showed a few patches; some weeks before it had fallen like snow upon the roofs and the lawns, the fields and streams.

No witchcraft, no enemy action had silenced the rebirth of new life in this stricken world. The people had done it themselves.

This town does not actually exist, but it might easily have a thousand counterparts in America or elsewhere in the world. I know of no community that has experienced all the misfortunes I describe. Yet every one of these disasters has actually happened somewhere, and many real communities have already suffered a substantial number of them. A grim specter has crept upon us almost unnoticed, and this imagined tragedy may easily become a stark reality we all shall know.

What has already silenced the voices of spring in countless towns in America? This book is an attempt to explain.

2. The Obligation to Endure

The history of life on earth has been a history of interaction between living things and their surroundings. To a large extent, the physical form and the habits of the earth's vegetation and its animal life have been molded by the environment. Considering the whole span of earthly time, the opposite effect, in which life actually modifies its surroundings, has been relatively slight. Only within the moment of time represented by the present century has one species—man—acquired significant power to alter the nature of his world.

During the past quarter century this power has not only increased to one of disturbing magnitude but it has changed in character. The most alarming of all man's assaults upon the environment is the contamination of air, earth, rivers, and sea with dangerous and even lethal materials. This pollution is for the most part irrecoverable; the chain of evil it initiates not only in the world that must support life but in living tissues is for the most part irreversible. In this now universal contamination of the environment, chemicals are the sinister and little-recognized partners of radiation in changing the very nature of the world—the very nature of its life. Strontium 90, released through nuclear explosions into the air, comes to earth in rain or drifts down as fallout, lodges in soil, enters into the grass or corn or wheat grown there, and in time takes up its abode in the bones of a human being, there to remain until his death. Similarly, chemicals sprayed on croplands or forests or gardens lie long in soil, entering into living organisms, passing from one to another in a chain of poisoning and death. Or they pass mysteriously by underground streams until they emerge and, through the alchemy of air and sunlight, combine into new forms that kill vegetation, sicken cattle, and work unknown harm on those who drink from once pure wells. As Albert Schweitzer has said, "Man can hardly even recognize the devils of his own creation."

It took hundreds of millions of years to produce the life that now inhabits the earth—eons of time in which that developing and evolving and diversifying life reached a state of adjustment and balance with its surroundings. The environment, rigorously shaping and directing the life it supported, contained elements that were hostile as well as supporting. Certain rocks gave out dangerous radiation; even within the light of the sun, from which all life draws its energy, there were short-wave radiations with power to injure. Given time—time not in years but in millennia—life adjusts, and a balance has been reached. For time is the essential ingredient; but in the modern world there is no time.

The rapidity of change and the speed with which new situations are created follow the impetuous and heedless pace of man rather than the deliberate pace of nature. Radiation is no longer merely the background radiation of rocks, the bombardment of cosmic rays, the ultraviolet of the sun that have existed before there was any life on earth; radiation is now the unnatural creation of man's tampering with the atom. The chemicals to which life is asked to make its adjustment are no longer merely the calcium and silica and copper and all the rest of the minerals washed out of the rocks and carried in rivers to the sea; they are the synthetic creations of man's inventive mind, brewed in his laboratories, and having no counterparts in nature.

To adjust to these chemicals would require time on the scale that is nature's; it would require not merely the years of a man's life but the life of generations. And even this, were it by some miracle possible, would be futile, for the new chemicals come from our laboratories in an endless stream; almost five hundred annually find their way into actual use in the United States alone. The figure is staggering and its implications are not easily grasped—500 new chemicals to which the bodies of men and animals are required somehow to adapt each year, chemicals totally outside the limits of biologic experience.

Among them are many that are used in man's war against nature. Since the mid-1940's over 200 basic chemicals have been created for use in killing insects, weeds, rodents, and other organisms described in the modern vernacular as "pests"; and they are sold under several thousand different brand names.

These sprays, dusts, and aerosols are now applied almost universally to farms, gardens, forests, and homes—nonselective chemicals that have the power to kill every insect, the "good" and the "bad," to still the song of birds and the leaping of fish in the streams, to coat the leaves with a deadly film, and to linger on in soil—all this though the intended target may be only a few weeds or insects. Can anyone believe it is possible to lay down such a barrage of poisons on the surface of the earth without making it unfit for all life? They should not be called "insecticides," but "biocides."

The whole process of spraying seems caught up in an endless spiral. Since DDT was released for civilian use, a process of escalation has been going on in which ever more toxic materials must be found. This has happened because insects, in a triumphant vindication of Darwin's principle of the survival of the fittest, have evolved super races immune to the particular insecticide used, hence a deadlier one has always to be developed—and then a deadlier one than that. It has happened also because, for reasons to be described later, destructive insects often undergo a "flareback," or resurgence, after spraying, in numbers greater than before. Thus the chemical war is never won, and all life is caught in its violent crossfire.

Along with the possibility of the extinction of mankind by nuclear war, the central problem of our age has therefore become the contamination of man's total environment with such substances of incredible potential for harm—substances that accumulate in the tissues of plants and animals and even penetrate the germ cells to shatter or alter the very material of heredity upon which the shape of the future depends.

Some would-be architects of our future look toward a time when it will be possible to alter the human germ plasm by design. But we may easily be doing so now by inadvertence, for many chemicals, like radiation, bring about gene mutations. It is ironic to think that man might determine his own future by something so seemingly trivial as the choice of an insect spray.

All this has been risked—for what? Future historians may well be amazed by our distorted sense of proportion. How could intelligent beings seek to control a few unwanted species by a method that contaminated the entire environment and brought the threat of disease and death even to their own kind? Yet this is precisely what we have done. We have done it, moreover, for reasons that collapse the moment we examine them. We are told that the enormous and expanding use of pesticides is necessary to maintain farm production. Yet is our real problem not one of *overproduction*? Our farms, despite measures to remove acreages from production and to pay farmers *not* to produce, have yielded such a staggering excess of crops that the American taxpayer in 1962 is paying out more than one billion dollars a year as the total carrying cost of the surplus-food storage program. And is the situation helped when one branch of the Agriculture Department tries to reduce production while another states, as it did in 1958, "It is believed generally that reduction of crop acreages under provisions of the Soil Bank will stimulate interest in use of chemicals to obtain maximum production on the land retained in crops."

All this is not to say there is no insect problem and no need of control. I am saying, rather, that control must be geared to realities, not to mythical situations, and that the methods employed must be such that they do not destroy us along with the insects.

The problem whose attempted solution has brought such a train of disaster in its wake is an accompaniment of our modern way of life. Long before the age of man, insects inhabited the earth—a group of extraordinarily varied and adaptable beings. Over the course of time since man's advent, a small percentage of the more than half a million species of insects have come into conflict with human welfare in two principal ways: as competitors for the food supply and as carriers of human disease.

Disease-carrying insects become important where human beings are crowded together, especially under conditions where sanitation is poor, as in time of natural disaster or war or in situations of extreme poverty and deprivation. Then control of some sort becomes necessary. It is a sobering fact, however, as we shall presently see, that the method of massive chemical control has had only limited success, and also threatens to worsen the very conditions it is intended to curb.

Under primitive agricultural conditions the farmer had few insect problems. These arose with the intensification of agriculture—the devotion of immense acreages to a single crop. Such a system set the stage for explosive increases in specific insect populations. Single-crop farming does not take advantage of the principles by which nature works; it is agriculture as an engineer might conceive it to be. Nature has introduced great variety into the landscape, but man has displayed a passion for simplifying it. Thus he undoes the built-in checks and balances by which nature holds the species within bounds. One important natural check is a limit on the amount of suitable habitat for each species. Obviously then, an insect that lives on wheat can build up its population to much higher levels on a farm devoted to wheat than on one in which wheat is intermingled with other crops to which the insect is not adapted.

The same thing happens in other situations. A generation or more ago, the towns of large areas of the United States lined their streets with the noble elm tree. Now the beauty they hopefully created is threatened with complete destruction as disease sweeps through the elms, carried by a beetle that would have only limited chance to build up large populations and to spread from tree to tree if the elms were only occasional trees in a richly diversified planting.

Another factor in the modern insect problem is one that must be viewed against a background of geologic and human history: the spreading of thousands of different kinds of organisms from their native homes to invade new territories. This worldwide migration has been studied and graphically described by the British ecologist Charles Elton in his recent book *The Ecology of Invasions*. During the Cretaceous Period, some hundred million years ago, flooding seas cut many land bridges between continents and living things found themselves confined in what Elton calls "colossal separate nature reserves." There, isolated from others of their kind, they developed many new species. When some of the land masses were joined again, about 15 million years ago, these species began to move out into new territories—a movement that is not only still in progress but is now receiving considerable assistance from man.

The importation of plants is the primary agent in the modern spread of species, for animals have almost invariably gone along with the plants, quarantine being a comparatively recent and not completely effective innovation. The United States Office of Plant Introduction alone has introduced almost 200,000 species and varieties of plants from all over the world. Nearly half of the 180 or so major insect enemies of plants in the United States are accidental imports from abroad, and most of them have come as hitchhikers on plants.

In new territory, out of reach of the restraining hand of the natural enemies that kept down its numbers in its native land, an invading plant or animal is able to become enormously abundant. Thus it is no accident that our most troublesome insects are introduced species.

These invasions, both the naturally occurring and those dependent on human assistance, are likely to continue indefinitely. Quarantine and massive chemical campaigns are only extremely expensive ways of buying time. We are faced, according to Dr. Elton, "with a life-and-death need not just to find new technological means of suppressing this plant or that animal"; instead we need the basic knowledge of animal populations and their relations to their surroundings that will "promote an even balance and damp down the explosive power of outbreaks and new invasions."

Much of the necessary knowledge is now available but we do not use it. We train ecologists in our universities and even employ them in our governmental agencies but we seldom take their advice. We allow the chemical death rain to fall as though there were no alternative, whereas in fact there are many, and our ingenuity could soon discover many more if given opportunity.

Have we fallen into a mesmerized state that makes us accept as inevitable that which is inferior or detrimental, as though having lost the will or the vision to demand that which is good? Such thinking, in the words of the ecologist Paul Shepard, "idealizes life with only its head out of water, inches above the limits of toleration of the corruption of its own environment . . . Why should we tolerate a diet of weak poisons, a home in insipid surroundings, a circle of acquaintances who are not quite our enemies, the noise of motors with just enough relief to prevent insanity? Who would want to live in a world which is just not quite fatal?"

Yet such a world is pressed upon us. The crusade to create a chemically sterile, insect-free world seems to have engendered a fanatic zeal on the part of many specialists and most of the so-called control agencies. On every hand there is evidence that those engaged in spraying operations exercise a ruthless power. "The regulatory entomologists . . . function as prosecutor, judge and jury, tax assessor and collector and sheriff to enforce their own orders," said Connecticut entomologist Neely Turner. The most flagrant abuses go unchecked in both state and federal agencies.

It is not my contention that chemical insecticides must never be used. I do contend that we have put poisonous and biologically potent chemicals indiscriminately into the hands of persons largely or wholly ignorant of their potentials for harm. We have subjected enormous numbers of people to contact with these poisons, without their consent and often without their knowledge. If the Bill of Rights contains no guarantee that a citizen shall be secure against lethal poisons distributed either by private individuals or by public officials, it is surely only because our forefathers, despite their considerable wisdom and foresight, could conceive of no such problem.

I contend, furthermore, that we have allowed these chemicals to be used with little or no advance investigation of their effect on soil, water, wildlife, and man himself. Future generations are unlikely to condone our lack of prudent concern for the integrity of the natural world that supports all life.

There is still very limited awareness of the nature of the threat. This is an era of specialists, each of whom sees his own problem and is unaware of or intolerant of the larger frame into which it fits. It is also an era dominated by industry, in which the right to make a dollar at whatever cost is seldom challenged. When the public protests, confronted with some obvious evidence of damaging results of pesticide applications, it is fed little tranquilizing pills of half truth. We urgently need an end to these false assurances, to the sugar coating of unpalatable facts. It is the public that is being asked to assume the risks that the insect controllers calculate. The public must decide whether it wishes to continue on the present road, and it can do so only when in full possession of the facts. In the words of Jean Rostand, "The obligation to endure gives us the right to know."

References

Commodity Stabilization Service. *The Pesticide Situation for 1957–58,* U.S. Department of Agriculture, April 1958.

Elton, Charles S. *The Ecology of Invasions by Animals and Plants.* New York: Wiley, 1958.

Report on Environmental Health Problems. *Hearings before the Subcommittee of the Committee on Appropriations.* House of Representatives, 86th Congress, 2nd Session, 1960.

Shepard, Paul. "The Place of Nature in Man's World." *Atlantic Naturalist,* Vol. 13 (1958): 85–89.

Ethical Duties to the Environment

Ethical Land Use: Principles of Policy and Planning (1994)

Timothy Beatley

The environmental impacts of land-use actions are substantial, and contemporary land-use practices threaten, in a variety of ways, the ecological integrity of our planet. Land-use practices and patterns can create and induce serious air and water pollution problems. Without significant safeguards, for example, site grading and land development can generate tremendous erosion and sedimentation problems. Urbanization, which usually results in the replacement of natural vegetation with pavement and other impervious surfaces, can create serious storm-water runoff problems as well as modifications to the microclimate. Other land-use practices, such as heavy reliance on septic tanks, lead directly to the degradation of water quality. Sprawling land-use patterns, which encourage the use of automobiles, contribute to urban air quality problems. Numerous metropolitan areas, for example, are in violation of minimum EPA ambient standards for ozone and carbon monoxide pollution.

As population growth and land consumption continue over time, there are fewer and fewer natural areas, areas largely untouched by human hands, and fewer opportunities to connect them through greenways and other green systems. A recent global analysis of existing wilderness areas undertaken by the Sierra Club found that there are, not surprisingly, relatively few places which do not bear human scars (McCloskey and Spalding, 1987). Wilderness and natural areas are increasingly lost to the human pressures to build and develop as if the frontier still exists in perpetuity. Globally, the planet is in the midst of an unprecedented period of species extinction and loss of biodiversity, and the chief cause is habitat loss (see Ehrlich and Ehrlich, 1981; Wilson, 1988). In many developing countries a primary cause of the loss of rainforests and natural areas is human settlement policy—and land tenure policies that encourage the settlement of rural areas and the decentralization of urban population (e.g., Gradwohl and Greenberg, 1988; Repetto, 1988). Loss of forestlands and other forms of vegetation in turn contributes to current global warming. (It is estimated that deforestation results in the emission of between one and two billion tons of carbon into the atmosphere each year; see Flaven, 1989.)

Justifications for land-use interventions to protect the environment have, in the past, relied heavily upon anthropocentric reasoning. Wetlands are preserved because they provide necessary functions beneficial to human beings— for instance, in the form of flood control, biological spawning grounds for commercially important fish, and important recreational uses. Restrictions are placed on the extent to which individuals and businesses are allowed to pollute, not primarily because such pollution is a priori immoral, but usually because such actions are allocatively inefficient: that is, if the free market could take such externalities into account, then pollution levels would tend to be much lower. The costs of unrestricted pollution, it is believed, when added up over the entire society, far exceed the benefits. . . . [W]e . . . explored nonutilitarian rationales; for instance, placing restrictions on the extent to which an individual is allowed to pollute surface waters not because such an outcome is inefficient, but rather because we believe it is wrong that an individual should be allowed to impose these kinds of harms on others and the general public.

Is it conceivable that certain ethical obligations may exist relative to the environment *itself*, rather than as instrumental to human beings who use or enjoy the environment? In this chapter we address this critical question, or what might be broadly described as the nonanthropocentric view. We will not disassociate ourselves completely from instrumental, anthropocentric views, but will find that certain types of environmental obligations may effectively advance both anthropocentric and nonanthropocentric moral obligations.

Before we address the matter of nonanthropocentric obligations, we shall briefly examine several special questions of environmental duty not previously taken up but which may figure prominently into any comprehensive treatment of land-use ethics. Specifically, we need to define the fundamental role of nature and the natural environment in human lives—not from a biological or ecological perspective, but from a psychological and emotional view.

The Role of Nature and Natural Areas in a Modern World

Very often land-use conflicts center around proposals to destroy or consume natural areas—whether a wild area or an urban park—and to put in their place human-made structures. This process raises a host of questions relating to equity and to expectations (e.g., citizens frequently feel shocked and surprised upon learning that a special patch of land they have come to appreciate and value will no longer be available to them); in addition, there is a broader question about the role and importance of such areas in human existence. As population growth continues to escalate and human pressures to build and develop continue to rise, it becomes increasingly difficult to preserve and protect these natural areas.

Do human beings really need to see and experience mountains, deserts, streams, and wildlife? Obviously we require certain environmental goods to survive, notably clean air, clean water, and productive soil. But is it not the case that most human beings can survive quite nicely—can live full and productive lives—without hiking in a forest, without watching a peregrine falcon fly, without walking along a seashore? Indeed, depending upon where one lives, few of these opportunities may currently be available.

Moreover, should our concern about the loss of nature, and natural areas, be lessened somewhat because of our ability to find replacements for nature? There is considerable evidence that, when we contemplate contemporary landscape architectural designs such as zoos, we increasingly see the replacement or substitution of pseudo-nature or natural artifacts in place of the real thing. And, if such artifacts can satisfy many of the same psychological and aesthetic needs as the real thing, why should we be concerned about the loss of nature? Several years ago Laurence Tribe fueled this debate by writing an article, "Ways Not to Think about Plastic Trees" (1974), in which he lambasts the increasing tendency to replace the real natural environment with fake substitutes, and the belief on the part of some (e.g., Krieger, 1973) that society can manipulate environments with such artifacts to create or simulate the experience of nature. Tribe argues that such trends are symptomatic of a narrowly utilitarian and anthropocentric view of nature. Even from a narrow anthropocentric view, it is apparent that plastic trees simply cannot replace the aesthetic and ecological functions of natural trees, but, to be sure, they "survive" the environs of smog-infested cities. . . .

It can be argued that human beings require natural areas, that they must be exposed to *real* nature, above and beyond the biological and ecological functions they provide, for psychological well-being. Whether we have ethical obligations to preserve natural areas is at the center of many land-use disputes. Should we save wilderness areas? Do they serve important human functions that artificial nature and recreation in civilized environs simply cannot provide? Do we have obligations to preserve natural wonders, such as virgin prairie or Mt. St. Helens, or landscapes of special visual and aesthetic importance, such as the Virginia Piedmont, or coastal shorelines such as Cape Cod?

Many have argued that such landscapes and natural areas are important for stimulating the human contemplative faculty. Joseph Sax, for instance, argues convincingly for the important role played by national parks in this regard. Such areas are especially suited to promoting contemplative and reflective forms of recreation, increasingly important in a technologically dominated society and landscape. . . . The natural world and natural landscapes promote wonder and fascination, and there is a genuineness about them which seems to heighten this wonder. Frederick Law Olmsted, the famous landscape architect, spoke of this well over a century ago.

It does seem that as human beings we require "other things" in our lives for psychological balance and well-being. Ernest Partridge refers to this as "self-transcending" and argues that for human beings to achieve personal fulfillment, and to prevent us from becoming alienated and narcissistic, we require things in our lives which are independent and external to us: "our personal and moral life is enriched to the degree that it is 'extended outward' in self-transcending enjoyment, cherishing and contemplating things, places and ideals that are remote in space and time—ever, in a sense *timeless*" (Partridge, 1984, p. 126). Through this self-transcendence humans are able to "identify with, and seek to further, the well-being, preservation, and endurance of communities, locations, causes, artifacts, institutions, ideals, etc., which are outside themselves and which they hope will flourish beyond their own lifetimes" (Partridge, 1984, p. 188). Thus, under such a theory nature and natural objects—mountains, trees, wildlife—may serve an important psychological function. If we are unable to preserve and conserve such resources, opportunities for self-transcendence will be difficult. Of course it can be argued that other opportunities outside of nature exist for self-transcendence. But can this basic need for cherishing and contemplating other things be directed toward aspects of the built environment—for instance, historic buildings or major public monuments (such as the Cliff Palace at Mesa Verde, the San Francisco Golden Gate Bridge, or the Vietnam Memorial)? Will the lives of people who reside in urban areas be substantially diminished by the loss of natural opportunities? How does one explain the intense popularity of Gateway National Recreation Area in New York City? Certainly by something other than human census data.

The Possibilities of a Nonanthropocentric Land-Use Ethic

Contemporary western attitudes about the environment have been heavily criticized for being overly anthropocentric—that is, attributing value to nature and the natural environment based exclusively on their utility to human beings. Considerable literary attention and debate have occurred, particularly within the environmental ethics community, about the possibilities of a different paradigm—one which recognizes that nature may have intrinsic value; that is, it may be seen to have value and worth in and of itself, irrespective of what human value might be given to it.

Economists have an especially difficult time accepting such a moral theory, since all decisions under their paradigm are based on assigning human value and expressing this value in the form of dollar votes and economic demand. If a wetland has value, we know this by referring to what people are willing to pay to buy it, or see it, or visit it, or hunt on it. One of the more vehement critics of the nonanthropocentric view of moral obligations to the environment is William Baxter. His now classic *People or Penguins: The Case for Optimal Pollution* (1974) presents the archetypal case for a system of human-centered valuation. Baxter has difficulty imagining how any ethical obligations to the environment might be acknowledged which do not relate to human needs and valuations. . . .

Arguing that there are moral and ethical obligations that derive from, and extend beyond, human interests immediately raises a host of difficult questions, perhaps most obviously, how inclusive should our conception of the moral community be? If certain things *other than human beings* have value in and of themselves, which *things* do? Do ethical obligations extend just to certain forms of intelligent life (say to primates or cetaceans)? Do they extend to all sentient creatures? Do these obligations extend to all other species of life (from plants to elephants)? Do ethical obligations extend as well to protecting the larger ecosystems upon which these other life-forms rely? A variety of positions can be taken, which we will survey.

We should remember that preservation and management of the natural environment can be, and often is, defended on utilitarian grounds. Many of the earliest proponents of conservation in the United States, including Gifford Pinchot, saw such efforts as essential to maximizing the benefits of such resources as forests, watersheds, and fisheries. Many supporters of the concept of stewardship follow a similar logic, arguing for moral responsibilities to manage carefully the natural environment so as to protect its long-term productivity, including scenic beauty. Recently there has been substantial interest in a Judeo-Christian notion of stewardship, which holds that similar obligations exist, primarily stemming from the fact that ultimate ownership resides with God.

Expanding the Moral Community

It is an empirical truth that, over the last several decades, citizens and elected officials have expanded the moral horizons to include "other" considerations besides narrow anthropocentric concerns. Laws have been passed to protect the welfare of animals used in research and the treatment of animals in society generally. Many wildlife conservation laws, including the federal Endangered Species Act (1973), have been enacted to protect other forms of life from the abuses and overexploitation of human beings. To be sure, much of the motivation behind these laws is indeed anthropocentric and utilitarian, but a significant degree of motivation has gone beyond this. Expanding the moral community to include other forms of life is seen by some as the result of a natural historical expansion of moral considerateness. Roderick Nash likens this expansion to a modern-day form of abolitionism. Expanding the moral community is entirely consistent, he argues, with the spirit and ideas of the American Revolution. This expansion of the moral community "fits quite squarely into the most traditional of all American ideals; the defense of minority rights and the liberation of exploited groups. Perhaps the gospel of ecology should not be seen so much as a revolt against American traditions as an extension and new application of them—as just another rounding out of the American Revolution" (Nash, 1985, p. 179). This incremental expansion of moral and legal rights is illustrated by Nash in figure 2-2, extending most recently to other forms of life, as expressed by the federal Endangered Species Act. In Nash's view it is natural that our moral journey begins with personal self-interest, and that gradually over time our moral community expands, considering family, tribe, nation, and ultimately nature and the larger environment. . . .

Obligations to Protect Species and Biodiversity

While some people would dispute whether ethical obligations exist to protect or prevent harm of individual organisms, many more are willing to acknowledge that it is morally wrong to jeopardize the continued existence of an entire species. This has become a particularly central issue in public land-use policy, as urban development and habitat loss have increasingly become major causes of species extinction, both in this country and abroad. In the United States severe conflicts are arising between demands for housing and development, and the habitat needs of endangered or threatened species. Examples of species-development conflicts are numerous (see Beatley, 1989a). A recent proposal to build a shopping center in Austin, Texas, threatens the survival of several cave-dwelling invertebrates found nowhere else in the world (a spider, two types of beetles, a pseudo-scorpion, and a cave-adapted daddy-longlegs). New housing

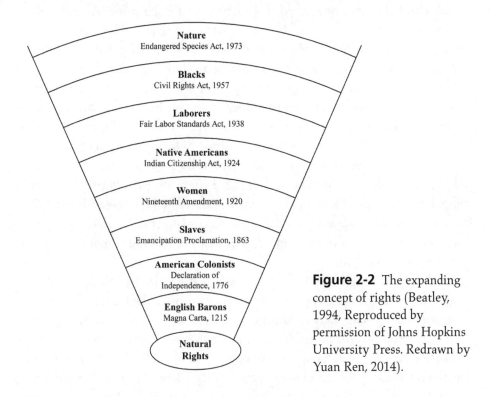

Figure 2-2 The expanding concept of rights (Beatley, 1994, Reproduced by permission of Johns Hopkins University Press. Redrawn by Yuan Ren, 2014).

projects in western Riverside County, California, threaten habitat of the endangered Stephens's kangaroo rat. Second-home development on Big Pine Key, Florida, threatens the existence of the dwindling population of the Key deer, which, among other things, has fallen victim to road-kills as a result of the dramatic increases in automobile traffic accompanying new development. Endangered sea turtles all along the Atlantic and Gulf coasts have difficulty nesting because of the explosive shoreline development and the bright lights typically associated with it. The least Bell's vireo, a western songbird, is threatened in the San Diego area as a result of development in, and destruction of, its riparian habitats. A recent study by the Center for Plant Conservation indicates that urban development is threatening hundreds of native American plants (Shabecoff, 1988). Neither land-use theory nor practice have adequately taken this issue into consideration.

Globally, species extinction and loss of biodiversity is perhaps the single most disturbing environmental trend of our time, with estimates that as much as one-quarter of all species on the earth will become extinct by the next century (see Reid and Miller, 1990). Some scientists estimate that we may already be losing more than 17,000 species per year.

Much of the reasoning used to justify concern about loss of endangered species in recent years has clearly been anthropocentric and largely utilitarian in nature. There are many important reasons for protecting endangered plant and animal species. They represent a tremendous biological storehouse, the loss of which may deprive us of substantial medical, scientific, and commercial benefits. It is estimated that the total number of species in the world ranges from ten to one hundred million (of this there is even considerable uncertainty; see Wilson, 1988, 1992). We are now in the position of losing many species we have yet to discover or even catalog or understand fully. A large portion of commercial pharmaceutical products are derived directly from wild plants and animals, and potential scientific and medical benefits are tremendous (see Myers, 1979). Protecting species diversity may also hold out the potential of discovering new disease-resistant crops, or crops better adjusted to changing climatic conditions (e.g., the Buffalo gourd).

Endangered and threatened species are also important indicators of how healthy and sustainable our planet really is. The loss of the least Bell's vireo, or other songbird species, may hold little direct impact to most people, yet it may be indicative of the broader environmental degradation occurring—a harbinger of worse environmental calamities to come. Biologists Paul and Anne Ehrlich use a vivid analogy for species extinction: they liken it to the rivets popping out of the wing of an airliner (see Ehrlich and Ehrlich, 1981). With each popped rivet (extinction), the structural integrity of the airliner (earth) is further undermined, until the plane will no longer fly: "unfortunately all of us are passengers on a very large spacecraft, one on which we have no option but to fly" (Ehrlich and Ehrlich, 1981, p. xii). Endangered species and their habitats can also provide substantial recreational, aesthetic, and other benefits for humans.

Nonanthropocentric arguments have also been offered. Similar to the positions embraced by animal rights supporters, the protection of species diversity is sometimes defended on the grounds that species have an inherent right to existence, regardless of the utility or value such species might hold for humans. Ehrenfeld, one of the more frequently cited authors, argues for such a right in his classic, *The Arrogance of Humanism* (1981). . . .

The willingness of *Homo sapiens* to acknowledge the existence rights of other forms of life is not uniform, however, but is biased in favor of certain types of species. Certain endangered species are clearly put at a marked disadvantage because they are not cute, cuddly, or otherwise visually attractive or appealing to the public. This explains why people express a disproportionately high level of concern and affection for bears but not bats, lions but not lizards, tigers but not tiger salamanders. The bias seems particularly evident in favor of large terrestrial mammals, especially those that are in some way anthropomorphic. . . .

. . . More fundamentally, no species should have to rely on its visual attractiveness to humans as a measure of its worth or right to exist.

Biocentric Approaches and Obligations to Ecosystems

Perhaps our ethical obligations extend not to individual organisms or natural
objects or to endangered species, but rather to a broader ecological plane. Can
it be argued that in the use of land the primary moral obligation is to protect
and sustain entire ecological systems rather than to single out any one or a
few components of this system? The emergence of the field of ecology during
the twentieth century, and especially the last thirty years, has done much to
promote these types of ethical viewpoints. During this period there has been
a growing recognition that the natural environment is an incredibly complex
and interwoven system, and that modifications to any part of the system may
impact other elements of the system, often (if not usually) in ways which are
not understood fully in advance. Different biocentric or ecosystem positions
have emerged in recent years, and I will briefly review the more central of
these below and speculate on their implications for land-use policy. I begin with
Aldo Leopold's land ethic, outlined over sixty years ago, which also serves as a
foundation for many of the more contemporary theories.

Leopold's Land Ethic

In many ways an eco-centric ethic of land use was first developed and argued
by Aldo Leopold, in an article first published in the *Journal of Forestry* (1933)
that later appeared in his now classic *A Sand County Almanac* (1949). This
book has, perhaps more than any other, crystallized, at least for those in the
land-use and environmental professions, the notion that there are fundamental
ethical issues involved in how we use, allocate, and appreciate land. Moreover, it
is an ethic based on an ecological premise; Leopold saw the need to protect the
integrity of the ecosystem as a whole. Indeed, Leopold views human beings as
part of this ecosystem with certain ethical obligations deriving from this relationship. Equally, it is an ethic based on an aesthetic premise; Leopold saw the
need to consider beauty in land-use decisions (see Little, 1992).

Leopold is particularly harsh to economists and those who hold that the
appropriate ethical posture toward the land is essentially economic. Recall his
oft-quoted passage that admonishes us to acknowledge other noneconomic factors: "quit thinking about decent land-use as solely an economic problem. Examine each question in terms of what is ethically and esthetically right, as well
as what is economically expedient. A thing is right when it tends to preserve

the integrity, stability and beauty of the biotic community. It is wrong when it tends otherwise" (1949, pp. 224–235).

Leopold is equally critical of our contemporary notions of progress. He questions whether, as a society and culture, we are indeed moving forward, given the types of choices we make in the process. Is it progress to forsake a marsh for a highway or a shopping center? Is it progress for people to recreate in automobiles at high speeds, failing to comprehend the beauty and wonder of the natural environment—an appreciation only available at a slower, more contemplative pace? Is it progress to permit the extinction of an animal species, or the destruction of wild lands, for the sake of material goods? Leopold raises the possibility that, rather than being in a period of *progress*, perhaps our current situation can better be described as *regress*. Here are three passages which, when linked together, form the core of his sermon:

> Our grandfathers were less well-housed, well-fed, well-clothed than we are. The strivings by which they bettered their lot are also those which deprived us of pigeons [referring to passenger pigeons]. Perhaps we now grieve because we are not sure, in our hearts, that we have gained by the exchange. The gadgets of industry bring us more comforts than the pigeons did, but do they add as much to the glory of the spring? (p. 109)
>
> Man always kills the thing he loves, and so we the pioneers have killed our wilderness. Some say we had to. Be that as it may, I am glad I shall never be young without wild country to be young in. Of what avail are forty freedoms without a blank spot on the map? (p. 149)
>
> In short, a land ethic changes the role of *Homo sapiens* from conqueror of the land-community to plain member and citizen of it. It implies respect for his fellow-members, and also respect for the community as such. (p. 204)

Primary to the development of Leopold's land ethic is the concept of community. He analogizes from the human community to the natural community. In a human community there are certain obligations that derive from the mutual interdependence of individuals. Individuals in the community benefit from the community as a whole, and thus in turn they have obligations to the community. Equally true, just as a person is a member of human communities, she or he is also a part of a larger biological community and as such has obligations to that community as well. "The land ethic simply enlarges the boundaries of the community to include soils, water, plants, and animals, or collectively: the land" (Leopold, 1949). The notion of people as "plain citizens" of earth, rather than its conquerors—plain members of an ecological community—is a powerful one with substantial implications for land-use policy. While Leopold offered few specifics concerning what such an ethical orientation requires, it is clear that major disruptions of the ecological community are unethical. It is also clear that, to Leopold, there is an ethical obligation to act as "stewards" of the land and not to waste its fruits or undermine its ecological integrity.

Holistic and Organic Ethics

In more recent years a number of environmental ethicists have further expanded and developed the Leopold land ethic. Some have argued that ethical obligations are owed to ecosystems qua ecosystems—not necessarily because ecosystems hold value to humans, or because they support other forms of life, but because of their complexity and uniqueness and thus their intrinsic value. . . .

There are, of course, practical difficulties in operationalizing an ethic based on obligations to ecosystems. Perhaps the most obvious difficulty is determining how ecosystems are to be defined. In reality the natural environment is comprised of a series of nested ecosystems—each smaller ecosystem is part of a larger one. On one level, a small five-acre wetland is clearly an ecosystem, and filling it in or otherwise destroying it might be considered immoral under an organic or holistic ethic. Such a wetland, however, is itself but one of many other similar eco-units which comprise and make up a larger ecosystem—an estuary, or a regional watershed, or ultimately a continental ecosystem. In the view of organic/holistic ethicists, which of these ecosystems are we obliged to protect? . . .

There are several problems with this interpretation, of course. One is that the same eco-dynamics and natural conditions which give rise to the ethical obligations at larger scales are present in the five-acre wetland case. On what grounds does the larger ecosystem have *intrinsic* value, while the smaller one does not? Furthermore, from an empirical point of view, destruction of the smaller ecosystem may have impacts on the integrity of the larger ecosystem, when the cumulative effects of such practices are considered. (Indeed this has been a major shortcoming of our current regulatory approach to wetlands management—we fail to consider adequately the long-term cumulative effects of the continual loss of a few acres at a time.)

The organic/holistic view appears to give greater ethical importance to preserving the integrity of the larger ecosystem but also questions land-use practices that jeopardize the natural functioning of smaller ecosystems. But having concluded this, the skeptic might wonder, How can it be possible to satisfy the organic/holistic ethic while permitting any significant use of the land? First, land development can occur in ways which respect and sustain ecosystems; as we have already discussed at numerous points in this book, land use and land development are not uniform in their environmental effects. Land development can occur in ways which minimize disruption to hydrological, geological, and biological systems. (Consider Ian McHarg's famous book *Design with Nature* [1969] and the land planning techniques argued for therein.) Second, implementing the organic view provides additional moral weight to avoidance and protection of certain lands and natural processes especially critical for ecosystem maintenance (e.g., wetlands, estuaries, riverine systems). Third, while some degree of ecosystem disruption may be required to accomplish certain necessary societal land-use objectives (e.g., provision of new housing), the organic/holistic ethic emphasizes the moral imperative of *minimizing* the extent of this alteration. This ethic would seem to strengthen the criteria found in some existing environmental laws and regulations that prevent environmental destruction when there are *practicable alternatives* (e.g., section 404 of the federal Clean Water Act, which restricts placement of dredge and fill materials on wetlands; for explanation, see Salvesen, 1990). It also lends further weight to the conclusions of some courts, as in the classic *Just v. Marinette County* (1974) case, which ruled that landowners have no inherent right to modify the basic natural dynamics of a parcel of land.

Taylor's Respect for Nature

While organicists such as Callicott and Rolston argue that it is the natural ecosystem to which environmental obligations are owed, Taylor has taken an interesting and different theoretical approach in developing his theory, "Respect for Nature" (1986). In his book of the same title, Taylor argues that it is not the ecosystem per se which we have obligations to protect and sustain, but rather other forms of life (see also Taylor, 1981, 1983, 1984). All living creatures in Taylor's framework have inherent worth, regardless of whether they are sentient or nonsentient, plant or animal, endangered or nonendangered. Taylor argues that this respect for nature flows directly from a "biocentric outlook on nature." While this biocentric outlook cannot itself be further justified or derived—one simply has to accept it or not—once the outlook is embraced the attitude of respect is the only consistent ethical posture. . . .

What Taylor argues for is a kind of bioegalitarianism, where all forms of life have inherent worth and must be considered equally in any decision-making about land or environment. Taylor argues, interestingly, that the proposition that all organisms are teleological centers of life can be demonstrated by mentally assuming the posture of such organisms. Only by appreciating the entirety of their lives (a "wholeness of vision") can we see this. . . .

A Hierarchical System of Environmental Land Duties?

The ethical obligations to protect natural environments and their constituent parts are extensive and compelling. Land-use activities and patterns have had, and continue to have, a tremendous impact on the environment, and they represent a major policy area in which these ethical duties come into play. Protecting the natural environment can certainly be defended on the grounds of human self-interest; it seems clear to me that the very survival of the human race depends on a fundamentally different ethical orientation to natural resources, one which degrades and consumes these resources only sparingly and only when other alternatives are first exhausted.

But irrespective of the benefits of the natural environment to humans, I find convincing the arguments that nature has certain inherent worth that demands respect, to use Taylor's terms. This derives in my view from the existence of life, both sentient and nonsentient. This life can be seen to have a good of its own, can be seen to have inherent worth. Inanimate objects in nature—rivers, rocks, mountains—have no inherent worth in themselves in my view, but demand our protection and conservation because they sustain and provide habitat for living creatures. Unlike Taylor, I find the distinction between sentient and nonsentient life-forms to be a morally relevant one. When one develops land there is a difference, in my view, between the felling of a tree and, say, the killing of a black bear or a golden eagle. Greater moral obligations and duties are owed to the latter than the former because of their sentience.

Similarly, I believe our moral obligations to larger categories of organisms—that is, to species or communities of organisms—are greater than to single organisms. The right of an entire species to exist must outweigh the rights of a single creature. We are sometimes faced with difficult choices between the interests of endangered and nonendangered species where such a prioritizing may be necessary. For instance, the endangered desert tortoise (particularly its young) have, in recent years, been heavily preyed upon by ravens (a nonendangered species). The killing of some ravens may be essential to ensure the very survival of the tortoise as a species. As figure 2-3 indicates, moral priority must also be given to protecting the larger ecosystems which sustain species and organisms. If confronted with a choice between preserving an endangered species and the larger ecosystem which sustains multiple species (many of which may be endangered), the duty to preserve the ecosystem, in my view, takes precedence.

At every biological level, ethical land use requires that all efforts be made to minimize the extent of damage and destruction to the natural environment, and such impacts are permissible only for *important* social purposes. "Important"

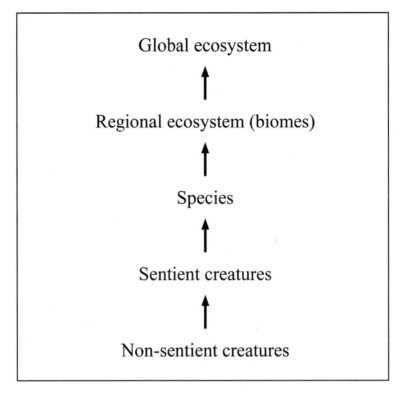

Figure 2-3 A hierarchy of environmental land obligations (Beatley, 1994, Reproduced by permission of Johns Hopkins University Press. Redrawn by Yuan Ren, 2014).

is, of course, open to substantial interpretation, but we must recognize that some degree of use and consumption of the natural commons is necessary. The strictest interpretation of "important" is to hold to the belief that destruction is only justified to promote the basic survival needs of human beings (e.g., to grow food, to build shelter and housing). I, like Taylor, however, recognize that for human existence to have value may require *other* land uses which extend beyond mere survival, and which promote such things as cultural values (e.g., from art museums to opera houses) and recreational values (e.g., from tennis courts to jogging trails). Beyond this, what is *necessary* or *essential* to human society is necessarily left to individual moral judgments.

Ethical land use requires, as well, serious efforts of good faith to discover and promote alternatives to environmental destruction and degradation. Different land-use configurations and plans may have dramatically different impacts on the natural environment. Satisfying the basic housing needs of our society, for example, need not be so land intensive. Land, moreover, is not uniform in its environmental features and characteristics, and development of certain areas (e.g., wetlands, shorelines, floodplains, and riverine areas) are particularly damaging from an ecological point of view. The availability of alternative sites for destructive or damaging land uses must be considered.

A special comment is also appropriate concerning the concepts of environmental *restoration* and *mitigation*. Ethical land use acknowledges that people have caused destruction to the natural environment for centuries, and with the development of technologies to restore (at least partially) degraded landscapes arises the moral obligation to restore the natural environment wherever possible. Ethical land use supports efforts to promote the recovery and reestablishment of populations of species, such as the red wolf, which have historically been eradicated over much of their original habitat. Ethical land use demands efforts to restore larger ecosystems, such as the hydrologic systems of the Florida Everglades and the Lower Mississippi Valley, to their natural conditions. Such actions seem consistent with our earlier notions of culpability and seem to be dictated even where the financial costs are high. Such restoration activities provide us with the opportunity to pass along a world and a common habitat which is in better condition than when it was inherited.

On the other hand, we should be realistic in recognizing the inherent limitations of human technology in this area. We should admit the great difficulties and uncertainties that exist in attempting to approximate the "natural" result. This issue is perhaps most clearly illustrated in the area of wetlands mitigation. It is a common practice today (at both federal and state levels) to permit the filling or degradation of *natural* wetlands in exchange for certain mitigation actions—either the restoration of degraded wetlands of an equal or greater acreage elsewhere, or the creation of new wetlands. The evidence is fairly convincing that, while it may be possible to restore or create certain functions of natural wetlands (e.g., their flood retention capacities), it is nearly impossible to replicate their full natural workings, especially their biological productivity (see Kusler and Kentula, 1989). If such natural systems are permitted to be damaged or degraded, some form of adequate compensation should be mandated, but ethical land use demands that all efforts be made to prevent the destruction in the first place. Mitigation and restoration cannot be used as an excuse to permit the destruction of such areas.

These environmental obligations, then, hold substantial implication for contemporary land-use policy and planning. A reverence for, and serious moral consideration of, the interests of other forms of life and the habitats upon and in which they rely, implies a new sense of caution about how natural lands are used. It implies the need to minimize the extent of the human "footprint." It implies, perhaps, a vision of a shared planet and an obligation not to squander the limited common habitat (see Beatley, 1989a). Among the specific land-use and planning policies that seem required by such an ethic are these: higher urban and suburban densities and more compact and contiguous development patterns; the redirection of growth back into existing urban centers and the revitalization of declining areas; in filling and utilizing already degraded and committed lands for new developments before encroaching on environmentally sensitive habitat areas; the creation of regional networks of green spaces connecting existing parks and open spaces, and protecting hydrological and other important elements of the ecosystem; and restricting the extent to which resorts, second homes, and other less essential forms of development are subsidized or permitted at all.

The vision of a shared planet may call for other changes in life-style that extend beyond simply the amount of land we directly consume for development. A number of contemporary threats to species in this country involve, for example, water projects (e.g., dams, reservoirs, diversion systems). The vision of a shared planet may necessitate sharply curtailing the extent to which we wastefully consume a scarce resource such as water (particularly for agricultural use in the arid West). The same can be said about energy consumption, when as a consequence we severely and irreparably damage the habitat of endangered and nonendangered species (e.g., the destruction of a riparian ecosystem as a result of a hydroelectric project, or the creation of acid deposition as a result of coalburning power plants, the tremendous damage done by the Exxon Valdez tanker in the recent Alaska oil spill). There are many ways in which being a plain citizen may require rethinking basic life-style and consumption patterns, many of which play themselves out in the land-use arena. And, perhaps most fundamentally, the notion of sharing the planet with fellow human beings and all life-forms will require serious efforts on a global scale to control population growth. Such strategies as higher densities, urban infilling, and energy conservation can do only so much to reduce the human impact when the quantity of people, their activities, and resource demands are expanding at exponential rates. The pressure on all environmental systems increases in relation to human demands for survival.

Summary

Ethical land use includes major duties to protect the natural environment. Ethical land-use policy acknowledges both the instrumental values served by and the inherent worth of the natural environment. Land-use ethics must acknowledge that humans are but plain citizens on the earth and have no right to use land and natural resources in a wasteful manner. Land-use ethics requires a basic respect for all forms of life, and a concerted and serious effort to minimize the impacts of human actions on the other members of the biotic community. These obligations extend to individual organisms, species, and the larger ecosystems which sustain them. While some degree of human intrusion on the natural environment is inevitable, there is an ethical obligation to ensure that the human footprint is a small one.

References

Baxter, William F. *People or Penguins: The Case for Optimal Pollution*. New York: Columbia University Press, 1974.

Beatley, Timothy. "Planning for Endangered Species: On the Possibilities of Sharing a Small Planet." *Carolina Planning* 15, no. 2 (1989): 32–41.

Booth, Annie L., and Harvey M. Jacobs. Forthcoming. "Ecofeminism: Connectedness and Wholeness in Human/Nature Relationships." *Environmental Ethics*.

Clark, Stephen R. L. *The Moral Status of Animals*. Oxford: Oxford University Press, 1977.

Devall, Bill. *Simple in Means, Rich in Ends: Practicing Deep Ecology*. Salt Lake City: Peregrine Smith Books, 1988.

Devall, Bill, and George Sessions. *Deep Ecology: Living As If Nature Mattered*. Salt Lake City: Peregrine Smith Books, 1985.

Ehrlich, Paul R., and Anne H. Ehrlich. *Extinction: the Causes and Consequences of the Disappearance of Species*. New York: Ballantine, 1981.

Flavin, Christopher. *Slowing Global Warming: A Worldwide Strategy*. Washington, DC: Worldwatch Institute, 1989.

Fox, Michael W. *Returning to Eden: Animal Rights and Human Responsibility*. New York: Viking, 1980.

Fretwell, Sammy. "General Assembly Debates Dolphin Rights." *Sun Myrtle Beach News* (1990).

Gradwohl, Judith, and Russell Greenberg. *Saving the Tropical Forests*. Washington, DC: Island Press, 1988.

Hare, Richard M. "Moral Reasoning about the Environment." *Journal of Applied Philosophy* 4, no. 1 (1987): 3–14.

Kellert, Stephen R. *Public Attitudes toward Critical Wildlife and Natural Habitat Issues*. Washington, DC: U.S. Fish and Wildlife Service, 1979.

Kheel, Marti. "Ecofeminism and Deep Ecology: Reflections on Identity and Difference." *Trumpeter* 8, no. 2 (1991): 62–71.

Krieger, Martin H. "What's Wrong with Plastic Trees?" *Science* 179 (1973): 446–55.

Kusler, Jon, and Mary Kentula, eds. *Wetland Creation and Restoration: The Status of the Science*. Washington, DC: Environmental Protection Agency, 1989.

Leopold, Aldo. *A Sand County Almanac, and Sketches Here and There*. Oxford: Oxford University Press, 1949.

Little, Charles E. "Commentary: On Loving the Land." *Journal of Soil and Water Conservation* 42, no. 4 (1987): 249–50.

McCloskey, J. Michael, and Heather Spalding. *A Reconnaissance-Level Inventory of the Amount of Wilderness Remaining in the World*. San Francisco: Sierra Club, 1987.

McHarg, Ian L. *Design with Nature*. Garden City, New York: Anchor Books, 1969.

Midgley, Mary. *Animals and Why They Matter*. Harmondsworth, England: Penguin, 1983.

Morris, Richard Knowles, and Michael W. Fox. *On the Fifth Day: Animal Rights & Human Ethics*. Washington, DC: Acropolis Books, 1978.

Myers, Norman. *The Sinking Ark. A New Look at the Problem of Disappearing Species*. New York: Pergamon Press, 1979.

Naess, Arne. "Self-Realization in Mixed Communities of Humans, Bears, Sheep, and Wolves." *Inquiry* 22 (1979): 231–41.

———. "The Shallow and the Deep, Long Range Ecology Movement, a Summary." *Inquiry* 16 (1973): 95–100.

Nash, Roderick F. "Rounding Out the American Revolution: Ethical Extension and the New Environmentalism." In *Deep Ecology*, edited by Michael Tobias, 170–81. San Diego: Avant Books, 1985.

Partridge, Ernest, ed. "Nature as a Moral Resource." *Environmental Ethics Albuquerque* 6, no. 2 (1984): 101–30.

Regan, Tom. *All That Dwell Therein*. Berkeley: University of California Press, 1982.

———. *The Case for Animal Rights*. Berkeley: University of California Press, 1983.

Regan, Tom, and Peter Singer, eds. *Animal Rights and Human Obligations*. Englewood Cliffs, NJ: Prentice Hall, 1976.

Reid, Walter V., and Kenton R. Miller. *Keeping Options Alive*. Washington, DC: World Resources Institute, 1990.

Repetto, Robert. *The Forest for the Trees. Government Policies and the Misuse of Forest Resources*. Washington, DC: World Resources Institute, 1988.

Rodman, John. "Animal Justice: The Counter Revolution in Natural Right and Law." *Inquiry* 22 (1980): 3–22.

———. "The Liberation of Nature?" *Inquiry* 20 (1977): 3–22.

Rolston, Holmes. *Environmental Ethics: Duties to and Values in the Natural World*. Philadelphia: Temple University Press, 1988.

Salvesen, David. *Wetlands: Mitigating and Regulating Development Impacts*. Washington, DC: Urban Land Institute, 1990.

Sax, Joseph L. *Mountains without Handrails: Reflections on the National Parks*. Ann Arbor: University of Michigan Press, 1980.

Shabecoff, Philip. "Survey Finds Native Plants in Imminent Peril." *New York Times* (December 6, 1988): C1, C11.

Singer, Peter. *In Defense of Animals*. Oxford: Basil Blackwell, 1985.

———. "Animal Liberation." In *People, Penguins, and Plastic Trees*, edited by Donald Van DeVeer and Christine Pierce, 24–31. Belmont, California: Wadsworth, 1986.

Singer, Peter. *Animal Liberation*. New York: Random House, 1975.

Stone, Christopher D. *Should Trees Have Standing? Toward Legal Rights for Natural Objects*. Chapel Hill: University of North Carolina Press, 1974.

Taylor, Paul W. *Respect for Nature: A Theory of Environmental Ethics*. Princeton, NJ: Princeton University Press, 1986.

———. "The Ethics of Respect for Nature." *Environmental Ethics* 3, no. 3 (2008): 197–218.

Tobias, Michael, ed. *Deep Ecology*. San Diego, California: Avant Press, 1985.

Tribe, Laurence H. "Ways Not to Think about Plastic Trees: New Foundations for Environmental Law." *The Yale Law Journal* 83, no. 7 (1974): 1315–48.

Van DeVeer, Donald, and Christine Pierce. *People, Penguins, and Plastic Trees: Basic Issues in Environmental Ethics*. Belmont, California: Wadsworth Publishing, 1986.

Warren, Karen J. "Feminism and Ecology: Making Connections." *Environmental Ethics* 9, no. 1 (1987): 3–20.

Wilson, Edward O. *Biodiversity*. Washington, DC: National Academy Press, 1988.

———. *The Diversity of Life*. Washington, DC: National Academy Press, 1992.

Zales, Joan. "Prairie Dogs Gassed Day before Planned Resource." *Boulder Daily Camera*, July 20 (1988): A1.

Whither Conservation Ethics?

Beyond the Land Ethic (1999)

J. Baird Callicott

Today we face an ever deepening environmental crisis, global in scope. What values and ideals, what vision of biotic health and wholeness should guide our response? American conservation began as an essentially moral movement and has, ever since, orbited around several ethical foci. Here I briefly review the history of American conservation ethics as a context for exploring a moral paradigm for twenty-first-century conservation biology.

Ralph Waldo Emerson and Henry David Thoreau were the first notable American thinkers to insist, a century and a half ago, that other uses might be made of nature than most of their fellow citizens had theretofore supposed (Nash, 1989). Nature can be a temple, Emerson (1836) enthused, in which to draw near and to commune with God or the "Oversoul" (Albanese, 1990). Too much civilized refinement, Thoreau (1863) argued, can overripen the human spirit; just as too little can coarsen it. In wildness, he thought, lay the preservation of the world.

John Muir (1894, 1901) took the romantic-transcendental nature philosophy of Emerson and Thoreau and made it the basis of a national, morally charged campaign for the appreciation and preservation of wild nature. The natural environment, especially in the New World, was vast enough and rich enough, he believed, to satisfy our deeper spiritual needs as well as our more manifest material needs. Amplifying Thoreau's countercultural theme, Muir strongly condemned prodigal destruction of nature in the service of profligate materialism and greed (Cohen, 1984). People going to forest groves, mountain scenery, and meandering streams for religious transcendence, aesthetic contemplation, and healing rest and relaxation put these resources to a "better"—i.e., morally superior—use, in Muir's opinion, than did the lumber barons, mineral kings, and captains of industry hell-bent upon little else than worshipping at the shrine of the Almighty Dollar and seizing the Main Chance (Fox, 1981).

Critics today, as formerly, may find an undemocratic and therefore un-American presumption lurking in the romantic-transcendental conservation ethic of Emerson, Thoreau, and Muir. To suggest that some of the human satisfactions that nature affords are morally superior to others may only reflect aristocratic biases and class prejudices (O'Conner, 1988). According to utilitarianism—a popular moral and political doctrine introduced by Jeremy Bentham (1823)—human happiness, defined ultimately in terms of pleasure and pain, should be the end of both individual and government action. And one person's pleasure is not necessarily another's. Landscape painters, romantic literati, and transcendental philosophers may find beauty, truth, and goodness in pristine alpine heights, deep forests, and solitary dales, but the vast majority of workaday Americans want affordable building material and building sites, unlimited tap water, cheap food and fiber and good land to raise it on, industrial progress and prosperity generally . . . , and, after all of this, maybe a little easily accessible outdoor recreation.

At the turn of the century, Gifford Pinchot, a younger contemporary of John Muir, formulated a resource conservation ethic reflecting the general tenets of progressivism—an American social and political movement then coming into its own. America's vast biological capital had been notoriously plundered and squandered for the benefit not of all its citizens, but for the profit of a few. Without direct reference to John Stuart Mill (1863)—Bentham's utilitarian protégé, whose summary moral maxim it echoes—Pinchot (1947, 325–326) crystallized the resource conservation ethic in a motto which he credits WJ McGee with formulating: "the greatest good of the greatest number for the longest time." He bluntly reduced the romantic poets' and transcendental philosophers' "Nature" to "natural resources." Indeed, Pinchot insisted that "there are just two things on this material earth—people and natural resources" (1947, 325). He even equated conservation with the systematic exploitation of natural resources. "The first great fact about conservation," Pinchot (1947, xix) enthused, "is that it stands for development." And it was Pinchot (1947, 263) who characterized the Muirian contingent of nature lovers as aiming to "lock up" resources in the national parks and other wilderness reserves.

The first moral principle of the resource conservation ethic is equity—the just or fair distribution of natural resources among present and also future generations of consumers and/or users. Its second moral principle, equal in importance to the first, is efficiency—a natural resource should not be wastefully exploited. Just slightly less obvious, the principle of efficient resource utilization involves the concepts of best or "highest use" and "multiple use."

The "gospel of efficiency," as Samuel Hays (1959) characterized the resource conservation ethic, also implies a sound scientific foundation. The resource conservation ethic thus became wedded to the eighteenth and nineteenth century scientific worldview in which nature is conceived to be a collection of bits of matter, assembled into a hierarchy of externally related chemical and organismic aggregates, which can be understood and successfully manipulated by analytic and reductive methods.

The resource conservation ethic is also wedded to the correlative social science of economics—the science of self-interested rational monads pursuing "preference satisfaction" in a free market. However, because the market, notoriously, does not take account of "externalities"—certain costs of doing business: soil erosion, for example, and environmental pollution—and because standard economic calculations discount the future dollar value of resources in comparison with present dollar value, the free market cannot be relied upon to achieve the most efficient, and certainly not the most prudent, use of natural resources. Pinchot (1947) persuasively argued, therefore, that government ownership and/or regulation of natural resources and resource exploitation is a necessary remedy. Federal and state bureaucracies, accordingly, were created to implement and administer conservation policy as the twentieth century advanced.

Since the resource conservation ethic was based so squarely upon Progressive democratic social philosophy and rhetorically associated with the Modern secular ethic of choice—utilitarianism—it triumphed politically and became institutionalized in the newly created government conservation agencies. The nonconsumptive uses of nature by aesthetes, transcendentalists, and wilderness recreationalists can be accommodated by assigning them a contingent market value or "shadow-price" (Krutilla and Fisher, 1985). In some circumstances such uses may turn out to be the highest or most efficient allocation of a given "resource." Thus, an occasional, otherwise worthless wild sop might be thrown to the genteel minority.

The celebrated Schism in the traditional American conservation movement —the schism between the conservationists proper and the preservationists, associated with the legendary names of Pinchot and Muir, respectively—was, thus, in the final analysis a matter of differing moral (metaphysical) philosophies. Both were essentially human-centered or "anthropocentric," to use the now standard terminology of contemporary environmental ethics. Both, in

other words, regarded human beings or human interests as the only legitimate ends and nonhuman natural entities and nature as a whole as means.
In the now standard terminology of contemporary environmental ethics, for
both conservationists and preservationists only people possess *intrinsic* value,
nature possesses merely *instrumental* value. The primary difference is that the
preservationists posited a higher transcendental reality above and beyond the
physical world and pitted the pychospiritual use of nature against its material
use. And they insisted that the one was incomparably superior to the other. The
conservationists were more materialistic and insisted, democratically, that all
competing uses of resources should be weighed impartially and that the fruits
of resource exploitation should be distributed broadly and equitably.

Although Muir's public campaign for the appreciation and preservation
of nature was cast largely in terms of the putative superiority of the human
spiritual values served by contact with undeveloped, wild nature, Muir also
seems to have been the first American conservationist privately to ponder the
proposition that nature itself possessed intrinsic value—value in and of itself—
quite apart from its human utilities (no matter whether of the more spiritual or
more material variety). To articulate this essentially nonanthropocentric intuition, Muir (1916) turned, ironically, to biblical fundamentals for the rhetorical
wherewithal (chapter 10). Very directly and plainly stated, God created man
and all the other creatures. Each of His creatures—man included, but not man
alone—and the creation as a whole are "good" in His eyes (i.e., in philosophical terms they have intrinsic value). Hence, to eradicate a species or to efface
nature is to undo God's creative work, and to subtract so much divinely imbued
inherent goodness from the world—a most impious and impertinent expression of human arrogance.

More radically than most contemporary exponents of the by-now-familiar
Judeo-Christian stewardship environmental ethic, Muir insisted that people
are just a part of nature on a par with other creatures and that all creatures (including ourselves) are valued equally by God, for the contribution we and they
make to the whole of His creation—whether we can understand that contribution or not. In Muir's own inimitable prose, "Why should man value himself
as more than a small part of the one great unit of creation? And what creature
of all that the Lord has taken the pains to make is not essential to the completeness of that unit—the cosmos? The universe would be incomplete without
man; but it would also be incomplete without the smallest transmicroscopic creature that dwells beyond our conceitful eyes and knowledge" (Muir, 1916, 139).

Reading between the lines, we can, I think, easily see that there was another
mind set animating Muir's moral vision—an evolutionary and ecological world
view. Darwin had unseated from his self-appointed throne the creature Muir

sometimes sarcastically called "lord man" and reduced him to but a "small part" of creation, and the likes of H. C. Cowles, S. A. Forbes, and F. E. Clements would soon validate Muir's intuition that there exists a unity and completeness—if not in the cosmos or universe at large, certainly in terrestrial nature—to which each creature, no matter how small, functionally contributes (McIntosh, 1985). This worldview held a profound but murky moral import. It fell to Aldo Leopold to bring the ethical implications of the ripening evolutionary-ecological paradigm clearly and fully to light.

Leopold began his career as a professional conservationist trained in the utilitarian Pinchot philosophy of the wise use of natural resources, for the satisfaction of the broadest possible spectrum of human interests, over the longest time (Meine, 1988). His ultimately successful struggle for a system of wilderness reserves in the national forests was consciously molded to the doctrine of highest use, and his new technique of game management essentially amounted to the direct transference of the principles of forestry from a standing crop of large plants to a standing crop of large animals (Leopold, 1919, 1921). But Leopold gradually came to the conclusion that the Pinchot resource conservation ethic was inadequate, because, in the last analysis, it untrue.

The resource conservation ethic's close alliance with science proved to be its undoing. Applied science cannot be thoroughly segregated from pure science. Knowledge of ecology is essential to efficient resource management, but during the first half of the twentieth century, ecology began to give shape to a radically different scientific paradigm than that which lay at the very foundations of Pinchot's philosophy. From an ecological perspective, nature is more than a collection of externally related useful, useless, and noxious species furnishing an elemental landscape of soils and waters. It is, rather, a vast, intricately organized and tightly integrated *system* of complex *processes*. As Leopold (1939a, 727) expressed it: "Ecology is a new fusion point for all the sciences. . . . The emergence of ecology has placed the economic biologist in a peculiar dilemma: with one hand he points out the accumulated findings of his search for utility, or lack of utility, in this or that species; with the other he lifts the veil from a biota so complex, so conditioned by interwoven cooperations and competitions, that no man can say where utility begins or ends."

Thus, we cannot remodel our natural *oikos* or household, as we do our artificial ones, without inducing unexpected disruptions. More especially, we cannot get rid of the Early American floral and faunal "furniture" (the prairie flora, bison, elk, wolves, bears) and randomly introduce exotic pieces (wheat, cattle, sheep, English sparrows, Chinese pheasants, German carp, and the like) that suit our fancy without risk of inducing destructive ecological chain reactions.

Conservation, Leopold came to realize, must aim at something larger and more comprehensive than a maximum sustained flow of desirable products (like lumber and game) and experiences (like sport hunting and fishing, wilderness travel, and solitude) garnered from an impassive nature (Flader, 1974). It must take care to ensure the continued function of natural processes and the integrity of natural systems. For it is upon these, ultimately, that human resources and human well-being depend.

The Pinchot resource conservation ethic is also untrue on the human side of its people/natural resources bifurcation. Human beings are not specially created and uniquely valuable demigods any more than nature itself is a vast emporium of goods and services, a mere pool of resources. We are, rather, very much a part of nature. Muir (1916) groped to express this bio-egalitarian concept in theological terms. Leopold did so in more honest ecological terms. Human beings are "members of a biotic team," plain members and citizens of one humming biotic community (Leopold, 1949, 205). We and the other citizen-members of the biotic community sink or swim together. Leopold's affirmation that plants and animals, soils and waters are entitled to full citizenship as fellow members of the biotic community is tantamount to the recognition that they too have intrinsic, not just instrumental, value. An evolutionary and ecological worldview, in short, implies a land ethic.

In sum, then, examining a core sample of the ethical sediments in the philosophical bedrock of American conservation, one may clearly discern three principal strata of laterally coherent moral ideals. They are the romantic-transcendental preservation ethic, the progressive-utilitarian resource conservation ethic, and the evolutionary-ecological land ethic. American conservation policy and the conservation profession reflect them all—thus giving rise to internal conflict and, from an external point of view, the appearance of confusion. The public agencies are still very much ruled by the turn-of-the-century resource conservation ethic; some of the most powerful and influential private conservation organizations remain firmly rooted in the even older romantic-transcendental philosophy; while contemporary conservation biology is clearly inspired and governed by the evolutionary-ecological land ethic (Soulé, 1985).

As we approach the end of the twentieth century, we face a situation today that is analogous to that faced by our forebears at the end of the nineteenth. Then, the American frontier had closed and what had once appeared to be an effectively boundless and superabundant New World suddenly had palpable limits. At present our generation is pressing hard against the ecological limits not just of the continent, but of the entire planet. We are witnessing the extension of the industrial juggernaut into every corner of the globe. Soils are washing into the sea; toxic chemicals are polluting surface water and groundwater; chain saws and bulldozers are wreaking havoc in tropical forests—and coincidentally exterminating a significant portion of Earth's complement of species—while acid rain is withering the forests and sterilizing the lakes in temperate regions of the Northern Hemisphere; chlorofluorocarbons are eroding the planet's protective ozone shield and fossil-fuel consumption is loading Earth's atmosphere with carbon dioxide. Since Leopold's land ethic is fully informed by and firmly grounded in evolutionary and ecological biology, it ought to supplant its nineteenth-century antecedents as our moral anchor in the face of the second wave of the environmental crisis looming threateningly on the horizon—but we need to be very clear about its implications.

The word *preserve* in Leopold's (1949, 224–225) famous summary moral maxim—"A thing is right when it tends to preserve the integrity, stability, and beauty of the biotic community; it is wrong when it tends otherwise"—is unfortunate because it seems to ally Leopold and the land ethic with the preservationists in the century-old preservation versus conservation conflict. We tend to think of Leopold as having begun his career in the latter camp and gradually come over, armed with new arguments, to the former. Leopold's historical association with the wilderness movement cements this impression. But Leopold was from first to last committed as much to active land management as to passive preservation, as a review of Leopold's unpublished papers and published but long-forgotten articles confirms (Flader, 1974; Meine, 1988). Leopold's vision went beyond the *either* efficiently develop *or* lock up and reserve dilemma of the modern conservation *problematique*. Indeed, Leopold himself was primarily concerned, on the ground as well as in theory, with integrating an optimal mix of wildlife—both floral and faunal—with human habitation and economic exploitation of land.

In a typescript composed shortly after a four-month trip to Germany in 1935—and ironically, but revealingly, entitled "Wilderness"—Leopold wrote,

> To an American conservationist, one of the most insistent impressions received from travel in Germany is the lack of wildness in the German landscape. Forests are there....Game is there....Streams and lakes are there....But yet, to the critical eye there is something lacking....I did not hope to find in Germany anything resembling the great "wilderness areas" which we dream about and talk about, and sometimes briefly set aside, in our National Forests and Parks....I speak rather of a certain quality which should be, but is not found in the ordinary landscape of producing forests and inhabited farms. (Leopold, 1991, 226–227)

In a more fully developed essay entitled "The Farmer as a Conservationist," Leopold (1939b) regales his reader with a rustic idyll in which the wild and domesticated floral and faunal denizens of a Wisconsin farmscape are feathered into one another to create a harmonious whole. In addition to cash and the usual supply of vegetables and meat, lumber and fuelwood, Leopold's envisioned farmstead affords its farm family venison, quail, and other small game, and a variety of fruit and nuts from its woodlot, wetlands, and fallow fields; and its pond and stream yield panfish and trout. It also affords intangibles—songbirds, wildflowers, the hoot of owls, the bugle of cranes, and intellectual adventures aplenty in natural history. To obtain this bounty, the farm family must do more than permanently set aside acreage, fence woodlots, and leave wetlands undrained. They must sow food and cover patches, plant trees, stock the stream and pond, and generally thoughtfully conceive and skillfully execute scores of other modifications, large and small, of the biota that they inhabit.

The pressure of growing human numbers and rapid development, especially in the Third World, implies, I think, that a global conservation strategy focused primarily on "wilderness" preservation and the establishment of nature reserves represents a holding action at best—and a losing proposition at last. I support wilderness and nature reserves—categorically—with my purse as well as my pen. But faced with the sobering realities of the coming century, the only viable philosophy of conservation is, I submit, a generalized version of Leopold's vision of a mutually beneficial and enhancing integration of the human economy with the economy of nature—*in addition to* holding on to as much untrammeled wilderness as we can.

Lack of theoretical justification complements the present sheer impracticability of conserving biodiversity solely by excluding man and his works. Change—not only evolutionary change, but climatic, successional, seasonal, and stochastic change—is natural (Botkin, 1990). And "man" is a part of nature. Therefore, it will no longer do to say, simply, that what existed before the agricultural-industrial variety of Homo sapiens evolved or arrived, as the case may be, is the ecological norm in comparison with which all anthropogenic modifications are degradations. To define environmental quality—the integrity, stability, and beauty of the biotic community—dynamically and positively, not statically and negatively, is part of the intellectual challenge that contemporary conservation biology confronts.

Happily, Leopold's conservation ideal of ecosystems that are at one productive and healthy is capable of generalization beyond the well-watered temperate latitudes and pastoral lifestyles characteristic of the upper Midwest. Charles M. Peters, Alwyn H. Gentry, and Robert O. Mendelsohn (1989) report that the nuts, fruits, oils, latex, fiber, and medicines annually harvested from a representative hectare of standing rain forest in Peru, for example, is of greater economic value than the sawlogs and pulpwood stripped from a similar hectare—greater even than if, following clear-cutting and slash-burning, the land is, in addition, converted to a forest monoculture or to a cattle pasture. They conclude that "without question, the sustainable exploitation of non-wood forest resources represents the most immediate and profitable method for integrating the use and conservation of Amazonian forests" (Peters et al., 1989, 656). Arturo Gomez-Pompa and Andrea Kaus (1988) argue that the greater incidence of trees bearing edible fruits than would occur naturally in the extant remnants of Central American rain forest suggests that these "pristine" habitats may once actually have been part of an extensive Maya permaculture.

Of course we must remember David Ehrenfeld's (1976) classic warning that we not put all our conservation eggs in the economic basket. It is too much to hope that a standard benefit-cost comparison will, in every case, indicate that the sustainable alternative to destructive development is more profitable. Certainly I am not here urging an unregenerate return to the economic determinism of the resource conservation ethic. Rather, I am simply pointing out that it is often possible for people to make a good living—and, in some instances, even the best living to be had—coexisting with rather than converting the indigenous biotic community. And I am urging that we strive to reconcile and integrate human economic activities with biological conservation. Expressed in the vernacular, I am urging that we think in terms of "win-win" rather than "zero sum." Further, I would like explicitly to state—and thereby invite critical discussion of—Leopold's more heretical, from the preservationist point of view, implied corollary proposition, viz., that human economic activities may not only coexist with healthy ecosystems, but that they may actually enhance them. Citing Gary Nabhan (1982), in a more recent discussion Ehrenfeld (1989, 9) provides a provocative example:

> In the Papago Indian Country of Arizona's and Mexico's Sonoran Desert . . . there are two oases only thirty miles apart. The northern one . . . is in the U.S. Organ Pipe Cactus National Monument, fully protected as a bird sanctuary, with no human activity except bird watching allowed. All Papago farming which has existed there since prehistory was stopped in 1957. The other oasis, . . . over the border in Mexico, is still being farmed in traditional Papago style. . . . Visiting the oases "on back-to-back days three times during one year," Nabhan, accompanied by ornithologists, found fewer than thirty-two species of birds at the Park Service's bird sanctuary but more than sixty-five species at the farmed oasis.

From this "modern parable of conservation," Ehrenfeld (1986, 9) concludes that "the presence of people may enhance the species richness of an area, rather than exert the effect that is more familiar to us." Is species richness a measure of ecological health? What other standards of ecosystem health can be formulated? How do these norms all fit together to form models of fit environments? Can we succeed, as the Papago seem to have done, in enriching the environment as we enrich ourselves? How does ecosystem health differ from and complement the conservation of biological integrity? These are some of the questions germane to a future conservation philosophy.

References

Allen, Timothy F. H., and Thomas W. Hoekstra. *Toward a Unified Ecology*. New York: Columbia University Press, 1992.

Allen, Timothy F. H., and Thomas B. Starr. *Hierarchy: Perspectives for Ecological Complexity*. Chicago: University of Chicago Press, 1982.

Alverson, William Surprison, Walter Kuhlmann, and Donald M. Waller. *Wild Forests: Conservation Biology and Public Policy*. Washington, DC: Island Press, 1994.

Angermeier, Paul L. "Does Biodiversity Include Artificial Diversity?" *Conservation Biology* (1994): 600–602.

Angermeier, Paul L., and James R. Karr. "Biological Integrity Versus Biological Diversity as Policy Directives." *BioScience* 44, no. 10 (1994): 690–97.

Barnett, Harold J., and Chandler Morse. *Scarcity and Growth: The Economics of Natural Resource Availability*. Baltimore: Johns Hopkins University Press, 1963.

Batisse, Michel. "Biosphere Reserves: An Overview." *Nature and Resources* 29, no. 1 (1993): 3–5.

Begon, M., J. L. Harper, and C. R. Townsend. *Ecology: Individuals, Populations and Communities*. Sunderland, MA.: Sinauer Associates, 1986.

Brown, J. H. "Alternative Conservation Priorities and Practices." In *73rd Annual Meeting, Ecological Society of America, Davis, California*. 1988.

Callicott, J. Baird. "A Review of Some Problems with the Concept of Ecosystem Health." *Ecosystem Health* 1, no. 2 (1995): 101–12.

———. "Standards of Conservation: Then and Now." *Conservation Biology* 4, no. 3 (1990): 229–32.

Charles, Anthony T. "Towards Sustainability: The Fishery Experience." *Ecological Economics* 11, no. 3 (1994): 201–11.

Clinton, Bill, and Albert Gore. *Putting People First: How We Can All Change America*. New York: Times Books, 1992.

Costanza, Robert, and Herman E. Daly. "Natural Capital and Sustainable Development." *Conservation Biology* 6, no. 1 (1992): 37–46.

Cronon, William. "The Trouble with Wilderness: Or, Getting Back to the Wrong Nature." In *Uncommon Ground: Toward Reinventing Nature*, edited by W. Cronon, New York: W. W. Norton (1995): 23–90.

Davis, Thomas. *Sustaining the Forest, the People, and the Spirit*. Albany: State University of New York Press, 1998.

Denevan, William M. "The Pristine Myth: The Landscape of the Americas in 1492." *Annals of the Association of American Geographers* 82, no. 3 (1992): 369–85.

Ehrenfeld, David W. "The Conservation of Non-Resources: Conservation Cannot Rely Solely on Economic and Ecological Justifications. There Is a More Reliable Criterion of the Value of Species and Communities." *American Scientist* 64, no. 6 (1976): 647–55.

Ehrlich, Paul R. "The Limits to Substitution: Meta-Resource Depletion and a New Economic-Ecological Paradigm." *Ecological Economics* 1, no. 1 (1989): 9–16.

———. "The Loss of Diversity: Causes and Consequences." *Biodiversity*. National Academy Press, Washington DC (1988): 21–27.

Elton, Charles S. *Animal Ecology*. London: Sidgwick and Jackson, 1927.

Foreman, Dave, John Davis, David Johns, Reed Noss, and Michael Soulé. "The Wildlands Project Mission Statement." *Wild Earth (Special Issue)* 3, no. 4 (1992).

Foreman, Dave. "Wilderness Areas and National Parks." *Wild Earth* 5 (1995): 8–16.

Gomez-Pompa, Arturo, and Andrea Kaus. "Taming the Wilderness Myth." *BioScience* 42, no. 4 (1992): 271–79.

Guha, Ramachandra. *The Unquiet Woods: Ecological Change and Peasant Resistance in the Himalaya*. Berkeley: University of California Press, 1989.

Jackson, Wes. *Altars of Unhewn Stone: Science and the Earth*. North Point Press, 1987.

———. *New Roots for Agriculture*. Lincoln, NE: University of Nebraska Press, 1980.

Kaufmann, Robert K. "The Economic Multiplier of Environmental Life Support: Can Capital Substitute for a Degraded Environment?" *Ecological Economics* 12, no. 1 (1995): 67–79.

Land Stewardship Project. *Biological, Financial, and Social Monitoring to Develop Highly Sustainable Farming System: Progress Report for 1995*. White Bear Lake, MN: Land Stewardship Project, 1995.

Larkin, Peter A. "An Epitaph for the Concept of Maximum Sustained Yield." *Transactions of the American Fisheries Society* 106, no. 1 (1977): 1–11.

Lélé, Sharachchandra, and Richard B. Norgaard. "Sustainability and the Scientist's Burden." *Conservation Biology* 10, no. 2 (1996): 354–65.

Lindeman, Raymond L. "The Trophic-Dynamic Aspect of Ecology." *Ecology* 23, no. 4 (1942): 399–418.

Muir, John. *A Thousand-mile Walk to the Gulf*. Edited by W. F. Bade. Boston: Houghton Mifflin Harcourt, 1916.

National Research Council. *Alternative Agriculture*. Washington, DC: National Academy Press, 1989.

———. *Sustainable Agriculture and the Environment in the Humid Tropics*. Washington, DC: National Academy Press, 1993.

Noss, Reed F. "Sustainability and Wilderness." *Conservation Biology* 5, no. 1 (1991): 120–22.

———. "Maintaining Ecological Integrity in Representative Reserve Networks: A World Wildlife Fund Canada." World Wildlife Fund-United States Discussion Paper (1995): 77–99.

O'Neil, A. E., A. S. Pandian, S. V. Rhodes-Conway, and A. H. Bornbush. "Human Economies, the Land Ethic, and Sustainable Conservation." *Conservation Biology* 9 (1995): 217–20.

O'Neill, Robert V., D. L. DeAngelis, J. B. Waide, and T. F. H. Allen. *A Hierarchical Concept of Ecosystems*. Vol. 23. Princeton University Press, 1986.

Plucknett, Donald L. "International Goals and the Role of the International Agricultural Research Centers." *Sustainable Agricultural Systems* (1990): 33–49.

Ramakrishnan, Palayanoor S. *Shifting Agriculture and Sustainable Development: An Interdisciplinary Study from North-Eastern India*. Park Ridge, NJ: Parthenon Publishing Group, 1992.

Rapport, David J. "Ecosystem Health: More Than A Metaphor?." *Environmental Values* 4, no. 4 (1995): 287–309.

———. "Ecosystem Health: an Emerging Integrative Science." In *Evaluating and Monitoring the Health of Large-Scale Ecosystems*, edited by D. J. Rapport, C. Gaudet, and P. Calow. Heidelberg: Springer-Verlag (1995): 5–32.

Robinson, John G. "The Limits to Caring: Sustainable Living and The Loss of Biodiversity." *Conservation Biology* 7, no. 1 (1993): 20–28.

———. "Believing What You Know Ain't So: Response to Holgate and Munro." *Conservation Biology* 7 (1993): 941–42.

Thomas, D. *Lake Trout Restoration Program: Who Profits, Who Pays?* Ann Arbor, MI: Special Publication of the Great Lakes Sport Fishing Council, 1995.

USDA Forest Service. *New Perspectives: An Ecological Path for Managing Forests*. Redding, Calif.: Pacific Northwest Research Station, Portland, Oregon, and Pacific Northwest Research Station, 1989.

Von Droste, Bernd. "The Role of Biosphere Reserves at a Time of Increasing Globalization." In *For the Conservation of Earth*. Fulcrum, Golden, Colorado. US Forest Service (1989): 89–93.

Westra, Laura. *An Environmental Proposal for Ethics: The Principle of Integrity*. Lanham, MD: Rowman & Littlefield, 1994.

Willers, Bill. "Sustainable Development: A New World Deception." *Conservation Biology* 8, no. 4 (1994): 1146–48.

Wilson, Edward O. *The Diversity of Life*. Cambridge: The Belknap Press of Harvard University Press, 1992.

Woodley, Stephen Jerome, James J. Kay, and George Francis, eds. *Ecological Integrity and the Management of Ecosystems*. CRC Press, 1993.

World Commission on Environment. *Our Common Future*. Oxford: Oxford University Press, 1987.

World Resources Institute. *World Resources, 1992–93*. Oxford: Oxford University Press, 1992.

Part Three

Substantive Theory

Introduction to Part Three

Substantive theory deals with the content theory in ecological design and planning, or, put differently, the theoretical foundation on which ecological planning is grounded. The selected readings in this section have been influential in advancing the theoretical foundations of ecological design and planning. The six readings address well-known themes, including aesthetics, culture, design, ecology, fitness, and place.

I begin with Catherine Howett's article "Systems, Signs, Sensibilities: Sources for a New Landscape Aesthetic," in *Landscape Journal* (1987),[1] because it sets the stage for understanding the emerging theoretical thinking within the profession of landscape architecture and its allied disciplines in the 1980s. Howett argued for the recognition of ecology as a way to better understand the interactions between organisms, including humans and their environment; semiotics as a mode of architectural communication; and place theory. Together, these contribute to the formation of a new intellectual synthesis and aesthetic for informing design decisions.

In the next reading, by Ian McHarg, "Open Space from Natural Processes" (1998),[2] the author makes a compelling case for the conservation of metropolitan open spaces for the ecosystem services they provide. McHarg proposed an ecological approach to protecting open spaces based on the intrinsic value they offer for human use.

A reading by architects Sim Van der Ryn and Stuart Cowan follows. In

"An Introduction to Ecological Design," from *Ecological Design* (1996),[3] they proposed a new approach to ecological design, discussed its key principles, and explained in a compelling way how it differs from conventional design.

The next article, by ecosystem ecologist Eugene Odum, "The Strategy for Ecosystem Development," has remained a masterpiece since its publication in 1969 in the journal *Science*.[4] Drawing on the knowledge of how ecosystems develop from youth to maturity, Odum proposed a compartment model for sorting landscapes according to the intrinsic ecological functions they serve. He then offered guidance on how the resultant information can be used to delineate the optimal uses of the landscape.

Landscape ecologist Richard T. T. Forman's article provides a wealth of information. "Foundations," from *Land Mosaics: The Ecology of Landscapes and Regions* (1995),[5] laid the foundation for understanding the ecology of regions with remarkable clarity.

There are other important contributions on substantive theory that deserve mention. Notable are the works of Marina Alberti, Michael Hough, Timothy Beatley, Joan Nassauer, Randy Hester, Robert Thayer, Frederick Steiner, and Laura Musacchio.

In "Urban Patterns and Ecosystem Functions" (2008), planner Marina Alberti provides an insightful analysis of the linkages between urban pattern and ecosystem dynamics, a relationship that is poorly understood.[6] She has been influential in the continued development of urban ecology.

In *Cities and Natural Process: A Basis for Sustainability* (2004), landscape architect Michael Hough recommended robust principles to link urbanism with nature at both the regional and local scales. He contended that an environmental view is essential in understanding the processes that shape cities and introduced natural process as an alternative basis for their design and planning.[7]

In "Place Basics: Concepts, Research, Literature" from *Native to Nowhere* (2004),[8] planner Timothy Beatley examined important concepts of place and place making in contemporary life and brought together succinctly the key thinking and research on the subject. He argued that meaningful places are critical, in light of the increasing homogeneity of landscapes today. He concluded that place is an important facet of human experience. Exposure to nature and the natural landscape are important place qualities. Similarly, in *Biophilic Cities: Integrating Nature into Urban Design* (2010), Beatley offered a wide array of principles for integrating nature and natural systems into design and planning across spatial scales, from the building to the region.[9]

Likewise, in *Placing Nature: Culture and Landscape Ecology* (1997), landscape architect Joan Nassauer brought together a collection of insightful essays that examine mechanisms essential in integrating culture into design and planning interventions in human-dominated landscapes. In her essay "Cultural Sustainability: Aligning Aesthetics and Ecology," Nassauer explored how to use the culture of nature in introducing ecological health into built landscapes.[10]

In *Design for Ecological Democracy* (2006), landscape architect Randy Hester offered insightful perspectives on how to build a sense of place as people create cities.[11] He emphasized a design process that is democratic and actively engages people in creating places that are *enabling, resilient,* and *impelling.*

Similarly, in *LifePlace: Bioregional Thought and Practice* (2003), Robert Thayer proposed a *bioregional approach* to creating and sustaining places.[12] The approach is rooted in a deep understanding, caring, and nurturing emotive feelings for a naturally bounded region. He contended that bioregions are becoming the most logical locale and scale for "a sustainable, regenerative community to take root and to take place."[13]

In "Fundamental Principles of Human Ecology," from the book *Human Ecology: Following Nature's Lead* (2002), Frederick Steiner provided a robust examination of the key concepts and principles of human ecology by drawing from diverse fields.[14] He succinctly synthesized the major principles in human ecology and revealed how human interactions can be comprehended as ecological relationships, and how an understanding of the latter can inform decision making about balancing human use with ecological concerns.

Lastly, landscape planner and ecologist Laura Musacchio examined *the scientific basis for the design of landscape sustainability* and introduced an extended definition of sustainability—the six E's of landscape sustainability: *environment, economic, equity, esthetics, experience,* and *ethics* (2009).[15]

The essays presented here represent only a small microcosm of the theoretical and conceptual contributions dealing with what should be investigated, in balancing human use with ecological concerns, and why. Not included here are important concepts drawn from fields including geography (e.g., how humanized landscapes evolve); wildlife and conservation biology (e.g., island biogeography and habitat networks); social and behavioral sciences (e.g., people's behavior in their social and physical environments); and the humanities (e.g., human values and aesthetic experiences).

The scope and complexity of ecological concerns continue to expand. Land, water, and air degradation were important ecological issues in the 1960s. Today, these same issues have intensified and even expanded to include landscape fragmentation, accelerated erosion of biological diversity, climate change, rising sea levels, heightened energy demands, placelessness, intense suburbanization, degradation of life-support systems, social inequity, and continued deterioration of environmental quality. There is an increased need to create adaptive systems and landscapes that are more resilient.

McHarg and Odum informed us of the benefits humans obtain from ecosystems, including the role ecosystems play and the ecological value they serve. These benefits or ecosystem services, such as air and water cleansing and nutrient cycling, are critical to the survival of species. McHarg and Odum advocate the need to conserve "protective ecosystems." Today, the idea of employing ecosystem services as the basis for design represents a profound shift in the ways that we have traditionally engaged in design and planning.

Population growth and migration to metropolitan areas will continue to increase. In 2010, for instance, more than 83 percent of the U.S. population lived in urban areas. Thus, insights into how people interact with urban environments will continue into be important. Alberti and her colleagues have provided valuable insights into understanding patterns, processes, and functions of urban ecosystems.[16] Steiner's ideas on employing a human ecological perspective in understanding human-landscape relationships are noteworthy. A human ecological perspective implies thinking ecologically, which, according to Van der Ryn and Cowan, becomes a way of strengthening the weave that links "nature and culture." Nassauer contended that strengthening the links may improve ecological health.

Beatley argued that reinforcing these linkages also helps to create landscapes that are meaningful to their inhabitants. He provided us with a rich understanding of places, their qualities, how they work, and how they can be sustained. A focus on place counteracts the current forces of urbanization and globalization, in which spaces are generalized rather than particularized. Strengthening places is embedded in Catherine Howett's proposition of an aesthetic norm capable of creating new forms and appropriate landscape design styles. Both Hester and Thayer offered informative perspectives on building and enriching places and proposed design principles for realizing them. For Hester, active engagement of affected interests is crucial, while Thayer emphasized bioregional thinking and action. Musacchio's expanded definition of sustainability that embraces aesthetics, experience, and ethics further enriches our understanding of places (figure 3-1).

Forman's propositions on understanding the ecology of cities and regions are relevant, especially if the regional scale, as he pointed out, is more appropriate than the local or site scale for attaining the sustainability of the landscape. Urban areas are intimately linked to their outlying areas or their regional setting. Examining urbanizing regions from an ecosystem ecological perspective still presents challenges. As such, along with the contributions of ecologists such as Forman and Odum and researchers such as Alberti, landscape architects and planners, such as Michael Hough in Ontario, Canada, are increasingly using such information in making urban design decisions.

Figure 3-1 Places are unique, memorable, and embodied with meaning. Downtown Cape Town, South Africa (Photograph by author).

The science of ecology is undergoing paradigm shifts. The ideas about ecology as adopted by McHarg and Odum continue to evolve. Traditional ecology emphasized equilibrium, in which local populations and ecosystems are in balance with local resources and conditions, but emerging ideas acknowledge an equilibrium point of view "where history matters and population and ecosystems are continuously being influenced by disturbances."[17] Contemporary ecology focuses on change and processes. History and heritage help in profound ways to define and strengthen places. We should strive to create resilient places that persist in the face of change.

Notes

1. Catherine Howett, "Systems, Signs, Sensibilities: Sources for a New Landscape Aesthetic," *Landscape Journal* 6, no. 1 (1987), 1–12.
2. McHarg, Ian L., *To Heal the Earth*, F. Steiner (ed.), (Washington, DC: Island Press, 1998), 108–131.
3. Sim Van der Ryn and Stuart Cowan, "An Introduction to Ecological Design," in *Ecological Design* (Washington, DC: Island Press, 1996), 32–49.

4. Eugene P. Odum, "The Strategy of Ecosystem Development," *Science* 164, no. 3877 (1969), 262–270.
5. Richard T. T. Forman, "Foundations," in *Land Mosaics: The Ecology of Landscapes and Regions* (New York: Cambridge University Press, 1995).
6. Marina Alberti, "Urban Patterns and Ecosystem Functions," in *Advances in Urban Ecology: Integrating Humans and Ecological Processes into Urban Ecosystems* (New York: Springer, 2008), 61–86.
7. Michael Hough, *Cities and Natural Process: A Basis for Sustainability* (London: Routledge, 2004).
8. Timothy Beatley, "Place Basics: Concepts, Research, Literature," in *Native to Nowhere* (Washington, DC: Island Press, 2004).
9. Timothy Beatley, *Biophilic Cities: Integrating Nature into Urban Design* (Washington, DC: Island Press, 2010).
10. Joan Nassauer, ed. *Placing Nature: Culture and Landscape Ecology* (Washington, DC: Island Press, 1997). In her essay "Landscape as Method and Medium for the Ecological Design of Cities," in *Resilience in Ecology and Urban Design: Linking Theory and Practice for Sustainable Cities* (Springer Netherlands, 2013), 79–98, Nassauer adopted the definition of "landscape" provided by noted landscape historian J. B. Jackson and argued that viewing the landscape as both an analytical framework and experiential space enables it [landscape] to be a catalyst for synthesis in science and ecological design.
11. Randy Hester, *Design for Ecological Democracy* (Cambridge, MA: MIT Press, 2006).
12. Robert Thayer, *LifePlace: Bioregional Thought and Practice* (Berkeley: University of California Press, 2003).
13. Ibid., 3.
14. Frederick Steiner, "Fundamental Principles of Human Ecology," in *Human Ecology: Following Nature's Lead* (Washington, DC: Island Press, 2002), 19–38.
15. Laura Musacchio, "The Scientific Basis of the Design of Landscape Sustainability: A Conceptual Framework for Translational Landscape Research and Practice of Designed Landscapes and the six Es of Landscape Sustainability," *Landscape Ecology* no. 24, 8 (2009), 993–1013.
16. See Alberti, M., P. Christie, J. Marzluff, and J. Tewksbury, "Interactions between Natural and Human Systems in Puget Sound," *Sound Science: Synthesizing Ecological and Socioeconomic Information about the Puget Sound* (2007); Shandas, V., and M. Alberti, "Exploring the Role of Vegetation Fragmentation on Aquatic Conditions: Linking Upland with Riparian Areas in Puget Sound Lowland Streams," *Landscape and Urban Planning* 90 (2009): 66–75; Blaco, H., M. Alberti, A. Forsyth, K. Krizek, D. Rodriguez, E. Talen, C. Ellis. "Hot, Congested, Crowded, and Diverse: Emerging Research Agendas in Planning," *Progress in Planning* 71 (2009): 153–205.
17. Ronald H. Pulliam and Bart R. Johnson, "Ecology's New Paradigm: What Does It Offer Designers and Planners?" in *Ecology and Design: Framework for Learning*, Bart Johnson and Kristina Hill (eds.), (Washington, DC: Island Press, 2002), 51.

Systems, Signs, Sensibilities: Sources for a New Landscape Aesthetic

Landscape Journal (1987)

Catherine Howett

In the history of American landscape architecture, Frederick Law Olmsted was a figure of heroic proportions, a man in whom great powers of intellect were combined with imaginative brilliance, a passionate heart, literary and artistic gifts, and a practical turn of mind. Yet though we honor him as the father-founder of the profession in the United States, it is important to remind ourselves that neither the style he worked in, nor the cause of urban environmental reform for which he became a leading spokesman, originated with him.

His biographer Laura Wood Roper tells us that Olmsted's experience of seeing Birkenhead Park while travelling in England in 1850 "broke on him like a revelation," crystallizing "his two absorbing interests—the one in landscape, the other in means of elevating the character and condition of the poorer classes." The park was the work of Joseph Paxton, renowned horticulturalist and architect who made his early reputation as head gardener at the Duke of Devonshire's estate, Chatsworth. Like others of the public and private parks and grounds that Olmsted visited in England, Birkenhead's design represented the continued viability, in the middle of the nineteenth century, of an aesthetic theory and principles of composition that had emerged more than a century earlier in the school of informal and picturesque landscape gardening represented by the practice of men such as William Kent, Lancelot "Capability" Brown, and Humphry Repton. This design tradition had for most of the eighteenth century found its principal form of expression in the laying out and embellishment of the great estates of England's landed aristocracy; what most impressed Olmsted was the application of that tradition at Birkenhead to a 120-acre recreational pleasure ground created by and for the working-class citizens of this planned suburb across the river from industrial Liverpool.

He knew that at home in America an active circle of religious leaders, writers, and liberal reformers was already seeking ways to address the social problems that rapid population growth and industrialization had visited upon such cities as New York and Boston. Among these, the poet William Cullen Bryant, in his role as editor of the New York *Evening Post,* and Andrew Jackson Downing—eminent horticulturalist, editor, and author of a series of popular books on rural architecture and landscape gardening—had been calling for a concerted municipal planning effort in New York. They argued for improving the quality of life of the city's inhabitants by making changes in their physical environment, especially by providing spacious public parks that would afford opportunities for relief from urban congestion, for recreation, and for spiritual refreshment through contact with nature. Olmsted was familiar, too, with Downing's 1841 *Treatise on the Theory and Practice of Landscape Gardening Adapted to North America,* which had, as the title suggests, interpreted the precepts of the English school in its late phase for an eager audience of American readers building suburban and country homes.

Not long before his early and tragic death, Downing had persuaded the English architect Calvert Vaux to come to America to practice in partnership with him; Olmsted and Vaux later combined their talents in producing the winning plan in the competition for the design of Central Park and began a partnership of their own. Olmsted thus assumed Downing's mantle as the person best suited to conceive an American version of the English urban park, using aesthetic principles and conventions of the English landscape gardening movement to develop naturalistic oases of pastoral landscape in the heart of the city's built environment.

Throughout a long career, Olmsted was as important an apologist for the wisdom of seeking a harmonious balance of the natural and built environments as he was artist and architect responsible—personally and by extension through the work of his own firm and those of his disciples—for literally thousands of well-designed public and private outdoor spaces in cities and towns across America. This union of a strong philosophic base and a design formula that produced landscapes manifestly beautiful, delightful, useful, environmentally sensitive, and life-enhancing—the Olmsted legacy—helped to lay the foundation for the City Beautiful movement at the turn of the century and has dominated the practice of landscape architecture even into our own day.

There have been stylistic counter-currents, of course, although Olmsted himself—in the campus plan for Stanford University, or the plan of the grounds at the World's Columbian Exposition at Chicago in 1893, or his development of the formal gardens at the Biltmore estate of George Vanderbilt in Asheville, North Carolina—also participated in the revival of a classicism based on Renaissance and Baroque design traditions. This shift in taste was, however, more of an enlargement and an evolution than a negative reaction against the informal paradigm; his parks, for example, had often contained formal elements, such as Bethesda Fountain and the mall in Central Park, that were justified, in Olmsted's view, by the nature of the civic function they served. Moreover for Olmsted, and even for many later designers who were more exclusively committed to the Classical Revival's stylistic canon, the ideal of the picturesque park landscape remained operative, either as a complement to formal landscapes or as the preferred treatment for particular landscape situations; one thinks, for example, of the curving drives and tree-formed expanses of lawn that were characteristic of many otherwise formal residential estates.

And so it is even today. However much we may want to perceive ourselves as contemporary designers who are inventors of original forms that express our own time and place and culture, we are, I would like to suggest, still haunted by Olmsted's vision of an idyllic pastoral park, quintessential emblem of a civilized, humanized natural world; and still influenced, in our judgments of what is beautiful or appropriate in the designed landscape, by the impress of those powerful inherited models. In the landscape architecture of the twentieth century, no movement and no defined style—equivalent in importance, let us say, to the Modernist movement in architecture—has yet achieved the same widespread acceptance and cultural dominance as the Olmstedian aesthetic and its visual imagery. . . .

This is not the place to offer a detailed analysis of the ways in which contemporary theory and practice demonstrate, in a wide variety of professional settings, a persistent and usually unreflective commitment to aesthetic values derived from the design tradition epitomized in Olmsted's career. I might propose, just as one example, that current efforts to quantify relative degrees of scenic value in selected landscapes—the methodology of "visual resource assessment" as it is employed in natural and recreational resource planning—generally depend upon criteria derived from this tradition, especially in the importance attached to abstract, format qualities of such visual features as topographic relief, vegetation, water bodies, etc. Neil Evernden has argued that the presumably "scientific" character of these evaluative techniques actually disguises a "quest for the picturesque" not very different from that of the nineteenth-century Romantics, with their penchant for seeing nature as a series of "views" worthy of being made into a picture. "To ask a viewer what scene is beautiful or admirable," Evernden warns, "is really to ask which scenes are of the type defined as 'the beautiful' by cultural tradition." ...

It might be argued that sympathy with the intentions and traditional design devices of picturesque landscape composition does no harm, and that furthermore the enduring primacy of scenographic values in landscape architecture might be justified, given the dreary ugliness of so much of today's built environment. But the discomfort of ecologists with the landscape model as an aesthetic approach to natural environments should give us pause, since it suggests that there might be analogous deficiencies in the picturesque aesthetic that continues to inform so much contemporary landscape architecture. A critique of certain fundamental preconceptions of the picturesque canon will be implied in the observations that follow, which point toward potential sources in three separate disciplines from which we might garner ideas and insights—into ourselves, our lives, the world we make and the world that nature presents to us—needed for a new and more appropriate landscape aesthetic. These three critical and theoretical currents, each of which is already at the center of research, experiment, and argument within the profession, are: (1) the new ecology, which over the last two decades has fundamentality recast our vision of the natural world and the human community's place within its systems; (2) semiotics, which in proposing analogies between language and architecture has forced a fresh understanding of the expressive meanings of built form and the devices of architectural communication—sign systems as critical to the designer of landscapes as natural systems; and finally, (3) environmental psychology, including as well the work of such geographers as Yi-Fu Tuan who speculate on the nature of place experience and the profound conscious and preconscious bonds that make us respond in specific ways to various environments.

Curiously, the very notion of aesthetic values has become suspect in the view of many within each of these three domains. For the ecologist, aesthetic concerns are frequently identified with high-art traditions that are perceived as having been ruthlessly insensitive to the effects of certain kinds of development upon vulnerable natural systems. Architectural theorists have deplored the elitist cast of judgments based on uncritically accepted, inherited aesthetic values—hence the studied embrace, in recent years, of vernacular buildings and landscapes and "pop art" iconography. Environmental psychologists, too, see aesthetic evaluations as too often favoring somewhat arbitrary visual criteria at the expense of other, less obvious but ultimately more important, experiential ones. This shared suspicion works against the possibility of developing mutually satisfactory aesthetic norms that might reflect a cross-fertilization of values important to all three of these constituencies.

This should not discourage us, however. Landscape architecture is by its very nature interdisciplinary, combining science and art, as we are fond of saying. It is up to us to forge an intellectual synthesis that can act as the foundation for an aesthetic canon capable of generating new forms, new landscape styles. Olmsted's strength, as we have seen, had as much to do with his energetic involvement in the intellectual, political, and social discourse of his day as it did with his literary and artistic genius. Albert Fein has suggested, in fact, that Olmsted's work is best understood as the expression of a social and institutional ideal that was the highest achievement of nineteenth-century America, as central to its cultural identity as was the Acropolis to Athens or the cathedral to medieval France. Our profession's historic isolation, since Olmsted, from the central philosophical, ideological, literary, and artistic debates of our own time must finally be overcome if a new generation of landscape architects is to be capable of imagining and creating the landscape forms that would similarly express the highest values and aspirations of American culture on the eve of the third millennium.

Until that dialogue has been engaged, however, it is absurd to ask what, exactly, these new landscape forms will look like, or how they will operate. Who can precisely describe the physical form of tomorrow's art? These forms will emerge from the play of mind and spirit, from risk-taking experiment and painstaking work. Our task right now is to lay the groundwork, seeking to discover what characteristics such a new art ought to have.

Surely these new forms must reflect the awakening of our generation to ecological consciousness, and the growing popular understanding of the degree to which the natural world is, in Aldo Leopold's words, "interlocked in one humming community of co-operations and competitions, one biota." Suppose we acknowledge this ecological awareness as the ground of values to which we want our society to be dedicated—a kind of "post-humanist" environmental consciousness defined by Del Janik as one that "values all living things and the inorganic environment on which they depend, recognizing that all life and the conditions that sustain life are interrelated. It asserts that man can be, if he abandons his anthropometric assumptions, a contributor to, rather than the destroyer of, the pattern of nature." The implications of this revaluation within the discipline of landscape architecture should be far-reaching. Baird Callicott, in an essay on what he termed the "land aesthetic" implicit in Leopold's writing, expressed regret that artists (he was speaking of painters) are not able, because of their medium, to awaken the public to a more holistic appreciation of the natural world; because it is not represented and interpreted through art, that more evolutionary-ecological aesthetic of nature remains unappreciated by the average person. It is the art of landscape architecture, obviously, that ought to take up this challenge. Ian McHarg's now classic *Design with Nature* (1969) revolutionized the way that we approach urban and regional planning, proposing a methodology marked by greater responsiveness to the environmental contexts in which human activity acts as a dynamic shaping force for good or ill. But we are still worlds away from achieving the widespread and consistent application and interpretation of ecological principles in the designed landscape that Callicott hints at. We have for the most part been guilty of turning our backs on this ethically compelling opportunity, and our addiction to the picturesque aesthetic is principally to blame.

Nan Fairbrother called this dominant model the "park-and-garden style" and tried to explain to the readers of *New Lives, New Landscapes,* how the conventional way of handling vegetation in a designed landscape differs from the way plants grow naturally. . . . She went on to recommend a more natural style of planting in "country areas"—one that took natural competition into account, depended on indigenous plant communities, and reflected the way plants grow in nature. . . . Fairbrother's recommendations for more natural planting compositions in rural areas offer a model that emphasizes process over time and authentic patterns of growth as an alternative to an artificial appearance of closure, of static and idealized perfection.

There is no reason why this more ecologically-based approach should not be used in urban areas as well. And indeed there have been encouraging signs, within the last few years, or a growing interest in planting design and vegetation management approaches that take their inspiration from natural associations and processes. Starting in 1982, the British journal *Landscape Design* published a series of essays under the title "New Directions: Ecological Approaches" that surveyed recent examples of alternative, "natural" landscapes, including significant numbers of fairly large-scale projects in Sweden and the Netherlands. One author, O. D. Manning, ventured a definition of ecological design as "an approach which seeks to substitute for the restricted, artificial and expensive creations of conventional design, a looser and apparently more natural landscape, marked by species-diversity, structural complexity and freedom of growth, and achieved above all by the use of indigenous vegetation sensitively managed in order to exploit natural growth processes (especially successional) and the natural potential of the site." Darrel Morrison's early work in replicating and restoring Midwestern prairie landscapes represents the most significant American expression of this new enthusiasm, and has helped to popularize in this country the idea of using native plant communities in what would normally be considered "ornamental" planting situations. Morrison's example represents the best possible thrust for this effort, because he begins by justifying the planting on ecological grounds, a lesson first patiently imparted to clients and then absorbed slowly, by observation over time, by the general public. . . .

It may seem at first as if the advocacy of more ecologically-based landscape design will demand the sacrifice of cherished and legitimate values, the simple pleasure taken in creating or experiencing compositions that please the eye. But what is being called for is an expansion, not a diminishment, of sensibility. We must come to see that we are trapped not just in a tyranny of the visual imposed by an inherited picturesque aesthetic, but that even the range of possibilities for visual stimulation and pleasure has been needlessly narrowed. And we have deprived our other senses and, indeed, our own minds and souls, of a potentially richer and more profound delight. Baird Callicott has made the point that just as we can develop the capacity to enjoy dissonance in music or "the clash of color and distortion of eidetic form in painting," we can come to appreciate qualities in a landscape that initially confound our preconceptions of what is pleasing.

A cognitive element must come into play, however; it is our understanding of what is at work that will enhance our pleasure in the denser, more complex images that an ecologically-grounded aesthetic will promote. To foster this deepened understanding, those of us who live in cities might begin by reading Anne Whiston Spirn's comprehensive study *The Granite Garden: Urban Nature and Human Design* (1984), a work that vividly conveys the awesome scale of our habitual indifference to critical ecological processes in the design of urban environments. . . .

This important consideration of the way in which our perceptual faculties must be expanded and our understanding deepened by increased knowledge of ecological processes is related to the next area in which we hope to find the seed-ideas of a new landscape aesthetic—the realm of signs and symbols, semiotics. Within the limits of this essay I can only hope to suggest the critical relevancy of this field of philosophical, linguistic, and literary analysis to the formation of a new aesthetic for landscape architecture. *Signs, Symbols, and Architecture,* edited by Charles Jencks, Geoffrey Broadbent, and Richard Bunt (1980), is a valuable study of some of the ways in which theory and principles borrowed from semiotics can be applied to the world of built form. Basically, scholars and critics pursuing this mode of analysis argue that architecture can communicate visual and conceptual messages according to the way a vocabulary of meaningful formal signs is ordered, much as a spoken or written language makes sense to us because it follows rules of syntax and grammar in the arrangement of words whose meaning we know. Semiotics provides a structural and analytic framework for a reality that is familiar to all of us, once intellectual and affective responses that are automatic and pre-conscious are called to our attention.

For example, when Marx suggests that part of the attraction that suburban life exercises for many of us may have to do with an unconscious nostalgia for a simpler way of life identified with rural America and opposed to our ideas about city life, he is implying that the suburban landscape communicates to us, that its winding roads and tree-dappled lawns say "country," say "retreat from the city," and say it deliberately. If a developer were to put up a steel and glass tower in the middle of a suburban neighborhood, it would "read" all wrong to us, and we would object to its presence in that context. Similarly, Sonfist's *Time Landscape* intends to communicate a message; the artist has told us that he wants to make the city-dwellers who see his wooded landscape aware of a past environment that time has erased but history has not. It is part of their own history, suddenly made real and present to them in the work.

A better understanding of the sign-systems available to us will contribute to a revitalized, freshened imagery in the landscapes we design. We do not, after all, want to express a more uncompromising commitment to the clear demonstration of ecological processes in even the most routine landscapes we design, by making every one of them into a fragment of wild nature. I see no reason, however, not to propose that at this juncture in our history every landscape we design ought to be in some measure an *icon* of the natural world as we have come to understand it—an ecological sign, or cluster of signs. Jencks uses the term "univalent" to describe the architecture "created around one (or a few) simplified values," the expressive possibilities of which have been severely reduced and impoverished. When landscape architects rely upon conventional compositional devices and use forms and materials in predictable ways to achieve nothing more than a pleasant or tasteful scenic effect, we are perpetuating a univalent, hackneyed design tradition. . . . We will need to create landscape forms that express a multivalent symbolism of the sort that Joseph Grange has recently described:

> When a designer looks at an environment, three principles must be foremost in his mind. First, things are *meanings*, not material objects. Second, these meanings are nodal points of expression that open out into a field of relationships. Third, the goal of environmental design is to knot together these concentrations of meaning so that the participant-dweller can experience the radical unity that binds up these different qualities. . . .

. . . Maya Ying Lin's design for the Vietnam Memorial possessed these qualities in sufficient measure to arouse critics of the work, who finally succeeded in their demand to have a second memorial erected nearby on the same site, a predictably univalent figural sculpture of three GIs by Frederick Hart.

Another work of contemporary landscape architecture that probed richer layers of meaning by seizing upon anti-picturesque visual metaphors was Richard Haag's Gas Works Park in Seattle, Washington, begun in 1972. Here, too, the designer called down upon himself the wrath of politicians, journalists, and other members of the community who were outraged by his intention to retain as the central feature of a new urban park the hulking ruins of an early twentieth-century industrial complex that occupied the site. Haag's plan forced people to consider not just the degree of positive visual and spatial interest possessed by this relic of an outdated technology, but what its meanings might be for the community it had served for fifty years. For one thing, the lakefront site had been severely polluted by the plant's operations, so that inevitably the labyrinth of rusting pipes, towers, and other remaining structures must have seemed haunted by the shadow of harm done to earth, air, and water. The aim of the design was to redeem this history by re-cycling the site as a playful place, a *sign* of wholesome life and health salvaged, literally, from an industrial wasteland. . . .

To speak of the ways in which landscapes can communicate values shared by our culture, meanings whose discovery is part of our aesthetic response to the places we inhabit or encounter, brings us quite naturally to the third subject area that can help us to frame a new landscape aesthetic, the world of environmental psychology. Scholars in many disciplines, but especially philosophy, psychology, and cultural geography, have in recent years contributed to a growing body of literature analyzing the nature of human place experience. The subject area ranges over a spectrum from the rigorous methodologies of scientific inquiry, measurement, and evaluation at one extreme, to highly subjective and intuitive speculation about affective responses to place on the other. All of it is concerned with helping us ultimately to understand better the dynamics of the myriad different kinds of relationships we humans can have with the environments we shape and that are shaped by us, including the natural world. It has been more than ten years now since the geographer Yi-Fu Tuan published a ground-breaking study in which he tried to bring together strands of inquiry and insight from many disciplines in order to provide an overview of the factors that contribute to what he called "topophilia," "the affective bond between people and place or setting." Tuan explored the compelling evidence for the essential role that culture plays in determining how we read and respond to environment; distinct cultures provide, as we know, the conceptual structures that imbue environments with meanings and values particular to a given group. He described as well a class of responses that all human beings seem to share by their very nature, such as our tendency to organize phenomena in binary pairs or to invent rational justifications for non-rational drives and aspirations; these physical and psychological characteristics of the human community also determine the character of the environments we favor. In a telling passage, Tuan explored the difference between the occasional naive response to environment, unmediated by culturally-imposed criteria, and the more distant, intellectualized experience that is especially common in advanced societies. A child, he observed, cares less for a composed picturesque view at the seashore than for the particular things and physical sensations he or she encounters there. "Visual appreciation, discerning and reflective," Tuan concluded, "creates aesthetic distance."

Within recent years a growing number of philosophers, psychologists, and designers have begun to challenge more forcefully the almost exclusive identification of aesthetic perception with visual (or, to a lesser degree, aural) norms and modes of experience. They want to overcome the conventional assumption of a contemplative distance that separates us in some way from the environments to which we respond aesthetically. Martin Heidegger's phenomenology, with its frontal assault upon Cartesian arguments positing a world of things—the "other"—arrayed outside a thinking self, has appealed strongly to those who see a need for re-shaping the philosophical premises underlying our culture's approach both to nature and to the built world. Heidegger's essay "Building/Dwelling/Thinking" has achieved the status of a cult classic in schools of architecture and environmental design. . . .

History teaches us that new world-views may be expressed in art even before an integrated vision is articulated through discursive modes of thought and language. Olmsted's urban parks served as iconic summations of currents of thought abroad in his day; in a real sense, the energy of that discourse charged his art and created the historic moment that allowed him to bring it into being. The landscape arts are still capable—perhaps more capable than any other of the arts—of giving expression to that new vision of the world and of our place in it whose outlines we now see emerging. We must begin by thinking, talking, struggling together to see in fresh ways, forcing ourselves to put aside, at least for the moment, scenographic conventions and aesthetic assumptions that derive from our inheritance of picturesque practice. We must design new kinds of places, landscapes that body forth our understanding of the astonishing complexity, fragility, and beauty of the world and celebrate the new, more caring and loving relationship into which we wish to enter.

References

Bartuska, Tom J., and Gerald L. Young. "Aesthetics and Ecology: Notes on the Circle and the Sphere." *Journal of Aesthetic Education* 9, no. 3 (1975): 78–91.

Becker, Ernest. *The Denial of Death.* New York: Free, 1973.

Berleant, Arnold. "Aesthetic Participation and the Urban Environment." *Urban Resources* 1, no. 4 (1984): 37.

————. "Toward a Phenomenological Aesthetics of Environment." In *Descriptions*. New York: State University of New York Press, 1985.

Bradshaw, A. D., and J. Handley. "An Ecological Approach to Landscape Design: Principles and Problems." *Landscape Design* 138 (1982): 30–34.

Callicott, J. Baird. "The Land Aesthetic." *Environmental History Review* 7, no. 4 (1983): 348–50.

Campbell, Craig. "Seattle's Gas Plant Park." *Landscape Architecture* July (1973): 338–42.

Carlson, Allen A. "Appreciation and the Natural Environment." *The Journal of Aesthetics and Art Criticism* 37, no. 3 (1979): 270.

————. "On the Possibility of Quantifying Scenic Beauty." *Landscape Planning* 4 (1977): 131–72.

Cole, Lyndis. "New Directions, 6: Design for Environmental Education." *Landscape Design* 145 (1983): 28–31.

Evernden, Neil. "The Ambiguous Landscape." *Geographical Review* 71, no. 2 (1981): 151.

————. *The Natural Alien: Humankind and Environment.* Toronto: University of Toronto Press, 1985.

Fairbrother, Nan. "New Lives, New Landscapes." In *New Lives, New Landscapes: Planning for the 21st Century*, with Foreword by Walter Muir Whitechill, 364–66. New York: Alfred A. Knopf, 1970.

Fein, Albert. "The American City: The Ideal and the Real." In *The Rise of an American Architecture*, edited by Edgar Kaufmann, Jr., 51. New York: Praeger Publishers and The Metropolitan Museum of Art, 1970.

Gilbert, O. L., "New Directions, 7: The Urban Common." *Landscape Design* 149 (1984): 35–36.

Grange, Joseph. "On the Way Towards Foundational Ecology." *Soundings* 60, no. 2 (1977): 135–49.

————. "Radiant Lessons from the Failed Landscape of Desire." *Places* 2, no. 2 (1984): 21.

Greenwood, Roger. "New Directions, 5: Gorse Covert, Warrington—Creating a More Natural Landscape." *Landscape Design* 143 (1983): 35–38.

Gustavsson, Roland. "New Directions, 2: Nature on Our Doorstep." *Landscape Design* 139 (1982): 21–23.

Halprin, Lawrence. *The RSVP Cycles: Creative Processes in The Human Environment.* New York: George Braziller, 1969.

Heidegger, Martin. "Building/Dwelling/Thinking." In *Basic Writings*, edited by Martin Krell, 319-339. New York: Harper & Row, 1977.

Hussey, Christopher. *The Picturesque: Studies in a Point of View.* London and New York: GP Putnam's Sons, 1927.

Janik, Del Ivan. "D.H. Lawrence and Environmental Consciousness." *Environmental Review* 7, no. 4 (1983): 3456–59.

Jencks, Charles. *The Language of Post-Modern Architecture.* Vol. 102. New York: Rizzoli, 1977.

Leighton, Ann. *American Gardens in the Eighteenth Century: For Use or For Delight*, 334–36. Boston: University of Massachusetts Press, 1976.

Lippard, Lucy R. *Overlay: Contemporary Art and the Art of Prehistory.* New York: Pantheon Books, 1983.

Manning, O. D., "New Directions, 3: Designing for Man and Nature." *Landscape Design* 140 (1982): 30–32.

Marx, Leo. "Pastoral Ideals and City Troubles." In *The Fitness of Man's Environment.* Washington, DC: Smithsonian Institution Press, 1968.

Morrison, Darrel G. "Restoring the Midwestern Landscape." *Landscape Architecture* 65, no. 4 (1975): 398–403.

————. "Tallgrass Prairie in the Landscape." *Landscape Architecture Review* 6, no. 2 (1985): 5–11.

Olmsted, Frederick Law. *Walks and Talks of an American Farmer in England.* Vol. 1. New York: GP Putnam, 1852.

Pevsner, Nikolaus. "The Genesis of the Picturesque." *Architectural Review* 96 (1944): 139–46.

Rapoport, Amos, and Robert E. Kantor. "Complexity and Ambiguity in Environmental Design." *Journal of the American Institute of Planners* 33, no. 4 (1967): 210.

Rettig, Stephen. "The Rise of the Ecological Approach to Landscape Design." *Landscape Design* 143 (1983): 40.

Roper, Laura Wood. *FLO: A Biography of Frederick Law Olmsted.* Baltimore, MD: Johns Hopkins University Press, 1973.

Ruff, Allan, and Robert Tregay. "An Ecological Approach to Urban Landscape Design." *Occasional Paper,* no. 8. Manchester: Department of Town and Country Planning, University of Manchester (1982).

Smithson, Robert. "A Sedimentation of the Mind: Earth Projects (1968)." In *The Writings of Robert Smithson: Essays with Illustrations,* edited by Nancy Holt, intro. by Philip Lieder. New York: New York University Press, 1979.

Tuan, Yi-Fu. *Topophilia: A Study of Environmental Perception, Attitudes, and Values.* Englewood Cliffs, NJ: Prentice-Hall, 1974.

Venturi, Robert. *Complexity & Contradiction in Architecture.* The Museum of Modern Art and the Graham Foundation for Advanced Studies in the Visual Arts, 1977.

Watkin, David. "The English Vision: The Picturesque in Architecture." In *Landscape Architecture and Garden Design.* London: Breslich and Foss, 1982.

Wells, Malcolm B. "The Absolutely Constant Incontestably Stable Architectural Value Scale." *Progressive Architecture* 52 (1971): 92–95.

Open Space from Natural Processes

To Heal the Earth: Selected Writings of Ian L. McHarg (1998), edited by Frederick R. Steiner

Ian L. McHarg

There is need for an objective and systematic method of identifying and evaluating land most suitable for metropolitan open space based on the natural roles that it performs. These roles can best be understood by examining the degree to which natural processes perform work for man without his intervention, and by studying the protection which is afforded and values which are derived when certain of these lands are undisturbed.

Introduction

A million acres of land each year are lost from prime farmland and forest to less sustainable and uglier land uses. There is little effective metropolitan planning and still less implementation of what is planned. Development occurs without reference to natural phenomena. Flood plains, marshes, steep slopes, woods, forests, and farmland are destroyed with little if any remorse; streams are culverted, groundwater, surface water, and atmosphere polluted, floods and droughts exacerbated, and beauty superseded by vulgarity and ugliness. Yet the instinct for suburbia which has resulted in this enormous despoliation of nature is based upon a pervasive and profoundly felt need for a more natural environment.

The paradox and tragedy of metropolitan growth and suburbanization is that it destroys many of its own objectives. The open countryside is subject to uncontrolled, sporadic, uncoordinated, unplanned development, representing the sum of isolated short-term private decisions of little taste or skill. Nature recedes under this careless assault, to be replaced usually by growing islands of developments. These quickly coalesce into a mass of low-grade urban tissue, which eliminate all natural beauty and diminish excellence, both historic and modern. The opportunity for realizing an important part of the "American dream" continually recedes to a more distant area and a future generation. For this is the characteristic pattern of metropolitan growth. Those who escape from the city to the country are often encased with their disillusions in the enveloping suburb.

The Hypothesis

This pattern of indiscriminate metropolitan urbanization dramatizes the need for an objective and systematic way of identifying and preserving land most suitable for open space, diverting growth from it, and directing development to land more suitable for urbanization. The assumption is that not all land in an urban area needs to be, or even ever is, all developed. Therefore choice is possible. The discrimination which is sought would select lands for open space which perform important work in their natural condition, are relatively unsuitable for development, are self-maintaining in the ecological sense, and occur in a desirable pattern of interfusion with the urban fabric. The optimum result would be a system of two intertwining webs, one composed of developed land and the second consisting of open space in a natural or near natural state.

Heretofore, urbanization has been a positive act of transformation. Open space has played a passive role. Little if any value has been attributed to the natural processes often because of the failure to understand their roles and values. This is all the more remarkable when we consider the high land values associated with urban open space—Central Park in New York, Rittenhouse Square in Philadelphia being obvious examples. This lack of understanding has militated against the preservation or creation of metropolitan open space systems complementary to metropolitan growth. In this situation, governmental restraints are necessary to protect the public from the damaging consequences of private acts which incur both costs and losses to the public, when these acts violate and interrupt natural processes and diminish social values. There is an urgent need for land-use regulations related to natural processes, based upon their intrinsic value and their permissiveness and limitations to development. This in turn requires general agreement as to the social values of natural process.

Planning that understands and properly values natural processes must start with the identification of the processes at work in nature. It must then determine the value of subprocesses to man, both in the parts and in the aggregate, and finally establish principles of development and non-development based on the tolerance and intolerance of the natural processes to various aspects of urbanization. It is presumed that when the operation of these processes is understood, and land-use policies reflect this understanding, it will be evidence that the processes can often be perpetuated at little cost.

The arguments for providing open space in the metropolitan region, usually dependent on amenity alone, can be substantially reinforced if policymakers understand and appreciate the operation of the major physical and biological processes at work. A structure for metropolitan growth can be combined with a network of open spaces that not only protects natural processes but also is of inestimable value for amenity and recreation.

In brief, it is hypothesized that the criteria for metropolitan open space should derive from an understanding of natural processes, their value to people, their permissiveness, and their prohibition to development. The method of physiographic analysis outlined here can lead to principles of land development and preservation for any metropolitan area. When applied as a part of the planning process, it can be a defensible basis for an open space system which goes far toward preserving the balance of natural processes and toward making our cities livable and beautiful.

Normal Metropolitan Growth Does Not Provide Open Space, Although Land Is Abundant

Without the use of such a method as described earlier, open space is infinitely vulnerable. An examination of the growth in this century of the major metropolitan areas of the United States demonstrates that urbanization develops primarily on open land rather than through redevelopment. The open space interspersed in areas of low-density development within the urban fabric is filled by more intensive uses and open space standards are lowered. Urban growth consumes open space both at the perimeter and within the urban fabric. The result is a scarcity of open space where population and demand are greatest. This phenomenon has aroused wide public concern as the growth of the cities, by accretion, has produced unattractive and unrelieved physical environments. Amenity, breathing space, recreational areas, and the opportunity for contact with nature for an expanding population are diminished. As important, it often exacerbates flood, drought, erosion, and humidity and it diminishes recreational opportunity, scenic, historic, and wildlife resources. Further, the absence of understanding of natural processes often leads to development in locations which are not propitious. When natural processes are interrupted, there are often resultant costs to society. . . .

Exceptions to the General Experience

While generally metropolitan growth has been unsympathetic to natural processes, there are exceptions. In the late nineteenth- and early twentieth-century park planning, water courses were an important basis for site selection. The Capper Cromptin Act selected river corridors in Washington, D.C. The Cook County Park System around Chicago consists of corridors of forests preponderantly based upon river valleys. The first metropolitan open space plan, developed for Boston by Charles Eliot in 1893, emphasized not only rivers, but also coastal islands, beaches, and forested hills as site selection criteria. In 1928 Benton MacKaye, the originator of the Appalachian Trail, proposed using open space to control metropolitan growth in America but did not base his open space on natural process.

Patrick Abercrombie's Greater London Plan pays implicit attention to natural process in the location for the satellite towns, in the insistence on open space breaks between nucleated growth, in the recommendation that prime agricultural land should not be urbanized, and in specifying that river courses should constitute a basis for the open space system.

In recent studies conducted by Philip Lewis on a state-wide basis for Illinois and Wisconsin (e.g., State of Wisconsin, 1962) physiographic determinants of land utilization have been carried beyond these earlier examples. Corridors have been identified which contain watercourses and their flood plains, steep slopes, forests, wildlife habitats, and historic areas. These characteristics are of value to a wide range of potential supporters—conservationists, historians, and the like—and the studies demonstrate the coincidence of their interests in the corridors. The expectation is that these groups will coordinate their efforts and combine their influence to retain the corridors as open space. Resource development and preservation is advocated for them. In another recent study, ecological principles were developed and tested as part of a planning process for the Green Spring and Worthington valleys, northwest of Baltimore Maryland. Here the design process later described was evolved. Two more elaborate ecological studies, the first for Staten Island (McHarg, 1969, pp. 103–115) and the second for the Twin Cities Metropolitan Region in Minnesota (Wallace, McHarg, Roberts, and Todd, 1969), have undertaken to analyze natural processes to reveal intrinsic suitabilities for all prospective land uses. These are shown as unitary, complementary, or in competition.

The present study of metropolitan Philadelphia open space is more general in its objective. It seeks to find the major structure of open space in the PSMSA based upon the intrinsic values of certain selected natural processes to set the stage for further investigations.

Need for the Ecological Approach

There are, of course, several possible approaches. The first of these, beloved of the economist, views land as a commodity and allocates acres of land per thousand persons. In this view nature is seen as a generally uniform commodity, appraised in terms of time-distance from consumers and the costs of acquisition and development. A second approach also falls within the orthodoxy of planning, and may be described as the geometrical method. Made popular by Patrick Abercrombie, the distinguished British planner, this consists of circumscribing a city with a green ring wherein green activities, agriculture, recreation, and the like, are preserved or introduced.

The ecological approach, however, would suggest quite a different method. Beginning from the proposition that nature is process and represents values, relative values would be ascribed to certain discernible processes. Then, operating upon the presumption that nature performs services for man without his intervention or effort, certain service-processes would be identified as social values. Yet further, recognizing that some natural processes are inhospitable to human use—floods, earthquakes, hurricanes—we would seem to discover intrinsic constraints or even prohibitions to man's use or to certain kinds of use.

Objective discussion between the ecologist and the economist would quickly reveal the fallacy of the commodity approach. Nature is by definition not a uniform commodity. In contrast, each and every area varies as a function of historical geology, climate, physiography, the water regimen, the pattern and distribution of soils, plants, and animals. Each area will vary as process, as value and in the opportunities and constraints which it proffers or withholds from human use.

In a similar discussion between ecologist and green belt advocate, the question which most embarrasses the latter is whether nature is uniform within the belt and different beyond it. The next question is unlikely to receive an affirmative answer, "Does nature perform particular roles within the belt to permit its definition?" Clearly the ecologist emerges a victor in these small skirmishes, but now the burden is upon him. What is the ecological approach to the selections of metropolitan open space?

The Value of Natural Process in the Ecosystem

There is, at present, no existing ecological model for a city or metropolitan region; it is necessary, therefore, to embark upon a theoretical analysis of natural process without the aid of such a model.

Plant and animal communities require solar energy, food, nutrients, water, protection from climate extremes, and shelter. These conditions must be substantially regular in their provision. In order to ensure these optimal conditions, non-human or primitive-human systems have adapted to the natural environment and its constituent organisms to ensure a complex process of energy utilization, based upon photosynthesis, descending through many food chains to final decomposition and nutrient recirculation. In response to the problem of climatic extremes these communities do modify the microclimate. Such natural systems have mechanisms whereby water movement is modified to perform the maximum work. The aggregate of these processes is a stable, complex ecosystem in which entropy is low and energy is conserved (Odum, 1959, ch. 3).

The net result is a system with high energy utilization and production, continuous soil formation, natural defenses against epidemic disease, microclimatic extremes diminished, minimal oscillation between flood and drought, minor erosion, and natural water purification. There obviously are many advantages which accrue to civilized man from this condition—a viable agriculture and forestry, abundant fish and wildlife, natural water purification, stability in the water system, defense against flood and drought, diminished erosion, sedimentation and silting, and a self-cleaning environment with high recreational potential and amenity.

The values of the natural processes far exceed the values which usually are attributed to them. Agriculture, forestry, and fisheries are taken into consideration in the evaluation of regional assets, but atmospheric oxygen, amelioration of climate and microclimate, water evaporation, precipitation, drainage, or the creation of soils tend to be disregarded. Yet the composite picture of the region's resources must include all natural processes. Beginning with the values of agriculture, forestry, and fisheries, the value of minerals and the value of the land for education, recreation, and amenity may be added. Agricultural land has an amenity which is not generally attributed, since it is also a landscape which is maintained as a byproduct. Forests equally have an amenity value and are self-cleaning environments, requiring little or no maintenance.

Water has values which transcend those related to certain discrete aspects of the hydrologic cycle. In this latter category are many important processes—water in agriculture, industry, commerce, recreation, education and amenity, consumption, cooling, hydroelectric generation, navigation, water transport and dilution, waste reduction, fisheries, and water recreation.

Value is seldom attributed to the atmosphere; yet the protection from lethal cosmic rays, insulation, the abundance of oxygen for animal metabolism and the carbon dioxide for plant metabolism which it affords, all demonstrate an indispensability equal to land and water. In terms of positive attributed value the atmosphere has been accorded virtually none. Only when atmosphere has become polluted are the cost and necessity of ensuring clean air recognized.

Even in the exceptional condition when natural processes are attributed value as in agriculture and forestry, these are generally held in such low esteem that they cannot endure in the face of competition from urban or industrial uses. It is impossible to construct a value system which includes the vast processes described. It is, however, quite possible to recognize the fundamental value of these processes, their characteristics, and their relationship to industrial and urban processes. This understanding should lead to a presumption in favor of nature rather than the prevailing disdain.

Working toward the goal of developing working principles for land-use planning in general and the selection of metropolitan open space in particular, it is advantageous to examine the degree to which natural processes perform work for man without his intervention and the protection achieved by leaving certain sub-processes in their natural state without development. While this cannot yet be demonstrated quantitatively, it can be described.

Natural processes which perform work for man include water purification, atmospheric pollution dispersal, microclimate amelioration, water storage and equalization, flood control, erosion control, topsoil accumulation, and the ensurance of wildlife populations.

Areas which are subject to volcanic action, earthquakes, tidal waves, tornadoes, hurricanes, floods, drought, forest fires, avalanches, mud slides, and subsidence, should be left undeveloped in order to avoid loss of life and property. In addition, there are other areas which are particularly vulnerable to human intervention; this category includes beach dunes, major animal habitats, breeding grounds, spawning grounds, and water catchment areas. There are also areas of unusual scenic, geological, biological, ecological, and historic importance. In each of these cases, it is apparent that wise land-use planning should recognize natural processes and respond to them. As many of these processes are water related, it would seem that water may be a useful indicator of these major physical and biological processes described as natural processes. . . .

Conclusions

In summary, it is proposed that the form of metropolitan growth and the distribution of metropolitan open space should respond to natural process. The phenomenal world is a process which operates within laws and responds to these laws. Interdependence is characteristic of this process, the seamless web of nature. Man is natural, as is the phenomenal world he inhabits, yet with greater power, mobility, and fewer genetic restraints; his impact upon this world exceeds that of any creature. The transformations he creates are often deleterious to other biological systems, but in this he is no different from many other creatures. However, these transformations are often needlessly destructive to other organisms and systems, and even more important, by conscious choice and inadvertence, also deleterious to man.

A generalized effect of human intervention is the tendency toward simplification of the ecosystems, which is equated with instability. Thus, the increased violence of climate and microclimate, oscillation between flood and drought, erosion and siltation, are all primary evidence of induced instability.

Human adaptations contain both benefits and costs, but natural processes are generally not attributed values, nor is there a generalized accounting system which reflects total costs and benefits. Natural processes are unitary whereas human interventions tend to be fragmentary and incremental. The effect of filling the estuarine marshes or of felling the upland forests is not perceived as related to the water regimen, to flood or drought; nor are both activities seen to be similar in their effect. The construction of outlying suburbs and siltation of river channels are not normally understood to be related as cause and effect; nor is waste disposal into rivers perceived to be connected with the pollution of distant wells.

Several factors can be observed. Normal growth tends to be incremental and unrelated to natural processes on the site. But the aggregate consequences of such development are not calculated nor are they allocated as costs to the individual incremental developments. While benefits do accrue to certain developments, which are deleterious to natural processes at large (for example, clear felling of forests or conversion of farmland into subdivisions), these benefits are *particular* (related in these examples to that landowner who chooses to fell trees or sterilize soil), while the results and costs are *general* in effect. Thus, costs and benefits are likely to be attributed to large numbers of different and unrelated persons, corporations, and levels of government. It is unprovable and unlikely that substantial benefits accrue from disdain of natural process; it is quite certain and provable that substantial costs do result from this disdain. Finally, in general, any benefits which do occur—usually economic—tend to accrue to the private sector, while remedies and long-range costs are usually the responsibility of the public domain.

The purpose of this study is to show that natural process, unitary in character, must be so considered in the planning process that changes to parts of the system affect the entire system, that natural processes do represent values, and that these values should be incorporated into a single accounting system. It is unfortunate that there is inadequate information on cost-benefit ratios of specific interventions to natural process. However, certain generalized relationships have been shown and presumptions advanced as the basis for judgment.

It seems clear that laws pertaining to land use and development need to be elaborated to reflect the public costs and consequences of private action. Present land-use regulations neither recognize natural processes, the public good in terms of flood, drought, water quality, agriculture, amenity, or recreational potential, nor allocate responsibility to the acts of landowner or developer.

We have seen that land is abundant, even within a metropolitan region confronting accelerated growth. There is, then, at least hypothetically, the opportunity of choice as to the location of development and locations of open space.

The hypothesis, central to this study, is that the distribution of open space must respond to natural process. The conception should hold true for any metropolitan area, irrespective of location. In this particular case study, directed to the Philadelphia metropolitan region, an attempt has been made to select certain fundamental aspects of natural process, which show the greatest relevance to the problem of determining the form of metropolitan growth and open space.

The problem of metropolitan open space lies then, not in absolute area, but in distribution. We seek a concept which can provide an interfusion of open space and population. The low attributed value of open space ensures that it is transformed into urban use within the urban area and at the perimeter. Normal urbanization excludes interfusion and consumes peripheral open space.

Yet as the area of a circle follows the square of the radius, large open space increments can exist within the urban perimeter without major increase to the radius or to the time distance from city center to urban fringe.

The major recommendation of this study is that the aggregate value of land, water, and air resources does justify a land-use policy which reflects both the value and operation of natural processes. Further, that the identification of natural processes, the permissiveness and prohibitions which they exhibit, reveals a system of open space which can direct metropolitan growth and offers sites for metropolitan open space.

The characteristics of natural processes have been examined; an attempt has been made to identify their values, intrinsic value, work performed and protection afforded. Large-scale functions have been identified with the major divisions of upland, coastal plain, and piedmont; smaller scale functions of air and water corridors have been identified; and, finally, eight discrete parameters have been selected for examination.

For each of the discrete phenomena and for each successive generalization, approximate permissiveness to other land uses and specific prohibitions have been suggested. While all are permissive to a greater or lesser degree, all perform their natural process best in an unspoiled condition. Clearly, if land is abundant and land-use planning can reflect natural process, a fabric of substantially natural land will remain either in low intensity use or undeveloped, interfused throughout the metropolitan region. It is from this land that public metropolitan open space may best be selected.

This case study reveals the application of the ecological view to the problem of selecting open space in a metropolitan region. It reflects the assumption that nature performs work for man and that certain natural processes can best perform this work in a natural or mainly natural condition. Clearly, this is a partial problem; one would wish that simultaneously, consideration were also given to those lands which man would select for various purposes, for settlements, recreation, agriculture, and forestry. Such a study would be more complete than the isolation of a single demand. Yet, it is likely that the same proposition would hold although the larger study would better reveal the degree of conflict. For the moment, it is enough to observe that the ecological view does represent a perceptive method and could considerably enhance the present mode of planning which disregards natural processes, all but completely, and which in selecting open space, is motivated more by standards of acres per thousand for organized sweating, than for the place and face of nature in man's world.

References

Burton, Ian. *Types of Agricultural Occupancy of Flood Plains in the U.S.A.* Chicago: Department of Geography, University of Chicago, 1962.

Gottmann, Jean. *Megalopolis.* New York: The Twentieth Century Fund, 1962.

Kates, C., and Robert William. *Hazard and Choice Perception in Flood Plain Management.* Chicago: Department of Geography, University of Chicago, 1962.

Kates, C., Robert William, and Gilbert F. White. "Flood Hazard Evaluation." Edited by Gilbert F. White. *Papers on Flood Problems*, 135–147. Chicago: Department of Geography, University of Chicago, 1962.

MacKaye, Benton. *The New Exploration: A Philosophy of Regional Planning.* New York: Harcourt Brace, 1928.

McHarg, Ian L. "Processes as Values." *Design with Nature.* Garden City, New York: Doubleday, Natural History Press, 1969.

Odum, Eugene P. *Fundamentals of Ecology.* Philadelphia: Saunders, 1959.

State of Wisconsin. *Recreation in Wisconsin.* Madison: Department of Resource Development, 1962.

Wallace, McHarg, Roberts, Todd. *An Ecological Study of the Twin Cities Metropolitan Region, Minnesota.* Prepared for Metropolitan Council of the Twin Cities Area. Philadelphia: U.S. Department of Commerce, National Technical Information Series, 1969.

Wiitala, Sulo Werner. *Some Aspects of the Effect of Urban and Suburban Development upon Runoff.* Lansing, MI: U.S. Department of the Interior, Geological Survey, 1961.

An Introduction to Ecological Design

Ecological Design (1996)

Sim Van der Ryn and Stuart Cowan

Overview

We live in two interpenetrating worlds. The first is the living world, which has been forged in an evolutionary crucible over a period of four billion years. The second is the world of roads and cities, farms and artifacts, that people have been designing for themselves over the last few millennia. The condition that threatens both worlds—unsustainability—results from a lack of integration between them.

Now imagine the natural world and the humanly designed world bound together in intersecting layers, the warp and woof that make up the fabric of our lives. Instead of a simple fabric of two layers, it is made up of dozens of layers with vastly different characteristics. How these layers are woven together determines whether the result will be a coherent fabric or a dysfunctional tangle.

We need to acquire the skills to effectively interweave human and natural design. The designed mess we have made of our neighborhoods, cities, and ecosystems owes much to the lack of a coherent philosophy, vision, and practice of design that is grounded in a rich understanding of ecology. Unfortunately, the guiding metaphors of those who shape the built environment still reflect a nineteenth-century epistemology. Until our everyday activities preserve ecological integrity *by design*, their cumulative impact will continue to be devastating.

Thinking ecologically about design is a way of strengthening the weave that links nature and culture. Just as architecture has traditionally concerned itself with problems of structure, form, and aesthetics, or as engineering has with safety and efficiency, we need to consciously cultivate an ecologically sound form of design that is consonant with the long-term survival of all species. We define *ecological design* as "any form of design that minimizes environmentally destructive impacts by integrating itself with living processes." This integration implies that the design respects species diversity, minimizes resource depletion, preserves nutrient and water cycles, maintains habitat quality, and attends to all the other preconditions of human and ecosystem health.

Ecological design explicitly addresses the design dimension of the environmental crisis. It is not a style. It is a form of engagement and partnership with nature that is not bound to a particular design profession. Its scope is rich enough to embrace the work of architects rethinking their choices of building materials, the Army Corps of Engineers reformulating its flood-control strategy, and industrial designers curtailing their use of toxic compounds. Ecological design provides a coherent framework for redesigning our landscapes, buildings, cities, and systems of energy, water, food, manufacturing, and waste.

Ecological design is simply the effective *adaptation to* and *integration with* nature's processes. It proceeds from considerations of health and wholeness, and tests its solutions with a careful accounting of their *full* environmental impacts. It compels us to ask new questions of each design: Does it enhance and heal the living world, or does it diminish it? Does it preserve relevant ecological structure and process, or does it degrade it?

We are just beginning to make a transition from conventional forms of design, with the destructive environmental impacts they entail, to ecologically sound forms of design. There are now sewage treatment plants that use constructed marshes to simultaneously purify water, reclaim nutrients, and provide habitat. There are agricultural systems that mimic natural ecosystems and merge with their surrounding landscapes. There are new kinds of industrial systems in which the waste streams from one process are *designed* to be useful inputs to the next, thus minimizing pollution. There are new kinds of nontoxic paints, glues, and finishes. Such examples are now rapidly multiplying. . . .

We have already made dramatic progress in many areas by substituting design intelligence for the extravagant use of energy and materials. Computing power that fifty years ago would fill a house full of vacuum tubes and wires can now be held in the palm of your hand. The old steelmills whose blast furnaces, slag heaps, and towering smokestacks dominated the industrial landscape have been replaced with efficient scaled-down facilities and processes. Drafty, polluting fireplaces have been replaced with compact, highly efficient ones that burn pelletized wood wastes. Many products and processes have been miniaturized, with the flow of energy and materials required to make and operate them often dramatically reduced.

These examples show that when we think differently about design, new solutions are often quick to emerge. By explicitly taking ecology as the basis of design, we can vastly diminish the environmental impacts of everything we make and build. While we've often done well in applying design intelligence to narrowly circumscribed problems, we now need to integrate ecologically sound technologies, planning methods, and policies across scales and professional boundaries.

The nutrients, energy, and information essential to life flow smoothly across scales ranging from microorganisms to continents; in contrast, design has become fragmented into dozens of separate technical disciplines, each with its own specialized language and tools. As the inventor Buckminster Fuller once noted, "Nature did not call a department heads' meeting when I threw a green apple into the pond, with the department heads having to make a decision about how to handle this biological encounter with chemistry's water and the unauthorized use of the physics department's waves." No amount of regulation, intervention, or standalone brilliance will bring us a healthier world until we begin to deliberately join design decisions into coherent patterns that are congruent with nature's own.

In a sense, evolution is nature's ongoing design process. The wonderful thing about this process is that it is happening continuously throughout the entire biosphere. A typical organism has undergone at least a million years of intensive research and development, and none of our own designs can match that standard. Evolution has endowed individual organisms with a wide range of abilities, from harvesting sunshine to perceiving the world. Further, it has enabled communities of organisms to collectively recycle nutrients, regulate water cycles, and maintain both structure and diversity. Evolution has patiently worked on the living world to create a nested series of coherent levels, from organism to planet, each manifesting its own design integrities.

A few years ago, two Norwegian researchers set out to determine the bacterial diversity of a pinch of beech-forest soil and a pinch of shallow coastal sediment. They found well over four thousand species in each sample, which more than equaled the number listed in the standard catalogue of bacterial diversity. Even more remarkably, the species present in the two samples were almost completely distinct. This extraordinary diversity pervades the Earth's manifold habitats, from deep-sea volcanic vents to mangrove swamps, from Arctic tundra to redwood forests. It is a diversity predicated on precise adaptation to underlying conditions. Within this diversity, within a hawk's wings or a nitrogen-fixing bacterium's enzymes, lies a rich kind of design competence. In nature, there is a careful choreograph of function and form bridging many scales. It is this dance that provides the wider context for our own designs. In the attempt to minimize environmental impacts, we are inevitably drawn to nature's own design strategies.

These strategies form a rich resource for design guidance and inspiration. Contemplating the patterns that sustain life, we are given crucial design clues. We learn that spider plants are particularly good at removing pollutants from the air and might serve as an effective component of a living system for purifying the confined air of office buildings. We discover that wetlands can remove vast quantities of nutrients, detoxify compounds, and neutralize pathogens, and therefore can play a role in an ecological wastewater treatment system. The sum of these simple lessons from nature's own exquisite design catalog is nothing less than a blueprint for our own survival.

Suppose we represent our working "natural capital"—forests, lakes, wetlands, salmon, and so on—with a stack of coins. This natural capital provides renewable interest in the form of sustainable fish and timber yields, crops, and clean air, water, and soil. At present, we are simply spending this capital, drawing it down to dangerously low levels, decreasing the ability of remaining ecosystems to assimilate ever-increasing quantities of waste. Such an approach cannot help but deplete natural capital.

Ecological design offers three critical strategies for addressing this loss: conservation, regeneration, and stewardship. Conservation slows the rate at which things are getting worse by allowing scarce resources to be stretched further. Typical conservation measures include recycling materials, building denser communities to preserve agricultural land, adding insulation, and designing fuel-efficient cars. Unfortunately, conservation implicitly assumes that damage must be done and that the only recourse is to somehow minimize this damage. Conservation alone cannot lead to sustainability since it still implies an annual natural-resource deficit.

In the years before his death, Robert Rodale, editor of Rodale Press, was very concerned with what he termed *regeneration*. In a literal sense, regeneration is the repair and renewal of living tissue. Ecological design works to regenerate a world deeply wounded by environmentally insensitive design. This may involve restoring an eroded stream to biological productivity, re-creating habitat, or renewing soil. Regeneration is an expansion of natural capital through the active restoration of degraded ecosystems and communities. It is a form of healing and renewal that embodies the richest possibilities of culture to harmonize with nature. Regeneration not only preserves and protects: It restores a lost plenitude.

Stewardship is a particular quality of care in our relations with other living creatures and with the landscape. It is a process of steady commitment informed by constant feedback—for example, the gully is eroding, or Joe's doing poorly in math. It requires the careful maintenance and continual reinvestment that a good gardener might practice through weeding, watering, watching for pests, enriching the soil with compost, or adding new varieties. Stewardship maintains natural capital by spending frugally and investing wisely.

Ecological design embraces conservation, regeneration, and stewardship alike. If conservation involves spending natural capital more slowly, and regeneration is the expansion of natural capital, then stewardship is the wisdom to live on renewable interest rather than eating into natural capital. Conservation is already well established in the engineering and resource-management professions, but regeneration is just beginning to be explored by restoration ecologists, organic farmers, and others. Stewardship is a quality that all of us already have to some degree. Together, conservation, regeneration, and stewardship remind us of both the technical and personal dimensions of sustainability. They open up new kinds of creative endeavor even as they reaffirm the need for limits.

Careful ecological design permits such a great reduction in energy and material flows that human communities can once again be deeply integrated into their surrounding ecological communities. By carefully tailoring the scale and composition of wastes to the ability of ecosystems to assimilate them, we may begin to re-create a symbiotic relationship between nature and culture. By letting nature do the work, we allow ecosystems to flourish even as they purify and reclaim wastes, ameliorate the climate, provide food, or control flooding. It is clear that "the world is a vast repository of unknown biological strategies that could have immense relevance should we develop a science of integrating the stories embedded in nature into the systems we design to sustain us." Ecological design begins to integrate these biological strategies by gently improvising upon life's own chemical vocabulary, geometry, flows, and patterns of community.

For example, if we wish to buttress a badly eroding hill, a conventional design might call for a concrete retaining wall many inches thick to hold the earth in place. Such a wall makes ostentatious use of matter and energy and does little to heal the land. In looking for an ecological design solution, we seek natural processes that perform this same work of holding the earth in place. We are led to trees, and a useful solution in practice has been to seed the hill with hundreds of willow branches. Within months the branches sprout, providing effective soil stabilization. The willow's articulated roots are far more adapted to keeping the soil in place than concrete, which bears only a superficial relationship to the soil.

Ecological design occurs in the context of specific places. It grows out of place the way the oak grows from an acorn. It responds to the particularities of place: the soils, vegetation, animals, climate, topography, water flows, and people lending it coherence. It seeks locally adapted solutions that can replace matter, energy, and waste with design intelligence. Such an approach matches biological diversity with cultural diversity rather than compromising both the way conventional solutions do.

To design with this kind of care, we need to rigorously assess a design's set of environmental impacts. To take a simple example, consider just a few of the impacts of a typical house. Carbon dioxide emissions from the manufacture of the cement in its foundation contribute to global warming. The production of the electricity used to heat the house may contribute to acid rain in the region. Altered topography and drainage on-site may cause erosion, impacting the immediate watershed. The house might displace existing wildlife habitat. Inside the house, the health of the occupants may be compromised by emissions from the various glues, resins, and finishes used during construction. The lumber may have hastened the destruction of distant ancient forests. We are left with a somewhat disheartening picture of the wider ecological costs of a single building.

Ecological design converts these impacts from invisible side effects into explicitly incorporated design constraints. If ordinary cement's contribution to global warming renders its large-scale use undesirable, this imposes a critical design constraint. Perhaps the house can be sited in a way that minimizes cement use, or alternative, less-destructive cements can be used. If heating the house requires excessive quantities of electricity or natural gas, it may be possible to use passive solar heating through careful orientation of the building and the proper choice of building materials. In a similar way, each of the impacts can be turned into a stimulus for ecological design innovation.

Ecological design brings natural flows to the foreground. It celebrates the flow of water on the landscape, the rushing wind, the fertility of the earth, the plurality of species, and the rhythms of the sun, moon, and tides. It renders the invisible visible, allowing us to speak of it and carry it in our lives. It brings us back home. As the elements of our survival—the provenance of our food and energy, the veins of our watershed, the contours of our mountains—become vivid and present once again, they ground us in our place. We are given news of our region and the comings and goings of our fellow species. Ultimately, ecological design deepens our sense of place, our knowledge of both its true abundance and its unsuspected fragility.

Ecological design is a way of integrating human purpose with nature's own flows, cycles, and patterns. It begins with the richest possible understanding of the ecological context of a given design problem and develops solutions that are consistent with the cultural context. Such design cannot be the work of experts only. It is ultimately the work of a sustainable culture, one skilled in reweaving the multiple layers of natural and human design. Ecological designers are facilitators and catalysts in the cultural processes underlying sustainability.

We are beginning to get the pieces right, from highly efficient appliances to organic farms. However, until the pieces constitute the *texture* of everyday life, they will remain insufficient. This book is about the design wherewithal necessary to create a sustainable world. It provides a new way of seeing and thinking about design. It suggests a new set of questions and themes to order the design process. It proposes a form of design that is able to translate the vision of sustainability into the everyday objects, buildings, and landscapes around us. It embraces the best of the new ecological technologies but also inquires into the cultural foundations of sustainability. In short, it is an exploration of practical harmonies between nature and culture.

Table 3-1 compares conventional and ecological design in relation to a number of relevant issues.

History and Background

Ecological design is not a new idea. By necessity, it has been brought to a high level of excellence by many different cultures faced with widely varying conditions. The Yanomamö, living with a refined knowledge of the Amazon rainforest, deliberately propagate hundreds of plant species, thereby enhancing biological diversity. Balinese aquaculture and rice terracing maintain soil fertility and pure water while feeding large numbers of people. Australian aborigines use stories and rituals to preserve an exquisitely detailed ecological map of their lands. The design rules embedded in each of these cultures have enabled them to persist for millennia.

Even during the most uncritical growth eras of the industrialized nations, there have been strong movements for ecologically sound town planning, healthy building, organic agriculture, appropriate technology, renewable energy, and interdisciplinary approaches to design. William Morris's Arts and Crafts Movement, Rudolph Steiner's biodynamic agriculture, Ebenezer Howard's garden cities, Patrick Geddes's and Lewis Mumford's regional planning, and Frank Lloyd Wright's organic architecture—each celebrated design at a human scale firmly situated in a wider ecological context. Buckminster Fuller, in an enormously productive five decades of work, tested the limits of ephemeralization—decreasing the use of materials and energy—while designing Dymaxion houses that could process their own wastes and be recycled at the end of their useful lives.

Table 3-1

Characteristics of conventional and ecological design (Van der Ryn and Cowan, 1996, Reproduced with permission of Island Press. Redrawn by Travis Witt, 2014).

Issue	Conventional Design	Ecological Design
Energy source	Usually nonrenewable and destructive, relying on fossil fuels or nuclear power; the design consumes natural capital	Whenever feasible, renewable: solar, wind, small-scale hydro, or biomass; the design lives off solar income
Materials use	High-quality materials are used clumsily, and resulting toxic and low-quality materials are discarded in soil, air, and water	Restorative materials cycles in which waste for one process becomes food for the next; designed-in reuse, recycling, flexibility, ease of repair, and durability
Pollution	Copious and endemic	Minimized; scale and composition of wastes conform to the ability of ecosystems to absorb them
Toxic substances	Common and destructive, ranging from pesticides to paints	Used extremely sparingly in very special circumstances
Ecological accounting	Limited to compliance with mandatory requirements like environmental impact reports	Sophisticated and built in; covers a wide range of ecological impacts over the entire life-cycle of the project, from extraction of materials to final recycling of components
Ecology and economics	Perceived as in opposition; short-run view	Perceived as compatible; long-run view
Design criteria	Economics, custom, and convenience	Human and ecosystem health, ecological economics
Sensitivity to ecological context	Standard templates are replicated all over the planet with little regard to culture or place; sky-scrapers look the same from New York to Cairo	Responds to bioregion; the design is integrated with local soils, vegetation, materials, culture, climate, topography; the solutions grow from place
Sensitivity to cultural context	Tends to build a homogeneous global culture; destroys local communities	Respects and nurtures traditional knowledge of place and local materials and technologies; fosters commons
Biological, cultural, and economic diversity	Employs standardized designs with high energy and material throughput, thereby eroding biological, cultural, and economic diversity	Maintains biodiversity and the locally adapted cultures and economies that support it
Knowledge base	Narrow disciplinary focus	Integrates multiple design disciplines and wide range of sciences; comprehensive
Spatial scales	Tends to work at one scale at a time	Integrates design across multiple scales, reflecting the influence of larger scales on smaller scales and smaller on larger

Table 3-1 (cont.)

Issue	Conventional Design	Ecological Design
Whole systems	Divides systems along boundaries that do not reflect the underlying natural processes	Works with whole systems; produces designs that provide the greatest possible degree of internal integrity and coherence
Role of nature	Design must be imposed on nature to provide control and predictability and meet narrowly defined human needs	Includes nature as a partner: whenever possible, substitutes nature's own design intelligence for a heavy reliance on materials and energy
Underlying metaphors	Machine, product, part	Cell, organism, ecosystem
Level of participation	Reliance on jargon and experts who are unwilling to communicate with public limits community involvement in critical design decisions	A commitment to clear discussion and debate; everyone is empowered to join the design process
Types of learning	Nature and technology are hidden; the design does not teach us over time	Nature and technology are made visible; the design draws us closer to the systems that ultimately sustain us
Response to sustainability crisis	Views culture and nature as inimical, tries to slow the rate at which things are getting worse by implementing mild conservation efforts without questioning underlying assumptions	Views culture and nature as potentially symbiotic; moves beyond triage to a search for practices that actively regenerate human and ecosystem health

By the 1960s, various streams of stubborn ethical and aesthetic opposition to unfettered industrialization coalesced into the first modem generation of ecological design. Designer Sean Wellesley-Miller and physicist Day Chahroudi designed building "skins" based on biological metaphors and principles but using newly available materials. John and Nancy Todd and their associates at the New Alchemy Institute designed solar Arks that grew their own food, provided their own energy, and recycled their own wastes. Other experimental houses and habitats were built all over the world, including the Ouroboros House in Minneapolis, the Autonomous House at Cambridge University, and the Farallones Institute's Integral Urban House in Berkeley, California. While different in form and purpose, all of these projects shared a similar vision: Biology and ecology are the key sciences in rethinking the design of habitat. Within these projects, the metaphor of a living organism or ecosystem replaced Le Corbusier's old image of a dwelling as a "machine for living."

The house, the habitat we are most familiar with, seemed to be a good place to start this first generation of ecological design. The rural or village homestead was once the center of a largely self-sufficient system that produced a family's livelihood, its food and fiber, and its tools and toys. Over a period of several hundred years, this homestead has become an anonymous mass-produced dwelling unit, its inhabitants members of a faceless consumershed, the house itself totally dependent on outside resources to sustain its inhabitants. Rethinking home metabolism became the mission of the first generation of ecological design.

The Integral Urban House, conceived by biologists Bill and Helga Olkowski and sponsored by the Farallones Institute, started in 1973 in a ramshackle Victorian house in Berkeley, California. The oil embargo had made many people aware for the first time of their almost total dependence on an oil economy. Designers were challenged to work with the sun, turning this house from a consumer of oil for heating, cooling, electricity, and food into a producer of thermal energy, food, and electricity.

The Integral Urban House was intended to restore its inhabitants to a measure of control over the basics of their life support, reduce the outflow of money to pay for resources and services that the home and local environment could provide, and encourage interaction with local ecosystems. The idea was to integrate energy and food production and waste and water recycling directly into the home design. The Integral Urban House featured composting toilets, an aquaculture pond, organic gardens, and advanced recycling. The guiding vision was a new synthesis of architecture and biology.

During these years of creative ferment, important theoretical advances were also made. In *Design with Nature*, Ian McHarg looked at the natural functioning of landscapes and proposed that intelligent land-use planning be based on "what a landscape wants to be." In *Small Is Beautiful*, Fritz Schumacher, drawing heavily on the ideas of Gandhi, persuasively argued that small-scale systems made economic sense, thus launching the appropriate-technology movement. Amory Lovins provided a coherent solar alternative to nuclear energy in *Soft Energy Paths*. John and Nancy Todd provided nine key precepts for "biological design" in *Bioshelters, Ocean Arks, City Farming: Ecology as the Basis of Design*, recently republished as *From Eco-Cities to Living Machines: Principles of Ecological Design*. Christopher Alexander and colleagues presented a powerful new theory of design with important ecological ramifications in *A Pattern Language* and *The Timeless Way of Building*.

In the 1980s, the environmental movement grew into a broad-based sustainability movement. Great technical advances were made in solar and wind energy. Lovins's Rocky Mountain Institute helped transform energy policy in many nations. Bill Mollison's "permaculture" approach to organic agriculture and healthy building gained a worldwide following from its modest start in

Tasmania. Fundamental research on sustainable agriculture was performed at the University of California, Santa Cruz, and the Land Institute in Salina, Kansas. Work in landscape ecology and conservation biology provided a new set of tools for preserving biodiversity that have been effectively used by Project Wild. Peter Calthorpe, Andres Duany, and Elizabeth Plater-Zyberk created renewed interest in pedestrian-oriented town planning.

The 1990s have seen the emergence of the international ecocities movement, which is working to create healthier, more resource-efficient cities. Constructed ecosystems—wetlands and contained microcosms—are rapidly becoming an important alternative to conventional wastewater treatment systems. Industrial ecology and life-cycle analysis are already key tools for minimizing pollution. New approaches to ecological restoration and toxic decontamination show great promise. Recent attempts to integrate ecology and economics are also beginning to bear fruit, including Pliny Fisk's approach to bioregional design at the Center for Maximum Potential Building Systems in Austin, Texas. Artists like Andy Goldsworthy and Mierle Ukeles are creating works that demonstrate a deep commitment to ecological ideas.

The 1980s and 1990s also saw the publication of a handful of important theoretical works related to ecological design. John Tillman Lyle's *Design for Human Ecosystems: Landscape, Land Use, and Natural Resources* and more recent *Regenerative Design for Sustainable Development* provide careful and comprehensive treatments of ecological design strategies. Robert L. Thayer, Jr.'s, *Gray World, Green Heart: Technology, Nature, and the Sustainable Landscape* is a more philosophical work that raises important issues. Sim Van der Ryn and Peter Calthorpe's *Sustainable Communities: A New Design Synthesis for Cities, Suburbs, and Towns* treats ecological design at the town scale. Paul Hawken's *The Ecology of Commerce: A Declaration of Sustainability* makes important connections between ecological design and business.

The first generation of ecological design was based on small-scale experiments with living lightly in place. Many of the technologies and ideas of this generation, such as alternative building materials, renewable energy, organic foods, conservation, and recycling have been widely adopted in piecemeal fashion. We now stand at the threshold of a second generation of ecological design. This second generation is not an alternative to dominant technology and design; it is the best path for their necessary evolution.

The second generation of ecological design must effectively weave the insights of literally dozens of disciplines. It must create a viable ecological design craft within a genuine culture of sustainability rather than getting entangled in interdisciplinary disputes and turf wars. It is time to bring forth new ecologies of design that are rich with cultural and epistemological diversity.

References

Fuller, R. Buckminster. *Synergetics. Explorations in the Geometry of Thinking*. New York: Macmillan, 1975.

Olkowski, Helga, William Olkowski, and Tom Javits. *The Integral Urban House: Self-Reliant Living in the City*. San Francisco: Sierra Club Books, 1979.

Schiechtl, Hugo. *Bioengineering for Land Reclamation and Conservation*. Edmonton: University of Alberta Press, 1980.

Todd, John, and Nancy Jack Todd. *Tomorrow is Our Permanent Address: The Search for an Ecological Science of Design as Embodied in the Bioshelter*. New York: Harper & Row, 1980.

Todd, John. *From Eco-Cities to Living Machines: Principles of Ecological Design*. Berkeley: North Atlantic Books, 1994.

Todd, Nancy Jack, and John Todd. *Bioshelters, Ocean Arks, City Farming: Ecology as the Basis of Design*. San Francisco: Sierra Club Books, 1984.

Wilson, Edward O. *The Diversity of Life*. Cambridge: Harvard University Press, 1992.

The Strategy of Ecosystem Development

Science (1969)

Eugene P. Odum

The principles of ecological succession bear importantly on the relationships between man and nature. The framework of successional theory needs to be examined as a basis for resolving man's present environmental crisis. Most ideas pertaining to the development of ecological systems are based on descriptive data obtained by observing changes in biotic communities over long periods, or on highly theoretical assumptions; very few of the generally accepted hypotheses have been tested experimentally. Some of the confusion, vagueness, and lack of experimental work in this area stems from the tendency of ecologists to regard "succession" as a single straightforward idea; in actual fact, it entails an interacting complex of processes, some of which counteract one another.

As viewed here, ecological succession involves the development of ecosystems; it has many parallels in the developmental biology of organisms, and also in the development of human society. The ecosystem, or ecological system, is considered to be a unit of biological organization made up of all of the organisms in a given area (that is, "community") interacting with the physical environment so that a flow of energy leads to characteristic trophic structure and material cycles within the system. It is the purpose of this article to summarize, in the form of a tabular model, components and stages of development at the ecosystem level as a means of emphasizing those aspects of ecological succession that can be accepted on the basis of present knowledge, those that require more study, and those that have special relevance to human ecology.

Definition of Succession

Ecological succession may be defined in terms of the following three parameters. (i) It is an orderly process of community development that is reasonably directional and, therefore, predictable. (ii) It results from modification of the physical environment by the community; that is, succession is community-controlled even though the physical environment determines the pattern, the rate of change, and often sets limits as to how far development can go. (iii) It culminates in a stabilized ecosystem in which maximum biomass (or high information content) and symbiotic function between organisms are maintained per unit of available energy flow. In a word, the "strategy" of succession as a short-term process is basically the same as the "strategy" of long-term evolutionary development of the biosphere—namely, increased control of, or homeostasis with, the physical environment in the sense of achieving maximum protection from its perturbations. As I illustrate below, the strategy of "maximum protection" (that is, trying to achieve maximum support of complex biomass structure) often conflicts with man's goal of "maximum production" (trying to obtain the highest possible yield). Recognition of the ecological basis for this conflict is, I believe, a first step in establishing rational land-use policies.

The earlier descriptive studies of succession on sand dunes, grasslands, forests, marine shores, or other sites, and more recent functional considerations, have led to the basic theory contained in the definition given above. H. T. Odum and Pinkerton, building on Lotka's "law of maximum energy in biological systems," were the first to point out that succession involves a fundamental shift in energy flows as increasing energy is relegated to maintenance. Margalef has recently documented this bioenergetic basis for succession and has extended the concept.

Changes that occur in major structural and functional characteristics of a developing ecosystem are listed in table 3-2. Twenty-four attributes of ecological systems are grouped, for convenience of discussion, under six headings. Trends are emphasized by contrasting the situation in early and late development. The degree of absolute change, the rate of change, and the time required to reach a steady state may vary not only with different climatic and physiographic situations but also with different ecosystem attributes in the same physical environment. Where good data are available, rate-of-change curves are usually convex, with changes occurring most rapidly at the beginning, but bimodal or cyclic patterns may also occur. . . .

Table 3-2

Tabular model of ecological succession: trends to be expected in the development of ecosystems (Odum, 1969, Reproduced with permission of American Association for the Advancement of Science, Redrawn by Yuan Ren, 2014).

Ecosystem attributes	Developmental stages	Mature stages
Community energetics		
1. Gross production/ community respiration (P/R ratio)	Greater or less than 1	Approaches 1
2. Gross production/standing crop biomass (P/B ratio)	High	Low
3. Biomass supported/unit energy flow *(B/E* ratio)	Low	High
4. Net community production (yield)	High	Low
5. Food chains	Linear, predominantly grazing	Weblike, predominantly detritus
Community structure		
6. Total organic matter	Small	Large
7. Inorganic nutrients	Extrabiotic	Intrabiotic
8. Species diversity—variety component	Low	High
9. Species diversity— equitability component	Low	High
10. Biochemical diversity	Low	High
11. Stratification and spatial heterogeneity (pattern diversity)	Poorly organized	Well-organized
Life history		
12. Niche specialization	Broad	Narrow
13. Size of organism	Small	Large
14. Life cycles	Short, simple	Long, complex
Nutrient cycling		
15. Mineral cycles	Open	Closed
16. Nutrient exchange rate, between organisms and environment	Rapid	Slow
17. Role of detritus in nutrient regeneration	Unimportant	Important

Table 3-2 (cont.)

Ecosystem attributes	Developmental stages	Mature stages
	Selection pressure	
18. Growth form	For rapid growth ("*r*-selection")	For feedback control ("*K*-selection")
19. Production	Quantity	Quality
	Overall homeostasis	
20. Internal symbiosis	Undeveloped	Developed
21. Nutrient conservation	Poor	Good
22. Stability (resistance to external perturbations)	Poor	Good
23. Entropy	High	Low
24. Information	Low	High

Overall Homeostasis

. . .While one may well question whether all the trends described are characteristic of all types of ecosystems, there can be little doubt that the net result of community actions is symbiosis, nutrient conservation, stability, a decrease in entropy, and an increase in information (table 3-2, items 20–24). The overall strategy is, as I stated at the beginning of this article, directed toward achieving as large and diverse an organic structure as is possible within the limits set by the available energy input and the prevailing physical conditions of existence (soil, water, climate, and so on). As studies of biotic communities become more functional and sophisticated, one is impressed with the importance of mutualism, parasitism, predation, commensalism, and other forms of symbiosis. Partnership between unrelated species is often noteworthy (for example, that between coral coelenterates and algae, or between mycorrhizae and trees). In many cases, at least, biotic control of grazing, population density, and nutrient cycling provide the chief positive-feedback mechanisms that contribute to stability in the mature system by preventing overshoots and destructive oscillations. The intriguing question is, Do mature ecosystems age, as organisms do? In other words, after a long period of relative stability or "adulthood," do ecosystems again develop unbalanced metabolism and become more vulnerable to diseases and other perturbations?

Relevance of Ecosystem Development Theory to Human Ecology

Figure 3-2 depicts a basic conflict between the strategies of man and of nature. The "bloom-type" relationships, as exhibited by the 30-day microcosm or the 30-year forest, illustrate man's present idea of how nature should be directed. For example, the goal of agriculture or intensive forestry, as now generally practiced, is to achieve high rates of production of readily harvestable products with little standing crop left to accumulate on the landscape—in other words, a high P/B efficiency. Nature's strategy, on the other hand, as seen in the outcome of the successional process, is directed toward the reverse efficiency—a high B/P ratio. . . .

Man has generally been preoccupied with obtaining as much "production" from the landscape as possible, by developing and maintaining early successional types of ecosystems, usually monocultures. But, of course, man does not live by food and fiber alone; he also needs a balanced CO_2–O_2 atmosphere, the climatic buffer provided by oceans and masses of vegetation, and clean (that is, unproductive) water for cultural and industrial uses. Many essential life-cycle resources, not to mention recreational and esthetic needs, are best provided man by the less "productive" landscapes. In other words, the landscape is not just a supply depot but is also the *oikos*—the home—in which we must live. Until recently mankind has more or less taken for granted the gas-exchange, water-purification, nutrient-cycling, and other protective functions of self-maintaining ecosystems, chiefly because neither his numbers nor his environmental manipulations have been great enough to affect regional and global balances. Now, of course, it is painfully evident that such balances are being affected, often detrimentally. The "one problem, one solution approach" is no longer adequate and must be replaced by some form of ecosystem analysis that considers man as a part of, not apart from, the environment.

The most pleasant and certainly the safest landscape to live in is one containing a variety of crops, forests, lakes, streams, roadsides, marshes, seashores, and "waste places"—in other words, a mixture of communities of different ecological ages. As individuals we more or less instinctively surround our houses with protective, nonedible cover (trees, shrubs, grass) at the same time that we strive to coax extra bushels from our cornfield. We all consider the cornfield a "good thing," of course, but most of us would not want to live there, and it would certainly be suicidal to cover the whole land area of the biosphere with cornfields, since the boom and bust oscillation in such a situation would be severe.

The basic problem facing organized society today boils down to determining in some objective manner when we are getting "too much of a good thing."

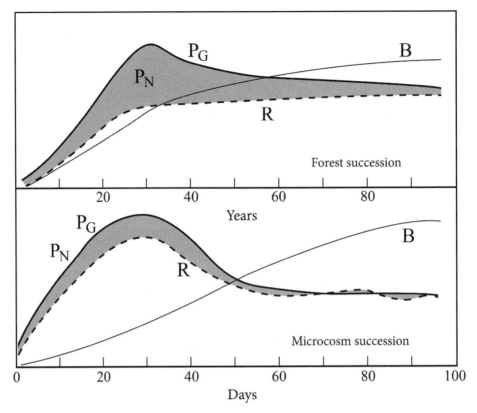

Figure 3-2 Comparison of the energetics of succession in a forest and laboratory microcosm. P_G, gross production; P_N, net production; R, total community respiration; B, total biomass (1969, Reproduced with permission of American Association for the Advancement of Science, Redrawn by Yuen Ren, 2014).

This is a completely new challenge to mankind because, up until now, he has had to be concerned largely with too little rather than too much. Thus, concrete is a "good thing," but not if half the world is covered with it. Insecticides are "good things," but not when used, as they now are, in an indiscriminate and wholesale manner. Likewise, water impoundments have proved to be very useful man-made additions to the landscape, but obviously we don't want the whole country inundated! Vast manmade lakes solve some problems, at least temporarily, but yield comparative little food or fiber, and, because of high evaporative losses, they may not even be the best device for storing water; it might better be stored in the watershed, or underground in aquifers. Also, the cost of building large dams is a drain on already overtaxed revenues. Although as individuals we readily recognize that we can have too many dams or other large-scale environmental changes, governments are so fragmented and lacking in systems-analysis capabilities that there is no effective mechanism whereby negative feedback signals can be received and acted on before there has been a serious overshoot. Thus, today there are governmental agencies, spurred on by popular and political enthusiasm for dams, that are putting on the drawing boards plans for damming every river and stream in North America!

Society needs, and must find as quickly as possible, a way to deal with the landscape as a whole, so that manipulative skills (that is, technology) will not run too far ahead of our understanding of the impact of change. Recently a national ecological center outside of government and a coalition of governmental agencies have been proposed as two possible steps in the establishment of a political control mechanism for dealing with major environmental questions. The soil conservation movement in America is an excellent example of a program dedicated to the consideration of the whole farm or the whole watershed as an ecological unit. Soil conservation is well understood and supported by the public. However, soil conservation organizations have remained too exclusively farm-oriented, and have not yet risen to the challenge of the urban-rural landscape, where lie today's most serious problems. We do, then, have potential mechanisms in American society that could speak for the ecosystem as a whole, but none of them are really operational.

The general relevance of ecosystem development theory to landscape planning can, perhaps, be emphasized by the "mini-model" of table 3-3, which contrasts the characteristics of young and mature-type ecosystems in more general terms than those provided by table 3-2. It is mathematically impossible to obtain a maximum for more than one thing at a time, so one cannot have both extremes at the same time and place. Since all six characteristics listed in table 3-3 are desirable in the aggregate, two possible solutions to the dilemma immediately suggest themselves. We can compromise so as to provide moderate quality and moderate yield on all the landscape, or we can deliberately plan to compartmentalize the landscape so as to simultaneously maintain highly productive and predominantly protective types as separate units subject to different management strategies (strategies ranging, for example, from intensive cropping on the one hand to wilderness management on the other). If ecosystem development theory is valid and applicable to planning, then the so-called multiple-use strategy, about which we hear so much, will work only through one or both of these approaches, because, in most cases, the projected multiple uses conflict with one another. It is appropriate, then, to examine some examples of the compromise and the compartmental strategies.

Table 3-3

Contrasting characteristics of young and mature-type ecosystems (Odum, 1969, Reproduced with permission of American Association for the Advancement of Science, Redrawn by Yuan Ren, 2014).

Young	Mature
Production	Protection
Growth	Stability
Quantity	Quality

Pulse Stability

A more or less regular but acute physical perturbation imposed from without can maintain an ecosystem at some intermediate point in the developmental sequence, resulting in, so to speak, a compromise between youth and maturity. What I would term "fluctuating water level ecosystems" are good examples. Estuaries, and intertidal zones in general, are maintained in an early, relatively fertile stage by the tides, which provide the energy for rapid nutrient cycling. Likewise, freshwater marshes, such as the Florida Everglades, are held at an early successional stage by the seasonal fluctuations in water levels. The dry-season drawdown speeds up aerobic decomposition of accumulated organic matter, releasing nutrients that, on reflooding, support a wet-season bloom in productivity. The life histories of many organisms are intimately coupled to this periodicity. The wood stork, for example, breeds when the water levels are falling and the small fish on which it feeds become concentrated and easy to catch in the drying pools. If the water level remains high during the usual dry season or fails to rise in the wet season, the stork will not nest. Stabilizing water levels in the Everglades by means of dikes, locks, and impoundments, as is now advocated by some, would, in my opinion, destroy rather than pre-serve the Everglades as we now know them just as surely as complete drainage would. Without periodic drawdowns and fires, the shallow basins would fill up with organic matter and succession would proceed from the present pond-and-prairie condition toward a scrub or swamp forest.

It is strange that man does not readily recognize the importance of recur-rent changes in water level in a natural situation such as the Everglades when similar pulses are the basis for some of his most enduring food culture sys-tems. Alternate filling and draining of ponds has been a standard procedure in fish culture for centuries in Europe and the Orient. The flooding, draining, and soil-aeration procedure in rice culture is another example. The rice paddy is thus the cultivated analogue of the natural marsh or the intertidal ecosystem.

Fire is another physical factor whose periodicity has been of vital importance to man and nature over the centuries. Whole biotas, such as those of the African grasslands and the California chaparral, have become adapted to periodic fires producing what ecologists often call "fire climaxes." Man uses fire deliberately to maintain such climaxes or to set back succession to some desired point. In the southeastern coastal plain, for example, light fires of moderate frequency can maintain a pine forest against the encroachment of older successional stages which, at the present time at least, are considered economically less desirable. The fire-controlled forest yields less wood than a tree farm does (that is, young trees, all of about the same age, planted in rows and harvested on a short rotation schedule), but it provides a greater protective cover for the landscape, wood of higher quality, and a home for game birds (quail, wild turkey, and so on) which could not survive in a tree farm. The fire climax, then, is an example of a compromise between production simplicity and protection diversity.

It should be emphasized that pulse stability works only if there is a complete community (including not only plants but animals and microorganisms) adapted to the particular intensity and frequency of the perturbation. Adaptation—operation of the selection process—requires times measurable on the evolutionary scale. Most physical stresses introduced by man are too sudden, too violent, or too arrhythmic for adaptation to occur at the ecosystem level, so severe oscillation rather than stability results. In many cases, at least, modification of naturally adapted ecosystems for cultural purposes would seem preferable to complete redesign. . . .

The Compartment Model

Successful though they often are, compromise systems are not suitable nor desirable for the whole landscape. More emphasis needs to be placed on compartmentalization, so that growth-type, steady-state, and intermediate-type ecosystems can be linked with urban and industrial areas for mutual benefit. Knowing the transfer coefficients that define the flow of energy and the movement of materials and organisms (including man) between compartments, it should be possible to determine, through analog-computer manipulation, rational limits for the size and capacity of each compartment. We might start, for example, with a simplified model, shown in figure 3-3, consisting of four compartments of equal area, partitioned according to the basic biotic-function criterion—that is, according to whether the area is (i) productive, (ii) protective,

(iii) a compromise between (i) and (ii), or (iv) urban-industrial. By continually refining the transfer coefficients on the basis of real world situations, and by increasing and decreasing the size and capacity of each compartment through computer simulation, it would be possible to determine objectively the limits that must eventually be imposed on each compartment in order to maintain regional and global balances in the exchange of vital energy and of materials. A systems-analysis procedure provides at least one approach to the solution of the basic dilemma posed by the question "How do we determine when we are getting too much of a good thing?" Also it provides a means of evaluating the energy drains imposed on ecosystems by pollution, radiation, harvest, and other stresses.

Implementing any kind of compartmentalization plan, of course, would require procedures for zoning the landscape and restricting the use of some land and water areas. While the principle of zoning in cities is universally accepted, the procedures now followed do not work very well because zoning restrictions are too easily overturned by short-term economic and population pressures. Zoning the landscape would require a whole new order of thinking. Greater use of legal measures providing for tax relief, restrictions on use, scenic easements, and public ownership will be required if appreciable land and water areas are to be held in the "protective" categories. Several states (for example, New Jersey and California), where pollution and population pressure are beginning to hurt, have made a start in this direction by enacting "open space" legislation designed to get as much unoccupied land as possible into a "protective" status so that future uses can be planned on a rational and scientific basis. The United States as a whole is fortunate in that large areas of the country are in national forests, parks, wildlife refuges, and so on. The fact that such areas, as well as the bordering oceans, are not quickly exploitable gives us time for the accelerated ecological study and programming needed to determine what proportions of different types of landscape provide a safe balance between man and nature. The open oceans, for example, should forever be allowed to remain protective rather than productive territory, if Alfred Redfield's assumptions are correct. Redfield views the oceans, the major part of the hydrosphere, as the biosphere's governor, which slows down and controls the rate of decomposition and nutrient regeneration, thereby creating and maintaining the highly aerobic terrestrial environment to which the higher forms of life, such as man, are adapted. Eutrophication of the ocean in a last-ditch effort to feed the populations of the land could well have an adverse effect on the oxygen reservoir in the atmosphere.

Until we can determine more precisely how far we may safely go in expanding intensive agriculture and urban sprawl at the expense of the protective

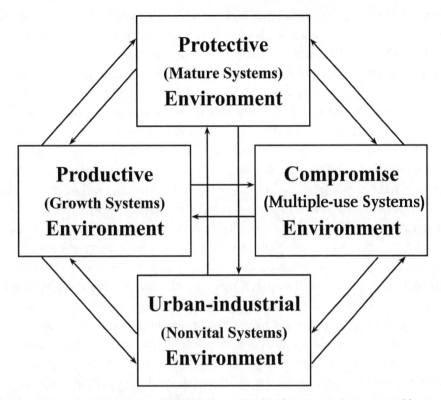

Figure 3-3 Compartment model of the basic kinds of environment required by man, partitioned according to ecosystem development and life-cycle resource constraints (1969, Reproduced with permission of American Association for the Advancement of Science, Redrawn by Yuan Ren, 2014).

landscape, it will be good insurance to hold inviolate as much of the latter as possible. Thus, the preservation of natural areas is not a peripheral luxury for society but a capital investment from which we expect to draw interest. Also, it may well be that restrictions in the use of land and water are our only practical means of avoiding overpopulation or too great an exploitation of resources, or both. Interestingly enough, restriction of land use is the analogue of a natural behavioral control mechanism known as "territoriality" by which many species of animals avoid crowding and social stress.

Since the legal and economic problems pertaining to zoning and compartmentalization are likely to be thorny, I urge law schools to establish departments, or institutes, of "landscape law" and to start training "landscape lawyers" who will be capable not only of clarifying existing procedures but also of drawing up new enabling legislation for consideration by state and national governing bodies. At present, society is concerned—and rightly so—with human rights, but environmental rights are equally vital. The "one man one vote" idea is important, but so also is a "one man one hectare" proposition.

Education, as always, must play a role in increasing man's awareness of his dependence on the natural environment. Perhaps we need to start teaching the principles of ecosystem in the third grade. A grammar school primer on man and his environment could logically consist of four chapters, one for each of the four essential kinds of environment, shown diagrammatically in figure 3-3.

Of the many books and articles that are being written these days about man's environmental crisis, I would like to cite two that go beyond "crying out in alarm" to suggestions for bringing about a reorientation of the goals of society. Garrett Hardin, in a recent article in *Science*, points out that, since the optimum population density is less than the maximum, there is no strictly technical solution to the problem of pollution caused by overpopulation; a solution, he suggests, can only be achieved through moral and legal means of "mutual coercion, mutually agreed upon by the majority of people." Earl F. Murphy, in a book entitled *Governing Nature*, emphasizes that the regulatory approach alone is not enough to protect life-cycle resources, such as air and water, that cannot be allowed to deteriorate. He discusses permit systems, effluent charges, receptor levies, assessment, and cost-internalizing procedures as economic incentives for achieving Hardin's "mutually agreed upon coercion."

It goes without saying that the tabular model for ecosystem development which I have presented here has many parallels in the development of human society itself. In the pioneer society, as in the pioneer ecosystem, high birth rates, rapid growth, high economic profits, and exploitation of accessible and unused resources are advantageous, but, as the saturation level is approached, these drives must be shifted to considerations of symbiosis (that is, "civil rights," "law and order," "education," and "culture"), birth control, and the recycling of resources. A balance between youth and maturity in the socio-environmental system is, therefore, the really basic goal that must be achieved if man as a species is to successfully pass through the present rapid-growth stage, to which he is clearly well adapted, to the ultimate equilibrium-density stage, of which he as yet shows little understanding and to which he now shows little tendency to adapt.

References

Ardrey, Robert. *The Territorial Imperative.* New York: Atheneum, 1967.

Ayala, Francisco J. "Genotype, Environment, and Population Numbers." *Science* 162, no. 3861 (1968): 1453–59.

Baltensweiler, W. "Zeiraphera griseana Hübner (Lepidoptera: Tortricidae) in the European Alps. A Contribution to the Problem of Cycles." *The Canadian Entomologist* 96, no. 5 (1964): 792–800.

Barrett, Gary W. "The Effects of an Acute Insecticide Stress on a Semi-Enclosed Grassland Ecosystem." *Ecology* 49 (1969): 1019–35.

Beyers, Robert J. "The Metabolism of Twelve Aquatic Laboratory Microecosystems." *Ecological Monographs* 33, no. 4 (1963): 281–306.

Bonner, John Tyler. "Size and Cycle—An Essay on the Structure of Biology." *American Scientist* 53, no. 4 (1965): 488–94.

Bormann, F. Herbert, and Gene E. Likens. "Nutrient Cycling." *Science* 155, no. 3761 (1967): 424–29.

Bray, J. R. "Measurement of Leaf Utilization as an Index of Minimum Level of Primary Consumption." *Oikos* 12, no. 1 (1961): 70–74.

Cooke, G. Dennis. "The Pattern of Autotrophic Succession in Laboratory Microcosms." *Bioscience* 17, no. 10 (1967): 717–21.

Cooper, Charles F. "The Ecology of Fire." *Scientific American* 204, no. 4 (1961): 150.

Frank, Peter W. "Life histories and community stability." *Ecology* (1968): 355–57.

Hairston, Nelson G. "Species Abundance and Community Organization." *Ecology* 40, no. 3 (1959): 404–16.

Hardin, Garrett. "The Tragedy of the Commons." *Science* 162 (1968): 1243–48.

Hibbert, A. R. "Forest Treatment Effects on Water Yield." *International Symposium on Forest Hydrology*. New York: Pergamon Press (1978): 813.

Hutchinson, G. Evelyn. "Homage to Santa Rosalia or Why Are There So Many Kinds of Animals?" *The American Naturalist* 93, no. 870 (1959): 145–59.

Johnston, David W., and Eugene P. Odum. "Breeding Bird Populations in Relation to Plant Succession on the Piedmont of Georgia." *Ecology* 37, no. 1 (1956): 50–62.

Kahl, M. Philip. "Food Ecology of the Wood Stork (*Mycteria americana*) in Florida." *Ecological Monographs* 34, no. 2 (1964): 98–117.

Kira, Tatuo, and Tsunahide Shidei. "Primary Production and Turnover of Organic Matter in Different Forest Ecosystems of the Western Pacific." *Japanese Journal of Ecology* 17, no. 2 (1967): 70–87.

Leopold, Aldo. "Lakes in Relation to Terrestrial Life Patterns." *A Symposium on Hydrobiology*. University of Wisconsin Press (1941): 17–42.

Lloyd, Monte, and Robert J. Ghelardi. "A Table for Calculating the Equitability' Component of Species Diversity." *The Journal of Animal Ecology* (1964): 217–25.

Lotka, Alfred James. *Elements of Physical Biology*. Baltimore: Williams & Wilkins, 1925.

MacArthur, Robert, and Edward O. Wilson. *The Theory of Island Biogeography*. Princeton, NJ: Princeton Press, 1967.

MacArthur, Robert H., and John W. MacArthur. "On Bird Species Diversity." *Ecology* 42, no. 3 (1961): 594–98.

Mackereth, F. J. H. "Chemical Investigation of Lake Sediments and Their Interpretation." *Proceedings of the Royal Society of London. Series B, Biological Sciences* 161, no. 984 (1965): 295–309.

Margalef, Ramon. "Correspondence between the Classic Types of Lakes and the Structural and Dynamic Properties of Their Populations." *Verh. Int. Verein. Limnol* 15 (1964): 169–75.

———. "Information Theory in Ecology." *General Systems: Yearbook of the International Society for the Systems Sciences* 3 (1958).

———. "On Certain Unifying Principles in Ecology." *American Naturalist* 97 (1963): 357–74.

———. "Some Concepts Relative to the Organization of Plankton." *Oceanography and Marine Biology: An Annual Review* 5 (1967): 257–89.

———. "Succession in Marine Populations." *Advancing Frontiers of Plant Sciences* 2 (1963): 137–88.

Murphy, Earl Finbar. *Governing Nature*. Chicago, Illinois: Quadrangle Books, 1967.

Odum, Eugene P. *Ecology*. New York: Holt, Rinehart and Winston, 1963.

Odum, Howard T. "Biological Circuits and the Marine Systems of Texas." *Pollution and Marine Ecology*. New York: Wiley (1967): 99–158.

————. "Work Circuits and System Stress." *Symposium on Primary Productivity and Mineral Cycling in Natural Ecosystems*. Orono: University of Maine Press (1967): 81–138.

Odum, Howard T., and Richard C. Pinkerton. "Time's Speed Regulator: The Optimum Efficiency for Maximum Power Output in Physical and Biological Systems." *American Scientist* 43, no. 2 (1955): 331–43.

Paine, Robert T. "Food Web Complexity and Species Diversity." *American Naturalist* (1966): 65–75.

Patten, B. C. "J. Marine Res. (Sears Found. Marine Res.), 20: 57 (1960); Leigh." *Proc. Nat. Acad. Sci. US* 55 (1965): 777.

Pianka, Eric R. "Latitudinal Gradients in Species Diversity: A Review of Concepts." *American Naturalist* (1966): 33–46.

Pielou, Evelyn C. "Species-diversity and Pattern-diversity in the Study of Ecological Succession." *Journal of Theoretical Biology* 10, no. 2 (1966): 370–83.

————. "The Measurement of Diversity in Different Types of Biological Collections." *Journal of Theoretical Biology* 13 (1966): 131–44.

Pimentel, David. "Animal Population Regulation by the Genetic Feed-Back Mechanism." *American Naturalist* (1961): 65–79.

Redfield, Alfred C. "The Biological Control of Chemical Factors in the Environment." *American Scientist* 46, no. 3 (1958): 205–21.

Simpson, Edward H. "Measurement of Diversity." *Nature* 163 (1949): 688.

Taub, F. B., and A. M. Dollar. "A Chlorella-Daphnia Food-Chain Study: The Design of a Compatible Chemically Defined Culture Medium." *Limnology Oceanography* 9 (1964): 61–74

Watt, Kenneth E. F. *Ecology and Resource Management: A Quantitative Approach*. New York: McGraw-Hill, 1968.

Wellington, W. G. "Individual Differences as a Factor in Population Dynamics: The Development of a Problem." *Canadian Journal of Zoology* 35, no. 3 (1957): 293–323.

Wiegert, Richard G., Eugene P. Odum, and Jay H. Schnell. "Forb-Arthropod Food Chains in a One-Year Experimental Field." *Ecology* (1967): 75–83.

Williams, C. B. "The Relative Abundance of Different Species in a Wild Animal Population." *Journal of Animal Ecology* 22, no. 1 (1953): 14–31.

Woodwell, George M. "Radiation and the Patterns of Nature." *Brookhaven National Laboratory Publisher* 924 (1965): 1–15.

Foundations

Land Mosaics: The Ecology of Landscapes and Regions (1995)

Richard T. T. Forman

Nature, the earth herself, is the only panacea.
—Henry David Thoreau, *Journal*, 1859

Five minutes after leaving a tropical city one of the plane's two engines dies. The plane begins dropping. Rich primeval rainforest awaits on one side, and town-dotted farmland on the other. Someone snaps an instant photograph, carries it to the open cockpit, and the pilot explodes in laughter. The passengers remain petrified until we slip over a ridge and bounce onto an unlighted runway.

The object spread out beneath an airplane window, or on an aerial photograph, is the subject of this book. Indeed, an aerial vantage provides a goldmine of information on the ecology of large land areas, such as landscapes and regions. For example in figure 3-4, one can predict with some confidence that the forest has many more interior species than the wooded patches on the right. Animal movement funnels through the lobes or peninsulas of the forest. Wind erosion is high in the corridor gaps on the left. Cool-water fish are probably missing from the stream in the far right. The clearing at the top has been expanding, while the clearing below it is contracting. The ecologically optimum location for a cluster of houses is by the field-forest edge in the upper right. The evidence for interpretations such as these and many more is presented in this book. Of course, dropping from the sky to examine the land closely is also essential.

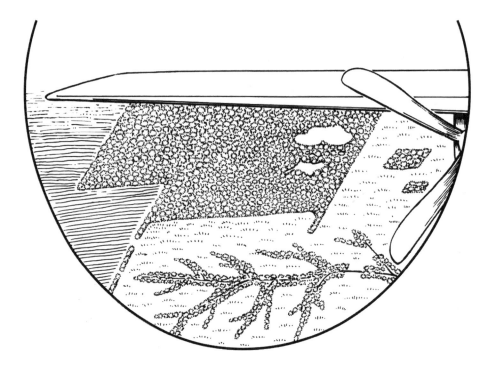

Figure 3-4 Looking only at pattern, "landscape detectives" gain extensive information about the ecology of the landscape (1995, Reproduced with permission of Cambridge University Press).

Mosaics and the Patch-Corridor-Matrix Model

From an airplane, land almost always appears as a *mosaic*. The glorious mosaics of St. Mark's in Venice or the University of Mexico appear as a pattern of colored patches and strips, usually with a background matrix. Tiny stones of different colors are aggregated to create the patches, strips, and matrix. The land appears much the same. Individual trees, rocks, houses, and so forth are the tiny stones. Woods, fields, and housing tracts are conspicuous patches. Roads, hedgerows, rivers, and power-lines are equally striking corridors. Grassland, forest, rice culture, or another land use often forms a background matrix. In short, the individual trees, shrubs, rice plants, and small buildings, analogous to the tiny stones in the artist's mosaic, are aggregated to form the pattern of patches, corridors, and matrix on land.

Mosaic patterns are found at all spatial scales, from submicroscopic to the planet and universe. Land mosaics, however, are at the "human scale", measured in kilometers to hundreds, even thousands, of kilometers. Thus, landscapes, regions, and continents are three scales of land mosaics.

What causes a mosaic? Much like a child's room with toys, a closed system with no energy input tends toward randomness. Such a lack of organization results in a fairly homogeneous mess throughout, and is expected according to the *second law* of thermodynamics. Without energy input, such as returning toys to their shelves, a system becomes more disorganized (gains entropy). But the land is always *spatially heterogeneous* (an uneven, non-random distribution of objects), that is, always has structure. The key is solar energy. Over geologic time it produces landforms, and today it grows different plants, which provide structure or heterogeneity to the land.

But spatial heterogeneity occurs in two flavors. A *gradient* or series of gradients has gradual variation over space in the objects present. Thus a gradient has no boundaries, no patches and no corridors, but is still heterogeneous. A portion of a moist tropical rainforest is an example where the assemblage of tree species changes gradually over the land. But gradient landscapes are scarce.

The alternative form of spatial heterogeneity is a mosaic, where objects are aggregated, forming distinct boundaries (figure 3-5). A land mosaic may contain only patches, or may also contain corridors. No spaghetti-like mosaic of only corridors is known. In short, the land mosaic is directly dependent on thermodynamically open conditions, with solar energy creating and maintaining structure.

More specifically, three mechanisms create the pattern. Substrate heterogeneity, such as hills, wet spots, and different soil types, causes vegetation patchiness. Natural disturbance, including fire, tornado, and pest explosions, creates heterogeneity. And human activity, such as plowing fields, cutting woodlots, and building roads, creates patches, corridors, boundaries, and mosaic pattern. Various biological processes commonly modify or enhance the patterns.

Understanding heterogeneity is only a first step. An infinite number of spatial arrangements can produce a particular level of heterogeneity, whether high or low. Specific spatial arrangements or configurations are ecologically much more important.

A more general way to understand form is to relate it to movements and change. One may say that "Form is the diagram of force". Form or structure, i.e., what we see today, was produced by flows yesterday. The curving sand dune was shaped by wind, the rectangular vineyards by tractors, and the dendritic stream corridor by water erosion. In addition, a linkage or feedback between structure and function is evident. Not only do flows create structure, but structure determines flows. For example, the arrangement of patches and corridors determines the movements of vertebrates, water, and humans across the land. Finally, movement and flows also change the land mosaic over time, much like turning a kaleidoscope to see different patterns.

Figure 3-5 Contrasting regions along the USA-Canada border (1995, Reproduced with permission of Cambridge University Press).

Therefore, like all living systems (those containing life), the landscape exhibits structure, function, and change. The plant cell has membranes and a nucleus which control the movement of molecules, and over time the cell's anatomy changes. The human body has organs and tubes through which fluids move, and over time the shape of the body changes in interesting ways.

Patches and corridors have long been a focus of human activity. Ecologists originally focused on patches and patchiness. Many became interested in corridors when discussing possible applications of island biogeographic theory on land, and the ecological roles of hedgerows and windbreaks.

The patch-corridor-matrix model coalesced when it was realized that a land mosaic is composed only of these three types of *spatial elements*. . . . Every point is either within a patch, a corridor, or a background matrix (figure 3-5), and this holds in any land mosaic, including forested, dry, cultivated, and suburban. This simple model provides a handle for analysis and comparison, plus the potential for detecting general patterns and principles.

Since a mosaic at any scale may be composed of patches, corridors, and matrix, they are the basic spatial elements of any pattern on land. Thus, *landscape elements* are simply spatial elements at the landscape scale. They may be of natural or human origin, and thus apply to the spatial pattern of different ecosystems, community types, successional stages, or land uses.

Because the key spatial attributes are so readily understood, the model has become a spatial language, enhancing communication among several disciplines and decision makers. For instance, patches vary from large to small, elongated to round, and convoluted to smooth. Corridors vary from wide to narrow, high to low connectivity, and meandering to straight. And a matrix is extensive to limited, continuous to perforated, and variegated to nearly homogeneous. These scientific descriptors are kept close to dictionary concepts.

Of course, the overall model can be elaborated to recognize additional spatial attributes. For example, *nodes* are patches attached to a corridor. *Boundaries* separate spatial elements and vary widely in structure. *Unusual features* are rare landscape-element types, such as a single major river or two mountains with particular functional significance.

The patch-corridor-matrix model has analogues in other disciplines. Point, line and plane are fundamental concepts in art and in architecture. Patch, matrix and mosaic are used in the medical field. The urban planner, Kevin Lynch (1960), recognized five spatial elements, based on what evokes a strong image in a person: district, edge, path, node, and landmark (C. Steinitz & M. W. Shippey, pers. commun.). They are similar to patch, boundary, corridor, node, and unusual feature. Finally, in addition to this foundation in spatial structure, insights are gained by studying spatial variations in movements and flows, different rates of pattern change over space, and scale (K. Hill & M. Roe, pers. commun.). . . .

The Hierarchy on Land

Suppose you had a giant zoom lens hooked up to your personal spaceship. You begin with a view of the whole planet, and slowly and evenly close the lens until you have a microscopic view of soil particles. At any point you would probably see a mosaic, a heterogeneous pattern of patches and corridors. But would the mosaic gradually change in form? Or would it remain for a period and then change suddenly to a new form, like a kaleidoscope that is turned abruptly at intervals? Probably the view through your zoom lens would resemble the kaleidoscope sequence. The quasi-stable mosaics separated by rapid changes would represent *domains of scale*. Thus, each domain exhibits a certain spatial pattern, which in turn is produced by a certain causative mechanism or group of processes. Overall a mosaic pattern is relatively stable from the beginning to the end of the scale domain, although minor changes are evident. With such a powerful lens you might wish to test the generality of this idea by zooming over a tropical rainforest, and then a desert.

The planet is spatially subdivided in many ways, including political, economic, climatic, and geographic, depending upon human objectives. The spatial hierarchy used here (figure 3-6) is selected because of its utility in meshing both human and ecological patterns, processes, and policies. David Miller (1978) further elucidates the following hierarchy levels in terms of energy and mass, including constraints and flows.

The *biosphere* or planet is subdivided into continents (and oceans). Continents are subdivided into regions, regions into landscapes, and landscapes into local ecosystems or land uses (figure 3-6). Local ecosystems, such as woodlots or fields, can, of course, be further subdivided to show their internal patchiness, and so on.

Each level in the hierarchy represents a single scale. Hence, at the scale below the East Anglia region (figure 3-6), landscapes differ in size, shape, and many other attributes, including from fine grained to coarse grained.

Continents usually have distinct boundaries, but in most cases are only loosely tied together by transportation, economics, and culture. Continents encompass extremely dissimilar areas of climate, soil, topography, vegetation, and land uses. Policies and political decision-making at the continental level have been much more often ineffective than effective. At present, an ecology of continents would be mainly an extrapolation from the subunits studied.

A *region* is a broad geographical area with a common macroclimate and sphere of human activity and interest. This concept links the physical environment of macroclimate, major soil groups, and biomes, with the human dimensions of politics, social structure, culture, and consciousness, expressed in the idea of regionalism. The southwestern USA, the Loire Valley of France, northern Queensland (Australia), the Andes of Venezuela, the Canadian maritime provinces, and East Anglia in Britain (figure 3-6) are regions. Some regions are international (e.g., Scandinavia and Central America), some within a country (Southern California and the Lake Baikal area of Russia), and some are predominantly urban and suburban (New Delhi and New Orleans). Regions often have diffuse boundaries determined by a complex of physiographic, cultural, economic, political, and climatic factors. A region is tied together relatively tightly by transportation, communication, and culture, but often is extremely diverse ecologically.

A *landscape*, in contrast, is a mosaic where the mix of local ecosystems or land uses is repeated in similar form over a kilometers-wide area. Familiar examples are forested, suburban, cultivated, and dry landscapes. Whereas

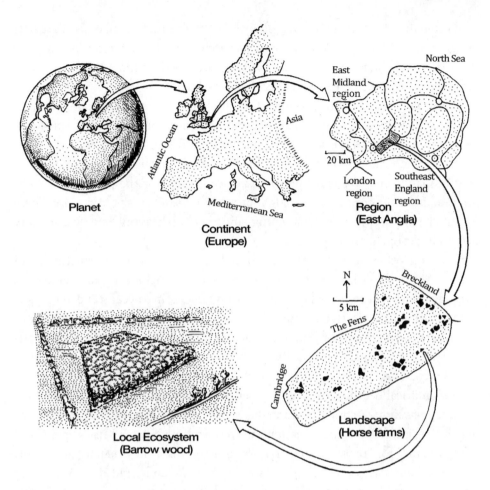

Figure 3-6 The spatial hierarchy on land (1995, Reproduced with permission of Cambridge University Press).

portions of a region ecologically are quite dissimilar, a landscape manifests an ecological unity throughout its area. Within a landscape several attributes tend to be similar and repeated across the whole area, including geologic land forms, soil types, vegetation types, local faunas, natural disturbance regimes, land uses, and human aggregation patterns. Thus, a repeated cluster of spatial elements characterizes a landscape.

Rooted in fields from geography to aesthetics, the term 'landscape' not surprisingly has been variously defined in hundreds of published papers. The above-described concept, now widely used, integrates a focus on (a) spatial pattern, (b) the area viewed in an aerial photograph or from a high point on the land, and (c) unity provided by repeated pattern.

The *local ecosystem* or land use as a spatial element within a landscape has been described earlier in this chapter. This element is relatively homogeneous and often distinct in its boundary (figure 3-6). Nevertheless, all objects are heterogeneous or variegated, composed of patches within patches. The internal heterogeneity, patchiness, and gap dynamic processes within a local ecosystem or land use are elucidated in most ecology textbooks.

Normally it is easy to distinguish individual patches and corridors as local ecosystems in a landscape, and also to distinguish different types of landscape, such as rangeland, suburbia, and rice-paddy land. But in the spatial hierarchy, is there a recognizable and useful intermediate level between the local ecosystem and the landscape? Several lines of evidence . . . suggest the presence of common stable *configurations* or neighborhoods of patches and corridors. These should be important in understanding landscape functioning, and be especially useful in design, planning, and management.

Several other spatial units have not been included in this hierarchy of scales. Although oceans (and "seascapes") are not included, many landscape ecology concepts are probably useful in understanding oceans and their bottoms. Nations are omitted because they vary so widely in size, from thousands of meters to thousands of kilometers across. *Biomes* and *ecoregions* are omitted because, by focusing primarily on the biological dimension, the boundaries usually correlate poorly with human-delimited administrative boundaries; effective political decision-making is essential for land planning and protection. *Drainage basins* (catchments, watersheds) are omitted because they too vary so widely in size, from a tiny stream basin to the whole Nile or Mississippi basin. They are nice for surface-water-driven processes. But watershed divides are often poor boundaries for delimiting animal, human, and wind-driven flows, or protecting home ranges, aquifers, ridges, and view-sheds.

Although boundaries determined by natural processes, such as drainage basins and bioregions, are theoretically optimum, it is not wise to wait for society to redraw the land. To accelerate the use of ecology in design, planning, conservation, management, and policy, we must use regions and landscapes that balance and integrate natural processes and human activities.

Natural Process and Human Activity

Some years ago an expert in forestry from a developed country was invited to advise in a developing country. A village leader welcomed the expert, and learned that productivity of the local wooded area could be tripled by gradually replacing the rather heterogeneous, scruffy-looking trees with a high-quality eucalypt or pine plantation. Pondering the many ramifications of this profound change, the two leaders strolled through the woods to look more closely. The host observed, "This tree provides nuts in the dry season; this clearing is where my ancestors won the final battle against invaders; this moist area protects our only clean drinking water; this grove provides the best firewood in the area; this tree is where I was married; this shrub is the only source of fibres for our unique dance; this vine provides the incense for our annual religious festival; this line of decrepit trees provides the children with flutes; this dense bushy area provides at least six major economic products; these virtually unburnable trees on the windward side are essential fireproofing; and these tall arching trees form the cathedral for reflection and inspiration." The two leaders embraced warmly, and the visitor returned home to take a closer look at the local tree plantations there.

The overall goal of science or scholarship is understanding, and concepts, models, theories, predictions, experiments, explanations, and so forth are used to gain understanding. Much of ecology, including landscape and regional ecology, is science. However, some ecological understanding (on interactions of organisms and their environment) comes from studies in social science and the humanities. In this book natural processes, including geomorphic, soil, atmospheric, hydrologic, fire, plant, and animal, receive emphasis. But human activities almost always interact with natural processes to produce the actual patterns, movements, and changes observed. As in the local woods example, these phenomena result from cultural, religious, social, and economic activities overlapping over historical time. Four brief examples from China, Eastern Europe, the USA, and Australia illustrate different ways that human activities and natural processes interact to produce pattern on the land.

Traditional Chinese philosophy focuses on the harmonious relationship among *Tian* (heaven or universe), *Di* (earth or resource), and *Ren* (people or society). Within this the *Yin* and *Yang* theory emphasizes the duality of natural forces acting upon and within a relationship or ecological system. The *Feng-shui* or wind-water theory expresses the spatial relationship between human settlements and the natural environment. For example, the main function of Feng-shui forests common in rural China is accumulating 'Qi' (or 'living energy'), the combined flow of energy, material, species, and information. Therefore, Feng-shui forests, as old as the villages, usually are in specific locations. The upper slopes and tops of hills, at water mouths where water enters or leaves a basin, and on steep erodible slopes fulfill the criteria for maintaining forests. . . .

Ecology of Landscapes

Ecology is generally defined as the study of the interactions among organisms and their environment. A landscape was described as a kilometers-wide mosaic over which local ecosystems recur. Thus, *landscape ecology* is simply the ecology of landscapes, and similarly, *regional ecology* is the ecology of regions. The spatial elements within landscapes have been called landscape elements, local ecosystems, ecotopes, biotopes, biogeocoenoses, geocomplexes, sites, and more. . . . The spatial elements within regions are landscapes. This land mosaic or "ecomosaic" paradigm has not only attracted scientists who see rich research opportunities, but also galvanized linkages among disciplines directly solving land use issues.

Nevertheless, various alternative perspectives on landscape ecology have appeared over the years. Carl Troll (1939, 1968) apparently first used the term when aerial photographs became widely available, and his concept evolved into: "Landscape ecology [is] the study of the entire complex cause-effect network between the living communities (biocoenoses) and their environmental conditions which prevails in [a] specific section of the landscape . . . [and] becomes apparent in a specific landscape pattern or in a natural space classification of different orders of size". V. Sukachev & N. Dylis (1964) described biogeocoenology as a similar concept. A. Vink (1975) considered landscape ecology to be "the study of the attributes of the land as objects and variables, including a special study of key variables to be controlled by human intelligence". I. Zonneveld (1979) indicated that "Landscape ecology is an aspect of geographical study, which considers the (land) as a holistic entity, made up of different elements, all influencing each other". Zev Naveh & Arthur Lieberman (1993) viewed landscape ecology as a transdisciplinary ecosystem-education approach based on general systems theory, biocybernetics, and ecosystemology as a branch of total human ecosystem science. Paul Risser et al. (1984) concluded that "landscape ecology considers the development and dynamics of spatial heterogeneity, spatial and temporal interactions and exchanges across heterogeneous landscapes, influences of spatial heterogeneity on biotic and abiotic processes, and management of spatial heterogeneity". Geography and geographic information systems also have been considered close to landscape ecology, and other diverse encapsulations of the field are available.

Based on the current prevalent concept of landscape ecology, several principles were outlined by Risser et al. (1984), Forman & Godron (1986), Risser (1987), and Turner (1989). These highlighted the distinctive nature of the questions being addressed, compared with those in ecosystem science, island biogeography and physical geography, for instance. But the field has moved ahead so rapidly, both empirically and in theory, that the present principles and theories are better absorbed in logical context than in an isolated list.

The repetition of a few characteristic ecosystems across a landscape means that there is a limit on the variety of habitats available for organisms. A landscape extends in any direction until the recurring cluster of ecosystems or site types significantly changes. For example, one moves from a cultivated landscape to a suburban landscape where the cluster of fields, hedgerows, farmsteads, farm roads, woodlots, and stream corridors changes to a cluster of housing tracts, grassy public spaces, shopping areas, woodlots, and stream corridors.

How sharp is the boundary of a landscape? In mountainous regions where landscape mosaics are usually relatively small, contrasts are great due to sharp boundaries. "A traveler crossing a mountain range moves into a new mix of ecosystems—that is, a new mosaic—every 20 to 50 km."

Where natural geomorphic and disturbance processes predominate in flatter terrain, boundaries of landscapes also tend to be rather sharp. Thus, rock types, soil types, flood regimes, and fire regimes often produce abrupt transitions on land at this scale. The same sharp boundaries of landscapes are observed where human land uses, such as agriculture and forestry, reflect the natural water, soil, and tree species distributions.

However, where human activities and land uses are more independent of the distribution of natural resources, boundaries of landscapes tend to be less distinct. Familiar examples are the boundary between suburbia and forest, agriculture, or dry land. In some areas houses and housing tracts are primarily located based on economic, social, and political criteria, with little regard for natural boundaries.

Often it is useful to observe part of a landscape or region, such as a representative or random sample (e.g., figure 3-4). This will be simply referred to as a *portion* of a landscape or region. Other than containing more than one local ecosystem of the landscape (or more than one landscape of the region), no structural unity, extent, or boundary is implied. It is analogous to a portion of a wood, town, or continent captured in a photograph.

Ecology of Regions
Concept of a Region

As the planet spins one feels that the atmosphere is circulating around the globe. Atmospheric "cells" form within this apparent overall circulation, due to differences in solar input and the configuration of continents, mountain ranges, and oceans. Each cell exhibits its own *macroclimate*, an essentially uniform weather history over a large area, and each contrasts with the surrounding cells. Some regions are the same size as, but many are a subset of, a macroclimatic cell. Thus, a region normally has a single macroclimate, which provides a region-wide control over the soils, ecosystems, and natural processes.

This climatic control of a region is illustrated in the southwestern United States, where scattered mountain ranges are surrounded by desert landscapes.

Major fires generally occur in the same year in many ranges. That is, though few fires can spread from one range to another, a drought affects all the mountain landscapes, and results in fires scattered throughout the region.

Some regions develop their own atmosphere though heat energy reflection (albedo), soil heat radiation, evapotranspiration of water, and air pollution. The Altiplano of Chile and Bolivia and the tropical rainforest of southern China are examples. Other regions are bathed more or less continually with outside air, and have energy and material flows determined mainly by other parts of the world. The mountains downwind of Los Angeles, the Gobi Desert east of the Himalayas, and the long diverse western half of Chile all have macroclimates determined by conditions to the west. Some regions, such as the North American Midwest and monsoonal areas of India, Indochina and China, are characterized by abrupt climatic changes, when one major air stream seasonally replaces another. Finally, human-caused climate change is increasingly considered at the regional scale.

In addition to macroclimate, human activities determine a region. Regions usually contain one major city, or occasionally a few. Transportation and communication usually tie a region together. In some cases, regional boundaries are relatively distinct, and act as strong filters of many inputs and outputs. In short, models of regional change must have an effective balance between nature and humans, or at least ecology and economics.

An example differentiating region and landscape is instructive. New England in the northeastern USA is a relatively distinct, widely recognized region. It is surrounded by two Canadian regions, two American regions, and an ocean. Except in the southwestern corner, its boundaries are quite distinct physically or culturally. New England is tied together by a cool climate, a tradition of governing by town meeting, a transportation network, and cultural nuances including architecture, religion, and language. However, different portions of the region differ markedly in their ecology, for instance, from wild spruce-fir (boreal) forests in high mountains to the housing tracts and exotic species of suburbia.

This region is composed of at least ten landscape types. Five cover large areas (oak forest, pitch pine, northern hardwoods, spruce-fir, and agricultural landscapes), and five more (suburban, urban, salt marsh, barrens, and industrial landscapes) are scattered within these. Some landscape types can be subdivided for special purposes, such as cultivated and pasture landscapes instead of agriculture, or oak, transition hardwood, and northern hardwood in lieu of simply oak and northern hardwood landscapes. Two important alpine areas (Mt. Washington and Mt. Katadin) do not extend for kilometers in width, and therefore are considered as unusual features within their respective spruce-fir landscapes. Overall, the New England region is composed of approximately 100 landscapes.

Spatial Arrangement of Landscapes

Just as in any level of the spatial hierarchy, the region is composed of patches, corridors and a matrix that vary widely in size and shape. In this case the spatial elements are whole landscapes. Unlike the recurring landscape elements in a landscape, a region does not exhibit a pattern of repeated landscapes.

Usually the distribution of landscapes simply mirrors the typically coarse-grained, geomorphic land surface. Thus, most regions are coarse-grained, or variable-grained with groups of small landscapes. Some common landscapes have distinctive shapes. For instance, "corridor landscapes" as kilometers-wide strips include major mountain ridges, wide river valleys, coastal strips, and suburbs along a major transportation route. A suburban ring or band, such as that around Paris, Sao Paolo, or Denver (USA), is also a distinctive landscape shape.

Not surprisingly, the arrangement of landscapes has a major effect on regional flows, and flows have an important feedback effect in producing the arrangement. A major urban center acts as a source of people, vehicles, information, and products. These disperse on radiating transportation and communication routes in all directions across the region. These routes help tie the landscapes together. Some objects, such as air and water pollutants, and people headed for recreation, move out in specific directions. Reverse flows of forest and agricultural products, water supply, and rural people head for the city.

The physical flows linking landscapes are conspicuous in a mountainous region. Here, landscapes, such as alpine, coniferous forest, basin grassland, and so forth, tend to be small and have sharp boundaries. It is a fine-grained region, or a portion of a variable-grained region that includes flatter landscapes. In the mountains gravity carries water overland, in streams, and in the ground to lower landscapes. Soil creeps overland or dashes down streams. Wind carries seeds and spores to higher landscapes, as well as downward and along ranges. Animals, often transporting seeds, move upward, downward, and along mountains. Water supplies rush downward in pipes and canals to agricultural and built landscapes.

In short, the spatial pattern or arrangement of landscapes in a region is just as important functionally as the pattern of continents on the globe, local ecosystems in a landscape, or gaps within a woods. Some flows are concentrated, such as water, silt, and industrial pollutants in rivers. Some flows are dispersed, including erosion, seeds, and vehicular pollutants. Some move rapidly and some slowly. And boundaries of landscapes are often filters or places where rates of movement change markedly, a distinctive pattern for fire or dispersing animals.

Wide-ranging species like caribou, tigers, black bears, and vultures are especially sensitive to the arrangement of landscapes. Such species commonly use, and perhaps require, two or more landscapes which cannot be too far apart. As suggested by island biogeography theory, landscapes of a particular type cannot be too far apart for dispersal of their species. For example, in the Southwest, a relatively distinct region in the USA, ski area development is damaging alpine landscapes, which in turn are limited to widely separated high mountain tops. Some alpine plants, invertebrates, and vertebrates may be significantly affected by this loss of stepping-stone landscapes.

Understanding the key flows and movements among landscapes permits us to search for an optimum spatial arrangement in a region. Simple geometric models readily understandable by decision-makers can be used for direct comparisons. For example, countless spatial arrangements of three common landscape types in a region, native vegetation, agriculture, and built area, are possible. Fifteen contrasting designs or arrangements are compared in figure 3-7 using a few simple assumptions. In these models the three key variables are the type of matrix, the sizes of landscapes, and their spatial arrangement.

Where native vegetation is the matrix (figure 3-7a), design number 2 exhibits the highest suitability for natural processes. Similarly, with this matrix (top graph) agricultural production appears best in design 1, and the built human community best in design 2. However, where agriculture is the matrix (figure 3-7b with middle graph), agriculture is best in arrangement 2, whereas both nature and the built area are best in design 1. Where the built area is the matrix (figure 3-7c), arrangement 5 appears optimum for the built human community, and arrangement 1 for natural process and agricultural production. Comparing all 15 models permits an estimate of the hypothesized, overall best designs and worst designs for natural process, agriculture, and the human community.

With such a simple modeling approach one could propose an optimum spatial design for sustainability of a region that integrates the three land-use objectives. Indeed, on average a region is a better bet for attaining sustainability than a landscape. This is because of its larger area, greater complementarity of resources, and a slower rate of change. The space-time relationship also supports this conclusion.

Linkages with Other Regions

The arrangement of landscapes in a region not only affects the region, but also neighboring regions. To illustrate, a century ago there was much discussion of how deforestation in the Pine Barrens landscape of New Jersey (USA) would affect climate change in the New York and Philadelphia metropolitan regions, some 50–100 km distant. The half-million-hectare forested landscape had been subjected to two and a half centuries of intense resource extraction and lack of

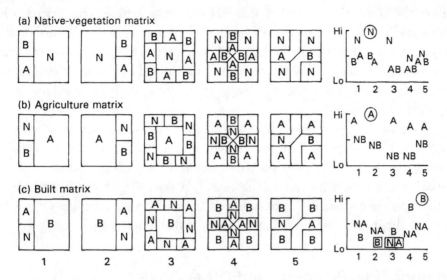

Figure 3-7 Comparison of spatial arrangements of three landscapes types, native vegetation (N), agriculture (A), and built area (B). Each square is a region composed of three to 12 landscapes. The graphs on the right have a horizontal axis representing the sequence of landscape patterns diagrammed on the left. The vertical axis is an overall measure of suitability (low to high) for maintaining natural ecosystems, agricultural productivity, and the built human community, respectively. Points circled in the graphs are the highest, and points enclosed in the boxes are the lowest, comparing all 15 regions. See text. Assumptions in these simple geometric models are: (1) the key variables examined are sensitive at the scale of these landscapes; (2) wind blows from the west, and upwind air is the same as that along the western edge; (3) native vegetation produces the cleanest air; (4) for the built area, only large landscapes produce air pollution; (5) for native vegetation, fragmentation into small landscapes is detrimental. The models could be modified with additional variables or different assumptions, and produce different results.

care. Exposed soil was extensive, shrublands were widespread, tree height had been halved, smoke from rampant fires persisted, and atmospheric heat and water balances were altered. During the ensuing few decades several events, technological developments, and policy changes led to a significant increase in land protection of the Pine Barrens. Fires decreased, the forest regrew, and threatened climate change evaporated.

This scenario also emphasizes that linkages between regions are generally both institutional and physical. Public policies plus wind determine flow rates of nitrogen and sulfur oxides between regions. Agricultural policies at a supra-regional level mean that the delta of the Rhone River receives chemicals from most of central France, and the Mississippi River delta receives chemicals from half of the USA. A boundary as sharp as a linear coastline formed across the plains between Canada and the USA (north of Montana) in five decades (figure 3-5). This was caused by big land-use policy change in far-off Ottawa, and little policy change in far-off Washington. The political and institutional change has effectively created a new region, where previously a single more extensive region had existed.

The remaining sections of this chapter introduce the history and research methods of landscape ecology, and its use in other fields. To provide both the appropriate breadth of vision and an entree into the rich literature available, the concepts and information will be densely packed. The reader is encouraged to focus on the overarching concepts or main points in each section. Of course, one may dip into important details in areas of special interest. . . .

Conservation, Planning, and Other Fields

Researchers, planners, designers, and managers in several fields related to ecology have become major contributors in landscape ecology. Inevitably, they have also integrated the basic theory and thinking of landscape ecology in their several fields. Foresters have incorporated bits into basic forestry planning and management, as have wildlife biologists. Landscape architects and regional planners have fit pieces into their repertoire of design techniques for parks, suburban development, and river corridors. Geographers have absorbed portions into their work in physical, biological, and historical geography. Park and recreation managers, and efforts in land restoration, use parts of it. Nature conservationists, conservation biologists, biological conservationists, and soil conservationists have found many portions to be useful. Landscape ecology should also be useful in range science, agronomy, urban planning, water management, climatology, industrial planning, transportation, and indeed in all fields concerned with land use. And of course ecology has incorporated major portions into its discipline.

The most obvious reason for the rapid expansion of landscape and regional ecology is the subject. It is at the human scale, where nature and people are seen to interact daily, and where land planning, design, conservation, management, and policy must take place. Society craves ecological understanding at this scale. A second reason is its analytic focus. It provides understanding and predictive ability useful for more wood products, species, game, clean water, housing, recreation, or other often-conflicting societal objectives. Advocacy focuses on the intelligent use of landscape and regional ecology in all land-use issues. A third reason is holistic; the mosaic emerges as much more than the sum of its parts.

The fourth reason is the assays or areas of ecological interest. The full meaning of ecology as interactions among organisms and the environment is included, rather than only current interests within ecology. Thus, four categories of ecological assays are recognized throughout, specifically production, biodiversity, soil, and water characteristics. . . .

Solutions to environmental ills such as wind erosion, species extinction, water pollution, septic leaching, aquifer pollution, and suburban sprawl have their roots in this field. Yet perhaps most important is its potential role in sustainability. . . . Designing a land that effectively meshes ecological integrity with basic human needs over human generations will only be accomplished with a healthy dose of landscape and regional ecology at the core.

References

Note: The list of references in Forman's essay "Foundations" is too extensive to be presented here in its entirety (298 articles). As such, I present his books and articles referenced in this essay and direct the reader to his book *Land Mosaics* (New York, NY: Cambridge University Press, 1995), 3–38, for a complete list of the references.

Cantwell, Margot D., and Richard T. T. Forman. "Landscape Graphs: Ecological Modeling with Graph Theory to Detect Configurations Common to Diverse Landscapes." *Landscape Ecology* 8, no. 4 (1993): 239–55.

Forman, Richard T. T. "Ecologically Sustainable Landscapes: The Role of Spatial Configuration." In *Changing Landscapes: An Ecological Perspective*, 261–78. New York: Springer-Verlag, 1990.

———. "Emerging Directions in Landscape Ecology and Applications in Natural Resource Management." *Proceedings of the Conference on Science in the National Parks: The Plenary Sessions*, vol. 1 (1986): 59–88.

———. "Growth under Controlled Conditions to Explain the Hierarchical Distributions of a Moss, *Tetraphis Pellucida*." *Ecological Monographs* (1964): 2–25.

———. "Landscape Corridors: from Theoretical Foundations to Public Policy." *Nature Conservation* 2 (1991): 71–84.

———. "Landscape Ecology Plans for Managing Forests." In *Proceedings of the Society of American Foresters*, 131–36. Bethesda, Maryland: Society of American Foresters, 1988.

———. "The Beginnings of Landscape Ecology in America." In *Changing Landscapes: An Ecological Perspective*, 35–41. New York: Springer-Verlag, 1990.

———. "The Pine Barrens of New Jersey: An Ecological Mosaic." *Pine Barrens: Ecosystem and Landscape* (1998): 569–85.

———, ed. *Pine Barrens: Ecosystem and Landscape*. New York: Academic Press, 1979.

Forman, Richard T. T., and Isaak Samuel Zonneveld. *Changing Landscapes: An Ecological Perspective*. New York: Springer-Verlag, 1990.

Forman, Richard T. T., and Michel Godron. "Patches and Structural Components for a Landscape Ecology." *BioScience* (1981): 733–40.

———. *Landscape Ecology*. New York: John Wiley, 1986.

Forman, Richard T. T., and Perry N. Moore. "Theoretical Foundations for Understanding Boundaries in Landscape Mosaics." In *Landscape Boundaries*, 236–58. New York: Springer, 1992.

Forman, Richard T. T., and Ralph E. Boerner. "Fire Frequency and the Pine Barrens of New Jersey." *Bulletin of the Torrey Botanical Club* (1981): 34–50.

Franklin, Jerry F., and Richard T. T. Forman. "Creating Landscape Patterns by Forest Cutting: Ecological Consequences and Principles." *Landscape Ecology* 1, no. 1 (1987): 5–18.

Hardt, Richard A., and Richard T. T. Forman. "Boundary Form Effects on Woody Colonization of Reclaimed Surface Mines." *Ecology* (1989): 1252–60.

Milne, Bruce T., Kevin M. Johnston, and Richard T. T. Forman. "Scale-Dependent Proximity of Wildlife Habitat in a Spatially-Neutral Bayesian Model." *Landscape Ecology* 2, no. 2 (1989): 101–10.

Part Four

Procedural Theory

Introduction to Part Four

Procedural theory deals with the methodological directives, processes, and principles for employing substantive knowledge in design and planning to manage landscape change. In the first of five readings in this part, I document and review an array of first-generation landscape suitability approaches that have served as models for the development of subsequent approaches in "The First Landscape-Suitability Approach" from *Ecological Planning: A Historical and Comparative Synthesis* (2002).[1] Landscape suitability is used to ascertain the *fitness* of a tract of land for a particular use (figure 4-1).

How human ecosystems work is the primary focus of the second reading, by architect and landscape architect John Tillman Lyle, from *Design for Human Ecosystems: Landscape, Land Use, and Natural Resources* (1985).[2] He proposed an ecosystematic approach to the design of human ecosystems and landscapes drawn from a deep understanding of their inner workings—their structure, function, and order. Lyle's emphasis on integrating ecosystem processes in design is an important contribution that advances the methodological foundation of land design and planning. It exemplifies a second-generation suitability approach.

The next two readings deal with guidelines and action-oriented principles for balancing human use with ecological concerns.[3] The reading by Virginia Dale and her colleagues, "Ecological Principles and Guidelines for Managing the Use of Land" (2000), is another important piece that brings together

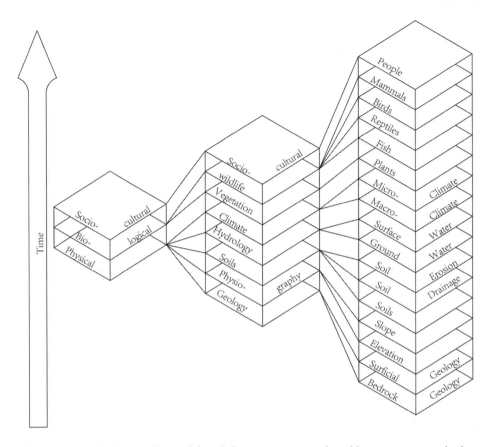

Figure 4-1 The layer-cake model (Ndubisi, 2002, Reproduced by permission of Johns Hopkins University Press. Redrawn by Yuan Ren, 2014).

substantial scientific evidence on how ecological principles can inform decisions about land use.[4] This work was commissioned by the Land Use Committee of the Ecological Society of America as part of their ongoing efforts to use the latest scientific evidence to channel the knowledge of the ecological-scientific community in understanding and solving pressing societal and environmental concerns.

Dale's piece is followed by landscape ecologist Richard Forman's work "Basic Principles for Molding Land Mosaics," from *Urban Regions: Ecology and Planning Beyond the City* (2008).[5] He introduced a palette of principles drawn from conservation biology, landscape ecology, transportation, water resources, and other fields that are intended to guide the use of landscapes. Importantly, these principles concentrate on urban regions, which has not been the major geographical focus of ecological studies in North America until recently.

Forman emphasized that these principles should be combined with creativity and imagination to produce effective results.

The last reading, by Jack Ahern, Elizabeth Leduc, and Marie Lee York, is the introduction to the book *Biodiversity Planning and Design: Sustainable Practices* (2007).[6] It provides a concise overview of recent efforts in conserving biodiversity. The authors reviewed the current state of protection, as well as the strategies for assessing and conserving biodiversity, and proposed alternative strategies. They concluded by reasserting the crucial importance of protecting biodiversity and the important role designers and planners can play.

There is a substantial and growing body of scholarly contributions to procedural theory in ecological design and planning. Other important contributions to procedural theory include the works of Nancy Jack Todd and John Todd, Pliny Fisk, David Orr, and John Brinckerhoff Jackson. In *From Eco-Cities to Living Machines* (1993), environmental activist Nancy Jack Todd and biologist John Todd proposed nine ecological design precepts, most of which have proven to be effective in providing sustainable and equitable means for guiding how people relate to the landscape.[7] Architect Pliny Fisk (2009) proposed principles for guiding the allocation of land uses in a regenerative way based on the footprints required for sustaining basic human life-support needs. These needs are air, water, food, energy, and materials.[8] David Orr (2004) assembled an impressive array of essays on "ecological design intelligence" and its potential for creating healthy, resilient, and livable communities.[9] Lastly, in "How to Study Landscape," noted landscape historian and writer John Brinckerhoff Jackson (1980) provided a compelling account of how to examine landscapes, drawing important distinctions between what, why, and how his approach differs from that of the conventional historian.[10]

If fitness implies searching for the fittest location of land uses while minimizing negative environmental impact and energy use, then all of the approaches advocated in these readings address fitness at some level. The first landscape-suitability approach relied on the natural features of a tract of land to estimate fitness, and by implication, land suitability. Subsequent theoretical-methodological advances to the approach resulted in employing a vast array of factors, including ecological, social, economic, and technological considerations to establish the optimal uses of the landscape. "Optimal" implies the best use of the land when everything is considered. With the exception of the reading on biodiversity conservation, economic and social considerations are evident implicitly or explicitly in estimating suitability. Moreover, Ahern, Leduc, and York's reading on biodiversity conservation is the only one so far that focuses on the preservation and conservation of species, as a use by right, irrespective of any human interests that may be implied. I draw the reader's attention to the readings in part 2 on ethical foundations, especially the essay by Timothy Beatley, "Ethical Duties to the Environment," in which he argued for the protection of all forms of life.

Understanding ecosystematic order is an important consideration in the ecological design and planning approach proposed by John Tillman Lyle. He employed three types of information to estimate the optimal uses of the landscape: ecosystem structure, processes, and location. The latter is the most visible of the three. He advocated utilizing suitability models to ascertain the most desirable location of land uses on a tract of land. According to Lyle, suitability provides the bridge between the considerations of ecological processes and their relative location on the landscape. Likewise, ascertaining the optimal uses of the landscape must account for the ecological footprints needed for sustaining basic life-support needs.

Pliny Fisk offered an innovative approach. He contended that the measurement of sustainability is an integral component of his proposed *ecobalance planning* method and suggested how the measurement should be accomplished. He suggested ascertaining the ratio of the *sourcing* requirements of a physical space, for instance, compared to the *resourcing* capacity of the life-support needs, or the ratio of the life-support needs provided on-site compared to the needs supplied off-site.[11]

The search for the optimal uses of the landscape is also evident in some of the ecological principles dealing with land-use allocation that Virginia Dale and her colleagues proposed, such as avoiding land uses that deplete natural resources, preserving rare landscapes, and retaining large contiguous areas that contain critical species. The same statement holds for the spatial principles offered by Richard Forman, as well as the precepts underlying sustainable ecological design proposed by Nancy Jack Todd and John Todd. [12] Some of the precepts have been validated empirically. Notable among them are the precepts that emphasize harmony with the laws of life, bioregionalism, renewable energy resources, and integration of living systems.[13] The essays compiled by David Orr represent an original voice in the pursuit of the healthy and sustainable uses of the landscape.

The strategies for biodiversity conservation discussed by Ahern and his colleagues rely on indicators, such as target or indicator species, to ascertain ecosystem quality and integrity. They usually focus on one ecosystem characteristic, such as dominant plant species or soil productivity. The use of indicators is based on the logic that the structural and functional characteristics of an ecosystem vary predictably with location and, as such, ecosystem quality and integrity can be inferred reliably from the indices.[14] Indicators can be used in ascertaining the optimal uses of the landscape as well, beyond their specific use in biodiversity conservation.

John Tillman Lyle's ecosystematic approach uses Eugene Odum's compartment model examined in part 3 as a theoretical base. Lyle's proposals focused exclusively on those landscapes Odum denoted as "compromise areas." Lyle referred to them as human ecosystems where the most land use conflicts occur. What are not obvious are his specific proposals for dealing with "productive" and "protective" landscapes in Odum's compartment model. Should they always be left in those states? Can their inherent capacities be enhanced? How and to what degree can "non-vital" landscapes be restored to productive and protective landscapes? These questions were not addressed in Lyle's work.

Moreover, it is not readily apparent how the spatial principles that Dale and her team proposed can embrace the aesthetic dimension of people's interactions with their environment. How can an understanding of human values and experiences be integrated into the spatial guidelines they proposed for managing land use, to create landscapes that are socially responsive, beautiful, and yet ecologically sound? How can these land use guidelines inform the creations of three-dimensional-volumetric spaces, which, in reality, are the spaces where human experiences occur, as opposed to two-dimensional spaces implied in the proposed guidelines? John Brinckerhoff Jackson's contributions are especially relevant here. He draws our attention to subtle but very significant aspects of the humanized landscape and ecological objects that ought to be examined to better understand those aesthetic and cultural dimensions that are so crucial in creating beautiful, sustainable landscapes. Lastly, it is not immediately clear that the guidelines offered by Dale were intended for dealing with degraded landscapes, or whether the guidelines were subsumed into those dealing with "preserving rare landscapes" and "avoiding land uses that deplete natural resources."

Certainly, each of the readings presented here, as well as other contributions briefly noted, has something to offer, in varying degrees, to the continued advancement of the theoretical-methodological base of ecological design and planning. Importantly, they reinforce the need for a comprehensive and interdisciplinary approach to its successful realization.

Notes

1. Forster Ndubisi, "The First Landscape-Suitability Approach," *Ecological Planning: A Historical and Comparative Synthesis* (Baltimore, MD: Johns Hopkins University Press, 2002).
2. John Tillman Lyle, *Design for Human Ecosystems: Landscape, Land Use, and Natural Resources* (Van Nostrand Reinhold, 1985). (Republished, Island Press, 1999).

3. These guidelines and principles are action-oriented and primarily serve to resolve problems, including the search for optimal uses of the landscape. Procedural frameworks rarely exist in a vacuum. In some cases, they may be intricately linked with action-oriented guidelines. We have encountered a situation with regard to these articles, where the dichotomy between substantive and procedural frameworks is not fine-grained. Because the principles are action-oriented and serve as a foundation for planning and design action, I lean more in favor of discussing them under procedural theory rather than substantive theory.

4. V. H. Dale, S. Brown, R. A. Haeuber, N. T. Hobbs, N. Huntley, R. J. Naiman, W. E. Riebsame, M. G. Turner, and T. J. Valone, "Ecological Principles and Guidelines for Managing the Use of Land," *Ecological Applications* 10, no. 3 (2000): 639–70.

5. Richard T. T. Forman, "Basic Principles for Molding Land Mosaics," in *Urban Regions: Ecology and Planning Beyond The City* (Cambridge: Cambridge University Press, 2008).

6. Jack Ahern, Elizabeth Leduc, and Mary Lee York, *Biodiversity Planning and Design: Sustainable Practices* (Washington, DC: Island Press, 2007).

7. Nancy Jack Todd and John Todd, "Emerging Precepts of Ecological Design," in *From Eco-Cities to Living Machines: Principles of Ecological Design* (Berkeley, CA: North Atlantic Books, 1993, first published in 1984).

8. Pliny Fisk III and Lovleen Gill Aulakh, *Ecobalance: A Sustainable Land Use Planning and Design Methodology* (Center for Maximum Potential Building Systems, 2009). http://www.cmpbs.org.

9. David Orr, *Earth in Mind: On Education, Environment, and the Human Prospect* (Washington, DC: Island Press, 2004).

10. John Brinckerhoff Jackson, "How to Study Landscape," in *The Necessity of Ruins and Other Topics* (Amherst: The University of Massachusetts Press, 1980), 113–26.

11. Center for Maximum Potential Building Systems, accessed October, 25, 2013, http://www.cmpbs.org.

12. Nancy Jack Todd and John Todd, "Emerging Precepts of Ecological Design."

13. Ibid.

14. Ndubisi, "The First Landscape-Suitability Approach," 147.

The First Landscape-Suitability Approach

Ecological Planning: A Historic and Comparative Synthesis (2002)

Forster Ndubisi

. . . I outlined six major approaches to ecological planning: landscape suitability 1 (pre-1969), landscape suitability 2 (post-1969), applied human ecology, applied ecosystem, applied landscape ecology, and landscape values and perception. These approaches have offered alternative ways to best manage human actions sustainably in the landscape. They differ in their philosophical outlooks and disciplinary origins, concepts for understanding and analyzing landscapes, data requirements, and techniques for putting the concepts into practice.

These ecological approaches have not evolved in isolation. In fact they have borrowed concepts and techniques from one another. Although at the level of practice the differences between these approaches are fuzzy, the differences at the level of theory are significant. . . . I provide an overview of landscape-suitability approach 1 (LSA 1) and landscape-suitability approach 2 (LSA 2). Landscape-suitability approaches (LSAs) have been explored by several people although not in the manner that I do here. My intent is to illuminate key principles and theoretical intent rather than to provide a comprehensive and exhaustive review.

I . . . [examine] landscape-suitability approaches [in detail] for three reasons. First, the LSA is the most widely used approach in professional practice and tends to be covered extensively in the curricula of landscape architecture and planning schools, as well as in environment-related courses offered in allied disciplines. Second, a comprehensive, systematic, and updated examination of the approaches is urgently needed to provide a common base of understanding. Third, the approaches to ecological planning . . . borrow concepts and techniques from LSAs.

The Landscape-Suitability Approaches

The LSA focuses on the *fitness* of a given tract of land for a particular use. It is chiefly concerned with finding the optimal location for different uses of the landscape. The earliest variations of the LSA were developed by soil scientists, though landscape architects began using hand-drawn, sieve-mapping overlays in the late nineteenth century. These scientists and landscape architects sought ways to understand and classify rural landscapes according to their natural features. The classification became the basis for assessing the ability of the land to support alternative land uses, such as agriculture, forestry, and outdoor recreation. The approach was subsequently refined and developed by others, especially landscape architects, who extended its application to include evaluation of the landscape for preservation, conservation, and development in both urbanizing and rural areas.

Initially, the LSA used the natural features of the landscape as the basis for determining land suitability. A growing public awareness of the negative environmental impacts of human actions in the past three decades, as well as increasing environmental legislation worldwide, made it necessary to develop methods that were both accurate and legally defensible. In turn, there were significant theoretical advancements in the LSA. Variations of LSAs are still perhaps the most widely used methods for ecological planning worldwide.

I have divided the LSA into two approaches to emphasize the theoretical-methodological advancements that have occurred as the LSA has evolved. *Landscape-suitability approach 1* (*LSA 1*) comprises methods developed prior to 1969, and *landscape-suitability approach 2* (*LSA 2*) includes methods proposed or developed after 1969. Nineteen sixty-nine was the year when the National Environmental Policy Act was passed; among other things, this act challenged federal agencies to develop effective methods and procedures for environmental assessment. Also, Ian McHarg's *Design with Nature*, which offered the most coherent synthesis yet of suitability analysis, was published that year.

All LSA 1 and LSA 2 methods operate on the same general logic and analytical base. They assume that the ability of the landscape to support a particular land use varies according to the physical, biological, and cultural resources that are distributed over a geographical area. By implication, if we understand the location, distribution, and interactions among these resources, it is then possible not only to determine the optimal location of land uses on a given tract of land but also to minimize the environmental impacts and the energy required to implement and maintain these proposed land uses.

Lewis Hopkins summarized suitability analysis as follows: "The output of a land suitability analysis is a set of maps, one for each land use, showing which level of suitability characterizes each parcel of land. This output requirement leads directly to two necessary components of any method: 1) a procedure for identifying parcels of land that are homogenous and 2) a procedure for rating these parcels with respect to suitability for each land use" (figure 4-2).

Methods of suitability analysis vary in terms of how they define the fitness of a particular tract of land for a given use; how they define and evaluate homogenous areas and how sophisticated they are; how and to what degree they consider social, cultural, economic, and political factors in assessing fitness; whether they use expert or nonexpert judgments to evaluate suitability; which factors they consider and the sophistication of the operations they use in selecting the preferred land-suitability option; and whether they specify strategies for implementation and administration. Other differences in LSAs include the type of the land-use issues they are used to address (e.g., development and conservation), as well as their ability to address effectively micro-scaled and/or macro-scaled issues and urban and/or rural issues.

A variation in LSAs that deserves further comment is the way they define fitness, a primary criterion for deciding on the best allocation of land uses. Fitness is often defined as capability or suitability, though they mean different things. *Capability* is defined in the *American College Dictionary* as "the ability or strength to be qualified or fitted for or to be susceptible or open to influence or effect of." Other definitions of capability emphasize the ability of a land resource to support potential land uses and the management practices required to sustain the uses; the ability of land to support land uses within a given level of geological and hydrological costs; and the potential of an area of land to allow the use of resources under a certain level of management intensity. *Suitability*, on the other hand, suggests "being appropriate, fitting, or becoming." Unlike *capability*, *suitability* suggests optimizing a tract of land for the best use, all things considered.

Implicit in these definitions are the ideas of *inherent capacity*, or the ability of the landscape to support a given use, and *sustained use*, the ability to support the use on a permanent basis without suffering degradation of its natural and cultural features. I therefore define fitness to imply the inherent capacity and sustained use of a tract of land for particular use(s). Sustained use also suggests optimization, implying that in addition to natural factors, social, economic, and political issues must be considered in suitability analysis.

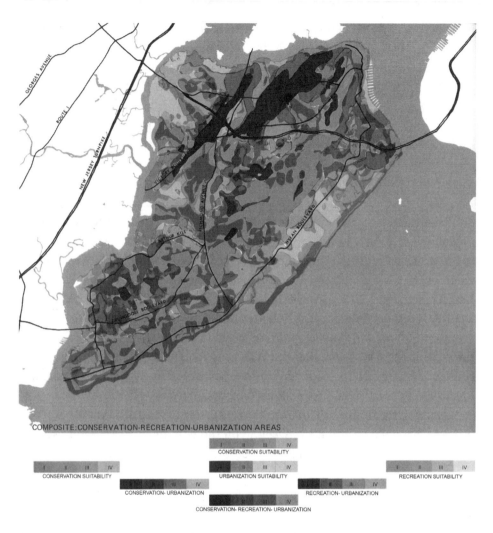

Figure 4-2 A composite suitability map for conservation, recreation, and urbanization (Ndubisi, 2002, Reproduced by permission of Johns Hopkins University Press).

Landscape-Suitability Approach 1

LSA 1 emphasizes the natural characteristics of the landscape in determining the fitness of a given tract of land for a defined use. The LSA 1 methods developed in an ad hoc manner, linked to specific problems, programs, and individuals. I discuss their ad hoc development in order to illuminate their historical evolution. The LSA 1 methods that merit a closer examination in this evolutionary overview are the seminal ones, mentioned in most discussions of approaches to ecological planning. They are: (1) the gestalt method,

(2) the Natural Resources Conservation Service (NRCS) capability system, (3) the Angus Hills, or physiographic-unit, method, (4) the Philip Lewis, or resource-pattern, method, and (5) the Ian McHarg, or University of Pennsylvania, suitability method. I discuss the latter as described in *Design with Nature* extensively because McHarg's discussion of landscape-suitability analysis was supported by a well-articulated philosophy and has been applied in a variety of urban, rural, and natural settings. Also discussed briefly are the suitability methods proposed by C. S. Christian, Ervin Zube, Richard Toth, and Carl Steinitz, methods also mentioned often in ecological-planning literature.

The Gestalt Method

The gestalt method was one of the first methods used to understand and analyze the ability of landscapes to support human uses. Lewis Hopkins used the term *gestalt* to explain a way of understanding and analyzing perceivable patterns in the landscape without considering compositional elements such as slope, soils, and vegetation. *Webster's Encyclopedic Unabridged Dictionary* defines gestalt as "a unified whole, a configuration, pattern, or organized field having scientific properties that cannot be derived from the summation of its parts." William Passons referred to music appreciation to illustrate the essence of the gestalt method: "Listening to a piece of music is a process which involves more than hearing the specific notes, just as melody is more than a constellation of notes." Experiential knowledge rather than technical knowledge is the point of departure in making gestalt judgments about landscape suitability. The philosopher John Dewey contended that "experience recognizes no division between act and material, subject and object, but contains both of them in an unanalyzed totality."

In using the gestalt method, the planner or designer makes observations about the landscape under study from aerial photographs and remote-sensing data or from personal observation of the landscape at different times of day. The planner then records patterns or areas of the landscape that are homogenous in one or more ways, such as a cornfield or lowland hardwood forest on wet soil, as well as unique qualities of the landscape, such as outstanding views. Having recorded these features, the planner describes the impacts of proposed land uses on the landscape patterns and draws inferences about the ability of the land depicted by the patterns to support potential uses. For instance, if the planner observes that a tract of land in the study area is wet upon each visits, he or she may conclude that the tract of land might not be able to support houses because of unstable soil conditions. Some of the patterns observed may be of equal suitability since they are based on perceived natural and cultural types rather than on the suitability for any one use. In that case the planner develops a set of maps for each land use to show the ability of each pattern to support a given use.

Gestalt judgment is arguably a feature of most suitability methods, at least at an elemental level. For example, a woodland identified on an aerial photograph may be regarded as a gestalt since it is a composite of a vegetation association made up of understory plants and ground covers. In this instance, the gestalt method is used to identify a particular landscape resource, vegetation, which will be combined with other resources to generate suitability maps. Hopkins adds that "once a factor [resource] such as cover type is identified . . . one can no longer use the gestalt method at some higher level because by definition it does not combine factors."

The Natural Resources Conservation Service (NRCS) Capability System

The soil-capability system is one of the most established methods for determining the ability of the soil to support different land uses. The system was developed by the NRCS (formerly the Soil Conservation Service), a division of the U.S. Department of Agriculture, to assist farmers with agricultural-management practices. As information about the linkages between soil behavior and the structural properties of soils became more readily available after World War II, the use of the capability system was extended to planning and resource management.

Soil represents a transitional zone that relates the physical and biological characteristics of the landscape. It has depth, shape, and boundaries. These boundaries are altered when one or more soil-forming factors change. These factors are climatic forces, the living matter that acts on the soil, and the parent material for the soil, modified by relief over time. The identified properties of soils—texture, depth to bedrock, profile or gradient of soil layers from the surface to the bedrock, slope, stoniness—derive from the interaction of these factors. The soil-capability system is a widely used system for classifying soils to determine the ability of the landscape to support various land uses. (Other classification systems developed by the NRCS are discussed later.) The underlying logic of the soil-capability system is that combinations of soil properties pose restrictions when they are manipulated and used for certain types of agricultural production. In other words, the classification system emphasizes the limitations rather than the attractiveness of soils for supporting various land uses.

The system focuses on the use of soil for field crops, the risk the soil poses for damage to crops, and the response of the soil to management practices when used for the production of particular crops. It does not take into account properties such as soil depth and slope or specific types of agricultural crops that require special types of management practices, such as horticultural crops.

The NRCS classifies soils according to three capability levels: class, subclass, and unit. It then ranks the levels based on the limitations the soil poses to land uses and uses the rankings to make evaluations for agricultural production, planning, and resource management.

The capability class is the broadest homogenous level. Soil classes are designated by the Roman numerals I through VIII, indicating progressively greater limitations for agricultural production in terms of the choice of plants, soil erodibility, and intensity of management practices. Class I soils have few limitations, while Class VIII soils have many restrictions, making them unsuitable for commercial production, wildlife, and water supply.

The second level is the subclass, which consists of soil groups within a soil class. Subclasses are indicated by the letter e (erosion), w (water), s (stoniness or shallowness), or c (climatic variations) following the Roman numeral to indicate limitations, for example, IIIs or IVe. Since the subclasses are based on limitations, it follows that Class I would have the least subclasses and Class VIII would have the most.

The third level, the subunit, consists of soils within a subclass that support similar crops, have similar agricultural productivity, and require similar management practices. Subunits are indicated by an Arabic numeral following the subclass symbol, for example, IIIs-2 or IVw-3.

In sum, the NRCS capability system helps individuals and organizations evaluate landscape suitability by using soil inventories. The information is readily available to the public at a mapping scale of 1:20,000, or 4 inches = 1 mile. The evaluation of the soil for land suitabilities is descriptive, as inferences about land capabilities for different uses can be drawn from the classification.

The Angus Hills, or Physiographic-Unit, Method

The physiographic-unit approach to landscape analysis was proposed in 1961 by the Canadian forester G. Angus Hills, the chief research scientist with the Ontario Department of Lands and Forests. The approach contributed to the development of the Canadian Land Inventory system. Initially, Hills focused on using soil associations to determine land capabilities, but over time his interest shifted to using landforms and vegetation associations.

The essence of Hills's method was to divide the landscape into physiographic homogenous units and then reaggregate them for planning purposes. The method addresses a number of questions to ensure that landscape resources are used in a renewable way. How can the time and money needed to collect ecological inventories be minimized? What is the most effective way of differentiating landscapes on a permanent basis for a variety of planning purposes? What is the ability of the landscape to support the highest intensity of human use? What is the relative advantage of maintaining that inherent ability given existing or projected social and economic conditions? What management practices may be required to put the proposed uses of the landscape into effect?

Hills contended that human use of the landscape must be based on the principles that relate organisms to their physical and biological environment. Classifying landscapes based on their biological productivity will help to ensure that landscape resources will be renewable. "Any area of land combined with the organism it supports constitutes a biological productivity system," wrote Hills. The system depends on the potential of the land to support energy and matter as well as on the ability of the crop systems to utilize it.

To ensure that resources will be renewable, land should be organized hierarchically based on a gradient of the most significant features governing biological productivity. Then the resultant units should be assessed based on their ability to support crop systems under an assumed set of circumstances. However, this ability is dynamic since humans change their minds about what is suitable whenever there is a change in their social or economic circumstances.

Hills proposed a five-step method for assessing landscape suitability. The first step is an ecological inventory that focuses on the physical and biological characteristics of the study area and on existing or projected social and economic conditions. To minimize the time and cost of data collection, representative areas that exhibit severe physiographic conditions are identified and used as reference points for collecting more detailed data. Next, the site area is divided hierarchically into homogenous physiographic units—site regions, landscape types, site classes, site types, and site units—based on a gradient of its biological productivity (climate and landforms features).

As the largest unit, the *site region* comprises land areas that display consistent patterns of vegetation and microclimatic conditions. The region is defined by the recorded succession of forest types on major landform classes. An example of this is a birch-poplar association on a glacial-outwash landform. Each site region is divided into distinct *landscape types* based on landforms, geological composition, and water regimes. The average size of a landscape type is approximately 1 square mile, or 0.631 square hectare. An example is a tract of land that has shallow sandy loam or sandy soil over granite bedrock.

Each landscape type is differentiated further into physiographic *site classes* that may be rated for their biological productivity. A site class is distinguished by variations in soil moisture, depth of bedrock, and local climate. The average size of a site class is approximately 10 acres. Poorly drained soil on a glacial-outwash bedrock and moderately drained soil on a glacial till represent different site classes. Various combinations of soil moisture, depth to bedrock, and local climate define different physiographic *site types*, such as moderately deep soil in a dry local climate. The smallest physiographic category is the *site unit*, a subdivision of the physiographic site type. The significant features of the site unit include soil profile, stoniness, slope, and aspect, which are useful in evaluating land uses.

The third step is to identify the characteristics and land requirements of the proposed land uses, such as forestry and agriculture. Hills suggested that a panel of experts evaluate the ability of the physiographic units to support the proposed land uses. The experts would conduct suitability, capability, and feasibility assessments at the broad ecological-planning level and also at the regional-planning level.

Suitability refers to the capacity of the site in its present condition to meet specific management practices. Suitability assessment involves determining the "actual use of an area of land for any specified period of time." Capability assessment entails ascertaining "the probable results, in terms of both crop production and land conservation, if a given body of land is put to a particular use." Feasibility assessment involves determining the relative advantage of managing a tract of land for specific land uses under existing or forecasted social and economic conditions. While suitability and capability assessment focus on the inherent features of a site, feasibility assessment emphasizes the social and economic conditions needed to ensure the continued use of a site for the proposed land uses. For each type of assessment the land is rated on a seven-point scale, ranging from excellent to extremely poor, based on the intensity and quality of the landscape resource rather than on its type. Emphasis is placed on the absence of potential site limitations.

To ensure that the outcome of the evaluation is used for a variety of planning purposes, Hills proposed ways to combine the smaller physiographic units into larger units. For example, if the study is to be conducted at the local level, then it is useful to combine physiographic site classes to create *landscape components*. Landscape components, approximately a quarter of an acre (0.15 ha.) in size, are convenient for rating land-use capability because they signify the biological productivity of the individual site and the effects of the distribution of crops on the site as well as of management practices. For studies conducted at the level of the community or the region Hills suggested combining the landscape components into landscape units, measuring approximately 16 square miles (10 sq. ha.). An example would be a shallow bedrock with shallow to moderately deep till.

The fourth step is to combine the suitability, capability, and feasibility assessments into a composite map depicting landscape units that may support multiple uses. The appropriate panel of experts then makes recommendations for the proposed land uses. Final recommendations are made by local decision makers to ensure that the social and economic needs of the community or region are met. In the fifth step, management guidelines prescribe how to put the proposed uses into effect.

The Philip Lewis, or Resource-Pattern, Method

Philip Lewis Jr. proposed a method for identifying patterns of unique perceptual qualities in the landscape and for integrating them into regional landscape plans and designs. Lewis developed and refined his method through numerous projects he directed between 1960 and 1970, including the Illinois Recreation and Open State Plan (1961), the Outdoor Recreation Plan for the state of Wisconsin (1965), and the Upper Mississippi River Comprehensive Basin Study (1970).

Lewis was primarily concerned with the haphazard patterns of urban growth in the Midwest, which occurred with little regard for the "intrinsic qualities inherent in nature's design." The growth patterns resulted in declining recreational spaces, which Lewis sought to discover, protect, and conserve. Lewis's work addressed such concerns as which recreational resources required protection and conservation; which ones were significant and why; what the geographical linkages were among these resources; how these linkages could be identified, analyzed, and integrated into regional planning and design; and how the value of these resources and the outcome of their assessment could be communicated to the public in order to gain support for implementation.

Lewis hypothesized the *environmental corridor* as the basic recreational-resource unit. They comprise significant, or *major*, natural and cultural resources that are connected in their distribution of such things as surface water, wetlands, and significant topographic features. The resources' significance rests in their ability to enhance and stabilize property values, provide recreational opportunities, and maintain the ecological and cultural integrity of the landscape. The major resources are enhanced by additional, *minor* resources that may not be distributed in a continuous manner but provide concentrations of ecological and cultural values. Lewis referred to the concentrations, such as rock outcrops, fish habitats, and picnic areas, as *resource nodes*. Resource nodes offered the greatest flexibility in ensuring that the environmental desires and needs of midwesterners were met. By focusing attention on environmental corridors and resource nodes, Lewis shifted attention from the protection of single resources to the protection of multiple ones. He explained the nature and significance of environmental corridors as follows:

> Looking beneath the Great Lake Canopy, it is apparent that the elements and glacial action through the ages have etched a treelike design pattern on the face of the landscape. The flat prairie farmlands, driftless hills and expansive northern forests have their share of beauty, but it is the stream valleys, mellow wetlands and sandy soils combined in elongated patterns that provide outstanding diversity, tying the landscape together in regional and statewide corridors. . . . Once inventoried and mapped, they suggest a framework for total environmental design. If protected and enhanced, the system provides a source of strength, spiritual and physical health and wisdom for the individual, in addition to open space for recreation and enjoyment.

Lewis's work on environmental corridors, especially his recognition of their visual, recreation, and ecological values, was an important contribution to the greenway movement. He further hypothesized a vital connection between the psychological health of humans and the visual quality of the prairie landscape. Lewis suggested that since the visual features of the landscape are most striking in environmental corridors, those corridors could be identified using visual indicators such as visual contrast and diversity.

Even though the procedures Lewis used in his numerous studies varied, they share some features in common. In the *Outdoor Recreation Plan* for the state of Wisconsin, which focused on identifying statewide recreational resource patterns, Lewis selected a pilot study area in order to identify the geographical relationships between the major and minor resources. The size of the area was approximately 100 square miles (259.07 sq. km). He then identified the key recreational uses and established land-use criteria. For example, recreational uses might include hiking, canoeing, fishing, and camping. The primary land-use criteria were visual contrast between landscape types and landscape diversity.

Lewis identified the major resources, such as water bodies and topographic features, that met the use criteria and then recorded each resource on a separate map to facilitate data collection. Using map overlays, he combined the individual resources into a composite pattern. He used the same procedure for identifying and mapping such minor resources as waterfalls, rock outcrops, and picnic areas. Symbols were used to denote the minor resources. The data were collected at a scale of 1 inch = 2,000 feet (1:24,000) by many people, including federal, state, and local officials, who worked closely with local people. Local inhabitants' awareness of the ecological and cultural values inherent in the major and minor resources was crucial for their successful identification, protection, and preservation.

Using overlay maps, Lewis correlated and compared the composite maps that displayed the major and minor resource patterns to establish the degree of congruence between them. Based on the outcome of the correlations, he confirmed that wetlands, water bodies, and significant topographic features constituted about 90 percent of the resources that were held in high esteem by the local people and located within the environmental corridors.

Lewis then proceeded to identify the major and minor resource patterns throughout the state of Wisconsin and to ascertain their location, distribution, and significance. To establish priorities for the preservation and conservation of these resource patterns, he developed a rating system and assigned points to the individual resources that made up the major and minor resource patterns. The locations that contained resources degraded irreversibly by human use, such as wetlands, received the highest scores. The resources that received the highest scores were designated as priority areas for protection.

This rating system was complemented by information on the demand for the recreational resources. Lewis examined the type and intensity of the demand, the degree of access to the recreational areas, and the patterns of land ownership. Once the priority areas were established, he conducted detailed soil surveys and visual studies to identify unique local features and to illuminate the limitations on development. The outcomes were used to provide preliminary estimates of the carrying capacity of the area since human use of recreational areas might have negative impacts, such as soil compaction. Lewis has conducted numerous studies since his outdoor recreation plan for Wisconsin, described here, which he documented in his 1996 book, *Tomorrow by Design*.

The McHarg, or University of Pennsylvania, Suitability Method

The McHarg method was described extensively in Ian McHarg's *Design with Nature*, a book that immensely influenced the environmental movement in the 1970s (figure 4-3). The McHarg method and its variations are arguably among the most widely used methods in professional landscape architecture and planning today. The method was refined through numerous projects McHarg conducted with his colleagues and students at the University of Pennsylvania as well as with his partners at Wallace, McHarg, Roberts, and Todd (WMRT). Examples of application in the 1960s include the New Jersey Shoreline Study (1962), the Plan for the Valley study (1963), the Richmond Parkway Study (1965), the Potomac River Basin Study (1965–66), and the Staten Island Study (1969). The method has undergone several revisions and has advanced beyond the theoretical conceptualizations presented in this chapter. . . .

Figure 4-3 Ian McHarg (Photograph by author, 2002. Reproduced by permission of Johns Hopkins University Press).

McHarg was deeply disturbed by patterns of population growth that resulted in degradation of the landscape. He promoted designs that integrated the city and countryside while preserving the features of nature that were crucial for the survival and well-being of humans. His interest was in understanding life processes and using them as limitations or opportunities for allocating human uses in the landscape.

McHarg believed firmly that the dialogue between humans and nature should be one of mutual interdependence. Humans are dependent on nature for air, water, food, and fiber, and nature also provides order, meaning, and dignity. Yet, the dialogue between humans and nature was turbulent, as evidenced by the ecological crises that were prevalent in Western industrialized societies by the 1960s. People sought to conquer rather than to seek unity with nature.

McHarg summarized his ideas about the relationship between humans and nature in a compelling fashion in his 1963 article "Man and Environment," published in Leonard Duhl and John Powell's book *Urban Condition*. He noted that a duality existed between man and nature. This duality, which was the basis of our ecological crisis, was firmly rooted in the religious tradition, Christianity, and was reinforced by economic determinism and the misuse of technology. The attitudes and technology that emerged from Christianity and Western philosophy promoted dominion and subjugation of nature by humans. McHarg contended that by using a system that used money as a yardstick of success, the Western mode of economic organization failed to take into account the physical and biological processes that are crucial for human evolution and survival. His ideas about the basis of ecological degradation were reinforced by Lynn White in his 1967 article "The Historical Roots of Our Ecological Crisis."

To address effectively the ecological crisis that confronted our society, McHarg forcefully proposed replacing our economic view of the world with an ecological one. An ecological view of the world measures success in terms of energy and evolutionary order rather than money. The ecological view also accepts human cooperation and biological partnership as points of departure in solving problems of human adaptation to the environment. The natural sciences in general and the field of ecology in particular offer the most useful insights into applying the ecological view to mediate the dialogue between humans and nature.

The fundamental question the McHarg method sought to address was how to achieve the fittest environment for the survival and evolutionary success of the organism, the species, the community, and the biosphere. For McHarg, suitability implies searching for this environment to ensure survival and evolutionary success. The next question was how to determine the fittest environment for human uses. McHarg proposed that the answer lay in understanding nature as an interactive process, one that responds to physical and natural laws and represents values. Together, nature's processes and values offer opportunities and limitations for human use.

Nature's values include the inherent characteristics of nature that endow it with the right to existence, such as natural beauty; the productive function that nature serves; nature's role in maintaining ecological processes, such as aquifer-recharge areas and flood plains; and the potential hazards that result from improper use of nature, such as flooding, erosion, and the degradation of water quality. The McHarg method seeks to understand nature's processes, interactions, and values as the basis for allocating human uses in the landscape. "In essence," he wrote, "the method consists of identifying the area of concern as consisting of certain processes, in land, water, and air—which represent values. These can be ranked—the most valuable land and the least, the most valuable water resources and the least, the most and least productive agricultural land, the richest wildlife habitats and those of no value, the areas of great or little scenic value, historic buildings and their absence, and so on."

Applications of the McHarg method usually include the following steps (figure 4-4).

1. The goals, objectives, and land use needs are defined, and study boundaries are established.

2. An ecological inventory of the relevant physical and biological processes is conducted. The processes are documented and mapped in chronological order and are related to the land-use needs. The chronological sequence of data collection and interpretation provides a causative explanation of landscape processes, culminating in a descriptive biophysical model of the landscape. For example, once the climate and historical geology of the landscape are understood, the ground-water hydrology and physiography can be explained.

3. The resultant inventory is mapped. Each factor, that is, each of the physical and biological characteristics of the landscape, such as slope or soil, is mapped and displayed in terms of homogenous areas. For example, if residential development is one of the land uses under consideration, soil drainage may be an important process to examine and map. In doing so, we might divide soil drainage into three subhomogenous areas: perfectly drained, moderately well drained, and poorly drained soils.

4. Each factor map is examined to determine which areas are suitable for each proposed land use. For example, the homogenous areas that represent perfectly drained soils, moderately well drained soils, and poorly drained soils are rated for their suitability for residential development. The output is a color-coded map, with the darkest color representing constraints, or poorly drained soils, and the lightest denoting opportunities, or perfectly drained soils.

5. All factor maps pertinent to determining the landscape suitability for a particular land use are overlaid using transparencies. Maps showing such characteristics as depth to bedrock, soil drainage, slope, and vegetation are combined to determine residential suitability. The outcome is a suitability map for each prospective land use under consideration.

6. The suitability maps for the individual land uses are combined into a composite map using transparent overlays. The composite map reflects a pattern of light and dark colors indicating the estimated suitability

for all prospective land uses. The interpretation and documentation of the composite map may be used in allocating land uses or may serve as an input into a larger ecological or land-use study.

A closer examination of McHarg's application of the suitability method in numerous projects reveals that there are two basic versions, quantitative and qualitative. The six steps described above are illustrative of the quantitative variation. The homogenous areas mentioned in step 3 are rated to obtain a grand index of suitability. The Richmond Parkway Study and the Staten Island Study, described in *Design with Nature*, exemplify the application of the quantitative version of McHarg's method. Even though overlays were used, the process of overlying maps to determine suitability was a mathematical operation equivalent to assigning weights to the subhomogenous areas and totaling the weights to obtain an index of suitability.

In contrast, the qualitative version follows a different path after step 3. The subhomogenous areas are not rated; in fact, they may be described in terms of ecological zones and key characteristics pertinent to land-use decisions. Experts then develop and apply land-use and ecological principles to relate suitability to the homogenous areas.

McHarg used the quantitative version in his 1963 Plan for the Valley study. McHarg and his colleagues assessed the suitability for urban development of 70 square miles (181 sq. km), or approximately 45,000 acres (18,225 ha.) within the greater Baltimore region. This area contained widespread valleys, plateaus, wooded ridges, and an intricate array of many land uses. Based on the social, economic, and physical characteristics of the region, McHarg and his colleagues made a number of propositions that guided the ecological study of the region. For example, they postulated that the region could accommodate all prospective growth without degrading the landscape. They then used two factors, topography and vegetation, to distinguish five ecological zones or homogenous areas: valley floors, unforested valley walls, forested valley walls, forested plateau, and unforested plateau.

Development guidelines were prescribed for each of these homogenous areas. In the valley-floor zone, for instance, McHarg and his partners proposed restrictions on development except for land uses that were compatible with the extant pastoral scenery, such as agriculture, very-low-density residential, and parks and recreation. In contrast, they designated the unforested plateau as the area to receive the most intensive development. To ensure that these guidelines were workable, McHarg and his colleagues projected future land-use demands in the region and correlated them with the proposed land suitability.

STEP 1
MAP DATA FACTORS BY TYPE

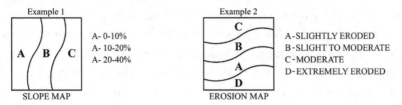

Example 1

A   B   C

A- 0-10%
A- 10-20%
A- 20-40%

SLOPE MAP

Example 2

C
B
A
D

A-SLIGHTLY ERODED
B-SLIGHT TO MODERATE
C-MODERATE
D-EXTREMELY ERODED

EROSION MAP

STEP 2
RATE EACH TYPE OF EACH FACTOR FOR EACH LAND USE

Factor Type	Agriculture	Housing
Example 1		
A	1	1
B	2	1
C	3	3
Example 2		
A	1	1
B	2	2
C	3	2
D	3	3

1- PRIME SUITABILITY
2- SECONDARY
3- TERTIARY

STEP 3
MAP RATINGS FOR EACH AND USE ONE SET OF MAPS FOR EACH LAND USE

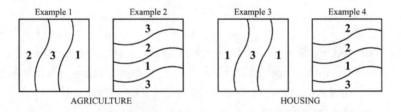

Example 1

2   3   1

Example 2

3
2
1
3

AGRICULTURE

Example 3

1   3   1

Example 4

2
2
1
3

HOUSING

STEP 4
OVERLAY SINGLE FACTOR SUITABILITY MAPS TO OBTAIN COMPOSITES.
ONE MAP FOR EACH LAND USE

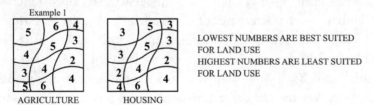

Example 1

5   6   4
      5   3
4
3   4   2
5   6   4

AGRICULTURE

3   5   3
      5   3
3
2   2
4   6   4

HOUSING

LOWEST NUMBERS ARE BEST SUITED
FOR LAND USE
HIGHEST NUMBERS ARE LEAST SUITED
FOR LAND USE

Figure 4-4 An example of a suitability-analysis procedure (Ndubisi, 2002, Reproduced by permission of Johns Hopkins University Press, Redrawn by Yuan Ren, 2014).

Other Methods

In the late 1950s C. S. Christian, an Australian who worked for the Commonwealth Scientific and Industrial Research Organization (CSIRO), developed a land-classification system for assessing the landscape's potential to support various uses. Similar to Angus Hills's classification system, Christian's broke the landscape into progressively smaller homogenous tracts of land using criteria such as variations in geological features and landforms. Christian's system, also known as the Australian system of classification, is useful in conducting preliminary appraisals for extremely large regions. Much of his work has been adapted by international organizations, including the International Union of Conservation for Nature and Natural Resources (IUCN).

Ervin Zube, formerly chair of the Department of Landscape Architecture and Regional Planning at the University of Massachusetts and now professor emeritus at the University of Arizona, considered both visual and cultural factors and natural-resource characteristics in order to understand and analyze landscapes. Parallel efforts took place in Britain in the mid- to late 1960s largely through the efforts of K. D. Fines and his colleagues in East Sussex. In the 1966 Nantucket Island Study, in Massachusetts, Zube, C. A. Carlozzi, and others identified significant landscape types on the island based on visual indicators. The landscape types were horizontal landscape; highest-quality landscape; linear pond, marshes, and meadows; and shoreline landscape. Experts and lay people ranked the landscape types according to their perceived value for public use, preservation, and conservation. This information was combined with natural-resource data to arrive at a composite landscape-synthesis map.

In addition, Zube, in his 1968 resource-assessment study of the U.S. Virgin Islands, classified the landscape hierarchically into visual units based on criteria such as visual differences in landforms, visual contrast and variety, and significant visual elements, such as bodies of water. The visual units were assessed by experts and lay people for protection, conservation, or development.

Another area in which important contributions were made in the 1960s was that of assessing the impact of development. Richard Toth, formerly at the University of Pennsylvania and now at Utah State University, developed a method for analyzing the natural characteristics of the landscape in order to estimate the impact of development. He used this method in the study he conducted for the Tock Island Regional Advisory Council in Pennsylvania in 1968. Toth used matrices to identify and display the frequency and the ecological consequences of interactions among key natural characteristics, such as topography and soils, and land-use needs. He summarized the predicted consequences of the interactions as a guide for future allocation of land uses.

Utilizing hand-drawn overlays to combine resource factor maps in suitability analysis may be cumbersome, expensive, and sometimes inefficient, especially when many options for land-use allocation are desired. Moreover, a limited number of variables can be included in formulating alternative land-use options. To address some of these problems, Carl Steinitz and his colleagues at Harvard University applied computer technology in numerous projects they conducted beginning in the mid-1960s in order to improve the efficiency and economy of managing information. Their use of computer technology also enabled the integration of social and economic considerations in suitability assessments and permitted the evaluation and prediction of the spatial consequences of alternative land-use options. The work of Steinitz and his colleagues marked the beginning of the use of interactive land-use-suitability models in the United States.

LSA 1 methods offer ways to evaluate the optimal uses of the landscape but predominately emphasize the natural characteristics. Even though these methods evolved in an ad hoc manner, linked to specific individuals and projects, they display an increasing level of sophistication based on substantive and procedural principles and on the techniques they offer for inventorying the relevant natural and cultural features of the landscape and assessing their suitability for varied uses. In order of increasing sophistication, the methods are: gestalt; landscape-unit and landscape-classification methods; landscape-resource survey and assessment; and allocation evaluation.

The gestalt method is used in making elemental judgments of suitability. Landscape-unit and landscape-classification methods divide the landscape into homogenous areas independent of the prospective land uses based on a single criterion (NRCS, Zube, Litton) or on multiple criteria (Hills, Christian). Resource-survey and resource-analysis methods define homogenous areas in order to determine their suitability for prospective land uses. Suitable lands are selected either by eliminating lands deemed unsuitable for the potential land uses (e.g., Lewis's delineation of environmental corridors and resource nodes) or by establishing compatibilities between the natural and cultural characteristics used in defining the homogenous areas (e.g., McHarg's Staten Island Study). In addition, suitability analysis may focus on a single use, such as recreation (Lewis), or on multiple land uses (as in numerous projects undertaken by McHarg and his colleagues, such as their 1967 Comprehensive Landscape Plan for Washington, D.C., or the 1969 Ecological Study for the Twin Cities Metropolitan Region in Minnesota).

Landscape-resource survey and assessment methods also permit the evaluation of environmental impacts. Examples include Toth's Tock Island Study and

McHarg's 1968 Least Social Cost Corridor Study for the Richmond Parkway. The Parkway study heavily influenced the articulation of the conceptual base of the environmental-impact assessment, which is the centerpiece of NEPA. However, the impacts are implied but not reported explicitly.

Allocation-evaluation methods, which were only in the formative stages in the late 1960s, assign land uses to different locations on a tract of land and assess the social, economic, and environmental consequences of alternative land-use options. Computer-assisted methods proposed by Steinitz and his colleagues, for instance, can be used to assess the landscape to determine suitability and to evaluate the impacts of alternative land-use options. These methods broaden the criteria traditionally used in determining landscape suitability to include social and economic criteria. In addition, they employ computer technology, which enhances the ability to manage complex and diverse information.

LSA 1 methods are also varied in their ability to address development and conservation or preservation issues in both urbanizing and natural or rural areas. Variations of the McHarg method can address both, as can other methods, such as computer-assisted methods. Some LSA 1 methods are useful in dealing with one specific type of land use, such as conservation or preservation; however, they may also be used to make informed judgments about suitability for other uses. Examples include the NRCS capability system, Hills's physiographic-unit method, Zube's visual-resource method, and Lewis's resource-pattern method. Other LSA 1 methods focus on ascertaining suitability for a specific land use; for example, the Lewis method emphasizes recreational land use.

Problems may arise when a method developed to establish landscape suitability for one type of use is adapted to establish landscape suitability for other types of uses. For example, the use of the NRCS classification for planning and resource-management purposes produces inconsistent results. While it accurately identifies septic-tank limitations, it is inconsistent in determining home sites and roads.

In general, LSA 1 methods are primarily used to address macro-scaled issues rather than site-specific projects. However, this does not mean that they cannot be adapted to deal with site-specific issues. For example, the NRCS soil-classification maps are usually published on a county-by-county basis, and the soils are mapped at a scale of 1:20,000, yet the soil information can be adapted to address site-specific conservation and development issues as long as on-site investigations are conducted to validate the data. In contrast, the gestalt method is useful in understanding and analyzing small tracts of land. As the size of the parcel of land increases, it becomes more difficult to fully comprehend the parcel in its entirety. Another notable exception is Hills's physiographic-unit method, which was designed to address multi-scaled issues. Since the method involves a hierarchical classification based on variations in landform and climate, it can be applied at a variety of scales by combining the appropriate physiographic units appropriate to the scale of the study area, for example, by combining physiographic site classes to create landscape components.

LSA 1 methods vary remarkably in the extent to which expert or nonexpert judgments are used to determine landscape suitability. For instance, the McHarg method relies predominantly on expert judgment or scientific knowledge to assess suitability, even though the logic of the process of establishing and ranking the interactions between homogenous areas and potential land uses suggests both objective and subjective judgments. In the NRCS and Christian classification schemes expert judgment was used to assign soils to various classes and to prescribe varied land uses.

Hills used expert judgment to assess the landscape's existing and true potential; however, the projected potential of the landscape to support varied uses was based on expert judgment and on the value-based opinions of policymakers. Similarly, Zube and Carlozzi used both expert and non-expert judgments to assess the visual units in their method. Lewis involved public officials and local inhabitants not only to collect and assess the pertinent data but also to increase their awareness of regional design values crucial to the successful protection of the environmental corridors. Although the LSA 1 methods make use of both expert and nonexpert judgment, they ultimately rely heavily on expert judgment to synthesize the outcome of suitability assessment.

With few exceptions, LSA 1 methods rarely take an active management orientation; that is, the outputs of suitability assessment rarely result in criteria for management actions. These methods rarely offer strategies for predicting the cumulative consequences of the outcomes of suitability assessments. However, some LSA 1 methods, such as Angus Hills's, suggest substantive management guidelines that would put the outcome of suitability assessment into effect. Rarely do LSA 1 methods recommend institutional arrangements or administrative strategies to implement the outcome of suitability assessments.

In conclusion, significant theoretical-methodological advances in landscape-suitability methods occurred in the 1960s. However, they only hinted at the developments in ecological-planning approaches that would occur subsequently. As the nature, scope, and complexity of ecological issues increased, and as public awareness of the negative environmental impacts of human actions rose worldwide, the need to develop accurate, legally defensible landscape-suitability methods strengthened.

References

Belknap, R., and J. Furtado. *Three Approaches to Environmental Resource Analysis.* Conservation Foundation, 1967.

Brady, Nyle C. *The Nature and Properties of Soils.* New York: Macmillan, 1974.

Christian, C. S. "The Concept of Land Units and Land Systems." *Proceedings of the Ninth Pacific Sciences Congress* 20 (1958): 74–81.

Davis, Paul E., N. Lerch, L. Tornes, J. Steiger, N. Smeck, H. Andrus, J. Trimmer, and G. Bottrell. "Soil Survey of Montgomery County, Ohio." *United States Department of Agriculture.* Soil Conservation Service (1976).

Denig, Nancy W. "'On Values' Revisited: A Judeo-Christian Theology of Man and Nature." *Landscape Journal* 4, no. 2 (1985): 97–105.

Dewey, John. *Experience and Nature.* Reprint. New York: Dover, 1958.

Gordon, Steven I., and Gaybrielle E. Gordon. "The Accuracy of Soil Survey Information for Urban Land Use Planning." *Journal of the American Planning Association* 47, no. 3 (1981): 301–12.

Hills, G. Angus. *The Ecological Basis for Land-Use Planning.* Ontario Department of Lands and Forests, Research Branch, 1961.

Hopkins, Lewis D. "Methods for Generating Land Suitability Maps: A Comparative Evaluation." *Journal of the American Institute of Planners* 43, no. 4 (1977): 386–400.

Kellogg, Charles E. "Soil Surveys for Community Planning." In *Soil Surveys and Land Use Planning,* 1–7. Soil Science Society of America, 1966.

Laird, Raymond T. *Quantitative Land-Capability Analysis: A Method of Applying Earth-Science Information to Planning and Decision-Making.* Vol. 945. Washington, DC: U.S Government Printing Office, 1979.

Lee, Brenda J. "An Ecological Comparison of the McHarg Method with Other Planning Initiatives in the Great Lakes Basin." *Landscape Planning* 9, no. 2 (1982): 147–69.

Lewis, Philip H. "Ecology." *AIA Journal* (1969): 59–63.

———. "Quality Corridors for Wisconsin." *Landscape Architecture* 54, no. 2 (1964): 100–107.

———. *Recreation and Open Space in Illinois.* University of Illinois, Bureau of Community Planning, 1962.

Lyle, John. *Design for Human Ecosystems: Landscape, Land Use, and Natural Resources.* 1985. Reprint. Washington, DC: Island Press, 1999.

McAllister, Donald M. *Evaluation in Environmental Planning: Assessing Environmental, Social, Economic, and Political Trade-Offs.* Cambridge: MIT Press, 1982.

McHarg, Ian L. "Ecological Determinism." In *The Future Environment of North America,* edited by F. Darling and J. Milton, 526–38. Garden City, New York: Natural History Press, 1966.

———. *Design with Nature.* Garden City, New York: Natural History Press, 1969.

———. *A Quest for Life: An Autobiography.* New York: John Wiley & Sons, 1996.

Passons, William R. *Gestalt Approaches in Counseling.* New York: Holt, Rinehart and Winston, 1975.

Steiner, Frederick. "Resource Suitability: Methods for Analyses." *Environmental Management* 7, no. 5 (1983): 401–20.

Steinitz, Carl. *Computers and Regional Planning: The DELMARVA Study.* Cambridge: Graduate School of Design, Harvard Graduate School of Design, 1967.

Steinitz, Carl, and Peter Rogers. *A Systems Analysis Model of Urbanization and Change.* Cambridge: Harvard University, Department of Landscape Architecture, 1968.

Toth, Richard E. *Criteria for Evaluating the Valuable Natural Resources of the TIRAC Region.* Pennsylvania: Tocks Island Regional Advisory Council, 1968.

U.S. Congress. "National Forest System Land and Resource Management Planning." *Federal Registrar* 44, no. 181 (1979).

White, Lynn Jr. "The Historical Roots of Our Ecologic Crisis." *Science* 155, no. 3767 (1967): 1203–07.

Zube, Ervin H. *The Islands: Selected Resources of the United States Virgin Islands and Their Relationships to Recreation, Tourism and Open Space*. Prepared in conjunction with the Department of Landscape Architecture, University of Massachusetts at Amherst. Washington, DC: United States Department of the Interior, 1968.

Zube, Ervin H., and Carl A. Carlozzi. *An Inventory and Interpretation: Selected Resources of the Island of Nantucket*. Cooperative Extension Service, no. 4. Amherst: University of Massachusetts, 1967.

Introduction

Design for Human Ecosystems: Landscape, Land Use, and Natural Resources (1985)

John Tillman Lyle

. . . Populations compete for limited supplies of the essential ingredients of life.

In its natural state, by contrast, the lagoon and the original community it supported never had the option of becoming dependent on distant sources. They had to live on the resources at hand. Over tens of thousands of years, the estuarine ecosystem gained coherence by adapting to the existing conditions of ocean and land. By trial and error, it evolved its own unique trophic structure, every niche filled, for the cycling of materials and the distribution of energy. It learned to share the energy of the tides, which one might expect to be an unsettling influence, to heighten growth and productivity. It found ways of mediating between land and sea, concentrating, controlling, and making the best of the effects of one or the other.

If one is to put all this experience to good use in creating a new natural urban environment—one that will help support the human community on its own local resources—we must search out the secrets of the lagoon's extraordinary productivity. Every ecosystem has certain motivating processes that define its essential character and that provide us with a key for understanding and working with it. Sometimes these processes are obvious from the start, but usually they emerge only after careful analysis. In the estuarine ecosystem, the keys lie in the flow of energy—particularly the tidal subsidy that spreads the food around the lagoon twice a day—and the food web. Together, they largely account for the lagoon's productivity. An essential first step toward reestablishing the essential flow for San Elijo, therefore, will be the restoration of tidal flushing. Given the fact that the existing bridges are there to stay, a built-in mechanical device for preventing the buildup of silt in the channel will probably have to be provided. Several practical techniques for doing so have been proposed. Once such a device is operating, the lagoon should continue flushing and scouring out collecting silts with little human intervention, although some initial dredging might be needed to provide an adequate tidal volume.

The necessary step for reestablishing the food web is the restoration of the marshgrasses. Once tidal flushing is in operation, the grasses will begin to recolonize the tidal areas naturally. Since the natural growth of an extensive population will take a number of years, however, it would be better to hasten the process by a heavy initial planting of the most valuable grass—the Spartina. Once the Spartina covers the tidal areas, the whole food chain, from algae to hawks, will soon reappear.

How Human Ecosystems Work

The pattern of uses we are envisioning here is far more complex than anyone might have imagined at the beginning when the issue was posed as a simple choice between preservation and development. In this sense, the issues at San Elijo are very much like most other landscape issues that we face in the ever more crowded environment of these last decades of the twentieth century. Though the clarity of an estuarine ecosystem makes the processes and possibilities involved more sharply defined than they are in most places, the issues are typical in that they involve the merging and interacting of human and natural processes.

The poles of preservation and development created by so many conflicts of the 1960s and 1970s are drastic oversimplifications. Without a doubt, there are large areas of the earth that should be preserved in their natural state, and this may very well be the most fundamental environmental issue of all. The wilderness is where our roots are. As Wendell Berry says, "Only if we know how the land was can we know how it is." Granting this, there may very well be other areas, albeit far less extensive, that could be developed in concrete with no great loss, areas that exclude nature entirely.

Eugene Odum has proposed compartmentalization of the total landscape into areas divided according to basic ecological roles. He argues that we need both successionally young ecosystems for their productive qualities and older natural ones for their protective qualities. According to Odum, ". . . the most pleasant and certainly the safest landscape to live in is the one containing a variety of crops, forests, lakes, streams, roadsides, marshes, seashores, and waste-places—in other words, a mixture of communities of different ecological ages." He might well have added houses, gardens, parks, playing fields, offices, and shops. In the interest of achieving or maintaining such a mix, Odum would classify all land in one of four categories:

1. The productive areas, where succession is continually retarded by human controls to maintain high levels of productivity.
2. The protective, or natural, areas, where succession is allowed or encouraged to proceed into the mature, and thus stable if not highly productive, stages.
3. The compromise areas, where some combination of the first two stages exists.
4. The urban industrial, or biologically nonvital, areas.

If we accept this schema a great many of the most pressing, most challenging, and probably even most important landscape issues fall into the third category. "Compromise areas," however, is hardly an adequate term for those places in which human beings and nature might be brought together again after a very long and dangerous period of estrangement. I prefer to call such places "human ecosystems."

. . . The ecosystems shaped by our changes of the landscape will invariably be different in structure and function from the previously existing natural ones, but they will continue to respond to exactly the same natural forces even though they may be more or less diverse, more or less stable, more or less productive, or have more or less of any number of other qualities. Our creation of new ecosystems has almost always been unintentional—that is, without conscious understanding of how natural processes work and therefore without any way of predicting how the new ecosystem would work, even without any comprehension of the fact that it was actually a system. Not surprisingly then, without conscious control, new systems usually do not work very well. In the San Elijo case, we might call the railroad, the freeway, and the sewage treatment plant all examples of unintentional ecosystem design, and we have seen the results. The developers' and the preservationists' proposals fall into the same general category because, although they do consider some aspects of the lagoon environment, they do not take into account its ecological processes and its interacting, systematic nature.

The point is that if we are going to design ecosystems (and we continually do so whether we want to face all of the implications or not) then it will be best to design them intentionally, making use of all the ecological understanding we can bring to bear. Only then can we shape ecosystems that manage to fulfill all their inherent potentials for contributing to human purposes, that are sustainable, and that support nonhuman communities as well. Not every landscape can fully accomplish all three of these goals, of course, and thus Odum's term, "compromise." There will always be conflicts to be resolved and priorities to be assigned. Intentional design means carrying out conscious choices. What we are trying to do, then, is to gain a measure of control, not in order to dominate nature but to participate creatively in its processes.

Ecosystem design is undoubtedly a difficult undertaking. Nature rarely reveals herself unequivocally, and there is always the risk that we will end up agreeing with Spinoza that ". . . the attempt to show that nature does nothing in vain . . . seems to end in showing that nature, the gods, and man are alike mad." We have to begin by admitting that our tools are still crude, and we do not know enough to do the job with absolute confidence, recognizing at the same time that we will have to do it anyway.

To participate creatively in natural processes and to do so with reasonable hope of success, we need to include as subjects of design not only the visible form of the landscape but its inner workings, the systems that motivate and maintain it. Natural systems are continuously self-organizing (there being nobody available to organize them), and we can draw upon the principles by which they work to make human ecosystems more sustainable. Such an aim requires a knowledge of these systems. Fortunately, the sciences provide a great deal of information, which, while far from complete, is yet enough to get us started.

Generally speaking, we can divide this scientific knowledge into two types. First, there are facts or data concerning the situation at hand. For any given landscape, a great many of these may be available, or very few, depending on how much research has been done. . . .

The second type of scientific knowledge might be loosely categorized under the heading of "concepts," a word the dictionary defines as general notions, ideas, or principles conceived in the mind. The science of ecology has developed a number of basic concepts—such as productivity, trophic levels, succession, and energy flow—that help unify and give coherence to the masses of otherwise unrelated facts produced by research. These concepts are large and inclusive and fit the known facts, but since they are conceived in the mind, it is virtually impossible to prove that any of them actually exist in nature. . . . For purposes of design, however, concepts are indispensable because they can be put to general use. In fact, utility is the criterion of value of a scientific concept but is rarely considered with respect to scientific facts or theories.

For purposes of design, concepts are useful because they provide access to the mechanisms that join all of the facts. They make it possible to work with the forest before the trees. They make it possible to gain a working understanding of an ecosystem even though many of the facts may be unknown. They give us handles with which to grasp the unseeable. They provide us with a basis for developing theories of ecosystem design that allow us to reach into and reshape the inner workings of the landscape. . . .

The Ecosystem Concept

The first concept is that of the ecosystem itself. It is a rather new concept, having been first advanced by A. G. Tansley in 1935, but an important one, having become since that time the fundamental principle of all ecological study. Simply defined, an ecosystem is the interacting assemblage of living things and their nonliving environment. Among living things are human beings themselves, although ecologists usually choose to study ecosystems that exclude man, and human beings usually choose to think of themselves as somehow set apart from ecosystems. This is an important point, and one that is implicit in everything that follows: We human beings are integral, interacting components of ecosystems at every level, and in order to deal adequately with these systems, we have to recognize that simple fact. In most situations, even at the level of the biosphere, we may be an overriding, controlling component, but we are a component nonetheless.

Another important characteristic of the ecosystem is that it can be of any size. That we can consider any landscape of any size is a great convenience for designers, but there are rules to be followed. No ecosystem stands alone. "All ranks of ecosystems are open systems, not closed ones. . . ." This implies that ecosystems are connected by flows of energy and materials. Each system draws in energy and materials from the systems around it and in turn exports to them. In drawing the boundaries of an ecosystem, therefore, we need to consider the flows that link it with its neighbors. Ignoring these connections—these imports and exports of energy and materials—has caused a great many of the disasters of unintentional ecosystem design.

In the shaping of ecosystems, three organizational concepts are of fundamental importance. The first is *scale*, or the relative size of the landscape in question and its connections with larger and smaller systems and ultimately with the whole. It is scale that provides us with an encompassing frame of reference. The second is *design process*, the pattern of thought that we follow in dealing with this frame of reference. The third is the underlying *order* that binds ecosystems together and makes them work. These constitute the three major subjects of this book, which is divided into three parts, each concerned with one of them. For the sake of orientation, I will introduce each concept briefly here before proceeding to treat it in greater detail.

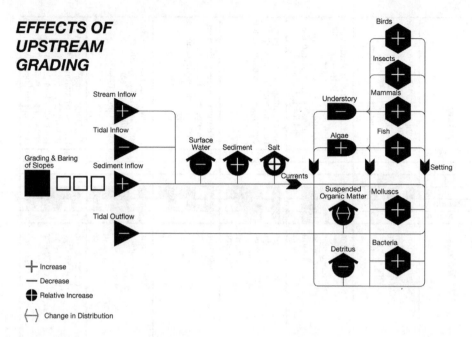

Figure 4-5 Effects of upstream grading (Lyle, 1999, Reprinted with permission of Island Press. Redrawn by Yuan Ren, 2014).

Scale

We need to recognize that every ecosystem is a part—or subsystem—of a larger system and that it in turn includes a number of yet smaller subsystems. It also has necessary linkages to both the larger and the smaller units. San Elijo lagoon, for example, is at the same time a component of a larger watershed unit and a component of an even larger oceanic unit. The water that runs off the land in this eighty-square-mile watershed eventually reaches the lagoon, bringing along everything it has picked up in the interim. This may include silts from eroding slopes, nitrates from fertilized agricultural lands, oil from roads, and any number of other substances that can seriously affect the life of the lagoon. If the lagoon is to operate as a healthy ecosystem, therefore, some control over land use in the watershed will be required. By the same token, all these materials finally flow from the lagoon into the Pacific Ocean, establishing yet another linkage. The lagoon is also linked to the San Diego urban region, even the entire Southern California region, because of all the people who come there for recreation. On a still larger scale, it is tied to Alaska and Central America by the Pacific Flyway. Events in San Elijo can thus seriously affect animal populations thousands of miles away.

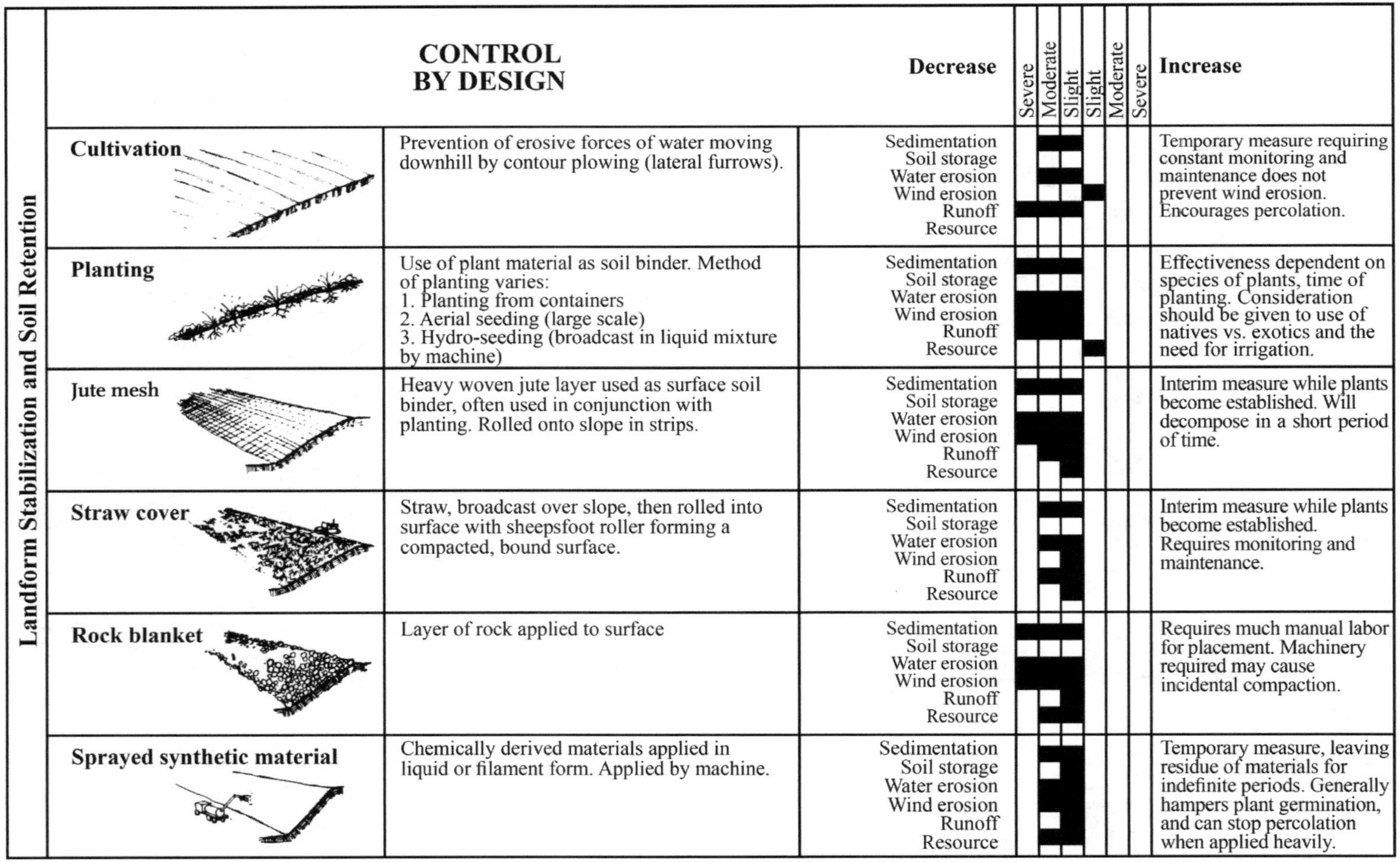

CONTROL BY DESIGN	Description	Decrease	Increase
Cultivation	Prevention of erosive forces of water moving downhill by contour plowing (lateral furrows).	Sedimentation, Soil storage, Water erosion, Wind erosion, Runoff, Resource	Temporary measure requiring constant monitoring and maintenance does not prevent wind erosion. Encourages percolation.
Planting	Use of plant material as soil binder. Method of planting varies: 1. Planting from containers 2. Aerial seeding (large scale) 3. Hydro-seeding (broadcast in liquid mixture by machine)	Sedimentation, Soil storage, Water erosion, Wind erosion, Runoff, Resource	Effectiveness dependent on species of plants, time of planting. Consideration should be given to use of natives vs. exotics and the need for irrigation.
Jute mesh	Heavy woven jute layer used as surface soil binder, often used in conjunction with planting. Rolled onto slope in strips.	Sedimentation, Soil storage, Water erosion, Wind erosion, Runoff, Resource	Interim measure while plants become established. Will decompose in a short period of time.
Straw cover	Straw, broadcast over slope, then rolled into surface with sheepsfoot roller forming a compacted, bound surface.	Sedimentation, Soil storage, Water erosion, Wind erosion, Runoff, Resource	Interim measure while plants become established. Requires monitoring and maintenance.
Rock blanket	Layer of rock applied to surface	Sedimentation, Soil storage, Water erosion, Wind erosion, Runoff, Resource	Requires much manual labor for placement. Machinery required may cause incidental compaction.
Sprayed synthetic material	Chemically derived materials applied in liquid or filament form. Applied by machine.	Sedimentation, Soil storage, Water erosion, Wind erosion, Runoff, Resource	Temporary measure, leaving residue of materials for indefinite periods. Generally hampers plant germination, and can stop percolation when applied heavily.

Landform Stabilization and Soil Retention

Figure 4-6 Control by design (Lyle, 1999, Reproduced with permission of Island Press, Redrawn by Yuan Ren, 2014).

Despite all these connections, San Elijo Lagoon is a limited unit of landscape, one of a certain size with definite boundaries, which means that we can deal with it only at a certain scale. The concerns that we can address in detail are likewise limited to those that are appropriate to that scale. Nevertheless, we need to work within the context, or framework, of the larger-scale unit, in this case the watershed, and we need to consider the proposed development projects as smaller-scale units within the framework of the lagoon. . . .

Design Processes

In part II, we will explore design processes, the vehicles for what we have called creative participation in natural processes. The ways in which we go about design will naturally vary according to the scale of concern and the situation at hand. At this point I will have to digress briefly in order to clear up a semantic difficulty. The activity of "design," as I am using the term here, means giving form to physical phenomena, and I will use it to represent such activity at every scale. The challenges we face require some broadening and redefinition of the activity of design. According to Erich Jantsch, "Design attempts to find, formalize, and bring optimally into play the innate forms of a process . . . [and] . . . focuses on finding and emphasizing internal factors in evolution, on making them conscious and effective."

This is a departure from the convention of using the term "planning" for landscape shaping at scales larger than that of construction detail. I believe the departure is justified by the very broad, rather indefinite inclusiveness of the term "planning," by the confusion that results from its use, and by the increasing tendency in the environmental design disciplines to associate planning with administrative activity rather than physical form-shaping. This book is about making physical changes in the landscape and not about administrative, legal, or policymaking activity, although, needless to say, it will usually take a great deal of the latter to bring about these changes. Planning and design are thus closely linked and work in tandem, sometimes to the point of being indistinguishable.

In using the term "design" in this sense, I believe I am following, not trying to initiate, a trend. More and more, we hear of "site design" rather than "site planning." Carl Steinitz refers to "regional landscape design" and justifies the usage of this term by defining design as "intentional change. . . . the landscape and its social patterns are altered by design." And Ian McHarg, of course, entitled his famous work "Design with Nature." In any event, the term "design" carries the connotations of intention, precision, and control that befit the approach I am describing. It also suggests emotional involvement. Jantsch speaks of design as being planning plus love. Consequently, I shall use the term with all these overtones in mind, although with apologies for any confusion it may cause. Likewise I shall use the term "planning" to refer to more strictly administrative and institutional activities, such as the articulation and implementation of policy.

Combining as it does two different modes of thought—analytical use of scientific information and creative exploration (or the left and right sides of the brain, if you will)—ecosystem design can get very complicated. The two modes can work together, but only if the roles of each are clearly established. Especially at the larger scales, design processes are further complicated by the involvement of considerable numbers of people—in some cases, as we shall see, huge numbers. To deal with this complexity in a rational manner, we shall break these processes down into component themes that are more or less common to all of them: formulation, information, models, possibilities, plan evaluation, and management. Then we will examine each of these themes with respect to its content and the analytical or creative orientation associated with it.

The inclusion of management is particularly important in ecosystem design because of the variable future that is a fact of life for any organic entity. The design of ecosystems is probabilistic in that we cannot say what will definitely happen in the future but only what will probably happen. Management deals with this uncertainty in the cybernetic manner, by observing what actually does happen and redesigning as necessary. Thus, being an essential continuation of design by other means, to paraphrase the famous statement on war and politics, management assumes a more creative role than has usually been expected. To repeat, the interlocking relationship between design and management is a *particularly* important feature of any ecosystematic design process.

Order

In the midst of complexity, with its many opportunities for diversion, we need to keep reminding ourselves that the purpose of creating order in human ecosystems is to enable them to fulfill the needs of both their human and other components. But how do we define "order"? There are a great many kinds and degrees of order, although in landscape design, we are most used to thinking in terms of visual order. Ecosystematic order is something else again, although it is usually reflected in what we see.

Here, to return to the concepts of ecology, we can identify three modes of order, each of which provides a key to one aspect of the inner workings of ecosystems. The three modes are structure, function, and location. Odum defines structure as ". . . the composition of the biological community, including species, their biomass, life histories and spatial distribution, the quantity and distribution of abiotic materials, and the range of conditions like light and climate." Margalef is more succinct: "If we consider the elements and the relations between the elements, we have the structure." . . .

The second mode of order, function, or the flow of energy and materials, is closely intertwined with structure. According to Odum, the ". . . complex biomass structure is maintained by the total community respiration which continually pumps out disorder." Respiration is fueled by the flow of energy, and keeping this flow going, distributing energy to all the members of the community, is a basic purpose of ecosystem function. At San Elijo, the tides add their force to the "pumping," thus speeding up the flow and increasing the rate of productivity. Every ecosystem has a characteristic pattern of energy flow that corresponds with its structure. . . .

Also essential to ecosystem function are the flows of water and the chemical elements essential to life. In contrast with energy, these are not continuously dissipated but circulate intact along more or less consistent pathways through storage to environment to organisms and back. Thus, the material flows, or biogeochemical cycles, as they are usually called, provide each organism with its needed chemicals and nutrients.

At San Elijo, as in most unintentionally designed manmade ecosystems, the material flows have long been in a state of perpetual dysfunction, not for lack of materials, but because they are directed to the wrong places. During the long period when primarily treated sewage effluent was dumped into the lagoon, the enormous concentration of nutrients from the sewage brought about rapid growth of algae, which used enormous quantities of oxygen from the water, thus denying it to fish and molluscs and depleting their populations. When the algae died at a faster rate than the waters could absorb them or the tides move them out, they decayed on the surface, causing unsightly masses of green scum and unpleasant odors. This is an example of a very common difficulty created by unintentional design. The solution eventually implemented for the "water pollution problem" was the four-mile-long ocean outfall. Now there are only a few occasional algae blooms on the lagoon's surface, mostly caused by fertilizer nitrates in runoff water. But it is not only the nutrients that have been lost for any human purpose; with the freshwater infusions from the sewage cut off as well, the surface level of the lagoon has dropped, leaving dried-up stretches of mudflat around some of its edges. The natural fresh water supply through Escondido Creek was long ago drastically reduced by upstream impoundments. . . .

The alternative that we propose would redirect the flows to reuse both water and nutrients through biological sewage treatment. Thus, by feeding the primarily treated effluent into a series of ponds in which water hyacinths and other aquatic plants will take up the nutrients, the water will eventually reach a level of purity that will permit its use for irrigating recreational areas and its eventual return to the lagoon. The hyacinths can be harvested for cattle feed and thus eventually be returned to the system as well. Such a pattern of water and nutrient flow is more like that of a natural ecosystem, more efficient and economical. The outfall, incidentally, would still be needed for overflows and emergencies.

One major consideration remains, however, at least for the predictable future. Such a system will not operate itself. Management will have to take the place of the self-regulating mechanisms of a natural estuarine system, which means that a high level of ongoing, creative management of the sort mentioned earlier will be needed. . . .

The third mode of ecosystematic order—locational patterns—usually receives far more attention in design than the other two, although it is less explored in the scientific literature. Usually, the proposed pattern of locations is considered *the* plan. Although this practice follows historical precedent and fits established decision-making patterns, it often results in the less visible aspects of structure and function being ignored. Ideally, the three modes would be considered equally important, so interrelated indeed, that one could not consider one mode without considering the others. Location, nevertheless, remains the most visible of the three, and "the plan" will probably remain the vehicle on which the design of ecosystem structure and function will ride.

The ideal pattern of locations is determined mostly by what is already there. The processes and organisms that we have described are distributed over the landscape in relation to climate and topography. If our purpose is to build on these to develop the sort of human ecosystem we have discussed, then that pattern will have to be respected. At San Elijo, the tidal areas where marshgrasses grow to support the food chain are essential parts of the picture, as are the mudflats where the shorebirds feed and the shallow waters and matted islands where they find cover for nesting. . . .

Perhaps most difficult to deal with is the pattern of private ownerships, which makes it necessary to show how the land can be used profitably. Whenever public acquisition is recommended, strong justification will be needed.

The most useful tool for sorting out the competing patterns is the *suitability model*, which consists of an analytically derived map showing the relative suitabilities of land increments for given human activities. In the case of San Elijo Lagoon, the complexity of the data made it convenient to use a computer-mapping technique for defining suitabilities. Whether it is produced by hand or by computer, however, there is nothing magical or definitive about a suitability model. The hand or the computer simply combines and aggregates the information that it is given in the ways it is told to and produces a graphic expression of the results. . . .

These estimates of suitability are based on predictions of future economic costs and environmental impacts. For the first model, that concerned with residential development, the most suitable locations were hypothesized to be those where development costs are likely to be lower, erosion rates less, landsliding improbable, and wildlife populations left undisturbed. Any number of other criteria might have been used, of course, but these were the ones judged most important in this particular case. The dark areas, then, assuming the technical reliability of the models, are those where some combination of high development costs, rapid erosion rates, probable landsliding, and wildlife disruption renders the land unsuitable for residential development.

The series of models that follow shows the relative suitability for various recreational and residential uses. The criteria for each model are different, but in each case the most and least suitable locations are defined.

Suitability models play a pivotal role in ecosystem design, providing a bridge between the consideration of processes and their location on the land. They aggregate complex collections of information concerning natural, social, and economic functions into usable forms. They disclose new patterns that are extremely difficult, if not impossible, to discern in any other way.

It sometimes happens that a model is used not as a basis for planning, but as a plan in itself. This is a serious mistake. Models are simply expressions of the interactions of clearly stated facts and values. Once they are made, there is still a creative leap to be taken to shape a plan. The models provide a firm footing for this leap, hut in the end, the plan will look quite different from the models.

From Models to Plan to Management

Witness the plan for San Elijo that emerged from the long process we have been describing here. It divides the lagoon and its watershed into seven distinct categories of land use. These generally follow the patterns of the suitability models, but the actual configurations are quite different. Moreover, the seven uses bear no resemblance to the traditional zoning categories, because the purpose of the zoning is quite different from that of traditional zoning. Here, we are not trying to promote uniformity of use, but to encourage the greatest diversity that is consistent with the healthy and productive functioning of lagoon processes. Consequently, the definition of uses is as general and as open to ideas as it can reasonably be. . . .

Such a system [design for San Elijo], however, will continue to work well only if it is managed—man-aged—well. Once the system begins to take shape, ongoing management is to be instituted as one of its essential components. Only management can control the feedback loops needed to augment those that have evolved as internally functioning mechanisms in natural systems.

Certain kinds of control are needed to prevent foreign and potentially damaging materials like fertilizers, pesticides, oil residues, or phosphates from entering the lagoon. Human activities can be regulated in such a way as to prevent their interfering with sensitive lagoon processes or populations. Critical indicators of environmental quality, especially water quality, in the lagoon need to be monitored to maintain the stability of the system. When an imbalance appears, or if there is evidence of deterioration or conflict somewhere, some corrective action can be taken. In the absence of such a program, however carefully the initial design may be conceived, the lagoon will eventually return to its present sorry state or worse.

This intentionally designed and managed ecosystem represents a symbiosis of urban and natural processes. Food production, wildlife habitats, recreation, dwelling, resource conservation, water and nutrient recycling, and visual amenity are joined in a network of interdependence. The composition as a whole is very different from the estuarine ecosystem that would still exist at San Elijo had man never arrived on the scene, being more varied in its forms and more intense in its activities. Although it is dependent on human energy and ingenuity for its stability, the reverse is also, to some degree, true. If all goes well, if our models are correct and our design works as it should, and, if the management is both imaginative and sound, then human and natural processes will merge indistinguishably into an organic whole, a human ecosystem in the best sense of the term. That, hard as it may be to achieve, is the ideal.

References

Berry, Wendell. *The Unsettling of America: Culture and Agriculture.* New York: Avon Books, 1977.

Evans, Francis C. "Ecosystem as the Basic Unit in Ecology." *Science* 123, no. 3208 (1956): 1127–28.

Jantsch, Erich. *Design for Evolution: Self-Organization and Planning in the Life of Human Systems.* New York: George Braziller, 1975.

Margalef, Ramon. "On Certain Unifying Principles in Ecology." *American Naturalist* 97 (1963): 357–4.

McHarg, Ian L. *Design with Nature.* New York: Natural History Press, 1969.

Odum, Eugene P. "The Strategy of Ecosystem Development." *Science* 164, no. 3877 (1969): 262–70.

———. *Fundamentals of Ecology, 3rd Edition.* Philadelphia: W. B. Saunders Company, 1971.

Rigler, F. H. "The Concept of Energy Flow and Nutrient Flow between Trophic Levels." In *Unifying Concepts in Ecology,* edited by W. H. Van Dobben and R. H. Lowe-McConnell. The Hague: Dr. W. Junk B.V. Publishers, 1975.

Steinitz, Carl. "Simulating Alternative Policies for Implementing the Massachusetts Scenic and Recreational Rivers Act: The North River Demonstration Project." *Landscape Planning* 6, no. 1 (1979): 51–89.

Van Dobben, W. H., and R. H. Lowe-McConnell. "Preface." In *Unifying Concepts in Ecology,* edited by W. H. Van Dobben and R.H. Lowe-McConnell. The Hague: Dr. W. Junk B.V. Publishers, 1975.

Ecological Principles and Guidelines for Managing the Use of the Land

Ecological Applications (2000)

V. H. Dale, S. Brown, R. A. Haeuber,
N. T. Hobbs, N. Huntly, R. J. Naiman,
W. E. Riebsame, M. G. Turner, and T. J. Valone

Introduction

Wake, now, my vision of ministry clear; Brighten my pathway with radiance here; Mingle my calling with all who will share; Work toward a planet transformed by our care.
—T. J. M. Mikelson, 1936

The words of the Irish hymn by Mikelson have been applied literally to the earth. During the past few millennia, humans have emerged as the major force of change around the globe. The large environmental changes wrought by our actions include modification of the global climate system, reduction in stratospheric ozone, alteration of Earth's biogeochemical cycles, changes in the distribution and abundance of biological resources, and decreasing water quality (Meyer and Turner, 1994; IPCC, 1996; Vitousek et al., 1997; Mahlman, 1997). However, one of the most pervasive aspects of human-induced change involves the widespread transformation of land through efforts to provide food, shelter, and products for our use. Land transformation is perhaps the most profound result of human actions because it affects so many of the planet's physical and biological systems (Kates et al., 1990). In fact, land-use changes directly impact the ability of Earth to continue providing the goods and services upon which humans depend.

Unfortunately, potential ecological consequences are not always considered in making decisions regarding land use. Moreover, the unique perspective and body of knowledge offered by ecological science rarely are brought to bear in decision-making processes on private lands. The purpose of this paper is to take an important step toward remedying this situation by identifying principles of ecological science that are relevant to land-use decisions and by proposing a set of guidelines for land-use decision making based on these principles (figure 4-7). This paper fulfills this purpose through four steps. (1) It describes the conceptual and institutional foundations of land-use decision making, outlining the implementation of U.S. land-use decisions [not included in the version of this article in this book]. (2) It identifies (a) ecological principles that are critical to sustaining the structure and function of ecosystems in the face of rapid land-use change and (b) the implications of these principles for land-use decision making. (3) It offers guidelines for using these principles in making decisions regarding land-use change. Finally, (4) it examines key factors and uncertainties in future patterns of land-use change. Throughout, the paper offers specific examples to illustrate decision-making processes, relevant ecological principles, and guidelines for making choices about land use at spatial scales ranging from the individual site to the landscape.

The paper focuses on the United States, which some may see as parochial; however, the incredible variety of political, economic, social, and cultural institutions encountered throughout the world make a thorough comparative study impossible in a single paper. More importantly, while the paper concentrates on land-use decisions in the United States, the principles and guidelines it describes are applicable worldwide.

In undertaking this paper, the Land Use Committee of the Ecological Society of America (ESA) continues an ongoing effort by the Society to marshal the resources and knowledge of the ecological-science community in understanding and resolving critical environmental-policy and resource-management issues. In 1991, for example, the Sustainable Biosphere Initiative (Lubchenco et al., 1991) established the priority research areas that must be explored if ecologists are to contribute in maintaining Earth's life-support systems. Similarly, the ESA Report on the Scientific Basis of Ecosystem Management (Christensen et al., 1996) focused on the application of ecological science in managing ecological systems for extractive uses. Our report continues that tradition, offering relevant ecological principles for making decisions regarding human actions that change the land from one category of use to another (e.g., from forests to agriculture or from agriculture to housing subdivisions). . . .

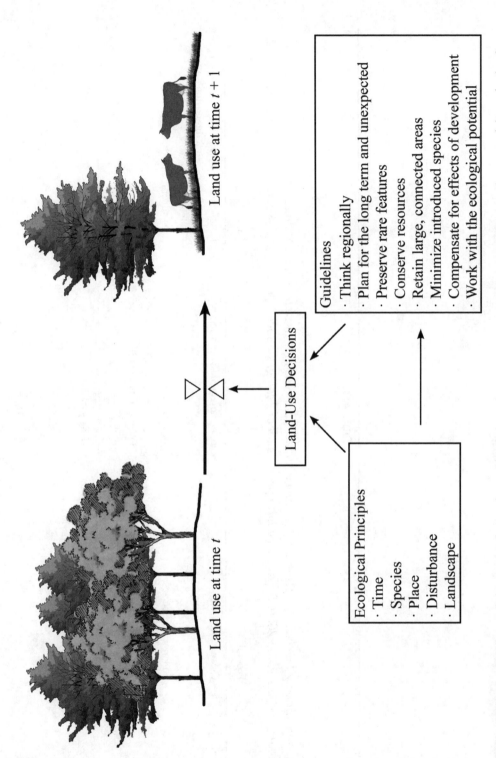

Figure 4-7 A roadmap to this paper shows that ecological principles relating to land use are developed into guidelines for land managers (Dale et al., 2000, Reproduced with permission of Ecological Society of America, Reproduced by Yuan Ren, 2014).

Table 4-1

Decision-making levels in the United States and examples of their land-use management powers, both regulatory and nonregulatory (Dale et al., 2000, Reproduced with permission of Ecological Society of America, Redrawn by Travis Witt, 2014).

Powers	Federal	State	Local
Direct regulatory	Clean Water Act	State endangered-species acts	Land-use zoning (e.g., lot size, housing density, structural dimensions, and landscaping)
	Endangered Species Act	Growth-management statutes	Agricultural land-use regulations
	National Flood Insurance Program	Regulation and permitting (e.g., siting power plants, landfills, reservoirs, and mines)	Stormwater management
	Surface mining reclamation	Programs (e.g., Coastal Zone Management)	
	Wetlands/Waterways Reclamation Act		

Indirect regulatory	Tax policy (e.g., estate taxes and home-mortgage deduction) Clean Air Act Transportation funding and development Agricultural programs (e.g., Conservation Reserve Program and Farmland Protection Program) Subsidies (e.g., gasohol program, land and production credit, and crop insurance)	Property-tax exemptions (e.g., for farmland or commercial property) Transportation policy Economic-development programs	Property-tax rates Water-use ordinances Local service placement and development (e.g., water and sewer systems, schools, and roads)
Management of publicly owned lands	Land-use planning (e.g., national parks, national forests, and BLM properties) National Wilderness Act Wild and Scenic Rivers Act Siting and design of roads and other facilities	State parks and forests State roads and rights-of-way Regulation of mining and reclamation activities	Municipal parks and recreation areas County roads and rights-of-way Green-space systems Greenways

Challenges of Ecologically Sustainable Land Use

A critical challenge for land use and management involves reconciling conflicting goals and uses of the land. The diverse goals for use of the land include resource-extractive activities, such as forestry, agriculture, grazing, and mining; infrastructure for human settlement, including housing, transportation, and industrial centers; recreational activities; services provided by ecological systems, such as flood control and water supply and filtration; support of aesthetic, cultural, and religious values; and sustaining the compositional and structural complexity of ecological systems. These goals often conflict with one another, and difficult land-use decisions may develop as stakeholders pursue different land-use goals. For example, conflicts often arise between those who want to extract timber and those who are interested in the scenic values of forests. Local vs. broad-scale perspectives on the benefits and costs of land management also provide different views of the implications of land actions. Understanding how land-use decisions affect the achievement of these goals can help achieve balance among the different goals. The focus of this paper is on the last goal: sustaining ecological systems, for land-use decisions and practices rarely are undertaken with ecological sustainability in mind. Sustaining ecological systems also indirectly supports other values, including ecosystem services, cultural and aesthetic values, recreation, and sustainable extractive uses of the land.

To meet the challenge of sustaining ecological systems, an ecological perspective must be incorporated into land-use and land-management decisions. Specifying ecological principles and understanding their implications for land-use and land-management decisions are essential steps on the path toward ecologically based land use. The resulting guidelines translate theory into practical steps for land managers. Ecological principles and guidelines for land use and management elucidate the consequences of land uses for ecological systems. Thus, a major intent of this paper is to set forth ecological principles relevant to land use and management and to develop them into guidelines for use of the land. . . .

Ecological Principles and Their Implications for Land Use

Changes in technology and modes of production have fundamentally altered the relationship between people and natural ecosystems. When people were sustained by hunting and gathering, the availability and distribution of plant and animal foods limited human population abundance and distribution; hunter-gatherers were tightly integrated into natural food webs. The dependence of humans on natural stocks of plants and animals declined with the advent of agriculture, which allowed people to concentrate in areas with high productivity, areas where soils were fertile and rainfall was abundant. No longer was the spatial distribution of people limited by the availability of "prey." Augmentation of rainfall with irrigation, and addition of fertilizers to natural stocks of nutrients, further reduced the spatial dependence of human population centers on the biotic and abiotic properties of ecosystems. The advent of extensive transportation networks and the development of food-preservation technologies during the Industrial Revolution extended the habitable area by allowing population of areas remote from agriculture.

These trends have reduced the interdependence of ecological and human systems, and the consequences of land-use decisions often are not felt immediately. Planning is needed to avert long-term or broad-scale harmful ecological effects resulting from unwise land-use choices. Therefore, planning should be based upon a sound ecological basis.

The major lessons of ecological science for land management can be summarized in numerous ways. This report organizes ecological information into five principles that have implications for land management. The principles deal with *time, place, species, disturbance,* and the *landscape.* The principles are presented as separate entities, although they interact in many ways. They are translated into specific guidelines in a later section.

Time principle: Ecological processes function at many time scales, some long, some short; and ecosystems change through time. . . . *Species principle:* Particular species and networks of interacting species have key, broad-scale ecosystem-level effects. . . . *Place principle:* Local climatic, hydrologic, edaphic, and geomorphologic factors as well as biotic interactions strongly affect ecological processes and the abundance and distribution of species at any one place. . . . *Disturbance principle:* The type, intensity, and duration of disturbance shape the characteristics of populations, communities, and ecosystems. Disturbances are events that disrupt ecological systems. . . . *Landscape principle:* The size, shape, and spatial relationships of land-cover types influence the dynamics of populations, communities, and ecosystems. . . .

Guidelines for Land Use

Ecologically based guidelines are proposed here as a way to facilitate land managers considering the ecological ramifications of land-use decisions. These guidelines are meant to be flexible and to apply to diverse land-use situations. The guidelines recognize that the same parcel of land can be used to accomplish multiple goals and require that decisions be made within an appropriate spatial and temporal context. For example, the ecological implications of a decision may last for decades or even centuries, long outliving the political effects and impacts. Furthermore, all aspects of a decision need to be considered in setting the time frame and spatial scale for impact analysis. In specific cases, the relevant guidelines can be developed into prescriptions for action. One could think of these guidelines as a checklist of factors to be considered in making a land-use decision:

1) Examine the impacts of local decisions in a regional context.
2) Plan for long-term change and unexpected events.
3) Preserve rare landscape elements, critical habitats, and associated species.
4) Avoid land uses that deplete natural resources over a broad area.
5) Retain large contiguous or connected areas that contain critical habitats.
6) Minimize the introduction and spread of nonnative species.
7) Avoid or compensate for effects of development on ecological processes.
8) Implement land-use and land-management practices that are compatible with the natural potential of the area.

Checking the applicability of each guideline to specific land-use decisions provides a means to translate the ecological principles described in the previous section into practice.

Examine Impacts of Local Decisions in a Regional Context

As embodied in the landscape principle, the spatial array of habitats and ecosystems shapes local conditions and responses (e.g., Risser, 1985; Patterson, 1987) and, by the same logic, local changes can have broad-scale impacts over the landscape. Therefore, it is critical to examine both the constraints placed on a location by the regional conditions and the implications of decisions for the larger area. This guideline dictates two considerations for planning land use: identifying the surrounding region that is likely to affect and be affected by the local project and examining how adjoining jurisdictions are using and managing their lands. Once the regional context is identified, regional data should be examined. Items to include in a regional data inventory include land-cover classes, soils, patterns of water movement, historical disturbance regimes, and habitats of focal species and other species of special concern (see Diaz and Apostol [1992] and Sessions et al. [1997] for a thorough discussion). The focal species typically represent a diversity of functional roles that are possible within a place and reflect the environmental fluctuations that provide opportunities and constraints for species. In some cases, an attribute (such as soils) can be used as a surrogate for other information that is dependent on that feature (such as vegetation). Recent technological advances—such as the development of geographic information systems (GIS) and the general availability of databases for soils, roads, and land cover on the Internet—make regional analysis a possibility even for small projects (e.g., Mann et al., 1999).

Where one has the luxury of planning land use and management in a pristine site, both local and broad-scale decisions can be considered simultaneously. Forman (1995) suggests that land-use planning begin with determining nature's arrangement of landscape elements and land cover and then considering models of optimal spatial arrangements and existing human uses. Following this initial step, he suggests that the desired landscape mosaic be planned first for water and biodiversity; then for cultivation, grazing, and wood products; then for sewage and other wastes; and finally for homes and industry. Planning under pristine conditions is typically not possible. Rather, the extant state of development of the region generally constrains opportunities for land management.

This guideline implies a hierarchy of flexibility in land uses, and it implicitly recognizes ecological constraints as the primary determinants in this hierarchy. A viable housing site is much more flexible in placement than an agricultural area or a wetland dedicated to improving water quality and sustaining wildlife. Optimizing concurrently for several objectives requires that planners recognize lower site flexibility of some uses than others. However, given that most situations involve existing land uses and built structures, this guideline calls for examining local decisions within the regional context of ecological concerns as well as in relation to the social, economic, and political perspectives that are typically considered.

Ideally, land-use models that incorporate both ecological and other concerns about impacts of land activities could be used to design and explore implications of land-use decisions in a regional context. Land-use models that truly integrate the social, economic, and ecological considerations are in their infancy, and no consensus has yet been reached about what approaches are best for this task. Therefore, many diverse approaches have been advanced (Wilkie and Finn, 1988; Southworth et al., 1991; Baker, 1992; Lee et al., 1992; Dale et al., 1993; 1994 a, b; Riebsame et al., 1994; Gilruth et al., 1995; Turner et al., 1996; Wear et al., 1996). Development and use of these models have improved understanding of the relationship between the many factors that affect land-use decisions and their impacts—including human perceptions, economic systems, market and resource demands, foreign relations (e.g., trade agreements), fluctuations in interest rates, and pressure for environmental conservation and maintenance of ecosystem goods and services. Understanding this interface between causality and effect of land-use decisions is a key challenge facing the scientific community and planners in the coming decades.

Plan for Long-Term Change and Unexpected Events

The time principle indicates that impacts of land-use decisions can, and often do, vary over time. Long-term changes that occur as a response to land-use decisions can be classified into two categories: delayed and cumulative. Delayed impacts may not be observed for years or decades. An example is the composition of forest communities in New England; today those forests differ substantially among areas that were previously woodlots, pasture, or croplands (Foster, 1992). Cumulative effects are illustrated by events that together determine a unique trajectory of effects that could not be predicted from any one event (Paine et al., 1998). For example, at Walker Branch Watershed in East Tennessee, patterns of calcium cycling are determined not only by past land uses (timber harvest vs. agriculture) but also by the history of insect outbreaks in the recovering forest (Dale et al., 1990).

Future options for land use are constrained by the decisions made today as well as by those made in the past. These constraints are conspicuous in forested systems, where options for areas to harvest may be limited by the pattern of available timber left from past cuts (Turner et al., 1996). In addition, areas that are urbanized are unlikely to be available for any other land uses because urbanization locks in a pattern on the landscape that is hard to reverse. This difficulty of reversal also holds for suburban sprawl and the development of vacation or retirement homes.

The concept of externalities, discussed earlier (see Land-use decision making in the United States: Private lands) as a foundation of government's role in private land use and management, needs to [be] considered within this guideline. Land actions should be implemented with some consideration as to the physical, biological, aesthetic, or economic constraints that are placed on future uses of the land. External effects can extend beyond the boundaries of individual ownership and thus have the potential to affect surrounding owners.

Planning for the long term requires consideration of the potential for unexpected events, such as variations in temperature or precipitation patterns or disturbances. Although disturbances shape the characteristics of ecosystems, estimating the occurrence and implications of these unanticipated events is difficult. Nevertheless, land-use plans must include them. For example, the western coast of the United States has a high potential for volcanic eruption, which would have severe effects. Yet, predicting exact impacts is not possible. Climate change is occurring, but global-climate-projection models cannot determine the temperature and precipitation changes that will happen in any one place. Thus, potential impacts of land-use changes on future dynamics should be recognized but cannot be precisely specified, as yet. Similarly, land-use changes that affect natural water drainages can cause catastrophic flooding during extreme rain events (Sparks, 1996). Although it will not be possible to foresee all extreme events or the effects of a land-use decision on natural variations, it is important to estimate likely changes.

Long-term planning must also recognize that one cannot simply extrapolate historical land-use impacts forward to predict future consequences of land use. The transitions of land from one use or cover type to another often are not stable from one period to another (Turner et al., 1996; Wear et al., 1996) because of changes in demographics, public policy, market economies, and technological and ecological factors. Thus, models produce projections of potential scenarios rather than predictions of future events. It is difficult to model (or even understand) the full complex of interactions among the factors that determine land-use patterns, yet models offer a useful tool to consider potential long-term and broad-scale implications of land-use decisions.

Preserve Rare Landscape Elements and Associated Species

Rare landscape elements often provide critical habitats. For example, in the Southern Appalachian Mountains, 84% of the federally listed terrestrial plant and animal species occur in rare communities (Southern Appalachian Assessment, 1996). While these communities occupy a small area of land, they contain features important for the region's biological diversity. Therefore, rare landscape elements need to be identified, usually via an inventory and analysis of vegetation types, hydrology, soils, and physical features that identifies the presence and location of rare landscape elements and, when possible, associated species (e.g., see Mann et al., 1999). Once the inventory is complete, effects of alternative land-use decisions on these landscape elements and species can be estimated. These effects can then be considered in view of the overall goal for the project, the distribution of elements and species across the landscape, and their susceptibility, given likely future land changes in the vicinity and region. Strategies to avoid or mitigate serious impacts can then be developed and implemented. This guideline to preserve rare landscape elements and associated species derives from both the species and place principles.

Avoid Land Uses That Deplete Natural Resources Over a Broad Area

Depletion of natural resources disrupts natural processes in ways that often are irreversible over long periods of time. The loss of soil via erosion that occurs during agriculture and the loss of wetlands and their associated ecological processes and species are two examples. This guideline entails prevention of the rapid or gradual diminishment of resources, such as water or soil. This task first requires the determination of resources at risk. For example, in the southwestern United States, water might be the most important resource; but elsewhere, water might not be a limiting factor, yet it may not be readily replaced. Evaluation of whether a resource is at risk is thus an ongoing process as the abundance and distribution of resources change.

This guideline also calls for the deliberation of ways to avoid actions that would jeopardize natural resources. Some land actions are inappropriate in a particular setting or time, and they should be avoided. Examples of inappropriate actions are farming on steep slopes, which might produce soil loss; logging on stream sides, which may jeopardize the habitat for aquatic organisms; and growing hydrophilic plants in areas that require substantial watering (e.g., lawns grown in arid areas).

Retain Large Contiguous or Connected Areas That Contain Critical Habitats

Large areas are often important to maintaining key organisms and ecosystem processes (e.g., Brown, 1978; Newmark, 1995). Habitats are places on the landscape that contain the unique set of physical and biological conditions necessary to support a species or guild. Thus, the features of a habitat must be interpreted in the context of the species or community that defines them. Habitat becomes critical to the survival of a species or population when it is rare or disconnected. Thus, this guideline derives from both the place and landscape principles. Size and connectivity of patches provide ecological benefits. The presence of animals in an area can be predicted by the size of their home range and their ability to cross gaps of inhospitable habitat. . . . However, habitat connectivity is not always a positive attribute for species and ecosystems. Land uses that serve as barriers to species' movement can have long-term negative effects on populations (e.g., Merriam et al., 1989); but, at the same time, corridors can facilitate the spread of nonnative species or diseases. (See the next guideline, below.) Additionally, habitats do not need to be in natural areas to provide benefits for wildlife. For example, golf courses in the southeastern United States often contain enough long-leaf pine (*Pinus palustris*) to provide habitat for the endangered Red-cockaded Woodpecker (*Pocoides borealis*).

Again, the importance of spatial connections depends on the priorities and elements of a situation. A first step in implementing the guideline is to examine the spatial connectivity of key habitats in an area, determining which patches are connected and whether the connectivity has a temporal component. Second, opportunities for connectivity must be promoted. Sometimes, those opportunities complement other planning needs. For instance, corridors along streams must be protected during timber extraction to provide benefits for aquatic species (Naiman and Décamps, 1997).

The term "connected" also should be defined in a manner specific to the situation. In some cases, two areas that are divided by a land-cover type may be artificially connected. For example, the habitat of panther (*Felis concolor coryi*) that is bisected by roads in Florida is now connected by tunnels under the highway (Foster and Humphrey, 1995). For other species, such as meadow voles (*Microtus pennsylvanicus*), roadside vegetation itself serves as a corridor between habitat sites (see Getz et al., 1978). In other cases, areas of similar habitat need not be directly adjacent but only need to be within the dispersal distance of the species of concern (e.g., migratory birds returning to nesting grounds [Robinson et al., 1995]). The connections provided by linear land-cover features, such as roads, may have both positive and negative effects (Forman and Alexander, 1998), and thus the broad-scale impacts of these features require careful consideration.

Minimize the Introduction and Spread of Nonnative Species

The species principle indicates that nonnative organisms often have negative effects on native species and the structure and functioning of ecological systems. Thus, land-use decisions must consider the potential for the introduction and spread of nonnative species. Land planning should consider vehicle movement along transportation routes, the planting of native species, and control of pets. For example, transportation routes have been very important in the spread of the spores of the pathogen *Phytophthora lateralis*, which kills Port Orford cedar (*Chamaecyparis lawsoniana*), an important timber species of southwestern Oregon (Harvey et al., 1985; Zobel et al., 1985). The USDA Forest Service has found that cleaning trucks or minimizing traffic during wet periods can dramatically reduce the transport of this pathogen between forests. Similarly, the spread of gypsy moth (*Lymantria dispar*) is correlated with overseas transportation of the eggs, larvae, and adults in the cargo holds of ships (Hofacker et al., 1993) or along roads when egg sacs are attached to vehicles (Sharov et al., 1997) or outdoor furniture. The great potential for vehicular transport of nonnative species was demonstrated by a case in which material was collected from the exterior surface of an automobile following a drive through central Europe; the collected matter represented 124 plant species and exhibited a high proportion of foreign propagules (Schmidt, 1989). The introduction of aquatic organisms transported incidentally with shipping traffic is a comparable example for aquatic ecosystems. Many of these introductions have had devastating effects. Waterways for shipping have impacts on the movement of introduced species not unlike those of roadways.

Often, growing native species reduces the need for planting nonnative species, particularly in urban, suburban, or other developed areas. The planted native species can then provide propagules that may disperse and establish. As an added benefit, the native species are adapted to the local conditions and frequently become established more readily and require less maintenance than nonnatives. Native species are also adapted to long-term variations in climate or disturbance regimes to which nonnative species often succumb. Terrestrial environmental conditions associated with native vegetation may also deter the spread of nonnatives. For example, in small forest islands interspersed among alien-dominated agroecosystems in Indiana, even the smallest forest remnants retained interior habitat conditions sufficient to resist invasion by the available nonnative plant species (Brothers and Spingharn, 1992). Introduced agricultural crops often result in less sustainable farming practices than does the use of native crops, as has been observed in the Brazilian Amazon (Soulé and Piper, 1992).

The control of pets is an essential aspect of reducing introductions. As suburbanization expands, one of the major effects on native fauna is the introduction of exotic pets. The mosquitofish (*Gambusia affinis*), swordtail (*Xiphophorus helleri*), and other species used as pets and then released into the wild have had a dramatic impact on the native fauna (Gamradt and Kats, 1996). In addition, cats (*Felis cattus*) kill birds and small mammals (Dunn and Tessaglia, 1994). In Australia, conservationists have worked with developers and the public to ban dogs from suburban development projects that contain koala habitat because dogs strongly contribute to koala mortality in developed areas.

Avoid or Compensate for Effects of Development on Ecological Processes

Negative impacts of development might be avoided or mitigated by some forethought. To do so, potential impacts need to be examined at the appropriate scale. At a fine scale, the design of a structure may interrupt regional processes. For example, dispersal patterns may be altered by a road, migrating birds may strike the reflective surfaces of a building, or fish may be entrained in a hydroelectric generator. At a broad scale, patterns of watershed processes may be altered, for example, by changing drainage patterns as part of the development.

Therefore, how proposed actions might affect other systems (or lands) should be examined. For example, landslides are generally site specific so that development of places with a high potential for landslides should be avoided. Also, human uses of the land should avoid structures and uses that might have a negative impact on other systems; at the very least, ways to compensate for those anticipated effects should be determined. It is useful to look for opportunities to design land use to benefit or enhance the ecological attributes of a region. For example, golf courses can be designed to serve as wildlife habitat (Terman,1997), or traffic in rural areas can be concentrated on fewer and more strategically placed roads, resulting in decreased traffic volumes and flows within the region as a whole and less impact on wildlife (Jaarsma, 1997).

Implement Land-Use and Land-Management Practices That Are Compatible with the Natural Potential of the Area

The place principle implies that local physical and biotic conditions affect ecological processes. Therefore, the natural potential for productivity and for nutrient and water cycling partially determine the appropriate land-use and land-management practices for a site. Land-use practices that fall within these limits are usually cost effective in terms of human resources and future costs caused by unwarranted changes on the land. Nevertheless, supplementing the natural resources of an area by adding nutrients through fertilization or water via irrigation is common. Even with such supplements, however, the natural limitations of the site must be recognized for cost-effective management. Implementing land-use and land-management practices that are compatible with the natural potential of the area requires that land managers have an understanding of the site potential. Traditional users of the land (e.g., native farmers) typically have a close relationship with the land. As farming and other resource extraction become larger and more intensive, the previous close association that managers had with the land is typically lost. Yet, land-management practices such as no-till farming reduce soil erosion or mitigate other resource losses. Often, however, land uses ignore site limitations or externalize site potential. For example, building shopping malls on prime agriculture land does not make the best use of the site potential. Also, establishing farms where irrigation is required or lawns where watering is necessary assumes that site constraints will be surmounted. Nevertheless, the land products are still limited by the natural potential of the site.

The Future: Predictions, Uncertainties, and Surprises

Land Use in a Future World

This paper began with a challenge for land use and management: to address the conflicting goals and desires for use of the land. To meet this challenge, ecological principles and their implications were identified, current processes for making land-use decisions were discussed, and guidelines were proposed for improving the process and for identifying the long-term effects on the landscape. Nevertheless, societies will continue to impose additional and increasingly complex impacts on the land. Environmental changes in the future will be driven by population growth and urbanization, economic expansion, resource consumption, technological development, and environmental attitudes and institutions (EPA, 1995; Naiman et al., 1998). Despite these pressures, further poorly planned land-use changes and their ecological consequences are not predestined or inevitable. Rather, policymakers will shape the future landscape, and scientists have a significant opportunity to help guide that process for the benefit of all creatures.

Predicting future patterns in land use requires knowledge of changing human demographics and patterns of resource consumption. For example, the aging of the U.S. population and the pending retirement surge among the baby-boom generation is likely to have a strong impact on patterns of settlement and recreation. The development of urban centers that will result from relocation patterns of humans should also be considered. Uncertainties abound regarding the future consumptive patterns and environmental attitudes of demographically influential segments of the population, and these uncertainties are likely to lead to surprises.

Patterns of our future landscapes will result not only from changes in land use but also from other broad-scale changes, especially those resulting from global warming (Santer et al., 1996). The implications of global climate change are profound for water availability, for the probability of natural-disturbance events such as fires or floods, and for the production of food and fiber (Watson et al., 1998). Because regional projections of climate change are uncertain, the implications of climate change for land-use patterns remain unclear. However, planning for future land uses should not be conducted under the assumption that today's climate and environmental conditions will persist, unaltered, into the future. The likelihood of substantial environmental changes should be considered in alternative future scenarios; lack of attention to such changes may result in land uses that are incompatible with future environmental conditions (e.g., increased density of residential development in locations where fire frequency will increase). In turn, patterns of land cover and the degree of fragmentation of natural habitats will influence the ability of ecological systems to respond to a changing climate. The interactions between land-use patterns and climate change are complex (Dale, 1997).

Emerging Technologies That May Change Land-Use and Land-Use Management Practices or Moderate Deleterious Effects

Examination of recent history provides many examples of how the emergence of new technologies has profoundly affected societal use of the landscape (Headrick, 1990). Inventions, such as powerful water pumps, labor-saving machinery, and the development of herbicides and pesticides, have fundamentally altered agriculture and forestry; construction of highways and river locks have forever altered the transportation and use of essential goods; and medical advances have reshaped the age structure and size of human populations. New technologies continue to emerge, and some will have strong influences either on the distribution of human populations or on land use. . . .

Telecommunications and the virtual office: Recent and emerging advances in telecommunications promise to change the way business is conducted and thereby influence patterns of human settlement. The spatial dispersion of human settlement will likely increase as proximity to urban centers or corporate offices becomes less critical. Professionals conducting business via electronic mail or the Internet may choose to live farther from urban centers on relatively larger home sites. Road density of rural areas and ownership of 1- to 3-ha parcels will likely increase, which could exacerbate (1) nonpoint-source erosion and nutrient pollution from intensive land use by domestic animals (horses, cattle, and sheep) and (2) the introduction of nonnative species. Exact patterns and uses are difficult to predict, but it is likely that widespread implementation of new telecommunication technologies will affect land patterns and uses. . . .

Technologies are already available to improve substantially the efficiencies of water and energy use with concomitant impacts on the land (McKinney and Schoch, 1996). In the United States, where agriculture is a large user of water, microirrigation is slowly gaining a foothold, especially in western regions where water is limited and the environmental costs of food production are high. In addition, conservation advances in personal water use include low-flush toilets, low-volume shower heads, and home landscaping designed for the climate. Collectively, these technological changes, along with behavioral adjustments, indicate that water-use impacts on the land will be different in the future.

Making Sustained Progress

Much progress has been made in managing land in ecologically sustainable ways. Often, these gains are made as a result of past mistakes. For example, in the aftermath of the Dust Bowl in the Great Plains of the United States, crops more compatible with site conditions were grown, and trees were planted in rows to provide windbreaks. Even so, as the memory of the Dust Bowl faded, unsustainable land-management practices returned, and more soil has been lost in recent dust storms.

Instead of just learning from past mistakes at a site, it is possible to synthesize the lessons from ecological science that relate to land use. This paper presents ecological principles relevant to land use and management and develops them into guidelines for use of the land. However, more actions are needed before ecologically based land management is broadly implemented. These guidelines must be translated to particular land uses. This translation can be done, for example, by using the principles and guidelines to shape municipal ordinances for land use practices. In addition, the guidelines can provide the basis for specifying and understanding ecological concerns relevant to the needs of specific types of land users, such as farmers or foresters.

Another important step in this process is to set scientifically based priorities for developing the ecological science necessary to meet the needs of land-use management. Unfortunately, the priorities are lacking at present. Other fields in environmental and human sciences have set priorities that have helped to shape their disciplines (Lubchenco et al., 1991; NRC, 1994; Naiman et al., 1995). It is important that ecologists, land planners, and decision makers (1) define priorities to sustain progress in developing the science needed by land managers and (2) revise them on a regular basis to reaffirm that these priorities are still valid. Therefore, we propose five actions to develop the science that is needed by land managers:

1) Apply ecological principles to land use and land management.
2) Explore ecological interactions in both pristine and heavily used areas.
3) Develop spatially explicit models that integrate social, economic, political, and ecological land-use issues.
4) Improve the use and interpretation of in situ and remotely sensed data to better understand and predict environmental changes and to monitor the environment.
5) Communicate relevant ecological science to users (which includes land owners and the general public). . . .

. . . Researchers and policy analysts recognize that most land-management decisions currently have little relation to ecological science, being influenced more strongly by economics, values, traditions, politics, and other factors. If ecological science is to guide land use and land management and to have a positive impact on resources and people, it must be clearly and reliably communicated. This requires scientists to identify relevant scientific issues and explain the importance of those issues within the decision-making process.

References

Note: The published works referenced in this essay are very rich but too extensive to be presented here entirely (222 articles). As such, I present those written by Dale and her team that were referenced in this essay and direct the reader to their article in *Ecological Applications* 10, no. 3 (2000), 639–670, for a complete reference list.

Bilby, Robert E., and Peter A. Bisson. "Function and Distribution of Large Woody Debris." In *River Ecology and Management*, edited by R. J. Naimand and R. E. Bilby, 324–46. New York: Springer-Verlag, 1998.

Dale, Virginia H., A. E. Lugo, J. A. MacMahon, and S. T. A. Pickett. "Management Implications of Large, Infrequent Disturbances." *Ecosystem* 1 (1998): 546–57.

Dale, Virginia H., L. K. Mann, R. J. Olson, D. W. Johnson, and K. C. Dearstone. "The Long-Term Influence of Past Land Use on the Walker Branch Forest." *Landscape Ecology* 4, no. 4 (1990): 211–24.

Dale, Virginia H., Robert V. O'Neill, Marcos Pedlowski, and F. Soutworth. "Causes and Effects of Land-Use Change in Central Rondônia, Brazil." *Photogrammetric Engineering and Remote Sensing* 59, no. 6 (1993): 997–1005.

Dale, Virginia H., Robert V. O'Neill, Frank Southworth, and Marcos Pedlowski. "Modeling Effects of Land Management in the Brazilian Amazonian settlement of Rondônia." *Conservation Biology* 8, no. 1 (1994): 196–206.

Dale, Virginia H., Scott M. Pearson, Holly L. Offerman, and Robert V. O'Neill. "Relating Patterns of Land-Use Change to Faunal Biodiversity in the Central Amazon." *Conservation Biology* 8, no. 4 (1994): 1027–36.

DeFerrari, Collette M., and Robert J. Naiman. "A Multi Scale Assessment of the Occurrence of Exotic Plants on the Olympic Peninsula, Washington." *Journal of Vegetation Science* 5, no. 2 (1994): 247–58.

Gardner, Robert H., Robert V. O'Neill, Monica G. Turner, and Virginia H. Dale. "Quantifying Scale-Dependent Effects of Animal Movement with Simple Percolation Models." *Landscape Ecology* 3, no. 3–4 (1989): 217–28.

Haeuber, Richard A., and William K. Michener. "Policy Implications of Recent Natural and Managed Floods." *BioScience* 48, no. 9 (1998): 765–72.

Lee, Robert G., Richard Flamm, Monica G. Turner, Carolyn Bledsoe, Paul Chandler, Collette DeFerrari, Robin Gottfried, Robert J. Naiman, Nathan Schumaker, and David Wear. "Integrating Sustainable Development and Environmental Vitality: A Landscape Ecology Approach." In *Watershed Management*, edited by Robert J. Naiman, 499–521. New York: Springer-Verlag, 1992.

Mann, Linda K., Anthony W. King, Virginia H. Dale, William W. Hargrove, Robert Washington-Allen, Larry R. Pounds, and Tom L. Ashwood. "The Role of Soil Classification in GIS Modeling of Habitat Pattern: Threatened Calcareous Ecosystems." *Ecosystems* 2, no. 6 (1999): 524–38.

Naiman, Robert J., and Henri Décamps. "The Ecology of Interfaces: Riparian Zones." *Annual Review of Ecology and Systematics* 28 (1997): 621–58.

Naiman, Robert J., D. M. McKnight, and J. A. Stanford. *The Freshwater Imperative: A Research Agenda*. Washington, DC: Island Press, 1995.

Naiman, Robert J., and Kevin H. Rogers. "Large Animals and System-Level Characteristics in River Corridors." *BioScience* 47, no. 8 (1997): 521–29.

Pearson, Scott M., Monica G. Turner, Robert H. Gardner, and Robert V. O'Neill. "An Organism-Based Perspective of Habitat Fragmentation." In *Biodiversity in Managed Landscapes: Theory and Practice*, edited by R. C. Szaro, 77–95. New York: Oxford University Press, 1996.

Richards, John F., and Elizabeth P. Flint. "A Century of Land-Use Change in South and Southeast Asia." In *Effects of Land-Use Change on Atmospheric CO_2 Concentrations*, edited by Virginia Dale, 15–66. New York: Springer-Verlag, 1994.

Riebsame, W. E., W. J. Parton, K. A. Galvin, I. C. Burke, L. Bohren, R. Young, and E. Knop. "Integrated Modeling of Land Use and Cover Change." *BioScience* 44, no. 5 (1994): 350–56.

Saunders, Denis A., Richard J. Hobbs, and Chris R. Margules. "Biological Consequences of Ecosystem Fragmentation: A Review." *Conservation Biology* 5, no. 1 (1991): 18–32.

Southworth, F., Virginia H. Dale, and R. V. O'Neill. "Contrasting Patterns of Land Use in Rondonia, Brazil: Simulating the Effects on Carbon Release." *International Social Science Journal* 43, no. 4 (1991): 681–98.

Turner, Monica G. *Landscape Heterogeneity and Disturbance*. New York: Springer-Verlag, 1987.

———. "Landscape Ecology: The Effect of Pattern on Process." *Annual Review of Ecology and Systematics* 20 (1989): 171–97.

Turner, Monica G., Virginia H. Dale, and Edwin H. Everham. "Fires, Hurricanes, and Volcanoes: Comparing Large Disturbances." *BioScience* 47, no. 11 (1997): 758–68.

Turner, Monica G., Robert H. Gardner, and Robert V. O'Neill. "Ecological Dynamics at Broad Scales." *BioScience* 45 (1995): S29–S35.

Turner, Monica G., William W. Hargrove, Robert H. Gardner, and William H. Romme. "Effects of Fire on Landscape Heterogeneity in Yellowstone National Park, Wyoming." *Journal of Vegetation Science* 5, no. 5 (1994): 731–42.

Turner, Monica G., William H. Romme, Robert H. Gardner, and William W. Hargrove. "Effects of Patch Size and Fire Pattern on Early Post-Fire Succession on Yellowstone National Park." *Ecological Monographs* 67, no. 4 (1997): 411–33.

Turner, Monica G., David N. Wear, and Richard O. Flamm. "Land Ownership and Land-Cover Change in the Southern Appalachian Highlands and the Olympic Peninsula." *Ecological Applications* 6, no. 4 (1996): 1150–72.

Valone, Thomas J., and James H. Brown. "Effects of Competition, Colonization, and Extinction on Rodent Species Diversity." *Science* 267 (1995): 880–83.

Wear, David N., Monica G. Turner, and Richard O. Flamm. "Ecosystem Management with Multiple Owners: Landscape Dynamics in a Southern Appalachian Watershed." *Ecological Applications* 6 (1996): 1173–88.

Basic Principles for Molding Land Mosaics

Urban Regions: Ecology and Planning Beyond the City (2008)

Richard T. T. Forman

An artist can translate a compelling inspiration into a painting or object that inspires the public, and even pleases the artist. In addition to inspiration and materials, skill is a key to success. Skill might be thought of as a set of principles, knowing what works and what doesn't—color mixtures, composition, types of lines, and much more. The artist has a palette of principles. When mixed with imagination and experimentation, they greatly increase the chance of a successful or inspiring result.

If one were designing wheels, using the known principles of wheel design greatly decreases the chance of producing square, oval, or one-spoked wheels. No matter how beautiful or well-made they are, such wheels do not work. If the land or an urban region is being planned or changed, we do not start from scratch. We use principles, subconsciously or specified. Water flows downward so streams are not designed flowing to hilltops. Trees require oxygen for their roots so we do not plant trees in water. People need security when asleep at night, so they are surrounded by shelter. Using known principles helps protect society from poor quality, and unethical, work.

Rather than simply ideas or hypotheses or even concepts, principles can be thought of as solid rigorous guidelines, a basis or foundation for planning and action. They do not apply everywhere anytime as we expect a universal law to do, but the often-considerable direct or indirect evidence supporting them is a basis for their widespread application (Dramstad et al., 1996; Forman, 2004a).

Principles alone, however, lead to generic solutions. Monotonous, out-of-date, or lack-of-creativity might describe designs and plans using only principles on our palette. Instead, as for the artist whom we so admire, principles are mixed with imagination and inspiration to produce solutions for the land. Results are both dependable and creative.

This chapter is a palette or treasure chest of principles. All deal with land use, most with nature and people, and many with urban regions. They are not to be blindly followed. If your guidebook says that bears avoid the habitat type you are in and you see a bear moving rapidly toward you, it is wise to think beyond the guideline. Principles are to be creatively and intelligently used.

The bear example emphasizes that planning or action is also based on characteristics of the land. Land is not a blank canvas or a homogenous space. Spatial patterns, as well as flows and movements across them, are always present. The big challenge, and opportunity, is the integration of those existing land patterns with both principles and creativity. The goal is to improve the pattern and set of flows, and have improvements continue into the future.

Thus a set of *principles* useful for land-use planning and derived from a range of fields is presented. Overall these are statements of importance, of wide applicability, and with predictive ability. All have at least some empirical evidence, fit with indirect lines of evidence, and in some cases also have a known theoretical basis. Other scholars and planners, of course, would pinpoint a somewhat different list, including additional points. Indeed the reader can doubtless add to the list. Nevertheless, the bulk of the principles here seem to represent a consensus within each of the fields represented. Cutting-edge hypotheses and results are absent, as are narrowly focused principles with limited applicability. As always, both ongoing research and special attributes in a region dictate caution in applying or extrapolating a principle.

Not surprisingly, with a focus on natural systems and their uses in a region, landscape ecology is a particularly important contributor to the list. Yet principles are also drawn from transportation, community development, economics, conservation biology, water resources, and other fields.

Principles are conveniently placed into five broad categories, though clearly much overlap exists among the categories: (1) patch sizes, edges, and habitats; (2) natural processes, corridors, and networks; (3) transportation modes; (4) communities and development; and (5) land mosaics and landscape change.

Patch Sizes, Edges, and Habitats

Principles in this first category focus on spatial pattern or structure of the land, especially relative to nature or greenspace. Consistent with the basic idea of nature conservation as a priority for society, rather than attempting to protect each species, the emphasis is on landscape patterns. The list of principles leans heavily on those presented in Schonewald-Cox and Bayless (1986), Salvesen (1994), Forman (1995, 2004a), Dramstad et al. (1996), Mitsch and Gosselink (2000), Farina (2005), Dale and Haeuber (2001), Opdam et al. (2002), Gutzwiller (2002), France (2003), Lindenmayer and Burgman (2005), Groom et al. (2006), Wiens and Moss (2005), Perlman and Milder (2005), Fischer et al. (2006), and Lindenmayer and Fischer (2006). . . .

These principles are listed in four groupings: (1) patch size and edge; (2) natural habitats for conservation; (3) species-focused conservation; and (4) wetlands.

Patch Size and Edge

(A) *Large-patch benefits.* Large patches of natural vegetation are the only structures in a landscape that protect aquifers and interconnected stream networks, sustain viable populations of many interior species, provide core habitat and escape cover for most large-home-range vertebrates, and support near-natural disturbance regimes and plants dependent on them.

(B) *Edge width of a natural community.* Edge width, which largely results from penetration of wind, solar energy, and human influence into a natural community, is the distance with significant effects on sensitive ecological variables, such as desiccation, seedling mortality, herbaceous species, and upper soil layer conditions.

(C) *Edge and interior species.* A more convoluted natural-vegetation patch, or one that has been subdivided into two smaller patches, will have a higher proportion of edge habitat with slightly more generalist edge species, but will contain significantly fewer and smaller populations of interior species, including those of conservation importance.

(D) *Small-patch benefits.* Small natural-vegetation patches scattered across a less-suitable matrix act as stepping stones enhancing the movement of some species, provide some protection for widely scattered uncommon species, and, if near a large patch, may enhance species richness and movement associated with the large patch.

(E) *Populations in small patches.* Small patches, especially if isolated, tend to have smaller populations which fluctuate more over time, more inbreeding and resulting genetic deficiencies, and therefore a greater chance of local extinction or disappearance.

(F) *Human impacts and protected areas.* Closing spur roads and roads that bisect the interior of a large protected patch, and concentrating recreational opportunities and facilities for people in the edge portion of a protected area are effective ways to protect resources, especially in the interior of a large protected patch.

(G) *Boundary characteristics.* Boundaries or edges of a habitat, including their three-dimensional structure, distinctive microclimate and soil, and high vegetational density and species richness, affect adjacent habitats by functioning as a source of effects and as a filter of movements between the habitats.

(H) *Degradation of a natural community or ecosystem.* Degradation by human activity reduces vertical and horizontal structure, such as foliage layers, tree holes, vegetation gradients, and soil horizons, and reduces functional interactions and flows, including food webs, water flows, and mineral nutrient cycles.

Natural Habitats for Conservation

(A) *Number of large patches.* Consistent with risk-spreading theory, if each large patch of a particular habitat type contains almost all of its characteristic species in a landscape, then two or three large patches are probably sufficient to sustain almost all the species, but if each patch has a limited portion of the characteristic species present, four or five large patches are probably required.

(B) *Especially valuable patches.* Natural vegetation patches that play a particularly important role in the overall system (such as a key link in the landscape pattern), or contain unusual or distinctive characteristics (such as an important aquifer or rare habitat), are especially valuable for minimizing degradation.

(C) *Economically productive areas.* Remnant natural habitats in particularly productive areas especially merit habitat expansion, because they tend to be rare and to contain many rare species that thrive on the rich environmental conditions.

(D) *Habitat diversity.* Increasing the number of habitat types, primarily by including more substrate and microclimatic conditions or secondarily by maintaining more successional stages (e.g., fallow fields, shrubby areas), increases the number of native species present.

(E) *Tree holes and dead wood.* Dead wood, both standing and fallen, and cavities in tree trunks tend to be scarce in built areas, yet are especially important for biodiversity benefits.

(F) *Rare and representative habitats.* By protecting reasonable numbers and sizes of rare and representative habitats, nature (including the bulk of the native species present) should persist long term.

(G) *A small isolated habitat.* To protect a small isolated habitat long term typically requires the presence of an important role played by the habitat within a larger landscape pattern, and may also require widespread public recognition.

(H) *Ecology, cost, and threat.* Successful long-term land protection particularly focuses on location of the land relative to other protected lands, plus three characteristics subject to rapid change: (1) present ecological attributes of the land; (2) land cost and subsequent management cost; and (3) threats (urgency) to the land.

Species-Focused Conservation

(A) *Species of small isolated habitats*. To provide some long-term protection for species of dispersed small distinct habitats requires protection of extensive heterogeneous areas, or of numerous small sites, or of several large patches with enough connections across the landscape that most species distributions will be included in the large patches.

(B) *Species "perception" and conservation priority*. Animals and plants "perceive" and respond to different-sized structures and patterns, and thus successful conservation focuses on species especially sensitive to large structures and patterns, which are most likely to be lost or degraded by human activities in the landscape.

(C) *Keystone species*. Landscape patterns that protect keystone species (those with disproportionately large effect on ecosystem function relative to their abundance or biomass), particularly predators, are likely to be especially effective in protecting biodiversity.

(D) *Species extinction proneness*. A landscape pattern that enhances the following species types—low mobility animal, large body size, low reproductive rate, top of food chain, large home-range size, hunted species, small population size, habitat specialist, and strong dependence on another species—reduces the chance of species loss.

(E) *Invasive species*. If an invasive non-native or feral species degrades a natural habitat, and ecological succession and other natural processes are unlikely to be an effective control, then carefully researched human control of the species is normally appropriate to restore the habitat.

Wetlands

(A) *Hydrologic functions of wetlands*. When not "full" of water, wetlands act as sponges slowing down and absorbing water flows, and then slowly releasing water through evaporation to air, percolation into ground, and runoff into surface water-bodies, that effectively reduces downstream peak flows and flooding (figure 4-8).

(B) *Pollutants and wetlands*. Particulate pollutants settle out in wetlands, dissolved substances are absorbed by plant roots, diverse pollutants are filtered as water moves through soil, and some pollutants are broken down by microorganisms, that together results in cleaner water flowing out of a wetland.

(C) *Plants in wetlands*. Because the water table level is close to the irregular

Figure 4-8 Tidal wetland and river spanned by multilane highway bridge that facilitates wildlife and floodwater passage (Forman, 2008, Reproduced with permission of Cambridge University Press, Redrawn by Yuan Ren, 2014).

soil surface in a wetland, considerable spatial microheterogeneity and temporal change in water conditions are the norm, often producing a high diversity and biomass of adaptable, seasonally changing species.

(D) *Wetland complexes.* A connected cluster or complex of wetlands normally provides the highest wetland biodiversity and stability.

(E) *Ephemeral ponds.* Ephemeral ponds (or vernal pools) which dry out for a period most years often contain a concentration of both rare plants that thrive with alternating inundation and dry soil, and rare animals which either burrow deeply into the soil during dry periods, or seasonally migrate some distance from and to the pond.

(F) *Wetland surroundings.* Natural vegetation surrounding a wetland or ephemeral pond reduces sediment and other pollutant inputs, and is intensively used by many wetland animals, which also tend to move longer distances in the direction of other wetlands and suitable habitat.

(G) *Wetland restoration and creation.* Restoration is typically more successful than wetland creation, and establishing the right hydrologic conditions and flows is normally more important for the formation and stability of wetlands than are soil conditions and vegetation, that will develop naturally over time.

(H) *Wetland as pollutant filter.* Wetlands tend to be effective filters for waterborne suspended sediment, phosphorus, and biological-oxygen-demand (BOD), but less so for bacteria and nitrogen, unless the water flows a long distance through a wetland.

(I) *Rare species in wetlands.* Because wetland removal by drainage and filling has been so pervasive in urban regions, the wetlands remaining typically have among the highest concentrations of rare species in the region.

Natural Processes, Corridors, and Networks

This second set of principles emphasizes function, the flows and movements across space, that in effect describes how the land or region works. Natural systems are the focus. The following references are especially useful for these principles: Forman (1995, 2004a), Dramstad et al. (1996), Harris et al. (1996), Ludwig et al. (1997), Beier and Noss (1998), Burel and Baudry (1999), Bennett (2003), Turner et al. (2001), Wiens (2002), Groom et al. (2006), Lindenmayer and Burgman (2005), Hilty et al. (2006), and Lindenmayer and Fischer (2006). . . .

Four groupings of principles are present: (1) natural processes and species movement; (2) water flows; (3) natural corridors and the matrix; and (4) natural networks.

Natural Processes and Species Movement

(A) *Form and function.* Compact forms effectively conserve internal resources, convoluted forms enhance interactions with the surroundings, and network forms serve as an internal transport system, so that a natural vegetation patch with a rounded core, some curvilinear boundaries, and a few long lobes or attached corridors provides a range of ecological benefits.

(B) *Interactions between patches.* Species interactions (movements) are greatest between a small patch or site and its adjacent land uses, somewhat lower with nearby patches of the same type, and lowest with distant patches of a different type.

(C) *Metapopulation arrangement.* Human activities in the urban region often subdivide a large natural population into spatially separate small populations with few individuals moving among them (a metapopulation), in which case a few large natural patches, each surrounded by small patches, is an excellent design for sustaining metapopulations.

(D) *Metapopulation dynamics.* Species disperse outward from a large patch, providing genetic variation and reducing local extinction in nearby small patches, whereas species that disappear from a small patch are less likely to return or recolonize, if the patch is isolated or surrounded by an inhospitable matrix.

(E) *Movement among small patches.* For a species that inhabits and moves among a few small patches, loss of a patch tends to reduce population size, movement, and stability.

(F) *Straight and convoluted boundaries.* A straight boundary tends to have more species movement along it, whereas a convoluted boundary with lobes and coves provides diverse wildlife habitat and facilitates boundary crossing between adjacent habitats.

Water Flows

(A) *Surface runoff.* Rainwater washing surfaces and soils of a land mosaic carries dissolved chemicals, erodes surface particles containing chemicals, and rapidly flows as stormwater into and along channels to cause a pulse of flooding, and to deposit its contents in gullies, streams, lakes, and other water-bodies. . . .

(B) *Groundwater flows.* Surfacewater carries dissolved chemicals down into the ground where they may accumulate and contaminate the typically slow-moving water of an aquifer, or groundwater may be partially cleaned by flowing through soil or wetlands to water bodies on the surface such as streams and lakes.

(C) *Stream corridor.* A ("blue-green") ribbon of dense natural vegetation that covers the floodplain, both hillslopes, and a strip of interior habitat on both adjoining upland areas will normally provide protection against erosion, dissolved mineral nutrients, and toxic chemicals from the matrix, especially if the vegetation widens to surround entering intermittent channels.

(D) *Vegetation along small channels.* Vegetation protecting intermittent channels and small (first-order) streams is especially important for minimizing downstream peak flows and flooding.

(E) *Floodplain or riparian vegetation.* Dense floodplain vegetation, especially shrub cover, provides friction to reduce downstream flooding, provides shade, dead leaves and wood to enhance fish and other aquatic organisms, and increases the rich floodplain habitat diversity of wetland depressions, streambanks, sandy ridges, and surface microheterogeneity.

(F) *River-ladder pattern.* A "river ladder" to protect rivers has vegetation strips along both sides of a floodplain to facilitate wildlife movement and protect hillslopes and adjacent upland, plus a sequence of large vegetation patches crossing the floodplain that reduce flooding, trap sediment, contribute wood for downriver fish habitat, provide organic matter for aquatic food chains, and maintain diverse habitats with rare floodplain species.

(G) *Drainage basin and stream corridor.* The hydrologic, physical, chemical, and biological characteristics of a stream/river can be modified or mitigated by the riparian or stream corridor, but are much more affected and effectively managed by the types and spatial arrangement of land use across the watershed or drainage basin.

(H) *Aquifer water.* Aquifer groundwater, which (except in limestone areas) moves very slowly and has little capacity to remove pollutants, is mainly kept clean by a complete cover of natural vegetation, particularly over its upslope portion.

Natural Corridors and the Matrix

(A) *Corridor functions and their control.* Width and connectivity are the primary controls on all five key roles or functions of natural-vegetation strips or corridors, i.e., conduit, filter (or barrier), source, sink, and habitat.

(B) *Small patches attached to corridors.* Small patches attached to natural corridors and networks provide "rest stops" for wildlife movement that, especially on long routes, typically increase the chance of a species reaching a destination.

(C) *Gap in a corridor.* The ability of an animal moving along a natural-vegetation corridor to cross a gap or break in the corridor especially improves as gap length relative to the spatial scale of species movement shortens, and with more suitable conditions in and around the gap.

(D) *Stepping stones between large patches.* For species movement between two large natural patches, a row of stepping stones (small patches) or a poor-quality corridor is normally better than no corridor, but a cluster of stepping stones with an overall linear alignment provides alternative routes and is likely to be more effective.

(E) *Habitat contrast.* Greater habitat contrast or difference between a patch and a corridor or matrix decreases movement of species between the patch and an adjoining corridor or matrix, and hence across a landscape.

(F) *Matrix heterogeneity.* Microhabitat heterogeneity increases the total species pool of the matrix and its role as a source of species, and if heterogeneity is arranged as a (gradual) gradient, rather than being patchy, species movement is either greater or less depending on gradient orientation relative to direction of movement.

Natural Networks

(A) *Major natural-vegetation network.* The primary network (emerald network) of large natural patches and connecting corridors helps maintain distinct sections across a landscape, preventing coalescence of development and promoting a sense of community, local culture, and care for the land.

(B) *Loops in a network.* Loops or circuits in a network provide alternative routes for movement, thus reducing the effects of gaps and less suitable spots, and increasing the chance of successfully reaching a destination.

(C) *Landscape connectivity.* Most species evolved in highly connected heterogeneous natural landscapes, have had relatively little time to adapt to human fragmented ones, and occur in greater numbers (species richness) in more connected areas.

(D) *Species dispersal.* Since species disperse different distances and directions, a natural corridor and patch network with a relatively high average number of linkages per patch provides good dispersal opportunities which enhance the persistence of most species.

Transportation Modes

This third set of principles involves highways and roads, commuter-rail lines, and walking. Transportation is a core spatial attribute and plays a major functional role in the urban region. It is a key factor in economic investment and development, as well as natural systems and their use. The following references are particularly useful for the principles here: National Research Council (1997), Warren (1998), Cervero (1998), Forman and Alexander (1998), Forman and Deblinger (2000), Ravetz (2000), Bullard et al. (2000), Simmonds and Hack (2000), Calthorpe and Fulton (2001), AASHTO (2001), Benfield et al. (2001), Willis et al. (2001), Forman et al. (2003), Forman (2004b), Dittmar and Ohland (2004), Handy (2005), Erickson (2006), Forman (2006), and Moore (2007). . . .

Four groupings are addressed: (a) highways; (b) commuter-rail lines and communities; (c) roads in communities; and (d) walking and park systems.

Highways

(A) *Highway as source of effects.* Wider and especially busier highways, as concentrated linear sources of ecological effects, increasingly alter local hydrology, wetlands and streams, block animal movement across the landscape, subdivide natural populations into smaller populations, road-kill animals, and disperse air pollutants into the environment. . . .

(B) *Degradation zones by highway.* Increased vehicular traffic on highways creates wider adjacent zones of degraded animal communities (presumably due to traffic noise), wider highways generally (often with more traffic) are greater sources of non-native species, eroded earth material, stormwater contaminants, and atmospheric pollutants.

(C) *Highway protection* of *the matrix*. A more concentrated, safe, and efficient transportation system to access resources, homes, and other human land uses is valuable for reducing dispersed human impacts on nature and natural systems across the landscape.

(D) *Highway network*. Busier and wider highway corridors increasingly reduce landscape connectivity and subdivide an urban region into sections, with a mesh size normally suitable for relatively separate small populations of large animals.

(E) *Perforated highway corridor*. Increasingly perforating a transportation corridor with passages, from tiny wildlife tunnels to culverts, underpasses, and overpasses, reduces habitat fragmentation by providing for relatively natural movements and flows of wildlife and water.

(F) *Closing roads*. Progressively closing spur roads and low-usage roads in and by medium-to-large natural patches is an especially effective way to create large natural patches and their many important benefits for nature and society.

(G) *Adding radial-route capacity*. Adding transportation capacity on a city's radial route stimulates growth and development in that direction.

(H) *Adding a ring road*. Adding an outer ring road provides flexibility in movement for suburban (peri-urban) residents and catalyzes growth and development over a broad outward zone.

(I) *Trucking center*. A truck (lorry) transportation terminal near the metro-area border facilitates the transfer of manufactured goods and agricultural products for long-distance trucks, as well as small-truck movement serving local farms, industries, markets and restaurants, in effect providing economic efficiency and better traffic flows on congested urban streets.

Commuter-Rail Lines and Communities

(A) *Commuter rail lines*. Light or heavy rail lines and streetcars/trollies that extend outward, offering convenient service beyond the metro area, provide greater modal (transportation types) flexibility for suburban residents and help limit vehicular traffic.

(B) *Transit-oriented development*. TOD that meshes mixed-use residential-shopping areas with local natural ecosystems within 800 m (half-mile) of a station on a commuter transit line has a higher proportion of people commuting to work on public transport, and also may have more walking, bicycling, and local shopping, a tighter community, and a greater sense of place by residents.

Roads in Communities

(A) *Traffic calming*. Traffic-calming techniques that slow vehicle movement increasingly provide safer, more convenient walking opportunities for children and the elderly, and enhance a sense of community in neighborhoods.

(B) *Accessibility and local spaces.* Road infrastructure which effectively provides for both accessibility and local community spaces and private spaces successfully addresses both broader social goals and narrower neighborhood and individual goals.

Walking and Park Systems

(A) *Park system.* Providing routes for movement of people and/or species among parks changes a group of parks into a park system, with consequent benefits to both nature and people.

(B) *Greenspaces and neighborhoods.* An effective urban park system has greenspaces conveniently walkable for residents of all neighborhoods.

(C) *Sustainable park system.* To establish a sustainable park system, each park and each connection is important, and both government and the public understand how the interdependent pieces fit together to work as a whole.

Communities and Development

In this fourth area of principles, the focus is a community, an aggregation of interacting residents in a city, town, or village. Development emphasizes the spread of built areas, including economic investment across the land. Both communities in place and the process of development strongly interact with natural systems. In contrast to the preceding section on human movement patterns, the social and economic focus here is where people live.

Principles here are largely extracted from Yaro et al. (1990), Sukopp and Hejny (1990), Bartuska (1994), Campbell (1996), Seddon (1997), Warren (1998), Donahue (1999), Atkinson et al. (1999), Ravetz (2000), Beatley (2000), Jacobi et al. (2000), Warner (2001), Willis et al. (2001), Macionis and Parillo (2001), Benfield et al. (2001), Peiser (2001), White (2002), Grimm et al. (2003), LeGates and Stout (2003), Campbell and Fainstein (2003), Nassauer (2005), Handy (2005), Kellert (2005), Hersperger (2006), Clark (2006), Moore (2007), and Robert Yaro (personal communication). The emphasis is much more on land planning than on management of existing land (Atkinson et al., 1999; Willis et al., 2001; White, 2002). . . .

Three subgroupings are useful for this topic: (a) locating development; (b) environment and community; and (c) social dimensions and sense of community.

Locating Development

(A) *Development and low-ecological-value areas.* Guiding potential growth and development to areas of low ecological value is a major step in protecting and sustaining natural systems.

(B) *Concentrating or dispersing development.* Concentrating rather than dispersing development greatly increases the protection of natural systems and reduces the dependence on transportation infrastructure and vehicular usage. . . .

(C) *Coalescence of communities.* Preventing the coalescence of adjoining communities, e.g., with greenspace strips, helps maintain the identity and distinctiveness of each community.

(D) *Mixed-use communities.* Intermixing residential, commercial, and light-industry areas in sections of a community reduces vehicular travel, but causes more nearby land-use conflicts than in single-use communities.

(E) *Edge nodes of industry and employment.* Concentrating light industry (and sometimes medium industry) in nodes on the edge of residential/commercial towns and small cities helps reduce both vehicular travel and land-use conflicts.

(F) *Heavy industry centers.* Aggregating compatible heavy industries on a site with efficient water, power, and waste-disposal plus convenient public transport for nearby employees, away from major rivers/streams, and downwind of population centers and valuable nature, minimizes environmental problems and maximizes benefits.

(G) *Land prices.* Overall, land prices decrease with distance from a city's central business district, a pattern mainly modified by geomorphology and by major nodes of public or private investment.

(H) *Radial transportation corridors.* Radial transportation corridors are major catalysts of commercial and residential expansion, either directly as strip development, or indirectly as nodal growth along a transportation corridor begins, elongates, and coalesces.

(I) *Strategic position.* The strategic position of a community conveys a commercial or other advantage over other places, though in time any advantage reflects the balance of changes in the community relative to those elsewhere.

(J) *Hazardous areas.* Establishing protected natural lands on high-hazard-risk areas helps avoid the social and economic disruptions of community "disasters."

(K) *Compact development.* Compact development enriches the sphere of an individual's social, cultural, employment, and other opportunities in a small area, reducing vehicular travel, and providing economic support for public transport and walking/biking paths.

(L) *Development density.* Residential development at sufficient density helps support public transport conveniently accessible for both residential and employment locations.

(M) *Geometry of a node (πr^2 problem).* Since area is scarce around the center of a circle and increases rapidly moving outward, a land price gradient tends to produce concentric land-use zones, which may be broken by convenient transportation radii and planned slices or nodes of different land use.

(N) *Infill.* Infill development on greenspaces in a built area is often beneficial for creating compact neighborhoods, but only up to the point where quality parks are too far apart for most residents to walk, and stepping stones too far apart for effective species movement across the built area.

Environment and Community

(A) *Metabolism/ecosystem/machine analogy.* Using the structure and flows of an organism, ecosystem, or machine to understand a city emphasizes the importance of limited diverse inputs and outputs, and maintaining a diverse, but not too complex, structure within the city, both of which provide stability and adaptability for the inevitable big surprises ahead.

(B) *Human–environment relationships.* In addition to social needs and economic opportunity, human–environment relationships are at the core of a community and are sustained by an effective mix of greenspaces, built areas, infrastructure, and institutions.

(C) *Environmental management.* Management of urban environmental resources and problems that places short-term crisis-prevention measures as part of long-term solutions for a larger potential future community is likely to save costs, maintain public support, and establish a more sustainable future.

(D) *Impermeable surfaces.* Limiting the amount of impermeable-surface area, especially in suburbs, reduces rapid-runoff peak-flow flooding, recharges groundwater, reduces pollutant levels reaching water bodies, and improves local streams and fish populations.

(E) *Drainage connection.* Drainage connection area (impermeable surface directly connected by pipes or ditches to water bodies) is reduced by channeling stormwater into vegetated depressions and drainage basins, which help reduce flooding, filter water pollutants through the soil, and improve water quality and fish populations in water bodies.

(F) *Wetland uses.* Multi-use wetlands with adequate water flow and attractive paths or boardwalks help provide recreation, biodiversity, aesthetics, flood control, and pollutant absorption, and can separate or center neighborhoods.

Social Dimensions and Sense of Community

(A) *A central park.* Parks in the center of communities normally are intensively used, serve as meeting places, receive considerable maintenance, and have severely degraded nature.

(B) *A linear edge park.* An edge park along the border of a community provides amenities for the existing community and for present or future outside communities, and, with limited human use, provides natural habitat and connectivity for movement of some species.

(C) *Market-gardens*. Market-gardening (truck farming) near a city provides fresh fruits and vegetables at low transport cost to city markets and restaurants, plus diverse environmental benefits on the city's outskirts.

(D) *Human habitat*. For planning purposes, a good human habitat is a community offering a choice in the diversity of frequently needed and used places (e.g., grocery, school, park, eatery) located in relative proximity to its residents.

(E) *Neighborhood units*. Neighborhoods serve as the basic social and planning units of a larger community or district, and several neighborhoods connected to a cultural and/or shopping center are likely to sustain the larger community.

(F) *Urban district*. An aggregation of interacting neighborhoods with a distinctive identity forms a district (or urban "village"), a place that residents identify with and that the broader city or metropolitan area uses for identification and planning.

(G) *Green, profitable, and fair*. Combining environmental protection, economic growth/efficiency, and social justice/economic opportunity/income equality as equal parts under the rubric of sustainable development still seems to be utopian, marketing, impossible, or a ruse, yet balancing such big human and environmental objectives is attainable and should be the norm.

(H) *Aesthetics and basics*. Adding aesthetic forms, after providing the basics of water, neighborhoods, jobs, natural areas, etc. for a community, enhances a sense of place and stimulates people to actively care for it.

(I) *Sense of place*. The intertwining of built structures and greenspaces that persist over time creates a place that people care for and remember.

(J) *Community gardens (allotments)*. Joining neighbors digging in the soil and growing their own plants and foods on tiny adjoining plots enhances an understanding of nature and creates valuable social bonds that strengthen a community.

(K) *Commuter-station areas for urban residents*. Community gardens, bicycle parks, walking paths, and recreation areas centered around commuter-rail stations provide important accessible resources and values for urban residents concentrated in high-density metro areas.

Land Mosaics and Landscape Change

This fifth and last category of principles highlights the big picture. Land mosaics emphasize the structure or spatial pattern of a landscape or urban region, including how nature and people are arranged. Land change then focuses on how the pattern is altered or changes, plus the associated functional changes over time. Change may be catalyzed by overall planning or decision, or produced by the multitude of little steps taken by people (Odum, 1982), or caused by natural systems. For these subjects, Pickett and White (1985), Zonneveld and Forman (1990), Forman (1995, 2004a), Dramstad et al. (1996), Ludwig et al. (1997), Losada et al. (1998), Dale and Haeuber (2001), Ingegnoli (2002), Gutzwiller (2002), Foster and Aber (2004), Chen et al. (2004), Lindenmayer and Fischer (2006), Erickson (2006), and Moore (2007) are particularly useful. . . .

The two subgroupings are: (a) land mosaics; and (b) landscape change.

Land Mosaics

(A) *Structure–function–change feedbacks.* Landscape structure or pattern controls landscape function (how the area works), which alters structure, in turn causing function to change.

(B) *Spatial scales.* Ecological and human conditions in an area (such as a landscape) are strongly affected by patterns and processes at three scales: the broader scale (e.g., region); the finer scale (e.g., large patches within the landscape); and surrounding areas (e.g., competing or collaborating) at the same scale.

(C) *Hierarchical structure.* A spatial hierarchy of habitat sizes, stream orders, and population sizes controls the amounts and directions of flows and movements across a landscape, and patterns and processes of a particular type tend to differ at different spatial scales.

(D) *Grain size of the mosaic.* A coarse-grained landscape (mainly composed of large patches) that contains fine-grained areas (mainly small patches) is better than either type alone, because it effectively provides for many large-patch benefits, multi-habitat species including humans, and a wide range of habitats and natural resources. . . .

(E) *Mosaic pattern and multi-habitat species.* Species (and people) that regularly use different habitats or land uses are favored by convergency points (junctions where three or more habitats converge), adjacencies (different combinations of adjoining habitat types), and habitat interspersion (habitat types scattered rather than aggregated).

(F) *Environmental gradients and patchiness.* Environmental gradients with gradual ecological change over space are sometimes evident, though patchiness with distinct boundaries predominates on land, because of patchy substrates and especially human activities that typically sharpen boundaries.

(G) *Nature and a grid.* A regular grid, such as of roads and strip development, may be the ecologically worst way to distribute a small amount of built area over a natural landscape, since the grid leaves only small natural patches, truncates connectivity, and removes much of the irregularity and heterogeneity characteristic of nature's species-rich communities.

(H) *Key variables of urban areas.* Human population density and spatial proximity are considered to be the two leading variables, with functionality the third, providing understanding and predictive ability for most human patterns and issues in urban areas.

Landscape Change

(A) *Ecologically optimum change.* The optimum way to change a large natural landscape to a less ecologically suitable one is to progressively remove vegetation in strips from two adjacent sides of the landscape, maintain a few large green patches in the middle phase, and then sequentially remove the patches.

(B) *Specific changes within an optimum sequence.* Determining an optimum spatial sequence for a changing landscape permits one to pinpoint at any stage the best and worst locations for a specific change, either deleterious or beneficial.

(C) *Spatial processes.* With the spread of human activities, natural areas may be perforated, dissected, fragmented, shrunk, and/or eliminated with quite different ecological consequences, even though habitat loss and isolation normally increase with all of the processes.

(D) *Change in mosaic pattern.* Ongoing human activities and natural disturbances keep the structure and habitat diversity of a land mosaic changing over time, as land uses and successional-stage habitats "move around," even though natural resources of the whole landscape may be in a degradation, meta-stable, or restoration trajectory.

(E) *Greenspace in a changing context.* All greenspaces change over time from interactions with adjacent and more-distant land uses, with the intensity or rate of flows/movements decreasing with distance and increasing with direction of incoming wind/water flows, animal locomotion, and human influences.

(F) *Worst urbanization.* Regional urbanization in dispersed sites surrounding a metropolitan area, and to a lesser extent along transportation corridors, appears to cause the most extensive nature-and-human resource degradation. . . .

(G) *Best urbanization.* Urbanization focused around satellite cities, which causes the least overall resource degradation, appears to be the best regional development pattern, though factors specific to a region may indicate a preference for combining satellite-city development with concentric-zone development adjacent to a metropolitan area. . . .

(H) *Cumulative effects.* Cumulative effects represent the combination of spatially separate effects, previous effects at different times, and different types of effects, and therefore a group of different and dispersed solutions is normally required to significantly reduce or mitigate cumulative effects.

(I) *Time lags.* Time lags reflecting the inertia or resilience of nature mean that some ecological responses (such as biological diversity and populations of long-lived species) are delayed after a change, that some ecological conditions today reflect earlier patterns, that mitigation may be effective well after landscape degradation, and that a successful response may be delayed after mitigation.

(J) *Plan/design for long term.* A land-use plan which provides an adaptable pattern to anticipate and respond to changes and which outlines broad land-use areas or zones, with only spots designed in detail, is more likely to be a successful long-term plan.

(K) *Region and local.* Planning regionally for broad-scale patterns (e.g., large greenspaces, highways) and then planning locally (e.g., neighborhoods, aesthetics) to effectively mesh with them is likely to successfully address both regional and local needs.

(L) *Communities and history.* Cities and towns are a product of historical development, yet they have also helped shape that history.

In conclusion, a treasure chest of principles has been opened. Many are or will become second nature to practitioners and scholars dealing with land use and urban regions. The list is also a handbook to be kept handy for solving problems. In effect, the principles are convenient handles for molding better urban regions where nature and people both thrive long term.

Such a cornucopia of riches calls out for a few governing principles or broad paradigms, from which the detailed statements or principles follow. Perhaps the patch–corridor–matrix model or pattern-process paradigm illustrates one of the broad paradigms (Forman, 1995; Turner et al., 2001; Robert McDonald, pers. comm.). Many of the principles, at least indirectly, follow from that. Articulating the few broad paradigms covering all principles awaits an exceptionally creative mind. At the other end of the conceptual scale, some of the principles articulated follow from more detailed or basic theories, such as central place and hierarchy theory (O'Neill et al., 1986; Hall, 2002).

Finally, experts in specific fields can and hopefully will delineate more, better, and fuller lists of principles in those fields. The value of the preceding treasure chest is to see the principles from different fields listed together, and to see some integrated principles that cross fields. Consider this list to be a palette, much in need for direct use today. But also consider it a work in progress, readily amenable to enhancement and enrichment on into the future.

References

AASHTO, *A Policy on Geometric Design of Highways and Streets: 2001.* Washington, DC: American Association of State Highway and Transportation Officials, 2001.

Atkinson, Adrian, E. Fernandes, and M. Mattingly. *The Challenge of Environmental Management in Urban Areas*. Aldershot, UK: Ashgate, 1999.

Bartuska, Tom J. "Cities Today: The Imprint of Human Needs in Urban Patterns and Form." In *The Built Environment: Creative Inquiry into Design and Planning*, edited by Wendy R. McClure and Tom J. Bartuska, 273–88. Menlo Park, CA: Crisp Publications, 1994.

Beatley, Timothy. *Green Urbanism: Learning from European Cities*. Washington, DC: Island Press, 2000.

Beier, Paul, and Reed F. Noss. "Do Habitat Corridors Provide Connectivity?" *Conservation Biology* 12, no. 6 (1998): 1241–52.

Benfield, F. Kaid, Jutka Terris, and Nancy Vorsanger. *Solving Sprawl: Models of Smart Growth in Communities Across America*. New York: Natural Resources Defense Council, 2001.

Bennett, Andrew Fawcett. *Linkages in the Landscape: The Role of Corridors and Connectivity in Wildlife Conservation*. No. 1. Gland, Switzerland and Cambridge, UK: IUCN-The World Conservation Union, 2003.

Bullard, Robert, Glenn S. Johnson, and Angel O. Torres, eds. *Sprawl City: Race, Politics, and Planning in Atlanta*. Washington, DC: Island Press, 2000.

Burel, Françoise, and Jacques Baudry. *Ecologie du Paysage: Concepts, Méthodes et Applications*. Paris: Tec & Doc, 1999.

Calthorpe, Peter, and William Fulton. *The Regional City*. Washington, DC: Island Press, 2001.

Campbell, Scott, and Susan S. Fainstein, eds. *Readings in Planning Theory*. Malden, MA: Blackwell, 2003.

Campbell, Scott. "Green Cities, Growing Cities, Just Cities? Urban Planning and the Contradictions of Sustainable Development." *Journal of the American Planning Association* 62, no. 3 (1996): 296–312.

Cervero, Robert. *The Transit Metropolis: A Global Inquiry*. Washington, DC: Island Press, 1998.

Chen, A., G. C. Liu, and K. H. Zhang. *Urban Transformation in China*. Aldershot, UK: Ashgate Publishing, 2004.

Clark, Peter, ed. *The European City and Green Space: London, Stockholm, Helsinki and St. Petersburg, 1850–2000*. Aldershot, UK: Ashgate Publishing, 2006.

Dale, Virginia H., and Richard A. Haeuber, eds. *Applying Ecological Principles to Land Management*. New York: Springer, 2001.

Dittmar, Hank, and Gloria Ohland, eds. *The New Transit Town: Best Practices in Transit-Oriented Development*. Washington, DC: Island Press, 2004.

Donahue, Brian. *Reclaiming the Commons: Community Farms and Forests in a New England Town*. New Haven, CT: Yale University Press, 1999.

Dramstad, W., J. D. Olson, and R. T. T. Forman *Landscape Ecology Principles in Landscape Architecture and Land-Use Planning*. Washington, DC: Island Press, 1996.

Farina, Almo. *Principles and Methods in Landscape Ecology: Towards a Science of the Landscape*. Berlin/New York: Springer, 2005.

Fischer, Joern, David B. Lindenmayer, and Adrian D. Manning. "Biodiversity, Ecosystem Function, and Resilience: Ten Guiding Principles for Commodity Production Landscapes." *Frontiers in Ecology and the Environment* 4, no. 2 (2006): 80–86.

Forman, Richard T. T., and Isaak Samuel Zonneveld. *Changing Landscapes: An Ecological Perspective*. New York: Springer-Verlag, 1990.

Forman, Richard T. T., and Lauren E. Alexander. "Roads and Their Major Ecological Effects." *Annual Review of Ecology and Systematics* 29 (1998): 207–31.

Forman, Richard T. T., and Robert D. Deblinger. "The Ecological Road Effect Zone of a Massachusetts (USA) Suburban Highway." *Conservation Biology* 14, no. 1 (2000): 36–46.

Forman, Richard T. T. "Road Ecology's Promise: What's Around the Bend?" *Environment: Science and Policy for Sustainable Development* 46, no. 4 (2004): 8–21.

———. *Land Mosaics: The Ecology of Landscapes and Regions*. New York: Cambridge University Press, 1995.

————. *Mosaico Territorial Para la Región Metropolitana de Barcelona*. Barcelona: Editorial Gustavo Grill, 2004.

Foster, David R., ed. *Forests in Time: The Environmental Consequences of 1,000 Years of Change in New England*. New Haven, CT: Yale University Press, 2006.

France, R. L. *Wetland Design Principles and Practices for Landscape Architects and Land-Use Planners*. New York: Norton, 2003.

Grimm, Nancy B., Lawrence J. Baker, and Diane Hope. "An Ecosystem Approach to Understanding Cities: Familiar Foundations and Uncharted Frontiers." In *Understanding Urban Ecosystems*, edited by Alan R. Berkowitz, Charles H. Nilon, and Karen S. Hollweg, 95–114. New York: Springer, 2003.

Groom, Martha J., Gary K. Meffe, and Carl Ronald Carroll. *Principles of Conservation Biology*. Sunderland: Sinauer Associates, 2006.

Gutzwiller, Kevin J., ed. *Applying Landscape Ecology in Biological Conservation*. New York: Springer, 2002.

Handy, Susan. "Critical Assessment of the Literature on the Relationships Among Transportation, Land Use, and Physical Activity." *Department of Environmental Science and Policy, University of California, Davis*. Washington, DC: Transportation Research Board (2005).

Harris, Larry D., Thomas S. Hoctor, and Sarah E. Gergel. "Landscape Processes and Their Significance to Biodiversity Conservation." *Population Dynamics in Ecological Space and Time* 1 (1996): 319–47.

Hersperger, Anna M. "Spatial Adjacencies and Interactions: Neighborhood Mosaics for Landscape Ecological Planning." *Landscape and Urban Planning* 77, no. 3 (2006): 227–39.

Hilty, Jodi A., William Z. Lidicker Jr, and Adina Merenlender. *Corridor Ecology: The Science and Practice of Linking Landscapes for Biodiversity Conservation*. Washington, DC: Island Press, 2006.

Ingegnoli, Vittorio. *Landscape Ecology: A Widening Foundation*. New York: Springer, 2002.

Jacobi, Petra, Axel W. Drescher, and Jörg Amend. "Urban Agriculture-Justification and Planning Guidelines." *GTZ, Eschborn*. Partly published in: *RUAF-Newsletter* 1, no. 1 (2000).

Kellert, Stephen R. *Building for Life: Designing and Understanding the Human-Nature Connection*. Washington, DC: Island Press, 2005.

LeGates, Richard T., and Frederic Stout, eds. *The City Reader*. New York: Routledge, 2003.

Lindenmayer, David B., and Joern Fischer. *Habitat Fragmentation and Landscape Change: An Ecological and Conservation Synthesis*. Washington, DC: Island Press, 2006.

Lindenmayer, David B., and Mark Burgman. *Practical Conservation Biology*. Collingwood, Australia: CSIRO Publishing, 2005.

Losada, H., H. Martinez, J. Vieyra, R. Pealing, R. Zavala, and J. Cortés. "Urban Agriculture in the Metropolitan Zone of Mexico City: Changes over Time in Urban, Suburban and Peri-Urban Areas." *Environment and Urbanization* 10, no. 2 (1998): 37–54.

Ludwig, John, D. Tongway, K. Hodgkinson, D. Freudenberger, and J. Noble. *Landscape Ecology, Function and Management: Principles from Australia's Rangelands*. Collingwood, Victoria: CSIRO Publishing, 1996.

Macionis, John J., and Vincent N. Parrillo. *Cities and Urban Life*. Upper Saddle River, NJ: Pearson Education, 2004.

Mitsch, W. J., and J. G. Gosselink. *Wetlands*. New York: John Wiley, 2000.

Moore, Steven A. *Alternative Routes to the Sustainable City: Austin, Curitiba, and Frankfurt*. Lanham, MD: Lexington Books, 2007.

Nassauer, Joan Iverson. "Using Cultural Knowledge to Make New Landscape Patterns." In *Issues and Perspectives in Landscape Ecology*, edited by John A. Wiens and Michael R. Moss, 274–80. Cambridge: Cambridge University Press, 2005.

National Research Council. *Toward a Sustainable Future: Addressing the Long-Term Effects of Motor Vehicle Transportation on Climate and Ecology*. Washington, DC: National Academy Press, 1997.

O'Neill, R. V., D. L. Deangelis, J. B. Waide, and T. F. H. Allen. *A Hierarchical Concept of Ecosystems*. Princeton, NJ: Princeton University Press, 1986.

Odum, William E. "Environmental Degradation and the Tyranny of Small Decisions." *BioScience* 32, no. 9 (1982): 728–29.

Opdam, Paul, Ruud Foppen, and Claire Vos. "Bridging the Gap between Ecology and Spatial Planning in Landscape Ecology." *Landscape Ecology* 16, no. 8 (2001): 767–79.

Peiser, Richard. "Decomposing Urban Sprawl." *The Town Planning Review* 72 (2001): 275–98.

Perlman, Dan L., and Jeffrey Milder. *Practical Ecology for Planners, Developers, and Citizens*. Washington, DC: Island Press, 2005.

Peter, Hall. *Cities of Tomorrow: An Intellectual History of Urban Planning and Design in the Twentieth Century*. Oxford: Blackwell, 2002.

Pickett, S. T. A. and P. S. White. *The Ecology of Natural Disturbance and Patch Dynamics*. New York: Academic Press, 1985.

Ravetz, Joe. *City-Region 2020: Integrated Planning for a Sustainable Environment*. London: Earthscan, 2000.

Salvesen, David. *Wetlands: Mitigating and Regulating Development Impacts*. Washington, DC: Urban Land Institute, 1994.

Schonewald-Cox, Christine M., and Jonathan W. Bayless. "The Boundary Model: A Geographical Analysis of Design and Conservation of Nature Reserves." *Biological Conservation* 38, no. 4 (1986): 305–22.

Seddon, George. *Landprints: Reflections on Place and Landscape*. Cambridge: Cambridge University Press, 1998.

Simmonds, Roger, and Gary Hack, eds. *Global City Regions: Their Emerging Forms*. Taylor & Francis, 2000.

Sukopp, Herbert, and Slavomil Hejný. *Urban Ecology: Plants and Plant Communities in Urban Environments*. The Hague, Netherlands: SPB Academic Publishing, 1990.

Turner, Monica G., Robert H. Gardner, and Robert V. O'Neill. *Landscape Ecology in Theory and Practice: Pattern and Process*. New York: Springer, 2001.

Warner, Sam Bass. *Greater Boston: Adapting Regional Traditions to the Present*. Philadelphia: University of Pennsylvania Press, 2001.

Warren, Roxanne. *The Urban Oasis: Guideways and Greenways in the Human Environment*. New York: McGraw-Hill, 1998.

White, Rodney. *Building the Ecological City*. Cambridge, UK: Woodhead Publishing, 2002.

Wiens, John A. "Riverine Landscapes: Taking Landscape Ecology into the Water." *Freshwater Biology* 47, no. 4 (2002): 501–15.

Wiens, John A., and Michael R. Moss, eds. *Issues and Perspectives in Landscape Ecology*. Cambridge: Cambridge University Press, 2005.

Willis, Kenneth George, R. Kerry Turner, and Ian Bateman, eds. *Urban Planning and Management*. Cheltenham, UK: Edward Elgar, 2001.

Yaro, R., R. Arendt, H. Dobson, and E. Brabec. *Dealing with Change in the Connecticut River Valley: A Design Manual for Conservation and Development*. Amherst, MA: Lincoln Institute of Land Policy, 1990.

Introduction

Biodiversity Planning and Design: Sustainable Practices (2007)

Jack Ahern, Elizabeth Leduc, and
Mary Lee York

The state of biodiversity is of increasing concern around the world. Considerable agreement exists among scientists that habitat loss and degradation are among the leading causes of global biodiversity decline. Renowned entomologist and champion of biodiversity awareness E. O. Wilson (1988, 3) claims: "Overall we are locked into a race. We must hurry to acquire the knowledge on which a wise policy of conservation and development can be based for centuries to come."

If habitat loss is the leading cause of biodiversity decline, it follows that planning and design will be essential in any viable solution by directly conserving, protecting, or managing landscapes and habitats. Planners set policy and make plans to organize land use to meet multiple goals. Landscape architects create designs that are realized in physical form, affecting protection, change, and restoration of land and habitat. Landscape architects and planners engage biodiversity by working independently or in interdisciplinary teams that include conservation biologists, restoration ecologists, and natural and social scientists. Some of these teams have very successfully addressed biodiversity across a range of scales and geographical contexts.

As part of its case study series, the Landscape Architecture Foundation (LAF) sponsored this issue-based research into how landscape architects and planners have addressed biodiversity in their work. This case study undertook to learn how biodiversity fits with other goals in professional planning and design work; the role(s) of landscape architects and planners in interdisciplinary teams; and strategies for moving forward with biodiversity planning and design when faced with uncertainty and incomplete knowledge. The study includes five biodiversity planning and design projects, arranged into a comparative, issue-based case study representing a range of scales and geographic locations across the United States. The projects include the following:

- The Woodland Park Zoo's long-range plan, by Jones & Jones, Architects and Landscape Architects, in Seattle, Washington.
- A storm water management and wetland restoration project by Carol R. Johnson and Associates in Devens, Massachusetts.
- The Crosswinds Marsh Wetland Mitigation project, in Wayne County, Michigan, by the Smith Group/JJR of Ann Arbor, Michigan.
- The Willamette River Basin Study in Oregon, by University of Oregon landscape architect David Hulse and colleagues.
- The Florida Statewide Greenways System Planning Project, by the University of Florida Department of Landscape Architecture.

Our research found that biodiversity planning best succeeds when it is integrated with other goals, including environmental education, environmental impact mitigation, and regulatory compliance. Achieving multiple goals requires an interdisciplinary approach, and planners and designers often excel in leading such teams. Landscape architects and planners offer the ability to synthesize and visualize complex information, a familiarity with construction processes, skills in facilitating public participation, and expertise in implementing and managing projects. Additionally, the case study found that, although important, biodiversity is often a secondary or minor project goal in planning and design projects. It becomes more important in broad-scale, public policy–related projects and when mandated by regulatory and permitting agencies.

Data for planning and designing biodiversity projects are often incomplete for explicitly supporting planning and design decisions—an inherent problem related to the site- and species-specific nature of the data required. Despite the lack of good data, however, monitoring has rarely been conducted, due mostly to cost and convenience. This limits the ongoing involvement of landscape architects and planners in the projects they conceive, design, and build and thus to learn if the intended results were achieved. The lack of monitoring misses opportunities to (1) contribute new knowledge to science, (2) afford planners and designers the chance to expand their interdisciplinary collaboration with scientists and decision makers, and (3) "to learn by doing" to develop and refine planning strategies and design responses to address biodiversity more effectively.

Biodiversity is implicit in virtually all of the work of planners and landscape architects, and many signs point toward increased global interest and support for biodiversity planning. Both disciplines—planning and landscape architecture—include principles guiding the treatment of the natural environment in the ethical codes put forth by their professional societies. . . .

Biodiversity represents a significant growth opportunity for planning and design professionals. To become more active players, landscape architects and planners need to: become more familiar with the issues, terminology, and methods for biodiversity planning and design; understand the complex issue of representative species selection and how to apply a method in the context of species/habitat associations and ecological models; and to develop advanced skills for leading interdisciplinary teams. By examining how planners and designers have been involved in five specific projects in the United States and by identifying areas of strength and points of weakness, this study seeks to identify specific ways these professionals can participate in and contribute to biodiversity conservation. The study is intended to not only encourage design and planning professionals to take a more active role in projects that involve biodiversity issues but also to better inform them about biodiversity and conservation efforts in general.

Definitions of Biodiversity

Biodiversity has many definitions in the current literature written by independent researchers, government agencies, and international organizations. The differences among the definitions emphasize the complexity of the issue. Some include detailed spatial or temporal considerations, whereas others are quite simple. For example, the Keystone Center (1991, 2) describes biodiversity as "the variety of life and its processes," while biologist B. A. Wilcox (1982, 640) calls it "the variety of life forms, the ecological roles they perform, and the genetic diversity they contain." These simple definitions recognize that both the quantity of species and the ecological processes that affect those species are important. Conservation biologists R. F. Noss and A. Y. Cooperrider (1994, 5) extend the Keystone Center's definition to say: "Biodiversity is the variety of life and its processes. It includes the variety of living organisms, the genetic differences among them, the communities and ecosystems in which they occur, and the ecological and evolutionary processes that keep them functioning, yet ever changing and adapting."

Similarly, the U.S. National Biological Information Infrastructure (NBII), an organization composed of a wide array of federal, state, international, nongovernmental, academic, and industry partners, states that "biodiversity or biological diversity is the sum total of the variety of life and its interactions and can be subdivided into 1) genetic diversity, 2) species diversity, and 3) ecological or ecosystem diversity" (NBII, 2003). In 1992 the World Resources Institute, the World Conservation Union (otherwise known as the IUCN, or International Union for Conservation of Nature and Natural Resources), and the United Nations Environment Programme (UNEP) produced a joint publication, *Global Biodiversity Strategy*, in which biodiversity is defined as "the variability among living organisms from all sources, including, *inter alia*, terrestrial, marine and other aquatic ecosystems and the ecological complexes of which they are part; this includes diversity within species, between species and of ecosystems" (WRI, 1992)....

The definitions above show three principal similarities: (1) biodiversity exists and needs to be understood at multiple scales, (2) biodiversity is inseparable from its physical environment, and (3) biodiversity is integral with ecological processes. For this study, we have integrated these similarities into the following working definition: *Biodiversity is the totality, over time, of genes, species, and ecosystems in an ecosystem or region, including the ecosystem structure and function that supports and sustains life.*

The Status of Biodiversity—Measurement and Trends

Whether or not such issues as spatial or temporal contexts or accompanying ecological processes are addressed, a general consensus exists that, at the very least, the concept of biodiversity rests on baseline knowledge of the number of species that exist on earth. This itself is a controversial topic; estimates of the number of species span orders of magnitude, ranging widely according to the method of calculation and the data used. E. O. Wilson (1988) suggests that the true number of species ranges anywhere from 5 to 30 million. In 1982, Terry L. Erwin's (1982) method of gassing and collecting insects from select trees in a Panamanian rain forest lead [sic] him to propose that, worldwide, there are 30 million species of tropical arthropods alone. Basing his estimates on the assumption that an inverse relationship exists between the numbers of species and body size, University of Oxford zoologist Robert M. May (1988) estimated global species richness to be between 10 and 50 million species. In 1995, the United Nations Environment Programme (UNEP) estimated that there are 13.6 million species on earth (Hammond, 1995). This figure—which is very close to that of 13.4 million species proposed by Nigel Stork (1999) for the "Living Planet in Crisis" conference sponsored by the American Museum of Natural History in 1995—is currently considered an acceptable working estimate....

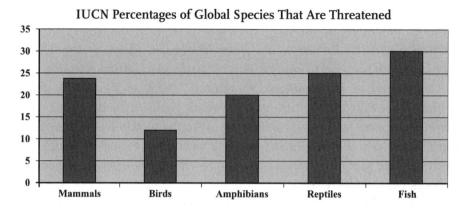

Figure 4-9 Percentages of global species that are threatened (Ahern, Leduc, and York, 2006, Reproduced with permission of Island Press, Redrawn by Yuan Ren, 2014).

Strategies for Assessing and Conserving Biodiversity

Landscape architects and planners must rely on the expertise of biologists to conduct biodiversity assessments, and it is important that they understand the pertinent concepts and terminology so they can collaborate effectively. Methods to assess and conserve biodiversity fall into two broad categories: reactive strategies, which are undertaken once a problem or issue has been identified, and proactive strategies, undertaken before a problem arises. Biodiversity plans that integrate both are likely to be more successful.

Biodiversity is commonly evaluated by either an "endangered species" reactive approach that addresses species that are already in trouble; or a "hot spot" proactive approach that focuses on protecting geographical areas with high concentrations of biodiversity. Historically in North America, species conservation methods were aimed at preserving single species that had some perceived value to humankind and whose declining numbers needed to be managed to ensure the species' future use by humans. Desirable species (such as deer and caribou) were managed, while undesirable species (such as wolves) were pushed to the brink of extinction. These early efforts tended to focus on large-game vertebrates that could be exploited for their meat or hides. Gradually, aided by the passage of the Endangered Species Act of 1973 (ESA), the scope of species to be conserved expanded to include invertebrates, plants, and other historically undervalued species (Noss and Cooperrider, 1994). Under the ESA, vulnerable species are those in danger of becoming extinct or those federally listed as being threatened or endangered (TES) (Feinsinger, 2001). This vulnerable species approach has several drawbacks:

- Until recently, it has focused on large vertebrates to the exclusion of plants and invertebrates.
- This fine filter, single-species approach cannot possibly keep tabs on the vast numbers of species in the world.
- Historically, this approach has addressed direct threats to species survival, such as poaching and hunting—a focus that has become increasingly misguided as habitat loss has eclipsed direct killing as the major threat to species.
- Most single-species efforts are reactive, coming into play only after a given species is imperiled (Noss and Cooperrider, 1994).

The endangered species approach came into fundamental conflict with development activities, leading to multispecies habitat conservation plans that attempted to negotiate a reasonable compromise between conservation and development, informed by species biology and development alternatives, while operating within the legal guidelines of the ESA. To the purist, habitat conservation plans represent an unacceptable weakening of the ESA; to others, they provide a model for sustainable "balancing" of conservation and development in which serious consideration is granted to biodiversity (Beatley, 1994).

Alternatively, a hotspot approach is more strategic and proactive in that it entails the protection of areas that help conserve overall diversity before the quality of the ecosystems and species within those areas degrades entirely. Generally, hotspots are high in species richness and endemic species (those species found only in a single location in the world). Hotspots may also be determined by the degree of threat to the area. For example, Conservation International, a U.S.-based, international nonprofit organization, uses a hotspot approach as its central strategy for preserving biodiversity. It has identified twenty-five hotspots worldwide, where it concentrates its efforts. According to Russell A. Mittermeier, president of Conservation International: "The hotspots strategy makes the extinction crisis more manageable by enabling us to prioritize and target conservation investments in order to have the greatest impact" (Conservation International, 2002).

Another example of the hotspot approach is the National Gap Analysis Program (GAP), conducted by the Biological Resource Division of the U.S. Geological Survey. It is used to analyze how well native animal species and natural plant communities are represented in the network of currently protected lands. In the GAP analysis, "gaps" are areas in which particular species or natural communities are not adequately represented in currently protected lands. GAP assessment classifies lands into four management classes, which range from permanently protected with natural disturbance regimes (class 1) to unprotected areas with extensive human changes allowed to existing eco-systems and plant communities (class 4) (Jennings, 2000). When "gaps" are identified, they may be targeted for acquisition or for alternative management approaches. GAP is a type of hotspot approach in which both ecological pro-cesses and species distribution are examined to determine which areas should receive protection before they become vulnerable. A stated goal of the project is "to ensure that all ecosystems and areas rich in species diversity are repre-sented adequately in biodiversity management areas" (Scott et al., 1993, 1). . . .

Another coarse filter, proactive conservation and planning approach that at-tempts to work at regional scales and over broader time periods is the ecoregion approach used by the World Wildlife Fund (WWF), based on the work of James Omernick of the U.S. Environmental Protection Agency (EPA) and Robert Bai-ley of the U.S. Forest Service (Stein et al., 2000). Ecoregions are broad regions of land or water that include "geographically distinct assemblage of natural communities," which contain many of the same ecological processes and spe-cies, exist under similar environmental conditions, and depend on ecological interactions for long-term survival (Dinerstein et al., 2000, 13). The WWF has identified more than two hundred ecoregions and uses them to set conserva-tion priorities. Ecoregions simplify landscapes to reveal underlying patterns. To address biodiversity with a more fine-grained, intermediate-scale approach, The Nature Conservancy and the National Heritage Network rely instead on mapping ecological communities which are assemblages of species that exist together in the same areas and whose life processes are potentially interrelated (McPeek and Miller, 1996).

Selecting species for biodiversity planning presents a great dilemma: to be truly inclusive many species need to be considered, yet there is rarely enough species-specific knowledge, information, or time to support this type of inclu-sive approach. As the number of species considered increases, so too do the time and cost of planning. In response to this dilemma, biodiversity planners often use representative, or indicator, species. An indicator species is a species whose status provides information on the overall condition of an ecosystem and of other species in that ecosystem. Indicator species flag changes in biotic or abiotic conditions. They reflect the quality of and changes in environmental conditions as well as aspects of community composition (Heywood and Wat-son, 1995).

Biodiversity planners commonly think of the term *indicator species* as syn-onymous with *target species*. However, some experts contend that target spe-cies are often chosen more for their value in conservation politics than for their validity as true biological indicators (Landres et al., 1988; Noss, 1990; Fein-singer, 2001; Storch and Bissonette, 2003). In this way, target species are used reactively. In addition, problems can arise in determining what species should serve as indicators; there appears to be little consensus in the literature regarding methods of selection for indicator fauna (Hilty and Merenlender, 2000). . . .

The use of target species is generally reactive, focusing on the species itself but not generally on the biota interacting with that species. Targets commonly receive attention because they are in some danger of extinction. Indicators, on the other hand, are more proactive because they are chosen to act as "signals" that change before change actually occurs. Finally, ecosystem patterns, processes, or relationships are receiving more attention as indicators to biodiversity, as "species based approaches have been criticized on the grounds that they do not provide whole-landscape solutions to conservation problems" (Lambeck, 1997, 850).

Because the design of a project may depend on the type of biodiversity strategy used, landscape architects must consult with ecologists before any planning or design process begins. We will now examine why landscape architects and planners should acknowledge biodiversity in their planning and design efforts.

Why Should Biodiversity Be Important to Landscape Architects and Planners?

All societies depend on biodiversity and biological resources either directly or indirectly. Humans rely directly on the diversity of life on earth as a source of air (plants produce oxygen through photosynthesis), fuel, fiber, medicines and, most importantly, for food. We also depend on microbes and scavengers to break down wastes, recycle nutrients, and replenish our soils (Miller et al., 1985). Placing a value on biodiversity is difficult because the many ecological services and functions performed by biodiversity, such as climate regulation, do not have explicit markets and are difficult to quantify. Often, the aesthetic or moral values associated with biodiversity are not explicitly acknowledged in ecological or economic assessments (Organisation for Economic Co-operation and Development, 2002). Today, justification of the importance of conserving biodiversity falls into three main categories:

1. The vast repository of genetic information stored in the diversity of the earth's organisms provides a buffer against disease and famine because it holds the building blocks for biotechnological discoveries (e.g., future foods and medicines).
2. Ecosystems provide services to the earth (e.g., filtering carbon dioxide), and we do not yet understand the full extent or economic value of the possible services.

3. Humans have a moral obligation to preserve the balance of life on earth (Gibbs, 2001). Ehrenfeld's "Noah principle" makes this point elegantly: "They [species] should be conserved because they exist and because this existence is itself but the present expression of a continued historical process of immense antiquity and majesty. Long-standing existence in nature is deemed to carry with it the unimpeachable right to continued existence" (quoted in Beatley, 1994, 9).

The state of biodiversity is currently fragile and is heavily influenced by land use decisions. Understanding biodiversity and its functions is important to landscape architects and planners because, by definition, planning and design change spatial configurations, ecological patterns, and the processes linked to these—often unintentionally. . . .

Conclusion

To be seen as leaders in the environmental community, landscape architects and planners cannot afford to dismiss the importance of biodiversity. They must recognize that the elements of biodiversity planning are interdependent and cannot be addressed in isolation. For example, decisions concerning types of linkages used to increase connectivity for a particular animal species may also increase the connectivity for the dispersal of an invasive plant. By acknowledging these connections, landscape architects and planners can potentially protect and restore biodiversity. Clearly, landscape architects and planners working in both the public and private sectors could have a large effect on the future of any unprotected landscape. They must examine how well they are able to adhere to the overarching priorities of sustainability in their daily work. The current state of biodiversity calls for a reevaluation of ethics and a return to Aldo Leopold's concept of human beings as stewards of the land, safeguarding resources for future generations:

All ethics so far evolved rest upon a single premise: that the individual is a member of a community of interdependent parts. His instincts prompt him to compete for his place in that community, but his ethics prompt him also to cooperate (perhaps in order that there may be a place to compete for). The land ethic simply enlarges the boundaries of the community to include soils, waters, plants, and animals, or collectively: the land. (Leopold, 1949, 203–204)

References

American Planning Association. "*Ethical Principles in Planning, 1992.*" Accessed July 18, 2006. http://www.planning.org/ethics/ethics.html

American Society of Landscape Architects. "*ASLA Code of Environmental Ethics, 2000.*" Accessed July 18, 2006. http://www.asla.org/about/codeenv.htm

Beatley, Timothy. *Habitat Conservation Planning: Endangered Species and Urban Growth.* Austin: University of Texas Press, 1994.

Benfield, F. Kaid, Matthew D. Raimi, and Donald D. D. T. Chen. *Once There Were Greenfields: How Urban Sprawl Is Undermining America's Environment, Economy, and Social Fabric.* New York: Natural Resources Defense Council, 1999.

Bissonette, John A., and Ilse Storch, eds. *Landscape Ecology and Resource Management: Linking Theory with Practice.* Washington, DC: Island Press, 2003.

Brown Jr., K. S., and G. G. Brown. "Habitat Alteration and Species Loss in Brazilian Forests." In *Tropical Deforestation and Species Extinction,* edited by T. C. Whitmore and J. A. Sayer, 119–142. London: Chapman and Hall, 1992.

Conservation International. *Conservation Strategies: Hotspots,* 2002. Accessed July 18, 2006. http://www.conservation.org/xp/CIWEB/home#

Dinerstein, E., G. Powell, D. Olson, E. Wikramanayake, R. Abell, C. Loucks, E. Underwood, et al. *A Workbook for Conducting Biological Assessments and Developing Biodiversity Visions for Ecoregion-Based Conservation. Part I: Terrestrial Ecoregions.* Washington, DC: Conservation Science Program, World Wildlife Fund, 2000.

Drake, J. A., H. A. Mooney, F. di Castri, R. H. Groves, and F. J. Kruger. *Biological Invasions: A Global Perspective.* New York: John Wiley and Sons, 1989.

Ehrlich, Paul R. "Biodiversity Studies: Science and Policy." *Science* 253, no. 5021 (1991): 758–62.

Erwin, Terry L. "Tropical Forests: Their Richness in Coleoptera and Other Arthropod Species." *Coleopterists Bulletin* 36, no. 1 (1982): 74–75.

Feinsinger, Peter. *Designing Field Studies for Biodiversity Conservation.* Washington, DC: Island Press, 2001.

Forman, Richard T. T. *Land Mosaics: The Ecology of Landscapes and Regions.* Cambridge: Cambridge University Press, 1995.

———, ed. *Road Ecology: Science and Solutions.* Washington, DC: Island Press, 2003.

Gibbs, W. Wayt. "On the Termination of Species." *Scientific American* 285, no. 5 (2001): 40–49.

Groves, Craig R., Lynn S. Kutner, David M. Stoms, Michael P. Murray, J. Michael Scott, Michael Schafale, Alan S. Weakley, and Robert L. Pressey. "Owning Up to Our Responsibilities: Who Owns Lands Important for Biodiversity?" In *Precious Heritage: The Status of Biodiversity in the United States,* edited by Bruce A. Stein and Lynn S. Kutner, 275–300. Oxford: Oxford University Press, 2000.

Hammond, P. M. "The Current Magnitude of Biodiversity." In *Global Biodiversity Assessment,* edited by V. H. Heywood and R. T. Watson, 113–38. Cambridge: Cambridge University Press for United Nations Environment Programme, 1995.

Heywood, Vernon H. *Global Biodiversity Assessment.* Cambridge: Cambridge University Press for the United Nations Environment Programme, 1995.

Heywood, Vernon H., Georgina M. Mace, Robert M. May, and S. N. Stuart. "Uncertainties in Extinction Rates." *Nature* 368 (1994): 105.

Hilty, Jodi, and Adina Merenlender. "Faunal Indicator Taxa Selection for Monitoring Ecosystem Health." *Biological Conservation* 92, no. 2 (2000): 185–97.

Jennings, Michael D. "Gap Analysis: Concepts, Methods, and Recent Results." *Landscape Ecology* 15, no. 1 (2000): 5–20.

Keystone Center. "Final Consensus Report of the Keystone Policy Dialogue on Biological Diversity on Federal Lands, 1991." Accessed July 18, 2006. http://ceres.ca.gov/ceres/calweb/biodiversity/def_KC.html

Kittredge, A. M., and T. F. O'Shea. "Forestry Practices on Wildlife Management Areas." *Massachusetts Wildlife* 49 (1999): 33–38.

Lambeck, Robert J. "Focal Species: A Multi-Species Umbrella for Nature Conservation." *Conservation Biology* 11, no. 4 (1997): 849–56.

Landres, Peter B., Jared Verner, and Jack Ward Thomas. "Ecological Uses of Vertebrate Indicator Species: A Critique." *Conservation Biology* 2, no. 4 (1988): 316–28.

Leopold, Aldo. *Sand County Almanac, and Sketches Here and There.* New York: Oxford University Press, 1949.

Lovejoy, Thomas E. "A Projection of Species Extinctions." In *The Global 2000 Report to the President*, 328–331. Washington, DC: US Government Printing Office, 2000.

Mac, M. J., P. A. Opler, C. E. P. Haecker, and P. D. Doran. *Status and Trends of the Nation's Biological Resources.* Reston, VA: US Department of the Interior, 1998.

MacArthur, Robert H., and Edward O. Wilson. *The Theory of Island Biogeography.* Princeton, NJ: Princeton University Press, 1967.

Massachusetts Executive Office of Environmental Affairs. *Biomap—Guiding Land Conservation for Biodiversity in Massachusetts.* Boston: Executive Office of Environmental Affairs, 2001.

Master, Lawrence L., Bruce A. Stein, Lynn S. Kutner, and Geoffrey A. Hammerson. "Vanishing Assets: Conservation Status of US Species." In *Precious Heritage: The Status of Biodiversity in the United States*, 93–118. New York: Oxford University, 2000.

Mawdsley, N. A., and N. E. Stork. "Species Extinctions in Insects: Ecological and Biogeographical Considerations." In *Insects in a Changing Environment*, 321–369. London: Academic Press, 1995.

May, Robert M. "How Many Species Are There on Earth?" *Science* (Washington) 241, no. 4872 (1988): 1441–49.

McPeek, Mark A., and Thomas E. Miller. "Evolutionary Biology and Community Ecology." *Ecology* 77, no. 5 (1996): 1319–20.

National Biological Information Infrastructure (NBII). "Biodiversity Definitions." Accessed September 6, 2004. http://www.nbii.gov/issues/biodiversity

Noss, Reed F. "Indicators for Monitoring Biodiversity: A Hierarchical Approach." *Conservation Biology* 4, no. 4 (1990): 355–64.

Noss, Reed F., and Allen Cooperrider. *Saving Nature's Legacy: Protecting and Restoring Biodiversity.* Washington, DC: Island Press, 1994.

Peck, Sheila. *Planning for Biodiversity: Issues and Examples.* Washington, DC: Island Press, 1998.

Raven, Peter H. "Our Diminishing Tropical Forests." In *Biodiversity*, edited by E. O. Wilson and F. M. Petter, 119–122. Washington, DC: National Academy Press, 1988.

Scott, J. Michael, Frank Davis, Blair Csuti, Reed Noss, Bart Butterfield, Craig Groves, Hal Anderson, et al. "Gap Analysis: A Geographic Approach to Protection of Biological Diversity." *Wildlife Monographs* (1993): 3–41.

Society for Ecological Restoration International. "*Mission Statement, 2004.*" Accessed July 18, 2006. http://www.ser.org/about.asp

Stein, Bruce A., and Lynn S. Kutner, eds. *Precious Heritage: The Status of Biodiversity in the United States.* Oxford: Oxford University Press, 2000.

Stork, Nigel E. "The Magnitude of Global Biodiversity and Its Decline." In *The Living Planet in Crisis: Biodiversity, Science and Policy*, edited by J. Cracraft and F. Grifo, 3–32. New York: Columbia University Press, 1999.

US Fish and Wildlife Service (USFWS). *Endangered Species Act of 1973, as Amended through the 100th Congress.* Washington, DC: US Department of the Interior, 1988.

Vitousek, Peter M. "Diversity and Biological Invasions of Oceanic Islands." In *Biodiversity*, edited by E. O. Wilson and F. M. Peter, 181–89. Washington, DC: National Academy Press, 1988.

Whittaker, Robert Harding. *Communities and Ecosystems.* New York: Macmillan, 1975.

Wilcove, David S., David Rothstein, Jason Dubow, Ali Phillips, and Elizabeth Losos. "Leading Threats to Biodiversity: What's Imperiling US Species." In *Precious Heritage: The Status of Biodiversity in the United States,* edited by Bruce A. Stein and Lynn S. Kutner, 239–54. Oxford: Oxford University Press, 2000.

Wilcox, Bruce A. "In Situ Conservation of Genetic Resources: Determinants of Minimum Area Requirements." In *National Parks, Conservation and Development: The Role of Protected Areas in Sustaining Society,* edited by J. A. McNeely and K. R. Miller, 639–647. Washington, DC: Smithsonian Institution Press, 1982.

Wilson, Edward O. "The Current State of Biological Diversity." In *Biodiversity,* edited by E. O. Wilson and F. M. Peter, 3–18. Washington, DC: National Academy Press, 1988.

World Conservation Union-IUCN. *Confirming the Global Extinction Crisis: A Call for International Action as the Most Authoritative Global Assessment of Species Loss Is Released.* IUCN-World Conservation List Program, 2000.

———. *Species Survival Commission.* The SSC Red List Programme, 2001.

World Resources Institute (WRI). *Global Biodiversity Strategy: Guidelines for Action to Save, Study and Use Earth's Biotic Wealth Sustainably and Equitably.* World Resources Institute, Washington, IUCN and UNEP, 1992.

Part Five

Methods and Processes

Introduction to Part Five

When Frederick Law Olmsted and his protégée Charles Eliot (1855–97) developed plans for the Fens and River Way in Boston (completed in 1891, resulting in the development of the first metropolitan park system planned around hydrological features and ecological ideas), the processes or methods they employed enabled them to effectively translate ecological ideas into design, although their directives were not as obvious as those that have been utilized over the past fifty years. Scottish biologist and planner Patrick Geddes proposed a regional survey method in 1915, which was refined subsequently by urban historian Lewis Mumford. Geddes's method was based on understanding the nature of the complexities between human action and the environment. *Survey before plan*—a maxim well known to planners even today—is a phrase attributed to Patrick Geddes. He contended that planning should be viewed as a problem-solving activity.

In the 1950s, landscape architects and planners espoused "staged models of design."[1] These models emphasized the design and planning processes as problem-solving activities, building on Geddes's earlier proposition. One of the most eloquent voices of this perspective was that of landscape architect Hideo Sasaki, as articulated in his paper "Design Process."[2] Sasaki viewed design as "relating all the operational factors into a comprehensive whole, including the factors of costs and effects."[3] Critical thinking when applied to design involves *research* to understand the factors involved; *analysis* to highlight the ideal functional relationships among the factors under consideration; and *synthesis* to articulate the complex relationships among the pertinent factors into some form of spatial organization (figure 5-1). This synoptic-rational view of design and planning, as it was later coined by planner Barclay M. Hudson, was prevalent when Ian McHarg proposed his method for landscape architecture in the mid-1960s.[4]

The seven readings presented in this part begin with the classic essay by Ian McHarg "An Ecological Method for Landscape Architecture," first published in *Landscape Architecture* in 1967.[5] He offered a method for landscape architecture grounded on ecology and interpreted nature as an interacting process that exhibits opportunities and limitations for human use. This work signifies an important phase in the evolution of ecological planning, characterized by methods that were increasingly defensible in public debates. Prior methods employed information and techniques that were covert and often ambiguous.

In the next reading, "Methods for Generating Land Suitability Maps: A Comparative Evaluation" (1977),[6] Lewis Hopkins systematically examined land suitability methods for their validity and reliability and offered guidance on when to use one method over another.

In the classic piece by Kevin Lynch and his colleague Gary Hack "The Art of Site Planning" (1962, 1984),[7] the authors described site planning both as a problem-solving activity and an art in which goals are based upon morals and aesthetics. The first edition of this reading, in 1962, filled a gap in planning education and practice by providing credible methods for transforming landscapes for human use and habitation at varied spatial scales.

The reading by Danilo Palazzo and Frederick Steiner follows. "Processes" (2012)[8] reviewed several methods and processes to determine their relevance to urban design. Palazzo and Steiner proposed an interdisciplinary approach for investigating the transformation of urban spaces, supported by theories, techniques, visual information, and case studies.

In the next reading, "On Teaching Ecological Principles to Designers,"[9] Carl Steinitz proposed a strategy that organizes six different questions framed within the context of problem solving, each of them emphasizing a "theory-driven answer or model." This reading contributed to the foundation of Steinitz's book *A Framework for Geodesign: Changing Geography by Design* (2012), in which he proposed a collaborative design process for transforming large landscapes.[10]

Next, in "Framing the Land Use Plan: A Systems Approach" (2012),[11] William M. Marsh proposed a conceptual model that employs a systems approach for framing land use. His basic idea was to identify and examine the types of landscape systems that shape the site or locale under consideration, and to use

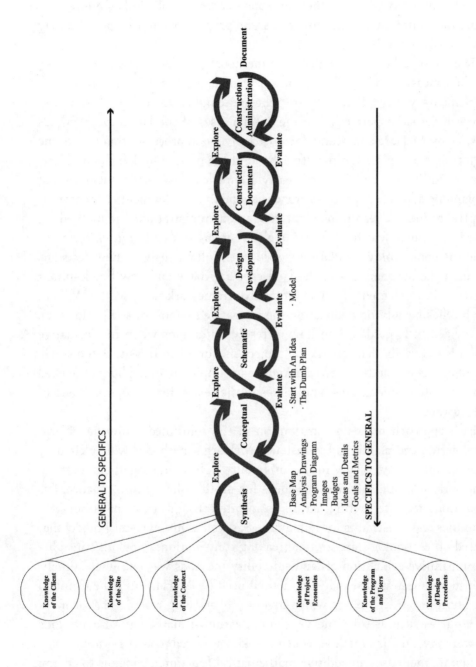

Figure 5-1 Design processes (Kurt Culbertson, 2002, Reproduced with permission of Design Workshop, Redrawn by Yuan Ren, 2014).

the resultant information to frame thinking and developing plans for the optimal uses of the landscape.

In the last reading, "A Synthesis of Approaches to Ecological Planning" (2002),[12] I offer a synthesis of the major approaches to ecological planning, illuminate their differences and similarities, and propose when one approach may be favored over another.

The ecological design and planning methods reviewed here strive to ascertain the fitness of a tract of land for a particular use but do so in diverse yet complementary ways. Each of them relies on employing ecological principles to inform decisions pertaining to the optimal uses of the landscape. Methods proposed by McHarg and Marsh focus exclusively on processes that lead to the development of a plan. On the other hand, those offered by Lynch and Hack, Palazzo and Steiner, and Steinitz clearly acknowledge to varying degrees that the planning and design process extends beyond the development of a master or site plan, to include plan implementation and administration. The method espoused by Steiner, which I referred to elsewhere as *strategic-suitability methods* in the book *Ecological Planning,* focuses simultaneously on how decisions regarding the optimal uses of the landscape are made and how the resultant decisions are implemented.[13] The innovative framework proposed by William Marsh relies heavily on delineating the formative systems of a site. However, he provided little guidance on how to resolve situations when the formative system is not easily delineated on a project site, or when the site is too small. Almost all the methods reviewed acknowledge implicitly or explicitly the need to incorporate public interest and values in the search for the optimal uses of the landscape.

Each approach makes a contribution in the continued evolution of ecological design and planning. For instance, McHarg's method is widely cited by the other authors, especially for his originality in bringing together an ethical framework, working theories, and ideas for putting theory into practice. His propositions for interpreting nature as an interacting system that offers opportunities and constraints for human uses, as well as his layer-cake model that is based on chronology, are groundbreaking contributions. Hopkins's insightful comparative evaluation of land suitability methods was extremely timely. For instance, he revealed that the method used by McHarg in his Richmond Park Study (McHarg, 1969), which involved overlaying resource factor maps for resources such as soils and vegetation, assumed mathematical operations that were invalid. This method, which Hopkins referred to as the *ordinal combination* method, uses an additive mathematical function analogous to adding apples and oranges. Yet the map overlay technique, similar to the one McHarg used, was an important and widely used technique employed in landscape architecture, land-use planning, and ecological design and planning practice during that era (1960s and 1970s).

Lynch and Hack revealed in ways few people before them had done that site planning involved the search for ways to most effectively accommodate human behavior and activities. Throughout their article, the authors emphasized the behavioral dimension of site planning. They were emphatic that site planning establishes a behavioral setting where "physical form and human activity are repeatedly associated."[14] Palazzo and Steiner's article, on the other hand, exposes the reader to a wide variety of methods that may be adapted to urban design, and also proposes an interdisciplinary framework for urban design that embraces the considerations of urban ecology and sustainability issues.

The framework proposed by Carl Steinitz has some noteworthy features. Take, for instance, the question that leads to implementing his *evaluation model*: Is the landscape functioning well? This question focuses on ascertaining the current state or well-being of an ecosystem as a point of departure in examining the landscape—an issue that is rarely addressed in ecological design and planning methods. My reading enables planners to be more informed of the theoretical and methodological assumptions made by these approaches in balancing human use with ecological concerns.

In conclusion, these methods illustrate some of the diversity in approaches. Advances will continue to be made to effectively respond to landscape change, especially by improving the technical validity and predictive capabilities of the analytical operations; incorporating advances in ecological sciences flawlessly in design; and skillfully integrating innovations in information, communication, visualization, remote sensing, and computing technologies. Other advances include increasing the involvement of affected interests to ensure that their values are reflected in design decisions, as well as seamlessly embracing culture and aesthetics and sustaining effective collaboration in balancing human use with ecological concerns.

Notes

1. Simon R. Swaffield (ed.), *Theory in Landscape Architecture: A Reader* (Philadelphia, PA: University of Pennsylvania Press, 2002).
2. Max Nicholson cites Hideo Sasaki's work in *The Environmental Revolution: A Guide for the Masters of the World* (New York: McGraw-Hill, 1970).
3. Swaffield (ed.), *Theory in Landscape Architecture: A Reader*, 35.
4. Barclay Hudson and Jerome Kaufman, "Comparison of Current Planning Theories: Counterparts and Contradictions," *Journal of the American Planning Association* 45 (1979), 387–406.

5. Ian McHarg, "An Ecological Method for Landscape Architecture," *Landscape Architecture* 57, no. 2 (1967), 105–07.

6. Lewis D. Hopkins, "Methods for Generating Land Suitability Maps: A Comparative Evaluation," *Journal of the American Planning Association* 43, no. 4 (1977), 386–400.

7. Kevin Lynch and Gary Hack, "The Art of Site Planning," in *Site Planning* (Cambridge, MA: MIT Press, 1984).

8. Danilo Palazzo and Frederick Steiner, "Processes," in *Urban Ecological Design: A Process for Regenerative Places* (Washington, DC: Island Press, 2011), 25–36.

9. Carl Steinitz, "On Teaching Ecological Principles to Designers," in *Ecology and Design: Frameworks for Learning*, B. Johnson and K. Hill (eds.) (Washington, DC: Island Press, 2002), 231–244.

10. Carl Steinitz, *A Framework for Geodesign: Changing Geography by Design* (New York: ESRI, 2012).

11. William M. Marsh, "Framing Land Use: A Systems Approach," in *Landscape Planning: Environmental Applications* (Hoboken, NJ: Wiley, 2010).

12. Forster Ndubisi, "A Synthesis of Approaches to Ecological Planning," in *Ecological Planning: A Historical and Comparative Synthesis* (Baltimore: Johns Hopkins University Press, 2002).

13. Ndubisi, "A Synthesis of Approaches to Ecological Planning," 95.

14. Lynch and Hack, "The Art of Site Planning," 8.

An Ecological Method for Landscape Architecture

Landscape Architecture (1967)

Ian L. McHarg

In many cases a qualified statement is, if not the most propitious, at least the most prudent. In this case it would only be gratuitous. I believe that ecology provides the single indispensible basis for landscape architecture and regional planning. I would state in addition that it has now, and will increasingly have, a profound relevance for both city planning and architecture.

Where the landscape architect commands ecology he is the only bridge between the natural sciences and the planning and design professions, the proprietor of the most perceptive view of the natural world which science or art has provided. This can be at once his unique attribute, his passport to relevance and productive social utility. With the acquisition of this competence the sad image of ornamental horticulture, handmaiden to architecture after the fact, the caprice and arbitrariness of "clever" designs can be dismissed forever. In short, ecology offers emancipation to landscape architecture.

This is not the place for a scholarly article on ecology. We are interested in it selfishly, as those who can and must apply it. Our concern is for a method which has the power to reveal nature as process, containing intrinsic form.

Ecology is generally described as the study of the interactions of organisms and environment which includes other organisms. The particular interests of landscape architecture are focused only upon a part of this great, synoptic concern. This might better be defined as the study of physical and biological processes, as dynamic and interacting, responsive to laws, having limiting factors and exhibiting certain opportunities and constraints, employed in planning and design for human use. At this juncture two possibilities present themselves. The first is to attempt to present a general theory of ecology and the planning processes. This is a venture which I long to undertake, but this is not the time nor place to attempt it. The other alternative is to present a method which has been tested empirically at many scales from a continent, a major region, a river basin, physiographic regions, sub-regional areas, and a metropolitan region town to a single city. In every case, I submit, it has been triumphantly revelatory.

First, it is necessary to submit a proposition to this effect: that the place, the plants, animals and men upon it are only comprehensible in terms of physical and biological evolution. Written on the place and upon its inhabitants lies mute all physical, biological and cultural history awaiting to be understood by those who can read it. It is thus necessary to begin at the beginning if we are to understand the place, the man, or his co-tenants of this phenomenal universe. This is the prerequisite for intelligent intervention and adaptation. So let us begin at the beginning. We start with historical geology. The place, any place, can only be understood through its physical evolution. What history of mountain building and ancient seas, uplifting, folding, sinking, erosion and glaciation have passed here and left their marks? These explain its present form. Yet the effects of climate and later of plants and animals have interacted upon geological processes and these too lie mute in the record of the rocks. Both climate and geology can be invoked to interpret physiography, the current configuration of the place. Arctic differs from tropics, desert from delta, the Himalayas from the Gangetic Plain. The Appalachian Plateau differs from the Ridge and Valley Province and all of these from the Piedmont and the Coastal Plain. If one now knows historical geology, climate and physiography then the water regimen becomes comprehensible—the pattern of rivers and aquifers, their physical properties and relative abundance, oscillation between flood and drought. Rivers are young or old, they vary by orders; their pattern and distribution, as for aquifers, is directly consequential upon geology, climate and physiography.

Knowing the foregoing and the prior history of plant evolution, we can now comprehend the nature and pattern of soils. As plants are highly selective to environmental factors, by identifying physiographic, climatic zones and soils we can perceive order and predictability in the distribution of constituent plant communities. Indeed, the plant communities are more perceptive to environmental variables than we can be with available data, and we can thus infer environmental factors from the presence of plants. Animals are fundamentally plant-related so that given the preceding information, with the addition of the stage of succession of the plant communities and their age, it is possible both to understand and to predict the species, abundance or scarcity of wild animal populations. If there are no acorns there will be no squirrels; an old forest will have few deer; an early succession can support many. Resources also exist where they do for good and sufficient reasons—coal, iron, limestone, productive soils, water in relative abundance, transportation routes, fall lines and the termini of water transport. And so the land use map becomes comprehensible when viewed through this perspective.

The information so acquired is a gross ecological inventory and contains the data bank for all further investigations. The next task is the interpretation of these data to analyze existing and propose future human land use and management. The first objective is the inventory of unique or scarce phenomena, the technique for which Philip Lewis is renowned. In this all sites of unique scenic, geological, ecological, or historical importance are located. Enlarging this category we can interpret the geological data to locate economic minerals. Geology, climate and physiography will locate dependable water resources. Physiography will reveal slope and exposure which, with soil and water, can be used to locate areas suitable for agriculture by types; the foregoing, with the addition of plant communities will reveal intrinsic suitabilities for both forestry and recreation. The entire body of data can be examined to reveal sites for urbanization, industry, transportation routes, indeed any human land-using activity. This interpretive sequence would produce a body of analytical material but the end product for a region would include a map of unique sites, the location of economic minerals, the location of water resources, a slope and exposure map, a map of agricultural suitabilities by types, a similar map for forestry, one each for recreation and urbanization.

These maps of intrinsic suitability would indicate highest and best uses for the entire study area. But this is not enough. These are single uses ascribed to discrete areas. In the forest there are likely to be dominant or co-dominant trees and other subordinate species. We must seek to prescribe all coexistent, compatible uses which may occupy each area. To this end it is necessary to develop a matrix in which all possible land uses are shown on each coordinate. Each is then examined against all others to determine the degree of compatibility or incompatibility. As an example, a single area of forest may be managed for forestry, either hardwood or pulp; it may be utilized for water management objectives; it may fulfill an erosion control function; it can be managed for wildlife and hunting, recreation, and for villages and hamlets. Here we have not land use in the normal sense but *communities* of land uses. The end product would be a map of present and prospective land uses, in communities of compatibilities, with dominants, co-dominants and subordinates derived from an understanding of nature as process responsive to laws, having limiting factors, constituting a value system and exhibiting opportunities and constraints to human use.

Now this is not a plan. It does not contain any information of demand. This last is the province of the regional scientist, the econometrician, the economic planner. The work is thus divided between the natural scientist, regional planner-landscape architect who interprets the land and its resources, and the economics-based planner who determines demand, locational preferences, investment and fiscal policies. If demand information is available, then the formulation of a plan is possible, and the demand components can be allocated for urban growth, for the nature and form of the metropolis, for the pattern of regional growth.

So what has our method revealed? First, it allows us to understand nature as process insofar as the natural sciences permit. Second, it reveals casuality [sic]. The place is because. Next it permits us to interpret natural processes as resources, to prescribe and even to predict for prospective land uses, not singly but in compatible communities. Finally, given information on demand and investment, we are enabled to produce a plan for a continent or a few hundred acres based upon natural process. That is not a small accomplishment.

You might well agree that this is a valuable and perhaps even indispensible method for regional planning but is it as valuable for landscape architecture? I say that any project, save a small garden or the raddled heart of a city where nature has long gone, which is undertaken without a full comprehension and employment of natural process as form-giver is suspect at best and capriciously irrelevant at worst. I submit that the ecological method is the sine qua non for all landscape architecture.

Yet, I hear you say, those who doubt, that the method may be extremely valuable for regional rural problems, but can it enter the city and reveal a comparable utility? Yes, indeed it can but in crossing this threshold the method changes. When used to examine metropolitan growth the data remains the same but the interpretation is focussed upon the overwhelming demand for urban land uses and it is oriented to the prohibitions and permissiveness exhibited by natural process to urbanization on the one hand and the presence of locational and resource factors which one would select for satisfactory urban environments on the other. But the litany remains the same: historical geology, climate, physiography, the water regimen, soils, plants, animals and land use. This is the source from which the interpretation is made although the grain becomes finer.

Yet you say, the method has not entered the city proper; you feel that it is still a device for protecting natural process against the blind despoliation of ignorance and Philistinism. But the method can enter the city and we can proceed with our now familiar body of information to examine the city in an ecological way. We have explained that the place was "because" and to explain "because," all of physical and biological evolution was invoked. So too with the city. But to explain "because" we invoke not only natural evolution but cultural evolution as well. To do this we make a distinction between the "given" and the "made" forms. The former is the natural landscape identity, the latter is the accumulation of the adaptations to the given form which constitute the present city. Rio is different from New Orleans, Kansas City from Lima, Amsterdam from San Francisco, because. By employing the ecological method we can discern the reason for the location of the city, comprehend its natural form, discern those elements of identity which are critical and expressive, both those of physiography and vegetation, and develop a program for the preservation and enhancement of that identity. The method is equally applicable when one confronts the made form. The successive stages of urbanization are examined as adaptations to the environment, some of which are successful, some not. Some enter the inventory of resources and contribute to the *genius loci*. As for the given form, this method allows us to perceive the elements of identity in a scale of values. One can then prepare a comprehensive landscape plan for a city and feed the elements of identity, natural process, and the palette for formal expression into the comprehensive planning process.

You still demur. The method has not yet entered into the putrid parts of the city. It needs rivers and palisades, hill and valleys, woodlands and parkland. When will it confront slums and overcrowding, congestion and pollution, anarchy and ugliness? Indeed the method can enter into the very heart of the city and by so doing may save us from the melancholy criteria of economic determinism which have proven so disappointing to the orthodoxy of city planning or the alterative of unbridled "design" which haunts architecture. But here again we must be selective as we return to the source in ecology. We will find little that is applicable in energy system ecology, analysis of food pyramids, relations defined in terms of predator-prey, competition, or those other analytical devices so efficacious for plant and animal ecology. But we can well turn to an ecological model which contains multi-faceted criteria for measuring ecosystems and we can select health as an encompassing criterion. The model is my own and as such it is suspect for I am not an ecologist, but each of the parts is the product of a distinguished ecologist. Let us hope that the assembly of the constituents does not diminish their veracity, for they have compelling value.

The most obvious example is life and death. Life is the evolution of a single egg into the complexity of the organism. Death is the retrogression of a complex organism into a few simple elements. If this model is true, it allows us to examine a city, neighborhood, community institution, family, city plan,

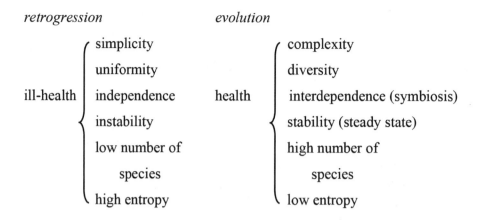

retrogression   *evolution*

ill-health ⎰ simplicity   health ⎰ complexity
          ⎱ uniformity   ⎱ diversity
            independence   interdependence (symbiosis)
            instability   stability (steady state)
            low number of   high number of
               species   species
            high entropy   low entropy

Figure 5-2 Retrogression versus evolution (McHarg, 1967, Reprinted with permission of American Society of Landscape Architects, Redrawn by Travis Witt, 2014).

architectural or landscape design in these terms. This model suggests that any system moving towards simplicity, uniformity, instability with a low number of species and high entropy is retrogressing; any system moving in that direction is moving towards ill health. Conversely, complexity, diversity, stability (steady state), with a high number of species and low entropy are indicators of health and systems moving in this direction are evolving. As a simple application let us map, in tones on transparencies, statistics of all physical disease, all mental disease and all social disease. If we also map income, age of population, density, ethnicity and quality of the physical environment we have on the one hand discerned the environment of health, the environment of pathology and we have accumulated the data which allow interpretation of the social and physical environmental components of health and pathology. Moreover, we have the other criteria of the model which permit examination from different directions. If this model is true and the method good, it may be the greatest contribution of the ecological method to diagnosis and prescription for the city.

But, you say, all this may be very fine but landscape architects are finally designers—when will you speak to ecology and design? I will. Lou Kahn, the most perceptive of men, foresaw the ecological method even through these intractable, inert materials which he infuses with life when he spoke of "existence will," the will to be. The place is because. It is and is in the process of becoming. This we must be able to read, and ecology provides the language. By being, the place or the creature has form. Form and process are indivisible aspects of a single phenomenon. The ecological method allows one to understand form as an explicit point in evolutionary process. Again, Lou Kahn has made clear to us the distinction between form and design. Cup is form and begins from the cupped hand. Design is the creation of the cup, transmuted by the artist, but never denying its formal origins. As a profession, landscape architecture has exploited a pliant earth, tractable and docile plants to make much that is arbitrary, capricious, and inconsequential. We could not see the cupped hand as giving form to the cup, the earth and its processes as giving form to our works. The ecological method is then also the perception of form, an insight to the given form, implication for the made form which is to say design, and this, for landscape architects, may be its greatest gift.

References

Lewis, Philip H. "Quality Corridors for Wisconsin." *Landscape Architecture* 54, no. 2 (1964): 100–107.

McHarg, Ian L., and David A. Wallace. "Plan for the Valleys vs. Spectre of Uncontrolled Growth." *Landscape Architecture* (1965): 11–26.

Methods for Generating Land Suitability Maps: A Comparative Evaluation

Journal of the American Planning Association (1977)

Lewis D. Hopkins

Land resource inventories to determine land suitabilities have become a standard part of planning analysis at many scales. Any attempt to review, compare, evaluate, or improve upon the myriad of case studies, many only partially documented and in limited circulation, suffers from the lack of reference to a common framework. This article develops a general statement of the purpose and character of land suitability analysis, a taxonomy of existing methods for identifying homogeneous areas and rating them as to suitability for specific uses, and a comparative evaluation of these methods.

A suitability map shows the spatial pattern of requirements, preferences, or predictors of some activity. Although the use of the word suitability is often restricted to analyses related to development, the analytical concepts involved are much more general. Using the word loosely, a suitability map for natural hazards (Patri et al., 1970) identifies the pattern of and characteristics associated with some hazard, such as earthquakes. A suitability map for vulnerability to impact (Murray et al., 1971) shows the pattern of characteristics that portend varying degrees or likelihoods of damage from some action elsewhere. For example, low lying lands near flood plains are vulnerable to flooding if there is additional development upstream. Suitability maps for natural hazards, vulnerability to impacts, or off-site impacts are usually preliminary steps in the development of suitability maps for the location of land uses, which might range from nature preserves to nuclear power plants. All of these applications of suitability mapping rest on the same general analytical base. The methods described here might be applied to any of them. For simplicity in this article, most of the discussion focuses on land use rather than in terms of hazard, vulnerability, or impact.

Determining the level of particular costs or impacts is not the central issue here. The primary issue is how such cost or impact information can be manipulated and combined to generate suitability maps for land uses. In this article *suitability* will be assumed to include market, nonmarket, and nonmonetary costs and impacts. The difficulties in obtaining such measures in practice, of course, remain; but discussing these difficulties simultaneously would muddle the attempt to distinguish among methods for generating suitability maps. MacDougall and Brandes (1974) provide a bibliography covering many of the aspects of land resource analysis not covered in this article.

The output of a land suitability analysis is a set of maps, one for each land use, showing which level of suitability characterizes each parcel of land. This output requirement leads directly to two necessary components of any method: (1) a procedure for identifying parcels of land that are homogeneous and (2) a procedure for rating these parcels with respect to suitability for each land use. The next section describes a method in which each of these components is carried out directly without any consideration of the factors that determine the homogeneity of regions and the suitability of land uses. This method sets the stage for considering other methods that explicitly combine factors.

Gestalt Method

The essence of the gestalt method is that the homogeneous regions are determined directly through field observation, or perhaps aerial photographs or topographic maps, without consideration of individual factors such as slope, soils, vegetation, and so on. A gestalt is a whole that cannot be derived through consideration of its parts. A strict interpretation of gestalt would mean that individual factors that could be manipulated to provide understanding of the whole do not even exist.

The gestalt method of suitability analysis can be described in three steps and is diagramed in figure 5-3. First, the study area is partitioned by implicit judgment into homogeneous regions, such as uplands and valley floors. Second, a table is developed that verbally describes the effects or problems that will occur in each of the regions if each of the potential land uses is located there— e.g., this region presents no construction problems, but has no amenities that would render it a pleasant place in which to live. Note from figure 5-3 that some regions identified in step 1 may be determined in step 2 to be of equal suitability for some uses, because the homogeneous regions in step 1 are based on perceived natural land types, not on suitabilities for any one land use. Third, a set of maps, one for each land use, is drawn to show the homogeneous regions in terms of their suitability. Graphic presentation of the map requires that each descriptive suitability comment be represented by some color or symbol as in figure 5-3.

It can be argued that any land suitability analysis must rely on gestalt judgments at some level of specificity. For example, vegetation cover types might be observed in the field and noted on aerial photographs. The determination of cover type is thus based on implicit judgment rather than on explicit rules. Cover types can be thought of as a combination of various lower level factors— age, understory species, canopy species, and management practices. In this case, a gestalt method is being used to generate vegetation cover type, a factor to be combined with other factors in a later step. Once a factor such as cover type is identified, however, one can no longer use the gestalt method at some higher level because by definition it does not combine factors. Thus, although the gestalt method may underlie any other method at the elemental level, in this article gestalt method refers to attempting to determine land suitability directly in one gestalt judgment.

Limitations of Gestalt Method

Few people have the capability, and planners seldom have the longstanding local experience, to deal with land classification and interpretation as a gestalt. Some land resource inventory processes are specifically intended as a means of immersing the planner in a study region, "understanding the place" as McHarg (1969) calls it, so that gestalt judgments can be made. However, land suitabilities generated without identification of the factors considered are difficult for other people to scrutinize or confirm. The results are therefore difficult to communicate convincingly to decision makers.

Given both the scarcity of people capable of using the gestalt method and the frequent necessity of communicating results in public forums, more explicit methods must be found for generating land suitability maps. More explicit methods inherently require the consideration of factors—the variables or dimensions such as soils, slope, vegetation, and existing land use—that enter into the determination of suitabilities. The remainder of this article is concerned with how such factors can be combined in relatively explicit ways to yield land suitability maps. . . .

Another general response to the difficulties of applying gestalt was to devise explicit methods of combining factors in order to *discover* suitabilities. The assumption in this case is that the method yields valid suitability ratings

Land types map

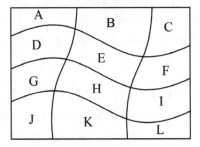

Step 1: partition land into homogenous regions by gestalt field observation

Land uses

Land types	R1	R2	R3	R4
A				

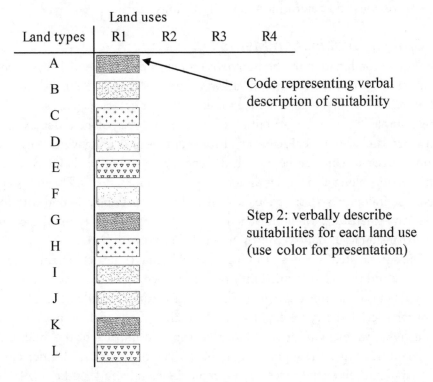

Code representing verbal description of suitability

Step 2: verbally describe suitabilities for each land use (use color for presentation)

Suitability map

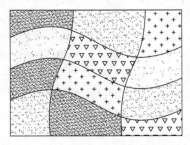

Step 3: map suitabilities by code for each land use, one map for each land use

Figure 5-3 Gestalt method (Hopkins, 1977, Reproduced by permission of the American Planning Association, Redrawn by Travis Witt, 2014).

because of the properties of the method itself. The results are not judged by conformation to some gestalt or empirical standard. This general approach was the one taken by McHarg. The ordinal and linear combination methods presented in the next section are generally perceived from this perspective.

Determining Suitabilities by Mathematical Combination

This section describes three general methods for generating suitability maps by mathematical operations. These operations simultaneously identify homogeneous regions and determine suitability ratings.

Ordinal Combination Method

The ordinal combination method, sometimes referred to as the McHarg method because of its use in the Richmond Parkway study (McHarg, 1969), is diagrammed in figure 5-4. The first step is to map for each of a set of factors (e.g., soils, slope, vegetation, land use) the distribution of types (soil types, slope classes, vegetation types, land use types). Factors are distinct dimensions along which variations among parcels of land can be described. Types are nominal labels for particular characteristics along a particular dimension (e.g., Drummer soil). The first step is illustrated in figure 5-4 using one factor with three types and a second with four types. An actual study would include many factors and more types of each, but such expansion leads only to confusion for the purposes at hand.

The second step consists of filling in a table that indicates (in this case by levels of gray) the relative suitability rating for each land use of each type (e.g., soil type) of each factor (e.g., soils). The ratings assume consideration of all the characteristics of the type (e.g., for soil type this might include permeability, productivity, water table, etc.) and all the costs and impacts of the land use if located on this type. These ratings may be derived through use of other tables, maps, and extensive study (see, for example, Lyle and von Wodtke, 1974), but the process of deriving them is not the central issue here.

The third step consists of making a suitability map for each land use based on each factor. For each land use the type designations on each factor map from step 1 are replaced with the appropriate gray levels from the particular land use column in the table from step 2. Step 3 is illustrated in figure 5-4 for land use R1.

The fourth step consists of overlaying, for each land use, the suitability maps of individual factors. A composite suitability map is thus obtained for each land use. Each of these composite maps shows the spatial pattern of levels of suitability for the given land use.

Step 1: map data factors by type

Factor 1 types map

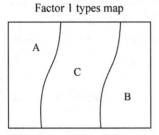

Factor 2 types map

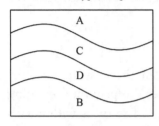

Step 2: rate each type of each factor for each land use

Factor type	Land uses			
	R1	R2	R3	R4
Factor 1				
Type A	▥	•	•	•
Type B	▦	•	•	•
Type C	▥	•	•	•
Factor 2				
Type A	▤	•	•	•
Type B	▤	•	•	•
Type C	▤	•	•	•
Type D	▤	•	•	•

Step 3: map ratings for each land use, one set of maps for each land use

Factor 1 suitability map

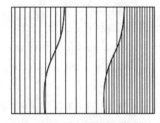

Factor 2 suitability map

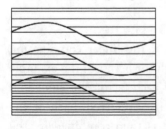

Step 4: overlay single-factor suitability maps to obtain composite map, one map for each land use

Composite suitability map

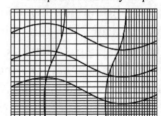

Figure 5-4 Ordinal combination methods with gray levels (Hopkins, 1977, Reproduced by permission of the American Planning Association, Redrawn by Travis Witt, 2014).

Limitations of ordinal combinations. By describing the same process using a numerical index to represent gray levels some assumptions emerge that implicitly underlie the ordinal combination. Figure 5-5 is identical to figure 5-4 except that gray levels have been replaced by an equivalent ordinal number system, an ordering of types for each factor. Step 4 in figure 5-5 involves the addition of what appear to be numbers on an ordinal scale. This addition is an invalid mathematical operation in the sense that the mathematical properties usually assumed do not hold. . . .

Ordinal combination is *not* a good method for generating suitability maps because of the implied addition of ordinal scale numbers and because of the implied independence of factors.

Linear Combination Method

The most frequent response to this understanding of the measurement assumptions of the ordinal combination method has been to play the weighting game. The usual procedure is illustrated in figure 5-6. The types within each factor are rated on separate interval scales. Then a multiplier—often identified as an *importance* weight—is assigned for each factor as shown in step 2. The ratings for each type are multiplied by the weight for the factor. The suitability rating for a particular region is then the sum of the multiplied ratings, or in mathematical terms, the linear combination. The effect of multiplication by the weights is merely to change the unit of measure of the ratings on each factor by the ratio of the multipliers so that all of the ratings are on the same interval scale (e.g., if one factor is in dollars and another in cents, then the first would be multiplied by 1 and the second by 0.01 to put both in dollars). The ratings can then be added. Thus, the units of measure for suitability with respect to each factor can be made equivalent after rating the types for each factor individually on interval scales with different measurement units.

Rating procedures. A straightforward explanation of the linear combination method is given by Ward and Grant (1971), although (or because) the example is entirely artificial as is the one here. Each type of each factor is assigned an interval rating from one to nine, where nine is most preferred. Each of the factors is then assigned a weight. The information is then combined by the standard formula for a weighted average: the sum of the products of the ratings multiplied by the respective weights for each factor, divided by the sum of the weights.

$$\text{Rating} = \frac{w_1 r_1 + w_2 r_2 + \dots + w_n r_n}{w_1 + w_2 + \dots w_n}$$

Step 1: map data factors by type

Factor 1 types map

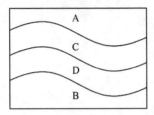

Factor 2 types map

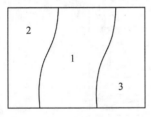

Step 2: rate each type of each factor for each land use

Land uses

Factor type	R1	R2	R3	R4	• • •
Factor 1					
Type A	2	•	•	•	
Type B	3	•	•	•	
Type C	1	•	•	•	
Factor 2					
Type A	2	•	•	•	
Type B	3	•	•	•	
Type C	1	•	•	•	
Type D	2	•	•	•	

Step 3: map ratings for each land use, one set of maps for each land use

Factor 1 suitability map

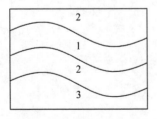

Factor 2 suitability map

Step 4: overlay single-factor suitability maps to obtain composite, one map for each land use

Composite suitability map

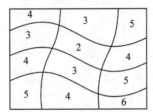

Figure 5-5 Ordinal combination methods with numerical index (Hopkins, 1977, Reproduced by permission of the American Planning Association, Redrawn by Travis Witt, 2014).

Step 1: map data factors by type

Factor 1 types map

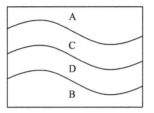

Factor 2 types map

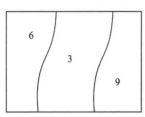

Step 2: rate each type of each factor and weight each factor for each land use

		Land uses			
	Factor types	R1	R2	R3	R4 ▪ ▪ ▪
Factor 1 weight		3			
	Type A	2	▪	▪	▪
	Type B	3	▪	▪	▪
	Type C	1	▪	▪	▪
Factor 2 weight		5			
	Type A	2	▪	▪	▪
	Type B	3	▪	▪	▪
	Type C	1	▪	▪	▪
	Type D	2	▪	▪	▪

Step 3: map ratings for each land use, one set of maps for each land use

Factor 1 suitability map

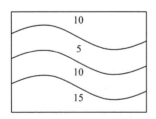

Factor 2 suitability map

Step 4: overlay single-factor suitability maps to obtain composite map, one map for each land use

Composite suitability map

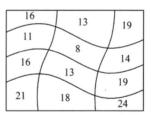

Figure 5-6 Linear combination method (Hopkins, 1977, Reproduced by permission of the American Planning Association, Redrawn by Travis Witt, 2014).

A *1* is the minimum rating permitted in the Ward and Grant example, suggesting that a system visualized as ordinal is being scaled by multiplication and addition. One therefore must assume, as is indicated implicitly, that *1* represents zero, and signifies no amenities and all costs. . . . The weights are merely relative proportions among the units in which the suitability within each factor was measured in the first place. One must be wary of using units of measure resulting in single factor ratings of 4, 6, and 8 with an importance of 1, versus ratings using units resulting in 2, 3, and 4 with an importance of 2. This ambiguity occurs in the Ward and Grant example. The importance weights are not independent of the units used to measure suitability in terms of the individual factors. . . .

The result of the weighted combination is a single measurement scale with a common unit. Some people find it easier to evaluate all the types of all the individual factors directly in a common unit rather than devising separate units of measure and weights for each factor. One way of initiating such an evaluation is to choose an arbitrary value, say 100, for the suitability of a certain type (e.g., Drummer-Flannagan soil) of a certain factor (soils) for a certain land use (e.g., row crop agriculture). All other evaluations are then made with reference to this standard, using the unit implied. The dollar is one unit of valuation that people are used to applying to a wide, but still limited, range of options. Therefore, another useful evaluation procedure is to express suitabilities by factor directly in estimated dollar units (Hopkins, 1975).

Although some people do not believe that such all-inclusive ratings can exist, the same thing is being accomplished through the weights in the usual linear combination method. The protection of not understanding exactly what the ultimate ratings will be has simply been removed. Freeman (1970) has provided a straightforward explanation of the necessity of valuation in making choices (see also Hopkins et al., 1973). One can do the valuation explicitly or implicitly, but any choice among alternatives with respect to a set of factors implies a relative valuation of factors at least sufficient to make that choice.

Independence of factors. The linear combination method corrects the measurement problems of the ordinal combination method, but the problem of handling interdependence among the factors still remains. The linear combination method cannot deal with the situation where the relative suitability for a given land use of a type on one factor depends on the type on any of the other factors. Despite its inability to handle interdependence among the factors, the linear combination approach is still frequently used, as implied for example by the discussion of weighted overlays in Steinitz, Parker, and Jordan (1976). . . .

Nonlinear Combination Method

Interdependence among the factors could be handled if the combination equation were not linear. If the appropriate relationships among the factors are known and can be expressed as mathematical functions, the nonlinear combination method is ideal. Instead of a linear combination (weighted addition) as in deriving step 4 in figure 5-6, the ratings of types are plugged into the nonlinear functions and results are obtained analytically for all factors combined. The only difference from figure 5-6 is that the combination equation to get from step 3 to step 4 contains a nonlinear relationship instead of addition. However, this method is not likely to be possible for studies of the kind under consideration, because the relationships required to deal with the full range of costs and impacts are now known. . . .

Most nonlinear equations that are widely used generate suitabilities regarding generating of impact, runoff for example, rather than suitabilities for land uses. As discussed at the beginning of this article, such impact suitability maps may be inputs to land suitability maps, but they constitute only one factor in the broader level of analysis that is required. The nonlinear combination method overcomes the problem of interdependence among factors, but so far it has not been operationally useful for generating overall land use suitabilities.

Explicit Identification of Regions

One way to avoid the problem of interdependence among the factors is to first identify homogeneous regions explicitly. The homogeneity of regions does not depend on the independence of factors. Given the homogeneous regions, the suitability ratings for each region can be determined by implicit judgment concerning the combinations of types that then define the regions.

Factor Combination Method

A straightforward modification of the gestalt method allows one to deal with interdependence among the factors but with a tremendous loss of efficiency compared to the method described in the previous section. Figure 5-7 describes the same artificial problem used for illustration previously, but in this case the order of steps 2 and 3 is reversed. Step 2 now consists of combining type maps for each of the factors to obtain a composite map of regions that are homogeneous with respect to all factors. No rating is implied; this map is merely a complete logical intersection or factor combination of the boundaries of the regions from each factor map. It is equivalent to a very complex Venn diagram in set theory.

Step 3 is now the derivation of the suitability ratings table. Instead of a list of factors and types for each, the vertical axis identified all the regions that

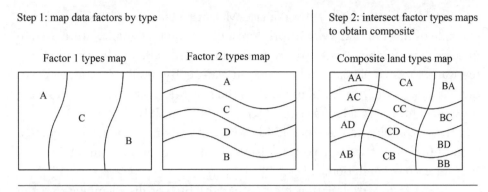

Step 1: map data factors by type

Step 2: intersect factor types maps to obtain composite

Factor 1 types map

Factor 2 types map

Composite land types map

Step 3: rate each region for each land use

Step 4: map suitability ratings for each land use, one map for each land use

Regions	Land uses			
	R1	R2	R3	R4
AA	10.0	•	•	•
AB	12.0	•	•	•
AC	22.0	•	•	•
AD	14.0	•	•	•
BA	40.0	•	•	•
BB	22.0	•	•	•
BC	35.0	•	•	•
BD	20.0	•	•	•
CA	8.0	•	•	•
CB	12.0	•	•	•
CC	14.0	•	•	•
CD	5.0	•	•	•

Composite suitability map

Figure 5-7 Factor combination method (Hopkins, 1977, Reproduced by permission of the American Planning Association, Redrawn by Travis Witt, 2014).

occur on the map. It is thus equivalent to the table for the gestalt method in figure 5-3, except that an explicit procedure has been used for deriving the homogeneous regions from the individual factors. One can now evaluate the suitability for each land use relative to each specific combination of types, without having to consider the general relationships among individual factors as in the linear combination and nonlinear combination methods. It is evident that, just as in the gestalt method, implicit judgments are used to determine the suitabilities. The determination of homogeneous regions has been made explicit; the determination of suitabilities has not.

The Plan for the Valleys by Wallace-McHarg Associates (1964) is a simple example of this method. Two factors, forest cover and topography, were used to generate five combinations: valley floors, unforested valley walls, forested valley walls, forested plateau, and unforested plateau. By implication, forest cover did not apply to any valley floor areas on the site. Management principles were prescribed for each region (see also McHarg 1969, pp. 79ff.).

Factor combination is suitable for studies involving only a few factors; a larger number of factors makes infeasible the determination of suitability ratings for each combination. . . .

. . . The factor combination method has the further disadvantage that the rating of regions in terms of suitability relies entirely on implicit judgment for the transformation of the types in the combination into a rating for the combination as a whole.

Cluster Analysis

Cluster analysis, used in the Rice Center (1974) study, also explicitly identifies homogeneous regions by successively pairing the most similar sites or groups of sites, based on an index of similarity across the set of factors. The process is stopped at some predetermined acceptable level of diversity within the clusters, resulting in a set of regions, each with a profile showing the range of types for each factor. As in the factor combination method, this profile still must be transformed into some aggregate rating by implicit judgment. The clustering does, however, serve to reduce explicitly the combinations of types to be considered.

One of the most interesting potentials of the cluster analysis method is the possibility of using the statistical measures of variation on factors within clusters as measures of suitability. Diversity within a homogeneous region is often a more useful measure of suitability for particular uses than a modal type or a specified range. For example, a region with diverse slopes makes a good site for a planned unit development; a region with all flat land or all steep slopes does not. However used, cluster analysis requires great care in interpretation and significant costs for computation. Cluster analysis can not be justified unless expected results are significantly better than from other methods; this case has not yet been demonstrated.

Suitabilities by Logical Combination

Rules of combination is a useful label for a class of methods that is, in a sense, a compromise between the nonlinear combination method and the factor combination method. The rules assign suitabilities to *sets* of combinations of types rather than to single combinations and are expressed in terms of verbal logic rather than in terms of numbers and arithmetic. It is then not necessary to evaluate each combination separately as in the factor combination method; nor is it necessary to find a precise mathematical statement of the relationships among factors as in the nonlinear combination method. In addition, the process of determining suitabilities is more explicit than in the factor combination method and can deal with interdependence. A final method, *hierarchical combination*, could be viewed as a special case of rules of combination. However, because it is an important case, with general properties of its own, hierarchical combination is treated separately.

Rules of Combination Method

A simple, clearcut example of the rules of combination method is given by Kiefer (1965). After mapping the factors, he rates the types within the factors in a process equivalent to step 2 in figure 5-5. He then states the general rule that the rating of the worst factor in a given region overrides the rating of all other factors. The rating of the worst factor is thus assigned as the rating of the combination of types for the given region, though often with exceptions. Kiefer, for instance, identifies sets of combinations that are to be rated by different rules, such as "a land unit rating 'optimum' in all factors except soil class and rating 'satisfactory' in soil class should be given an overall rating of 'optimum.'" Instead of a linear combination to map step 2 into steps 3 and 4 as in figure 5-5, the verbally expressed rules determine the composite ratings for the map in step 4.

The early warning system (Patri et al., 1970; Ingmire and Patri, 1971) uses the rules of combination approach in deriving the "critical factor" map for rock and soil dynamics, which is essentially a suitability map for the likelihood of geologic activity. Rules of the following sort were used to define suitability levels.

> This broad category includes all cells which are scored in excess of 10% slope and are of a high erosion hazard category. They are outside of critical formations and expansive soil zones. They may include all but "active" and "major" faults (Patri et al., 1970, p. 132).

Although McHarg's work is usually associated with the ordinal combination method described in figure 5-4, many of his studies are more accurately described in terms of rules of combination. A frequently used graphic procedure begins by following the factor combination method illustrated in figure 5-7. Each of the factor maps is drawn with nominal data types. A code sheet is made by placing a piece of tracing paper on each of the factor maps in succession, outlining areas bounding each type and identifying them with a sequential code of letters of numbers as illustrated for the two-factor case in step 2 of figure 5-7. This paint-by-number sheet is then printed as a base map for drawing suitability maps for various land use activities. However, instead of developing suitabilities through implicit judgment of each of the combinations at this stage, as in the factor combination method, a set of explicit rules of combination is developed. The map of step 4 is then colored to show suitability for a particular use by applying the rules to each combination on the coded base map. The only difference from figure 5-7 is that rules are used to generate the ratings in step 3. The Medford study (Juneja, 1974) provides a well-documented example of this approach, although the rules of combination follow a very simplistic and rigid form. The general rule used is not specific to the set of combinations, nor does it have any very convincing basis in terms of the natural relationships among factors. A single rule of this type is unlikely to be valid for the many different factors and land uses, because it is unlikely that the natural relationships involved will be so nearly the same. . . .

Rules of combination can be applied to construct the composite suitability ratings map without having to deal with each possible combination individually. If the rules are stated explicitly, they can be used to generate maps directly without compiling a suitability table for all possible combinations. This is an obvious saving of effort compared to the factor combination approach. In addition, such rules are explicit and thus subject to scrutiny. The rules, if carefully devised, can also handle interdependence among factors.

Hierarchical Combination

A more structured approach to rules of combination is based on the work of Alexander (1964). The basic concept is that a composite rating can be generated hierarchically. First, the combinations of types from each subset of strongly interdependent factors are rated for suitability as combinations, which thus permits consideration of interdependence among the factors within each subset. Then higher order combinations of the combinations from these subsets of factors are rated, with each lower order combination now treated as an integrated whole. This sequence of hierarchical combinations is repeated until a rating is achieved that includes all relevant factors. In this approach a combination of types in a subset is evaluated only once, rather than being evaluated each time it appears as part of a combination of types for all factors. The increase in efficiency over evaluating all possible combinations depends on the number of relatively independent subsets of factors that can be identified. Alexander and Manheim (1962) applied this concept in a somewhat different fashion for the location of a highway corridor. . . .

Comparison, Integration of Methods

A comparison of some important characteristics of the eight general methods —gestalt, ordinal combination, linear combination, nonlinear combination, factor combination, cluster analysis, rules of combination, and hierarchical combination—is presented in table 5-1. Because of the complementary characteristics of several of the methods, it is useful to apply more than one method in carrying out a land suitability analysis. This summary and comparison outlines circumstances in which the various methods are appropriate either alone or in conjunction with other methods.

Recommended Methods

For simple, small, land resource inventories, the gestalt method is quite acceptable if qualified field personnel are available. A typical application would be a site visit, enhanced by making notes on aerial photographs, to determine land suitabilities for a small planned unit development. The disadvantage of the gestalt method is the implicit identification of regions and determination of ratings. It would be difficult to convince others of the validity of the suitability results if, for example, a change in zoning were required.

The three mathematical combination methods are either invalid or insufficient by themselves. The ordinal combination method is invalid and should not be used because of its assumptions and its inability to handle interdependence. The linear combination method should not be used as a general method for developing suitability maps because of its inability to handle interdependence. For particular sets of factors that can be shown to be independent, however, it is perfectly appropriate and relatively easy to use. The nonlinear combination method is generally insufficient by itself because the required mathematical relationships for the full range of costs and impacts are not known.

The factor combination and cluster analysis methods do not include explicit means for determining suitability ratings. The factor combination method is sometimes useful when an analyst is not sufficiently familiar with an area to make gestalt judgments to identify land types. If the study is otherwise relatively simple, it may then be reasonable to make implicit judgments as to the relative suitabilities of the regions. Although cluster analysis has been used in a few research studies for reducing the number of suitability evaluations required, it has not yet been shown to be worthwhile compared to the costs and benefits of using other methods.

For most studies, the best approach is to use the linear and nonlinear combination methods as a first stage, followed by rules of combination. First, incorporate the relationships among factors for which mathematical functions, either linear or nonlinear, are known by using the particular functions that apply. For example, soil loss and runoff can be computed from nonlinear relationships of soil type, vegetation cover, and slope. Also, certain construction costs associated with soil characteristics, vegetation, and slope can be summed as a

Table 5-1

Summary comparison of methods (Hopkins 1977, Reproduced by permission of the American Planning Association, Redrawn by Travis Witt, 2014).

Method	Handles inter-dependence of factors	Explicit identification of regions	Explicit determina-tion of ratings	Additional comments	Example
Gestalt	Yes	No	No		Hills (1961)
Mathematical combination					
Ordinal combination	No	Yes	Yes	Involves invalid mathematical operations	McHarg (1969), pp. 31–41
Linear combination	No	Yes	Yes		Ward and Grant (1971)
Nonlinear combination	Yes	Yes	Yes	Required functional relationships generally not known	Voelker (1976), pp. 49 ff..
Identification of regions					
Factor combination	Yes	Yes	No	Requires a very large number of evaluative judgments	Wallace-McHarg (1964)
Cluster analysis	Yes	Yes	No		Rice Center (1974)
Logical combination					
Rules of combination	Yes	Yes	Yes		Kiefer (1965)
Hierarchical combination	Yes	Yes	Yes		Murray et al. (1971), pp. 131–174

linear combination to yield a construction cost figure. This preliminary stage yields additional factors—in this example soil loss, runoff, and construction costs. These new factors can then be combined with each other and the original factors (exclusive of their contribution to soil loss, runoff, and construction costs) using rules of combination. This second stage considers costs and impacts for which precise mathematical relationships are not known and yields an overall suitability rating for a land use. Extensive research projects at Harvard (Landscape Architecture Research Office, 1974), the University of Massachusetts (Fabos and Caswell, 1977) and Oak Ridge National Laboratories (Voelker, 1976) include examples of the general approach of using linear, nonlinear, and rules of combination for appropriate components of a suitability analysis.

The approach just described involves a hierarchical sequence of combinations. First, a set of relationships is used to yield a new factor, runoff. Other relationships are used to yield other new factors such as soil loss. Then these new factors (or a subset of them) are combined. In this combination of new factors the relationships that yielded the runoff are *not* considered. The relationships between runoff and the other new factors are considered at the more general level. Hierarchy is a pervasive structure in thinking and accumulating knowledge (Simon, 1969). It is therefore inherent in any complex procedure for generating suitability maps.

Interpretation of Land Suitability

No matter how obtained, land suitability maps provide information only about the supply of land at various levels of suitability for different uses. It is not possible to make evaluative, predictive, or normative statements about allocations of several uses to sites without also making some assumptions about the relative demands for the alternative uses. The necessity of dealing with both supply and demand in order to consider questions of land resource allocation is basic to land resource economics (Barlowe, 1972). Gold (1974) has presented the argument for simple, artificial examples in the context of land suitability analysis. Some land suitability studies pretend, or at least appear to pretend, to yield immediate implications for allocation of land uses without recourse to explicit assumptions about relative demand for various land uses. It is on this point that the land suitability inventory work of the past two decades must be integrated with other land use modeling and analysis, which has been developed primarily in the context of economic analysis. Many experiments already have been conducted in pursuit of analytical models capable of considering not only transportation and demand assumptions but also the site variations and environmental effects. (See, for example, Schlager, 1965; Southeastern Wisconsin Regional Planning Commission, 1968, 1969, 1973; Hopkins, 1973; Landscape Architecture Research Office, 1974; Hopkins, 1975).

This taxonomy of methods points up the inappropriateness of the frequently cited ordinal combination method, the limitations of the linear and nonlinear combination methods, and the advantages of the general class of methods called rules of combination. It is hoped that the attempt to draw meaningful distinctions among frequently used methods will provide a basis on which further development of land suitability analysis techniques can take place. . . .

Author's Note

An article of this nature relies on the work of others. In this case, particular acknowledgments must be made of the author's experiences working with Ian McHarg, Narendra Juneja, E. Bruce MacDougall, Charles Brandes (who was persuaded to write his master's thesis on this topic), and other colleagues and students at the University of Pennsylvania and the University of Illinois. Referees' comments on an earlier draft led to clarification of several points.

References

Alexander, Christopher. *Notes on the Synthesis of Form*. Vol. 5. Cambridge, MA: Harvard University Press, 1964.

Alexander, Christopher, and Marvin L. Manheim. "The Use of Diagrams in Highway Route Location: An Experiment." Research Report R62-3. Cambridge, MA: Department of Civil Engineering, MIT, 1962.

Barlowe, Raleigh. *Land Resource Economics*. Englewood Cliffs, NJ: Prentice Hall, 1972.

Brandes, Charles. *Methods of Synthesis for Ecological Planning*. Master's thesis, Department of Landscape Architecture and Regional Planning, University of Pennsylvania, 1973.

Buyhoff, G., P. Miller, J. Roach, D. Zhou, and L. Fuller. "An Artificial Intelligence Methodology for Landscape Visual Assessment." *Artifical Intelligence Applications Journal* 8, no. 1 (1994): 1–2.

Carmone, Frank J., and Paul E. Green. *Multidimensional Scaling and Related Techniques in Marketing Analysis*. Boston: Allyn and Bacon, 2009.

Durfee, R. C. *The Use of Factor and Cluster Analysis in Regional Modeling*. ORNL-TM-3720. Oak Ridge, TN: Oak Ridge National Laboratory, 1972.

Fabos, Julius Gy, and Stephanie J. Caswell. "Composite Landscape Assessment." Research Bulletin no. 637. Amherst: Massachusetts Agricultural Experiment Station, 1977.

Freeman, Myrick. "Project Design and Evaluation with Multiple Objectives." In *Public Expenditures and Policy Analysis*, edited by Robert H. Haveman and Julius Margolis. Chicago: Markham, 1970.

Gold, Andrew J. "Design with Nature: A Critique." *Journal of the American Institute of Planners* 40, no. 4 (1974): 284–86.

Hill, Morris, and Yigal Tzamir. "Multidimensional Evaluation of Regional Plans Serving Multiple Objectives." *Papers in Regional Science* 29, no. 1 (1972): 139–65.

Hills, G. Angus. *The Ecological Basis for Land-Use Planning*. Ontario Department of Lands and Forests, Research Branch, 1961.

Hopkins, Lewis D. "Design Method Evaluation—An Experiment with Corridor Selection." *Socio-Economic Planning Sciences* 7, no. 5 (1973): 423–36.

Hopkins, Lewis D., R. Bruce Wood, Debra Brochmann, and Louis Messina. *Environmental Impact Statements: A Handbook for Writers and Reviewers.* No. IIEQ-73-8. Illinois Institute for Environmental Quality. Report no. PB 226 276/AS. Springfield, VA: National Technical Information Service, 1973.

Ingmire, Thomas J., and Tito Patri. "An Early Warning System for Regional Planning." *Journal of the American Institute of Planners* 37, no. 6 (1971): 403–10.

Juneja, Narendra. *Medford, Performance Requirements for the Maintenance of Social Values Represented by the Natural Environment of Medford Township, NJ.* Center for Ecological Research in Planning and Design, Department of Landscape Architecture and Regional Planning, University of Pennsylvania, 1974.

Kiefer, Ralph W. "Land Evaluation for Land Use Planning." *Building Sciences* 1, no. 2 (1965): 109–25.

Landscape Architecture Research Office. *The Interaction between Urbanization and Land: Quality and Quantity in Environmental Plannin and Design—Progress Report for Years One, Two and Three, Proposal for Year Four.* Cambridge, MA: Gradaute School of Design, Harvard University, 1974.

Lewis, Philip H. "Ecology: The Inland Water Tree." *Journal of the American Institute of Architects* 51, no. 8 (1969): 59–63.

Lyle, John, and Mark Von Wodtke. "An Information System for Environmental Planning." *Journal of the American Institute of Planners* 40, no. 6 (1974): 394–413.

MacDougall, E. Bruce, and Charles E. Brandes. "A Selected Annotated Bibliography on Land Resource Inventory and Analysis for Planning." Harrisburg, PA: Department of Environmental Resources, Commonwealth of Pennsylvania, 1974

Maranell, Gary Michael. *Scaling: A Sourcebook for Behavioral Scientists.* Chicago: Aldine, 1974.

McHarg, Ian L. *Design with Nature.* New York: American Museum of Natural History, 1969.

Murray, Timothy, Peter Rogers, David Sinton, Carl Steinitz, Richard Toth, and Douglas Way. *Honey Hill: A Systems Analysis for Planning the Multiple Use of Controlled Water Areas.* 2 vols. Report nos. AD 736343 and AD 736344. Springfield, VA: National Technical Information Service, 1971.

Patri, Tito, David C. Streatfield, and Thomas J. Ingmire. *The Santa Cruz Mountains Regional Pilot Study: Early Warning System.* Berkeley: Deparment of Landscape Architecture, University of California, 1970.

Rice Center for Community Design and Research. *An Approach to Natural Environmental Analysis.* Houston: The Center, 1974

Schlager, Kenneth J. "A Land Use Plan Design Model." *Journal of the American Institute of Planners* 31, no. 2 (1965): 103–11.

Simon, Herbert A. *The Sciences of the Artificial.* Cambridge, MA: MIT Press. 1969.

Southeastern Wisconsin Regional Planning Commission. *A Land Use Plan Design Model: Volume 1; Model Development: Volume 2; Model Test: Volume 3: Final Report.* Waukesha WI: Southeastern Wisconsin Regional Planning Commission, 1968, 1969, 1973.

Steinitz, Carl, Paul Parker, and Lawrie Jordan. "Hand-Drawn Overlays: Their History and Prospective Uses." *Landscape Architecture* 66, no. 5 (1976): 444–55.

Storie, R. Earl. "An Index for Rating the Agricultural Value of Soils." *Bulletin 556.* Berkeley: California Agricultural Experiment Station, 1933.

Voelker, A. H. *Indices: A Technique for Using Large Spatial Databases.* ORNL/RUS-15. Oak Ridge, TN: Oak Ridge National Laboratory, 1976.

Wallace-McHarg Associates. *Technical Report on the Plan for the Valleys.* 2 vols. Philadelphia: Wallace-McHarg Associates, 1964.

Ward, Wesley, and Donald P. Grant. "A Computer-Aided Spatial Allocation Technique." In *Proceedings of the Kentucky Workshop on Computer Applications to Environmental Design,* edited by Michael Kennedy. Lexington, KY: College of Architecture, University of Kentucky, 1971.

Whitman, Ira L. "Design of an Environmental Evaluation System." *National Technical Information Service,* no. PB 201 (1971): 743.

The Art of Site Planning
Site Planning (1984)
Kevin Lynch and Gary Hack

Site planning is the art of arranging structures on the land and shaping the spaces between, an art linked to architecture, engineering, landscape architecture, and city planning. Site plans locate objects and activities in space and time. These plans may concern a small cluster of houses, a single building and its grounds, or something as extensive as a small community built in a single operation.

Site planning is more than a practical art, however complex its technical apparatus. Its aim is moral and esthetic: to make places which enhance everyday life—which liberate their inhabitants and give them a sense of the world they live in. Professional skill—that easy familiarity with behavior settings, grading, planting, drainage, circulation, microclimates, or survey—is only a path to that result.

Roads and buildings, even gardens, do not grow by themselves. They are shaped by someone's decision, however limited or careless. The economic and technical advantages of large-scale development incline us to organize sites in a more comprehensive and convulsive way than when there was time for the gradual adjustment of use and structure. But regardless of scale or the degree of deliberation, any human site is somehow planned, whether piecemeal or at one sweep, whether by convention or by conscious choice.

Site planning has a new importance, but it is an old art. One thinks of such magnificent places as the Katsura Palace, the Italian squares and hilltowns, the crescents of Bath, Wright's Taliesin, or the New England town green. By contrast, most site planning in our country today is shallow, careless, and ugly. This reflects a lack of skill, but also the stubborn structural problems of our society, which are political, economic, and institutional. Place making is divided from place using; purposes change, conflict, and are not well understood. Site planning may be a hurried layout, in which details are left to chance; or a cursory subdivision, to which buildings will be added later; or a last-minute effort to fit a previously designed building onto some available piece of land. Site plans are seen as minor adjuncts to the dominant decisions of developers, engineers, architects, and builders. At the same time, they are the subject of significant public regulations.

This neglect is a dangerous error, since the site is a crucial aspect of environment. It has a biological, social, and psychological impact that goes far beyond its more obvious influence on cost and technical function. It limits what people can do, and yet also opens new opportunities to them. For some groups—small children, for example—it can be the dominant feature of their world. Its influence outlives that of most buildings, since site organization persists for generations. What we do to our habitat has an enduring effect on our lives.

Normal Process

Site planning is usually accomplished in a regular sequence, a sequence around which we organize this text. This typical process has its flaws and admits of variations, as we will explain. But we begin by mapping that normal stream, and comment later on its inadequacies. . . .

In the most common case, a site plan is made by a professional for some paying client, who has the power to carry it out. The development is to consist of a collection of buildings, which will be built on some largely open piece of ground, already chosen for the purpose. In a project of moderate size, site planning and the design of the buildings will be done simultaneously, preferably in a single office. Development will be completed in a few year's time. Once occupied, the site will continue to be used in the same way, as far as can be foreseen. For a larger and more complex work to be created over a longer period of time, the site plan may be prepared first and the building designs later.

What Is the Problem?

Let this stand as the normal case. The first step—the most difficult and most often bungled step—is to ask what the problem is. Defining the problem means making a whole cluster of decisions: For whom is the place being made? For what purpose? Who will decide what the form is to be? What resources can be used? What type of solution is expected? In what location will it be built? These decisions set the stage for the entire process to come. Although they will to some extent be modified as the process develops—and should be modified more frequently than they are—later changes are painful and confusing.

The purpose of the development depends on the situation and on the values of the influential clients. But some of those who will be affected by the plans are absent, or uninformed, or voiceless. There usually are conflicts among the various clients. There may be sharp distinctions between the future users and those who pay for the professional services. In this touchy situation, the designer (if he has the opportunity) has the responsibility to clarify the given objectives, raise hidden ones for debate, reveal new possibilities and unexpected costs, and even speak for absent or voiceless clients. More often, however, designers will simply speak for their own values—an aggravated error, since most of them are members of a particular social class.

The decisions which define the problem are so closely interrelated as to be circular: the clients determine the purposes, and yet the purposes indicate the proper clients; the probable solution determines the resources required, and yet the resources available limit the possible solutions. This ring of decisions is fashioned according to the limits and the possibilities which the initiator of the project sees before her, but the designer can also enter this ring and affect its shape. More often, he fails to do so, and the ring is forged by customary solutions and by the prevailing distribution of power.

In embryo, the problem statement contains the final design, and any alert designer is anxious to play a role in making it: to comment on site, purpose, and user, to consider the type of solution required, and whether the resources are sufficient to accomplish it. Commonly, however, the problem is determined by the client before the site designer is brought in. As a minimum, in that case, the latter is responsible for seeing that the problem has been explicitly set out, that its parts are internally consistent (sufficient resources, solution appropriate to purpose, adequate site, etc.), and that he can in conscience work for the clients and purposes given. To do that, he must run through the entire site planning process in his mind, using his experience and judgment to guess at its outcome.

Assume that the problem is properly set out and the site planner is willing to begin. The principal objectives of the work are stated, as well as the expected users and their needs. The site is chosen, and so is the type of development and activity intended to occupy it. The basic character of the new environment has been proposed. A budget has been provided to carry it out, including the time and resources necessary to make the plan. The planner begins by analyzing the future use and users, on the one hand, and the given site, on the other.

Site and User Analysis

Every site, natural or man-made, is to some degree unique, a connected web of things and activities. That web imposes limitations and offers possibilities. Any plan, however radical, maintains some continuity with the preexisting locale. Understanding a locality demands time and effort. The skilled site planner suffers a constant anxiety about the "spirit of place."

Analysis of the site begins with a personal reconnaissance, which permits a grasp of the essential character of the place and allows the planner to become familiar with its features. Later, then, she can recall mental images of those features as she manipulates them. Analysis proceeds to a more systematic data collection, which may follow some standard list, but lists are treacherous. Certain information, such as a topographic base map, is almost always required. Other data are special to particular places. Some data are best gathered early, and some later. No data should be gathered unless they will have a significant influence on the design. New and unforeseen information will be needed as the design progresses.

The site is analyzed for its fitness for the purpose of the plan, and so it will be seen differently by people who are considering different uses for it. But the designer must also look at the site in its own right, as a living community of plants and animals (including human animals)—a community with its own interests that may, if ignored, respond in unsettling ways to any reorganization.

Through her analysis, the designer looks for patterns and essences to guide her plan, as well as simply for facts that she must take into account. She ends with a graphic summary, which communicates the fundamental character of the place, as well as how it will most likely respond to the proposed intervention. The study concludes with a statement of problems and potentials. . . .

How future users will act in the new configuration is the second pillar of knowledge. Frequently ignored, or simply drawn from intuition or personal experience, an understanding of future behavior is critical. When he can, the designer observes, and talks directly with, the actual people who will use the new place. Even better, these people may themselves participate in the design. This is the most straightforward way of making an effective plan.

At other times, future users will be dispersed, or unknown, or transient, complex, or conflicting, and indirect methods of study must be employed. Requirements may be taken from the literature, which is now becoming extensive. The functioning of analogous places may be studied. Surrogate users may be analyzed or simulated environments presented for discussion. But people can be unaware of their own purposes and problems or be unable to predict how they would act under different circumstances. Behavioral studies can also be misused in attempts to control other people. How people use their physical environment is a new field of study. The site designer must be familiar with the methods of that field and be able to employ them. . . .

Program

When the problem has been set and site and users analyzed, then a detailed program can be made out. Traditionally this has been a perfunctory affair: no more than a list of the number and size of required spaces and structures ("twelve one-bedroom apartments, a common laundry room, a tot lot, parking for twenty cars, and a management office of 200 square feet"). The paying client presents this to the designer, who fits it onto the site. The quality of those spaces, the behavior expected to occur in them, and how they will match the purposes of their users, are not mentioned. This quantitative schedule is confined to routine categories of form and neglects much that will make for success or failure of the plan. Unwittingly, the site has been predesigned by a narrow set of financial and administrative considerations. Important purposes are not served; trivia are overemphasized. Freedom of solution is restricted, and unforeseen consequences develop.

Properly prepared, on the other hand, the program will play a central and decisive role in the design. It explicitly connects the designer to objectives and to behavioral information. It begins with the actions that are expected to take place, by whom, and with what purpose. It then proposes a schedule of "behavior settings," or places where physical form and human activity are repeatedly associated ("a compact cooking place," "a mysterious place for exploration," "a dust-free space for assembling electronic parts"). The program gives the required character and equipment for each setting and specifies how form should connect with action and purpose. But it does not fix concrete shape or exact size. It may also specify the intensity and timing of use, the desirable connections between settings, and the expected management and service support. However detailed or generalized, the program expresses environment, management, and behavior as one connected whole and also describes how the attainment of that whole will be organized, including its timing and financing.

This program is the first act of design. It is built in a dialogue between client and designer, based on the knowledge of site and user, and expressed in diagrams and verbal statements. It is the proposed outcome, a hypothesis of how the design will work when finally occupied, an understanding of what the client will receive for his outlay and what the designer promises to deliver. The program changes as design proceeds, since design is a process of learning about possibilities, but the changes can then be made explicitly. . . .

Schematic Plan

Once the program has been defined, designing in the conventional sense begins, although images of form have been latent in all the preceding stages, and program and design interact continuously throughout the remaining process. Here we are at the creative center. It is a mystery, like all human thought, and yet it is something that everyone does to some degree, and its techniques can be taught, again to some degree.

Design is the imaginative creation of possible form and is done in many ways. It develops clouds of possibilities, both fragments and whole systems, in places vague, in others precise, in a state of mind which alternates between childish suggestibility and stern criticism. It is a dialogue between the designer and the growing, shifting forms that she is developing—not a determinate, logical process but an irrational search over a ground prepared by a knowledge of principles, of prototypes and the characteristics of site and users.

In our case, design consists of imagining patterns of activity, circulation, and physical form, as they will occur in some particular place. It is expressed in freely drawn plans, sections, and activity diagrams, and perhaps also in sketch views and rough models. As these possibilities drift and accumulate, the program is redefined and the site and its users are reanalyzed. There are various strategies for entering and then mastering this play with complexity. . . .

At the end of this phase, the designer has developed one or more complete schematic plans, showing building form and location, outdoor activity, surface circulation, ground form, and general landscaping. . . . Rough cost estimates are made for each plan. . . . Plans and costs are linked to a revised program.

This material is now presented to the paying client for her review and decision. She may choose one alternative; she may reject them all; she may direct that one of them be modified; or she may revise her program or her financial plan. At this point, the whole project may be recycled back to programming or design or even be abandoned. If it goes forward, it is on the basis of one schematic plan, chosen by the client, together with its program and its estimated cost. This choice is founded on a prediction of future behavior and performance, a prediction that will be confirmed only when the project is occupied.

Detailed Plan and Contract Documents

Given that choice, the designer now proceeds to a detailed development of the plan, which will allow more exact cost estimates and final client approval. Plan development produces an accurate site plan, showing the location of all buildings, roads, and paved surfaces; the planted areas by type; the existing and proposed ground contours; the location and capacity of utilities; and the location and nature of site details. These plan drawings will be accompanied by sections, studies of detailed areas, typical views, and outline specifications. Any detailed tests of the plan—such as of wind effect—are made, and any formal impact analyses are prepared. An accurate cost estimate is drawn up, covering both construction and maintenance. Program and construction schedule are adjusted to fit this detailed plan.

Once the detailed plan is approved, the site planner goes on to make the contract documents, on which bids can be based. These usually consist of a precise layout of roads and structures, sufficient for their location by survey on the site; a complete grading plan and earthwork computation, with spot elevations for all major features; a utility layout and road and utility profiles; a planting plan; and plans and sections of site details and site furniture. . . . Complete specifications are drawn up, as well as the conditions of work and bid procedures. The documents distinguish the "add-ons"—features that may or may not be part of the final contract and should be priced separately to allow a last-minute adjustment between budget and contract price. These contract documents may be incorporated in the architectural or engineering documents or be independent, in the form of land development plans, landscape plans, or urban designs.

The client now asks for bids by contractors, based on these drawings and specifications. If there is an acceptable bid, the drawings and specifications become the contract documents, and construction begins. If the bids are not acceptable, plan and program must be revised once more. Careful planning and accurate costing help to avert this painful outcome, but not always.

Supervision and Occupation

Normally, the last professional step is to supervise construction on the ground, in order to ensure compliance, but also to make detailed adjustments as unexpected problems and opportunities arise. If properly made, the plans were based on a thorough knowledge of construction procedure and equipment, and so they allowed for the movement of machinery, the storage of material, the succession of site operations, and similar events. The inevitable disruptions of the construction period have already been discounted and provided for.

But the designer is also responsible for helping to make a smooth transition between construction and management of the site. Management support should have been part of the program from the beginning and is just as essential to success as the form itself. Ideally, the future managers of the site have already been involved in the creation of its form, and, at the latter end of the sequence, the site designer should continue to consult with management as use of the site builds up a pattern and momentum of its own. By watching how people use the place he has imagined, the designer learns something for his next endeavor. He compares the predictions of the program with actual events, and his inevitable mistakes are powerful lessons. In the typical case, unfortunately, designers rarely have a systematic opportunity to learn from their mistakes, and managers are rarely involved in the early stages of design. The transition to use is abrupt, and little information flows across the break.

To summarize, there are eight stages in the typical site planning cycle in which the designer is properly involved. (But often, alas, the designer has little to do with the first and the last.) Beyond this cycle of events, of course, other actors are engaged in other actions: the consideration and approval of plans, for example, or the securing of financing. Nevertheless the stages of site planning proper are:

1. defining the problem;
2. programming and the analysis of site and user;
3. schematic design and the preliminary cost estimate;
4. developed design and detailed costing;
5. contract documents;
6. bidding and contracting;
7. construction; and
8. occupation and management.

Reciting these stages makes them sound logical and linear, but the recital is only conventional; the real process is looping and cyclical. Knowledge of a later phase influences conduct of an earlier one, and early decisions are later reworked. Site design is a process of learning in which a coherent system of form, client, program, and site gradually emerges. Even after decisions are made and building begins—even after the site is occupied—the feedback from experience continues to modify the plan. . . . The designer thinks that her organization will have an absolute, permanent influence on all later occupants. In reality, this is only partly so, since whatever she does will soon undergo some modification. Every site has a long history that bears on its present. Every site will have a long future, over which the designer exerts only partial control. The new site form is one episode in a continuous interplay of space and people. Sooner or later, it will be succeeded by another cycle of adaptation.

Environment and Quality of Life

Some critics assert that our physical settings determine the quality of our lives. That view collapses under careful scrutiny, and then it is a natural reaction to

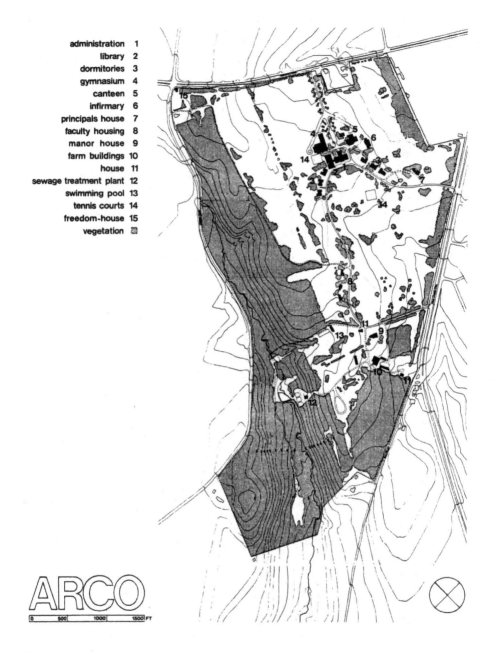

administration 1
library 2
dormitories 3
gymnasium 4
canteen 5
infirmary 6
principals house 7
faculty housing 8
manor house 9
farm buildings 10
house 11
sewage treatment plant 12
swimming pool 13
tennis courts 14
freedom-house 15
vegetation

ARCO

0 500 1000 1500 FT

Figure 5-8 A base map was prepared, and existing features were plotted from aerial photographs and an initial field survey (Lynch and Hack, 1984, Reproduced with permission of the MIT Press).

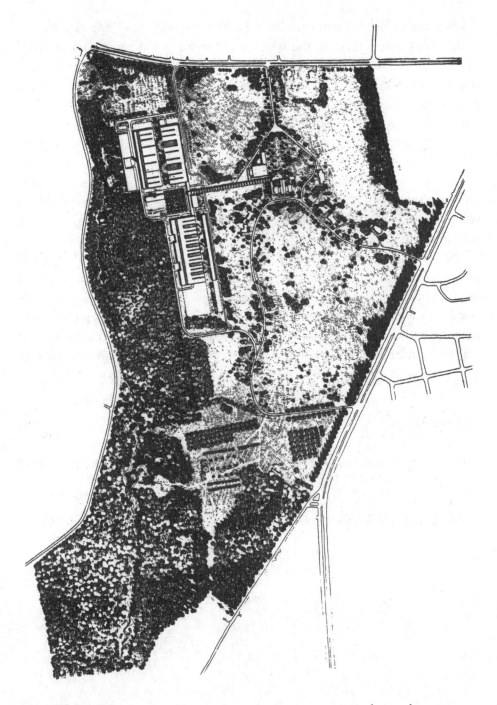

Figure 5-9 After selecting the most promising options, an initial site scheme was prepared for discussion and criticism (Lynch and Hack, 1984, Reproduced with permission of the MIT Press).

say that the spatial environment has no critical bearing on human satisfaction. Each extreme view rests on the fallacies of the other. Organism and environment interact, and environment is both social and physical. You cannot predict the happiness of anyone from the landscape he lives in (although you might predict his unhappiness), but neither can you predict what he will do or feel without knowing his landscape and others he has experienced. People and their habitat coexist. As humans multiply and their technology comes to dominate the earth, the conscious organization of the land becomes more important to the quality of life. Pollution impairs the living system, and some of our technical feats threaten all life. Careless disturbance of the landscape harms us; skilled siting enhances us. Well-organized, productive living space is a resource for humanity, just as are energy, air, and water.

Site planning, then, is the organization of the external physical environment to accommodate human behavior. It deals with the qualities and locations of structures, land, activities, and living things. It creates a pattern of those elements in space and time, which will be subject to continuous future management and change. The technical output—the grading plans, utility layouts, survey locations, planting plans, sketches, diagrams, and specifications—are simply a conventional way of specifying this complex organization. . . .

References

Fairbrother, Nan. *New Lives, New Landscapes*. New York: Knopf, 1970.

Hubbard, Henry Vincent, and Theodora Kimball Hubbard. *An Introduction to the Study of Landscape Design*. New York: Macmillan Company, 1917.

Shoemaker, Morrell M., ed. *The Building Estimator's Reference Book*. Chicago: Frank R. Walker, 1980.

Suttles, Gerald D. *The Social Order of the Slum*. Chicago: University of Chicago Press, 1970.

Processes

Urban Ecological Design: A Process for Regenerative Places (2011)

Danilo Palazzo and Frederick Steiner

Urban design connects knowledge to action through a systematic process that adapts to the specific circumstances of the project. The urban designer brings knowledge from previous experience, generates new intelligence about the project, and guides the process through to its realization.

We apply a model to urban design to help designers be more effective project managers. In this capacity, the designer glans, controls, and coordinates "a project from conception to completion . . . on behalf of a client [and] is concerned with the identification of the client's objectives in terms of utility, function, quality, time, and cost and in the establishment of relationships between [available] resources" (Blyth and Worthington, 2001).

Sticking to a process does not necessarily guarantee a successful project. However, an organized process can aid in collaboration and can clarify expectations of all involved parties. It can also help to make the best use of available resources, including time and money.

In the design and planning literature, several examples of processes and models are useful in considering a specific process for urban design. Michael Brawne (2003) investigates the architectural design process or, to say it in a different way, how architects and designers "proceed from the past and present to a forecast of the future." Brawne assumes that the way architects proceed can be assimilated to sequence in the same way Karl Popper explained how scientific theories come into being. Popper's explanation appeared mainly in *The Logic of Scientific Discovery*, first published in German in 1935 and then in English in

1959. Brawne described the Popper sequence as a process that starts with "the recognition of a problem, then put[s] forward a hypothesis, a kind of tentative theory which need[s] to be tested in order to eliminate errors and end[s] with a corroborated theory which is, however, the start of a new sequence in which it becomes the initial problem" (Brawne, 2003). Brawne then concludes that "although clearly architecture is not a scientific pursuit . . . I nevertheless believe that the problem, tentative solution, error elimination, problem sequence is the most accurate description of the design process."

In the field of planning, a well-known and heavily discussed dictum is *survey before plan*, coined by Scottish biologist and planner Patrick Geddes and then further elaborated on by English planner Patrick Abercrombie (Hall, 1995). This succinct dictum establishes the framework for linking knowledge to action in the process. Theoretical reflections on planning and design, particularly after the Second World War, have resulted in many examples of processes applied to planning and design. Some examples, in order of appearance in the literature, follow.

In 1980, the Royal Institute of British Architects, in the *Handbook of Architectural Practice and Management*, proposed in the field of urban design a process model divided into four phases (RIBA, 1980, quoted in Moughtin et al., 2004):

1. *Assimilation*—the accumulation of general information and information specifically related to the problem
2. *General Study*—the investigation of the nature of the problem; the investigation of a possible solution
3. *Development*—the development of one or more solutions
4. *Communication*—the communication of the chosen solution/s to the client

Hamid Shirvani (1985) distinguishes six groups of design methods: internalized, synoptic, incremental, fragmental, pluralistic, and radical. The *internalized* method is the intuitive one: "The designer who uses the intuitive method first develops a design for the project in his or her mind, with the benefit and assistance of memory, training, and experience."

The *synoptic* method, which is also commonly described as "rational" or "comprehensive," is usually composed of seven steps (Shirvani 1985):

1. Data collection, survey of existing conditions (natural, built, and socioeconomic);
2. Data analysis, identification of all opportunities and limitations;
3. Formulation of goals and objectives;
4. Generation of alternative concepts;

5. Elaboration of each concept into workable solutions;

6. Evaluation of alternative solutions; and

7. Translation of solutions into policies, plans, guidelines, and programs.

The *incremental* method is described by Shirvani as another version of the synoptic method in which "the designer establishes a goal and then develops incremental steps to achieve it." The fragmental process is similar to the synoptic, except that it is incomplete. The designer can "go through four out of the total *seven* steps suggested for the synoptic process." The *pluralistic* process is an approach that incorporates into the design process the inhabitants' value system and the functional/social structure of the urban area involved in the design. Shirvani's final approach, the *radical* process, has as an underlying concept that "in order to understand and design for a complex urban setting, social processes must be understood first."

A process of ecological planning, consisting of eleven steps, was proposed by Frederick Steiner in *The Living Landscape* (2008) (figure 5-10). These eleven interacting steps are as follows:

Step 1. Problem and/or opportunity identification

Step 2. Goal establishment

Step 3. Regional-level inventory and analysis

Step 4. Local-level inventory and analysis

Step 5. Detailed studies

Step 6. Planning concept

Step 7. Landscape plan

Step 8. Education and citizen involvement

Step 9. Detailed designs

Step 10. Plan and design implementation

Step 11. Administration

This ecological planning model synthesizes other processes of regional and landscape planning. Its main references are the ecological methods for design and planning formulated since the 1960s by Ian McHarg (1966, 1969, 1981). . . . The principal idea links environmental information through ecological knowledge to design and planning decisions by what McHarg called the "layer-cake model."

In the field of urban planning, Larz Anderson, on behalf of the American Planning Association (1995), defines an urban planning process as composed of nine strongly interconnected phases. The process of plan making was viewed as a continuous cycle that recognizes the iterative and interactive nature of planning (figure 5-11; Steiner and Butler, 2007):

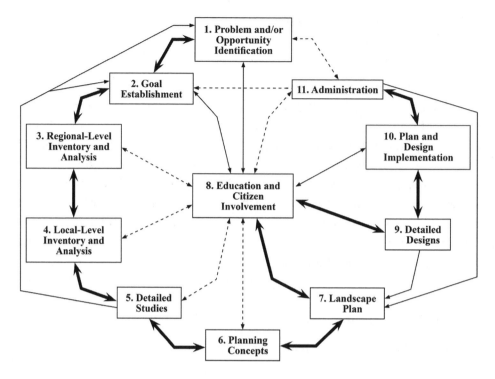

Figure 5-10 Ecological planning model (Palazzo and Steiner, 2011, Reproduced with permission of Island Press, Redrawn by Yuan Ren, 2014).

1. Identify issues.
2. State goals, objectives, and priorities.
3. Collect and interpret data.
4. Prepare plans.
5. Draft programs for plan implementation.
6. Evaluate impacts of plans and implementation programs.
7. Review and adopt plans.
8. Review and adopt implementation programs.
9. Administer implementation programs.

Planning involves managing land uses in cities, agricultural areas, and forests. Planning is studied and practiced in terms of process. The planning and management of natural resources can be accomplished using the principles of *stewardship*, which can be defined as "the call to care for the Earth," counting on human and individual responsibility to "guide individuals toward the common goal [of the preservation of] Earth's beauty and productivity for future generations" (President's Council on Sustainable Development, 1996) and can

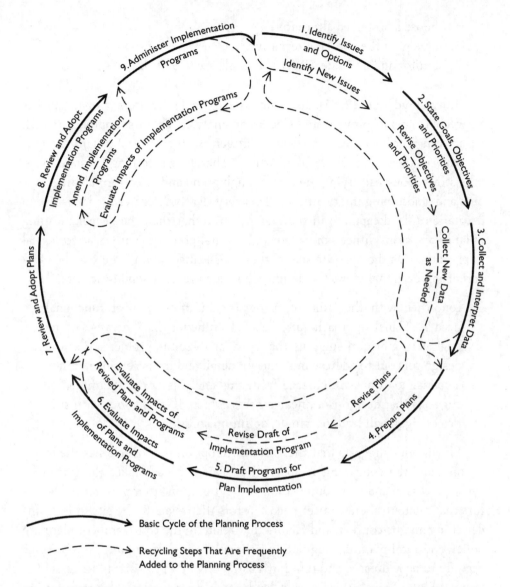

Figure 5-11 The process of plan making as a continuous cycle (Palazzo and Steiner, 2011, Reproduced with permission of Island Press).

be undertaken, according to Sexton et al. (1999), using the seven-step process summarized below:

1. Identify the problem, decision makers, their authorities, the stakeholders, and the decision-making process.
2. Define the problem and refine the objectives.
3. Develop alternative actions to achieve the objectives.
4. Compare each alternative with the objective.

5. Choose a preferred alternative.
6. Implement the chosen alternative.
7. Monitor and evaluate. (Reynolds et al., 1999, 690–92)

Tony Lloyd Jones (2001), discussing the urban design process, distinguishes between artistic inspiration and Geddesian analysis. The first approach (which barely can be considered a process) is driven by the view of "many designers who see themselves as . . . gifted artists." Therefore, according to Lloyd Jones, "the stress is on beautifying the city through grand and often formal street layouts and landscaping interventions." This very clearly relegates the landscape to decoration ("landscaping") in the grand plan, rather than the deeper meaning of landscape as a synthesis of nature and cultural processes with clear ecological implications. On the opposite side of the "artistic inspiration," there is the Geddesian approach that views the design action as a problem-solving activity

> concerned with the issue of spatial organisation to meet functional need. . . . [This] approach [also labeled "functionalist" because of its engineering origin] suggests that if we analyze the problems that the design sets out to address in sufficient detail and in a scientific manner, a spatial solution will emerge from this analysis or "programme." It suggests that design is a linear process, which, if carried out with sufficient rigor, will lead to a single, optimum solution.

Lloyd Jones suggests that there is a third option that overcomes the inspirational and the deterministic approaches. This approach takes the form of a cyclic process of analysis-composition-evaluation: "an attempt to reconcile factors that relate to client or user needs, factors that relate to the site or area under study and its context, and factors that relate to the constraints of planning policy and local planning regulation. It involves understanding the problems that are to be addressed and refining, abstracting and prioritizing the essential issues." Lloyd Jones's third option lends itself to an ecological interpretation that emphasizes cyclic process and interaction.

Following are the four steps of the urban design process:

1. *Defining the problem*—starting from a study area appraisal and the project brief
2. *Developing a rationale*—taking into account summary analysis on planning/socioeconomic context; built form/townscape; land use/activity; movement and access; physical and natural environment; public realm and social space; and perceptual and cultural factors
3. *Summarizing development opportunities and constraints*—balancing the potentials of the site for its projected uses

4. *Conceptualizing and evaluating design options*—envisioning the possibilities for the study area with relative merits and shortcomings

Urban design can be considered "a continuous process of trial-test-change, involving imaging (thinking in terms of solutions), presenting, evaluating, and reimagining (reconsidering or developing alternative solutions)" (Carmona et al., 2003, 55), a process characterized by cycles and iterations "by which solutions are gradually refined through a series of creative leaps or conceptual shifts."

Process Strategies

As the process begins, it helps to provide an outline of future steps that should be considered during the project development. Available time, project character, and necessary materials to achieve the briefs requirements are important criteria for defining the process scope. In environmental impact assessments, scoping is used to define the proposed action, identify significant issues, eliminate peripheral issues, identify project requirements, indicate the decision-making schedule, and identify cooperating agencies. These activities are generally relevant to many urban design projects as well (especially if an environmental assessment is required by law).

The urban design process described in this book can be used as a reference basis, but every design project will possess its own particular characteristics (see figure 5-12). Defining the times, responsibilities, meeting schedules, and interim deadlines is useful. However, as the project progresses, the outline will need to be amended as a result of factors that are often unpredictable in the idealized planned process.

Any urban design process should have a strategy, as Kevin Lynch and Gary Hack explain (1984, 369):

> Plans imply agreements. Without the agreement of those with the power to make changes, and at least the passive assent of those who could stop them, plans remain on paper. To have an effect beyond that of an influential intellectual model, the process of site planning must follow a strategy: it must organize the analysis, programming, design, and implementation so that ideas and decisions are meshed. A strategy includes many choices: how to define the problem, the particular design approach, the use of intuition or rationality, the response to uncertainty, the technique of learning, the degree of participation, the linking of form and management, the use of professionals, and the relation to the client and other decision makers. A good many of these decisions are in the usual case simply customary. But . . . such choices should be made explicitly.

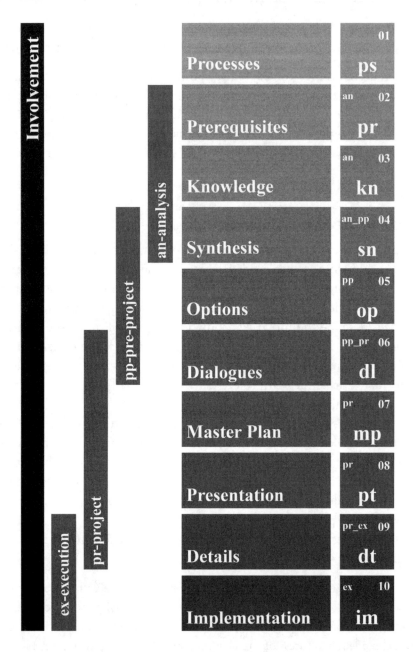

Figure 5-12 The not-only-one solution process and its ten phases (Palazzo and Steiner, 2011, Reproduced with permission of Island Press, Redrawn by Yuan Ren, 2014).

The Process Strategy in the Workshop on Chisinau, Moldova

Organizing the design process takes into consideration the time available, the competencies, the prerequisites, and the nature of the assignment. When time is particularly short, as is usually the case in a workshop, the process organization has a significant value. In 2007, an urban design workshop was conducted in Lecco, Italy, for a strategic area of Chisinau, the capital of Moldova, the Eastern European state that borders Romania to the west and the Ukraine to the east. . . .

Chisinau is the political, industrial, and commercial center of Moldova. Located on the Bîc River in the center of the country, it is the largest city of Moldova, with 650,000 inhabitants. During the Soviet domination (1944–1991), the heavy industry of the country was located along the Bîc River. Today, the industrial areas have been largely abandoned. Some buildings were demolished and replaced by retail centers; others are only partially used. The Bîc River and its adjacent soils are heavily polluted.

The municipality of Chisinau and Milan Polytechnic promoted a design initiative to define some ideas for the area along the river. A two-week workshop was organized to produce a proposal for the City of Chisinau. The workshop was held with practitioners from the London office of Skidmore, Owings & Merrill (SOM), with academics from the Universidat Autònoma de Barcelona (Autonomous University of Barcelona) and Milan Polytechnic, and with students from various European and Asian countries. In addition, four design and planning professionals from Chisinau communicated daily via computer with this group of twenty-one people. To redefine the function of the whole area (7,400 acres, or 3,000 hectares), the team decided to work on different issues:

- *Transportation* at national, regional, and urban levels
- *Mobility* of people and goods
- *Environment and landscape,* including the pollution of the river and soils and the need to redesign the areas along the river in terms of hydraulics and for recreational uses
- *Agriculture,* one of the most important resources of the nation and the major land use outside Chisinau
- *Energy,* the need to understand how to reduce natural gas use by introducing biomass plants
- *Finance,* finding the financial sources to implement the workshop proposals
- *Administration and management* of the whole project

To perform these tasks, the twenty-five-member team was split into different groups focusing on specific issues. A phasing table was proposed to organize the process and to give the team pace and rhythm. The process was determined at the very beginning of the two-week workshop on the basis of the time available, the strengths of the team, the request of the "client," and a rational organization of the steps from initial research and analysis (which correspond to the "knowledge" and "synthesis" steps described in this book) to preliminary concepts ("options") to final plan ("master plan") and then the final presentation. The "prerequisites" were contained in a briefing book prepared in advance and distributed to workshop participants and in "dialogue" between the Milan team and the local participants in Chisinau.

Summary

Usually, the designer provides an early version of the project plan, perhaps only roughly sketched. The idea is to begin imagining the final outcome but to avoid getting locked into a fixed solution. This "open-endedness" permeates the entire process and is indeed important, even if it is difficult to manage. The project is the process target, its goal. It is therefore natural and expected that designers direct individual thought, their own actions, toward that final outcome during all the steps of the process.

In the design process, as in planning, improvisation can occur so that information is synthesized before the data survey is completed as part of the knowledge phase.

References

Anderson, Larz T. *Guidelines for Preparing Urban Plans*. Washington, DC: American Planning Association Press, 1995.

Blyth, Alastair, and John Worthington. *Managing the Brief for Better Design*. London: SPON Press, 2001.

Brawne, Michael. *Architectural Thoughts: The Design Process and the Expected Eye*. Amsterdam: Elsevier, 2003.

Carmona, Matthew, Tim Heath, Taner Oc, and Steve Tiesdell. *Public Places-Urban Spaces*. The Dimensions of Urban Design. Oxford, United Kingdom: Architecture Press, 2003.

Hall, Peter. "Bringing Abercrombie Back from the Shades: A Look Forward and Back." *Town Planning Review* 66, no. 3 (1995): 227–41.

Johnson, Nels, Robert C. Szaro, and William T. Sexton. *Ecological Stewardship: A Common Reference for Ecosystem Management*. Oxford: Elsevier Science, 1999.

Lloyd Jones, Tony. "The Design Process." In *Approaching Urban Design: The Design Process*, 51–56. Harlow, United Kingdom: Pearson Education Limited, 2001.

Lynch, Kevin, and Gary Hack. *Site Planning*. 3rd ed. Cambridge, MA: MIT Press, 1984.

Moughtin, Clifford, Rafael Cuesta, Christine Sarris, and Paola Signoretta. *Urban Design: Method and Techniques*. Amsterdam: Architectural Press/Elsevier, 2004.

Popper, Karl. *The Logic of Scientific Discovery*. New York: Basic Books, 1959.

Reynolds, Keith, Jennifer Bjork, Rachel R. Hershey, Dan Schmoldt, John Payne, Susan King, Lee DeCola, Mark Twery, and Pat Cunningham. "Decision Support for Ecosystem Management." In *Ecological Stewardship: A Common Reference for Ecosystem Management*, vol. 3 (2000): 687–721.

Shirvani, Hamid. *The Urban Design Process*. New York: Van Nostrand Reinhold, 1985.

Steiner, Frederick R. *The Living Landscape: An Ecological Approach to Landscape Planning*. Washington, DC: Island Press, 2008.

Steiner, Frederick, and Kent Butler, eds. *Planning and Urban Design Standards (Student Edition)*. Hoboken, NJ: John Wiley & Sons, 2007.

On Teaching Ecological Principles to Designers

Ecology and Design: Frameworks for Learning (2002)

Carl Steinitz

This [reading] presents the framework within which I have organized the teaching of ecological principles to designers, and which I have used for many years to integrate lectures, studios, and research. For more than thirty years, I have been teaching in the Department of Landscape Architecture of the Harvard Graduate School of Design. During this time, I have visited almost all of the landscape programs in North America and Europe, and many in the rest of the world. I certainly comprehend the great variety of institutional settings from which the subject of this book is derived and in which its findings will have influence. I am sure that there is no single and appropriate set of conclusions, and I am absolutely certain that my experiences at Harvard have limits to their transferability. Nonetheless, I hope that my contribution will be of interest, use, and perhaps of influence.

This contribution must be seen in the context of my personal experience. I entered this field from its edge, bringing some ideas, but without substantial prior education or experience in either landscape architecture or ecology. In retrospect, I was fortunate, curious, energetic, somewhat iconoclastic, seriously interested in teaching and a broad range of major environmental issues, and at an institution that valued and supported my personal and academic "research and development." I always had very good students and collaborating faculty. And I learned much of what I now think I know in large part from these other people. In short, I am a consumer of ecology, not a producer.

I appreciate Herbert Simon's (1969) definition of design, and especially when the word "design" is seen as an active verb:

> Everyone designs who devises courses of action aimed at changing existing conditions into preferred ones.

Surely all of us can relate to this definition.

In "Design Is a Verb; Design Is a Noun" (Steinitz, 1995), I argued that both ecology and art are defined in human terms. They are different, they can be in conflict and frequently are, but they can also be symbiotic. The sad fact is that all too often our field can be seen as dividing between the two conflicting cultures—art and ecology. However, in my view, "design" as a noun should be an idea made tangible, but also more than that; it should be a social communication that is experienced and understood. As George Santayana reminds us,

> When creative genius neglects to ally itself to some public interest, it hardly gives birth to wide or perennial influence. Imagination needs a soil in history, tradition or human institutions, else its random growths are not significant enough and, like trivial melodies, go immediately out of fashion.

A related point is made in a commentary on *Exodus,* chapter XXV,

> The true artist possesses the power to inspire others. A light that cannot kindle other lights is but a feeble flame. The core of art is its teaching and ennobling influence not only on other artists, but on humanity.

Some might argue that the primary objectives of landscape architecture are aesthetic, others that they are ecological, and others that they are relationships between ecology and perception. My view is that because landscape architecture is the result of design as a verb, of an anthropocentric process of intentional change, its primary aims and decision criteria are social relationships. The primary means of design, the materiality and the organization of experience, are the appropriate roles of ecology and perception (Steinitz, 1995). Thus, regardless of whether design is directed toward intentional change or intentional conservation, it has the primary social objective of changing people's lives by changing their environment and its processes, including its ecological processes.

The teaching of design "as a verb and as a noun" is a very difficult task, and in recent years I have become a critic of the ways in which we teach (speaking broadly and not ad hominem). I have written and lectured on the subject (Steinitz 1990, 1993, 1995), and I have formulated a framework both for design and for education that tries to sharpen the questions that we pose to our students. I have found the framework to be both robust and useful in organizing my academic activities, and I think that it is germane to the issues posed by the organizers of this volume. I know that it is familiar to some readers, but it may be worthwhile to repeat the short description for others.

My proposed framework (figure 5-13) organizes six different questions, each of which is related to a type of theory-driven answer or model. The framework is "passed through" at least three times in any project: first, downward in defining the context and scope of a project—defining the questions; second, upward in specifying the project's methods—how to answer the questions; and third, downward in carrying the project forward to its conclusion—getting the answers. The six questions with their associated modeling types are listed downward, in the order in which they are usually considered when initially defining a landscape project.

I. How should the state of the landscape be described; in content, boundaries, space, and time? This level of inquiry leads to Representation models.

II. How does the landscape operate? What are the functional and structural relationships among its elements? This level of inquiry leads to Process models.

III. Is the current landscape functioning well? The metrics of judgment, whether health, beauty, cost, nutrient flow, or user satisfaction, lead to Evaluation models.

IV. How might the landscape be altered; by what actions, where, and when? This is directly related to level I, in that both are data; vocabulary and syntax. This fourth level of inquiry leads to Change models. At least two important types of change should be considered: change by current projected trends, and change by implementable design, such as plans, investments, regulations, and construction.

V. What predictable differences might the changes cause? This is directly related to level II, in that both are based on information; on predictive theory. This fifth level of inquiry shapes Impact models, in which the Process models (II) are used to simulate change.

VI. Should the landscape be changed? How is a comparative evaluation among the impacts of alternative changes to be made? This is directly related to level III, in that both are based on knowledge; on cultural values. This sixth level of inquiry leads to Decision models. (Implementation could be considered another level, but this framework considers it as a forward-in-time feedback to level I, the creation of a changed representation model.)

Note that the six levels have been presented in the order in which they are normally recognized. However, I believe that it is more important to consider

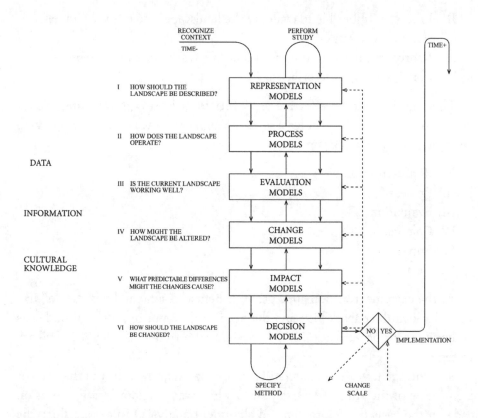

Figure 5-13 A framework for design (Steinitz, 2002, Reproduced with permission of Island Press, Redrawn by Yuan Ren, 2014).

them in reverse order, both as a more effective way of organizing a landscape planning study and specifying its method (which I consider the key strategic phase) and as a more effective educational approach. A design method for a project should be organized and specified upward through the levels of inquiry, with each level defining its necessary contributing products from the models next above in the framework.

VI. Decision—To be able to decide to propose or to make a change (or not), one needs to know how to compare alternatives.

V. Impact—To be able to compare alternatives, one needs to predict their impacts from having simulated changes.

IV. Change—To be able to simulate change, one needs to specify (or design) the changes to be simulated.

III. Evaluation—To be able to specify potential changes (if any), one needs to evaluate the current conditions.

II. Process—To be able to evaluate the landscape, one needs to understand how it works.

I. Representation—To understand how it works, one needs representational schema to describe it.

Then, in order to be effective and efficient, a landscape-planning project should progress downward at least once through each level of inquiry, applying the appropriate modeling types:

I. Representation
II. Process
III. Evaluation
IV. Change
V. Impact
VI. Decision

At the extreme, two decisions present themselves: no and yes. A "no" implies a backward feedback loop and the need to alter a prior level. All six levels can be the focus of feedback; (IV), "redesign," is a frequently applied feedback strategy.

A "contingent yes" decision (still a "no") may require a shift in the scale or size or time of the study. (An example is a highway corridor location decision made on the basis of a more detailed alignment analysis.) In a scale shift, the study will again proceed through the six levels of the framework, as previously described.

A project should normally continue until it achieves a positive "yes" decision. (In my area of application, a "do not build" conclusion can be a positive decision.) A "yes" decision implies implementation and (one assumes) a forward-in-time change to new representation models.

While the framework and its set of questions looks orderly and sequential, it frequently is not so in application. The line through any project is not a smooth path: It has false starts, dead ends, serendipitous discoveries—but our activities do pass through the questions and models of the framework as I have described it, before a "yes" can be achieved. The same questions are posed again and again. However, the models, which are the answers, vary according to the context (Steinitz et al., 1996).

The framework in figure 5-13 can be recognized as both a scientific research process and as a simulation model, and these are how I present it to my students. The framework has been useful in organizing studios, advising doctoral students, and structuring case study papers by masters students. I have also used it to organize large interdisciplinary research programs. For three landscape planning examples that combine research with teaching, and with major ecological components, see the following on my Web site http://www.gsd .harvard.edu/info/directory/faculty/steinitz/steinitz.html.

References

Carroll, Allen. *The Developer's Handbook*. Connecticut Dept. of Transportation, Hartford, Connecticut, 1972.

Collinge, Sharon Kay. "Ecological Consequences of Habitat Fragmentation: Implications for Landscape Architecture and Planning." *Landscape and Urban Planning 36*, no. 1 (1996): 59-77.

———. "Spacial Arrangement of Patches and Corridors in the Landscape: Consequences for Biological Diversity and Implications for Landscape Architecture." PhD dissertation. Harvard University, 1995.

Dramstad, Wenche E., James D. Olson, and Richard T. T. Forman. "Landscape Ecology Principles in Landscape Architecture and Land-Use Planning." In *Landscape Architecture and Land-Use Planning*, 1–40. Washington, DC: Harvard Graduate School of Design, Amercian Society of Landscape Architects, and Island Press, 1996.

Hendler, Bruce. *Caring for the Land: Environmental Principles for Site Design and Review*. No. 328. Chicago, Illinois: American Society of Planning Officials, 1977.

Hill, Kristina Elizabeth. "The Representation of Categorical Ambiguity: A Comparison of Fuzzy, Probabilistic, Boolean, and Index Approaches in Suitability Analysis." PhD dissertation, Harvard University, 1997.

Lowry, Ira S. "A Short Course in Model Design." *Journal of the American Institute of Planners* 31, no. 2 (1965): 158–66.

Simon, Herbert Alexander. *The Sciences of the Artificial*. Cambridge: MIT Press, 1996.

Steinitz, Carl. "A Framework for Theory and Practice in Landscape Planning." *GIS Europe* (1993): 42–45.

———. "A Framework for Theory Applicable to the Education of Landscape Architects (and Other Environmental Design Professionals)." *Landscape journal* 9, no. 2 (1990): 136–43.

———. "Design is a Verb; Design is a Noun." *Landscape Journal 14*, no. 2 (1995): 188–200.

———. *Alternative Futures for Monroe County, Pennsylvania*. Harvard University, Cambridge, MA, 1994.

———. Planning and Design of Landscapes. GSD 1212, 1998. http://www.gsd.harvard.edu./info /directory/faculty/steinitz/steinitz.html.

———. Theories and Methods of Landscape Planning, GSD 3307, 1998. http://www.gsd.harvard .edu./info/directory/faculty/steinitz/steinitz.html.

Steinitz, Carl, Michael Binford, Paul Cote, Thomas Edwards Jr, and Stephen Ervin. *Biodiversity and Landscape Planning: Alternative Futures for the Region of Camp Pendleton, California*. Harvard University, Cambridge, MA, 1996.

Yu, Kongjian. "Security Patterns and Surface Model in Landscape Ecological Planning." *Landscape and Urban Planning 36*, no. 1 (1996): 1–17.

———. "Security Patterns in Landscape Planning: with a Case in South China." PhD dissertation, Harvard University, 1995.

Framing the Land Use Plan: A Systems Approach

Landscape Planning: Environmental Applications (2010)

William M. Marsh

Introduction

When Ian L. McHarg first published his classic statement, *Design with Nature*, in 1969, and the U.S. Congress passed the National Environmental Policy Act a year later, we in academia and the professions were hopeful that a new era of landscape planning and design had emerged, one that would see the rise of environmentally responsive land use development. Happily some progress did take place in the ensuing decades. Today almost everywhere we give consideration to floodplains, wetlands, air quality, and stormwater management. Species protection is given national attention in both the United States and Canada, and many jurisdictions have enacted policies concerning streams, shorelands, watersheds, groundwater, and open space. Unfortunately, however, the character of development, as well as how it relates to the landscapes it occupies, has not changed much, and on some fronts has declined over the past 40 years. All the while, our knowledge base on the North American landscape and our technical and economic power as individuals, communities, and nations have grown substantially.

Modern land use in North America tends to occupy the landscape rather than live within it as other life-forms must do. But if we quiz citizens about their habitat preferences, invariability [*sic*] we find the desire to live with the landscape, even to embrace it and celebrate it. Why, then, can we not design and build communities, neighborhoods, and homes to satisfy that desire? We have the knowledge to do it and a clientele with open arms. Perhaps the clientele does not quite offer open arms because the desire to "live with nature" carries a variety of meanings in North America. But even if we assume that society's notion of living with nature is broadly similar to ours, we must agree that barriers, often substantial ones, stand in the way of designing and building with nature. The proof is in the human landscape around us. . . .

Some of these barriers are mentioned in the opening chapters of the book. High on the list is the absence of a basic understanding of landscape among community officials, developers, and their agents followed by the assumption that one landscape is pretty much like another, especially in how they function. Granted, recognition is usually accorded to extremes in the landscape such as between seashore and floodplain, but less salient phenomena—especially those at the site scale, such as hill-slopes, swales, seasonal streams, rock outcrops, and wet pockets—are usually written off as so much noise with little or no meaning in a functional sense. . . . This sort of thinking has, in many quarters, given tacit endorsement to shoddy site planning and design practices that ignore most form and function details and that replace thoughtful attempts at understanding sites as part of the larger working landscape—as parts of systems—with various shorthand approaches involving simple checklists, templates borrowed from other projects, makeover engineering schemes, and so on.

This chapter presents an approach to building landscape plans that draws on systems concepts. It follows, more or less, the main thread of the book, arguing that landscape planning and design schemes must extend into the arena of landscape dynamics and grapple with the systems and processes that shape sites and their settings, for unless we address systems, there is little chance of achieving sustainability in the landscape. The approach outlined is not intended as a methodology but more as a conceptual model aimed at providing a rationale for framing the plan and providing perspective. We begin with systems.

Getting a Handle on Systems

Using systems as a beginning point in landscape planning might, on first thought, appear a bit daunting, implying the need for all sorts of scientific knowledge and detailed field investigations. But for planning purposes, we are not after an analytical understanding of systems. Our objective, rather, is more contextual: first to identify the kind of landscape system we are dealing with and second to use that information to frame our thinking in the early stages of the planning process. Of course, analytical insight into landscape systems is not to be ignored if it is available. But the process of designing a land use plan is usually not an analytical one, as preparers of environmental impact statements have come to learn over the years. Rather, the process, we argue, involves responding to the system (or systems) that drives, or shapes, the landscape, what we call the formative system. Table 5-2 lists a number of major formative systems, headed by the principal landscape system, watersheds and drainage nets.

Identifying Formative Systems

Formative systems consist of the systems and related conditions that govern the character and operation of a site and its contextual space. The opening challenge to planners and designers is to identify which among the candidate landscape systems is the formative one or ones at a given location—the one or ones that deliver the forces that most shape a site's essential character. The route to the answer lies in first finding the *geographic context* of a site, or more precisely, defining the site's physiographic character.

Every site has a place, and every place is the product of the systems and processes that operate there. All places have *physiographic character*, and it is that character that leads us to the identity of the formative systems. . . . [We] discussed the broadly regional physiography of North America, but here we are interested more in local physiography and what it means in terms of defining formative systems. For example, if the site's physiographic setting is the floor of a stream valley, then the formative system is the stream, its drainage net, and the watershed that feeds them. If the physiographic setting is in the coastal zone, then the longshore (drift) system, driven by wind, waves, and currents, is the likely candidate. To most coastal sites, drainage nets and watersheds are probably of little or no consequence compared to longshore systems, unless, of course, the site lies on or near a delta, river mouth, or major stormwater outfall.

A surprising amount of insight can be gained from this simple step. Among other things, it tells us what to put on the list of planning considerations, that is, what to look for, examine, and address. Many communities miss this point because they prepare standardized inventory lists that usually ask about things such as wetlands and floodplains, no matter where the site is located, while completely ignoring other systems that operate in and around their jurisdiction.

The Significance of Location

The next step is determining *where* you are in the system. All landscape systems function as *open systems*, meaning they receive inputs of matter and/or energy and release outputs of matter and/or energy. Within the system, work may be performed, and energy and matter may be stored. In a watershed, work is performed when water and sediment are moved downstream. Storage takes place when water is taken up in aquifers as groundwater or when sediment is deposited in floodplains and locked in place by vegetation. Generally speaking

Table 5-2

Major formative landscape systems and their components (Marsh 2010, Reproduced with permission of John Wiley & Sons, Inc., Redrawn by Yuan Ren, 2014).

System Component

System	Contributing/Input	Transport/storage	Receiving/Output
Watershed and drainage net	Headwaters, uplands, wetlands, lakes, springs	Stream channels, floodplains, swales, wetlands	Deltas, bays, estuaries, wetlands, ponds, reservoirs
Groundwater	Recharge zones: valley floors, basins, floodplains, wetlands, lakes	Transmission zones, aquifers	Discharge zone: stream channels, springs, lakes, wetlands, wells
Longshore (drift)	Source areas: deltas, shores, banks, bluffs, cliffs	Transport zone (current and beach drift)	Sediment sinks: bays, spits, bars, beaches, barrier islands
Wind	Source areas: beaches, denuded soil, floodplains, deflation hollows	Transport zone (e.g., wind corridors)	Sand dunes, loess deposits, beach ridges
Wetland	Watershed, aquifer, precipitation, flood flows	Stream channels, interflow, groundwater transmission	Stream discharge, springs, groundwater seepage, evapotranspiration
Terrestrial ecosystem	Climate (light and heat), soil (water and nutrients)	Flood chains, biomass, topsoil	Organic matter, heat, water vapor, nutrients

every site in a watershed belongs to one of the following: (a) a zone that gives up (or contributes) water and sediment, (b) a zone that collects water and sediment and/or conveys it downslope or stores it, and (c) a zone that releases water and sediment at the output end of the system (figure 5-14a).

Consider the significance of location for the sites at (a), (b), and (c) in figure 5-14b. A site located in a zone that gives up water [a headwaters setting at location (a), for example] must be given serious consideration with regard to actions that alter system performance and cause impacts downstream. To maintain the system's long-term performance, that is, to achieve sustainability in the watershed system, a land use plan should be designed to mimic the natural performance of the site (or predevelopment performance, whichever is used

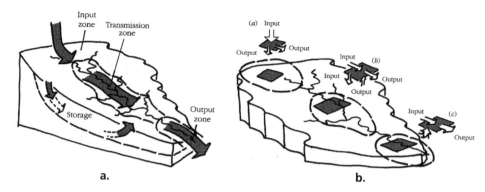

a.   b.

Figures 5-14a and 5-14b The basic components and functions of an open system using the watershed as an example (left image). Sites at three different locations in the watershed (right image) (Marsh 2010, Reproduced with permission of John Wiley & Sons, Inc. Redrawn by Yuan Ren, 2014).

as a performance target). That is, if the site discharged no overland flow into surface channels before development, then it should not release surface runoff (stormwater) into natural channels after development.

The same objective holds for a site located in the transmission (or conveyance) zone (in figure 5-14b). The continuity of flow—that is, allowances for inputs and outputs—should be the same after development as before. At the output end of the system, a critical concern should be the performance of the entire system upstream because a change in the rate and amount of water delivery, for example, may have serious effects on flood magnitude and frequency, water supply, and other consequences. In a functional sense, sites at the output end of a system should be thought of as extending way beyond the site's formal boundaries, all the way to the head of the system where the inputs begin. The whole system, then, is the planning arena for such sites.

The significance of location in the system is easily demonstrated for watersheds, which are the systems of greatest concern in most areas, but the concept is equally applicable to other landscape systems. Groundwater is also a three-part system, as are longshore (drift) systems, wind systems, wetland systems, and others. . . . The geographic configurations of some are more easily defined than others, of course, but at the very least it is important to remember that even though some systems defy precise definitions, all systems operate according to a definable order that is usually represented by *vectors* (directions) of motion in matter and energy. Vectors enable us to delineate patterns, trends, and linkages in the landscape. *Linkages*, in turn, lead to observations about the connections among different places and ultimately to inferences about cause-and-effect relationships.

Application to a Segment of Coastline

Let us examine a segment of coast where the formative system is a longshore (or drift) cell. Figure 5-15 shows a typical longshore system setup in the Puget Sound–Georgia Strait region of Washington and British Columbia. The coast here is composed of glacial deposits, mostly sand and gravel with a small percentage of cobbles and boulders. The shoreline in this area has a northeast-southwest orientation, which is close to perpendicular to the force of winter storm waves (from the southeast) that drive the coastal currents and that, in turn, do the lion's share of the work in moving sediment down the shore.

The resultant longshore system has two arms or cells: one that moves sediment northeastward and the other that moves sediment southwestward. Since no streams supply sediment to the shore here, there is only one source of sediment for the longshore system, namely, the glacial deposits that make up the shore and the banks behind it. Storm waves erode this material and feed it to the longshore system. From the source area (the in situ deposits), the sediment is moved downshore, both to the northeast and to the southwest, forming two cells. At the end of each cell, the coastline breaks (turns abruptly) into two bays, and the sediment load is deposited, forming large bars on one end and a long spit on the other.

The configuration and operation of these two drift cells are easy enough to identify, and their implications for planning and design are no mystery. In the source area, the shore is giving up sediment and slowly retreating. In the transport zone, the sediment is mainly passing by, en route downshore. From year to year, the beach in this zone may fluctuate, shifting seaward in some years and landward in others, but as a whole the action is overwhelmingly lateral. By contrast in the sinks at the ends of the cells, the shore is growing as sediment fills in the bays. So, on balance, the character and behavior of the shoreline are best explained by examining the form and work of the longshore system. The operative word here is "behavior" because understanding the coastline is impossible without a basic appreciation of its dynamics. Unfortunately, landscape dynamics is something rarely entertained in land use planning.

As for land use along this coastline, the entire area, save for two small parks and two military installations, is dedicated to residential development, and, according to existing policy, the only planning regulation that applies to site design is setback distance from the shore. Residential structures must be at least 15 meters (50 feet) back from the high-water mark unless the applicant builds an erosion protection wall, and in that case, the required minimum setback can be reduced to 7.5 meters (25 feet). No mention is made of the longshore system.

If the system *were* considered, the first response would be to vary setback distance according to the site's location in the system. Setbacks should be much

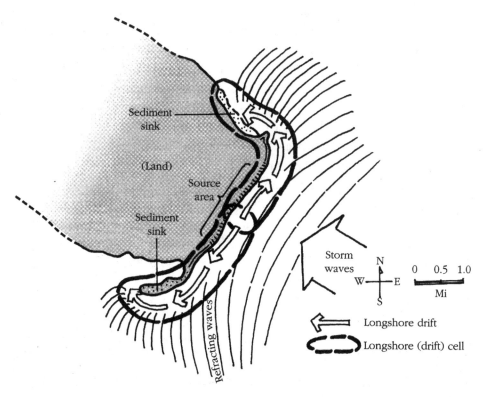

Figure 5-15 Map showing wind, wave, and current patterns that produce systems of longshore drift at one location in the Puget Sound–Georgia Strait region (Marsh 2010, Reproduced with permission of John Wiley & Sons, Inc. Redrawn by Yuan Ren, 2014).

larger in sediment source areas to accommodate the inevitable shoreline retreat there. Provision for erosion protection structures and sediment control structures should be eliminated throughout both cells, especially in transport zones, to maintain the continuity of flow. In sink zones, the requirement for erosion protection structures is probably meaningless because such facilities will end up lying idle behind accreting beaches or, in the case of the spit, repeatedly covered and exposed because this narrow neck of sand shifts about over time. Beyond site-scale considerations, however, there is a more meaningful level of planning to consider.

Implications for Community Planning

Recognition of the broader patterns and features of systems early in the planning process could have helped guide planners toward more prudent zoning decisions. From a system's perspective, where, for example, should residential land use and public open space be assigned? What better land use to allocate to the sediment source area (where the shore is retreating) than, say, public park with large setbacks and modest, low-cost facilities, such as trails, decking, and parking? Let the shore retreat its few inches a year while the sediment produced feeds the rest of the system.

Further downshore, residential zoning is appropriate, but only with provisions for setbacks large enough to accommodate shoreline fluctuation and rules against clearing and manipulation of the backshore to guard against the destabilization of banks and bluffs. Near the sinks, at the beginning of the accretion zones, residential zoning can be considered, but setback distances should take into account another system—onshore wind and sand dune formation—with development restrictions on landforms such as dunes, fore dunes, and beach ridges. With respect to the spit itself, development there would be highly risky in light of the fact that these long, narrow features are prone to major shoreline shifts and breaches by stormwaves. . . .

References

Beatley, Timothy, and K. Manning. *The Ecology of Place: Planning for Environment, Economy, and Community*. Washington, DC: Island Press, 1997.

Beer, Anne R. *Environmental Planning for Site Development*. London: E. & F. N. Spon, 1990.

Bookout, Lloyd W. *Value by Design: Landscape, Site Planning, and Amenities*. Washington, DC: Urban Land Institute, 1994.

Capra, Fritjof. *The Web of Life: A New Scientific Understanding of Living Systems*. New York: Anchor., 1996.

DeFries, Ruth S., Gregory P. Asner, and Richard A. Houghton. *Ecosystems and Land Use Change*. Vol. 153. Washington, DC: American Geophysical Union, 2004.

LaGro, James A. *Site Analysis: Linking Program and Concept in Land Planning and Design*. New York: John Wiley & Sons, 2001.

Lynch, Kevin. *Site Planning*. Cambridge, Mass.: MIT Press, 1971.

Waugh, Frank. "Physical Aspects of Country Planning." *The Journal of Land and Public Utility Economics* 13, no. 3, 1937.

Woldenberg, Michael J. "Horton's Laws Justified in Terms of Allometric Growth and Steady State in Open Systems." *Geological Society of America Bulletin* 77, no. 4 (1966): 431–34.

A Synthesis of Approaches to Ecological Planning

Ecological Planning: A Historical and Comparative Synthesis (2002)

Forster Ndubisi

We have come a long way from the nineteenth century, when the likes of Thoreau, Olmsted, and Muir reminded us about the inevitable ramifications of human abuse of landscapes. The evolution of ecological planning as a philosophy and framework for managing change to bring human actions into tune with natural processes has been slow, incremental, and sometimes disjointed. New ideas have been proposed and debated, and some have been refined for subsequent use. From the late 1950s to the present the evolutionary progression has intensified, almost surpassing that during the era of awakening, the formative era, and consolidation. Unlike in the earlier eras, when evolutionary progression elaborated and clarified the theme of planning with nature, the progression over the past four decades has been in more divergent but related directions. The field of ecological planning and design has expanded, not only in the type, scale, and scope of issues addressed but also in the diversity of approaches used.

With the expanded scope of ecological planning comes an increased need to make explicit the theoretical and methodological assumptions that lead us to choose one approach over another. Each approach reflects a particular way of understanding the problems arising from human-landscape interactions and provides guidance for their resolution. In this chapter I propose a tentative classification of the five approaches to ecological planning—*landscape suitability (LSA 1 and LSA 2), applied human ecology, applied ecosystem ecology, applied landscape ecology,* and *assessment of landscape values and perception*—as a way to systematically examine the linkages among them and to explore their similarities and differences. I review their similarities and differences by exploring three questions: What are their major concerns? How do they propose that the concerns be addressed? What are the anticipated outcomes? Based on a review of their relative strengths and weaknesses, I argue that none by itself can adequately address the whole spectrum of ecological-planning issues. I then speculate on when landscape architects and planners may lean toward one approach rather than another for guidance.

Undertaking a comparative synthesis of these approaches is perhaps a risky venture given the diverse methods and techniques of each approach; therefore, I risk the criticism of overgeneralization. I therefore explore the central tendency or bias, as statisticians would call it, of each approach's responses to the questions. In a strict sense, studies of landscape values and perception should not be included as an ecological-planning approach, but they are relevant to ecological planning because knowledge about the values held by people is "essential to the development of socially responsive and supportive landscapes." . . .

Substantive and Procedural Theory in Ecological Planning

In the discussion that follows, I argue that there are two types of theories in ecological planning: substantive and procedural. *Substantive theories* of ecological planning permit an in-depth understanding of the landscape as the interface between human and natural processes. These theories, which are descriptive and predictive, originate from the social and natural sciences, as well as the humanities, including such fields as anthropology, biology, ecology, fine arts, geography, geology, and history. When we seek to understand the landscape as a reflection of culture, we turn to the works of J. B. Jackson, John Stilgoe, David Schuyler, Denis Wood, Neil Evernden, Cotton Mather, and the like. When we want to understand soils, we turn to a pedologist. The intellectual traditions depicted in figure 5-16 indicate the disciplinary origins of the substantive theories that inform each approach.

Procedural theories focus on the ideology, purposes, and principles of ecological planning. They explicate the functional relationships that permit the application of the knowledge of human and natural processes in resolving human conflicts in the landscape. The five approaches examined in this book are procedural theories of ecological planning. Each offers a working theory and procedural recommendations for putting the theory into practice. Thus, in ecological planning we draw upon substantive theories for content knowledge but use procedural theories as a framework for organizing the pertinent knowledge to address ecological-planning problems.

A Tentative Classification

I propose figure 5-16 as a tentative classification of the major approaches to ecological planning. The classification is intended to provide a common base of understanding. "If such a base can be established, then future programs can be built on past experience, rather than starting over from scratch," remarked Frederick Steiner. Not surprisingly, some methods do not fit neatly into the classification. It is evident that substantial overlap exists, suggesting that in practice methods draw relevant principles from one another. All the approaches share a common concern: how knowledge of the interdependent relationship between people and the landscape should properly inform the process of managing change while maintaining regard for its wise and sustained use. In using the phrase *between people and the landscape* I do not mean to imply a separation. Rather, it acknowledges that humans have the capacity to modify the relationship through conscious choice, much more than other members of Aldo Leopold's biotic community, "soils, water, plants, and animals, or collectively the land."

Each approach defines the knowledge and how it should be used. The approaches span the entire spectrum, from those that view the interactions as heavily influenced by the natural environment, such as LSA 1; to those that see them as a potential tension to be resolved, for example, the applied-ecosystem approach; to studies of landscape values and perception, which focus entirely on the perceptions, values, and experiences of individuals and groups in the interactions.

Some approaches are more developed than others. The oldest, LSA 1, reaches back into the nineteenth century, rooted in the wisdom of such visionaries as Emerson, Olmsted, and George Perkin [sic] Marsh. In the twentieth century, Manning, Geddes, the NRCS, Hills, McHarg, Steinitz, and others provided methodological directions. LSA 1 evolved into LSA 2 in the late 1960s and early 1970s in response to increased pressure on resource-management professionals to develop methods that were systematic, technically, and ecologically sound, as well as legally defensible. LSA 2, the well-established applied-ecosystem approach, and the assessment of landscape values and perception are arguably the most widely used. In contrast, the applied-human-ecology and applied-landscape-ecology approaches have not yet developed a coherent body of knowledge to give them a clear identity and direction.

Some approaches have distinct subgroups, reflecting an increased sophistication in their way of executing tasks typically associated with steps in the conventional planning process. Distinctions within LSA 1 occur at a rudimentary level, linked to individuals and projects. The gestalt method is used in making

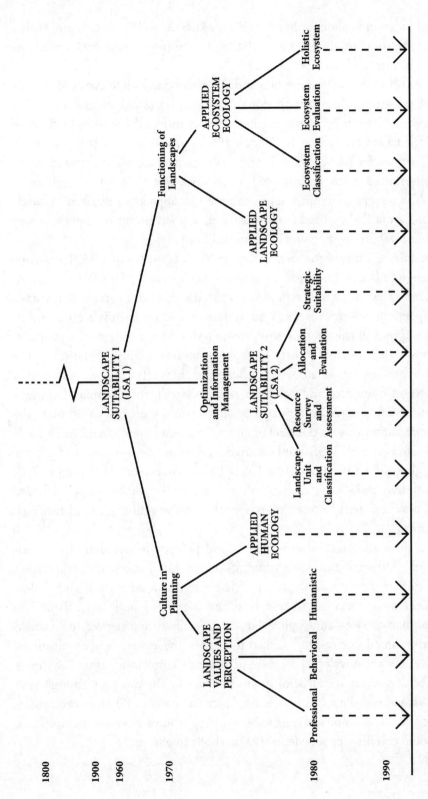

Figure 5-16 Ecological planning practice: plural approaches (Ndubisi, 2002, Reproduced by permission of Johns Hopkins University Press, Redrawn by Yuan Ren, 2014).

elemental judgments about suitability. The NRCS capability system and Hills's physiographic-unit method classify the landscape into homogenous areas irrespective of intended uses.

Lewis's resource-pattern method and the method associated with McHarg's Staten Island study define homogenous areas in order to judge their suitability for prospective land uses. Some methods, for example, those used in Richard Toth's Tock Island study and McHarg's 1968 least-social-cost corridor study for the Richmond Parkway, permit the evaluation of environmental impacts. Computer-assisted methods proposed by Steinitz and his Harvard colleagues can assess landscape suitability and evaluate the impacts of alternative land-use options. In fact, they used biophysical and socioeconomic considerations to determine suitability, which was atypical of LSA 1.

Since LSA 2 reflects the next phase in the evolution of LSA 1, its sub-groupings—*landscape-unit and landscape-classification, landscape-resource survey and assessment, allocation-and-evaluation*, and *strategic landscape-suitability methods*—are distinct and systematic. A similar division exists in the subgroupings of the applied-ecosystem approach: *ecosystem-classification, ecosystem-evaluation*, and *holistic-ecosystem methods*. The evaluation methods are further distinguished based on whether they rely on indices to evaluate ecosystem dynamics and behavior (*index-based*), for example, Dorney's abiotic-biotic-cultural (ABC) strategy, or on a modeling process to simulate the effects of perturbations on the flow of energy, materials, and nutrients (*model-based*), such as the S-RESS method used as one of the numerous strategies for managing the Laurentian Great Lakes Basin ecosystems. Unlike in LSA 2, the cumulative tasks that distinguish the applied-ecosystem approach are based on a system perspective that emphasizes cause-and-effect and feedback relationships.

The assessment of Landscape values and perception has definitive theoretical and methodological subgroupings based on disciplinary orientation and on whether the intended use is problem solving or advancing knowledge: *professional, behavioral (psychophysical and cognitive)*, and *humanistic*. The applied-human-ecology and applied-landscape-ecology approaches, in contrast, developed in an ad hoc fashion, linked to specific individuals and applications. They have not yet developed a coherent body of empirically tested methods that can be organized systematically around specific themes even though several well-documented applications exist. Since the early 1980s, however, rigorous theoretical and empirical landscape-ecology studies have been conducted, so we should certainly expect definitive methods to emerge.

Major Concerns

The landscape-suitability approaches seek to determine the *fitness* of a given tract of land for a particular use. Their conceptual base is drawn from the arts, design, and natural sciences, including community ecology and ecosystem ecology, as well as plant and soil sciences. LSA 1 leans heavily on the natural features of the landscape to ascertain fitness.

LSA 2 defines fitness as optimization, that is, revealing the optimal uses of a given tract of land in a manner that sustains its ecological stability and productivity in the face of changing natural, social, economic, political, and technological forces. Consequently, the conceptual base expanded as professionals with expertise in resource management, recreation, and the social sciences (e.g., economics, geography, and policy sciences) became increasingly involved in ecological planning in the late 1960s and early 1970s. Some LSA 2 methods address additional issues. The allocation-evaluation methods are concerned with selecting and evaluating competing suitability options. Strategic suitability methods address these concerns but also examine the programs, strategies, and institutional arrangements for implementing the optimal plan.

The applied-human-ecology approach views fitness as resulting from the congruence between ecologically suitable and culturally desirable locations maximized for the adaptive strengths of the various users of an area. More specifically, it is concerned with how people use, value, and adapt to the landscape and how they influence land-use allocation. It is interdisciplinary, originating from social and ecological sciences, especially cultural anthropology, ecology, ecological psychology, economics, human geography, and sociology.

The applied-ecosystem approach is primarily concerned with examining the structure and function of landscapes and exploring how they respond to human and natural influences. Its intellectual roots lie in ecosystem sciences, especially ecosystem ecology, systems theory, economics, and policy sciences. It also draws on landscape-suitability studies for techniques that link ecological processes to their specific locations in the landscape. The approach assumes that ecosystems are responsive to human and natural influences. The purpose of intervention, therefore, is to identify the current state of the ecosystems studied, to assess their capability for self-sustenance, and to propose appropriate management goals and actions. Additionally, the holistic-ecosystem methods address institutional considerations to ensure that the resultant management criteria are implemented.

The primary concern of the applied-landscape-ecology approach is to understand how landscape structure evolves along with relevant ecological processes in response to natural and human influences. It uses this knowledge to seek sustainable spatial arrangements of land uses in the landscape. Adherents of this approach view the landscape as a mosaic of interacting ecosystems connected by the flows of materials, energy, and species across spatial scales. It is an interdisciplinary area of inquiry with the intellectual roots primarily in ecosystem ecology and geography. However, other fields have contributed immensely to its theoretical base, especially soil science, geomorphology, and vegetation sciences. The applied-landscape-ecology approach has two branches with different but related focuses. The European branch emphasizes the identification and naming of landscape elements, reflecting an interest in vegetation sciences and in applications. The North American branch focuses on patterns and processes. But this distinction has become blurred because of an increased fusion of ideas between European and American landscape ecologists since the early 1980s.

Studies of landscape values and perception attempt to understand aesthetic experiences—preferences, values, meanings, and experiences encountered in human-landscape interactions. The three major paradigms emphasize different aspects of aesthetic experiences. The professional paradigm, rooted in the arts, design, and ecology, focuses primarily on visual experiences. The behavioral paradigm, rooted in the social and behavioral sciences, especially psychology, emphasizes both visual and other affective responses. And the humanistic paradigm, with roots in human geography, cultural anthropology, and phenomenological studies, stresses experiences encountered in human-landscape interactions.

Organizing Principles

Each approach uses ecological principles and related concepts to make the relations between people and the landscape more understandable and to define problems arising from the relations in ways that make them amenable to intervention. The ecosystem is a fundamental concept used by all the approaches to conceptualize the landscape as a system of interacting physical, biological, and cultural factors connected through the flow of material, energy, and species. Equilibrium is the fundamental force that drives the organization and maintains the stability of ecosystems. Under certain conditions, minimal disturbances enhance the stability and productivity of ecosystems. Stable ecosystems recover from disturbances and establish new equilibriums. Hence, ecosystems have developed varying abilities to recover from disturbances. Ecological-planning approaches seek to sustain the stability of ecosystems while maximizing their productivity.

Frank Golley noted that the ecosystem concept has been treated as the *object* under investigation or a *framework* for understanding how the components interact. I argue that the LSA and applied-human-ecology approaches use the ecosystem more as a framework for understanding ecological interactions and less as object. Except in specific applications, they rarely redefine a study area in terms of ecosystems to permit a more precise empirical understanding of how the components interact. In contrast, the concept is used as both a framework and an object in the ecosystem and landscape-ecology approaches, which attempt to redefine a study site explicitly as interacting ecosystems with boundaries whose properties and behavior can be studied empirically. In a strict sense, the usage of the ecosystem concept as object is more often associated with empirical research in ecosystem sciences, which enrich the substantive theory of ecological planning.

Hierarchy theory, general systems theory (GST), and the related concepts of holism, cybernetics, homeostasis, feedbacks, cause and effect, and self-regulation are important principles that make ecological knowledge more comprehensible. These principles help us understand the landscape as interacting ecological systems that display an increasing level of organization and complexity. Ecosystems at each level of organization are always in a state of flux that entails social and physical conditions, inputs, system changes, outputs, and complex feedback mechanisms.

This perspective on the organization of ecological systems is fundamental to how the applied-ecosystem and landscape-ecology approaches conceptualize the relations between people and the landscape; what their primary concerns should be; and how problems arising from the relations should be resolved. However, landscape ecology is more holistic because it deals with three inseparable perspectives: the aesthetic, focusing on visual concerns; the chorological; and the ecosystemic. Aesthetic concerns are equally important in the landscape-suitability and applied-human-ecology approaches but are often deemphasized in the applied-ecosystem approach. They are the primary focus of assessments of landscape values and perception.

The applied-human-ecology approach adopts a parallel systemic and hierarchically ordered viewpoint on ecological relations, but the degree of emphasis depends on the human-ecology framework employed. Place constructs, for instance, acknowledge that the past, present, and future of a place are linked and that places are also connected to larger places. The human-ecology framework proposed by Young and others uses interaction, hierarchy, functionalism, and holism in a way parallel to the way they are used in the applied-ecosystem and landscape-ecology approaches, but from a social perspective. According to G. Young and his colleagues, interaction implies "reciprocal action, the action or influence of persons or things on each other. . . . It is nature and frequency of interaction that most strongly affects relationships and associations, including those with the landscape or environment. . . . Interaction provides the medium through which systems, including ecosystems and regional systems, perform functions and, in terms of human systems, carry out intended purposes. Unless interaction takes place, no system can continue to exist."

Flowing from the concept of interaction are the notions of hierarchy, functionalism, and holism. These help explain the interactions between parts and wholes and among components in social processes. John Bennett's human-ecology framework, for instance, is based on a systemic view of people's adaptation to landscapes. It regards the landscape as comprising human ecosystems that are open and linked through resource use, organizations, and technology to ecosystems at lower and higher levels of the hierarchy.

LSA 1 and LSA 2 adopt this systemic, hierarchically ordered perspective on ecological relations philosophically. In other words, many LSA methods and techniques have adopted this perspective, but they are inconsistent in how they use it to define and solve problems. Hills's physiographic-unit method, for instance, uses the concept of hierarchy to delineate levels of productivity at varied spatial scales. Lyle and von Wodtke's information system for planning illustrates an LSA 2 method that regards the landscape as comprising ecological systems with input-output relations. This enabled them to model the effects of developmental activities on the flow of nutrients and materials in numerous projects they conducted in San Diego County in the 1970s.

In a similar vein, Steiner's strategic suitability method employs the concept of hierarchy in resource survey and assessment. He recommended three scales—region, locality, and specific site—with an emphasis on the local. He noted that "the use of different scales is consistent with the concept of levels-of-organization used by ecologists. According to this concept, each level of organization has special properties." In contrast, theories on design, arousal, prospect and refuge, information processing, and sense of place are more relevant in understanding the organization of aesthetic experiences in the assessment of landscape values and perception.

The extent to which human-cultural considerations are emphasized deserves further elaboration because it helps define more precisely the nature of the concerns addressed by the approaches and has direct bearing on how they should be resolved. Information on the physical and biological features of the landscape has reduced meaning when it is separated from human concerns. . . .

Procedural Directives

All the approaches to ecological planning use an organizational framework that parallels the sequence of activities used in conventional planning, but with an ecological perspective. The landscape-suitability approaches define the landscape in terms of its structural biophysical and sociocultural attributes. Fitness is established through some surrogate that assumes a dialectic balance between ecosystem stability, self-sustenance, and productivity. Such surrogates are opportunities and constraints, carrying capacity, and indices of attractiveness, vulnerability, and capability.

The judgment of fitness proceeds in a number of ways: by eliminating lands deemed unsuitable for the potential land uses; by identifying both the attractive and vulnerable features of the site; or by analyzing compatibilities among biophysical and sociocultural factors and aggregating them using logical combination rules or rating functions. Some LSA 2 methods, for example, Lyle and von Wodtke's information system, process models used by Carl Steinitz in the Upper San Pedro Watershed study, and the environmental-management-decision-assistance system (a network-impact model for predicting suitability) simulate descriptively the effects of land disturbances on the flows of energy and materials. What is not known, and must be assumed, is how materials, energy, or organisms actually flow among the landscape elements under study.

The human-ecology approach scrutinizes the underlying social structure of the landscape—values, needs, desires, and adaptation mechanisms and then matches the structure with the opportunities and constraints offered by the natural and biological environment using qualitative techniques such as verbal descriptions, texts, and matrices. According to Berger, the underlying structure is better understood by "getting closer to people to discover their definitions of the world . . . and the chosen method is flexible, technically pragmatic, self-discovering, and capable of providing feedback in the course of an investigation." Additionally, because the degree to which we can understand people's values and adaptation to the landscape is limited, most human-ecological-planning methods also provide explicit avenues for ongoing involvement of the affected interests.

The applied-ecosystem and landscape-ecology approaches regard ecological units as having structural properties organized in terms of parts and wholes. Consequently, they first attempt to redefine a study area in terms of ecosystems and input-output relations. They then use pertinent ecological indicators and modeling techniques to examine the ecosystems properties and behavior in response to human actions and natural influences. Some of the indicators deal with the properties of the ecosystems, such as thresholds, lags, and feedbacks; others focus on ecological processes, for example, resiliency, replacement time, feeding relationships, and the efficiency of energy transfer and nutrient cycling.

The use of indicators is exemplified in the studies conducted by Bastedo and Therberge in the 1980s using the ABC strategy and in Cooper and Zedler's location of power lines in southern California in 1980. These indicators can also be aggregated to establish an environmental index, such as the water-quality index developed by the EPA. But there is disagreement about what constitutes sensitive, valid, and reliable indicators of ecosystem quality and integrity.

Some modeling procedures, such as the IBP studies, compartment-flow models used in determining phosphorous levels in the Great Lakes, and nutrient-enrichment landscape-ecology studies of freshwater wetlands in the Netherlands, can manipulate quantitative data. Others are descriptive, such as the process model that Lyle used to simulate material and energy exchanges in his design of the Center for Regenerative Studies at California State Polytechnic University and the land-use studies in Western Massachusetts conducted by Hendrix, Fabos, and Price using Odum's compartment model.

Except when ecosystem boundaries can be fitted nicely around convenient landscape units such as watersheds and drainage basins, defining study areas in terms of ecosystems is still problematic. Additionally, because ecosystems are complex and we know only so much about how they respond to human-induced and natural stresses, the most significant questions asked in using the applied-ecosystem and landscape-ecology approaches relate to which abiotic, biotic, and cultural characteristics of ecosystems should be described; which interactions among them should be emphasized; which stresses affect what ecosystem characteristics and processes, in what ways (temporal and spatial occurrences of stress symptoms), and to what degree; which ecosystem processes are able to withstand extreme stress; and which indicators best measure the short- and long-term effects of these stresses. But while the ecosystem approach examines a study area at the organizational level of the ecosystem, landscape ecology focuses on spatial scales that are much larger than those of traditional ecology, usually on the landscape scale from the human perspective.

The landscape-ecology approach extends the interest in ecological functioning by attempting to understand the spatial resolution and temporal scale that is appropriate in examining patterns and processes. Unlike the other approaches, it explores how the spatial configurations of landscape elements and ecological objects affect function. From landscape-ecology studies, we now know more precisely how linear elements such as stream corridors serve as conduits for water, mineral nutrients, and species or as filters for the protection of water quality. We are also better informed about how patch size, shape, and edge influence the composition, amount, and diversity of interior and edge plant and animal species.

The landscape-ecology approach also examines the horizontal and vertical heterogeneity formed by all land attributes. The other approaches stress the vertical relationships within biophysical and sociocultural elements in relatively homogenous units, including the ecosystem-approach, with which it shares so much. The assumption is that horizontal relationships will be revealed through an examination of the vertical elements. Yet the horizontal relations—patches, corridors, matrices, or ecotopes—possess distinctive characteristics and serve specific ecological functions.

The applied-landscape-ecology approach acknowledges that the structure of the whole landscape and the specific location of the tract of land under consideration are more important than its internal characteristics. Species, energy, and materials move across the patches, corridors, and matrix that make up the tract of land and into other ones. Additionally, landscape change involving interacting abiotic, biotic, and cultural factors suggests that the tract of land must be examined in relation to its context. The tract's formative processes, previous human influence, and natural disturbances also influence its ability to sustain prospective uses. Moreover, one direction of the European branch of landscape ecology is toward the classification and assessment of ecotope assemblages, combining as appropriate the procedures used in the landscape-suitability and ecosystem approaches.

Except for the humanistic paradigm, assessments of landscape values and perception attempt to identify aesthetic landscape units using physical, artistic, and psychological descriptors. Professionals and public groups judge the units based on the preferences, values, and meanings assigned to the descriptors or on their overall aesthetic quality. The behavioral paradigm uses quantitative analytical techniques to link the judgments to descriptors in order to develop statistical models of preferences. In contrast, the humanistic paradigm employs phenomenological explorations to understand people's values and behavior, using qualitative techniques such as open-ended interviews and reviews of literary and creative works.

The classification of landscape resources is one important characteristic of all approaches. Some LSA 1 methods categorize the landscape into homogenous spatial units independent of the prospective land uses by using either a single criterion, such as the NRCS soil survey or Litton's visual classification, or multiple criteria, such as the criteria in Hills's physiographic-unit scheme. The classification methods in the other approaches do the same. Examples in LSA 2 include Holdridge's bioclimatic life zones, the U.S. Fish and Wildlife classification of wetlands, and LESA. In the ecosystem approach they include compartment flow, energy flux, and physiographic-biotic-cultural site types. Illustrative examples in applied landscape ecology are the Canadian ecological land classification, the land facet–land system–main landscape configuration, and the patch-corridor-matrix scheme. While the LSA approaches focus on the structural ecosystem characteristics, the ecosystem and landscape-ecology methods emphasize their interactions.

The applied-human-ecology approach also classifies the landscape, but in a very general way, such as in the geographer Wilbur Zelinsky's vernacular regions, which reflect an embodiment of the spatial perceptions of indigenous people, and the geographer Donald Meinig's cultural regions, defined in terms of cores, domains, and spheres, the core being an extension of the anthropologist Julian Steward's cultural-core concept. . . .

Quantitative Versus Qualitative Techniques

All the ecological-planning approaches employ both qualitative and quantitative techniques. If there is a leaning toward one or the other, the applied-ecosystem approach and landscape-ecology approaches are biased toward quantitative techniques. The suitability and perception studies are clearly divided, and the applied-human-ecology approach favors qualitative analysis.

The inclination toward quantification is hardly surprising; the scientific approach employed in the natural and physical sciences often strives for objectivity, which requires that issues underlying a phenomenon be made explicit. Scientific rigor is strongly associated with the ability to organize data around measurable units so that they can be manipulated to make predictions about hypothesized relationships. The likelihood of obtaining more accurate results is high as well. Proponents of qualitative assessments, however, argue that the complexity of ecosystems and the nature of social values are not understood well enough to be reduced to precise mathematical formulas and equations. Even so, the rules used to derive the mathematical formulas are greatly influenced by value judgments.

Advances in ecological sciences, information and computer technologies, as well as geographical information systems in the past three decades have led to an increased leaning toward describing and analyzing the landscape in ways that facilitate quantitative assessments. While a case can be made for the dominance of quantitative assessments in the applied-ecosystem and landscape-ecology approaches, I review qualitative ones as well. The division is more obvious within landscape-ecological-planning studies. Being an interdisciplinary area of inquiry, the field is dominated by ecologists, geographers, landscape architects, vegetation scientists, wildlife biologists, and so forth. Since each professional brings the orientation of his or her disciplinary approach to problem solving, there is a mix of quantitative and qualitative studies, though the former outnumber the latter. For instance, at the sixteenth annual symposium of the U.S. Regional Association of the International Association of Landscape Ecology, in 2001, more than 70 percent of the papers presented were based on quantitative studies. The topics ranged from quantitative modeling of vegetation and animal-habitat patterns to qualitative descriptions of cultural and aesthetic issues in landscape ecology. Monica Turner and Robert Gardner's *Quantitative Methods in Landscape Ecology* (1991), A. Farina's *Principles and Methods in Landscape Ecology* (1988), as well as Turner, Gardner, and Robert O'Neill's *Landscape Ecology in Theory and Practice* (2001) are testimonies to the dominance of quantitative methods in analyzing landscape heterogeneity in North American landscape-ecology studies. These studies are oriented toward spatial patterns and processes.

LSA methods use quantitative and qualitative assessments or combine them to ascertain suitability. In general, when quantitative techniques are used in suitability analysis, for example, in McHarg's Richmond Parkway study, Steinitz's Boston information system and Upper San Pedro Watershed study, the METLAND model, and LUPLAN, the computerized programming modules used by many Australian planning agencies, a rating function is used to synthesize biophysical and sociocultural data to obtain a grand index of suitability. In contrast, qualitative assessments involve allocation rules judged by planners and landscape architects to be suitable to the objectives of the project and to the natural and cultural features of the landscape. In practice, most LSA studies involve both quantitative and qualitative judgments.

The quantification of aesthetic values is largely a philosophical question on which landscape values and perception scholars fiercely disagree. Proponents of the professional paradigm are divided. Most of them agree that qualitative descriptions are useful when the primary objective is simply to describe the appearance of landscapes, but they disagree on whether the evaluation of their quality should be based on quantitative or qualitative judgments.

The behavioral paradigm assumes that quantification is not only feasible but necessary for accurate estimates of landscape preferences and quality. Social and behavioral scientists have traditionally used quantitative analysis to evaluate similar values. G. Dearden and P. Miller asserted that "public perceptions can be related and, in fact, predicted from environmental attributes of a more tangible nature."

In contrast, humanists contend very strongly that since judgments about people's aesthetic values are inherently subjective in nature, the reasoning behind describing, weighing, comparing, and aggregating them is inherently flawed. We know little about the interactions of the components of aesthetic values. Isolation of one component for further scrutiny is suspect, especially in quantitative terms. Moreover, since landscape descriptors are defined subjectively, judgments about aesthetic preferences and quality are likely to be questionable when these subjectively defined categories are weighted and aggregated to build statistical models. Humanistic studies therefore favor qualitative assessments and tend to be nonjudgmental.

The applied-human-ecology approach also relies mainly on qualitative assessments to examine human-cultural processes. Numerous applications use a repertoire of techniques that include key-informant interviews, participant observation, site reconnaissance, historical surveys, and interpretations of literary and artistic works. The information gained through these techniques complements information obtained from social, economic, and demographic profiles and assessments typically gathered from census data. Because many human-ecological-planning studies synthesize independent assessments of biophysical and human-cultural processes, the evaluation of the biophysical component may involve quantitative and qualitative analysis.

Outputs

The outputs of ecological-planning studies reflect the project goals, the type of approach, and the functions performed. In classification methods across the approaches the outputs are maps accompanied by explanatory text that display homogenous spatial units based on ecosystem characteristics, as in the LSA approaches, or based on interactions, as in the ecosystem and landscape-ecology approaches. In the LSA, the maps may contain data on individual resources, such as soils and vegetation, for example, maps generated using data from the NRCS soil survey or from the U.S. Fish and Wildlife classification hierarchy of wetlands and deepwater habitats; or on multiple resources, such as maps using WMRT's layer-cake model and Holdridge's bioclimatic life-zones classification. The results from using the LSA 2 classification methods usually include social, cultural, and economic information, exemplified by LESA.

The outputs of the ecosystem and landscape-ecology methods can only be based on multiple resources since by definition they focus on processes rather than on structural characteristics. It follows also that the data in the maps can only be presented in an interpretive format, unlike the LSA maps, which can be either interpretive (e.g., Hills's physiographic-unit scheme, the NRCS soil maps, and the Canadian land-inventory maps) or raw (e.g., vegetation and wildlife field surveys, which provide baseline data that are interpreted later for specific purposes).

The primary output of LSA resource survey-and-assessment methods is a series of maps or a single composite map, often accompanied by text, depicting the suitability of each tract of land for single or multiple land uses. The allocation and evaluation methods also provide information on the rationale for selecting among competing suitability options. A part of the rationale is a statement of the environmental effects, as well as the social costs and benefits of each option. Additionally, the outputs of strategic suitability methods, such as Steiner's ecological method or the SIROPLAN method, include information on the programs, institutional arrangements, and resources required to implement the selected suitability option.

The results of human-ecological-planning studies are similar to those of suitability studies. The difference is that the suitabilities reflect a gradient of homogenous spatial areas where culturally preferred locations coincide with ecologically suitable lands. Some studies, such as Berger and Sinton's work on the New Jersey Pinelands, also provide detailed information on organizations and institutional arrangements required for implementation since these are examined as a part of people's adaptive strategies.

Ecosystem-planning studies present information in maps depicting spatial units, accompanied by text. The specific outputs largely depend on project goals and objectives since they address issues beyond the spatial allocation of land uses. The goal may be to decrease non-source [sic] pollution, to rehabilitate ecosystems to allocate land uses, or to assess the effects of fragmentation on animal populations. The outputs often include one or more of the following: a description of ecosystem quality and value to distinguish ecosystems that are valuable from those that may require modifications under management practices; the rationale for selecting appropriate indicators for evaluating ecosystem behavior; and a description of the appropriate management goals—protection (conservation, maintenance, or preservation), correction (restoration or rehabilitation), exploitation (land-disturbing activities such as residential and commercial development), or a combination of these. The outputs of the holistic-ecosystem methods are similar to those of the strategic suitability methods in that they include a statement of the institutional arrangements and resources for implementation.

Because the applied-landscape-ecology approach does not yet have a substantial body of empirically tested methods, the outputs are varied. Some are similar to those of ecosystem-planning studies, such as hydrological-modeling studies. Others produce maps comparable to those resulting from suitability studies, with accompanying texts that explain landscape processes. Moreover, the products of methods such as LANDEP contain descriptions of the rationale for selecting the preferred land-use allocation options and the mechanisms for implementation.

The outcomes of assessments of landscape values and perception depend on the paradigm. The professional paradigm provides statements of visual preferences and quality. The behavioral paradigm produces numerical estimates of preferences, quality, meanings, and other affective responses to landscapes. The output of the humanist paradigm is somewhat similar to the outputs of human-ecology studies, including statement of tastes, ideas about beauty, valued landscapes, and in general the experience of landscapes and the accompanying changes in both people and landscapes. The difference is that the outcomes of the humanistic paradigm are primarily oriented toward advancing knowledge, while human ecology uses outputs as an input in ascertaining landscape suitability.

It is obvious that no single approach can address all ecological problems. Each approach has its strengths and weaknesses. Planners and landscape architects can draw on the strong features of each approach and ignore the less desirable aspects.

When the emphasis is on seeking the optimal fitness of human and other uses in the landscape, we turn to LSA 1 and LSA 2. The earlier of these, LSA 1, stressed natural factors. The significant theoretical and methodological advances in landscape-suitability methods since the early 1970s are reflected in LSA 2. Important advances were: embracing sociocultural information systematically in establishing the optimal uses of the landscape; improving the technical validity of the analytical operations; placing more emphasis on ecological processes; increasing the scope of functions performed to include evaluation and implementation; and making the outputs more defensible in a public debate. Moreover, LSA 2 methods developed within the past twenty years have integrated innovations in information, remote-sensing, and computer technologies, including visual simulation and geographic information systems, making them more powerful and efficient in storing, processing, and displaying information. Sophisticated LSA 2 methods address the six questions Carl Steinitz proposed, as well as a seventh added by me, that are essential in addressing problems of any scale: How should the landscape be represented? How does the landscape function? Is the landscape functioning well? How might the landscape be changed? What predictable differences might the changes cause? How should the landscape be changed? How can the proposed changes in the landscape become a reality?

LSA methods are arguably the most widely used in ecological planning. They are capable of addressing conservation and development issues in urban, rural, and natural areas. Some methods are tailored to deal with single-resource allocation and management issues, such as the siting of a highway corridor; others can address multiple-resource issues. Moreover, they perform a wide range of functions. The LSA 1 gestalt method, for instance, is useful in analyzing small tracts of land. As the size of the parcel of land increases, it becomes more difficult to comprehend it fully in its entirety. Gestalt analysis is integrated in most ecological-planning methods. When the cost of data collection is a limiting factor, planners and designers may decide to use the landscape-unit and landscape-classification method as a first step in establishing suitability.

When the evaluation of alternative landscape allocation options is a major consideration, allocation-evaluation methods may serve the purpose. With rapid advances in ecosystem sciences as well as in information and computer technologies, the models have become more sophisticated in terms of the evaluative tasks they perform, as is evident from the study of the upper San Pedro region conducted by Carl Steinitz and his colleagues. They employed a series of process and analytical models to evaluate the effects of urban development on the hydrological regime and biodiversity in the region over the next twenty years. But LSA methods still examine ecological functions in a static way except when the database has a strong dynamic component, as in the investigation of hydrological relations in the study for The Woodlands. Also, since the methods focus on fitness for human and other uses, landscape characteristics that do not have direct use implications are often neglected, unless the use is an objective of the study, such as protecting biodiversity.

The human-ecology approach is especially useful when cultural matters are important. It provides an explicit way of understanding human-cultural processes beyond the typical social and economic analyses associated with most ecological-planning studies. One direction in its evolution may be viewed as an extension of LSA 2 to explicitly include human processes by way of adaptation mechanisms and postures. The other emphasizes the scrutiny of landscapes as places where human values and experiences coincide with biophysical processes. Unfortunately, this approach has not evolved with the same theoretical rigor that characterizes the other approaches.

Recent ecological-planning literature rarely uses the term *human-ecological planning and design*. Instead, fashionable terms are employed even though what is really meant is human-ecological planning. Examples of substitute terms are *human-ecology bias, sustainable design, place making, focus groups, historicism,* and *phenomenology*. Human ecology is still located in the margins of many disciplines. Additionally, while cultural adaptation and similar concepts are useful in explaining human-environment interactions, their translation into planning and design are somewhat cumbersome. For example, ethnographic-survey and related techniques are not mainstream techniques that planners and designers often use for data gathering and analysis. Planners may be concerned about justifying the outputs in a public debate. A related but important issue is that despite the power of cultural-adaptation models to explain how people use and adapt to the landscape, they generalize about the spatial distribution of human-cultural processes. Many planners and designers find place constructs very appealing, but as we have seen, putting the constructs into practice has occurred on a project-by-project basis. Consequently, the reliability and validity of the place constructs are questionable.

The applied-ecosystem and applied-landscape-ecology approaches bring more scientific rigor to the examination of landscapes. They use a system perspective to define ecological problems. Moreover, their interest in examining the landscape in terms of input-transformation-output relations makes explicit the tracking of the specific effects of human and natural disturbances on ecological processes. Their emphasis on ecosystem quality and response is important for suggesting appropriate management actions more systematically

The landscape-ecology approach has additional strengths. It reveals explicitly how the structure of ecological systems changes along with relevant functional processes; how these changes enable ecosystems to develop identifiable visual and cultural identity; and how ecological systems are linked both vertically and horizontally through the flow of nutrients, energy, and materials. The approach can also be used to study large landscapes, such as the Columbia Basin. We are only beginning to understand how the spatial configurations of landscape elements affect function. Perhaps the most definitive contributions of landscape ecology to planning are bridging concepts, spatial frameworks for describing the functional components of any landscape and explicit principles for creating sustainable spatial arrangements of the landscape. The principles seek to maintain the ecological integrity of landscapes characterized by natural levels of plant productivity; minimum disruption of the flows of nutrients, energy, and species; increased soil productivity; and sustained healthy aquatic communities.

The applied-ecosystem approach is used mostly in dealing with development, conservation, restoration, and rehabilitation concerns in urbanizing and natural-rural landscapes. Landscape-ecological planning has been applied in similar settings, including urban environments. In Europe applications have focused on ecological problems arising from rapid intensification of land uses, which creates extreme competition for space among agriculture, forestry, industry, and urban development and redevelopment. This is not surprising since landscapes in Europe have long been dominated or influenced by humans. In contrast, applications in North America focus on habitat-network planning and wildlife conservation in rural and natural areas, with special emphasis on the conservation of biological diversity and on sustainable land use. Very few applications in urban areas are documented, though the potential exists.

The Central Arizona–Phoenix Long-Term Ecological Research (CAP LTER), for instance, is a promising research project that is likely to yield data and information that planners and designers can use in addressing ecological-planning issues in urban areas. Led by Charles Redman and Nancy Grimm, CAP LTER is a multifaceted study directed at understanding how the development patterns of the central Arizona and Phoenix area alter the area's ecological conditions, and vice versa. It is one of the two long-term ecological sites currently supported by the U.S. National Science Foundation to study the city as a mosaic of interacting ecosystems; the other study is located in Baltimore.

Assessments of landscape values and perception are useful when human values, meanings, and experiences are the major considerations. The paradigms differ on what aesthetic values should be addressed, who should be involved in aesthetic judgments, and how. The professional paradigm is arguably the most widely used and documented, but the results have low reliability and are less defensible in a public debate. Regardless of whether qualitative or quantitative techniques are used, their effectiveness is heavily dependent on the perceptions, technical expertise, and the sociocultural conditioning of the evaluators.

The behavioral paradigm, with its emphasis on objectivity and quantification, is usually subjected to the rigorous tests of validity and reliability associated with the empirical methods of the social and behavioral sciences. The humanistic paradigm produces a rich source of qualitative information about landscape values and preferences, but it has low validity and reliability. The studies often take a long time to complete, and the results may be difficult to justify in a public debate. Generalization of the results for problem solving is restricted. But since landscape perception is a continuum without boundaries, many studies combine elements from different paradigms.

Because of the paradigms' distinctive theoretical positions on human-landscape interactions, which in turn are strongly aligned with the orientations of participating disciplines, it has been extremely difficult to articulate a unified theory of landscape perception. This issue was raised twenty years ago by Jay Appleton, and it is still very much alive, despite concerted efforts to develop such a theory. Zube and others remarked that when such a theoretical foundation is lacking, questions "of why some landscapes are valued more than the others and the significance of those values remain largely unanswered."

The aesthetician Allen Carson adds that what is needed is a theory that addresses very fundamental issues about human-landscape interactions. Such a theory would simultaneously explain and justify. Explanatory theory allows us to identify "things and state of things . . . and allows us to explain, predict, and control." Justification theory provides us with a normative framework to "clarify our ideas . . . formulate our positions, argue for them, and justify them." If it does not define our position on "things and their states, explanatory theory will have nothing to explain." One thing is certain: such a theory has not been formulated.

References

Baschak, Lawrence, and Robert Brown. "River Systems and Landscape Networks." *Landscape Planning and Ecological Networks.* Elsevier, Amsterdam (1994): 179–99.

Bastedo, Jamie D., J. Gordon Nelson, and John B. Theberge. "Ecological Approach to Resource Survey and Planning for Environmentally Significant Areas: The ABC Method." *Environmental Management* 8, no. 2 (1984): 125–34.

Bastedo, Jamie D., and University of Waterloo. Dept. of Geography. *An ABC Resource Survey Method for Environmentally Significant Areas with Special Reference to Biotic Surveys in Canada's North.* Department of Geography, 1986.

Bennett, John William. *The Ecological Transition.* New Brunswick, NJ: Transaction Books, 1976.

Berger, Jonathan. "Landscape Patterns of Local Social Organization and Their Importance for Land Use Planning." *Landscape Planning* 8, no. 2 (1981): 193–232.

Berger, Jonathan, and John W. Sinton. *Water, Earth, and Fire: Land Use and Environmental Planning in the New Jersey Pine Barrens.* Baltimore, MD: Johns Hopkins University Press, 1985.

Carlson, Allen. "On the Theoretical Vacuum in Landscape Assessment." *Landscape Journal* 12, no. 1 (1993): 51–6.

Cooper, Charles F., and Paul H. Zedler. "Ecological Assessment for Regional Development." *Journal of Environmental Management* 10, no. 3 (1980): 285–96.

Cowardin, Lewis M. *Classification of Wetlands and Deepwater Habitats of the US.* Collingdale, PA: Diane Publishing, 1979.

Dansereau, P., and G. Pare. *Ecological Grading and Classification of Landscape Occupation and Land-Use Mosaics.* Geographic paper no. 58. Ottawa, Ont.: Fisheries and Environment Canada, 1977.

Deithlem and Bressler. *Mount Bachelor Recreation Area: Proposed Master Plan.* Eugene, Oregon, 1980.

Forman, Richard T. T. *Land Mosaics: The Ecology of Landscapes and Regions.* Cambridge University Press, 1995.

Forman, Richard T. T., and M. Godron. *Landscape Ecology.* New York: John Wiley, 1986.

Francis, G., J. Magnuson, H. Reiger, and D. Talhelm, eds. *Rehabilitating Great Lakes Ecosystems.* Technical Report 37. Ann Arbor, MI.: Great Lakes Fisheries Commission, 1979.

Haber, Wolfgang. "Using Landscape Ecology in Planning and Management." In *Changing Landscapes: An Ecological Perspective,* Springer New York, 1990.

Hills, G. Angus. "A Philosophical Approach to Landscape Planning." *Landscape Planning* 1 (1974): 339–71.

Holdridge, Leslie. *Life Zone Ecology.* San Jose, Costa Rica: Tropical Science Center, 1967.

Hopkins, Lewis D. "Methods for Generating Land Suitability Maps: A Comparative Evaluation." *Journal of the American Institute of Planners* 43, no. 4 (1977): 386–400.

Ingmire, Thomas J., and Tito Patri. "An Early Warning System for Regional Planning." *Journal of the American Institute of Planners* 37, no. 6 (1971): 403–10.

International Joint Commission. *Environmental Management Strategy for the Great Lakes System.* Windsor, Ont., 1978.

Ive, J. R., and K. D. Cocks. "SIRO-PLAN and LUPLAN: an Australian Approach to Land-Use Planning. 2. The LUPLAN Land-Use Planning Package." *Environment and Planning B: Planning and Design* 10, no. 3 (1983): 347–55.

Jacobs, Peter. "Landscape Development in the Urban Fringe. A Case Study of the Site Planning Process." *Town Planning Review* 42, no. 4 (1971): 342.

Juneja, N. "Medford." Center for Ecological Research in Planning and Design, University of Pennsylvania, Philadelphia, PA (1974).

Klign, F. "Spatially Nested Ecosystems: Guidelines for Classification from a Hierarchical Perspective." In *Ecosystem Classification for Environmental Management,* 85–116. Berlin: Springer-Verlag, 1994.

Lenz, Roman J. M. "Ecosystem Classification by Budget of Material: The Example of Forest Ecosystems Classified as Proton Budget Types." In *Ecosystem Classification for Environmental Management*, 117–37. Springer Netherlands, 1994.

Leopold, Aldo. *A Sand County Almanac*. New York: Ballantine Books, 1949.

Lewis, Philip H. "Quality Corridors for Wisconsin." *Landscape Architecture* 54, no. 2 (1964): 100–107.

Linton, R. Burton. *Forest Landscape Description and Inventories: A Basis for Land Planning and Design*. Pacific Southwest Forest and Range Experiment Station, U.S. Department of Agriculture, 1968.

Lyle, John Tillman. *Regenerative Design for Sustainable Development*. John Wiley & Sons Incorporated, 1996.

Lyle, John Tilman, and Mark Von Wodtke. "An Information System for Environmental Planning." *Journal of the American Institute of Planners* 40, no. 6 (1974): 394–413.

McHarg, Ian L. "Human Ecological Planning at Pennsylvania." *Landscape Planning* 8, no. 2 (1981): 109-20.

Meinig, Donald W. "The Mormon Culture Region: Strategies and Patterns in the Geography of the American West, 1847–1964." *Annals of the Association of American Geographers* 55, no. 2 (1965): 191–219.

Odum, Eugene P. "The Strategy of Ecosystem Development." *Science* (New York, NY) 164, no. 3877 (1969): 262.

Odum, Howard T. *Systems Ecology: An Introduction*. New York: John Wiley & Sons, 1983.

Opdam, Paul, Rob van Apeldoorn, Alex Schotman, and Jan Kalkhoven. "Population Responses to Landscape Fragmentation." In *Landscape Ecology of a Stressed Environment*, 147–71. Springer Netherlands, 1993.

Rapport, David, and Anthony Friend. "Towards a Comprehensive Framework for Environmental Statistics: A Stress Response Approach." Vol. 11, no. 510. Ottawa, Ont.: Statistics Canada, 1979.

Rice Center for Community Design and Research. *Environmental Analysis for Development Planning, Chambers County, Texas*. Houston: Southwest Center for Urban Research, Rice University, 1974.

Ruzicka, Milan, and Ladislav Miklos. "Basic Premises and Methods in Landscape Ecological Planning and Optimization." In *Changing Landscapes: An Ecological Perspective*, 233–60. Springer New York, 1990.

Selman, Paul. "Landscape Ecology and Countryside Planning: Vision, Theory and Practice." *Journal of Rural studies* 9, no. 1 (1993): 1–21.

Steiner, Frederick R. *The Living Landscape: An Ecological Approach to Landscape Planning*. 2nd edn. McGraw-Hill, New York, 2000.

———. "Resource Suitability: Methods for Analyses." *Environmental Management* 7, no. 5 (1983): 401–20.

Steinitz, Carl. "Landscape Change: Models, Alternatives, and Levels of Complexity." Summarized and presented by Stephen Ervin at the Workshop in Landscape Change, 25–27 January 2001, Santa Barbara, Calif.

———. *Computers and Regional Planning: The DELMARVA Study*. Cambridge: Graduate School of Design, Harvard University, 1967.

Steinitz, Carl, and Peter Rogers. *A Systems Analysis Model of Urbanization and Change: An Experiment in Interdisciplinary Education*. Cambridge, MA: MIT Press, 1970.

The Netherlands Ministry of Housing, Spatial Planning and Environment. *Summary of General Ecological Model*. Study Report 5.3.B. The Hague: National Physical Planning Agency, 1977.

Theberge, John, James Nelson, and Terry Fenge. *Environmentally Significant Areas of the Yukon Territory*. Ottawa, Ont.: Arctic Resources Committee, 1980.

Thie, J., and G. Ironside. *Ecological (Biophysical) Land Classification in Canada*. Ecological Land Classification Series, no. 1. Ottawa, Ont.: Land Directorate, Environment Canada, 1976.

Thorne, James F. "Landscape Ecology." *Landscape Journal* 6, no. 2 (1987): 153–54.

Toth, Richard. *Criteria for Evaluating the Valuable Natural Resource of the TIRAC Region.* Stroudsburg, Pa.: Tocks Island Regional Advisory Council, 1968.

U.S. Department of Agriculture, Forest Service. *Land Capability Classification.* Agricultural Handbook No 210. Washington, DC, 1961.

U.S. Department of Agriculture, Soil Conservation Service. *National Agriculture Land Evaluation and Site Assessment Handbook.* Washington, DC, 1961.

Van Buuren, Michael, and Klaas Kerkstra. "The Framework Concept and the Hydrological Landscape Structure: A New Perspective in the Design of Multifunctional Landscapes." In *Landscape Ecology of a Stressed Environment,* 219–243. Springer Netherlands, 1993.

Wallace, D., I. McHarg, W. Roberts, and T. Todd. *Woodlands New Community.* 4 vols. Philadelphia, 1971–74.

Young, Gerald, Frederick Steiner, Kenneth Brooks, and Kenneth Struckmeyer. "Determining the Regional Context for Landscape Planning." *Landscape Planning* 10, no. 4 (1983): 269–96.

Zelinsky, Wilbur. "North America's Vernacular Regions." *Annals of the Association of American Geographers* 70, no. 1 (1980): 1–16.

Zonneveld, Isaak S. "Scope and Concepts of Landscape Ecology as an Emerging Science." In *Changing Landscapes: An Ecological Perspective,* 3–20. New York: Springer, 1990.

———. "The Land Unit—A Fundamental Concept in Landscape Ecology, and Its Applications." *Landscape Ecology* 3, no. 2 (1989): 67–86.

Zube, Ervin H. "Perceived Land Use Patterns and Landscape Values." *Landscape Ecology* 1, no. 1 (1987): 37–45.

Zube, Ervin H., James L. Sell, and Jonathan G. Taylor. "Landscape Perception: Research, Application and Theory." *Landscape Planning* 9, no. 1 (1982): 1–33.

Part Six

Dimensions of Practice

Introduction to Part Six

To illustrate the wide spectrum of global ecological design and planning practices, seven case studies of exemplary practice are examined in this section. These practices are noteworthy applications of substantive and procedural ecological planning theories and principles that sustainably balance human use with ecological concerns in the research environment and professional practice.

In the first reading, by Arthur Johnson, Jonathan Berger, and Ian McHarg, "A Case Study in Ecological Planning," from *Planning the Uses and Management of Land* (1979), the authors examined a method for establishing the inherent suitabilities of the landscape for human uses and its application in The Woodlands, Texas, located twenty-five miles north of Houston.[1]

The approach depicts a notable theoretical-methodological advancement over McHarg's earlier methods examined in part 5. Its fundamental logic and conceptual and analytical base are still as valid and relevant today as they were thirty-five years ago. It is still one of the most widely used methods in professional practice today, although newer ones have enhanced its capabilities remarkably, particularly in the context of technological, modeling, and visualization advances.

The next reading is a case study by the design and planning firm Design Workshop, Inc., "Project Discussion: Aguas Claras, Belo Horizonte" (2007).[2] It is a successful example of reclamation and transformation of a derelict iron-ore mine in a satellite village for the Belo Horizonte metropolitan area (Brazil's third largest city with a population of more than three million people). The firm was effective in implementing a holistic approach and philosophy that sought to synthesize environment, community, economics, and arts with the "dictates of land and needs of society." They skillfully blended diverse knowledge bases to develop an adaptive-reuse master plan for Aguas Claras. Knowledge bases included those of the client, site, context, project economics, program and users, and design precedent.[3] This project was featured as an exemplary sustainable mining reclamation project in the Brazilian exhibit at the 1992 Earth Summit in Rio de Janeiro.

Next is the "Foreword" of Chris Mulder's book *Thesen Islands* (2008), which documents the transformation of a hundred-year-old polluting, contaminated, and derelict lumber processing landscape into a vibrant and highly successful mixed-use community in Knysna, Western Cape Province, South Africa.[4] The island is located in the heart of the serene waters of one the most ecologically sensitive ecosystems in South Africa. The project has received numerous awards for excellence in design and environmental stewardship.

The next two readings are case studies focused on the conservation of natural and cultural values and resources. The first is by Carl Steinitz and colleagues, "The Upper San Pedro River Basin" (2003), which documents the application of his framework reviewed in part 5 for delineating alternative futures for the Upper San Pedro River Basin.[5] The authors applied his six-question framework through a series of iterations and identified ten alternative futures for the basin, as well as the direct and indirect effects of these scenarios on issues such as biodiversity, hydrological processes, flora and fauna habitats, and scenic resources. The outcome of the study did not lead to a specific plan but rather to an array of alternative futures and their effects on important landscape processes such as hydrology and wildlife. The alternative scenarios are intended to guide decision makers in delineating an appropriate course of action.

The next reading is a case study focusing on the collaborative work of landscape architect Kongjian Yu, dean of the College of Architecture and Landscape Architecture at Peking University, and head of the landscape architecture and planning firm Turenscape.[6] The study, "Reinvent the Good Earth: National Ecological Security Pattern Plan, China" (2012), examined the critical landscape infrastructure for conserving ecological values and resources and proposed a national strategy for their conservation. Yu's ambitious plan was based on the conservation of ecosystem infrastructure and services, especially the protection of river source or "head water," storm water management, flood control, reversal of desertification, soil and erosion prevention, and biodiversity conservation.

Each of these factors constitutes a "security pattern." The scale of the project is noteworthy in its comprehensiveness.

The last two readings focus on creating places. In "From Regional Planning to Site Design: The Application of 'Shan-shui City' Concept in Multi-scale Landscape Planning of New Cities in China" (2010), landscape architect Jie Hu documents successful efforts at integrating Chinese philosophy and cultural traditions into the design and planning of new towns in China.[7] Hu argued that landscape planning, which seeks to address tensions between "urban-artificial ecosystems and natural-ecosystems," must involve both the regional and the local scales to create "ecologically secure landscapes" that meet aesthetic and urban requirements at the site scale but are also informed by the assessment of landscape-ecostructure at the regional scale.

The last reading, by architect and University of Washington professor David Miller, "Site: Building through Ecological Planning," from *Toward a New Regionalism: Environmental Architecture in the Pacific Northwest*, presents case studies demonstrating excellent environmental design practices in the Pacific Northwest, with special emphasis on the Cedar River Watershed Education Center in King County, Washington State.[8] The project designers, the award-winning firm of Jones and Jones Architects and Landscape Architects, envisioned the project as an opportunity to reveal the site's hydrological processes to the public while cultivating public appreciation for the source of the city's drinking water and nurturing ecological stewardship.[9] Today, many of the ecological design features and strategies that Jones and Jones had introduced are only now beginning to be used widely in professional practice.

Though not included in the readings for lack of space, I discuss my coauthored article in the synthesis. The article, "Environmentally Sensitive Areas: A Template for Developing Greenway Corridors," published in *Landscape and Urban Planning* (1995), presents a pilot study on creating greenway corridors.[10] Unlike other readings presented here, an abiotic-biotic-cultural method was used that enabled the investigation of abiotic (e.g., bedrock and hydrology), biotic (flora and fauna), and cultural (human activities) phenomena in terms of their structural (descriptive) and functional (relational) attributes. The outcomes are interpreted for their relative ecological values and employed subsequently as the basis for creating greenway corridors in Walton County, Georgia.

The readings display a wide array of case studies in global ecological design and planning practices. The case studies span from those originating in the research environment, such as Carl Steinitz's San Pedro River Basin study and my Walton County environmentally sensitive areas (ESA) study, to others originating from private practice, like Design Workshop's Aguas Claras mining reclamation and satellite community scheme or Chris Mulder's Thesen Islands reclamation and new settlement project. The ecological problem types addressed traverse new community and restoration schemes and biodiversity and resource conservation proposals, as seen in Kongjian Yu's national ecological security, Carl Steinitz's San Pedro Basin, and the Walton County ESA project. The spatial scale of the projects examined ranges from national to local levels. Also represented is a diversity of global practices from Africa, China, South America, and the United States.

Each case study makes a unique contribution to the continued development of ecological design and planning, but the extent to which the case studies explicitly embrace aesthetic considerations is mixed. It is especially obvious in the Aguas Claras, Thesen Islands, and Cedar River Watershed Education Center projects, and less so but implied in the national ecological security and Walton County ESA projects. The San Pedro Basin study modeled the visual impacts of alternative futures for the study area. As George Thompson and Frederick Steiner remarked, successfully designed places blend aesthetic foundation with ecological processes.[11]

Jie Hu's multiscale landscape planning project in China sought to integrate the "Shan-shui City" concept into landscape design and new town planning. The concept is essentially an aesthetic founded on the Taoist philosophy that can enhance the creation of places that are enriching and meaningful to their inhabitants.

Hu's design is clearly consistent with Catherine Howett's proposition in part 3 for a new aesthetic that combines ecological thinking and place theory, while forging expressive meanings of the built environment. Hu was insistent that incorporating visual resources in design alone is not enough, and stated that, "Healthy urban development should support a secure ecological environment in the creation of a Shan-shui City that is appropriate for its location. Landscape design that considers only visual effects is not advisable."[12]

This case study arguably exemplifies an effective implementation of culturally informed ecological design and planning. It challenges us to reflect deeply on the user groups' or the clients' cultural traditions, values, and motifs that may be relevant to ecological design and planning, especially in cross-cultural settings in which the designer comes from a social group whose culture is different from that of the client group. In addition, Hu's project does a much better job than others in embracing the consideration of multiple spatial scales when defining and solving landscape planning problems (e.g., region, local, and site). As Richard Forman affirmed, contextual forces are sometimes more important than internal dynamics in influencing how a landscape functions.[13]

Suitability analysis and the use of overlays are inherent features of the methods employed in each of the case studies examined here, but with varying degrees of emphasis. Today, overlays are used primarily via geographical information systems, with their advanced capabilities in modeling and visualization. The suitability method employed in The Woodlands study clearly represents a major methodological innovation in suitability analysis for the 1970s, with its focus on seeking optimal uses of the landscape based on a dialectic balance between ecological, economic, and social factors. This demonstrated a shift away from considering only biophysical factors in determining suitability—a major feature of first-generation landscape-suitability methods.

Moreover, the method employed matrices, tables, and flow diagrams to explore the impacts of prospective uses in The Woodlands on landscape factors such as soils and vegetation, and conversely, the impact of these resource factors on each of the uses. Arthur Johnson and his colleagues suggested the viability of deriving performance measures from suitability analysis, which is extremely useful in ascertaining how well a design or plan has performed in reaching its targeted goals.

The management of storm water based on the natural processes of the landscape, as practiced in The Woodlands, marked an important milestone in ecological design and planning. The Woodlands has become a global model for storm water management and has provided the impetus for the evolution of low-impact development practices today. Dr. Ming-Han Li at Texas A&M University and his protégée, Dr. Bo Yang at Utah State University, provided the most compelling empirical evidence to date affirming that storm water management that utilizes a system of natural swales and corridors is an effective, economical, and efficient strategy.[14]

The methods employed in the aforementioned case studies seek to embrace ecological functioning in determining the optimal uses of the landscape. They have done so with varied degrees of effectiveness. Most of the case studies essentially model ecological processes by using matrices (such as in The Woodlands), process models (as employed in Steinitz's San Pedro River Basin study), or graphic overlay (as implied in Yu's ecological security pattern project) in making such determinations. In my Walton County ESA study, I used the abiotic-biotic-cultural strategy, which permitted biophysical and sociocultural resources to be described first in terms of their structural (descriptive) attributes, such as plant communities, followed by functional (relational) characteristics— for example, successional patterns. The outcomes are synthesized to establish ecological significance and constraints.

Steinitz's framework further permits the advanced modeling of cause-effect relationships. It also enables an examination of the current health, value, or

Figures 6-1a and 6-1b Preliminary master plan for the Thompson and Grace Medical City, Akwa Ibom, Nigeria. Designed by Texas A&M University. The award winning international design firm, HKS, contributed in finalizing the master plan (2014, Courtesy of Chanam Lee, Forster Ndubisi, Weyan Ji, Yue Li, and Sinan Zhong).

functioning of the landscape as a point of departure in conducting the assessment of landscape resources, which many of the methods rarely do. Exceptions exist, especially when restoration or reclamation is the explicit focus of the study.

In conclusion, there are many exemplary case studies of ecological design and planning practice. The material presented here acknowledges the growing body of works that make a significant stride in effectively balancing human use with ecological concerns (figures 6-1a, b).

Notes

1. Arthur H. Johnson, Jonathan Berger, and Ian McHarg, "A Case Study in Ecological Planning: The Woodlands, Texas," in *Planning the Uses and Management of Land*, M. T. Beaty, G. W. Petersen, and L. D. Swindale (eds.) (Madison, WI: American Society of Agronomy, Crop Science Society of America, and Soil Science Society of America, 1979), 935–955.
2. Design Workshop, Inc., "Essay on the Restorative Power of Nature by Richard Shaw," and "Project Discussion on the Aguas Claras Project in Brazil," in *Toward Legacy: Design Workshop's Pursuit of Ideals in Landscape Architecture, Planning, and Urban Design* (Washington, DC: Grayson Publishing, 2007): 21–41.
3. Design Workshop, Inc., "Project Discussion on the Aguas Claras Project in Brazil," In *Toward Legacy: Design Workshop's Pursuit of Ideals in Landscape Architecture, Planning, and Urban Design.* (Washington, DC.: Grayson Publishing, 2007), 38.
4. Chris Mulder, "Foreword," in *Thesen Islands* (Cape Town, South Africa: Quivertree Publications, 2008), 10–17.
5. Carl Steinitz, Hector Arias, Scott Bassett, Michael Flaxman, Tomas Goode, Thomas Maddock III, David Mouat, Richard Peiser, and Allan Shearer, "The Upper San Pedro River Basin," and "The Framework for Alternative Futures Studies," in *Alternative Futures for Changing Landscapes: The Upper San Pedro River Basin in Arizona and Sonora* (Washington, DC: Island Press, 2003).
6. William Saunders, "Reinvent the Good Earth: National Ecological Security Pattern Plan, China" in *Designed Ecologies: The Landscape Architecture of Kongjian Yu* (Birkhauser Basel, 2012).
7. Jie Hu, "From Regional Planning to Site Design: The Application of 'Shan-shui City' Concept in Multi-scale Landscape Planning of New Cities in China," in *International Federation of Landscape Architects World Congress* (2010).
8. David E. Miller, "Site Building Through Ecological Planning," in *Toward a New Regionalism: Environmental Architecture in the Pacific Northwest* (Seattle, WA: University of Washington Press, 2005).
9. Ibid.
10. Forster Ndubisi, Terry DeMeo, and Niels D. Ditto, "Environmentally Sensitive Areas: A Template for Developing Greenway Corridors," *Landscape and Urban Planning* 33, no. 1 (1995), 159–177.
11. George Thompson and Frederick Steiner, *Ecological Design and Planning* (New York: John Wiley & Sons, 2007).
12. Hu, "From Regional Planning to Site Design: The Application of 'Shan-shui City' Concept in Multi-scale Landscape Planning of New Cities in China," 5.
13. Richard Forman, *Land Mosaics: The Ecology of Landscapes and Regions* (New York: Cambridge University Press, 1995).
14. Bo Yang and Ming-Han Li, "Ecological Engineering in a New Town Development: Drainage Design in Woodlands, TX." *Ecological Engineering* 36, no. 12 (2010), 1639–1650.

A Case Study in Ecological Planning: The Woodlands, Texas

Planning the Uses and Management of Land (1979)

Arthur H. Johnson, Jonathan Berger, and Ian L. McHarg

I. Introduction

In reviewing the publications and reports in the regional and landscape planning literature and project reports from the profession, one finds a lack of uniformity in methodology, with ad hoc procedures "suited to the particular problem" a common approach. A method is presented in this chapter for determining the inherent suitability of a landscape for assimilating human activities and their artifacts. The approach is suggested in the writings of McHarg (1969) and exemplified by Juneja (1974), and has been applied professionally to a wide array of sites and locations. The method of landscape analysis described here is one part of a more comprehensive planning process which includes the social, legal, and economic factors which must be melded into a comprehensive plan that responds to the needs, desires, and perceptions of the people for whom the planning is being done. In developing an area, one would like to achieve the best fit between each human activity and the portion of the landscape to which that activity is assigned. As a starting point, a landscape may be thought of as being comprised of elements or components which may be labeled *geology, physiography, soils, hydrology, vegetation, wildlife,* and *climate.* Each landscape element may provide opportunities for certain land uses, and likewise, there may be constraints to each kind of desired land use imposed by components of the landscape. Areas which are most suitable for a specific use will have the greatest number of opportunities provided by the landscape and the least number of, or least severe, constraints imposed by the landscape on that particular use.

By using the approach of combining analyses of opportunities and constraints, the environmental impacts of the planned uses can be minimized, and the energy required to implement and maintain the proposed uses and artifacts can likewise be minimized. For example, areas where the water table is near the surface frequently or for extended periods provide an obvious constraint to subdivision housing in unsewered areas. This property of the landscape lowers the inherent suitability of such areas for that use. The situation can be ameliorated by the addition of sewers or by other engineering solutions, but costs, either economic or ecological, will be incurred, and additional energy will be required for installation and maintenance. This same area may provide little constraint to a golf course or park. Areas which are on the lee side of vegetative or physiographic barriers to winter winds provide a slight advantage for housing as energy costs for winter heating will be somewhat reduced. This same property of a site produces little opportunity for a park or golf course if the use is confined to the warm seasons. Thus the pattern of land uses assigned to the landscape could be controlled to a large degree by the characteristics and properties of the landscape. To this end, a careful analysis of the physiography, geology, soils, hydrology, plants, animals, and climate-microclimate of an area should be carried out and the implications for specified land uses determined by trained scientists.

The approach outlined here is designed to be flexible. It has been applied to areas ranging in size from a few hectares to a few hundred square kilometers and to urban, suburban, and rural areas.

There are also mechanisms to incorporate new data which may be generated after an initial plan has been formulated. Although flexible, the method is designed to be as objective as possible. The solutions are replicable and the methods of analysis overt and explicit.

Additionally, the method may be used to derive performance requirements (i.e., conditions which must be met by the developers) for the development of areas of less than prime suitability. The impact of any use on the landscape (or the impact of the landscape on the land use) can be mitigated by engineering to have the same result as the same development in the most suitable areas. The areas of prime suitability thus may become a "meter stick" for specifying what additional measures should be taken to minimize impacts on the land-use by the landscape, and on the landscape by the land use.

II. Outline of the Methods

A flow chart of the planning process of which this method of landscape analysis is a part is given in figure 6-2. The stream of landscape analysis identified by the box in figure 6-2 is the subject of this chapter and this part of the process is dependent upon the input of natural scientists. Clearly, the assembly of scientific data and its interpretation requires the perceptions and expertise of soil scientists, geologists, meteorologists, hydrologists, and ecologists. For a plan to be sound, the interpretations for opportunities and constraints must be suitable for the level of information obtained. The judgment and experience of trained scientists is necessary in collecting and interpreting data from the landscape. It should be the planners' charge to combine the natural scientists' perceptions with those of social scientists and engineers to cast these into a comprehensive plan within a sound legal and economic framework.

The first step in this holistic approach to analyzing a particular landscape is to collect information and map the components of the landscape. Some representative inventory maps which have generally been proven useful are listed in table 6-1. The level of detail of the data will be determined by the available information, time, and available resources which are related to the size of the area. . . .

The next step is to determine how the landscape functions as an interacting system of related components. . . . Knowledge of how the various components of the landscape affect and are affected by one another leads to an understanding of how the whole system works. This should indicate chains of events which might occur due to some proposed land uses. The completeness of understanding will, of course, depend upon the level of information used and the perceptions and abilities of the scientists who contribute to the understanding of the natural system. It is safe to assume that a complete understanding of a landscape and its processes is never achieved—the planner must deal with incomplete information, and care must be taken that the inferences drawn from the data are justifiable given the detail and completeness of the data base from which they are made. . . .

To understand the links between landscape elements and proposed land uses the set of matrices shown in figure 6-3b may be useful if there are a number of land uses which need to be considered. Matrix I describes the relationship between land uses and development activities. Matrix II describes the relationship between development activities and the landscape. Matrix III is the same as figure 6-3a. These arrays are one way of organizing the information which is brought to bear on the final land use plan, helping to make the assimilation of a large amount of information orderly and explicit. . . .

The information assembled in the planning process amounts to someone's interpretation and synthesis of information compiled and arrayed in map and matrix form to define the landscape components. Given sufficient information of this type at an appropriate level of detail, there is a basis for interpreting the assembled information to understand the opportunities afforded by the landscape for specified activities, and the constraints imposed by the landscape.

Determination of opportunities begins with a specific set of land uses which are desired by the users. Such uses have optimal or prerequisite conditions for their implementation and these must be defined, i.e., swimming areas require good water quality, appropriate bottom material and topography, and accessibility. Houses optimally need stable material beneath, well-drained soils for onsite sewage disposal, gentle to moderate slopes, and perhaps a good view and protection from winter winds. For each desired land use, the geology, soils, vegetation, hydrology, and/or other inventory maps are interpreted for the opportunities they afford, producing a set of opportunity maps which show the best areas for each land use individually based on the landscape components which afford opportunity. For each land use, the individual opportunity maps derived from each of the pertinent landscape components are combined by overlay techniques to produce a composite opportunity map which shows the opportunities afforded by the whole landscape for each desired land use.

In most cases the greater the number of concurrences of opportunities found in a particular environment, the higher the capability of that environment for the defined use. The trade-off between the environments of higher and lower capability will be increased capital costs of design and construction as well as increased energy costs for construction and maintenance if performance requirements are met. Users can decide between the possible trade-offs. Using the method outlined in figure 6-3b, the consultant scientists can demonstrate the attendant environmental costs and benefits of any desired scheme.

Constraints, defined here as adverse impacts of the land upon the land use and adverse impacts of the land use upon the land, are best expressed using the vocabulary of the National Environmental Policy Act and the health and welfare provisions of the states' and federal constitutions (table 6-2). Some land forms because of the natural processes are "inherently hazardous to life and health." Examples would be flood-prone areas, areas subject to landslides, areas subject to collapse, and areas of fire-prone vegetation.

Other natural factors present "to life and health through specific human action." Examples are the pollution of ground and surface waters from septic tanks in soils with a seasonally high water table, or the pollution of domestic ground water supplies through construction or waste disposal on an aquifer recharge area. Certain land forms with associated vegetation and land use can

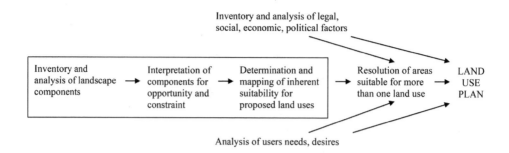

Figure 6-2 Flow chart of the ecological planning process (Johnson, Berger, and McHarg, 1979, Reproduced with permission of American Society of Agronomy, Redrawn by Travis Witt, 2014).

Table 6-1

Some useful inventory maps (Johnson, Berger, and McHarg, 1979, Redrawn by Travis Witt).

1. Physiography	Elevation, slope
2. Geology	Bedrock or subsurface geology, surficial deposits, geologic cross-sections.
3. Soils	Series or phases, drainage classes, hydrologic groups, capability group, depth to seasonal high water table, etc., as applicable.
4. Hydrology	Depth to water table, aquifer yields, direction of ground water movement recharge areas, water quality, surface waters (lakes, streams, wetlands), flood zones, drainage basins, etc.
5. Vegetation	Distribution of associations, communities, and habitats as identifiable, areas important as noise buffers, food supplies for wildlife, nesting areas, etc.
6. Wildlife	Identification of species and their habitats and ranges, movement corridors, etc.
7. Climate	Macro- and microclimate parameters (temperature, moisture, wind). Ventilation and insolation may be determined in conjunction with physiography.
8. Resources	Mineral or other valuable natural resources.

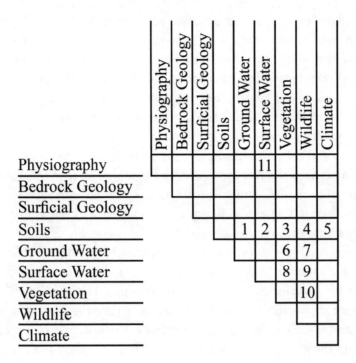

Figure 6-3a Simple version of a matrix arraying landscape components (Johnson, Berger, and McHarg, 1979, Reproduced with permission of American Society of Agronomy, Redrawn by Yuan Ren, 2014).

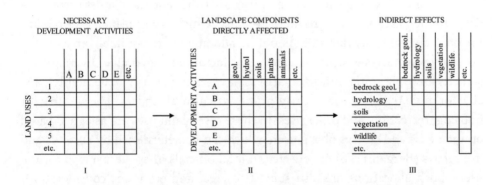

Figure 6-3b Organization of information for assessing the relationship between a set of desired land uses and the impacts they have on the landscape (Johnson, Berger, and McHarg, 1979, Reproduced with permission of American Society of Agronomy, Redrawn by Travis Witt, 2014).

be classified as "unique, scarce, or rare." Alteration of these areas through development would mean the loss to society of irreplaceable features. Social scientists (historians, ethnographers, archaeologists, folklorists, and art historians) and natural scientists value such areas. Finally, particular landforms may be "vulnerable resources" which need regulation to "avoid social costs." Depending on the environment under study, these would include prime agricultural soils, high quality gravel deposits, and scenic features, among others.

Planners and their consultant scientists can evaluate every inventory map and determine from the categories of data the relevant set of constraints. These constraints are mapped. Unlike opportunities, the concurrence of numerous constraints may not be as significant as the existence of one constraint which represents a "hazard to life and health."

The next step in the procedure is a synthesis of opportunities and constraints for a selected land use to produce a suitability map which identifies a gradient of suitabilities for that prospective use. The areas with the greatest number of opportunities and least constraints are the most suitable for the specified land use. The method of combining the opportunities and constraints and ranking the suitability may be arbitrary but is explicit if an array is used to show how decisions of suitability were made. The matrix in the figure shows the determination of most suitable land and land of secondary suitability for housing with septic tanks. The example is oversimplified, but the method has been applied successfully to complex landscapes. The reliability and accuracy of the map overlay techniques this method employs are discussed by McDougal (1975).

The suitability maps for the land uses that the landscape must accommodate are then assessed. Where there are areas which are of primary suitability for only a single use, that use should be allocated to the suitable areas if the other relevant social, economic, and legal factors are favorable. In many instances, multiple suitabilities will arise. That is, some areas will be highly suitable for more than one use. Clearly, prime agricultural lands will be suitable for housing, recreation, and other uses. In these cases, land uses are assigned based on the needs and desires of the users which can be determined by surveys and interviews (Berger, 1978) or reflected in local officials or spokespersons for the users. Such allocations are also subject to legal and economic considerations which should also be incorporated into a land use plan.

III. Application

A simplified example is given below which is a summary of a portion of the plan for the new city called *The Woodlands*, now being developed just north of

Table 6-2

Types of constraints (Johnson, Berger, and McHarg, 1979, Reproduced with permission of American Society of Agronomy, Redrawn by Yuan Ren, 2014).

Legally defined constraint	Rules of combination with other uses
Inherently hazardous to life and health	Preempts nearly all development
Hazardous to life and health through specific human action	Allows some land uses but not others
Unique, scarce or rare ⎫ Vulnerable resource ⎭	Requires regulation through performance requirements

Houston, Texas. . . . The site presented many problems for such a development. It was entirely forest—a pleasant place to live, but a difficult environment to build in. It is extremely flat with few slopes greater than 5%. As a result of the topographic and rainfall characteristics, nearly a third of the site is in the 100-year flood plain of Panther, Bear, and Spring Creeks. Drainage of storm runoff was poor. Many depressions exist on the flat terrain which is dominated by impermeable soils, and standing water was common. The determination of housing sites and housing densities in the Woodlands is used as an example of the method of landscape analysis outlined above.

A. Nature of the Site

The Woodlands is located in the Gulf Coastal Plain and is underlain by unconsolidated formations comprised of Quaternary and Tertiary age gravels, sand, silt, and clay, in various combinations and proportions. The formations strike northeast, roughly parallel to the coast, and dip southeast at 1 to 2 m/km. Several of the units are good aquifers and are sources of high-quality water. The bearing strength of the geologic units underlying the site is adequate for most development purposes. There are subsidence problems in the Houston area, but subsidence should not affect the Woodlands; ground water withdrawals and recharge have been carefully determined in the planning for the area, as described in more detail below.

The hydrologic regime was an extremely important consideration in designing the plan for the Woodlands community. There were flooding and storm drainage problems to be dealt with and a water supply to be developed.

Recharge of water was of primary importance to diminish the risk of subsidence on the site as well as down dip in Houston, which pumps from the same aquifers. Additionally, ground water was planned as a means of augmenting base flow in the creeks to enhance the amenity value of artificial lakes to be constructed on the site. . . .

The site is a mixed woodland dominated by loblolly pine. In mature stands, the pines are associated with oaks, sweet gum, hickories, tupelo, magnolia, and sycamore. The woodlands provide an amenity for development as well as limiting runoff and erosion. Additionally, the forest provides habitats for wildlife. Eight major vegetation associations were recognized: (i) shortleaf pine–hardwood; (ii) loblolly pine–hardwood; (iii) loblolly pine–oak–gum; (iv) pine–oak; (v) mixed mesic woodland; (vi) pine–hardwood; (vii) floodplain vegetation; and (viii) wet weather pond. Much of the forest has been logged at one time or another.

There are a multitude of types of wildlife present on the site. Those types which are abundant include songbirds, rabbits, raccoon, squirrels, opossum, armadillo, white-tailed deer, and wild turkey. The persistence of most of these types can be promoted by careful management and by maintaining suitable habitats and territories and movement corridors which are large enough to suit the species. Floodplain areas in the Woodlands provide a diversity of habitats suitable for several desirable forms of wildlife, so that type of vegetation association has a high value for wildlife preservation. Forest edge conditions provide a diversity of habitats and also encourage a diversity of wildlife. These edge conditions occur around wet weather ponds, which increases their value for wildlife protection. The ponds also serve as sediment traps and temporary shortage basins during storm periods, amounting to a significant value for the ponds.

The climate of the area is subtropical with warm, moist summers and mild winters. The climate factors were used in site planning but were not of overriding importance in determining suitability for development and so will not be discussed here.

B. Planning for Development

An overall plan for locating best areas for development including high- and low-density residential, commercial, recreational, municipal, industrial and open space land uses was derived from the inventory of the landscape. Economic consultants produced a housing market analysis for the Houston Region which showed seven feasible housing types for the Woodlands New Town. Engineers and landscape architects described the attributes of each development type in terms of space occupied by buildings, space covered by other impervious surfaces, and vegetation cleared. . . .

C. Relationship of Development Activities to Landscape Processes

The desired land uses and their attendant development activities would affect soils, vegetation, ground water levels, stream flow, and stream channel form. Modification of these landscape elements would affect the following processes: the balance between infiltration and overland flow, channel deposition and erosion, storage and movement of ground water, and the regenerative capacity of the forest and wildlife communities. . . .

Given these forecasted impacts of urbanization, several interest groups wished to mitigate potential adverse environmental impacts. The regional water management commission wanted to maintain the recharge of the city of Houston's ground water supply. The new town developers wanted to maintain a healthy forest as the prime marketing element of the new town. The Department of Housing and Urban Development had environmental guidelines for the processing of guaranteed loans. In response to these different interests the five guidelines listed below for the plan and design of the new town were established:

1) Minimize disruption of the hydrologic regime by creation of a natural drainage system which allowed removal of the low-frequency event runoff and recharged as much precipitation as possible from high- and low-frequency storms to maintain ground water reserves.
2) Preservation of the woodland environment.
3) Preservation of vegetation providing wildlife habitats and movement corridors.
4) Minimization of development costs.
5) Avoidance of hazards to life and health.

1. Requirements to Minimize Disruption of the Hydrologic Regime

Since the Woodlands site is a flat landscape with large areas of impermeable soils and streams of low gradient, conventional means of storm water management called for site drainage through a large and expensive network of concrete drainage channels. These would decrease recharge to the ground water reservoir, and call for the removal of vegetation. To avoid these environmentally and economically expensive problems a "natural" drainage system was devised.

Calculations of cleared area and impervious area for typical Woodland's residential clusters indicated the magnitude of development impacts on surface runoff, soil storage capacity, and forest cover. The design aim was to promote infiltration of high-frequency, low-volume storm water (up to 25 mm of precipitation in 6 hours) in order to reduce the period of standing water and increase movement into the ground water reservoir. For purposes of this design storm (25 mm in 6 hours), the soils were assumed to be at field capacity and flood plains were assumed to be left in their naturally forested state.

As a design tool to promote percolation, the most abundant soils were grouped according to their capacity to accommodate water from the high-frequency storm. Available storage capacity was calculated from the depth of the permeable soil layer, the depth to the seasonal high water table, and the air-filled pore space at field capacity. The proportion of each soil map unit which needed to be left undisturbed to absorb runoff from the cleared portion was calculated. . . .

With the onsite recharge capacity of the soils known, the capability of any soil environment to handle any development type could be determined. In some cases higher densities on lower recharge capacity soils were possible if adjacent land had a moderate to high storage capacity to handle the storm runoff not recharged by the lower capacity soil. Housing densities could be increased in this case, since all of an area of high recharge capacity soil could be used as a sump for the runoff from adjacent areas developed on soils not suitable for storage of storm runoff.

Given the need to "borrow" recharge capacity from adjacent soils the juxtaposition of soil types on the landscape became important in addition to the on-site recharge capability of a soil in determining housing suitability. Soil patterns based on drainage relationships were identified for their suitability for the different development types. Figure 6-4 shows one example. For each drainage relationship, management guidelines, housing suitabilities, and siting considerations were specified.

2. Requirements to Preserve the Woodland Environment

Different vegetation types gave rise to different levels of clearing. Based on their desirability to the projected residents, their tolerance to disturbance, the soils on which they grow, and their regenerative requirements, the forest types were rated somewhat subjectively on a scale of allowable clearing. For example, large pure hardwood or nearly pure hardwood stands are relatively scarce in the region, attractive to the residents, intolerant of soil compaction and change in ground water levels, better landscape shade trees, and slower to regenerate than pure pine stands which abound in the area. Clearing of hardwood stands was considered less desirable than clearing of pine stands. . . .

The gradient of tolerance from pure hardwood to pure pine is a gradient of opportunity and constraint for the development types. The more tolerant the vegetation to clearing the greater the opportunity for higher density housing.

The lower the tolerance to clearing the greater the opportunity for lower housing densities.

3. Movement Corridors

Wildlife needs cover, food, and water. The design objective was to provide for wildlife needs so that a maximum number of species present on the site could remain after development. Large areas offering diverse vegetation and water would make suitable wildlife refuges. These refuges would be connected by corridors of vegetation. Vegetation in refuges and corridors would be preempted from development. The corridors were provided by the design of a natural drainage system as described below.

4. Requirements to Avoid Hazards to Life and Health and Cost Savings for Construction

The ecological inventory of the Woodlands showed that flood hazard was the only natural hazard to life and health. Development in the area along major streams inundated by the projected 100-year flood (under development conditions) was preempted. In addition to the use of some soils as sinks for high-frequency storm drainage, a system of naturally occurring swales and stream corridors supplemented with man-made swales was designed to carry storm runoff from the low-frequency events. Development in the 25-year flood zone of the smaller drainage ways was also preempted. The swales and stream corridors were left in a vegetated condition which helped preserve the woodland environment and maintain corridors for wildlife movement. Wherever possible, the drainage system was routed over permeable soils to further increase the infiltration of storm runoff. Coupling this with the siting plan for infiltration of storm runoff, the need for conventional storm sewers was eliminated. This saved an incredible $14 million dollars in development costs and raised land values due to the elimination of unsightly concrete ditches, in addition to minimizing the disruption of runoff-recharge relationships, helping preserve the woodland environment, and helping to provide for the maintenance of wildlife on the site.

D. Opportunities and Constraints

The constraints to housing were the flood zones and restrictions placed on clearance by the vegetation analysis. This meant that areas prone to flooding, wetland areas, and hardwood areas were considered restrictions to development. . . . Opportunities for various housing types were determined from the allowed clearance of vegetation and the impermeable surface allowed by the soil groups so as to allow infiltration of the high-frequency storm. . . . For those

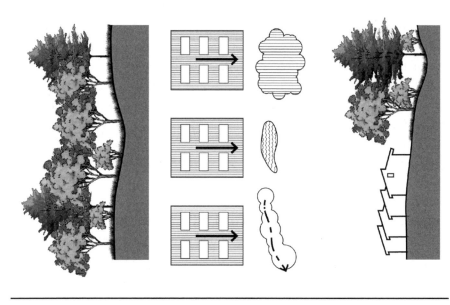

D Soils with slope greater than 1% are impermeable and therefore have minimal recharge capacity. When runoff from these soils cannot be recharged on A, B, or C Soils, it should be directed to a swale, water storage area, or area of uncleared D Soil with slope less than 1% which can be temporarily flooded.

Management Guidelines

The extent of clearing and the amount of impervious surface are not restricted except for limitations established by existing vegetation. (See vegetation guidelines.)

Housing Suitability

Since D Soils are already impervious they are especially suited to high density development.

Siting Consideration

Situate and design buildings, roads, and paths so as not to impound runoff.

Major pedestrian traffic should be on fill parallel to the line of slope, or raised on posts if traffic is perpendicular to the line of slope.

Figure 6-4 Management guidelines, housing suitability, and citing considerations for group D soils (effectively impermeable) (Johnson, Berger, and McHarg, 1979, Reproduced with permission of American Society of Agronomy. Redrawn by Yuan Ren, 2014).

areas that are not restricted by the defined constraints, a certain percentage of clearance was allowed, based on the vegetation present, a maximum amount of coverage by impermeable surfaces was set by the water-holding capacity of soils, and a certain type of housing with its characteristic density could be accommodated. . . .

E. Summary

The development will surely have impacts on the landscape and the natural processes occurring within it, but the development scheme allows for minimum disruption of the hydrologic cycle—recharge is maximized, exacerbation of flooding by development minimized, the ground water and base flow to streams augmented vis-a-vis conventional drainage, and erosion hazard reduced due to vegetated drainage ways. Desirable wildlife and vegetation are also preserved. Planning for the Woodlands encompassed far more. Site planning and phasing were considered in detail, as were the location of roads and industrial, commercial, and recreational areas. Engineering and economic considerations were incorporated into the overall development plan. Wildlife and the other components of the landscape were treated in much more detail than described here. The scope of the example is limited, as the inclusion of larger areas and more land uses greatly increases the complexity, and would require a great deal more space to describe.

An understanding of the features of a landscape, i.e., the soils geology, hydrology, vegetation, and wildlife, as well as how they interact or are linked by natural processes, allows some understanding of the effects specified types of development will have on the whole ecosystem. Certain elements of the landscape may therefore become determinants of the pattern of planned land uses so as to minimize the adverse affects on the landscape. In the Woodlands example, vegetation, soils, and the nature of the hydrologic conditions of the site were the most important determinants in the siting of residences. In other areas, certain other natural features may be more important determinants of planned land use patterns. For instance, areas underlain by cavernous limestone bedrock, fault zones, or areas of vertisols may preclude building, or the ameliorative design strategies necessary to protect lives, property, or natural resources will be costly. Ecological planning as it is described here is sound in practice as well as in concept. In the case of the Woodlands, this type of planning saved the development corporation money in construction costs.

Presently there are 2,500 residents in the Woodlands, and the first phase of development is underway. The ecological plan was submitted to HUD in 1972 and led to a $50,000,000 loan guarantee, the largest under Title VII provisions.

References

Berger, Jon. "Towards an Applied Human Ecology for Landscape Architecture and Regional Planning." *Human Ecology* 6, no. 2 (1978): 179–99.

Juneja, Narendra. *Medford: Performance Requirements for the Maintenance of Social Values Represented by the Natural Environment of Medford Township, NJ.* Center for Ecological Research in Planning and Design, Department of Landscape Architecture and Regional Planning, University of Pennsylvania, 1974.

Leopold, Luna B. *Hydrology for Urban Land Planning: A Guidebook on the Hydrologic Effects of Urban Land Use.* U.S. Geology Surv. Circ. 554. 1968.

MacDougall, E. Bruce. "The Accuracy of Map Overlays." *Landscape Planning* 2 (1975): 23–31.

McHarg, Ian L. *Design with Nature.* New York: Doubleday Natural History Press, 1969.

Project Discussion: Aguas Claras, Belo Horizonte, Brazil

Toward Legacy: Design Workshop's Pursuit of Ideals in Landscape Architecture, Planning, and Urban Design (2007)

Design Workshop

Owners of this iron-ore mine in Brazil saw mining as a temporary use of the land and began planning in the early 1990s to reuse the excavated pit once mineral resources are depleted. The master plan transforms the massive open pit and waste areas into a satellite village for a metropolitan region.

An Iron-Ore Mine Is Configured as a Community in Its Next Life

In recent decades, leading mining companies have begun at the start of mining operations to design end-use plans as part of their mining plans. Company officials realize it is more cost-effective to mine with a plan for reuse and that the future of the industry depends on its ability to look beyond compliance and come to grips with issues of economics, environment, community and the aesthetics of what they leave. The Aguas Claras mine demonstrates an approach to planning the reuse of more destructive mines from an older era.

Brazil's second-largest iron-ore mining company, Mineração Brasileiras Reunidas (MBR), has mined the rich iron-ore quadrangle southeast of the city of Belo Horizonte in southern Brazil since the 1940s, including the Aguas Claras mine, which was opened in 1965. Officials calculated in the early 1990s that they would be closing the mine in the next decade. The company was dedicated to efficient and profitable mining, which is critical to the country's economy, but officials also acknowledged that the land should have a life after mining, one that restored and protected the environment and contributed to the area economy. Design Workshop prepared a master plan for MBR to rehabilitate and reuse the land at a later time.

Land analysis revealed that the mine presented no issues of toxicity that would prohibit human use. Aguas Claras is an ideal location for a village since the mine is on the rear slope of mountains that form the southern boundary of the burgeoning city of Belo Horizonte, which at more than three million people is Brazil's third largest city.

The design team and operations managers collaborated to prepare a redevelopment plan that would ultimately transform the site into a new mixed-use village as a model for how walkable satellite villages can accommodate growth demands in the region with minimal disturbance to the environment. The plan places a nucleus of community life at its center, including a church, a school, shops, restaurants, a recreation club and conference and office centers, to provide an economic base for the village and to place jobs and services within walking distance of homes. The village plan also minimizes the need for cars and gives middle-class residents all alternative to automobile-oriented suburban living, which is beginning to choke the region with traffic.

The plan utilizes principles of adaptive reuse to apply elements of the mine and mining process to urbanization. The design creates a beautiful and functional garden setting for the village, using design standards for future development projects, site design and architectural standards for the community and revegetation strategies to add biodiversity to the massive site. The central feature of the village design is a lake created out of the mine pit, which is to be slowly filled with groundwater and surface runoff. Water-treatment facilities, once used to purify runoff from the mine, were incorporated into the plan as a means of protecting Aguas Claras Creek from village construction and urban runoff. The plan also called for contouring the tops of waste areas during the last phases of mining to better accommodate village development. MBR began implementation of the plan with construction of its own office building in a planned office park on the site.

MBR originally anticipated it would close the mine in 1997, but mining operations continued until December 2003. The company was acquired in 2001 by CVRD, another Brazilian iron-ore producer, and Japanese trading company Mitsui. Company and government officials are continuing to explore options and detail plans for reuse of the site. The Aguas Claras master plan was featured as an example of sustainable mining in the Brazil exhibit at the Earth Summit in Rio de Janeiro in 1992.

Project Credits

Planning/Design: Design Workshop, Inc.
    PIC: Joe Porter, Sergio Santana
    Designer: Sergio Santana
    Project Advisor: Kurt Culbertson
Client: Mineraçãos Brasileiras Reunidas (MBR), a division of Caemi Mineração
e Metalurgia SA

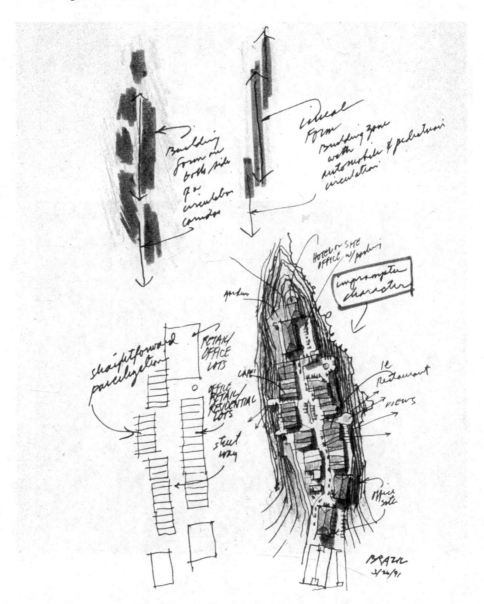

Figure 6-5a An early sketch fitted the Aguas Claras Village Center to the mine-processing area (Design Workshop, 2007, Reproduced with the permission of Design Workshop).

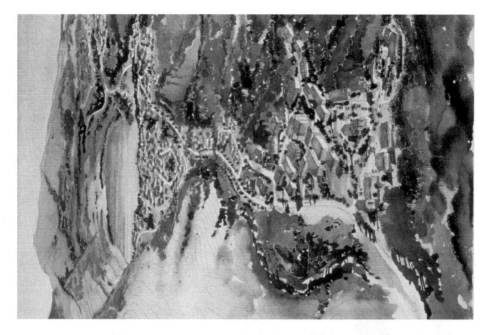

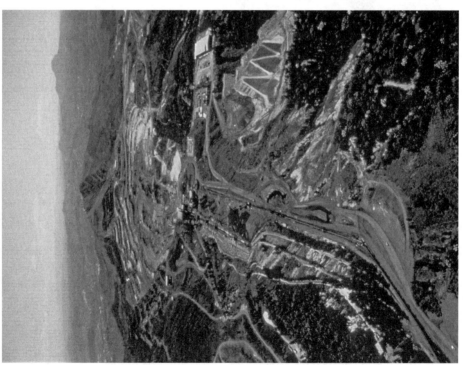

Figure 6-5b A comparison of existing conditions and vision for the site (Design Workshop, 2007, Reproduced with the permission of Design Workshop).

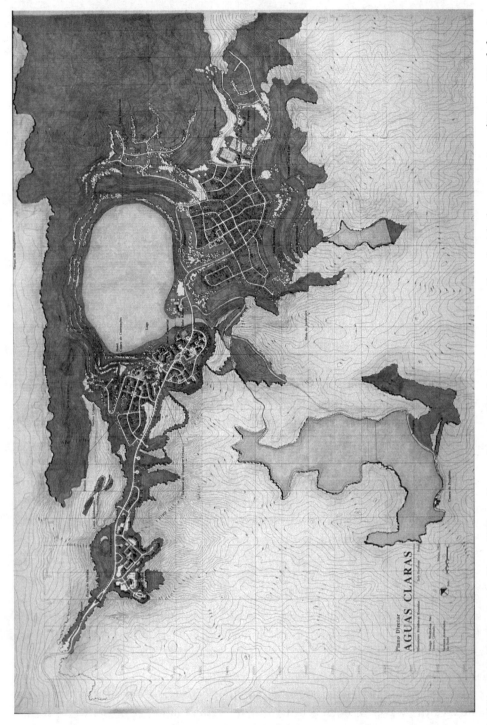

Figure 6-6 The Aguas Claras Village Center (Design Workshop 2007, Reproduced with the permission of Design Workshop).

Foreword

Thesen Islands (2008)

Chris Mulder

Sometimes in life you are faced with an opportunity and risk, and you have to decide to dare to take a risk or risk losing an opportunity. To dare is to risk losing your foothold for a moment. Not to dare is to risk losing yourself.

The concept, design and creation of Thesen Islands offered opportunity and risk. It was an opportunity to dare and, with creative design, to redevelop a 100-year-old polluting, smoky and dilapidated factory site into something quite unique.

Thesen Islands is steeped in the history of the Western Cape Province and particularly the Southern Cape. It is situated in the midst of the tranquil waters of one of the richest biologically and ecologically productive estuaries in South Africa. Host to a rich ecosystem of marine organisms, it is home to the rare and endangered Knysna sea horse *Hippocampus capensis*.

Legend has it that the San were the earliest inhabitants of the island. Later, settlers made the area their home, drawn by the rich indigenous forests that yielded treasures to be exported and where herds of the famous Knysna elephant roamed. (By all accounts, they did not find the 102 hectares in the northwest corner of the lagoon particularly inviting.) The elephant herds did not survive the waves of encroaching human settlers but the forests were to sustain a thriving timber industry for more than a century.

The island became the home of an ever-expanding timber factory and lumber mill with the Thesen Jetty the only berthing place for Thesen and Company steamers and sailing vessels ferrying their cargo of mostly indigenous wood.

By the early 1980s, Barlows (now Barloworld), one of the largest industrial conglomerates in South Africa, had purchased Thesen Island from Thesen and Company, and in doing so terminated the era of Thesen and Company, which had played such an important part in the development of the town.

Barloworld soon decided that the lumber and timber industry could not survive on an island in the midst of sensitive lagoon ecology. To continue with the timber processing, wood preserving and the chemical treatment of wood meant more air pollution emanating from the steam-driven boilers on the island. It was simply too great an environmental risk.

Something Extraordinary Had to Be Done. What Were the Challenges? What Were the Alternatives?

In 1990, Barloworld commissioned land development planners and urban designers Chris Mulder Associates Inc (CMAI) to investigate appropriate alternatives for Thesen Island.

The ultimate challenge was to create a viable plan for the 92-hectare factory site (the other 10 hectares, largely salt marsh, was government land), one that would be environmentally acceptable and economically sustainable.

The environmental challenges seemed insurmountable. Unknown quantities of contaminated soil as a result of 80 years of wood treatment with creosote and copper, chrome and arsenic (CCA), low-lying land an average of 1.3 metres above sea level and no provision of bulk services (i.e., no existing sewer system) and air pollution made rehabilitation a formidable task. The factory had grown haphazardly over a century and tens of thousands of cubic metres of wood waste had been dumped all over the island. An unknown quantity of chemicals had been buried and there were surface ponds of toxic creosote leachate in the pole yards. Ever increasing traffic congestion, including lumber trucks rumbling through Knysna, threatened to have an adverse impact on what was fast becoming South Africa's favourite tourist town.

However, the challenge went further than cleaning up the environment and placating a local tourism association. The factory was the single largest employer in the town of Knysna and in the region. More than 800 people worked there each day. What would happen to these people once redevelopment of the island began?

Those were the challenges that faced us all—developers, the team of professional urban designers, architects, landscape architects and appointed specialist consultants.

We immediately began to investigate alternative concepts for the redevelopment and commenced the research work with the baseline studies on the lagoon.

Figure 6-7 Thesen Islands master plan (Mulder, 2008, Reproduced with the permission of Chris Mulder).

The research was the "ground zero" of the project. We were faced with the fact that there was no general management plan for the lagoon and no data that showed the impact of the existing sources of pollution from the town into the lagoon. Before one clod of soil was turned, it was important to have an accurate, scientific profile of the lagoon. The baseline studies and status quo of the lagoon had to be established and presented to the authorities. If this process was not followed to the letter, it would be an easy matter to blame the new development for any environmental impact or ecological disturbance.

A second important concept had to be agreed on. There were no islands in South Africa that lent themselves to residential or resort development, much less an island in the protected waters of an estuary.

Fate had played a hand in keeping Thesen Island a single, private and industrial-owned entity for more than a century. It was a century in which sailing vessels and steamships were slowly but surely superseded by a railroad system and highway corridors, rendering the former modes of transport obsolete. A century passed in which no residential development, except staff accommodation, was even contemplated on the island because of the existing zoning.

These historic facts created an opportunity for prime waterfront living with the proviso that the environmental issues could be resolved satisfactorily and the ruling guide plan for the region and the zoning could be changed.

Large-scale, virtually uncontrolled harvesting of indigenous hardwood had been abandoned 50 years earlier. *The way was open for an exciting opportunity: what to do with Thesen Island.*

Slowly and painstakingly the development concept and my vision for the island evolved on the CMAI drawing boards. Each one had to be tested, evaluated and critiqued from a practical and construction viewpoint. Each one had to be assessed from a marketing and financial viewpoint. The team also had to come up with minimum finished floor levels of at least 1.7 metres higher than the then 1.3 metres above sea level of the island. The options? Either the houses had to be built on stilts or on landfill.

The evaluation continued and *to maximize the waterfront opportunities, the concept of canals was introduced.* Soil from this huge excavation would provide the landfill.

One scenario after the other was entertained and each time the feasibilities and evaluations were assessed critically.

While the practicalities of literally changing the topography of the island were pursued, there remained an issue of confidence that had nothing to do with environment or engineering issues. The history of waterfront developments and marinas outside of Cape Town was not good. They were beset by environmental and monetary problems, and public sentiment ran against the proposals. Financial institutions were extremely wary of backing this project because of previous disasters that had plagued marinas and waterfront developments in South Africa.

In December 1998, eight years after beginning the project planning, design and approval process, the CMAI team obtained approval from all the authorities to proceed with Concept Design Number 26.

The concept design called for the creation of 19 individual islands separated by canals or waterways and connected via bridges. A range of waterfront living options were developed to allow for a wide variety of buyer choices within a rigorously controlled architectural theme.

The concept further called for a mixed-use waterfront development consisting of 605 residential units and a commercial-retail component, to be dubbed Thesen Harbour Town. Retaining historically important buildings would create a link with the past.

Thesen Island Development Company (TIDC) was formed by six investors and the island was purchased from Barloworld. TIDC reached agreement with Investec Bank on the financing, and the project was on its way. Before development finance would be released, we had to obtain pre-sales of R70 million with a secured deposit in the bank. The first sales campaign was launched on 16 December 1998 and five years later the residential component of the project was sold out.

Construction of the waterways and canals commenced in September 2000 and all the major civil works were completed by the end of 2005.

Out of nowhere a wonderful community was created—a community of people gathered from all parts of South Africa and abroad who realized the value of what could be created on Thesen Islands. It had become a true waterfront community based on the traditional neighbourhood concept that evolved in the Southern states of the USA, a neighbourhood where people could walk to work, walk to shop, walk to visit one another—*a community where strangers become neighbours and where neighbours become friends.*

— Chris Mulder, 2008

Figure 6-8 Sunset on the Island (Mulder, 2008, Reproduced with the permission of Chris Mulder).

The Upper San Pedro River Basin

Alternative Futures for Changing Landscapes: The Upper San Pedro River Basin in Arizona and Sonora (2003)

Carl Steinitz, Hector Arias, Scott Bassett, Michael Flaxman, Thomas Goode, Thomas Maddock III, David Mouat, Richard Peiser, and Allan Shearer

The San Pedro River begins in Sonora, Mexico, and flows northward through Arizona, United States, before joining the Gila River, which flows into the Colorado, and finally empties into the Gulf of California. . . . The Upper San Pedro River Basin in Sonora and Arizona is the focus of a number of urgent, complex, interrelated, and controversial issues, including its international importance as bird habitat, its attractiveness to development, and the vulnerability of its landscape to changes caused directly by development and indirectly via continued lowering of the groundwater table.

The Upper San Pedro River Basin is located within an extremely diverse semiarid environment. It is diverse not only in terms of its abiotic geologic, geomorphic, and climatic environment, but also in terms of the associated edaphic and vegetation characteristics. This unique biogeographic setting defines habitat for a unique faunal assemblage. The basin provides breeding or migration habitat for 389 bird species (almost half of those seen in North America), 84 species of mammals (second in diversity only to those found in the rainforests of Costa Rica), and 47 species of reptiles and amphibians (Kunzmann, n.d.). Several are listed as threatened or endangered species. Most of these species are completely dependent on the continued functioning of this rare ecosystem. In 1988, the San Pedro Riparian National Conservation Area (SPRNCA) was established by the United States Congress. So important is the region—the last free-flowing river in the Southwest—that the Nature Conservancy has placed the San Pedro River Basin on its list of "Last Great Places in the Western Hemisphere." *Wild Bird Digest* lists the area as the number one birding site in the United States (U.S. Dept. of Interior, 1998). The potential disruption of this system by future patterns of land use and their anticipated effects forms the basis for intense debate among the various stakeholders in the region.

The San Pedro River can be characterized in part by the presence of shallow groundwater and intermittent stream flows. Small changes in either the groundwater level or river flow can greatly impact riparian vegetation and the animal species of the region. Water extraction and the concomitant lowering of the water table are threatening critical habitat and other environmental concerns.

In addition to the San Pedro riparian corridor, the uplands of the Upper San Pedro River Basin are also of value. The native perennial grasslands, along with the unique woodlands and forests of the higher elevations, are of significant importance in supporting the region's high biodiversity.

There are major policy and legal conflicts in the region over water use and water rights in the Upper San Pedro River Basin. In Sonora, the mining at Cananea pumps groundwater, uses it in its several mining processes, and discharges wastewater outside the San Pedro River Basin and into the south-flowing Rio de Sonora River Basin. In Arizona, and under Arizona law, surface water must be appropriated and uses must not interfere with those of senior or prior appropriations. However, in most of the rural areas of the state, including the basin, groundwater does not require appropriation. Irrigated agriculture and some domestic water users are of long standing, as is Fort Huachuca. An explicit federal reserved right to enough water for the Bureau of Land Management to fulfill the purposes of the San Pedro Riparian National Conservation Area was granted by Congress in 1988 (USDI BLM, 1998).

The Gila River Indian Community is also a claimant to the San Pedro Subbasin water. Although they draw water from far downstream on the Gila River, they consider that all water in the Upper San Pedro River Basin contributes to the supply of water to their reservation, and they include it in their very senior claims.

In Arizona, the pace of development is increasing. Fort Huachuca is unavoidably enmeshed in the controversy surrounding the fate of the San Pedro River. Local perception places much of the responsibility for growth and water impacts on the fort due to its link to 38 percent of Cochise County's employment (Crandall et al., 1992). The fort has been the subject of lawsuits alleging that it stimulates regional growth that in turn threatens endangered species by lowering the level of the aquifer supplying the San Pedro River.

Understanding the hydrologic processes that define the relationships between land use changes, ground water recharge, stream flow, vegetation, and habitat is of critical importance to the decision makers responsible for land management throughout the region.

These and other land use–related issues require integrated planning for long-term management. To deal with the decisions at hand, the United States and Mexico, Arizona and Sonora, their counties and towns, and Fort Huachuca need a long-term regional planning approach based on knowledge of local ecosystems.

This study is designed to develop an array of possible alternative future patterns of land uses for the region of the Upper San Pedro River Basin, Arizona, and Sonora, and to assess the resultant impacts that these alternative futures might have on patterns of biodiversity and related environmental factors, including vegetation, hydrology, and visual preference. A basic premise of the research is that issues related to land use and ecosystem planning can best be understood on a regional basis.

The research area (figure 6-9) includes the Upper San Pedro River Basin from its headwaters near Cananea, Sonora, to Redington, Arizona. Areas adjacent to the basin that are integral for the maintenance of regional biodiversity are also included in the investigation. In total, the study includes 10,660 sq km (nearly 4100 sq mi). Arizona encompasses 74 percent of the study area, and the remaining 26 percent is in Sonora.

This research on the Upper San Pedro River Basin builds on earlier work on biodiversity and related issues in southeast Arizona, carried out by Mexican and American government agencies, universities, research institutions, and other groups such as the Nature Conservancy. Paramount among the research efforts is the coordinated investigations of the Semi-Arid Land-Surface-Atmosphere (SALSA) program. SALSA is an international effort that includes government agencies, universities, and research centers working to evaluate the consequences of natural and human-induced changes in semiarid environments focused on the Upper San Pedro River Basin. The San Pedro River Basin has been the focus of several prior regional planning studies, most recently by the Commission on Environmental Cooperation (CEC, 1999) created by the North American Free Trade Agreement. The CEC report *Ribbon of Life* (1999) makes several conservation, planning, and related recommendations that are based principally on current conditions and the foresight of the several expert authors.

It is the aim of this study of alternative futures for the Upper San Pedro River Basin to investigate issues relating to possible future development in Arizona and Sonora and its potential impacts on regional hydrology and

Figure 6-9 Study area of the Upper San Pedro River Basin (Steinitz et al., 2003, Reproduced with permission of Island Press).

biodiversity. The study is solely a research project and should not be considered to be a part of a consulting or planning service. The study can aid decision making by identifying and evaluating regional ecosystem and water management options, by assessing the impacts of future land use patterns on the environment, and by demonstrating a flexible and practical planning approach to aid cooperative decision making in the region. The objective of this research is increased understanding of the risks and benefits implicit in a range of policy decisions for the Upper San Pedro River Basin.

The products of this research, including the scenarios and alternative futures, are not intended to be comprehensive analyses of the region. The planning assumptions used in this study rely mainly on publicly available documents and on local peoples' responses to policy choices as contained in the Scenario Guide (appendix A). There were six public presentations and many meetings, but the study did not include widespread community consultation in Arizona and in Sonora. Individual private property boundaries and local government jurisdictions are not considered except as related to hypothetical future development patterns. There are several important projects that have been proposed in the study area that have not been considered, including several very large private development proposals in Arizona; water recharge proposals related to Fort Huachuca and Sierra Vista; changes in water use related to mining in Sonora; and the importation of water into the San Pedro River Basin from outside sources.

In summary, there are many reasons to study the Upper San Pedro region. First, it has some of the highest levels of biodiversity in North America. Second, it is experiencing dramatic change and will have to manage increasing development pressures. Third, much information about the area had been complied, but had not yet been assessed across international boundaries or applied to regional management of hydrology and biodiversity. Fourth, there is still time to make a difference.

References

Bredehoeft, J., R. Lacewell, J. Price, H. Arias Rojo, J. Stromberg, and G. Thomas. *Ribbon of Life: An Agenda for Preserving Transboundary Migratory Bird Habitat on the Upper San Pedro River*. Commission for Environmental Cooperation, Montréal, Qué, 1999.

Crandall, Kristine, Julie Leones, and Bonnie G. Colby. *Nature-Based Tourism and the Economy of Southeastern Arizona: Economic Impacts of Visitation to Ramsey Canyon Preserve and the San Pedro Riparian National Conservation Area*, Ph.D. dissertation, Department of Agricultural and Resource Economics, University of Arizona, 1992.

Reinvent the Good Earth: National Ecological Security Pattern Plan, China

Designed Ecologies: The Landscape Architecture of Kongjian Yu (2012), edited by William Saunders

Kongjian Yu

This planning research project, the National Ecological Security Pattern Plan, was commissioned by the Chinese Ministry of Environmental Protection and was carried out by the Graduate School of Landscape Architecture (now the College of Architecture and Landscape Architecture) at Peking University in association with Turenscape. It identifies critical strategic landscape structures for safeguarding natural, biological, cultural, and recreational processes, thus securing the wide range of ecosystem functions essential for sustaining human society. In China during the pre-scientific period, critical landscape patterns such as "dragon hills" (sacred hills) or "feng shui forests" were protected. In the last three decades, as population, economic development, and urbanization have significantly increased, people have altered the landscape to an unprecedented extent. This, along with global climate change, has profoundly disrupted the structure and function of ecosystems, resulting in increased ecological and environmental problems such as the melting of glaciers and permafrost, wetland degradation, soil erosion, desertification, flood intensification, loss of biodiversity, and degradation of water conservation capacity.

Establishing the capacity for sustainable development is the challenge of China. Its population grew from 542 million in 1949 to 1.3 billion in 2008. The total population will reach 1.4 billion by 2050, and 70 percent will live in urban areas. The ecological environment will continue to face tremendous pressure. Regional land-use and urban planning (an extension of social and economic

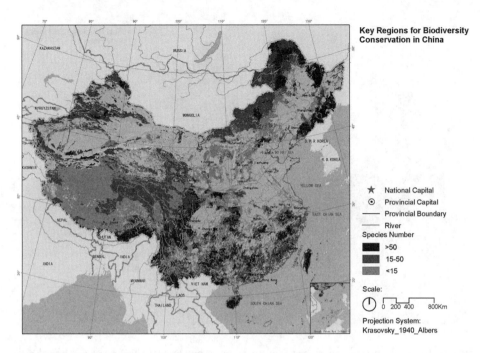

Key Regions for Biodiversity Conservation in China

★ National Capital
⊙ Provincial Capital
─ Provincial Boundary
─ River
Species Number
■ >50
■ 15-50
■ <15

Scale:
0 200 400   800Km

Projection System:
Krasovsky_1940_Albers

Figure 6-10 Key regions for biodiversity conservation (Saunders, 2012, Reproduced with permission of Kongjian Yu).

development planning in China) has seldom recognized the interrelationship of the natural environment to regional development. Instead population projections drive urban land use, resource allocation, functional zoning, and built infrastructure plans. Heritage protection planning, green space system planning, and even flood control planning have been subordinate to a *development* master plan. Now ecological security has become a key area of scientific research for a strategy of *sustainable* development.

Chinese researchers have done a great deal of work in this field and have succeeded especially in the theory and methods of ecological security evaluation. Yet research in the optimization and control of regional landscape patterns is still in an exploratory stage. The theory and practice of establishing landscape security patterns and regional ecological security patterns carried out in recent years has created a communication framework uniting the abstract concept of ecosystem services with implementable spatial planning.

Based on natural zoning and agricultural zoning research, the Chinese scientific community has developed spatial zoning research in recent years, including that for ecological zoning, and national major function zoning, and these are playing a positive role in promoting nature conservation regulations.

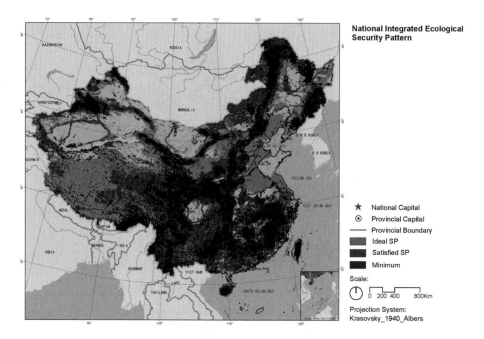

Figure 6-11 Proposed integrated map of areas to be conserved to promote healthy ecological systems (Saunders 2012, Reproduced with permission of Kongjian Yu).

Ecological protection is the central part of the newly constituted "Urban and Rural Planning Law of the People's Republic of China" and the newly promoted "Notice of the State Council on Issuing the Outline of the National Overall Planning on Land Use, 2006–2020." But under the present administrative system in which each ecological factor is managed by an individual department, how to build a comprehensive framework, and develop tools to serve as guidelines for major function-oriented zoning, land use planning and urban planning, has become an urgent problem for scientific research and practice.

Worldwide, research in the protection of critical natural landscape started at least a century ago. American landscape planner W. H. Manning published a National Plan in 1923, the aim of which was to establish strategies for the protection and use of natural resources. He introduced land classification on the basis of natural resources and natural systems. Ecological network planning and construction, which started in the United States in 1950 and was represented by the Greenway Movement, gradually became a rallying point for protecting natural resources. The American Greenway system promised to provide 220,000 kilometers (137,000 miles) of greenways and 5 million square kilometers (1.9 million square miles) of protected green space. Conceptions of greenway, ecological network, habitat network, and flood buffer zone also appeared in Europe. In Asia, recently Singapore and other countries have begun research on greenway planning. And in China, the planting of protective forests can be seen as the first step in the establishment of a greenway network in national planning.

Since the 1990s, the concept of green ecological infrastructure has gradually increased worldwide and has been developed into a widely recognized planning tool for natural conservation and regional and city development. In the United States, green infrastructure planning has been carried out gradually in Maryland, Minnesota, Illinois, Florida, Georgia, Alabama, Mississippi, South Carolina, Tennessee, and Kentucky. In China, exploratory research on ecological infrastructure planning is also in process at Taizhou in Zhejiang Province and at Weihai and Heze in Shandong Province. The case studies on these areas have provided guidelines for developing ecological security pattern planning at various scales.

The aim of Peking University and Turenscape's research here is to establish a national ecological security pattern plan based on addressing the main ecological problems in China through headwater conservation, storm water management and flood control, remediation of desertification, soil erosion prevention, and biodiversity conservation.

Using each individual ecological process analysis and evaluation, Yu's team integrated all the individual ecological security patterns into an overall national ecological security pattern that could help establish a healthy and secure life-supporting system.

References

"Interview with Kongjian Yu," American Society of Landscape Architects 2008. http://www.asla .org/contentdetail.aspx?id=20124.

Yu, Kongjian, and Birgit Linder. "Vernacular Cities and Vernacular Landscapes: The Legacy of the May Fourth Movement in Chinese Landscape Architecture," in Kongjian Yu and Mary Padua, eds., *The Art of Survival: Recovering Landscape Architecture*, 31–32. Mulgrave, Victoria: Images Publishing, and Beijing: China Architecture & Building Press, 2006.

Yu, Kongjian, and Dihua Li. *The Road to Urban Landscape: Talks to Mayors*. Beijing: China Architecture & Building Press, 2003.

Yu, Kongjian, and Mary G. Padua. "China's Cosmetic Cities: Urban Fever and Superficiality." *Landscape Research* 32, no. 2 (2007): 255–72.

Yu, Kongjian, and Wei Pang. *The Culture Being Ignored and the Beauty of Weeds: The Regenerative Design of an Industrial Site—The Zhongshan Shipyard Park*. Beijing: China Architecture & Building Press, 2003.

From Regional Planning to Site Design—The Application of the "Shan-shui City" Concept in Multi-scale Landscape Planning of New Cities in China

International Federation of Landscape Architects World Congress (2011)

Jie Hu

1. Foreword

Reducing the conflict between economic development and protection of the ecological environment is key to a city's sustainable development. A large number of new cities are being constructed every year in China—an inevitable outcome of the rapid economic growth and urbanization process. In addition to all the benefits that cities provide, numerous environmental problems have been emerging, the majority of which relate to pollution and the loss and fragmentation of natural habitats. Balancing economic growth with ecosystem demands in the development of new cities has become increasingly critical, requiring urgent solutions. Balanced urban development requires meeting both natural and urban demands, and therefore early stages of new city planning should be directed by low impact, sustainable development and ecological planning concepts.

Historically, new city development was based on human needs, ignoring ways in which an active response to nature's needs could benefit both people and the environment. Integration of the Shan-shui City concept into planning considerations not only preserves invaluable natural resources by recognizing both their ecological and cultural significance, it also promotes the establishment of a spiritual connection between people and the environment. This proto-planning process, as exhibited by New Harbour City, has the potential to become a better precedent for future urban green space planning, creating cities with a greater degree of ecological security and a better dwelling environment for people. "Shan-shui city is a city with an oriental quality. It keeps historical textures, protects landmarks while restoring them in ways that are applicable to modern urban construction, understanding local architecture while looking for contemporary expressions. Local governments should be encouraged to embody local architectural traditions in new public architecture" (Bao Shixing, 2010).

2. Interpretation of "Shan-shui City" Concept

The "Shan-shui City" concept originates from the perspective of the Chinese traditional living environment—"man is an integral part of nature" and "harmonious co-existence between man and nature", advocating ideas of "adjusting measures to local demands" and "design with nature", which includes comprehensive consideration of the relationship between urban and peripheral ecological areas at multi-scales, displaying an organically holistic philosophy of urban planning and design, architecture and landscape while interpreting the ancient ideal habitat condition of living embraced by a mountain-water environment.

"Shan-shui City is 'a sustainable city' and a city regarding 'man as an integral part of nature'. The planning process of Shan-shui City respects Taoist philosophy and laws of ecology, which clearly understands the natural alteration process, carrying capacity of land, the efficient management of urban waste problems, and encouraging recycling of water and other resources" (Yujiang Wu, 2010). The essence of the "Shan-shui City" concept can be summarized as "Natural State", "Picturesque State" and "Ideal State". "Natural State" requires the demands from ecosystems be fulfilled and key landscape resources preserved. "Picturesque State" aims to create picturesque art from the major preserved landscape elements. "Ideal State" refers to the creation of an imaginative artistic atmosphere in which people perceive and communicate with the picturesque urban landscape with their soul, in addition to their senses of sight and hearing.

Utilizing GIS and RS techniques, the multi-scale landscape planning process guided by the "Shan-shui City" concept is based on aerial remote sensing information that is collected through dynamic monitoring of ecological conditions and urban features of eco-regions, the city and the site. The process helps estimate ecological, cultural and economic values at different scales.

Establishing ecological security as the threshold for urban development, the mountain-water-city structure and landscape design concept based on Chinese traditional cultural principles results in a landscape structure that considers requirements for open space functions in the context of urban land-use. Blending objective analysis and artistic design, this approach to urban landscape planning provides a case study for the integration of landscape planning with eco-functions, aesthetic vision and urban requirements in other cities.

3. Application of "Shan-shui City" Concept in Multi-scale Landscape Planning

3.1 Yulong New City Area Landscape Planning and Design in Fuxin City, Liaoning Province

3.1.1 Existing Context and Problems

Fuxin City in Liaoning Province, China, is an important component of the Shenyang Economic Zone. With more than 7600 years of history, the city is experiencing rapid economic growth. A piece of pottery with dragon patterns excavated from the site and named "the first dragon of China", is a powerful impetus for recognizing the history of Chinese "dragon adoration" 3000 years earlier. Yulong New City, with Jiuyingzi River as its main ecological corridor, has an excellent location and sound ecological basis. With the expansion of urban development, the new city has become an important element in the old city's northward expansion. However, potential ecological problems still existed in the development of the new city, such as the maintenance of flood storage capacity after the original natural river was reformed as a central urban river; the degradation of polluted agricultural land at its upper reach; the protection of existing riverside forest land; and the use and protection of water resources in Yulong Mountain, adjacent to the new city. Comprehensive consideration and the development of appropriate solutions to these problems in the planning and design phase will have a decisive effect on the future sustainable development of Yulong New City.

3.1.2 Planning Concepts and Methods

Reducing the conflict between the requirements for sustaining a healthy ecological system and the demands of urban activity on the new city and creating a base on which to create and promote cultural meaning was an urgent problem that needed to be solved through landscape planning and design of the Fuxin Yulong New City core area.

The "Shan-shui City" concept is interpreted according to the characteristics of the site. Given the prerequisite of combining mountain-water factors and dragon cultural imageries at a regional scale, a natural mountain-water structure and abstracted urban Shan-shui culture has been considered to create an urban landscape with local Shan-shui characteristics. In the mountain-water structure of the new city, a real landscape axis has been formed, related primarily to the organization of the administrative business district while an imaginary axis has been abstracted through fictional factors from the ancient "Yulong (jade dragon)" culture, integrating both natural and man-made axes, which includes:

3.1.2.1 Selecting plant communities appropriate for preservation, according to survey results of existing plants and the river;

3.1.2.2 Using the large river corridor of Jiuyingzi River as an ecological axis to connect Fuxin old city and Yulong Mountain, blending the final landscape axis into the wide natural mountain forest environment.

3.1.2.3 Taking full advantage of existing trees and river resources to establish a new river system, and taking advantage of the mountain landscape of Yulong Mountain to create a northern Shan-shui City.

3.1.2.4 Forming a real landscape axis composed mainly by the administrative business district while abstracting an imaginary axis through fictional factors from the ancient "Yulong (jade dragon)" culture, in order to integrate both natural and man-made axes; establishing an urban development link from the old city to the new city and expressing the important administrative business function of the new city by creating a formal axis composed of the administrative core area, Longshou Lake and Jiefang Avenue (the main street).

3.1.2.5 Arranging a mountain-water relationship between the city and nature, making both the natural and man-made axes reach the core area of the new city, which is not only the heart of new city development, but also the key area for landscape planning.

3.1.2.6 Bringing the sense of natural mountains into the architectural design of landscape structures, strengthening natural mountain-water relationships through the creation of landscape corridors inside and through building forms, putting into practice the "Shan-shui City" concept.

3.1.3 Planning Innovation

Landscape planning and design of Yulong New City along the Jiuyingzi River in Fuxin City, Liaoning Province, combines a natural Shan-shui layout,

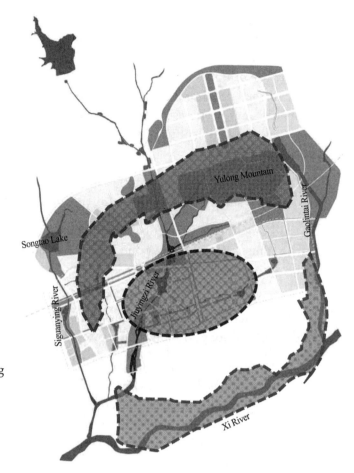

Figure 6-12 Planning objectives diagram for Yulong New City Area (Jie Hu, 2011, Reproduced with the permission of Jie Hu).

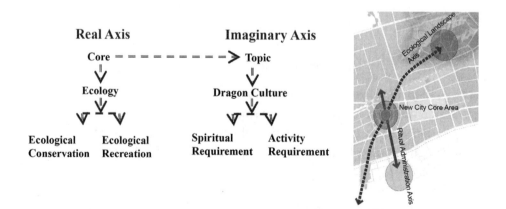

Figure 6-13 Landscape nodes and axis diagram of Yulong New City Area (Jie Hu, 2011, Reproduced with the permission of Jie Hu).

abstraction of Yulong (jade dragon) culture, local characteristics, and the human desire for health and happiness, while taking into account the unique glamour of a characteristic Chinese "Shan-shui City". Applying artificial measures to connect natural mountains and water with the city emphasizes an ideal living environment with local Shan-shui features. The planning innovation can be summarized as follows:

Using existing vegetation: taking account of the environmental conditions to maximize preservation and make best use of original plant communities and the region's existing landscape.

Flexible axes design: integrating artificial axis into natural axis while designing a cultural axis for the new city. Buildings on or beside the axis are distributed in an asymmetric pattern, making the urban design more artistic and flexible to attract public interest and participation.

Fully considering the peripheral land-use: taking into account human activity requirements in the peripheral areas, designing a variety of open spaces for different uses.

Reflecting outlines of natural mountains in architectural forms in the design concepts for individual buildings or building complexes, taking full advantage of the relationship between forms and outlines of artificial buildings and natural mountains in order to make artificial structures blend into the natural environment. Considering the local climate, patios are incorporated into building designs to create indoor recreation space.

Incorporating green building concepts: green roof energy saving concepts are integrated with architectural design, benefiting environmental beautification, and reducing urban pollution and noise.

The existing economic evaluation system should enhance both the biological evolution system and human aspirations in order to maintain a natural environment and improve the health and happiness of people living in the new city. Healthy urban development should support a secure ecological environment in the creation of a Shan-shui city that is appropriate for the location. Landscape design that considers only visual effects is not advisable.

3.2 Dalian New Harbor City Core Area Landscape Planning

3.2.1 Existing Context and Problems

Located in western Lushunkou Port in Dalian City, the landscape planning scope of the core area of New Harbor City is 7.48 km². To the north of the site are existing harbours and to the south is the business district of the old city. The core area of New Harbour City is a major port that makes significant contributions to the harbour economy of northeastern China in particular, and northeastern Asia as a whole. In recent years, the local government has been striving to establish a large industrial base in this location to include shipbuilding, manufacturing, and petrochemical industries in order to take advantage of existing infrastructure such as harbours, highways, and train ferries.

Economic development and construction of New Harbour City are expected to cause many environmental problems in the near future.

3.2.1.1 Construction and development of the existing agricultural land surrounding the mountains would cause serious fragmentation of forests that are significant for water conservation. Ecological flows from the mountains to the planned urban green networks would potentially be blocked by the built land in between.

3.2.1.2 Urban heat island effect will be intensified in certain areas.

3.2.1.3 The topographic characteristics of the site, i.e., low hills and steep slopes, result in low storage capacities or streams, which would be aggravated by future industrial water use.

3.2.1.4 Existing combined drainage systems and lack of sewage treatment facilities present major challenges for the planned industrial base in the north.

Consequently, the plan for the New City urgently requires consideration in terms of both urban development and ecological security.

3.2.2 Planning Concept and Methods

A core principle for the planning of Dalian Lushun New Harbour City was to embed the "Shan-shui City" concept . . . into a spatial organization that considers both human and ecosystem demands. Planning concepts include:

3.2.2.1 Establishing an Ecological Pattern: Three spatial scales, i.e., the Dalian Peninsula scale, the Western Dalian scale, and the New Harbour City scale, have been explored to determine the overall ecosystem structure of the New Harbour City. The regional ecosystem structure was determined at larger scale and characterization of specific ecosystem functions and development of protection strategies were established at smaller scale. . . .

3.2.2.2 Revealing the Shan-shui Landscape: The traditional Chinese "ideal dwelling environment" concept, landscape poetry and painting, and Fengshui geomancy provide various ways to identify ideal spatial organizations for the Shan-shui elements. These concepts and theories are the cultural foundations for green space planning that artistically incorporates surrounding mountains, bays and rivers into the overall layout of the city. . . .

3.2.2.3 Analyzing Urban Economic Organization: Land use structure based on economic growth patterns, area requirements for various land uses, and corresponding human activity characteristics have been analyzed to obtain spatial requirements for people.

3.2.2.4 Constructing "Shan-shui City": By overlapping the ecosystem structure, the Shan-shui cultural landscape layout, and the land use distribution required for human needs, an urban green network was established according to a spatial framework of "core, ring, corridor and patch". Green spaces within the network can be further categorized according to their functions or locations, e.g., public park, protective buffer, residential green space, subsidiary green space, etc.

Planning process measures included: 1. Analyzing a number of remote sensing pictures and dynamically monitoring eco-region and urban ecological systems and land-use conditions at multi-scales, based on GIS and RS techniques, then summarizing characteristics of urban land-use and ecological conditions; 2. Overlying spatial analysis results from eco-region to urban multi-scale eco-system and socio-economic system, obtaining spatial requirements for human activities and natural systems at various scales; 3. Estimating ecological and economic structure at regional scale, classifying landscapes and measuring at urban scale; 4. Integrating suggestions from expert consultants in urban planning, ecology, cultural art, architectural design and collecting input from local residents.

3.2.3 Planning Innovation
Landscape planning considered the relationship between natural and human requirements through:

Identification and creation of a regional scale urban eco-system among mountains, i.e., creating ecological corridors by connecting north-south and east-west mountain sides to form an ecological supply for urban space.

Design of a landscape structure that combines mountain-water visual corridors at regional scale with artificial mountains and water at urban scale, i.e., strengthening the connection between north-south flowing water and the surrounding mountains makes the mountain-water-city relationship consistent with traditional Chinese Fengshui principles.

Identification of urban landscape functional requirements according to the new city's future land-use requirements, i.e., functional green space planning including protecting forests from urban industrial, residential and transportation related development and creating recreational parks and related green fields.

Modification of landscape planning concepts, as appropriate, according to response from multi-disciplinary experts, i.e., adjusting number and location of recreational spaces in residential areas, changing paving colors in sports parks, and transforming southern undeveloped land into useful green space, strengthening ecological system connections.

In the planning and design of Dalian New Harbor City Core Area, human space needs have been coordinated with requirements for natural open space at many scales. Preliminary locations were determined at large scale while detailed design was completed at small scale. The low impact landscape design was completed strictly on a scientific basis, in accordance with the expectations of local people who aspire to the Chinese ideal living spatial structure of "Shanshui City".

3.3 Landscape Planning and Design of Longwan New Central Business District in Huludao City

3.3.1 Existing Context and Problems

Huludao City, located in southwest Liaoning Province, is a new growth center in the Bohai Economic Circle. Enjoying a unique strategic location, the city is at the intersection of the Northeast Asia Economic Circle, Beijing-Tianjin-Hebei Economic Circle and Northeast Economic Circle. Longwan New Central Business District is located in the southerly part of Longwan District, with a designated area of 7.63 km². The site is bordered on the north by the new city of Huludao, to the south by Xingcheng City, on the east by the Longwan coastline, and on the west by a natural boundary formed by mountains surrounding Dongyao Village. The site is framed by mountains on three sides and faces the sea on the fourth side, with excellent natural resources and beautiful mountain-water patterns. Since the integration of regional tourist resources will provide powerful support for the economic growth of Longwan Central Business District, the local government decided to transform the site into a coastal eco-city for business, holiday and residential use. However, finding ways to best preserve the existing good mountain-water qualities in the urban development scheme, integrate Shan-shui cultural concepts and organically blend both urban artificial and natural environments was a key challenge to project landscape planning.

3.3.2 Planning Concept and Methods

The planning concept is based on respect for, and preservation of, the existing natural mountain-water context, abstracting urban historical and regional characteristics to create an urban landscape structure. The plan is focused on the structure and significance of Shan-shui culture from Chinese traditional living environment concepts in urban human settlements, including:

Assessing landforms and site vegetation: the project team used total station, GPS and unmanned aircraft remote sensing modeling to obtain detailed features of the ecological environment. A data base was established based on serious investigation of natural mountain-water structures, shoals, and the diverse animal and plant habitats of the Moon River area, which provides an objective basis for future landscape planning and design and helps designers to comprehensively understand the mountain-water structure and degree of human activity within the site.

Organizing visual relationships between natural mountain-water elements and new urban development: preserving ecological corridors and sightline access according to sightline analysis and vertical overlay analysis regarding the natural environment and architectural spaces. The analysis helped to coordinate proposed architectural massing and building heights with the natural landforms that are embraced by mountains on three sides. The design of the mountain-water structure at large scale has been enhanced at urban scale, integrating artificial forms into natural mountain-water patterns. Accordingly, the city image becomes a tangible interpretation of Chinese traditional living environment concepts.

Preserving natural rivers and creating relationships between river and urban functions: Moon River flows west to east through the middle of the site and there are many natural forests, wetlands and estuary shoal landscapes along its edge. The preservation of these natural features and their relationship to the various adjacent urban development land is one of the most important design considerations. Maintaining a mutually beneficial relationship involves a number of issues, such as preservation of water conservation forests that rely on the river as a supply resource, water purification benefits provided by vegetation, flood control design, educational opportunities regarding ecological systems and interrelationships, creation of desirable urban waterfront open space, opportunities to create coastal recreational landscapes, etc. The river flowing through the center of the city is connected to human activities, maximizing the benefits from retaining its natural characteristics and providing places for waterfront activities.

Extracting elements of applicable Shan-shui culture in historical Shan-shui poems and paintings as well as from historical cultural traces within the development area: Huludao has a long history and the city has seen the footprints of several great men, such as the First Emperor of Qin, Emperor Wu of Han, Cao Cao in the Three Kingdoms and the great chairman Mao Zedong. Design elements with local historical significance have been abstracted from their poems, palace relics, etc.

Creating appropriate landscape design based on a Shan-shui cultural context and urban requirements for habitation:

As a river flowing through the city center, Moon River's natural landscape has been preserved. Robust vegetation in the upper reach close to the mountainous area was used to form a wetland park, primarily for water purification purposes, which serves as a good quality water resource; the middle reach running through the corn area of the city was designed to be a riverside recreational area that preserves the natural river pattern; and a natural tidal wetland was formed at the estuary of the lower reach. The diverse ecological environment maintains the river in its natural state.

Existing vegetation and areas in healthy ecological condition have been preserved to form urban green fields as part of planning and design. Agricultural land in poor condition was converted to buildable land, and large trees and native plants on the site have been conserved in order to retain the local character of the site.

The two mountains in the city were determined to be focal points for organization of the landscape design and structuring of scenic views. Views are an important consideration in the design of core area open spaces and green corridors extend to the peak of Dagu Mountain, which is a sightseeing platform.

A scenic location named "Longhuitou" which means a dragon is turning its head to look back, provides a picturesque podium for viewing the entire new area, the old city, mountains to the west and the sea to the east. It is an important landscape node that combines mountain, sea and city.

The planning and design of Longwan New Central Business District in Huludao City fully abstracts existing mountain-water site patterns, providing the basis for creating an urban green system and mountain-water landscape axis. It emphasizes the preservation of existing vegetation and restoration of river purification and biological diversity maintenance functions, providing a comfortable place for human activities in an area surrounded by mountains and water.

3.3.3 Planning Innovation

3.3.3.1 Site survey and investigation: the goal was to preserve natural features from the beginning, making best use of and protecting the natural elements through thorough investigation and survey of the site's natural characteristics.

3.3.3.2 Comprehensive and multi-scale site analysis utilizing GIS techniques: specialized methods were used to resolve the site's ecological problems. The status of ecological systems was studied at a regional scale to broaden the development plan's ecological benefit.

Combining the essence of Chinese Shan-shui painting in urban planning and design: by connecting the ideal state of Chinese Shan-shui poems and paintings with the actual mountain-water patterns of the site, the landscape planning and design creates an urban landscape with Shan-shui picturesque states by creating harmonious relationships between urban development and peripheral mountain-water textures.

4. Conclusions

The concept of "Shan-shui City" implies a complementary relationship between urban planning and Chinese traditional garden art. In previous new city development in China, urban landscape planning was a final step that focused on requirements for urban development and building while weakening the connection to natural mountain-water environments and the spiritual cultivation of Shan-shui culture. This fault can be corrected by urban landscape planning directed by the "Shan-shui City" concept. It assimilates the functional requirements for urban construction, environmental requirements and the abstraction of Shan-shui cultural textures as a whole, providing a livable, beautiful and comfortable environment for residents.

An ideal livable city should develop by embracing the natural environment, not in conflict with nature, creating a sustainable, livable and dynamic city. This "Shan-shui City" will provide for harmonious co-existence between man and nature, interpreting the Chinese "Shan-shui Complex" as the basis for creating an ideal human settlement.

The Chinese "Shan-shui City" concept integrates urban planning, architecture, and landscape architecture in total, embodying the holistic design idea of oriental philosophies. In these three new city landscape planning case studies, abstraction of regional Shan-shui cultural attributes and the objective of maintaining the existing eco-system have been combined as a premise for beginning new city landscape long-range planning, in order to achieve long-term merging and unification of urban human and ecological demands. Based on this prerequisite, the design process is the fusion of rational analysis and perceptual design and is a meaningful basis for regional sustainable development.

References

Belovsky, Gary E. "Ecological Stability: Reality, Misconceptions, and Implications for Risk Assessment." *Human and Ecological Risk Assessment* 8, no. 1 (2002): 99–108.

Deumlich, Detlef, J. Kiesel, J. Thiere, H. I. Reuter, L. Völker, and R. Funk. "Application of the Site Comparison Method (SICOM) to Assess the Potential Erosion Risk—A Basis for the Evaluation of Spatial Equivalence of Agri-Environmental Measures." *Catena* 68, no. 2 (2006): 141–52.

Forman, Richard T. T. "The Missing Catalyst: Design and Planning with Ecology Roots." *Ecology and Design: Frameworks for Learning* (2002): 85–109.

Judd, Nancy L., James R. Karr, William C. Griffith, and Elaine M. Faustman. "Challenges in Defining Background Levels for Human and Ecological Risk Assessments." *Human and Ecological Risk Assessment* 9, no. 7 (2003): 1623–32.

Li, Hui, and Zhiying Li. *Green Space Systematic Planning of Human Settlements*. China Architecture and Building Press, 2009, 36–38.

Robertson, David P., and R. Bruce Hull. "Which Nature? A Case Study of Whitetop Mountain." *Landscape Journal* 20, no. 2 (2001): 176–85.

Shixing, Bao. *Qian Xuesen Discusses Shan-shui City*. China Architecture and Building Press, 2010.

Site: Building through Ecological Planning

Toward a New Regionalism: Environmental Architecture in the Pacific Northwest (2005)

David E. Miller

Let us accept the proposition that nature is process, that it is interacting, that it responds to laws, representing values and opportunities for human use with certain limitations and even prohibitions to certain of these. We can take this proposition to confront and resolve many problems.
—Ian McHarg, *Design with Nature*

General Description

The Cedar River Watershed receives one and a half times the amount of Seattle's annual rainfall and is the main source for the city's drinking water. The Cedar River Watershed Education Center was created as a result of 1988 legislation to protect the watershed and educate the public about its value as a resource. The Seattle City Council has since designated the watershed an ecological preserve, to be managed for public use, habitat, and water supply. The Rattlesnake Lake recreation area just outside the boundary of the protected watershed was selected as the site for the Watershed Education Center. As a popular recreational area, it required upgrading and environmental repair.

Jones & Jones Architects and Landscape Architects began master planning in 1991. Early goals included siting the education center, programming a new administrative headquarters, and upgrading the park at Rattlesnake Lake. Throughout the design process, the firm viewed the project as an opportunity to reveal hydrological processes to the public, foster appreciation for the source

Figure 6-14 The Cedar River Watershed Education Center, Seattle (Miller, 2005, Reproduced with permission of University of Washington Press).

of the city's drinking water, and instill a sense of ecological stewardship. The eco-revelatory theme became the inspiration for the center, which was envisioned as a microcosm of the larger watershed.

The Education Center is a rhythmic arrangement of interior and exterior spaces that encourages movement and invites exploration. Jones & Jones nestled the complex of structures into the site, referencing its historical significance as a railroad route, offering framed views and glimpses of Rattlesnake Ledge and Rattlesnake Lake, and fostering an experience accessible to people of all abilities. The set of buildings clusters around a series of courtyards, generating a dialogue between architecture and landscape. The forest courtyards are receptacles for roof runoff and hold a sequence of inviting, exploratory spaces woven together by a stream and native plants.

Site History

The Cedar River Watershed has a rich history. Although archaeologists have documented Native American occupation in the upper watershed basins as early as 7400 B.C., railroads and small company towns associated with coal and clay mining produced settlement and industrial impacts beginning in the late 1800s. Logging activity, including two substantial logging camps, followed from the mid-1890s into the 1940s, greatly altering the landscape in the watershed.

The City of Seattle began acquiring land and developing the area as a municipal water source in the early twentieth century, damming the Cedar River in two places to provide water storage in Chester Morse Lake. However, some of the impounded water infiltrated the glacial moraine and reappeared as hillside springs, and in 1916, following construction of the second dam, water filled a valley depression to form Rattlesnake Lake. Rattlesnake Lake became a popular recreational destination, and active use led to substantial degradation of the lake edge and surrounding landscape.

By the mid-1900s, most of the settlements in the watershed had been dismantled in order to protect drinking water quality. By 1996, the City of Seattle had acquired the entire 90,000 acres as the primary source of water for the city and more than two-thirds of King County. For the last ten years, the Seattle city government and the Jones & Jones design team have worked diligently to repair the site. At the same time, they strove to create an unobtrusive vocabulary of intervention within the landscape that aims to foster educational opportunities and encourage environmental stewardship.

The site of the Watershed Education Center was a support station on a railroad line that connected Renton with Milwaukee during the first half of the twentieth century. A settlement of small bungalows housed railroad workers. The legacy of this settlement is a grand allée of native big-leaf maples parallel to the road as well as a compacted site infested with invasive (non-native) plants. The maples and railroad alignment provide an organizing datum, the small building volumes and forms recall the former residential settlement, historic tile artifacts manufactured in the watershed are displayed and used as paving, and thriving watershed plant communities have replaced the invasive landscape.

Climate

The Cedar River Watershed Education Center, located in the forest and mountains between Seattle and Snoqualmie Pass, receives sixty-one inches of rainfall each year. Marine air traveling eastward moves up and over the Cascades; as the air rises, it cools, reducing its capacity to hold moisture and generating significant precipitation. In addition, temperatures at the center are significantly cooler than temperatures in Seattle. This is due to the location's elevation and vegetative cover, as opposed to the concrete and asphalt of Seattle, which has the effect of creating an urban heat island. Rattlesnake Lake also tends to have a positive cooling effect in the summer, as air moves over the water before reaching the center along its shore. Jones & Jones employed simple, low-tech strategies to match the architectural response to local conditions.

Earth Strategies

The master plan and design for the Cedar River Watershed Education Center included restoration of the native landscape. Invasive plants, introduced during the site's use as a railroad support station, had caused extensive damage to the land surrounding the visitors center and along Rattlesnake Lake. Non-native plant species were cleared and replaced with indigenous plant communities that include habitat layers, from moss groundcovers to tree canopies. Although the complete eradication of foreign species has proved challenging, mast of the site has been restored. Careful planning and diligent follow-through minimized disturbance to healthy native vegetation during construction.

Rattlesnake Lake has been an extremely popular place to picnic, swim, boat, and fish and was in need of infrastructure improvements and environmental restoration. The edge of the lake was deteriorating from poorly delineated parking accommodation and road use. As a solution, Jones & Jones realigned the entrance road and parking areas and restored the park and shoreline with native vegetation, simultaneously benefiting the lake and its users. Soil contamination from former uses was cleaned and mitigated. The new road and parking areas blend gracefully into the landscape, and vehicles no longer barricade the lake edge.

A number of architectural decisions conscientiously consider the earth and its resources. Jones & Jones used component dimensioning to minimize waste from the buildings at the visitors center. Green roofs on some of the structures blend into the environment, reduce runoff, and help insulate the interior spaces underneath (some of the green roofs cover exterior walkways, and others cover restrooms). The architecture utilizes natural and recycled materials including 98 percent FSC-certified wood, recycled-wood flooring, minimally processed materials, water-based clear finishes, and fly-ash-component concrete slabs and outdoor terraces. Jones & Jones looked far into the future and designed the buildings so that they could all be disassembled, moved, and reassembled elsewhere later.

Fire Strategies

Although the architects examined multiple strategies for both heating and cooling the buildings, the design team found that the most basic solutions were best suited to the situation. The heating system relies on good-quality residential-scale heat pumps with economizers for greater efficiency. The buildings are exceptionally well insulated, so supplied heat is maintained longer. Insulated headers and rigid insulation above the exposed roof framing eliminate thermal bridging. Walls are well insulated also, and windows filled with argon gas minimize heat loss. Daylight enters the interior spaces through generous wood-framed side windows positioned both high and low for an even balance of light. Deep overhangs provide shade, and trees become light fixtures as they filter the direct rays of the sun and glow with dappled light.

Air Strategies

Nights at the Cedar River Watershed are always cool, and daytime air moves across water and through vegetation before reaching the center. The ventilation strategy capitalizes on the availability of fresh cool air. Operable double-hung windows provide natural cross ventilation, and generous overhangs protect against overheating in summer. The deep overhangs also create cool, sheltered spaces for mingling outside the buildings.

Water Strategies

One of the primary goals of the Watershed Education Center is to teach visitors about water and human interactions with it. A series of transitional spaces throughout the center allows a variety of relationships with water and nature, from completely exposed, to semi-sheltered, to enclosed. Water is revealed as an artistic element, a playful and interactive component that animates each space. Movement through the site enables the visitor to experience the watershed in microcosm. A stream greets visitors as they arrive. Following the stream to its source leads them through artful demonstrations that quietly teach about interconnectedness—the water cycle and how humans have interacted with patterns of water within the watershed. The sounds and rhythms of water create an engaging journey.

The education center has three sources of water. The first is a well that supplies potable water. The second source, the Cedar River, supplies non-potable water for the fire suppression system and irrigation. Huge penstocks siphon water from upstream (the same penstocks that pull water for the City of Seattle), which is then diverted to the fire suppression system. The non-potable system requires continuous flushing, so the water flows through it, and then through the center's stream and down to Rattlesnake Lake, where it rejoins the river through the groundwater. This detour models the pattern and flow of streams in the watershed, a beneficial scenario. The third source of water

Figure 6-15 Downspouts serve as an artistic element in the courtyard (Miller, 2005, Reprinted with permission of University of Washington Press).

is precipitation, and a variety of strategies address the path of this water as it moves from the sky to the earth. Two types of roofs intercept water as it falls from the sky. Green roofs, the first type, absorb much of the precipitation directly and support raised parcels of habitat for birds, insects, and plant communities. Steeply sloped metal roofs, the second type, direct water through carefully designed gutters and downspouts, which channel it into the stream, artful catchment basins, and a series of bioswales and infiltration basins. Pollutants from the road and parking area are treated in a chain of bioswales that release clean water back to the earth. Sand-set paving, where possible, further reduces runoff, increasing the opportunity for groundwater replenishment. With the exception of a demonstration area that includes a home-scale rain barrel for rainwater harvesting, water is not collected and stored on-site, since it is abundantly available year-round.

Postscript

An ecological project requires a change in our way of thinking about design, implementation, and ongoing operations and maintenance. Planning for the Cedar River Watershed Education Center began well before the concept of sustainability was widespread. In this sense, the center embraces sustainable strategies to a remarkable degree. Along the way, Jones & Jones, a firm long noted for its commitment to working within the earth's capacity to renew itself, educated the client, the contractors, the staff, and now the public about opportunities for reducing our impact on natural resources and, moreover, on becoming stewards of the environment.

While the Watershed Education Center deftly illustrates a myriad of strategies that we can all use to conserve resources, perhaps a few areas could have been pushed further during the design phase, given a different political construct or a more flexible budget. Passive (solar) strategies and ground-source heat, initially suggested by the design team, were rejected early on, because the systems and methods were unconventional, costly, and at the time viewed as tangential to the focused interpretive mission of the center. The simple, familiar technology of residential construction seemed the best fit for a project that was meant to resonate with homeowners and demonstrate strategies that people could apply in their daily lives.

During the construction phase, contractors needed to understand the intent of the project and adjust their accustomed patterns of work. Tree protection, green materials, and component dimensioning all minimized the project's resource impact. Though straightforward, these strategies were not standard practice, and proper implementation required good communication by all team members. This level of design team attention carried through to the essential details that reinforced the eco-friendly theme. Interconnections between the buildings and the exterior courtyards were integral to the success of the design; for example, gutters and downspouts that displayed the path of water from the roof to the earth were key aspects. Considered within the context of the whole project, the slope of a gutter is normally a minor detail, but to effectively display the flow of water it required special attention at all levels for successful implementation throughout the project.

Once built, a project emphasizing ecology requires stewardship. Standard maintenance and operations practices are often somewhat at odds with the larger goals of a sustainable project. The forest ecosystem of the watershed, for example, requires a different type of maintenance than does a typical urban park. Education efforts continue to include maintenance personnel and staff members, who soon embrace the sustainable strategies and systems.

Inherent to sustainability is the idea of interconnectedness in both built and natural systems, from the smallest details to the whole. Each component of a project affects the others, just as the project itself affects the world around it. The Cedar River Watershed Education Center shows that the ongoing success of a sustainable project hinges upon good communication and judicious education at every level, from inception to occupation and continuing stewardship.

Cedar River Watershed Education Center
King County, WA
Jones & Jones Architects and Landscape Architects, Ltd.

Part Seven

Emerging Frameworks

Introduction to Part Seven

Promising conceptual and procedural theoretical frameworks have been proposed for sustainably balancing human use with ecological concerns. In the first reading, "Ecological Footprints for Beginners," published in *Our Ecological Footprint: Reducing Human Impact on the Earth*,[1] Mathis Wackernagel and William Rees offer a useful accounting tool and form of impact capacity analysis. The ecological footprint is useful for estimating the resource consumption of an urban landscape and the capacity to absorb the corresponding waste generated by the residents, compared with a similar landscape. The authors introduce a preliminary framework for estimating the "ecological bottom line of sustainability"[2] and conclude that we tend to underestimate the ecosystem services or benefits we receive from nature.

In a condensed essay that follows, "The Region," from *The New Urbanism: Toward an Architecture of Community*,[3] architect and planner Peter Calthorpe examine how the principles of the *New Urbanism* design and planning framework, as they are typically implemented in cities, can be applied effectively in suburbs and the metropolitan region.

The next reading by planner Anthony Downs, "Smart Growth: Why We Discuss It More than We Do It," published in the *Journal of the American Planning Association*,[4] raises important policy issues in relation to the challenges and opportunities in implementing the *Smart Growth* model for mitigating suburban sprawl. The policy issues Downs examines are particularly relevant to the other emerging design and planning frameworks that are examined here, especially those addressing growth containment.

In the next reading, "Landscape Ecological Urbanism: Origins and Trajectories," from *Landscape and Urban Planning*,[5] Frederick Steiner explores how developments in *landscape urbanism* and *urban ecology* hold possibilities in restructuring the way we understand ecosystems and the ramifications for the design of cities.

Resilience is a concept that has a growing appeal to ecologists and planners alike. It is "a measure of the ability of these systems to absorb changes of state variables, driving variables, and parameters, and still persist. In this definition, *resilience* is a property of the system and *persistence or probability of extinction* is the result."[6]

In the next reading, "Ecological Resilience as a Foundation for Urban Design and Sustainability," from *Resilience in Ecology and Urban Design: Linking Theory and Practice for Sustainable Cities*,[7] planners Jianguo Wu and Tong Wu argue that many cities and regions are unsustainable. This is in part due to our lack of scientific understanding of how nature works and our misuse of ecological theory in action. They examine the key principles and developments behind the theory of ecological resilience since the seminal work by ecologist C. S. Holling was published in 1973, as well as their importance for sustainability and creating resilient urban communities.

In the last essay, "Ecological Urbanism: A Framework for the Design of Resilient Cities,"[8] noted landscape architect and planner Anne Whiston Spirn at Massachusetts Institute of Technology introduces *ecological urbanism* as another form of intervention that connects urban design with ecology. She traces its intellectual roots, discusses the key concepts and principles, and demonstrates how these can be used to create and sustain livable yet resilient cities. This piece builds upon concepts from her award-winning book, *The Granite Garden: Urban Nature and Human Design*.[9]

In "Sustainable Regionalism: Evolutionary Framework and Prospects for Managing Metropolitan Landscapes," published in *Landscape Journal*,[10] I look at this spatial framework for managing metropolitan growth. Unlike the other readings, this article explicitly examines urbanism from the perspective of a "regional-city;" however, regional thinking is implied in some of the frameworks proposed in the readings, especially Peter Calthorpe's essay on extending urbanism to the region. Sustainable regionalism is complementary to frameworks such as Smart Growth, New Urbanism, landscape ecological urbanism, and sustainable development.

The authors of the readings in part 7 agree that the problems—economic, social, and environmental—related to urbanization are becoming increasingly complex. Although each of the authors has offered solutions or insights to the ways in which we may comprehend or even resolve these concerns, it is best to think of the many contributions as "promising works-in-progress," some of which have yet to be validated in practice (figures 7-1 and 7-2).

Regarding cities as an integral part of the natural world is a consistent theme found in all of the articles. Spirn mentions, and I concur, that the "idea of nature as consisting of the biological, physical, and chemical processes that create life, the earth, and the universe is fundamental to ecological urbanism."[11] Spirn reveals that nature is neither a specific location, such as a wilderness area or countryside, nor an object, such as a mountain, river, or tree. She adds that "if one embraces this idea, then the false oppositions between city and nature, the given and the built, fall away."[12] This statement also helps to reconcile a theoretical divide, real or perceived, that has plagued the design disciplines, in regard to the nature–culture dichotomy or ecology–arts divide.

The Long-Term Ecological Research (LTER) projects in Baltimore and Phoenix funded by the U.S. National Science Foundation provided additional impetus in regarding cities as an integral part of the natural world. The purpose of these projects was to "document, analyze, and understand ecological processes and patterns that change over long temporal and large spatial scales."[13] Prior to 1997, LTERs were located outside urban areas.

The authors of these readings seem to agree that urban landscapes are complex, heterogeneous, and interacting ecological systems. Comprehending them and proposing sustainable solutions to urban problems require an interdisciplinary perspective. As landscape architect Meg Calkins puts it: "The environmental and social issues that must be addressed in sustainable design are too complex for just landscape architects or engineers [and planners]. By necessity, the sustainable site design process must include multiple disciplines that will collaborate on complex, interrelated systems."[14]

A point of departure in understanding the threats and risks to valued ecosystems as posed by continued urban growth is to undertake an ecological accounting of the state or health of such ecosystems. *Ecological footprint analysis* (EFA) is one way to conduct the accounting, and doing so helps to "determine the ecological constraints within which society operates; to shape policy to avoid or reduce overshoot; and to monitor progress towards achieving sustainability."[15] I recommend that the outcome of EFA should always be one of the policy options in making land-use decisions. EFA assigns monetary values to ecosystem services as well. In the absence of a definite way to compare resource demands on ecological systems, policy debates on the effective use of land and water resources have tended to emphasize ideological issues. EFA has enabled the development of widely used metrics that turn land use allocation decisions

Figures 7-1, 7-2 Bryant Park, New York City—a model of urban park restoration (Reproduced with permission of Olin/Karl-Rainer Blumenthal).

that are based on ideological grounds into discussions that are based on empirical evidence.[16] Ecological accounting via EFA or life-cycling costing is an issue that the proponents of the ecological design and planning frameworks reviewed here should seriously consider adopting, if they are not already doing so.

Peter Calthorpe argued that New Urbanism can be extended effectively into the design and planning of regions, and views regional design as one option for

containing the growth of urban areas. In addition, Calthorpe urged that the quality of new development in the region should follow town-like principles emphasizing urban growth boundaries, a diversity of uses, transit orientation, accessible open space, and ecological and conservation values that define the region's character. I offered a similar proposal, focused on designing and planning compact, place-based, hierarchical, interconnected communities. The connectivity of place-specific compact settlements is a defining feature of Sustainable Regionalism Framework (SRF).

The idea of a regional approach has also been implied in the writings of authors who advocated creating resilient communities, including Steiner, Spirn, and Wu and Wu. In his formulation of the resilience theory, Holling contended that a management approach based on resiliency needs to view activities and events in a regional rather than local context. Ecologist Richard Forman reminded us in part 3 that sustainability works best in regional landscapes due to their large scale and complementarity of resources. Ecological processes change more slowly at the regional scale in comparison with the site or local level as well. Except for Wackernagel and Rees, whose article focused on ecological accounting, all of the other authors in this part advocated (or implied in their writings) that increasing density through infill, redevelopment, or controlled growth is a strategy for managing the expansion of urban areas.

Economist Anthony Downs cautioned that proposals involving limiting the outward expansion of new developments and raising densities in both new-growth areas and existing neighborhoods are *very unlikely to be* implemented. They require a shift in power and authority from the local to regional levels of governance in the United States, which tends to be vigorously opposed by local governments. Proposals that involve shifting the public infrastructure costs to new residents, as well as providing more mixed uses, pedestrian-based environments, and diverse regulations on aesthetics, continue to enjoy public support and are likely to be implemented. The Envision Utah and Envision Central Texas coalitions represent successful efforts by a coalition of local governments in Utah and the Austin region, respectively, to formulate and implement a regional Smart Growth agenda. Steiner was heavily involved in this initiative.

Ecologists and planners are fascinated with the resiliency theory. Cities are increasingly viewed as resilient ecosystems. Steiner pointed out that stronger connections between planning and resilience research emerged post–September 11, 2001, through the leading efforts of Lawrence Vale of the Massachusetts Institute of Technology, Thomas Campanella of the University of North Carolina, now at Cornell, and, I might add, the research conducted by Marina Alberti and her colleagues at the University of Washington.[17] The application of resilience to urban ecosystems is largely a result of the two National Science Foundation–funded LTERs in Baltimore and Phoenix, as well as projects conducted by researchers including Alberti.

Resilience theory is embedded in the ecological design and planning frameworks proposed by Wu and Wu, Spirn, and Steiner, and is implied by mine. It offers refreshing insights into how we think about creating sustainable communities. Should design and planning continue to emphasize the maintenance of ecological stability of landscapes or sustenance of their adaptive capacities? Is seeking the stability of an ecological system mutually exclusive from strengthening its adaptive capacity? Can we strive for a workable blend of both? Or is one approach appropriate in some cases but not for others? How does resilience contribute to our understanding of regenerative systems and vice versa? These are emerging issues that designers and planners have to address.

Another related concept that is suggested in some of the articles is the idea of employing *ecosystem services* as a basis for design and planning. Ecosystem services are those "benefits humans obtain from ecosystems."[18] They comprise a range of benefits such as air and water cleansing, waste decomposition, erosion control and climate regulation, and spiritual and recreational values.[19] EFA may be viewed as a basic assessment of ecosystem services for a given landscape, as it strives to estimate the biologically productive ecosystems that are necessary to support the consumption of energy, biomass (food and fiber), water, and other resources needed by human populations in a location, and the corresponding waste assimilation capacity.

In the bigger picture, EFA suggests that it is necessary to perform more robust performance measurements of ecosystem services. The outcomes could serve as baseline data for estimating current performance and projecting future expectations for designed landscapes. Steiner recommended that the goal of landscape ecological urbanism should be to design and plan cities that increase ecosystem services. Wu and Wu suggested that increasing ecosystem services may be a way to establish resilient cities.

Many of the articles champion the establishment of ecological networks and green infrastructure, which arguably are strategies for conserving ecosystem services. Networks are composed of systems of fragile and valued natural and cultural resources such as conservation areas, hydrologic systems and wildlife habitats, and distinctive historical sites. In *Green Infrastructure: A Landscape Approach* (2013), planner Davis Rouse and landscape architect Ignacio Bunster-Ossa examine the concept of landscape as green infrastructure. They say green infrastructure "is the visible expression of natural and human ecosystem processes at work across scales and contexts to provide multiple benefits [or services] for people and their environments."[20]

Spirn indicates that many successful models of ecological urbanism currently exist, as is evident in the articles examined, namely New Urbanism, sustainable regionalism, landscape urbanism, ecological urbanism, and landscape ecological urbanism. She argues that what is needed, and I concur, is an authoritative documentation and critical review of ecological urbanism and its subfields to identify philosophical threads, key themes and concepts as well as the contributions of each, ways for putting ideas into practice, models of exemplary practice, and domains of similarities and differences.

To conclude, the readings presented in part 7 have revealed numerous themes in the search for solutions to ecological problems. These include ecological and life-cost accounting, resilience, regeneration, sustainability, ecosystem services, regionalism, landscapes as form givers, low-impact development, evidence-based interventions, spatial hierarchy, and aesthetic appreciation of landscapes. These themes will continue to be important as we seek to effectively balance human use with ecological concerns.

Notes

1. Mathis Wackernagel and William Rees, "Ecological Footprints for Beginners," in *Our Ecological Footprint: Reducing Human Impact on the Earth* (Philadelphia: New Society Publishers, 1996).
2. Ibid., 57.

3. Peter Calthorpe, "The Region," in *The New Urbanism: Toward Architecture of Community*, Peter Katz (ed.) (New York: McGraw-Hill, 1994).

4. Anthony Downs, "Smart Growth: Why We Discuss It More Than We Do It," *Journal of the American Planning Association* 71, no. 4 (2005), 367–378.

5. Frederick Steiner, "Landscape Ecological Urbanism: Origins and Trajectories," *Landscape and Urban Planning* 100, no. 4 (2011), 333–337.

6. Crawford S. Holling, "Resilience and Stability of Ecological Systems," *Annual Review of Ecology and Systematics* 4 (1973), 41–42. In 1973, ecologist Holling at the University of British Columbia published his pioneering article, "Resilience and Stability of Ecological Systems," in which he introduced a new perspective on understanding the behavior of ecological systems. He proposed that their performance could be established by two distinct properties: *resilience* and *stability*. Resilience "determines the persistence of relationships within a system and is a measure of the ability of these systems to absorb changes of state variables, driving variables, and parameters, and still persist. In this definition, *resilience* is a property of the system and *persistence or probability of extinction* is the result. Stability, on the other hand, is the ability of a system to return to an equilibrium state after a temporary disturbance. The more rapidly it returns, and with the least fluctuation the more stable it is. In this definition *stability* is the property of the system and the *degree of fluctuation* around specific states the result."

   Since Holling's publication, new thinking has emerged about how we grasp the behavior of ecosystems. Holling revealed that the stability and resilience perspectives on the behavior of ecological systems might produce very different approaches to the management of landscape resources (Holling, 1993). A management strategy based on the stability viewpoint emphasizes the equilibrium and maintenance of the structure and function of the ecosystems. On the other hand, the resilience viewpoint stresses the need for their persistence by keeping options open and recognizing that ecosystems comprise interacting heterogeneous elements connected by the flows of energy, materials, and species. Resilience theory is becoming very appealing to the disciplines of ecology and planning.

7. Jianguo Wu and Tong Wu, "Ecological Resilience as a Foundation for Urban Design and Sustainability," in *Resilience in Ecology and Urban Design: Linking Theory and Practice for Sustainable Cities* (New York: Springer, 2013), 211–229.

8. Anne Whiston Spirn, "Ecological Urbanism: A Framework for the Design of Resilient Cities," working paper (Cambridge: MIT, 2013).

9. Anne Whiston Spirn, *The Granite Garden, Urban Nature and Human Design* (New York: Basic Books, 1984).

10. Forster Ndubisi, "Sustainable Regionalism: Evolutionary Framework and Prospects for Managing Metropolitan Landscapes," *Landscape Journal* 27, no. 1 (2008), 51–68.

11. Anne Spirn, "Ecological Urbanism: A Framework for the Design of Resilient Cities," 4.

12. Ibid.

13. Steiner, "Landscape Ecological Urbanism: Origins and Trajectories," 333–337.

14. Meg Calkins, *The Sustainable Sites Handbook: A Complete Guide to the Principles, Strategies, and Best Practices for Sustainable Landscapes* (New Jersey: Wiley, 2012).

15. Wackernagel and Rees, "Ecological Footprints for Beginners," 56.

16. Ewing, B., D. Moore, S. Goldfinger, A. Oursler, A. Reed, and M. Wackernagel, *The Ecological Footprint Atlas 2010* (Oakland, CA: Global Footprint Network, 2010).

17. Steiner, "Landscape Ecological Urbanism: Origins and Trajectories," 333–337.

18. Millennium Ecosystem Assessment, "The Millennium Ecosystem Assessment," (2005), accessed June 19, 2013, http://www.unep.org/maweb/en/index.aspx.

19. Ibid.

20. David C. Rouse and Ignacio F. Bunster-Ossa, *Green Infrastructure: A Landscape Approach* (Chicago, IL: APA Planning Advisory Service, 2013), 1.

Ecological Footprints for Beginners

Our Ecological Footprint: Reducing Human Impact on the Earth (1996)

Mathis Wackernagel and William Rees

Many of us live in cities where we easily forget that nature works in closed loops. We go to the store to buy food with money from the bank machine and, later, get rid of the waste either by depositing it in the back alley or flushing it down the toilet. Big city life breaks natural material cycles and provides little sense of our intimate connection with nature.

Obvious but Profound: We Depend on Nature

Despite this estrangement, we are not just *connected* to nature—we *are* nature. As we eat, drink and breathe, we constantly exchange energy and matter with our environment. The human body is continuously wearing out and rebuilding itself—in fact, we replace almost all the molecules in our bodies about once a year. The atoms of which we are made have already been part of many other living beings. Particles of us once roamed about in a dinosaur, and some of us may well carry an atom of Caesar or Cleopatra.

Nature provides us with a steady supply of the basic requirements for life. We need energy for heat and mobility, wood for housing and paper products, and nutritious food and clean water for healthy living. Through photosynthesis green plants convert sunlight, carbon dioxide (CO_2), nutrients and water into chemical energy (such as fruit and vegetables), and all the food chains that support animal life—including our own—are based on this plant material. Nature also absorbs our wastes and provides life-support services such as climate stability and protection from ultraviolet radiation. Finally, the sheer exuberance and beauty of nature is a source of joy and spiritual inspiration. Since most of us spend our lives in cities and consume goods imported from all over the world, we tend to experience nature merely as a collection of commodities or a place for recreation, rather than the very source of our lives and well-being. . . .

What *Is* an Ecological Footprint?

Ecological footprint analysis is an accounting tool that enables us to estimate the resource consumption and waste assimilation requirements of a defined human population or economy in terms of a corresponding productive land area. Typical questions we can ask with this tool include: how dependent is our study population on resource imports from "elsewhere" and on the waste assimilation capacity of the global commons?, and will nature's productivity be adequate to satisfy the rising material expectations of a growing human population into the next century? William Rees has been teaching the basic concept to planning students for 20 years and it has been developed further since 1990 by Mathis Wackernagel and other students working with Bill on UBC's Healthy and Sustainable Communities Task Force.

To introduce the thinking behind Ecological Footprint analysis, let's explore how our society perceives that pinnacle of human achievement, "the city." Ask for a definition, and most people will talk about a concentrated population or an area dominated by buildings, streets and other human-made artifacts (this is the architect's "built environment"); some will refer to the city as a political entity with a defined boundary containing the area over which the municipal government has jurisdiction; still others may see the city mainly as a concentration of cultural, social and educational facilities that would simply not be possible in a smaller settlement; and, finally, the economically-minded see the city as a node of intense exchange among individuals and firms and as the engine of production and economic growth.

No question, cities are among the most spectacular achievements of human civilization. In every country cities serve as the social, cultural, communications and commercial centers of national life. But something fundamental is missing from the popular perception of the city, something that has so long been taken for granted it has simply slipped from consciousness.

We can get at this missing element by performing a mental experiment based on two simple questions designed to force our thinking beyond conventional limits. First, imagine what would happen to any modem city or urban region—Vancouver, Philadelphia or London—as defined by its political boundaries, the area of built-up land, or the concentration of socioeconomic activities, if it were enclosed in a glass or plastic hemisphere that let in light but prevented material things of any kind from entering or leaving—like the "Biosphere II" project in Arizona. . . . The health and integrity of the entire human system so contained would depend entirely on whatever was initially trapped within the hemisphere. It is obvious to most people that such a city would cease to function and its inhabitants would perish within a few days. The population and the economy contained by the capsule would have been cut off from vital resources and essential waste sinks, leaving it both to starve and to suffocate at the same time! In other words, the ecosystems contained within our imaginary human terrarium would have insufficient "carrying capacity" to support the ecological load imposed by the contained human population. This mental model of a glass hemisphere reminds us rather abruptly of humankind's continuing ecological vulnerability.

The second question pushes us to contemplate this hidden reality in more concrete terms. Let's assume that our experimental city is surrounded by a diverse landscape in which cropland and pasture, forests and watersheds—all the different ecologically productive land-types—are represented in proportion to their actual abundance on the Earth, and that adequate fossil energy is available to support current levels of consumption using prevailing technology. Let's also assume our imaginary glass enclosure is elastically expandable. The question now becomes: how large would the hemisphere have to become before the city at its center could sustain itself indefinitely and exclusively on the land and water ecosystems and the energy resources contained within the capsule? In other words, what is the total area of terrestrial ecosystem types needed continuously to support all the social and economic activities carried out by the people of our city as they go about their daily activities? Keep in mind that land with its ecosystems is needed to produce resources, to assimilate wastes, and to perform various invisible life-support functions. Keep in mind too, that for simplicity's sake, the question as posed does not include the ecologically productive land area needed to support other species independent of any service they may provide to humans.

For any set of specified circumstances—the present example assumes current population, prevailing material standards, existing technologies, etc.—it should be possible to produce a reasonable estimate of the land/water area required by the city concerned to sustain itself. By definition, the total ecosystem area that is essential to the continued existence of the city is its *de facto* Ecological Footprint on the Earth. It should be obvious that the Ecological Footprint of a city will be proportional to both population and *per capita* material consumption. Our estimates show for modern industrial cities the area involved is orders of magnitude larger than the area physically occupied by the city. Clearly, too, the Ecological Footprint includes all land required by the defined population wherever on Earth that land is located. Modern cities and whole countries survive on ecological goods and services appropriated from natural flows or acquired through commercial trade from all over the world. The Ecological Footprint therefore also represents the corresponding population's total "appropriated carrying capacity."

By revealing how much land is required to support any specified lifestyle indefinitely, the Ecological Footprint concept demonstrates the continuing material dependence of human beings on nature. For example, table 7-1 shows the Ecological Footprint of an average Canadian, i.e., the amount of land required from nature to support a typical individual's present consumption. This adds up to almost 4.3 hectares, or a 207 metre square. This is roughly comparable to the area of three city blocks. The column on the left shows various consumption categories and the headings across the top show corresponding land-use categories.

"Energy" land as used in the table means the area of carbon sink land required to absorb the carbon dioxide released by *per capita* fossil fuel consumption (coal, oil and natural gas) assuming atmospheric stability as a goal. Alternatively, this entry could be calculated according to the area of cropland necessary to produce a contemporary biological fuel such as ethanol to substitute for fossil fuel. This alternative produces even higher energy land requirements. "Degraded Land" means land that is no longer available for nature's production because it has been paved over or used for buildings. Examples of the resources in "Services" are the fuel needed to heat hospitals, or the paper and electricity used to produce a bank statement.

To use table 7-1 to find out how much agricultural land is required to produce food for the average Canadian, for example, you would read across the "Food" row to the "Crop" and "Pasture" columns. The table shows that, on average, 0.95 hectares of garden, cropland and pasture is needed for a typical Canadian. Note that none of the entries in the table is a fixed, necessary, or recommended land area. They are simply our estimates of the 1990s ecological demands of typical Canadians. The Ecological Footprints of individuals and whole economies will vary depending on income, prices, personal and prevailing social values as they affect consumer behavior, and technological sophistication—e.g., the energy and material content of goods and services.

Table 7-1

The consumption–land-use matrix for the average Canadian, with 1991 data (Wackernagel and Rees, 1996, Reprinted with permission of New Society Publishers, Redrawn by Yuan Ren, 2014).

Cell Entries = Ecologically Productive Land in [ha/capita]	A Energy	B Degraded Land	C Garden	D Crop	E Pasture	F Forest	Total
1. FOOD	**0.33**		**0.02**	**0.60**	**0.33**	**0.02**	**1.30**
11 fruit, vegs., grain	0.14		0.02	0.18		0.01?	
12 animal products	0.19			0.42	0.33	0.01?	
2. HOUSING	**0.41**	**0.08**	**0.002?**			**0.40**	**0.89**
21 const./maint.	0.06					0.35	
22 operation	0.35					0.05	
3. TRANSPORTATION	**0.79**	**0.10**					**0.89**
31 motorized private	0.60						
32 motorized public	0.07						
33 transp'n of goods	0.12						
4. CONSUMER GOODS	**0.52**	**0.01**		**0.06**	**0.13**	**0.17**	**0.89**
40 packaging	0.10					0.04	
41 clothing	0.11			0.02	0.13		
42 furniture & appli.	0.06					0.03?	
43 books/magazines	0.06					0.10	
44 tobacco & alcohol	0.06			0.04			
45 personal care	0.03						
46 recreation equip	0.10						
47 other goods	0.00						
5. SERVICES	**0.29**	**0.01**					**0.30**
51 gov't (+ military)	0.06						
52 education	0.08						
53 health care	0.08						
54 social services	0.00						
55 tourism	0.01						
56 entertainment	0.01						
57 bank/insurance	0.00						
58 other services	0.05						
TOTAL	**2.34**	**0.20**	**0.02**	**0.66**	**0.46**	**0.59**	**4.27**

The Region

The New Urbanism: Toward Architecture of Community (1994)

Peter Calthorpe

The New Urbanism is concerned with both the pieces and the whole. It applies principles of urban design to the region in two ways. First, urbanism—defined by its diversity, pedestrian scale, public space and structure of bounded neighborhoods—should be applied throughout a metropolitan region regardless of location: in suburbs and new growth areas as well as within the city. And second, the entire region should be "designed" according to similar urban principles. It should, like a neighborhood, be structured by public space, its circulation system should support the pedestrian, it should be both diverse and hierarchical and it should have discernible edges.

The first application is a simple but unique contribution of this movement. Urbanism is now well understood in the city, but rarely applied to the suburb. Although there have been many transgressions over the post war period, the principles of urbanism have clearly reemerged since Jane Jacobs, Vincent Scully, Aldo Rossi, Leon Krier and many others have articulated the traditions. What is new is the application of these principles in suburbia and beyond. Too often we think of these aesthetic, spatial and programmatic principles in terms of density and the inner-city context. But the New Urbanism demonstrates how such ideas can be realized in the contemporary suburban condition and formalized at any density. It shows that the relationship between architecture and public space can be "urban" regardless of building height or mass; that spatial hierarchy and connectedness can be rendered regardless of land-use intensity;

and that pedestrian life can exist in single-family neighborhoods as well as on tenement streets. Applying these principles in the unlikely areas of the modern suburb, while coping with its economic and social imperatives, is one important contribution of the New Urbanism.

The second application acknowledges that the city, its suburbs and their natural environment should be treated as a whole—socially, economically and ecologically. Treating them separately is endemic to many of the problems we now face, and our lack of governance at this scale is a direct manifestation of this disaggregation. Seen as a whole, the American metropolis should be designed with much the same attitude as we design a neighborhood: There should be defined edges (i.e., Urban Growth Boundaries), the circulation system should function for the pedestrian (i.e., supported by regional transit systems), public space should be formative rather than residual (i.e., preservation of major open-space networks), civic and private domains should form a complementary hierarchy (i.e., related cultural centers, commercial districts and residential neighborhoods) and population and use should be diverse (i.e., created by adequate affordable housing and a jobs/housing balance). Developing such an architecture of the region creates the context for a healthy urbanism in neighborhoods, districts and at the city center. The two forms of urbanism work together.

The Crisis of Growth

To understand how the New Urbanism works in a regional context, the evolution of the modern American metropolis must be understood (even if in sketch form as it must be here). For the last 40 years growth has been largely directed by suburban flight, highway capacity and federal government mortgage policy. The typical development cycle started with bedroom communities pioneering the most remote sectors of the metropolitan region.

With federal and state highway investments, such seemingly remote suburbs and small towns became commute-accessible to the existing major job centers. They offered low-cost land and affordable housing for the regional work force. Retail, services, recreation and civic uses followed in proportion to the demand created by the housing.

When they reached critical mass, the new suburban areas began to attract jobs. "Edge Cities," as author Joel Garreau calls them, were soon formed. As these new decentralized job centers grew, the process began again—creating another layer of sprawl extending out from the decentralized job centers. Today, the suburb-to-suburb commute represents 40 percent of total commute trips while suburb-to-city comprises only 20 percent.

Out of this evolution of the modern metropolis there has grown a profound sense of frustration and placelessness. A homogeneous quality overlays the unique nature of each place with chain-store architecture, scaleless office parks and monotonous subdivisions. Even these qualities are easily blurred by the speed at which we move and the isolation we feel in our cars and in our dwellings. At their extreme, the new forms seem to have an empty feeling, reinforcing our mobile state and the instability of our families. Moving at a speed which allows only generic symbols to be recognized, we cannot wonder that the man-made environment seems trite and overstated.

Americans initially moved to the suburbs for privacy, mobility, security and home ownership. What we now have is isolation, congestion, rising crime, pollution and overwhelming costs—costs that ultimately must be paid by taxpayers, businesses and the environment. This sprawling pattern of growth at the edge now produces conditions which frustrate rather than enhance daily life. Meanwhile, our city centers have deteriorated because much of their economic vitality has decanted to the suburbs.

Ironically, the American Dream is now increasingly out of sync with today's culture. Our household makeup has changed dramatically, the workplace and work force have been transformed, family wealth is shrinking and grave environmental concerns have surfaced. But we continue to build post–World War II suburbs as if families were large and had only one breadwinner, the jobs were all downtown, land and energy were endless and another lane on the freeway would end traffic congestion.

Settlement patterns are the physical foundation of our society and, like our society, they are becoming more and more fractured. Development patterns and local zoning laws segregate age groups, income groups, ethnic groups and family types. They isolate people and activities in an inefficient network of congestion and pollution, rather than joining them in diverse and human-scaled communities. Our faith in government and the fundamental sense of commonality at the center of any vital democracy is seeping away in suburbs designed more for cars than people, more for market segments than real communities. Special interest groups now replace the larger community within our political landscape, just as gated subdivisions have replaced neighborhoods.

Our communities historically were embedded in nature, helping set both the unique identity of each place and the physical limits of the community. Local climate, plants, vistas, harbors and ridge lands once defined the special qualities of every memorable place. Today, smog, pavement, toxic soil, receding natural habitats and polluted water contribute to the destruction of neighborhood and home in the largest sense.

We threaten nature and nature now threatens us in return: sunlight causes cancer, air threatens our lungs, rain burns the trees, streams are polluted and soils are toxic. Understanding the qualities of nature in each place, expressing it in the design of communities, integrating it within our towns and respecting its balance are critical to making the human place sustainable and spiritually nourishing.

A Taxonomy of Growth

The problems of growth are not to be solved by limiting the scope, program or location of development. They must be resolved by rethinking the nature and quality of growth itself, in every context. People argue heatedly about growth: where, how much, what type, what density and if it is really necessary at all. Sprawl is bad, infill is good (if it is not in our neighborhood), new towns destroy open space, master-planned communities are sterile and urban redevelopment is fine for "other people." Any region with a high growth demand has several options. It can 1) try to limit overall growth; 2) let the towns and suburbs surrounding the metropolitan center grow uncontrollably until they become a continuous mass; 3) attempt to accommodate growth in redevelopment and infill locations; or 4) plan new towns and new growth areas within reasonable transit proximity of the city center.

Every region needs to find an appropriate mix of these very different options. Each strategy has inherent advantages and problems, which need to be understood.

Limiting growth on a local level without the appropriate regional controls often spreads development into remote areas that are more receptive to sprawl. This increases commuting distances and creates our well known hopscotch land-use patterns.

Sometimes called "managed" or "slow" growth, this strategy is often used by a jurisdiction seeking to avoid its fair share of affordable housing or the expansion of transit. Unless there is a strategy for limiting growth at a regional level, local attempts will only extend and displace the problem.

At the other extreme, allowing the uncontrolled growth of existing suburbs and towns is our most common growth strategy. It has the most familiar results: sprawl, traffic and a loss of the identity for what historically may have been distinct neighborhoods, villages and towns. And it is an approach which seems inevitably to lead to powerful citizens' no-growth movements and growth limitations, thus fueling the cycle of regional sprawl.

Infill and Redevelopment

The best utilization of existing infrastructure and the best opportunity to preserve our open space will come from infill and redevelopment. Therefore it should always be a central part of a region's growth policy. But to expect infill sites to absorb all or even most new development is unrealistic. This is sometimes because there are not enough sites to accommodate the demand, and partly because no-growth neighborhood groups often resist such infill. Once again, without a political force to balance the larger economic and environmental needs of a region against the anti-infill tendency of individual communities, there is little hope such growth will reach even its limited potential. Both urban and suburban infill sites have special concerns and constraints beyond the generic and widespread political problems of NIMBYism (not in my backyard syndrome).

Over the last 30 years, urban infill and redevelopment has been a prime objective for most cities. There have been some successes but many failures. The list of problems and constraints is long: racial tension, gentrification, economic stagnation, bureaucracy, deteriorating schools and red-line appraisals to name a few. There are many ways to resolve or reduce the magnitude of these constraints, and they all need to be considered in future urban infill efforts. But it is clear that such strategies are falling short and additional means to advance urban infill are needed.

Portland, Oregon, is an example of a city and region which has gone beyond the traditional programs for urban infill and revitalization. It has successfully supported infill in two progressive ways: an Urban Growth Boundary (UGB) and zoning that supports a transit system that is focused on the central city. The UGB is a state-mandated limit to growth around the metropolitan region which was established in 1972. Both strategies are central to the thesis of a New Urbanism—that a regional system of open space and transit complemented with pedestrian-friendly development patterns can help revitalize an urban center at the same time it helps to order suburban growth. Downtown Portland, because of its light-rail system, sensitive urban planning and regional limits is now growing in a healthy relationship to its suburbs. Both the UGB and Portland's expanding light-rail system have helped to direct new development and economic activity back into its thriving downtown.

Suburban infill represents a different set of problems and constraints. Typically, no-growth and slow-growth neighborhood groups inhibit the density and mix of uses while driving the cost of suburban development ever upward. The existing street systems and zoning codes stand as further blocks to creating walkable communities. Finally, the density and configurations typical of suburban sprawl make transit a heavily subsidized safety net rather than a real alternative to the car. If we are to have significant growth as suburban infill, much needs to change. Foremost, local citizens must understand that there are options beyond no-growth or sprawl. Local concerns must be tempered with regional needs—an equitable distribution of affordable housing and jobs, preservation of open space and agriculture lands and a viable transit system. This calls for policies and governance which can both educate and guide the complex interaction of economics, ecology, technology, jurisdiction and social equity.

New Growth and Satellite Towns

When urban and suburban infill cannot accommodate the quantity or rate of growth of a region, new growth areas and satellite towns may be considered.

New growth areas are the easiest to develop with transit- and pedestrian-oriented patterns. However there is one caveat: They also may spread the city's size. Satellite towns are typically larger than new growth areas and provide a complete spectrum of shopping, jobs and civic facilities. But both, if well planned and transit-oriented, can complement infill and help to structure and revitalize the metropolitan region.

An effective transit system accomplishes many things. It can invigorate downtown, as transit invariably focuses on the central business district. Adding more sprawling suburbs to a metropolitan area only increases pressure for parking and freeways downtown, while competing with the city for jobs and retail activity.

By contrast, transit delivers people to the heart of our cities, reducing the need for parking and avoiding destructive urban freeway projects. Adding transit-oriented new growth areas and satellite towns can reinforce the city's role as the region's cultural and economic center. The transit system that is supported at the edge with new growth can also become the catalyst for redevelopment and infill at the regional center.

Recent experiences with "new towns" and new growth areas (sometimes called master-planned communities) have given such developments a bad name. In Europe, with some notable exceptions, new towns are predominantly sterile and suburban in character. In America they are sterile, suburban and—even worse—economic failures. But the questions remain: Are these qualities inherent or products of a dysfunctional design philosophy? And if new towns could be designed more intelligently, would they be justified or necessary?

To answer these questions it is useful to understand the history of new town planning. At the turn of the century and during the great depression the theory of new towns evolved in several directions. Ebenezer Howard and the Garden City movement defined a Luddite's vision of small towns built for workers surrounded by a greenbelt, combining the best of city and country. These towns were formed around rail stations and formally configured with a combination of the Romantic and Beaux Arts urban traditions: powerful civic spaces surrounded by village-scaled neighborhoods. In the same period Tony Garnier developed the first Modernist approach to town planning, segregating industry, isolating different uses and freeing buildings from the street. His was the first such vision of the 20th century city. During the depression Le Corbusier and Frank Lloyd Wright expanded this vision in the urban and suburban context while retaining fundamental Modernist principles: segregation of use, love of the auto and dominance of private over public space. In these utopias (which after World War II came to guide our development patterns) the street as the community's habitable common ground disintegrated. Even in the most progressive of the post–World War II new towns and master-planned communities, these basic Modernist concepts have compromised, if not completely destroyed, their ability to evolve into vital communities. The task of the New Urbanism is to learn from these failures, avoiding their sterile and suburban character while defining a form of growth which can help mend the metropolis.

Urbanism of the Pieces

The specific nature of a metropolitan region will dictate which growth strategies are necessary and useful. Some regions with a very slow growth rate may only need incremental infill. Some regions with fast growth and much undeveloped suburban land may benefit from both infill and new growth area projects. Other regions may require all three strategies, including satellite towns, to absorb massive growth without destroying the identity of existing places. One thing is certain: With any blend of these forms, it is the quality of development, not just its location or size that is the principal problem and opportunity of growth.

Sprawl is destructive in any growth strategy. Contemporary suburbs have failed because they lack, as do many of the so-called "modern" new towns and edge cities, the fundamental qualities of real towns: pedestrian scale, an identifiable center and edge, integrated diversity of use and population and defined public space. They may have diversity in use and user, but these diverse elements are segregated by the car. They have none of the places for casual and spontaneous interaction which create vital neighborhoods, quarters or towns. Unless urban infill sites, suburban new development areas and satellite towns embody the qualities of the New Urbanism, they will fail too. In every context, therefore, the quality of new development in a region should follow town-like principles—housing for a diverse population, a full mix of uses, walkable streets, positive public space, integrated civic and commercial centers, transit orientation and accessible open space.

Urban infill often succeeds because those urban qualities pre-exist and need only be preserved, not necessarily created. Nevertheless we see many urban infill projects which succeed in destroying these desirable pre-existing qualities. For smaller parcels in existing urban neighborhoods the task is to complete the mix of a community while honoring the unique qualities of the place. For suburban sites, even with the political constraints, mixed-use neighborhoods can be infilled. Far from being blank slates, these suburban infill sites sometimes offer rich histories to build on as well as debilitating sprawl to overcome.

Satellite towns at the outer edge of the metropolitan region can easily afford features that more expensive areas cannot provide—greenbelts, transit and affordable housing to name a few. At the same time they buffer their own edges with greenbelts, they can help establish permanent edges for the region. Without greenbelted satellite towns or stable Urban Growth Boundaries, a fast growing region will continually expand into and threaten close-in natural edges and open space. Additionally, satellite towns can help manage the growth of older suburbs and towns by absorbing excess development.

Urbanism of the Whole

The way these pieces are woven together into a whole is also part of the New Urbanism. Beyond resolving the balance between new growth and infill, and controlling the urban qualities of both, there is the challenge of creating a truly urban metropolitan form—oriented to public rather than private space, diverse, hierarchical and pedestrian-scaled.

Clearly, the Urban Growth Boundary is the regional equivalent of a defined neighborhood edge. These boundaries create identity for the whole and express the need to preserve nature as a limit to human habitat. Similarly, major open space within the region can be seen as a "village green" at a mega-scale. This internal commons, like the boundaries, establishes the ecological and conservation values which can help form the basis of regional character.

Urbanism at the regional scale has other parallels. Pedestrian scale translates into transit systems. Transit can order and formalize the region in much the same way a street network orders a neighborhood. It supports the life of the pedestrian throughout the region.

Diversity is a fundamental component of urbanism at both the neighborhood and regional scale. At the regional scale it is too often taken for granted—but diversity without connections (segregated diversity) is not urban at any scale. The diverse population and functions within a region should have a connecting fabric which makes the region vital and inclusionary. Our freeway and arterial networks now seem to privatize and isolate the components of a region more than connect them.

Finally, urbanism articulates the hierarchy of public and private, of civic and commercial. At the regional scale this means that the diversity and differences throughout the region should find a complementary and grand order. By this I mean that neighborhoods and districts should not just repeat one another but, much like the private and civic buildings of a neighborhood, find appropriate locations to express relative focus and importance.

These two dimensions—urbanism within neighborhoods and urbanism as regional form giver—are meant to inform and direct interventions within the existing framework of our cities, suburbs and towns. Infill, new development or reconstruction can and inevitably will shape the principles of a New Urbanism.

The goal is to apply the best of urban design to both the region and the neighborhood—applying them to a new context and at a new scale. The New Urbanism is not just about the city or the suburb. It is about the way we conceive of community and how we form the region—it is about diversity, scale and public space in every context.

Smart Growth: Why We Discuss It More than We Do It

Journal of the American Planning Association (2005)

Anthony Downs

As I speak to audiences around the country about how to cope with growth, people often ask me, "Where is Smart Growth being implemented most effectively?" I usually reply, "Smart Growth is much more talked about than actually carried out in practice." That does not mean no regions are actually using Smart Growth policies. But it does mean that such regions are greatly outnumbered by others where Smart Growth principles are commonly discussed but not actually put into effect. Why is that the case?

The basic reason is that carrying out Smart Growth principles encounters many obstacles that are not obvious at the outset, but emerge strongly as advocates try to apply those principles. Those obstacles have inhibited the ability of urban planners, government officials, environmentalists, and real estate developers who promote Smart Growth to achieve their initial objectives. This article explores why I believe that is the case.

The Genesis and Nature of Smart Growth

Smart Growth was originally conceived as a reaction to what many planners believed were undesirable features of continuing growth through "suburban sprawl" (Burchell, Listokin, et al., 2000; Burchell, Lowenstein, et al., 2002; Downs, 2001a). Those undesirable features included the following:

- Unlimited outward and "leapfrog" expansion of low-density new development.
- Large-scale conversion of open space and environmentally sensitive lands to urban uses.
- Lack of choice among housing types and neighborhood configurations.
- Worsening traffic congestion and air pollution caused by more intensive use of automotive vehicles for ground travel.
- Costly requirements to expand roads, sewers, water systems, and other infrastructures outward rather than repairing and using those already in place.
- Failure to redevelop existing older neighborhoods.
- Segregation of land uses rather than a mixing of uses that reduces the need for travel.

Since Smart Growth was created to reduce or eliminate these perceived ills, its advocates tend to promote opposite principles of action. Thus, the most common principles of Smart Growth are the following:

1. Limiting outward extension of new development in order to make settlements more compact and preserve open spaces. This can be done via urban growth boundaries or utility districts.
2. Raising residential densities in both new-growth areas and existing neighborhoods.
3. Providing for more mixed land uses and pedestrian-friendly layouts to minimize the use of cars on short trips.
4. Loading the public costs of new development onto its consumers via impact fees rather than having those costs paid by the community in general.
5. Emphasizing public transit to reduce the use of private vehicles.
6. Revitalizing older existing neighborhoods.

Other Smart Growth principles less universally advocated include these:

7. Creating more affordable housing.
8. Reducing obstacles to developer entitlement.
9. Adopting more diverse regulations concerning aesthetics, street layouts, and design.

In reality, different groups in society emphasize different constellations of these elements, depending upon their own perspectives. Thus, the real estate development community plays down limitations on outward development, big-city officials strongly favor redeveloping existing older areas plus repairing existing infrastructures, and urban planners and environmentalists accept all the above principles and stress using more public transit to cut down on vehicle trips and miles of travel. Thus, Smart Growth does not mean the same thing to everyone. In reality, it has almost come to stand for "whatever form of growth I like best" in the opinion of whoever is speaking. Nevertheless, the first six principles set forth above are generally considered key elements of most Smart Growth programs actually being promoted across the nation.

Who Actually Originates Pressures to Implement Smart Growth Principles?

Pressures to put Smart Growth principles into practice tend to originate from three different groups. . . . *nongovernment environmentalists* who are appalled by sprawl and want to stop its absorption of so much open land [. . .] *urban planners and other local public officials* . . . seek to preserve local government fiscal resources and keep local taxes low. . . . *innovative private real estate developers* who are trying to get permission from local governments to build specific new projects. They promote Smart Growth principles to support their desires to create large-scale mixed-use projects, use higher densities than in surrounding areas, and create a variety of housing types in a single project. . . .

One thing these three main sources of promotion for Smart Growth have in common is that they do *not* include significant numbers of plain citizens—especially local homeowners, who are the majority in most suburban communities. To put it another way, *most pressures to adopt Smart Growth policies do not come from the citizenry at large but from one or more of these special interest groups.* In almost every community, all three of these promotional groups are relatively small compared to the general citizenry. Hence these groups are all challenged by the need to persuade lots of "plain citizens" to agree with their views. Such persuasion is necessary in our democracy in order to shift a powerfully entrenched set of policies like those embodied in suburban sprawl to something quite different. It is a wise old saying that "You can't beat something with nothing!" Therefore, to beat sprawl, these groups must persuade significant numbers of local citizens to support adoption of a new and different set of growth-related policies—that is, Smart Growth policies. How to accomplish such persuasion is a critical aspect of getting Smart Growth policies actually put into practice.

How Applying Smart Growth Principles Generates Problems

Given the widespread hostility to continued suburban sprawl in America among professional planners and environmentalists, and even among many real estate developers, it seems that the major principles of Smart Growth ought to be in the process of being vigorously applied in most metropolitan areas. Yet I do not believe that is the case. True, quite a few areas have effectively implemented one or two principles of Smart Growth—the ones least difficult to implement. But few regions have put into practice the most problematic principles. And almost no areas (not even Portland, Oregon) have implemented all of Smart Growth's principles. The main reason is that carrying out those principles requires adopting one or more of eight other principles of action that are not nearly as widely praised nor as readily accepted by the American public. These obstacles are described below.

Redistributing Benefits and Costs of Developments

Smart Growth policies differ fundamentally from the sprawl-related development processes long dominant in almost all U.S. metropolitan areas. Therefore, changing from sprawl to Smart Growth almost inevitably involves redistributing the benefits and costs associated with urban development generally. For example, preventing growth from moving outward without limits from built-up areas by shifting to more compact growth concentrated very close to built-up areas changes the location of future subdivisions. It reduces the chances that owners of far-outlying parcels will "capture" future subdivisions, thereby profiting from big increases in land values. At the same time, this shift increases the chances that owners of close-in sites will capture higher density projects, thereby benefiting from large increases in land values. In short, it greatly alters the potential benefit structure currently embodied in the status quo, turning some now-likely future gainers into losers, and vice versa. But every basic change in development strategy that causes such major shifts in who gains and who loses upsets widespread expectations among yesterday's potential gainers, thereby alienating them. This naturally makes those once-potential gainers hostile to the idea of such change. Moreover, a loss of a potential future benefit tends to be felt more intensely than the gain of such an uncertain benefit. True, this is nothing new; even just building a new highway also generates winners and losers among land owners affected by that road. . . .

Shifting Power and Authority from Local to Regional Levels

Several key Smart Growth principles require government action at the regional or state level, not at the local government level where most powers over land use planning now reside. But achieving regional action requires shifting a significant degree of existing land use planning authority from local governments to some higher-level organization. In most metropolitan areas, no such higher-level organization exists, short of the state government itself. And even where such an organization does exist, most local governments do not want to yield any of their existing power over land use decisions to anyone else. "Home rule" powers are among the most vigorously defended of any authorities entrusted to local governments.

Yet this kind of power shift would be necessary for any real check on the outward expansion of urban development far beyond presently built-up areas. Although individual communities can adopt local urban growth boundaries, unless all such communities within a region adopt such boundaries that are closely coordinated (which almost never happens), no one community alone can stop growth from leaping out into open country beyond its boundaries. And even if all the localities in a metropolitan area adopted a coordinated set of urban growth limits, that would not prevent private developers from going outside the boundaries of that metropolitan area and starting new subdivisions in farther-out counties. This is precisely what is now happening in both the Washington, DC, and Minneapolis/St. Paul metropolitan areas. Only state governments are capable of *both* creating regional urban growth boundaries *and* stringently limiting growth outside those boundaries (as in Oregon), which can stop such long-distance "leapfrog" developments. But if these developments are not stopped, urban growth boundaries have only limited power to halt sprawl. . . .

Increasing Residential Density

A second critical problem in carrying out Smart Growth principles involves an inherent conflict of views within the minds of millions of American homeowners. In 2004, homeowning households comprised 69% of all American households, according to the U.S. Census Bureau (2004). In most suburbs, they form a significant majority of all voters. Nearly all such households strongly desire to maintain the market values of the homes they occupy. In most cases, those homes are their largest single asset, and those assets have been rising in value significantly in the past few years. Thus, from 1999 to 2004, the median value of single-family homes sold across the U.S. rose from $133,300 to $184,100, or by 38.1% (National Association of Realtors, 2005).

In order to protect the values of their homes from possibly declining, most homeowners (especially in the suburbs) are reluctant to permit into their existing neighborhoods any entry of additional housing units that would sell for lower prices than their own homes. They fear such lower-cost homes would reduce the desirability (and therefore the prices) of their homes too. This normally means they do not want any additional low-cost for-sale units built there, or any rental units built in primarily ownership neighborhoods.

This economic motive for preventing such changes in their neighborhoods is reinforced by the widespread American view that it is undesirable for lower-income households to move near them for social, educational, and security reasons. In addition, many households fear higher density would mean more traffic congestion and more crowded schools and other facilities.

These sources of hostility to local changes that might reduce home values are the foundation of NIMBYism. It is the belief that "although some changes in society are necessary, Not In My Back Yard please!" This attitude frequently surfaces whenever any increases in neighborhood density are proposed in built-up areas.

On the other hand, many suburban homeowners are also opposed to continued expansion of their metropolitan regions through more sprawl. They believe sprawl results in costlier tax bills to pay for the provision of infrastructures stretching out into open spaces. They also oppose more absorption of open land that they would like to have readily available to them. This hostility towards more sprawl is more general and abstract, however, than their hostility towards any increases in residential density near them. Thus, many suburban homeowners are likely to support Smart Growth in the abstract, but oppose its specific manifestations when the increases in density it calls for are planned near them (Fischel, 2001). . . .

Raising Housing Prices

Yet another problem caused by Smart Growth policies is a tendency to raise housing prices. After all, Smart Growth proposes to locate more housing units on smaller total amounts of land than in the past as part of its making future growth more compact. Smart Growth also seeks to set aside large amounts of open space as unavailable for housing purposes. And Smart Growth wants to prevent "leapfrog" subdivisions where households looking for low-cost homes on inexpensive far-out land can "keep driving until they qualify." This removes the least expensive land from availability for housing.

The resulting higher density on land still usable for housing is normally accompanied by higher land prices per gross acre. True, those higher land prices can be offset by smaller lots per dwelling, but there is no certainty that this will be the case. If the proportion of all housing units built shifts markedly towards higher shares of multifamily dwellings, as has happened in Portland, Oregon, then land costs per dwelling may not necessarily rise. But they still could rise even in that case. And if many residents continue to prefer detached single-family homes on their own lots, the land price per dwelling may rise considerably. . . .

Failing to Reduce Traffic Congestion

A fourth problem generated by some Smart Growth policies is their inherent inability to achieve the results they promise. This defect is especially true concerning policies that promise to reduce traffic congestion by increasing public reliance upon public transit. My own extensive analysis of traffic congestion in *Still Stuck in Traffic* (Downs, 2004b) convinced me that such congestion is likely to get worse throughout the world as societies become wealthier and more populous. Experience in the United States in particular shows that building additional public transit facilities almost never reduces traffic congestion in a region, once that congestion has reached the point of serious slowdowns during major rush hours. For example, although Portland, Oregon, doubled the extent of its light rail system's tracks in the 1990s, and significantly increased ridership on that system, traffic congestion became more intense than before. Why? First, a high percentage of the new light rail riders shifted from buses rather than private vehicles. Second, population growth in the region overcame any slight improvements in traffic congestion caused by the added light rail facilities. Similarly, additions of light rail systems in San Diego, San Jose, Denver, Dallas, and many other American communities have not reduced the intensity of traffic congestion there. In the period from 1980 to 2000, the U.S. added 1.2 additional cars, trucks, or buses to the existing vehicle population for every 1.0 additional man, woman, or child added to the human population. As long as that ratio continues, and our human population keeps growing around 30 million per decade, no policies are likely to reduce traffic congestion in any major U.S. metropolitan areas. . . .

Increasing the "Red Tape" of New Development

Shifting new development from an outward-oriented sprawl pattern into a more inward-oriented compact pattern typically increases the amount of "red tape" that developers must go through to complete projects, such as preparing environmental impact, endangered species, and historical preservation studies; getting applications processed by multiple departments in the local government; etc. This occurs because larger cities tend to have much more detailed and onerous permission processes for new projects than those outlying suburbs in which sprawl normally occurs. Moreover, many big cities also have strong construction labor unions that may impose higher wage costs upon projects within their boundaries than for projects in outlying suburban communities, where most housing is built with nonunion labor. These conditions increase the resistance of developers to adopting more compact development strategies, other things equal. More compact development also favors large-scale real estate developers, who have deeper pockets than small-scale developers with which to bear the greater delays and higher costs of new in-city projects. That is why developers promoting projects based upon Smart Growth values tend to be larger-scale developers. Small-scale developers are more likely to want to stick to building on suburban greenfield sites.

Restricting Profits for Owners of Outlying Land

The compact growth pattern dictated by Smart Growth principles restricts the ability of farmers and other owners of outlying land to take advantage of the higher land prices they could obtain from further sprawl development. By confining a lot of open outlying land to farming or open space. Smart Growth diminishes the capital gains the owners of such land can expect to receive from future development. On the other hand. Smart Growth increases the capital gains that owners of vacant land, or land covered with obsolete structures, within built-up areas are likely to receive from in-fill projects. However, the number of persons owning open land outside built-up areas who *might* profit from further sprawl is normally much larger than the number owning in-fill sites within built-up areas likely to profit from Smart Growth. That is because the amount of undeveloped open land outside built-up areas greatly exceeds the amount of land on usable in-fill or other close-in sites. Therefore, this obstacle tends to generate more voters resistant to Smart Growth strategies than voters supporting them.

In some regions, planners have attempted to offset the loss of potential gains from new development for owners of outlying land by creating transferable development rights (TDRs) for such owners. Under this arrangement, owners of outlying sites agree to limit future development on their land in return for receiving TDRs. The owners can then sell those TDRs to owners of closer-in land as a means of allowing the latter to increase permissible densities on their sites. However, this arrangement has not fully compensated most owners of outlying land for what they believe is the loss of future development profits when Smart Growth blocks development on their sites.

Replacing "Disjointed Incrementalism" with Regional Planning

There is a fundamental conflict between developing a single, overall plan to direct future population growth within a region and permitting such growth to occur through an unplanned, decentralized process of "disjointed incrementalism." Many Americans consider the first approach to be excessively socialistic in nature. They prefer the traditional American method of allowing individual developers, landowners, and local communities to make unrelated choices of where to put future growth. The resulting absence of regional planning makes it difficult to carry out Smart Growth policies that depend on such planning, such as limiting outward expansion of new development, preserving outlying open space, and creating new high-density development clusters around fixed-rail transit stations. But others think such an unplanned approach will only exacerbate existing undesirable conditions generated by past sprawl, such as "excessive" absorption of open space by urbanization. This is not a purely ideological argument. Its outcome partly hinges on whether centralized or regional planners can anticipate future trends in population growth, technological change, and the market's locational preferences as well as, or better than, individual entrepreneurs creating particular new subdivisions without any overall plan. There is no clear evidence regarding which approach is more effective in the long run, partly because so few U.S. regions have tried any regional planning of their growth. However, up to now, the disjointed incrementalism approach to future growth remains the overwhelmingly dominant method used in American metropolitan areas, mainly because there are very few effective regional bodies with the authority to influence where future growth will occur.

How These Obstacles Inhibit Implementation of Smart Growth Policies

The eight obstacles to implementing Smart Growth policies set forth above have quite different impacts upon each of the nine Smart Growth policies described earlier. The resulting relationships are briefly described in table 7-2. Each row in this chart represents one of the nine Smart Growth policies frequently advocated in various regions. Each column represents one of the eight obstacles to such policies that arise when trying to implement them. Therefore, each cell represents the probable interaction of one policy and one obstacle. Dark squares indicate that the particular obstacle concerned normally has a significant negative impact on implementation of that particular policy. For example, the first policy, limiting outward extension of growth, is strongly negatively affected by the second obstacle, the need to shift power from local to

Table 7-2

Obstacles to implementing Smart Growth policies (Downs, 2005, Reprinted with the permission of American Planning Association).

Smart growth policy	Redistributing benefits/costs	Shifting power	Increasing density	Raising housing prices	Failing to reduce congestion	Increasing red tape	Restricting profits	Establishing regional planning
1. Limiting outward extension of new developments	■	■	○	▨	○	○	■	▨
2. Raising densities in both new-growth and existing neighborhoods	○	▨	■	▨	○	○	○	○
3. Providing for more mixed land uses and pedestrian-friendly environments	○	▨	○	○	▨	○	○	○
4. Loading public costs of new development onto residents of growth areas	■	○	○	■	○	▨	▨	○
5. Emphasizing public transit to reduce the use of private vehicles	○	▨	○	○	▨	○	○	○
6. Revitalizing older existing neighborhoods	▨	○	▨	▨	○	○	○	○
7. Creating more affordable housing	▨	■	○	◆	○	▨	○	▨
8. Reducing obstacles to developer entitlement	▨	■	○	◆	○	○	◆	○
9. Adopting more diverse regulations on aesthetics, street layouts, and design	○	○	◆	○	◆	○	○	○

■ Large negative impact   ▨ Some negative impact   ◆ Policy reduces obstacle   ○ Not related regional authorities. This occurs because so many local officials and other citizens are opposed to shifting any of their local government authority over land use decisions to any regional or higher-level agency. So they tend to oppose limiting outward extensions of growth because doing so requires such a power shift.

Lighter squares indicate that the obstacle in that column has some negative impact on implementing the policy in that row, but not necessarily a decisively prohibitive impact. Diamonds show that the policy in that row actually reduces the negative impact of that obstacle on the implementation of that policy. Thus, the policy of creating more affordable housing tends to offset the impact of Smart Growth in raising housing prices, though that policy may also arouse hostility among homeowners who want home prices to rise higher.

Circles indicate no significant relationship between the policy in that row and the obstacle in that column. A significant relationship is lacking in 43 of the 72 cells in this matrix. Of course, the relationships described in all 72 cells represent my views—other observers may arrive at different conclusions concerning specific cells. Nevertheless, this matrix provides a clear way of relating each obstacle to each proposed Smart Growth policy.

This chart clearly shows that certain obstacles affect the implementation of far more Smart Growth policies than others. Thus, the obstacle "Shifting power" negatively affects implementation of six out of the nine Smart Growth policies. All six of those policies require some movement of power from local governments to more regional agencies. At the other extreme, the obstacle "Increasing red tape" only inhibits implementation of two Smart Growth policies, and then only partly. The obstacle "Raising housing prices" negatively affects four Smart Growth policies because they tend to raise housing prices. But the same obstacle also positively helps in the implementation of two other policies ("Creating more affordable housing" and "Reducing obstacles to developer entitlement") because they tend to reduce housing prices.

This chart also clearly shows that some Smart Growth policies are likely to encounter much more difficulty getting implemented than others. The policy of "Limiting outward extension of new developments" is likely to be hindered by five out of the eight obstacles, three of which will impose serious negative impacts. Conversely, the policy "Adopting more diverse regulations on aesthetics, street layouts, and design" is far more likely to be implemented because it helps reduce two obstacles and is not hindered by any others.

However, this matrix does not provide clear guidance about the degree of difficulty each Smart Growth policy is likely to encounter when advocates try to implement it. Why not? Because it does not quantify the interplay of different obstacles in relation to each specific policy. To provide more definite guidance of that type, a second chart is also presented. In table 7-3, the rows again

Table 7-3

Likelihood of implementing Smart Growth policies (Downs, 2005, Reprinted with the permission of American Planning Association).

Smart Growth policy	Arouses opposition among these	Garners support among these	Opposition vs. support	Likelihood of implementation
1. Limiting outward extension of new developments	Owners of land in outlying areas now blocked form development; real estate developers	Owners of close-in in-fill parcels not emphasized for higher-density development	Losers likely to vastly outnumber winners, and may feel their losses more strongly than winners feel their gains	Very unlikely
2. Raising densities in both new-growth and existing neighborhoods	Homeowners living near where higher density is proposed in both new and existing neighborhoods	Environmentalists; owners of in-fill sites where high density is proposed	Local NIMBYs intensely oppose any higher densities near them, pressuring local officials to block higher densities	Very unlikely
3. Providing for more mixed land uses and pedestrian-friendly environments	Only a few residents who dislike mixed-use environments; also retail chain operating firms	New Urbanism supporters; public transit supporters; many existing residents	Opposition likely to be weak except for unwillingness of retail chain operators to run small neighborhood outlets	Likely
4. Loading public costs of new development onto residents of growth areas	Renters wanting to restrain housing costs; households seeking to buy first homes	Residents of most existing neighborhoods; local government officials	Supporters of passing most public costs onto new residents will almost always outnumber those who pay because they live in new areas	Very likely

Policy	Opponents	Supporters	Analysis	Likelihood
5. Emphasizing public transit to reduce the use of private vehicles	Road builders who lose funds shifted to transit; trucking firms and auto companies	Supporters of more public transit facilities; builders of transit-oriented developments	Urban planners who favor transit tend to dominate MPOs; users of private vehicles do not feel harmed if more others shift to transit	Somewhat likely
6. Revitalizing older existing neighborhoods	Developers of outlying sites competing with older neighborhoods for funds	Big-city labor union workers; big-city local officials; owners of in-fill sites and sites in older areas	Key factor is size of financing available to revitalize older areas; if it is great, resistance to revitalization will be low	Somewhat likely
7. Creating more affordable housing	Homeowners fearing lower-cost housing will reduce values of their homes; local officials responding to them	Renters and low-income households needing housing assistance; low-income housing advocates	Resistance to any large amount of relatively low-cost housing is likely to be great because of homeowner attitudes	Unlikely
8. Reducing obstacles to developer entitlement	Environmentalists; home-owners seeking to keep local prices rising; historic preservationists; big-city labor unions	Home builders and real estate developers; landowners of sites on which developers want to create new projects	Not clear which group will have the greatest political power, though changing existing rules is different	Unclear
9. Adopting more diverse regulations on aesthetics, street layouts, and design	Historic preservationists	New Urbanists; real estate developers; home builders; urban planners	The cost of broadening existing regulations is very low and supporters are strong	Very likely

represent the nine Smart Growth policies described earlier, while the columns present a calculation of the resistance or support each policy is likely to encounter. The second column indicates which groups in society are likely to oppose each policy, while the third shows which groups are likely to support each one. The fourth column compares the strength of opposition and support among these groups, and the fifth arrives at a conclusion concerning how favorable the prospects for implementing each policy are likely to be. Again, the cells in this matrix represent only my best judgment, based upon my past experience and the literature on Smart Growth. Other observers may reach quite different conclusions. But this matrix should help anyone interested in this subject arrive at systematic conclusions about the likelihood any one policy will be adopted under "normal" circumstances.

This admittedly rough analysis shows the following results:

- Two Smart Growth policies—"Limiting outward extension of new developments" and "Raising densities in both new-growth and existing neighborhoods"—are *Very unlikely* to be implemented. Both require shifting considerable authority from local to regional bodies and would generate strong opposition from heavily affected groups.
- Implementation of "Creating more affordable housing" is considered *Unlikely* because it would arouse opposition from local homeowners trying to prevent the values of their own homes from being weakened by the appearance of lower-cost housing nearby.
- Two other Smart Growth policies—"Loading public costs of new development onto residents of growth areas" and "Adopting more diverse regulations on street layouts, aesthetics, and design"—are *Very likely* to be implemented. The first benefits existing residents, who vastly outnumber potential newcomers. The second has no significant negative costs.
- Implementation of three other Smart Growth policies is considered either *Likely* or *Somewhat likely*. "Providing for mixed land uses and pedestrian friendly environments," "Emphasizing public transit to reduce the use of private vehicles," and "Revitalizing older existing neighborhoods." However, the last is likely only when adequate public funds are available, and the second is not likely to change commuting behavior very much.
- Whether "Reducing obstacles to developer entitlement" will be readily implemented or not is *Unclear*.

This analysis indicates that prospects for a metropolitan area adopting an entire broad Smart Growth strategy are very low. The political resistance likely to be generated by shifting the requisite authority from local to regional bodies, by raising densities in most neighborhoods, and by blocking outward extension of future growth is too great to be easily overcome. Thus, the central idea of Smart Growth—constraining future development into more compact, higher-density patterns—is not very likely to be adopted by many regions.

On the other hand, changes in certain development rules within local governments designed to broaden housing styles, permit more mixed uses, create more pedestrian ways, and push most of the public costs of new development onto residents of new-growth areas are far more likely to be implemented. These policies can be carried out without having local governments lose any of their existing land use powers.

The Crucial Role of State Governments

An overall Smart Growth strategy that encompasses most of the specific policies discussed above cannot really be carried out in any U.S. metropolitan area without the active advocacy and strong support of the state government concerned. Only the state government has the Constitutional power to shift authority over certain types of land use planning from local governments to regional or statewide agencies with the scope to carry out many Smart Growth policies. Only the state government can both pressure metropolitan areas to agree upon a single urban growth boundary for the entire region, and then prohibit further development outside that boundary within reasonable commuting distance of the region. Without such a prohibition, developers will quickly leapfrog new subdivisions beyond the urban growth boundary into nearby counties outside the metropolitan area's legal limits. That will soon undermine the whole idea of confining future growth into a more compact area.

The state government's powers are also necessary for many other aspects of Smart Growth policies. Raising densities in both existing and new-growth areas on a consistent basis throughout a metropolitan area requires powers that go beyond those of individual local governments, which cannot alter what neighboring governments do. So does locating affordable housing throughout many parts of a region, rather than concentrating it within older central cities, as has often occurred in the past. Any attempts to shift more ground movement to public transit requires a regional plan for where new transit facilities should be located. That is in theory within the jurisdiction of the regional Metropolitan Planning Organization, but the state government's planning and condemnation powers will also be critical.

Past experience shows that state government is likely to become actively involved in implementing Smart Growth policies only if the state's governor assumes a powerful leadership role. The governor is best situated to coordinate the efforts of myriad state agencies related to growth, and to provide them with the incentives to make Smart Growth a reality. Even then, gubernatorial leadership may not be enough to overcome all the obstacles to implementing Smart Growth, as has been shown in Maryland. Yet without such leadership, chances of getting any specific region within a state to adopt an overall Smart Growth strategy are dim indeed.

This analysis also shows that getting effective Smart Growth policies adopted in a multistate metropolitan area will be extraordinarily difficult. Although individual county governments can try such policies, as in the Washington, DC, area, their efforts are likely to be undermined by the failure of all their neighboring counties to do likewise.

Conclusion

Many Americans unhappy with several past results of sprawl development have devised an alternative approach that has come to be known as Smart Growth. The policies incorporated into the Smart Growth vision have a strong intellectual and emotional appeal, compared to more sprawl. But trying to implement those policies requires adopting a whole set of additional policies that are much less appealing to most Americans. Those intermediary policies include changing the powers and scope of long-established governmental traditions, especially local home rule and relatively low-density living patterns. Unless the proponents of Smart Growth realize the necessity of carrying out such intermediary policies and devise ways of getting more political support for doing so. Smart Growth is likely to remain a vision that is much more talked about than carried out in practice.

References

Advisory Commission on Regulatory Barriers to Affordable Housing. *Not in My Back Yard: Removing Barriers to Affordable Housing.* Washington, DC: Government Printing Office, 1991.

American Planning Association. *Policy Guide on Smart Growth.* The Association, 2001.

Beaumont, Constance Epton, ed. *Challenging Sprawl: Organizational Responses to a National Problem.* Washington, DC: National Trust for Historic Preservation, 1999.

Benfield, F. Kaid, Matthew D. Raimi, and Donald D.T. Chen. *Once There Were Greenfields: How Urban Sprawl Is Undermining America's Environment, Economy and Social Fabric.* Washington, DC: Natural Resources Defense Council and Surface Transportation Policy Project.

Braybrooke, David, and Charles Edward Lindblom. *A Strategy of Decision: Policy Evaluation as a Social Process.* New York: Free Press of Glencoe, 1963.

Burchell, Robert W., David Listokin, and Catherine C. Galley. "Smart Growth: More Than A Ghost of Urban Policy Past, Less than a Bold New Horizon." *Housing Policy Debate* 11, no. 4 (2000): 821–79.

Burchell, Robert W., George Lowenstein, William R. Dolphin, Catherine C. Galley, Anthony Downs, Samuel Seskin, Katherine Gray Still, and Terry Moore. "Costs of Sprawl 2000." *Transit Cooperative Research Program Report* 74. Washington, DC: National Academy Press (2002).

Craig, T. "Maryland Panel Backs Study of Route 32 Widening; Vote to By-Pass "Smart Growth" Angers Activists." *Washington Post* (2004): B04.

Downs, Anthony, R. Burchell, C. Galley, and D. Listokin. "The Activities and Benefits of Smart Growth." *Wharton Real Estate Review* 6, no. 1 (2002): 86–93.

Downs, Anthony, ed. *Growth Management and Affordable Housing: Do They Conflict?* Washington, DC: Brookings Institution Press, 2004.

———. "An Approach to Analyzing the Impacts of 'Smart Growth' upon Economic Development." *Economic Development Review* 17, no. 4 (2001): 9–17.

———. "Growth Management, Smart Growth, and Affordable Housing." *Growth Management and Affordable Housing: Do They Conflict?* (2004): 264–74.

———. "What Does 'Smart Growth' Really Mean?" *Planning* 67, no. 4 (2001): 20–25.

———. *The Impacts of Smart Growth upon the Economy*. Land Use Institute of the New Jersey Institute for Continuing Legal Education, New Brunswick, NJ, 2003.

———. *Dealing Effectively with Fast Growth*. Washington, DC: Brookings Institution Policy Brief no. 67, 2000.

———. *New Visions for Metropolitan America*. Washington, DC: Brookings Institution Press, 1994.

———. *Opening Up the Suburbs: An Urban Strategy for America*. New Haven, CT: Yale University Press, 1973.

———. *Still Stuck in Traffic: Coping with Peak-Hour Traffic Congestion*. Washington, DC: Brookings Institution Press, 2004.

Fischel, William A. *The Homevoter Hypothesis: How Home Values Influence Local Government Taxation, School Finance, and Land-Use Policies*. Cambridge, MA: Harvard University Press, 2001.

Goldberg, Steven D. "Smart Growth Techniques Pave the Way for Affordable Housing." On Common Ground, 2003. 18–23.

Governor's Sustainable Washington Advisory Panel. *A New Path Forward: Action Plan for a Sustainable Washington: Achieve Long-term Economic, Social, and Environmental Vitality* (2003).

Lewis, Roger K. "Sprawl Is Here to Stay as Long as Suburbs Represent the American Dream." *Washington Post* (2004): F05.

Meck, Stuart. "Growing Smart Legislative Guidebook: Model Statutes for Planning and the Management of Change." *National Resources & Environment* 17 (2002): 175.

National Association of Home Builders. *Smart Growth Policy Statement: Building Better Places to Live, Work, and Play*. Washington, DC: Author, 1999.

National Association of Industrial and Office Parks. *Growing to Greatness: Creating America's Quality Work Places*. Herndon, VA: Author, 1999.

Nelson, Arthur C., and S. Wachter. "Growth Management and Affordable Housing Policy." *Journal of Affordable Homing and Community Development Law* 12, no. 1(2003): 173–87.

Orfield, Myron. *Metropolitics: A Regional Agenda for Community and Sustainability*. Washington, DC: Brookings Institution Press, 1997.

Pendall, Rolf. "Local Land Use Regulation and the Chain of Exclusion." *Journal of the American Planning Association* 66, no. 2 (2000): 125–42.

Porter, Douglas R. *Managing Growth in America's Communities*. Washington, DC: Island Press, 1997.

Urban Land Institute. *Smart Growth: Economy, Community, Environment*. Washington, DC, 1998.

Voith, Richard P., and David Crawford. "Smart Growth and Affordable Housing." *Growth Management and Affordable Housing: Do They Conflict?* (2004): 82–117.

Warbach, John D., and Donald F. Holecek. *Overcoming Impediments to Smart Growth: Finding Ways for Land Development Professionals to Help Achieve Sustainability*. Michigan Travel, Tourism and Recreation Resource Center at Michigan State University, 2004.

Whoriskey, Peter. "Space for Employers, Not for Homes: Residents Driven Farther Out as DC Suburbs Lure Business and Limit Housing." *Washington Post*, August 8 (2004): A01.

———. "Washington's Road to Outward Growth: Far-Off Houses Are Cheap, but Drive Carries Costs: Time, Traffic, and Pollution." *Washington Post* (2004): A01.

Landscape Ecological Urbanism: Origins and Trajectories

Landscape and Urban Planning (2011)

Frederick Steiner

1. Introduction

City design and planning are especially important in what has been called the "first urban century," with a majority of people on the planet living in city-regions for the first time in history. Since the mid-1990s, two ideas emerged with implications for how we design and plan cities in the twenty-first century: landscape urbanism and urban ecology. Landscape urbanism evolved from design theory within both architecture and landscape architecture. It melds high-style design and ecology. More traditional ecological design is perceived as messier (some detractors call ecological design practitioners 'weedies') and, as a result, less appealing to international design elites. Thus far, landscape urbanism is largely theoretical, with a few, highly visible actual projects.

Urban ecology evolved from science-based research. Scholars apply ecological methods, largely developed in non-urban places, to metropolitan regions. To date, urban ecology exists primarily within the world of academic journals and books. Policy and design implications have been suggested but not yet implemented.

Landscape ecological urbanism offers a potential strategy to bring ideas from landscape urbanism and urban ecology together to create new territories that reflect cultural and natural processes. This synthesis also suggests some possible research directions.

2. Landscape Urbanism

The basic premise of landscape urbanism holds that landscape should be the fundamental building block for city design. In traditional urbanism, some structure—a wall, roads, or buildings—led development. Green spaces were relegated to left-over areas, unsuited for building, or were used for ornament. Through landscape urbanism, cultural and natural processes help the designer to organize urban form.

Landscape urbanism is largely the invention of Charles Waldheim, who coined the term (Waldheim, 2006, see also Almy, 2007). As a student of architecture at the University of Pennsylvania in the 1980s, Waldheim was influenced by both James Corner and Ian McHarg, who were at the time engaged in a vigorous debate about the future of landscape architecture. Waldheim identified common ground, integrating McHarg's ecological advocacy with Corner's urban design vision.

Landscape urbanism remains a relatively new concept with few realized works. The plan for New York City's Fresh Kills provides an example of a project moving toward realization. . . . A key innovation is that James Corner and his Field Operations colleagues embraced long-term change in their design, eschewing a set end state for a more dynamic, flexible framework of possibilities grounded in an initial "seeding." Located in Staten Island, Fresh Kills covers some 2200 acres (890 ha) and was formerly the largest landfill in the world. Much of the debris resulting from the 11 September 2001 terrorist attacks on the World Trade Center was deposited there. The Field Operations plan suggests how the landfill can be converted into a park three times larger than Central Park. The 30-year plan involves the restoration of a large landscape and includes reclaiming much of the toxic wetlands that surround and penetrate the former landfill.

Another recent landscape urbanist example is the High Line Project in Manhattan (figures 7-3 and 7-4). The Regional Plan Association and the Friends of the High Line advocated that an abandoned rail line weaving through 22 blocks in New York City be converted into a 6.7-acre (2.7-ha) park. They promote the 1.45-mile (2.33-km) long corridor as a recreational amenity, a tourist attraction, and a generator of economic development. In 2004, the Friends of the High Line and the City of New York selected Field Operations and Diller Scofidio + Renfro to design the project. The designers proposed a linear walkway that blurred the boundaries between paved and planted surfaces while suggesting evolutions in human use plus plant and bird life. The first phase of the High Line opened to much acclaim in June 2009. Its success suggests a model for how abandoned urban territories can be transformed into community assets.

Figures 7-3, 7-4 The High Line, New York City, 2013 (Photograph courtesy of Yuan Ren, 2014).

As Field Operations advances landscape urbanism on the ground, others continue to refine the concept theoretically through competitions and proposals. For instance, Chris Reed and his StossLU colleagues presented many fresh ideas in their proposal for the 2007 Lower Don Lands invited design competition organized by the Toronto Waterfront Revitalization Corporation. . . . The site covers 300 acres (121.4 ha) of mostly vacated, former port lands, just east of downtown Toronto. StossLU's approach considered flood protection, habitat restoration, and the naturalization of the Don River mouth. They also proposed new development areas and an integrated transportation system. The Canadian ecologist Nina-Marie Lister joined the StossLU team, and her contribution is evident in proposals for restoring the fish ecology. The approach suggested restoration and renewal strategies for both the Don River and Lake Ontario, with the river marsh envisioned as a breeding ground for fish.

The broader regional planning lessons of Ian McHarg (1969) are at the base of landscape urbanism. The approach involves understanding large-scale systems first and allowing them to inform and even structure proposals in order to develop schemes that engage and inaugurate ecological and social dynamics. However, landscape urbanism departs from McHarg in the ways its proponents allow multiple functions to be hybridized or to occupy the same territory simultaneously. McHarg's approaches brought people closer to nature. For example, McHarg's plan for The Woodlands in Texas successfully used storm drainage systems to structure the master plan, making water an organizing principle. Protected hydrologic corridors form green ribbons weaving through the urban fabric of The Woodlands. In contrast, landscape urbanists are interested in having people and nature occupy the same space—and to construct new urban ecologies that tap into social, cultural, and environmental dynamics playing off one another. This is E. O. Wilson's concept of 'consilience', insofar as urban natural systems and human systems interact and alter one another, producing an energetic synthesis in the process. Landscape urbanism adds to this the often unfathomable flows of cultural and economic data, updating, if not negating, McHarg's original vision.

3. Urban Ecology

Ecology is an evolving discipline with an increasing focus on landscapes and urban regions. Forman and Godron (1981, 1986) are responsible for defining the field of landscape ecology and illustrating its potential for planning. They explain: "Landscapes as ecological units with structure and function are composed primarily of patches in a matrix. Patches differ fundamentally in origin and dynamics, while size, shape, and spatial configuration are also important. Line corridors, strip corridors, stream corridors, networks, and habitations are major integrative structural characteristics of landscapes" (Forman and Godron, 1981, 733). Forman expanded the field to address regions and planning. His particular interest addresses the ecology of landscapes and regions "beyond the city." Meanwhile, ecologists have also begun to refocus their science inside the city.

The U.S. National Science Foundation (NSF) supports a network of 26 Long Term Ecological Research (LTER) projects. The NSF initiated the LTER program in 1980 to support research on long-term ecological phenomena. The LTER mission is to document, analyze, and understand ecological processes and patterns that change over long temporal and large spatial scales. Until 1997, these LTERs were located outside urban regions. After an intense competition, the NSF selected the contrasting American cities of Phoenix (http://caplter .asu.edu) and Baltimore (http://www.beslter.org) for its first urban LTERs. Baltimore has a longer European settlement history and is located in a humid, coastal region. Although there were ancient native settlements, the Phoenix region has grown rapidly since World War II and is located in a desert.

The Baltimore LTER aims to understand the metropolitan region as an ecological system. The Baltimore Ecosystem Study team of cross-disciplinary researchers explores complex interactions between the built and the natural environments with ecological, social, economic, and hydrological processes (Pickett et al., 2007). The Baltimore LTER attempts to advance both ecological research and environmental policy. For example, "Our finding that urban riparian zones experiencing hydrologically-induced drought are not sinks for nitrate, but in fact may be nitrate sources, helped lead policy makers concerned with the water quality of the Chesapeake Bay to reduce their reliance on stream corridor tree planting as a primary mitigation strategy" (Pickett et al., 2007, 51). In addition, the Baltimore LTER team has suggested how science might be used in urban landscape design.

The Central Arizona-Phoenix LTER also includes an interdisciplinary team of researchers at Arizona State University (ASU). They study the interactions of ecological and socio-economic systems in a rapidly growing urban environment. They have especially advanced our understanding of land-use change on ecological patterns and processes (Grimm et al., 2000, 2008). Such understanding is important as cities in the Southwest United States continue to grow rapidly in an environmentally sensitive context.

In addition to the formal NSF-backed urban LTERs, other U.S. scholars are advancing urban ecology research across disciplines, most notably in the Puget Sound region of the Pacific Northwest (Alberti and Marzluff, 2004). The Puget Sound group from the University of Washington has contributed to our understanding of ecological resilience in urban ecosystems. Resilience, from the

Latin *resilire* meaning to spring back or rebound, is a concept and a theory with growing appeal in the disciplines of ecology and planning. When rising from traditional concepts in ecology, resilience emphasizes equilibrium and stability. The United Nations defines resilience as the ability to absorb disturbances while retaining the same basic structure and ways of functioning, the capacity for self-organization, and the capacity to adapt to stress and change.

As a result of urban-based ecological studies, urban ecology is emerging as a field that emphasizes an interdisciplinary approach to understanding the drivers, patterns, processes, and outcomes associated with urban and urbanizing landscapes. Alberti (2008) conceives of urban ecosystems as complex coupled human-natural systems where people are the dominant modifiers of ecosystems, thus producing hybrid social-ecological landscape patterns and processes. Some urban ecology research focuses on the impact of habitat fragmentation on suburban and urban housing development patterns for avian species productivity; other research focuses on the integration of scientific analyses into growth-management strategies. Such diverse research agendas are united in their recognition that urban ecosystems are characterized by complexity, heterogeneity, and hybridity, and are therefore best analyzed within an interdisciplinary approach.

4. Landscape Ecological Urbanism

Recently, Mohsen Mostafavi promoted the concept of "ecological urbanism" to imagine an approach "that has the capacity to incorporate the inherent conflictual conditions between ecology and urbanism" Mostafavi and Doherty (2010, 17). Mostafavi and his colleagues draw strongly on landscape urbanism, but pay scant attention to the advances made in urban ecology. If those ecological advances were incorporated, then one might imagine a truly new synthesis: landscape ecological urbanism.

New ideas about city design and planning are necessary because urbanization poses significant social and environmental challenges. As the number of people in the world increases in this first urban century, the percentage of those dwelling in large city-regions is also expected to increase. The consequences of continuing to develop as we have in the past are clear: energy use and greenhouse gas production for buildings and transportation systems increase; water and air pollution spreads; valuable habitat and prime farmland are lost; social issues, such as crime and poverty, are exacerbated.

Urban ecology research indicates what should be obvious: people interact with other humans and with other species as well as their built and natural environments. The city is a human-dominated ecosystem. Landscape urbanism projects, such as the High Line and the Toronto waterfront, illustrate how designing with nature can improve the quality of cities for people, plants, and animals.

In doing so, ecosystem services can be enhanced. Ecosystem services can be defined as the benefits we receive from nature: resource services, such as food, water, and energy; regulatory services, such as purification of water, carbon sequestration and climate regulation, waste decomposition and detoxification, crop pollination, and pest and disease control; support services, such as nutrient dispersal and cycling, and seed dispersal; and cultural services, including cultural, intellectual, and spiritual inspiration, recreational experiences, ecotourism, and scientific discovery. The concept has evolved in the Unite[d] States to provide a basis for measuring landscape design efficiency. For instance, the Sustainable Sites Initiative (SITES) has developed a measurement system for evaluating landscape performance. SITES is led by the American Society of Landscape Architects, the Lady Bird Johnson Wildflower Center of the University of Texas, and the U.S. Botanic Garden (www.sustainablesites.org). Its goal is to be the equivalent of the U.S. Green Building Council's LEED system for the outdoors. The SITES pilot projects currently underway suggest that ecosystem services can actually be enhanced and created through landscape design.

A goal of landscape ecological urbanism might be to design and plan cities to increase, rather than to decrease, ecosystem services. This suggests exciting new areas of research in landscape and urban planning, from ways to measure landscape performance to case studies of successful and not-so-successful projects.

5. Conclusions and Research Directions

Landscape ecological urbanism suggests three possible research directions: an evolution of aesthetic understanding, a deeper understanding of human agency in ecology, and reflective learning through practice. Humanities-based design theory can be a powerful force in how places are created. Traditional ecological design fell short in creating an alternative aesthetic to modernism (or its romantic offspring, postmodernism). Landscape urbanism, if nothing else, has succeeded in exciting architects, landscape architects, and urban designers about how city futures can be viewed.

Meanwhile, as ecological research has moved into cities, the role of people in urban ecosystems could not be ignored. Geographers and other social scientists have played a leadership role in urban ecology research, underscoring the dual cultural and natural foundations of human settlement. Concepts such as sustainability, regeneration, resilience, and ecosystem services hold the potential for advancing human ecology.

Projects such as Fresh Kills, the High Line, and the Lower Don Lands provide helpful lessons about what works and what does not through actual experience. Reflective practice and case studies have a strong heritage within city planning, landscape architecture, and urban design. Case studies can build on reflective practice by incorporating ecological research and design theory. In the process, new ways to design and plan city-regions with nature and culture can result.

References

Alberti, Marina. *Advances in Urban Ecology: Integrating Humans and Ecological Processes in Urban Ecosystems.* Springer Science, New York, 2008.

Alberti, Marina, and John M. Marzluff. "Ecological Resilience in Urban Ecosystems: Linking Urban Patterns to Human and Ecological Functions." *Urban Ecosystems* 7, no. 3 (2004): 241–65.

Almy, Dean. "Center 14: On Landscape Urbanism." Austin: Center for American Architecture and Design, School of Architecture, the University of Texas at Austin (2007).

Doherty, Gareth, ed. *Ecological Urbanism.* Baden, Switzerland: Lars Müller Publishers, 2010.

Forman, Richard T.T., and Michel Godron. "Patches and Structural Components for a Landscape Ecology." *BioScience* (1981): 733–40.

———. *Landscape Ecology.* John Wiley and Sons, New York, 1986.

Grimm, Nancy B., Stanley H. Faeth, Nancy E. Golubiewski, Charles L. Redman, Jianguo Wu, Xuemei Bai, and John M. Briggs. "Global Change and the Ecology of Cities." *Science* 319, no. 5864 (2008): 756–60.

Pickett, Steward T.A., Kenneth T. Belt, Michael F. Galvin, Peter M. Groffman, J. Morgan Grove, Donald C. Outen, Richard V. Pouyat, William P. Stack, and Mary L. Cadenasso. "Watersheds in Baltimore, Maryland: Understanding and Application of Integrated Ecological and Social Processes." *Journal of Contemporary Water Research & Education* 136, no. 1 (2007): 44–55.

Waldheim, Charles, ed. *The Landscape Urbanism Reader.* Princeton Architectural Press, 2006.

Ecological Resilience as a Foundation for Urban Design and Sustainability

Resiliency in Ecology and Urban Design: Linking Theory and Practice for Sustainable Cities (2013)

Jianguo Wu and Tong Wu

Introduction

As humans have transformed themselves from a predominantly agrarian to urban species, the world has become increasingly planned and designed (Wu 2008a, b). Human domination has become the prevailing theme in society's interactions with nature for more than two centuries, particularly since the Industrial Revolution in the eighteenth century. With growing human dominance in the biosphere, nature has become increasingly "domesticated" (Kareiva et al. 2007). As Herbert Simon (1996) put it, "The world we live in today is much more a man-made, or artificial, world than it is a natural world."

Our increasingly managed and designed ecosystems and landscapes are met with an increasing number of problems, which can be summarized in one word—unsustainable. Cities now account for about 75% of the energy use, 60% of the residential water use, 80% of the wood used for industrial purposes, and 80% of the greenhouse gas emissions of the entire world (Grimm et al. 2008; Newman et al. 2009). The environmental problems associated with urbanization have been well recognized in both the fields of ecology and design. In a broad sense, the state of the world is a consequence of the faulty design activities of humanity. . . .

A myriad of factors are responsible for the current unsustainable state of the world. Two of them are particularly relevant to mention here: our inadequate or incorrect understanding of how nature works in science and our inadequate or misuse of ecological knowledge in action. Our perception of nature has often been shaped by myths and beliefs, such as the balance of nature, which has been an important background assumption in ecology (Botkin 1990; Pickett et al. 1992; Wu and Loucks 1992, 1995). Until recently, it was common to view biological populations, communities, and ecosystems as ordered systems that were kept at a constant stable equilibrium by homeostatic controls. This way of thinking may be attributed partly to the human tendency to seek order in everything, including nature (Wu and Loucks 1992, 1995). Also, confined by the balance of nature notion and the natural history tradition, mainstream ecology had long overlooked cities (Collins et al. 2000). Ecology and design did not seem compatible because almost everything that humans did to nature was perceived to be ecologically negative. For decades ecology was viewed as a "subversive science" because it was perceived as being the advocate of nature as against the actions of humans (Shepard and McKinley 1969; Kingsland 2005).

However, mounting evidence from ecological research in the past few decades indicates that nature is not in constant balance, but rather in eternal flux. This recent discovery has led to a fundamental transformation in ecological thinking from emphasizing equilibrium, homogeneity, and determinism to non-equilibrium, heterogeneity, and stochasticity—or a shift from the balance of nature/equilibrium paradigm to the hierarchical patch dynamics paradigm (Pickett et al. 1992; Wu and Loucks 1992, 1995). Wu and Loucks (1995) articulated five key elements of hierarchical patch dynamics: (1) ecological systems are spatially nested patch hierarchies, (2) dynamics of an ecological system can be studied as the composite dynamics of individual patches and their interactions, (3) pattern and process are scale dependent, (4) non-equilibrium and random processes are essential to ecosystem structure and function, and (5) ecological (meta)stability is often achieved through structural and functional redundancy and spatial and temporal incorporation of dynamic patches. Only recently have these ideas of patch dynamics been applied in urban ecological studies (e.g., Pickett et al. 1997; Grimm et al. 2000; Zipperer et al. 2000; Wu and David 2002) and begun to find their way into urban design (McGrath et al. 2007).

In general, ecological principles have not been adequately incorporated in the theory and practice of design and engineering, and those principles that are applied tend to be outdated (Holling 1987; Pickett et al. 2004). Holling (1996) identified four such misunderstandings in design sciences: (1) changes in ecosystem structure and function are continuous and gradual, (2) ecosystems are spatially uniform and scale invariant, (3) ecosystems have a single equilibrium point, with stabilizing functions to keep them at this homeostatic state, and

(4) policies and management practices based on such equilibrium-centered and "linear" thinking inevitably lead to applying fixed rules, looking for constant carrying capacity or constant sustainable yield, and ignoring scale dependence. To overcome these problems, resilience theory, an emerging body of ideas, principles, and knowledge for understanding, managing, and designing socio-ecological systems (Levin et al. 1998; Holling 2001; Walker and Salt 2006), can provide a comprehensive and powerful framework.

The objectives of this chapter, therefore, are to provide an overview of the essential elements of resilience theory, and then explore how it can guide the science and practice of urban design. We will elucidate the complex and adaptive properties of cities as socio-ecological systems, and examine why the agenda of urban sustainable development entails the adoption of resilience as a guiding principle.

Key Elements of Resilience Theory

The emerging theory of resilience, or resilience thinking, is based on several key concepts and ideas, including thresholds or tipping points, alternate stable states or regimes, regime shifts, complex adaptive systems, adaptive cycles, panarchy, and transformability (Holling 2001; Folke 2006; Walker and Salt 2006). In this section, we discuss how these concepts are defined and interpreted in the context of understanding and managing social-ecological systems.

What Is Resilience?

Engineering Resilience vs. Ecological Resilience

Resilience has been defined differently in ecology, with two contrasting connotations. Consistent with the classic ecological paradigm that presumes a single equilibrium state, the first connotation of resilience refers to the rapidity with which a system returns to its equilibrium after a disturbance, usually measured in time units (Innis 1975; Pimm 1984). In contrast, based on the observation that ecosystems often have multiple stable states, Holling (1973) defined resilience as the ability of a system to absorb change and disturbance without changing its basic structure and function or shifting into a qualitatively different state. The resilience concept based on multiple alternate states has been called "ecological resilience" or "ecosystem resilience," which stresses persistence, change, and unpredictability (Holling 1996). It differs from the classical equilibrium-centered resilience concept, termed "engineering resilience," which focuses on efficiency, constancy, and predictability (Holling 1996).

The modern discourse on resilience hinges on ecological, rather than engineering, resilience. More recent work has further expanded and elaborated

Holling's (1973) original definition of ecosystem or ecological resilience. These revisions usually include the system's abilities to self-organize and adapt to changes, and also contributions that make resilience more pertinent to social and social-ecological systems (e.g., Holling 1996, 2001; Levin et al. 1998; Carpenter et al. 2001; Folke 2006). For example, social resilience is defined as the ability of a human community to withstand, and to recover from, external environmental, socioeconomic, and political shocks or perturbations (Adger 2000). The popularization of the term resilience across disparate fields seems to have made it increasingly removed from its original ecological meaning and more ambivalent in some cases (Brand and Jax 2007). Much of the recent research on resilience has been done in association with the Resilience Alliance, an international network of scientists, practitioners, universities, and government and non-government agencies, which was established in 1999 to promote resilience research in social-ecological systems (http://www.resalliance.org).

Multiple Stable States, Thresholds, and Regime Shifts

A critical assumption behind the concept of ecological resilience is the existence of multiple stable states, also known as basins of attraction, multiple equilibria, or regimes (figure 7-5). Thresholds—a concept similar to tipping points—refer to the boundaries between the basins of attraction, crossing which leads the system to a different regime. Such transitions of social-ecological systems between alternate stable states are known as "regime shifts" (Scheffer et al. 2001; Folke 2006). Regime shifts may result in abrupt and dramatic changes in system structure and function in some cases, or more continuous and gradual changes in other situations (figure 7-5). Examples of regime shifts are ubiquitous in environmental and human systems. For instance, a grassland may change to a shrubland due to overgrazing or climate change that pushes the system over a threshold in terms of vegetation cover and soil properties (Walker and Salt 2006). A productive lake with clear water can quickly become turbid upon reaching a tipping point from a steady influx of pollutants (Carpenter et al. 1999; Scheffer et al. 2000). Such dynamics illustrate the interplay of "slow" versus "fast" variables in the nonlinear dynamics of social-ecological systems. A slow moving attribute, such as a gradual stream of pollutants, can cause rapid shifts into a new state that is more visibly captured by the fast variable, such as lake nutrient concentration. Nonlinear dynamics, and regime shifts in particular, can result in a substantial element of surprise.

Specified and General Resilience

A system's resilience can also be discussed in terms of "specified resilience" (or "targeted resilience") and "general resilience" (Walker and Salt 2006; Walker

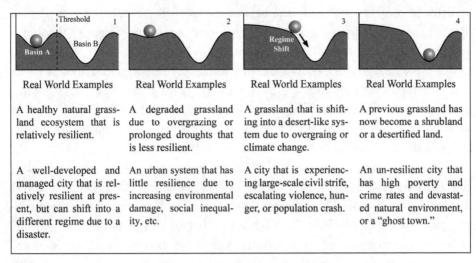

Figure 7-5 Illustration of some key concepts of ecological resilience (Wu and Wu, 2013, Reproduced with permission of Springer, Redrawn by Yuan Ren, 2014).

and Pearson 2007). Specified resilience is the resilience "of what, to what," i.e., the resilience of a specified system response variable to a known disturbance (e.g., the resilience of human and ecosystem health to increased temperatures caused by urban heat islands). General resilience refers to the overall resilience of a system to withstand unforeseen disturbances, which does not specify any particular kind of shock or any particular system response variable. An example of this could be the overall capacity of a city to persist in a rapidly and unpredictably changing world. Walker and Salt (2006) have pointed out that specified resilience, although important, is not adequate alone, and that optimizing specified resilience may actually undermine the general resilience of a social-ecological system. This is mainly because too much focus on specified resilience tends to make the whole system less diverse, less flexible, and less responsive in terms of cross-sector actions (Walker and Salt 2006).

Complex Adaptive Systems

Recent developments in resilience research have emphatically recognized social-ecological systems as "Complex Adaptive Systems" (CAS). Insights from the study of CAS have been increasingly incorporated into the theory of resilience (Holling 2001; Walker and Salt 2006). While various definitions of CAS exist (Cowan et al. 1994; Holland 1995; Lansing 2003), the one by Levin (1999) has been widely used in the resilience literature: a complex adaptive system is "a system composed of a heterogeneous assemblage of types, in which structure and functioning emerge from the balance between the constant production of diversity, due to various forces, and the winnowing of that diversity through a selection process mediated by local interactions."

Complex adaptive systems are characterized by self-organization, in which local interactions at small scales result in emergent patterns at larger scales. They are also characterized by adaptive processes, which typically produce multiple outcomes depending on accidents of history—a phenomenon known as "path dependence" (Kauffman 1993; Levin 1998, 1999). . . .

Natural, human, and coupled natural-human systems are complex adaptive systems (Holland 1995; Levin 1998, 1999; Holling 2001; Lansing 2003). Brown (1994) discussed five characteristics of ecosystems that make them prototypical examples of CAS: (1) a large number of components, (2) open and far-from-thermodynamic-equilibrium, maintained through exchanges of energy, materials, and information with the environment, (3) adaptive, i.e., able to respond to changes behaviorally or genetically, (4) irreversible histories, and (5) capable of a variety of complex, nonlinear dynamics. While human systems have features similar to these, they also possess at least three unique characteristics: foresight and intentionality, communication capacities, and technological advances that influence every aspect of human society (Holling 2001). As socio-ecological systems, cities represent a quintessential example of complex adaptive systems, which are heterogeneous in space, dynamic in time, and integrative in function (Wu and David 2002).

Adaptive Cycles and Panarchy

From the theory of resilience, complex adaptive systems often exhibit recurring dynamics, moving through four phases: (1) an r phase of growth or exploitation, (2) a K phase of conservation or consolidation, (3) an Ω. phase of release or collapse, and (4) an α phase of reorganization or renewal. These four phases are collectively known as the adaptive cycle, which is represented commonly by a ∞-shaped diagram (Holling 1986, 2001). While the r and K phases are two aspects of ecosystem dynamics that have long been studied in the context of ecological succession, the two additional phases were introduced into the adaptive cycle to highlight the importance of the interplay between growth and maintenance, between innovation and conservation, and between change and stability (Holling 1986, 2001).

Holling (1986) introduced the concept of the adaptive cycle with the example of ecosystem succession. After a disturbance an ecosystem starts recolonization and biomass accumulation with opportunistic and pioneer species (r-strategists) predominant in the early succession stage (r phase), and then gradually reaches maturity with locally competitive climax species (K-strategists) dominant in the late succession stage (K phase). During this process, biomass and nutrients accrue and become progressively more bound within the existing vegetation, and the ecosystem becomes increasingly more connected in structure, more rigid in regulatory control, and thus more brittle as a whole. Thus, a system in the K phase is characterized by high capital (or potential for other use), over-connectedness, and rigidity, representing a period of "an accident waiting to happen" (Holling 2001). For example, disturbances such as fires, storms, or pest outbreaks may trigger an abrupt collapse of the ecosystem, during which the tight regulatory control is broken up and the resources accumulated in the transition from r to K phases are released in the Ω phase. This sudden collapse, also known as "creative destruction" (sensu Schumpeter 1950), leads to an open and loosely organized situation with abundant opportunities, high uncertainties, and strong external influences. Resources are mobilized, and the ecosystem starts the process of reorganization (α). This leads back to the r phase, but there is no guarantee that the ecosystem will return to its previous state. As the adaptive cycle unfolds, system resilience expands and contracts: resilience is high in the α phase when potential (or capital) and connectedness (or controllability) are low, and low in the Ω phase when potential and connectedness are high.

Ecosystems that are unblemished by human encroachment adhere to a natural and salubrious cycle of growth and renewal. Dramatic events such as wildfires, while destructive, unleash the potential for revitalization and are a boon to the system's long-term health. Anthropogenic intrusions, however, can displace an ecosystem from its natural rhythm, resulting in collapses that are significantly more dramatic and potentially irreversible. In many parts of the United States, for instance, practices of fire suppression have disturbed naturally occurring fire regimes that are essential to the long-term health of forest ecosystems. Consequently, tree density and the accumulation of fuel loads now precipitate much more destructive fires that inflict long-term damage to both the ecosystem and adjacent communities (Covington 2000). . . .

Resilience and Sustainability

From a resilience perspective, sustainability is not about maintaining a system at its equilibrium state by reducing the variability in system dynamics or optimizing a system's performance, but rather sustainability should focus on the system's capacity to create and test opportunities and maintain adaptive capabilities (Holling 2001). Thus, resilience is the key to the sustainability in social-ecological systems (Walker and Salt 2006). This shift from a perspective oriented around stability, optimality and predictability to a perspective focusing on inherent uncertainty is in favor of a "risk management" approach to sustainability—avoiding potentially catastrophic regime shifts. Adaptability is promoted by self-organization. Preserving the ability to self-organize in the face of disturbances is a crucial characteristic of resilient systems. Thus, we may argue that all sustainable systems must be resilient, but not necessarily always stable. Indeed, in the face of social and environmental disturbances—from changing climatic conditions to geopolitical struggles, destructive hurricanes to armed conflicts—the ability to self-organize and preserve system integrity is crucial to realizing long-term sustainable development.

From a panarchical perspective, sustainability is inherently a multiple-scale concept. To achieve sustainability is not to get stuck in the conservation phase within an adaptive cycle, but rather to maintain proper operations of all four phases within each cycle as well as harmonic linkages between adjacent cycles across scales in space, time, and organization. Through a panarchical analysis, we may identify breaking points at which a social-ecological system are more brittle and leverage points at which positive changes are most effective for fostering resilience and sustainability (Holling 2000). As the expanding scale of human enterprise generates more and more coupled socio-ecological systems on a range of scales, we expect that the resilience perspective will play an increasingly important role in the science and practice of sustainability.

Resilience Thinking of Urban Design and Urban Sustainability

Cities are quintessential examples of complex adaptive systems. . . . [E]cological resilience is the key to the sustainability of such systems. Several attempts have been made to apply the concept of resilience to urban systems in recent years (Pickett et al. 2004; Vale and Campanella 2005; Wallace and Wallace 2008). For example, Alberti et al. (2003) discussed urban resilience as "cities—the degree to which cities tolerate alteration before reorganizing around a new set of structures and processes." Pickett et al. (2004) articulated the use of ecological (rather than engineering) resilience as a powerful metaphor for bridging ecology with urban planning. Vale and Campanella (2005) defined urban resilience as the capacity of a city to rebound from a disaster, which is an engineering resilience perspective as per Gunderson (2010).

Applying the theory of ecological resilience in urban design can result in design principles that are quite different from the traditional ones that emphasize stability, optimality, and efficiency. In this section, we explore several aspects of resilience thinking in the context of urban design and urban sustainability. These are neither specific guidelines nor actionable recipes for urban design, but rather are pointers that are useful for developing such guidelines and recipes for designing resilient cities.

Cities as Panarchies

Key to understanding the behavior of cities as complex adaptive systems is to study the interactions between spatial patterns and ecological and socioeconomic processes operating at differing temporal, spatial, and organizational scales. Thus, it is useful to think of cities as panarchies with nested adaptive cycles of characteristic scales in space and time. In an urban environment, panarchical dynamics, as illustrated through the example of fire in a forest ecosystem, also take place. For instance, a protest originally confined to a single neighborhood or locality may gain momentum and spread to other parts of the city, eventually evolving into a large-scale constructive reform or destructive revolt. The case of constructive reform is often indicative of a resilient political system that encourages healthy democratic participation and local feedbacks. The case of revolt may be due to a lack of social resilience, as law enforcement and the broader infrastructure fail to temper the contagion of uprising activities. Once the revolt has dissipated, administrators can rely on the social capital of the local community and the financial and political support from higher levels of government to clean up the resultant messes and help with reconstruction efforts. . . .

Climate change presents one of the greatest challenges to urban sustainability, which has cross-scale implications. With urban populations swelling, cities will continue to be the primary contributors of greenhouse gases to the atmosphere. As the planet warms, urban regions will then have to adapt to the consequences of the human-altered climate system, such as rising sea levels and higher occurrences of hurricanes. As we saw with the Asian Tsunami of 2004 and Hurricane Katrina of 2005, the effects of natural disturbances on heavily populated regions can be devastating. Thus, as the effects of urbanization continue to motivate biophysical changes at the global scale, resultant consequences of altered climatic conditions will feed back to create novel environmental conditions to which cities must inevitably adapt (Newman et al. 2009).

Connectedness, Modularity, and Tight Feedbacks

Resilient social-ecological systems usually have high diversity and individuality of components, local interactions, and an autonomous process that selects certain components for replication or enhancement based on the outcomes of the local interactions (Levin 1998, 1999; Holling 2001). Hierarchical or modular structure can facilitate all these three important features of complex adaptive systems. This has immediate implications for urban design. Cities can become more spatially homogenous when urbanized areas expand and coalesce. Correspondingly, a higher connectivity of the urban land cover can decrease modularity, resulting in more rapid distribution of the effects of a disturbance. . . .

Accounting for Nature's Services in Cities

As humanity becomes an increasingly urban enterprise, it is important to consider cities as socio-ecological systems, supported by ecosystem services. Ecosystem services refer to the benefits that humans derive from the natural environment, including provisioning services such as food and water; regulating services such as regulation of floods, drought, and disease; supporting services such as soil formation and nutrient cycling; and cultural services such as recreational, spiritual, religious and other nonmaterial benefits (Millennium Ecosystem Assessment 2005). The economic and social wellbeing of a society is inextricably tied to the availability of these ecosystem services or "natural capital." Urban development, however, can result in a significant loss of ecosystem services and thus a decrease in the city's cross-scale resilience.

Many urban ecosystem services are well-known to planners and city dwellers at large. Urban forests, for example, contribute numerous services such as air quality control and real estate appreciation (McPherson 1992; Wu 2008a, b). With regard to the pressing challenges of climate change, urban carbon sequestration is a service of great significance. While the importance of "natural" ecosystems such as forests and grasslands are well noted, there is less focus on the role of urban ecosystems in this regard. Recent studies have shown that urbanization of cities in arid environments can increase net primary production substantially (Buyantuyev and Wu 2009). This has significant implications for carbon sequestration capacity at a region scale. Another important way in which urban "nature" contributes to a city's wellbeing is in the form of "cultural services." Urban greenspaces, such as open and park-like spaces, are a hallmark of modern cities, offering a sense of place and opportunities for recreation. These spaces should be integrated into the urban context, and form a mainstay of social interactions and a diverse repository of species and other natural elements. These services should be considered in any sustainable design agenda (Chen and Wu 2009). To build resilient cities, urban designers and planners should properly account for nature's services to a city by investing in its natural capital. . . .

Developing Capacities for Urban Transformability

It is crucial to note that there can also be a negative dimension of having high resilience. A system can sometimes become resilient in a less desirable regime. For instance, urban regions besieged by impoverishment may be stuck in "poverty traps," where a suite of socioeconomic factors have induced a highly robust state of squalor. Low levels of education, endemism of substance abuse, and poor quality of governance can generate a series of tight feedback loops that prove immensely difficult to be overcome. The same genre of dynamics can also affect rural regions, urban fringes, and other socio-ecological systems, manifesting in environmental degradation and the depletion of valuable eco-system services. This is the case in many urban areas of the developing world, and illustrates that resilience can work as both a vehicle of sustainability and an agent of destitution. In such situations, the primary motivation of under-standing resilience and employing adaptive strategies is reversed—sustainable development then means finding ways of overcoming the robustness of unde-sirable regimes.

The capacity to overcome the obstacles of an undesirable regime to create a fundamentally new system is called transformability (Walker et al. 2004; Folke 2006; Walker and Salt 2006). Configuring an entirely new system means in-troducing new state variables—the attributes and processes that determine the qualitative character of the system. For instance, when dealing with deep urban poverty traps of high robustness, "urban renewal" may call upon the obsoles-cence of the underlying social, political, or economic determinants of the cur-rent condition. Social pathologies such as rampant drug use or a fundamentally flawed educational system may underpin the squalor at hand, perpetuating vi-cious cycles of impoverishment and disenfranchisement. In this case, it may become necessary to overhaul the administrative and incentive structure of the city's school districts, crack down on a multinational drug-based economy, and introduce rehabilitative opportunities to promote more productive activities.

Concluding Remarks

The world is dynamic, and change is ubiquitous. Cities, as prototypical complex adaptive systems, are not only dynamic but also self-organizing and actively adjusting to cope with change. These changes include a myriad of disturbances, some of which are known and predictable, but most of which are unforeseen and unpredictable. Urban design can play a critically important role in the self-organization and adaptive progression of cities. How urban design affects urban sustainability, however, depends heavily on design principles that are increasingly influenced by ecological theory. We have discussed that the tradi-tional equilibrium paradigm in ecology presumes homogeneity, predictability, and inherent stability of ecosystems, suggesting that the focus of sustaining a system should be on keeping it at stasis. In sharp contrast, the hierarchi-cal patch dynamics paradigm explicitly recognizes heterogeneity, nonlinearity, and multiple stable states, suggesting "flux of nature" and "order out of dis-order" (Pickett et al. 1992; Wu and Loucks 1992, 1995). The ideas of heteroge-neity, non-linearity, hierarchy, and multiple stable states are also essential in the theory of ecological resilience, which has emerged as a major approach to understanding and managing social-ecological systems, including urban design. This theory suggests that, to design sustainable cities, our emphasis should be on creating and maintaining urban resilience—the ability of a city to persist without qualitative change in structure and function in spite of disturbances. Pickett et al. (2004) have argued that "cities of resilience" can be a powerful metaphor for drawing together insights from both ecology and planning.

What would a resilient city look like? We do not believe that there is a universal model. Nevertheless, we believe that the features of "a resilient world," as envisioned by Walker and Salt (2006), may provide some clues:

1. Diversity: Promoting diversity in all its dimensions, from biological to economic, and encourage multiple components and resource uses to balance and complement homogenizing trends.
2. Ecological variability: Seeking to understand and work with the boundaries of the inherent variability of ecological and socio-ecological systems; attempting to tame such variability is often a recipe for disaster.
3. Modularity: Maintaining modularity can help hedge against dangers of low resilience caused by over-connectedness in system structure and function.
4. Acknowledging slow variables: Managing for resilience means understanding the "slow" or controlling variables that underpin the condition of a system, especially in relation to thresholds. By recognizing the importance of these critical variables, we can better avoid shifts to undesirable stable states and possibly enhance the capacity of a desirable regime to deal with disturbances.
5. Tight feedbacks: Tightening or maintaining the strength of feedback loops allows us to better detect thresholds. The weakening of feedback loops can result in an asymmetry between our actions and the consequences stemming from them. Salient examples of such dynamics include pollution and overconsumption.
6. Social capital: Promoting trust, social networks, and leadership to enhance the adaptive capacity for better dealing with the effects of disturbance.
7. Innovation: Embracing change through learning, experimentation, and promoting locally developed rules. Instead of narrowing our range of activities and opportunities, we should be seeking to explore and cultivate new ones.
8. Overlap in governance: Developing institutional arrangements that manage for cross-scale influences. Developing "redundancy" and overlap in governance frameworks enhances response diversity and flexibility.

9. Ecosystem services: Recognizing and accounting for ecosystem services when managing and designing for resilience. The benefits society derives from nature are regularly underpriced and ignored. Such services are often lost as socio-ecological systems shift into different, less desirable regimes.

At the heart of the resilience perspective on urban design is its focus on change instead of stasis—"to withstand change with adaptive change," not to deal with change by resisting or diminishing change. This is in the same spirit of "progress" as defined by Herbert Spencer (1857)—change underlies progress, which is "a beneficent necessity." Resilience theory suggests that what underlies a truly resilient city is not how stable it has appeared or how many little disturbances it has absorbed, but whether it can withstand an unforeseen shock that would fundamentally alter or erase the city's identity. For modern cities to be truly sustainable, therefore, urban design must explicitly account for the influence of both internal and external changes. Only by viewing urban regions as complex socio-ecological systems with feedback loops, cross-scale interactions, and inherent uncertainties can we design resilient cities. We argue that in applying the key ideas and principles of resilience, it is important to think of the seemingly opposing processes, such as change vs. stability, creativity vs. conservation, and flexibility vs. efficiency, not as paradoxes but dialectical duals that must coexist to achieve a synthesis of urban resilience.

References

Adger, W. Neil. "Social and Ecological Resilience: Are They Related?" *Progress in Human Geography* 24, no. 3 (2000): 347–64.

Alberti, Marina, John M. Marzluff, Eric Shulenberger, Gordon Bradley, Clare Ryan, and Craig Zumbrunnen. "Integrating Humans into Ecology: Opportunities and Challenges for Studying Urban Ecosystems." *BioScience* 53: 1169–79.

Botkin, Daniel B. *Discordant Harmonies: A New Ecology for the Twenty-First Century*. Oxford: Oxford University Press, 1990.

Brand, Fridolin Simon, and Kurt Jax. "Focusing the Meaning(s) of Resilience: Resilience as a Descriptive Concept and a Boundary Object." *Ecology and Society* 12, no. 1 (2007): 23.

Brown, James. "Complex Ecological Systems." In *Complexity: Metaphors, Models, and Reality*, edited by George Cowan, David Pines, and David Meltzer. Reading: Addison-Wesley, 1994.

Buyantuyev, A., and J. Wu. "Urbanization Alters Spatiotemporal Patterns of Ecosystem Primary Production: A Case Study of the Phoenix Metropolitan Region, USA." *Journal of Arid Environments* 73, no. 4 (2009): 512–20.

Carpenter, Stephen R., Carl Folke, Marten Scheffer, and Frances Westley. "Resilience: Accounting for the Noncomputable." *Ecology & Society* 14, no. 1 (2009): 13.

Carpenter, Stephen R., Donald Ludwig, and William A. Brock. "Management of Eutrophication for Lakes Subject to Potentially Irreversible Change." *Ecological Applications* 9, no. 3 (1999): 751–71.

Carpenter, Steve, Brian Walker, J. Marty Anderies, and Nick Abel. "From Metaphor to Measurement: Resilience of What to What?" *Ecosystems* 4, no. 8 (2001): 765–81.

Chen, Xiangqiao, and Jianguo Wu. "Sustainable Landscape Architecture: Implications of the Chinese Philosophy of 'Unity of Man with Nature' and Beyond." *Landscape Ecology* 24, no. 8 (2009): 1015–26.

Collins, James P., Ann Kinzig, Nancy B. Grimm, William F. Fagan, Diane Hope, Jianguo Wu, and Elizabeth T. Borer. "A New Urban Ecology Modeling Human Communities as Integral Parts of Ecosystems Poses Special Problems for the Development and Testing of Ecological Theory." *American Scientist* 88, no. 5 (2000): 416–25.

Covington, William Wallace. "Helping Western Forests Heal." *Nature* 408, no. 6809 (2000): 135–36.

Cowan, G. A., D. Pines, and D. Meltzer. *Complexity: Metaphors, Models, and Reality*. Reading: Perseus Books, 1994.

Dasgupta, Partha, and Ismail Serageldin. *Social Capital: A Multifaceted Perspective*. Washington, DC: World Bank Publications, 2001.

Folke, Carl. "Resilience: The Emergence of a Perspective for Social-Ecological Systems Analyses." *Global Environmental Change* 16, no. 3 (2006): 253–67.

Glanville, Ranulph. "Researching Design and Designing Research." *Design Issues* 13 (1999): 80–91.

Grimm, Nancy B., J. Morgan Grove, Steward T. A. Pickett, and Charles L. Redman. "Integrated Approaches to Long-Term Studies of Urban Ecological Systems." *BioScience* 50, no. 7 (2000): 571–84.

Grimm, Nancy B., Stanley H. Faeth, Nancy E. Golubiewski, Charles L. Redman, Jianguo Wu, Xuemei Bai, and John M. Briggs. "Global Change and the Ecology of Cities." *Science* 319, no. 5864 (2008): 756–60.

Gunderson, Lance H. "Resilience in Theory and Practice." *Annual Review of Ecology and Systematics* (2000): 425–39.

———. *Panarchy: Understanding Transformations in Human and Natural Systems*. Washington, DC: Island Press, 2002.

———. "Ecological and Human Community Resilience in Response to Natural Disasters." *Ecology and Society* 15, no. 2 (2010): 18.

Holland, John Henry. *Hidden Order: How Adaptation Builds Complexity*. Reading: Perseus Books, 1995.

Holling, Crawford S. "Engineering Resilience versus Ecological Resilience." *Foundations of Ecological Resilience* (1996): 51–66.

———. "Resilience and Stability of Ecological Systems." *Annual Review of Ecology and Systematics* 4 (1973): 1–23.

———. "Simplifying the Complex: The Paradigms of Ecological Function and Structure." *European Journal of Operational Research* 30, no. 2 (1987): 139–46.

———. "The Resilience of Terrestrial Ecosystems: Local Surprise and Global Change." *Sustainable Development of the Biosphere* (1986): 292–317.

———. "Theories for Sustainable Futures." *Conservation Ecology* 4, no. 2 (2000): 7.

———. "Understanding the Complexity of Economic, Ecological, and Social Systems." *Ecosystems* 4, no. 5 (2001): 390–405.

Innis, George. "Stability, Sensitivity, Resilience, Persistence. What Is of Interest?" *Ecosystem Analysis and Prediction* (1975): 131–40.

Kareiva, Peter, Sean Watts, Robert McDonald, and Tim Boucher. "Domesticated Nature: Shaping Landscapes and Ecosystems for Human Welfare." *Science* 316, no. 5833 (2007): 1866–69.

Kaufmann, S. A. *The Origins of Order*. Oxford: Oxford University Press, 1993.

Kingsland, Sharon E. *The Evolution of American Ecology: 1890-2000*. Johns Hopkins University Press, 2005.

Lansing, J. Stephen. "Complex Adaptive Systems." *Annual Review of Anthropology* (2003): 183–204.

Levin, Simon A. "Ecosystems and the Biosphere as Complex Adaptive Systems." *Ecosystems* 1, no. 5 (1998): 431–36.

———. "Learning to Live in a Global Commons: Socioeconomic Challenges for a Sustainable Environment." *Ecological Research* 21, no. 3 (2006): 328–33.

———. *Fragile Dominion: Complexity and the Commons*. Reading: Perseus, 1999.

Levin, Simon A., Scott Barrett, Sara Aniyar, William Baumol, Christopher Bliss, Bert Bolin, Partha Dasgupta, et al. "Resilience in Natural and Socioeconomic Systems." *Environment and Development Economics* 3, no. 2 (1998): 222–36.

McGrath, B., M. L. Cadenasso, J. M. Grove, V. Marshall, S. T. A. Pickett, and J. Towers. *Designing Patch Dynamics*. New York: Graduate School of Architecture, Planning and Preservation of Columbia University, 2007.

McPherson, Gregory E. "Accounting for Benefits and Costs of Urban Greenspace." *Landscape and Urban Planning* 22, no. 1 (1992): 41–51.

Millennium Ecosystem Assessment. *Ecosystems and Human Well-Being: Biodiversity Synthesis*. Washington DC: Island Press, 2005.

Newman, Peter, Timothy Beatley, and Heather Boyer. *Resilient Cities: Responding to Peak Oil and Climate Change*. Washington, DC: Island Press, 2009.

Ostrom, Elinor. "A General Framework for Analyzing Sustainability of Social-Ecological Systems." *Science* 325 (2009): 419–22.

Pendall, Rolf, and Jonathan Martin. *From Traditional to Reformed: A Review of the Land Use Regulations in the Nation's 50 Largest Metropolitan Areas*. Washington, DC: The Brookings Institution, 2006.

Pickett, Steward T.A., and Mary L. Cadenasso. "The Ecosystem as a Multidimensional Concept: Meaning, Model, and Metaphor." *Ecosystems* 5, no. 1 (2002): 1–10.

Pickett, Steward T.A., Mary L. Cadenasso, and J. Morgan Grove. "Resilient Cities: Meaning, Models, and Metaphor for Integrating the Ecological, Socio-Economic, and Planning Realms." *Landscape and Urban Planning* 69, no. 4 (2004): 369–84.

Pickett, Steward T.A., V. Thomas Parker, and Peggy L. Fiedler. "The New Paradigm in Ecology: Implications for Conservation Biology above the Species Level." In *Conservation Biology*, 65–88. Springer, 1992.

Pickett, Steward T.A., William R. Burch Jr., Shawn E. Dalton, Timothy W. Foresman, J. Morgan Grove, and Rowan Rowntree. "A Conceptual Framework for the Study of Human Ecosystems in Urban Areas." *Urban Ecosystems* 1, no. 4 (1997): 185–99.

Pimm, Stuart L. "The Complexity and Stability of Ecosystems." *Nature* 307, no. 5949 (1984): 321–26.

Redman, Charles L. *Human Impact on Ancient Environments*. Tucson: University of Arizona Press, 1999.

Rockström, Johan, Will Steffen, Kevin Noone, Åsa Persson, F. Stuart Chapin, Eric F. Lambin, Timothy M. Lenton, et al. "A Safe Operating Space for Humanity." *Nature* 461, no. 7263 (2009): 472–75.

Scheffer, Marten, Steve Carpenter, Jonathan A. Foley, Carl Folke, and Brian Walker. "Catastrophic Shifts in Ecosystems." *Nature* 413, no. 6856 (2001): 591–96.

Scheffer, Marten, William Brock, and Frances Westley. "Socioeconomic Mechanisms Preventing Optimum Use of Ecosystem Services: An Interdisciplinary Theoretical Analysis." *Ecosystems* 3, no. 5 (2000): 451–71.

Schumpeter, Joseph A. *Capitalism, Socialism, and Democracy*. New York: Harper & Row, 1950.

Shepard, Paul, and Daniel McKinley. *Subversive Science: Essays toward an Ecology of Man*. Boston: Houghton Mifflin, 1969.

Simon, Herbert Alexander. *The Sciences of the Artificial*. Cambridge: MIT Press, 1996.

Spencer, Herbert. *Progress: Its Law and Cause. Essays: Scientific, Political and Speculative*. (Reprinted in 1915) New York: Appleton, 1857.

Vale, Lawrence J., and Thomas J. Campanella. *The Resilient City: How Modern Cities Recover from Disaster*. New York: Oxford University Press, 2005.

Van der Ryn, Sim. *Ecological Design*. Washington, DC: Island Press, 1995.

Walker, Brian H., and Leonie Pearson. "A Resilience Perspective of the SEEA." *Ecological Economics* 61, no. 4 (2007): 708-15.

Walker, Brian H., and David Salt. *Resilience Thinking: Sustaining Ecosystems and People in a Changing World*. Washington, DC: Island Press, 2006.

Walker, Brian H., Crawford S. Holling, Stephen R. Carpenter, and Ann Kinzig. "Resilience, Adaptability and Transformability in Social-Ecological Systems." *Ecology and Society* 9, no. 2 (2004): 5.

Wallace, Deborah, and Rodrick Wallace. "Urban Systems during Disasters: Factors for Resilience." *Ecology and Society* 13, no. 1 (2008): 18.

Wu, Jianguo. "Making the Case for Landscape Ecology an Effective Approach to Urban Sustainability." *Landscape Journal* 27, no. 1 (2008): 41–50.

———. "Hierarchy and Scaling: Extrapolating Information along a Scaling Ladder." *Canadian Journal of Remote Sensing* 25, no. 4 (1999): 367–80.

———. "Toward a Landscape Ecology of Cities: Beyond Buildings, Trees, and Urban Forests." In *Ecology, Planning, and Management of Urban Forests*, 10–28. New York: Springer, 2008.

Wu, Jianguo, and John L. David. "A Spatially Explicit Hierarchical Approach to Modeling Complex Ecological Systems: Theory and Applications." *Ecological Modelling* 153, no. 1 (2002): 7–26.

Wu, Jianguo, and Orie L. Loucks. "From Balance of Nature to Hierarchical Patch Dynamics: A Paradigm Shift in Ecology." *Quarterly Review of Biology* (1995): 439–66.

Zipperer, Wayne C., Jianguo Wu, Richard V. Pouyat, and Steward T.A. Pickett. "The Application of Ecological Principles to Urban and Urbanizing Landscapes." *Ecological Applications* 10, no. 3 (2000): 685–88.

Ecological Urbanism: A Framework for the Design of Resilient Cities (2014)

Anne Whiston Spirn

Humans' survival as a species depends upon adapting ourselves and our . . . settlements in new life-sustaining ways, shaping contexts that acknowledge connections to air, earth, water, life, and to each other, and that help us feel and understand these connections, landscapes that are functional, sustainable, meaningful, and artful (Spirn 1998, 26).

Ecological urbanism aims to advance this goal. It weds the theory and practice of urban design and planning, as a means of adaptation, with the insights of ecology and other environmental disciplines. Ecological urbanism is critical to the future of the city: it provides a framework for addressing challenges that threaten humanity (climate change, environmental justice) while fulfilling human needs for health, safety, and welfare, meaning, and delight. This overview describes the roots of ecological urbanism, with an emphasis on the Anglo-American tradition, and identifies fundamental concepts and principles. The literature is vast, and a detailed review is impossible here (for more references, see Spirn 2012). This introduction provides historical context and a framework to guide more focused research and more comprehensive reviews of the literature and to advance the practice of ecological urbanism.

Ecological Urbanism: Historic Roots and Current Trends

The roots of ecological urbanism in Western culture are ancient (for a review, see Spirn 1985). Hippocrates described the effects of "airs, waters, and places" on public health, and Vitruvius (ca. first century B.C.) described how the layout of streets and the orientation and arrangement of buildings should respond to sun and wind. Leon Battista Alberti in 1485 proposed that cities should be adapted to the natural environment to promote health, safety, convenience, dignity, and pleasure and catalogued the disasters suffered by cities that had disregarded the power of nature (Alberti 1485), a warning issued several centuries later by George Perkins Marsh, who proposed that "in reclaiming and reoccupying lands laid waste by human improvidence or malice . . . the task . . . is to become a co-worker with nature in the reconstruction of the damaged fabric" (Marsh 1865). This was an approach embraced by Marsh's contemporary, Frederick Law Olmsted, who sought to "hasten the process already begun" by nature, thereby achieving more than the "unassisted processes of nature" in his designs for landscape infrastructure (Olmsted and Vaux 1887, pp. 19, 8). By 1915, Patrick Geddes advocated "regional surveys" as a way to comprehend each city and region as an evolving whole and to plan a future based on an understanding of its natural and cultural history and its "life-processes" (Geddes 1915, p. 2). Lewis Mumford, like Geddes, advocated an integrative approach to cities and their regions that "must include the form-shaping contributions of nature, of river, bay, hill, forest, vegetation, climate, as well as those of human history and culture" (Mumford 1968, p. 164). Mumford influenced Kevin Lynch and Ian McHarg, who shared the conviction that the natural environment has a social value to be cultivated in urban design.

Lynch judged "good city form" by how well it sustains human life and explored the role that natural features play in enhancing the identity, legibility, coherence, and immediacy of urban form (Lynch 1981). His last book, *Wasting Away*, takes an ecological approach to managing resources and waste (Lynch 1990). McHarg's point of departure was nature as "process," that is "interacting," "representing values and opportunities for human use with certain limitations and even prohibitions" (McHarg 1969, p. 7). As a prerequisite for planning and design, McHarg advocated the "ecological inventory" of interrelated systems. For McHarg, design was an evolutionary strategy, a means of adaptation (Spirn 2000). For Jane Jacobs, another important thinker in the history of ecological urbanism, "human beings are . . . part of nature" as are cities (Jacobs 1961, p. 446). Jacobs advocated an ecological approach to designing and managing cities, arguing that cities are problems of organized complexity, akin to living organisms where "half-dozen or even several dozen quantities are all varying simultaneously and in subtly interconnected ways" (Jacobs 1961, p. 433).

Jacobs's, McHarg's, Lynch's, and Mumford's ideas about an ecological approach to the design of cities were supported by scientific knowledge about the place of cities in the natural world (Thomas 1955). By 1980 there was a body of knowledge on urban nature and a growing interest in an ecological approach to urban design. My own book *The Granite Garden* described and applied that knowledge to demonstrate how cities can be designed in concert with natural processes (Spirn 1984). Michael Hough's book *City Form and Natural Process* presented a wealth of additional cases (Hough 1984).

Many others have contributed to the theory and practice of ecological urbanism, far too many to treat in this summary. Ecological urbanism is a broad approach to urban design and planning; related to it are aspects of several contemporary movements: ecological design and planning (Van der Ryn and Cowan 1996, Thompson and Steiner 1997, Johnson and Hill 2002, Ndubisi 2002 and 2008, Berger 2008, Palazzo and Steiner 2011), sustainable design (Calthorpe and Van der Ryn 1986, Lyle 1994, Hester 2006), green architecture (Wines 2000, Fromonot 2003), green infrastructure (Wenk 2002, Benedict and McMahon 2006), landscape urbanism (Mohstafavi 2003, Waldheim 2006, Almy 2007), industrial ecology (Graedel and Allenby 2003), and urban metabolism (Ferrão and Fernandez 2013). Not all the works produced under these rubrics, however, qualify as ecological urbanism; they belong to the extent that they embody key concepts and principles.

Ecological Urbanism: Key Concepts and Principles for Urban Design

Important concepts of ecological urbanism are the foundation from which principles for urban design and planning derive. The principles described here—and the citations of contributions—are illustrative not exhaustive.

Cities Are Part of the Natural World

Human activities interact with natural processes to create a typical urban climate (except under certain conditions), urban soils, urban hydrology, urban plant and animal communities, and characteristic flows of energy and materials. Conflicting ideas of nature coexist, however, and they affect perception and action (Cronon 1996, Spirn 1997). The idea of nature as consisting of the biological, physical, and chemical processes that create and sustain life, the earth, and the universe is fundamental to ecological urbanism. If one embraces this idea, then the false oppositions between city and nature, the given and the built, fall away. The idea of nature as a nexus of processes resonates with the approach of contemporary ecological science (Botkin 1990, Pulliam and Johnson 2001). In this view of the natural world as shaped and structured by processes, ecology has much to offer urban design (Johnson and Hill 2001, Leitão and Ahern 2002, Reed 2011).

Recognize cities as part of the natural world and design them accordingly.

The key is to think in terms of the ways that human activities and urban form interact with natural processes of air, earth, water, life, and ecosystems. This is not just a matter of imitating or echoing the *shape* of natural features or of using indigenous materials, but of adapting urban form to natural processes. By focusing on the processes that shape and structure the environment, designers and planners can accommodate dynamic change, make connections among seemingly unrelated elements and issues, and can realize opportunities. Many authors and practitioners have demonstrated how this might be accomplished: from projects by the offices of Olmsted and McHarg to those of contemporary designers such as James Corner, Anuradha Mathur and Dilip da Cunha, Alan Berger, Herbert Dreiseitl, and Kongjian Yu.

Cities Are Habitats

Cities are places for living, for humans and other species. As habitats, they must provide settings for the biological and social needs of the organisms who dwell there. What could be more obvious? And yet, cities are full of places that are ill-adapted to the needs of their inhabitants: dysfunctional, contaminated, and vulnerable to natural hazards, exposing residents to discomfort, inconvenience, and even to danger. Cities provide habitats for many nonhuman species and mammals, some are indigenous, others are typical urban species, some are central to human health and prosperity, a few are hostile (Sukopp et al. 1990, Burger 1999, Adams et al. 2005). Urban development tends to reduce biodiversity, with far-reaching adverse effects (McKinney 2008, Shochat et al. 2010). Enhancing biodiversity is not just important for plants and animals; Vandruff et al. (1995) have argued that the presence of urban wildlife is closely linked to human well-being.

Design the city as a life-sustaining and life-enhancing habitat.

Every urban design project should enhance the quality of the urban habitat for humans and other species. Kevin Lynch provides measures of "good city form" in terms of how well urban form sustains life, by how clearly it is perceived, how well environment and behavior "fit," and by whether it provides "access," "control," "efficiency," and "justice" (Lynch 1981). Many others have elaborated on how this might be accomplished (e.g., Alexander et al. 1977, Steiner 2002, Hill 2002, Hester 2006). Like humans, each species has specific needs, and the most effective way to enhance their survival or establish control is often through the design and management of their habitat (Adams et al. 2005, Mc-Donnell et al. 2009).

> *Celebrate the natural processes that shape the urban habitat and that sustain life, make them tangible and understandable.*

Pleasure and meaning are basic human needs, and "the mental sense of connection with nature is a basic human satisfaction, the most profound aspect of sensibility" (Lynch 1981, p. 257). Wilson's biophilia hypothesis argues that humans have an innate attraction to life and life's processes (Wilson 1984). Urban design that fosters and intensifies the experience of the natural processes that sustain life fulfills this need (Koh 1982, Howett 1987, Spirn 1988b and 1998, Gobster et al. 2007, Beatley 2011). Aesthetic experience of such places has the potential for "recentering human consciousness from an egocentric to a more bio-centric perspective" (Meyer 2008, p. 6).

Cities Are Ecosystems

The urban ecosystem consists of all the organisms that dwell within it and their interactions with each other and with their physical environment, which comprises built artifacts like buildings, roads, and sewers, as well as water, soil, and plants (Pickett and Grove 2009). The urban ecosystem is an open system: energy, material, and information flow through it as resources are imported, transformed, and consumed, then exported as wastes and goods (Brunner 2007). The less efficiently resources are used, the more wastes are produced and contamination increased. The urban ecosystem encompasses all the processes which flow within and through the city: cultural processes as well as natural processes, flows of capital, people, and goods, as well as flows of water, air, nutrients, and pollutants (Pickett et al. 1997). The city as a whole, itself an ecosystem, is composed of many smaller ecosystems: of ponds and river corridors, parks, buildings and neighborhoods. Landscape ecology and urban ecology have matured as fields in recent decades (Forman 2008, Pickett et al. 2010). Both fields offer insight and inspiration to the planners and designers of cities.

Design the city and its rural periphery, as well as every park, building, and district within that larger whole, as ecosystems that require minimal inputs of energy and resources to build and sustain.

The design of an urban ecosystem entails not just the composition of its structure, shape, and materials, but should include as well the means by which it will be built and maintained over time. The city, and every building, park, and infrastructure system within it, should be designed as much as possible to import and consume fewer resources, produce fewer wastes, and to recycle wastes as resources. This goal is most easily understood and achieved at the scale of a park or a building and its immediate surroundings, and there are good examples (Lyle 1994, Wines 2000, Fromonot 2003). At the district scale, increasing the density of urban development can make energy-conserving strategies such as shared transportation systems and district heating more feasible. At all scales from house to metropolitan region, wastes—the by-products of one activity—may be a resource for another. Industrial ecology brings together industries whose waste and resource streams are symbiotic (Lynch 1990, Graedel and Allenby 2003).

Preservation, conservation, restoration, reconstruction, and renewal are distinct approaches to managing an ecosystem. Preservation and conservation are most appropriate when the ecosystem is vital and intact and the task is to manage it. The goal of restoration is to reconstruct or repair a damaged ecosystem in order to return it to a former, healthy condition. The purpose of renewal, unlike the other three approaches, is to improve the condition of an ecosystem through the introduction of a wholly new element: a building, a park or reserve, or a neighborhood. Frederick Law Olmsted's proposal for Yosemite is an example of conservation, his design for Niagara Falls and plan for Biltmore's forest, examples of both restoration and conservation. His projects for the Fens and Riverway called for wholesale reconstruction (Spirn 1995). James Wescoat has applied the conservation approach to water systems in South Asian cities (Wescoat 2009), Kongjian Yu that of both conservation and renewal to new landscapes in China (Saunders 2012).

Urban Ecosystems Are Connected and Dynamic

The many ecosystems that comprise the larger urban ecosystem are linked by physical space and by the channels through which energy, material, and information flow. There are ecosystems within ecosystems. A pond ecosystem, for example, exists within the larger ecosystem of its watershed (and there are watersheds within watersheds, from that of a small stream to a continental river basin); a building is an ecosystem within a neighborhood. Given this connectivity, changes to one ecosystem may produce repercussions in many others, and an ecosystem may be externally regulated (Pickett et al. 2004).

Address social and environmental challenges within appropriate boundaries at the appropriate spatial and temporal scales.

Problems felt in one place may be caused by activities that take place elsewhere: strong winds at the base of a tall building aggravated by conditions upwind, floods and pollution by discharge upstream, vulnerability to hurricane-driven waves by erosion of marshes and swamps. Environmental and social problems in low-income neighborhoods are often created or aggravated by flows of capital and wastes to and from suburban communities (Spirn 2005). In these and many other cases, local intervention alone is doomed to failure. Solutions may require taking action in a different location than where the problem is felt. Designers should identify the systems to which their project site is connected and track the flows of energy, materials, information, and capital. No matter how small or large the project, the designer's responsibility is to address the impact on the ecosystems to which it is connected. Design proposals should not be limited to the area enclosed by the client's boundaries, but should be expanded to include that area necessary to effectively address the challenges posed by site, program, and context.

Define multi-purpose solutions to comprehensively defined problems.

The "three E's" of sustainable development—environment, economics, and equity—emerged in the 1980s (Brundtland et al. 1987). This recognition for the need to integrate the three "E's" was matched in practice, by proposals such as those for Boston in 1985 (Spirn 2000a), Philadelphia in 1991 (Spirn 1991 and 2005), and New York City in 1996 (Yaro and Hiss 1996). Increasingly, designers and planners of cities are seeking integrated solutions to social, economic, cultural, and environmental challenges (Hester 2006, Bargmann 2012). The integration of open urban land into a "green" infrastructure promises to extend the aesthetic and recreational value of parks and parkways to a crucial role in health, safety and welfare. Parks and plazas, rivers, streams, and floodplains, steep hillsides, and even parking lots and highway corridors could be part of a cohesive system to improve air quality and climate, to reduce flooding and improve water quality, to limit the impact of geological hazards such as earthquakes, subsidence, and landslides, to provide a diverse community of plants and animals within the city, to conserve energy, water and mineral resources, and to enhance the safe assimilation of the city's wastes

(Spirn 1984 and 1988, Wenk 2002, Benedict and MacMahon 2006, Ahern 2007, Dreiseitl 2009).

Take account of history.
Urban design is an art of time as well as space; it is a projection into the future, complicated by the fact that the urban ecosystem constantly changes in unpredictable ways. Knowing how a place has been shaped over time is essential to understanding its present and possible future. What is this place in the process of becoming? Which of its features are clues to ongoing processes that continue to exert a decisive influence, and which are merely artifacts of the past that assert little influence now? Which features are amenable to change and which are resistant? It is difficult to answer such questions without understanding how a place evolved, through what processes and actions, when, and which of its features have had a sustained impact on their surroundings over time. The environmental history of a place provides a window into the ways natural and social processes interact through time, and how planners have intervened, for good or bad effect (Cronon 1991, White 1996, Klingle 2007). This has little to do with imitating historic built form. Taking account of history means more than conserving historical structures and using history as a source of formal precedent. History is a way of extending human memory beyond the human life span.

Every City Has a Deep Structure or Enduring Context
Not all features of the urban natural environment are equally significant; some are ephemeral, others more enduring (Spirn 1993). While urbanization radically changes the surface of the landscape, the deep structure of a city, with its distinctive rhythms, is expressed in that city's climate (hot, cold, or temperate; humid or arid), geology (rock type and structure, seismic and volcanic activity), physiography (plain, basin, piedmont, or mountain), and bio-climatic zone (tundra, forest, prairie, or desert). Deep structure remains crucial to the history and future of a place—why it was settled, its initial location, its transportation routes, its economic development and population distribution, the character of its buildings, streets, and parks, and the health and safety of its residents. The design of cities that are in agreement with their region's deep structure, rather than counter to it, fosters resilient urban form. The work of Anuradha Mathur and Dilip da Cunha in the low-lying, "aqueous terrain" of Mumbai is a model for this approach. Their proposal, *Soak*, "is about making peace with the sea; about designing with the monsoon in an estuary" (Mathur and da Cunha 2009).

Adapt the physical shape and structure of a city—the infrastructure of roads and sewers, the buildings and parks—to its deep structure.

Planting trees and lawn in a desert or burying a river in a sewer and filling in its floodplain are examples of urban form that obscures or opposes a city's deep structure. In contrast, urban form that reveals and responds to deep structure is likely to be more functional, more economical, and more resilient than design that disregards it. This is especially important for the design of the infrastructure (water, sewer, power, transportation) that supports the city, whether at the scale of building, neighborhood, city, or region. Such design may also afford an aesthetic experience of unity with the processes which shape the landscape and which sustain life (Spirn 1988b, Brown 1998, Meyer 2008, Bargmann 2011).

Anticipate and exploit catastrophic events.

As a function of its deep structure, every city is prone to specific natural hazards whose precise timing is unknown. San Francisco will experience a major earthquake; Las Vegas and Phoenix, severe drought; St. Louis and Pittsburgh, major floods. It was inevitable that a major hurricane would strike New Orleans. After a catastrophe, there is a will to rebuild and to "do things right," but that window of opportunity is small. Urban designers should anticipate future redesign and rebuilding in order to seize the opportunity when catastrophe strikes; historical examples provide lessons of failure and success (Vale and Campanella 2005).

Urban Design is a Powerful Tool of Adaptation

Most humans now live in cities, and urban design is a powerful tool of adaptation. No matter how well one understands a city's history, its ecosystems, and its enduring context, no matter how carefully one tries to anticipate the future, there will always be unforeseen circumstances to which a city must adapt.

Design resilient cities.

The concept of resilience (as opposed to the concept of sustainability, for example, which implies maintenance of a stable state) is useful for urban designers who strive to create cities that are adaptable to changing conditions and needs (Gunderson et al. 2010, Pickett et al. 2004, Vale and Campanella 2005). The risk of earthquakes, hurricanes, floods, and drought in a particular place are well known, but "natural" hazards are also the product of human activities: e. g. the location of vulnerable land uses, the design and construction of buildings, actions that trigger an event, and, ironically, even the very measures designed to mitigate certain catastrophes (Cutter 2001, Mileti 2008, Mathur and da Cunha

2001 and 2009). Urban form that is congruent with the "deep structure" or enduring context of a city's natural environment will be more resilient.

Unlike certain natural hazards, phenomena like shifts in economy and culture, new technology, and changes in the global environment are relatively unpredictable. Kevin Lynch describes a range of additional physical design strategies for enhancing the ability of urban form to adapt to future change: avoid urban form that is too narrowly specialized such as districts that consist entirely of a single, specialized land-use; encourage a diversity of buildings and neighborhoods; adopt an additive structure, such as a grid, that can accommodate growth or decline at the periphery without major change to the overall structure at the center of a neighborhood or city; employ temporary structures or uses, when appropriate, especially true for uses in which technology is changing rapidly; utilize communication systems to accommodate changing needs rather than radical alteration of the city's physical structure (Lynch 1958).

Act comprehensively and incrementally.
Major challenges like climate change may require a comprehensive and rapid response, but it is dangerous to implement a single model for change. Massive large-scale interventions often produce unforeseen effects, which may be devastating. Diverse approaches, implemented incrementally, provide the opportunity to learn from failure and success and to respond; such solutions should fit local conditions, tailored to the needs of specific people in particular places. But incremental projects should be undertaken as part of a comprehensive framework for large-scale investment that addresses regional needs. The local view gives an intimate view of the habitat of individuals and small groups; an overview gives a broader perspective of larger systems. *The Granite Garden* offers a checklist for the designers and planners of cities; each section of the book concludes with suggestions for "What Every City Should Do," which range from the scale of the street corner to the scale of the region (Spirn 1984).

Ecological Urbanism and the Future of Urban Design

Much is known about the urban natural and social environment, and there exist many successful models of ecological urbanism. Yet most of these examples are not known to the public, to natural and social scientists, or even to urban designers and planners. Ignorant of existing knowledge and precedents, researchers and practitioners repeatedly reinvent the wheel. What is needed is a series of literature reviews on ecological urbanism and its subfields, which provide a critical, comprehensive overview of what is known: the principle themes and threads of inquiry; the keys works and contributions in each area; regions of agreement and the disputed territories; gaps in knowledge; potentially fertile areas of inquiry; and models of practice that deserve to be replicated.

Much is still not known about the urban natural environment and the processes that shape it, and there is great opportunity for future research. Particularly promising are recent collaborations between urban designers and experts in other disciplines, such as ecology, economics, engineering, and art. Landscape architect Alex Felson and ecologist Steward Pickett, for example, describe design projects that are also ecological experiments (Felson and Pickett 2005), and Joan Nassauer and Paul Opdam make a case for the incorporation of design into ecological research (Nassauer and Opdam 2008).

The reasons for embracing and promoting ecological urbanism are compelling. At stake is the future of humanity and the human habitat and whether we can adapt our behavior and settlements to meet the challenges we face (those posed by climate change and environmental contamination, for example, and by inequities in exposure to the hazards they represent) and whether we can do so in ways that are life-enhancing and life-expanding. Urban designers have an essential role, not merely in producing safer and healthier urban habitats, but in making legible and tangible the systems that support life, and in changing the perception of what is possible.

Acknowledgments

This is an abridged, revised version of a chapter in the *Routledge Companion to Urban Design*, edited by Tridib Banerjee and Anastasia Loukaitou-Sideris (London: Routledge, 2011). I regret that it was not possible to provide a more comprehensive review of the many authors who have contributed to the evolution and development of this tradition. That must wait for an in-depth review of the literature. Meanwhile, a much enlarged version is available at http://www.annewhistonspirn.com/pdf/Spirn-EcoUrbanism-2012.pdf.

References

Adams, Clark E., Kieran J. Lindsey, and J. Sarah Ash. *Urban Wildlife Management*. CRC Press, 2005.

Ahern, Jack. "Green Infrastructure for Cities: The Spatial Dimension." *Cities of the Future: Towards Integrated Sustainable Water and Landscape Management*, edited by V. B. P. Novotny. IWA Publishing, London (2007): 267–283.

Alberti, Leon Battista. *On the Art of Building in Ten Books*. Translated by Joseph Rykwert, Neil Leach, and Robert Tavernor. Cambridge, MA.: MIT Press, 1988.

Alexander, Christopher, Sara Ishikawa, and Murray Silverstein. *A Pattern Language: Towns, Buildings, Construction*. New York: Oxford University Press, 1978.

Almy, Dean. *On Landscape Urbanism*. Austin, TX: Center for American Architecture and Design, University of Texas at Austin School of Architecture, 2007.

Bargmann, Julie. "Just Ground: A Social Infrastructure for Urban Landscape Regeneration." *Resilience in Ecology and Urban Design*, Springer Netherlands (2012): 347–54.

Beatley, Timothy. *Biophilic Cities: Integrating Nature into Urban Design and Planning*. Washington, DC: Island Press, 2010.

———. *Green Urbanism: Learning from European Cities*. Washington, DC: Island Press, 2000.

Benedict, Mark A., and Edward T. McMahon. *Green Infrastructure: Linking Landscapes and Communities*. Washington, DC: Island Press, 2006.

Berger, Alan, and C. Brown. "A New Systemic Nature for Mussolini's Landscape Urbanism." *VIA: DIRT* (2009): 27–36.

Berger, Alan. *Drosscape: Wasting Land in Urban America*. New York: Princeton Architectural Press, 2006.

Botequilha Leitão, André, and Jack Ahern. "Applying Landscape Ecological Concepts and Metrics in Sustainable Landscape Planning." *Landscape and Urban Planning* 59, no. 2 (2002): 65–93.

Botkin, Daniel B. *Discordant Harmonies: A New Ecology for the Twenty-First Century*. Oxford University Press, 1990.

Brown, B., T. Harkness, and D. M. Johnston. "Eco-Revelatory Design." *Special Issue of Landscape Journal* 17 (1998): 2

Brundtland, Gro H. *Our Common Future*. New York: Oxford University Press, 1987.

Brunner, Paul H. "Reshaping Urban Metabolism." *Journal of Industrial Ecology* 1, no. 2 (2007): 3–19.

Burger, Joanna. *Animals in Towns and Cities*. Dubuque: Kendall/Hunt Publishing Company, 1999.

Calthorpe, Peter, and Sim Van der Ryn. *Sustainable Communities*. San Francisco: Sierra Club, 1986.

Cronon, William, ed. *Nature's Metropolis: Chicago and the Great West*. New York: W. W. Norton & Company, 1991.

———. *Uncommon Ground: Toward Rethinking the Human Place in Nature*. New York: W. W. Norton & Company, 1995.

Cutter, Susan L. *American Hazardscapes: The Regionalization of Hazards and Disasters*. Washington, DC: Joseph Henry Press, 2001.

Dreiseitl, H. *Recent Waterscapes: Planning, Building, and Designing with Water*. Basel: Birkhäuser, 2009.

Felson, Alexander J., and Steward T. A. Pickett. "Designed Experiments: New Approaches to Studying Urban Ecosystems." *Frontiers in Ecology and the Environment* 3, no. 10 (2005): 549–56.

Ferrão, Paulo, and John E. Fernández. *Sustainable Urban Metabolism*. Cambridge: MIT Press, 2013.

Forman, Richard T. T. *Urban Regions: Ecology and Planning Beyond the City*. New York: Cambridge University Press, 2008.

Fromonot, Françoise. *Glenn Murcutt: Buildings and Projects 1962–2003*. London: Thames and Hudson, 2003.

Geddes, Patrick, Richard T. LeGates, and Frederic Stout. *Cities in Evolution*. Vol. 27. London: Williams & Norgate, 1949.

Gobster, Paul H., Joan I. Nassauer, Terry C. Daniel, and Gary Fry. "The Shared Landscape: What Does Aesthetics Have to Do with Ecology?" *Landscape Ecology* 22, no. 7 (2007): 959–72.

Graedel, Thomas E., and Braden R. Allenby. *Industrial Ecology*. Upper Saddle River, NJ: Prentice Hall, 2003.

Hester, Randolph T. *Design for Ecological Democracy*. Cambridge: MIT Press, 2006.

Hill, Kristina. "Design and Planning as Arts: The Broader Context of Health and Environment." In *Ecology and Design: Frameworks for Learning*, Washington, DC: Island Press, 2002.

————. "Urban Ecological Design and Urban Ecology: An Assessment of the State of Current Knowledge and a Suggested Research Agenda." *Cities of the Future: Towards Integrated Sustainable Water and Landscape Management* (2007): 251–66.

Hippocrates (ca. fifth century B.C.). "Airs, Waters, Places." In *Hippocrates*, vol. 1, The Loeb Classical Library, Cambridge: Harvard University Press, 1962.

Hough, Michael. *Cities and Natural Process*. London: Routledge, 1995.

Howett, Catherine. "Systems, Signs, Sensibilities: Sources for a New Landscape Aesthetic." *Landscape Journal* 6, no. 1 (1987): 1–12.

Johnson, Bart, and Kristina Hill, eds. *Ecology and Design: Frameworks for Learning*. Vol. 1. Washington, DC: Island Press, 2002.

Klingle, M. *Emerald City: An Environmental History of Seattle*. New Haven: Yale University Press, 2007.

Koh, Jusuck. "Ecological Design: A Post-Modern Design Paradigm of Holistic Philosophy and Evolutionary Ethic." *Landscape Journal* 1, no. 2 (1982): 76–84.

Lyle, John Tillman. *Regenerative Design for Sustainable Development*. New York: John Wiley & Sons Incorporated, 1994.

Lynch, Kevin. "Environmental Adaptability." *Journal of the American Institute of Planners* 24, no. 1 (1958): 16–24.

————. *A Theory of Good City Form*. Cambridge: MIT Press, 1981.

————. *Wasting Away: An Exploration of Waste: What It Is, How It Happens, Why We Fear It, How to Do It Well*. San Francisco: Sierra Club Books, 1990.

Mathur, Anuradha, and Dilip Da Cunha. *Mississippi Floods: Designing a Shifting Landscape*. New Haven: Yale University Press, 2001.

McDonnell, Mark J., Amy K. Hahs, and Jürgen H. Breuste, eds. *Ecology of Cities and Towns: A Comparative Approach*. Cambridge: Cambridge University Press, 2009.

McHarg, Ian L. *Design with Nature*. Garden City: Natural History Press, 1969.

McKinney, Michael L. "Effects of Urbanization on Species Richness: A Review of Plants and Animals." *Urban Ecosystems* 11, no. 2 (2008): 161–76.

Meyer, Elizabeth K. "Sustaining Beauty. The Performance of Appearance: A Manifesto in Three Parts." *Journal of Landscape Architecture* 3, no. 1 (2008): 6–23.

Mileti, Dennis S. *Disasters by Design*. Washington, DC: Joseph Henry Press, 2008.

Mostafavi, M., and C. Najle, eds. *Landscape Urbanism*. London: Architectural Association, 2003.

Mumford, Lewis. *The Urban Prospect*. New York: Harcourt Brace Jovanovich, 1968.

Nassauer, Joan Iverson, ed. *Placing Nature: Culture and Landscape Ecology*. Washington, DC: Island Press, 1997.

Nassauer, Joan Iverson, and Paul Opdam. "Design in Science: Extending the Landscape Ecology Paradigm." *Landscape Ecology* 23, no. 6 (2008): 633–44.

Ndubisi, Forster. *Ecological Planning: A Historical and Comparative Synthesis*. Baltimore, MD: The John Hopkins University Press, 2002.

————. "Sustainable Regionalism Evolutionary Framework and Prospects for Managing Metropolitan Landscapes." *Landscape Journal* 27, no. 1 (2008): 51–68.

Olmsted, Frederick Law, and Calvert Vaux. *General Plan for the Improvement of the Niagara Reservation*. Gazette Book and Job Office, 1887.

Palazzo, Danilo S., and Frederick Steiner. *Urban Ecological Design*. Washington, DC: Island Press, 2011.

Pickett, Steward T.A., Mary L. Cadenasso, and Brian McGrath. *Resilience in Ecology and Urban Design*. New York: Springer, 2013.

Pickett, Steward T.A., Mary L. Cadenasso, J. Morgan Grove, Christopher G. Boone, Peter M. Groffman, Elena Irwin, Sujay S. Kaushal et al. "Urban Ecological Systems: Scientific Foundations and a Decade of Progress." *Journal of Environmental Management* 92, no. 3 (2011): 331–62.

Pickett, Steward T.A., Mary L. Cadenasso, and J. Morgan Grove. "Resilient Cities: Meaning, Models, and Metaphor for Integrating the Ecological, Socio-Economic, and Planning Realms." *Landscape and Urban Planning* 69, no. 4 (2004): 369–84.

Pickett, Steward T.A., William R. Burch Jr., Shawn E. Dalton, Timothy W. Foresman, J. Morgan Grove, and Rowan Rowntree. "A Conceptual Framework for the Study of Human Ecosystems in Urban Areas." *Urban Ecosystems* 1, no. 4 (1997): 185–99.

Pulliam, H. Ronald, and Bart R. Johnson. "Ecology's New Paradigm: What Does It Offer Designers and Planners?" *Ecology and Design: Frameworks for Learning*. Washington, DC: Island Press (2002): 51–84.

Reed, C. "The Agency of Ecology." In *Ecological Urbanism*, edited by M. Mostafavi and G. Doherty. Baden, Switzerland: Lars Müller, 2011.

Saunders, W., ed. *Designed Ecologies*. Basel: Birkhauser, 2012.

Shochat, Eyal, Susannah B. Lerman, John M. Anderies, Paige S. Warren, Stanley H. Faeth, and Charles H. Nilon. "Invasion, Competition, and Biodiversity Loss in Urban Ecosystems." *BioScience* 60, no. 3 (2010): 199–208.

Spirn, Anne Whiston. "Constructing Nature: The Legacy of Frederick Law Olmsted." *Uncommon Ground: Rethinking the Human Place in Nature* (1996): 91-113.

———. "Ian McHarg, Landscape Architecture, and Environmentalism: Ideas and Methods in Context." *Environmentalism in Landscape Architecture*, vol. 22. Washington, DC: Dumbarton Oaks (2000): 97–114.

———. "Restoring Mill Creek: Landscape Literacy, Environmental Justice and City Planning and Design." *Landscape Research* 30, no. 3 (2005): 395–413.

———. "The Authority of Nature: Conflict and Confusion in Landscape Architecture." *Nature and Ideology: Natural Garden Design in the Twentieth Century* (1997): 253–54.

———. "The Poetics of City and Nature: Towards a New Aesthetic for Urban Design." *Landscape Journal* 7, no. 2 (1988): 108–26.

———. "Urban Nature and Human Design: Renewing the Great Tradition." *Journal of Planning Education and Research* 5, no. 1 (1985): 39–51.

———. *The Granite Garden: Urban Nature and Human Design*. New York: Basic Books, 1984.

———. *The Language of Landscape*. New Haven: Yale University Press, 1998.

Sukopp, Herbert, Slavomil Hejný, and I. Kowarik. *Urban Ecology: Plants and Plant Communities in Urban Environments*. The Hague: SPB Academic Publishers, 1990.

Thomas, William Leroy. *Man's Role in Changing the Face of the Earth*. Chicago: University of Chicago Press, 1955.

Thompson, George F., and Frederick R. Steiner. *Ecological Design and Planning*. New York: John Wiley, 1997.

Tourbier, Joachim Toby, and Richard Noble Westmacott. *Water Resources Protection Technology: A Handbook of Measures to Protect Water Resources in Land Development*. Washington, DC: Urban Land Institute, 1981.

Vale, Lawrence J., and Thomas J. Campanella, eds. *The Resilient City: How Modern Cities Recover from Disaster*. New York: Oxford University Press, 2005.

Van der Ryn, Sim, and Peter Calthorpe. *Sustainable Communities: A New Design Synthesis for Cities, Suburbs and Towns*. Gabriola Island, BC: New Catalyst Books, 1986.

Vandruff, Larry W., Daniel L. Leedy, and Forest W. Stearns. "Urban Wildlife and Human Well-Being." *Urban Ecology as the Basis of Urban Planning*. The Hague: SPB Academic Publishing (1995): 203–11.

Waldheim, Charles, ed. *The Landscape Urbanism Reader*. New York: Princeton Architectural Press, 2006.

Wenk, William E. "Toward an Inclusive Concept of Infrastructure." *Ecology and Design: Frameworks for Learning* (2002): 173–90.

Wescoat Jr., James L. "Water Shortages and Water-Conserving Urban Design in Pakistan." *Running on Empty*. Washington, DC: Woodrow Wilson Center (2009): 129–52.

White, Richard. *The Organic Machine*. New York: Hill and Wang, 1996.

Wines, James. *Green Architecture*. New York: Taschen, 2000.

Yaro, Robert, and Tony Hiss. *A Region at Risk: The Third Regional Plan for the New York-New Jersey-Connecticut Metropolitan Area*. Washington, DC: Island Press, 1996.

Conclusion
Maintaining Adaptive and Regenerative Places

New ideas on how to effectively balance human use with ecological concerns are necessary because of the increasing extent, diversity, magnitude, urgency, and complexity of ecological problems arising from changing demographic, social, economic, and technological forces (figure 8-1).

To respond to this challenge, I ask four major questions to guide deliberations on their resolution.

- How can we create and maintain livable, healthy, and sustainable places that are resilient? In other words, how do we ensure that the sustainable solutions currently in practice will continue to be "sustainable" in the face of human and naturally induced disturbances?
- How can we ensure that the quality of landscapes that serve as life-support systems for people and other organisms does not degrade over time, and might even be enhanced?
- How do we best manage a warmer climate that creates rising coastlines, poses risks to valued and fragile plant and animal habitats, and threatens human health through intensified heat island effects?
- How might we conserve prime farmlands, valued natural and cultural resources, and rural values and character in the face of rapidly accelerated urbanization?

I do not intend to offer solutions to these questions. Certainly, it is evident from the other parts of this book that there has been a long history of research,

Figure 8-1 Effects of landscape change: air pollution typical in many cities worldwide (Photograph from http://toglobalist.org/wp-content/uploads/2010/11/Factory.jpg, accessed March 10, 2014).

scholarly work, and exemplary professional practice on resolving these problems. What follows is an attempt to acknowledge and to add to this enormous and rich body of contributions. I prescribe the following ideas and principles as a vehicle for framing meaningful and productive deliberations, as they pertain to ecological problems and the search for their resolution.

Framing Deliberations for an Evolutionary-Ecological Land Ethic

In thinking about the four questions above, I propose that we subscribe to a conservation-based ethical position founded upon the *evolutionary-ecological land ethic* as espoused in the writings of Aldo Leopold, Rachel Carson, and Ian McHarg. This ethical position is anchored in an interdependency view in which the survival of people depends on the continued existence of other species.[1] It emphasizes maintaining the continued "functioning of natural process and the integrity of natural systems"[2] (figure 8-2). Thus, nature—as an object, a place, and a value system—deserves protection.[3]

The evolutionary-ecological land ethic implies that we have an obligation to protect entire ecosystems for their continued right to existence, not just for

Figure 8-2 We have an interdependent relationship with the landscape. Landscape in western Cape, South Africa, 2012 (Photograph by author).

the instrumental benefits they provide to humans (i.e., biological, psychological, and emotional).[4] When conflicts arise in protecting or conserving natural ecosystems, and maintaining and enhancing their integrity is not feasible, the next level of priority would be to protect intelligent forms of life, followed by other forms of life.[5] Leopold and others make a plea for the aesthetic appreciation of land.[6] The conservation of valued natural resources in the context of balancing competing uses becomes increasingly difficult if the general populace does not appreciate its value and beauty. This appreciation is a learned behavior that may require intentional and continuous education.[7]

I propose that this educational component should be integral in efforts to foster environmental stewardship. An educational component should include continuous opportunities for people to *experience* and be inspired by nature.[8] This is an important feature in gaining appreciation for natural systems and processes.[9] If the proposed ethical position is to serve as a useful moral standard to guide the optimal uses of the landscape, it must embrace economic considerations as well.[10] Promising ideas have emerged in this arena, and people are learning in public debates the economic benefits that ecosystems provide, such as flood protection and well water storage and purification.[11]

Life-Support Systems: Ecosystem Services

It is unrealistic to expect to preserve or conserve every ecosystem, especially in free market economies. In the United States, for instance, a significant amount of land is owned by individuals and corporations. Private property rights are entrenched in the legal and economic fabric. People have a long-established tradition of making individual choices about the use of their land, tempered to varying degrees by federal, state, and local regulations, as well as by land-use laws and policies.

Therefore, we must establish priorities for conserving ecosystems. Those that serve as "life-support systems" and provide a variety of services and benefits to humans should receive the highest priority for preservation.[12] Such ecosystems consist of interacting networks of topography, water, soil, plants, and animals that are constantly in flux.

Ecosystem services have been referred to as "those benefits we [including other organisms] acquire from ecosystems."[13] These include *resource* services such as the processes for purifying water and air; *support* services such as waste decomposition and nutrient cycling; *regulation* services, for instance carbon sequestration and climate regulation, as well as erosion control; and *cultural* services, such as recreational, spiritual, and health benefits. Some ecosystems provide multiple benefits. Wetlands, for instance, help to remove pollutants from storm waters before they flow into streams, serve as habitats for some threatened flora and fauna, and reduce vulnerability to damage from storm surge and flooding.

Ecosystems that provide such services are distributed spatially and temporally in urban, suburban, and rural landscapes. They include environmentally sensitive areas that are vital to the long-term maintenance of biological diversity, soil, water, or other natural resources, locally and regionally.[14] Although these environmentally sensitive areas occur within every landscape, their importance in maintaining the health of a locality is relative to their ecological values, and to the type and management regime of adjacent landscapes (figure 8-3).[15]

We have an ethical obligation to ensure the continuity and persistence of these ecosystems that provide a variety of services to human and other organisms beyond the utilitarian requirement to ensure our own health and survival. One goal is to restore, protect, conserve, and enhance these ecosystems as appropriate, to increase rather than decrease the services they provide.[16] In addition, designed landscapes "can protect, sustain, and even provide these critical

Figure 8-3 Thesen Islands, Kynsa, South Africa, 2012 (Photograph by author).

ecosystems services."[17] If we are serious about employing the idea of ecosystem services as a basis for design, we need "to shift our focus from creating and maintaining static, isolated landscapes to that of designing and managing complex, interrelated living systems of the built environment and natural environments,"[18] employing principles that are "inherent in our planet's ecosystems, principles that include zero waste, adaptation, and resiliency."[19] Related and pertinent principles include input management (e.g., reducing the input needed for maintaining human ecosystems such as through reuse and recycling of resources) and integrated management of ecosystem resources (e.g., management of storm water through *low-impact development* principles) (figure 8-4).

Employing ecosystem services as a design and planning goal will involve, among other things, establishing baseline data and performance measures for ascertaining the current value or health of these ecosystems, and for estimating their anticipated performance in response to design and planning interventions.[20] Employing ecosystem services as a design and planning goal will entail paying heightened attention to cause-effect relationships because ecosystems are complex interrelated systems in which one action may trigger numerous reciprocal actions; ascertaining the aesthetic potential of landscapes

Figure 8-4 A multifunctional landscape in Mueller, Texas, 2012, site of former airport serving Austin, Texas (Photograph by author).

and employing the outcomes as an input in creating designed landscapes (input management); adopting a holistic, multidisciplinary, and interdisciplinary approach given the complexity and interdependence of ecosystems; recognizing that ecosystems can have a variety of functions and thus designing accordingly;[21] and lastly, planning and designing for change and adaptation given that ecosystems change over time.[22]

Adaptive-Regenerative Landscapes

How can we create predictably resilient landscapes that conserve and improve ecosystem services? As planners and ecologists become increasingly captivated with resilience theory, there have been a growing number of efforts to integrate ecological resilience theory into ecological design and planning. Indeed, numerous frameworks have been proposed, such as those suggested by Jianguo Wu and Tong Wu, Anne Whiston Spirn, and Frederick Steiner in part 7. The result has been a growing and robust body of work focused on creating systems that enhance the ability of the landscape to absorb change and disturbance, without modifying its basic structure and function, or transforming it into a new state.[23] Such systems emphasize "persistence, change, and unpredictability."[24]

These are some common themes in the frameworks:

- A goal of ecological design and planning should be to manage predictable and unpredictable changes in the landscape, which would ultimately necessitate the development of self-organizing mechanisms to enable landscapes to adapt effectively.
- Adaptive systems work best within the regional rather than local spatial scales and are characterized by intense and persistent feedback loops.
- Change, if guided properly, may lead to innovation and result in the creation of new opportunities for the continuing adaptation of the landscape.
- Landscapes are composed of spatially heterogeneous elements, thus inviting the need to promote diversity in all of its dimensions and to formulate design and planning proposals that are specific in content, rather than overly general.

Design and planning interventions should, therefore, be undertaken in recognizing the possibility of eventual change. Many individuals have offered insightful suggestions to how this might be achieved. These range from creating a first-order organization of space and infrastructure in a landscape and allowing the details to be filled in over time;[25] planning simultaneously for large-scale change and incremental opportunities while employing the "underlying structures" of the landscape as the foundation for shaping urban form, because they change slowly;[26] and targeting interventions to critical ecosystem variables that underpin the effective performance of a system, as well as developing governance structures that manage for cross-scale influences.[27] Other suggestions include adopting design and management processes that nurture reflective learning; acknowledging and accounting for ecosystem services;[28] and establishing tight feedback loops and monitoring protocols for designed landscapes that connect design intentions seamlessly to on-going management activities.[29]

There is an urgent need for continued monitoring of how ecosystems are evolving, as well as research on ways to create and sustain resilient landscapes that fulfill their intended purposes and that have been validated in practice. To ensure that resilience qualities hold over time, I suggest that the methods for creating resilient landscapes should be permanently *linked* or *coupled* with goals for developing regenerative systems. One outcome is a reformulated or emergent ecological design and planning goal focused on creating and maintaining *adaptive regenerative landscapes*.

Regeneration is the "renewal or restoration of a body, bodily part, or biological system (as a forest) after an injury or as a normal process."[30] It implies renewal, restoration, and repair that enable ecosystems to be resilient to natural and human-induced events that bring about disturbance or damage. The concept of regeneration relies heavily on modeling in systems ecology with its emphasis on using input-output models to evaluate the behavior of ecological systems. For regeneration to be effective, the output of the system should exceed the input, with all of the outputs viable and each input accounted for. The flow of materials and minerals occurs in a closed loop in which the outputs of one system become the input of the next system. This progressively results in an overall reduction of energy and material inputs into successive cycles or systems.

There is a growing body of knowledge on regenerative systems and strategies in applied ecological sciences, natural resource planning and management, and ecological planning.[31] A noted advocate for the creation of regenerative systems, John Tillman Lyle, proposed numerous insightful strategies for sustainable design in the early 1990s,[32] including allowing nature to do the work before engineering intervention occurs; employing nature as both model and context; providing multiple pathways for achieving the same goal; shaping form to guide flow; and managing *storage*. I find that targeting regeneration actions to critical points in the ecosystem's adaptive process is crucial to creating successful adaptive regenerative landscapes.

From resilience theory, we know that the adaptive cycle involves four stages that may occur after the disturbance of an ecosystem.[33] The first is a *growth* or *exploitation* phase, in which ecosystems begin recolonizing with pioneer species [r phase]. The ecosystem gradually reaches maturity with locally adapted climax or mature species, which represents the *conservation* or *consolidation* phase [K phase]. Biomass and nutrients accrue during this phase and are progressively integrated within the tissues of the plants. Nutrient cycling is efficient, with tightly closed mineral loops. Energy inputs are primarily directed toward maintaining the ecosystem.[34]

When a severe disturbance occurs, such as a major fire, flood, or hurricane, the ecosystem may collapse, especially if it is "over-connected" and rigid. The tight regulatory controls are then broken up and the resources that have accumulated during the previous two phases [r and K] are released. The overall ecosystem becomes loosely organized in terms of regulatory controls. This represents a phase of *collapse* that is characterized by a high degree of uncertainty, strong external influences, and abundant opportunities for the ecosystem to regroup creatively. Over time, resources can be remobilized, and the ecosystems may move toward a phase of *reorganization*. This move may result in another growth or exploitation [r] phase, but not necessarily. As the ecosystem moves through these phases of adaptation, resilience increases during the phase of reorganization or renewal, when tight controls and connectivity are low, and shrinks in the phase of consolidation [K], when connectedness is high and the system is rigid.[35] The first two phases, *growth* and *consolidation*, are typically reported in traditional ecological studies.

If resiliency and regenerative strategies are permanently coupled, corrective regenerative actions would "ease the likelihood of collapse" of an ecosystem after a major unpredictable disturbance, facilitating the healing or repair process and moving it toward the *creative reorganization* phase. Regeneration provides opportunities to reduce the energy and material inputs needed for the long-term maintenance of landscapes because wastes from one cycle of ecological transactions become inputs into the next cycle of transaction.

Regenerative strategies could be targeted to repair the stressed structural components of ecological systems from wear and tear typically associated with normal operations; to ensure that damaged components of the ecosystem are healing properly, for example by repairing the weak structural links in the system, thereby bolstering the system's elasticity; and to solidify the smooth flow of energy, materials, and species across the landscape mosaic via the removal of blockages in connectivity pathways (i.e., as ecological networks). Establishing adaptive regenerative landscapes opens up new areas of research in ecological design and planning, including:

- on-going monitoring of ecosystems so that we may better model their behavior,
- the search for new theoretical approaches, methods, and strategies for understanding coupled socio-ecological systems,
- the validation of approaches in practice, and
- the development of valid and reliable performance metrics for estimating the quality, value, and health of ecosystems prior to and after disturbances.

Commitment to Place

How might adaptive regenerative landscapes be transformed into "places" rather than remain as "spaces"? Space is an abstract concept that is called a "place" when it has meaning to its users. Places emerge from the interactions between environmental forces and human actions.[36] There is a long history of documented scholarship about place, place qualities, place making, place assets, and placelessness.[37] Definitions emphasize giving meaning to spaces through personal, group, or cultural processes;[38] getting to know a location better through associations;[39] frequent associations with a geographic space; and recurrent experiences in specific landscapes.[40] Individuals derive significant emotional and psychological satisfaction when they feel connected to a place.[41] Moreover, one's identification with a place extends beyond the given area to embrace broader geographic, historical, social, and cultural contexts. But places are not static. They change constantly as people adapt to them. They are also linked through time (natural and cultural history) and space (connection to larger places).[42]

Placelessness is increasingly becoming a feature of our current urban landscapes. Contemporary forces of change (i.e., urbanization, globalization, technological advances, increased mobility, and growing consumerism) progressively lead to the homogeneity of landscapes. The particulars that make places unique have gradually eroded. Take, for instance, advances in technology. They have improved our lives significantly but have also had "community-distant impacts."[43] We can now know a great deal about many geographic locations today via the Internet without ever having experienced them firsthand. Given the transitory nature of Americans and the opportunities afforded to us to move around in search of wealth, employment, and recreation, it is not surprising that we often fail to develop strong emotional attachments to specific places. Certainly, "the growing uniformity and anonymity of contemporary settlement patterns beget an attitude that they are disposable and interchangeable. One is just like, or as good as, another. Without intimate contact with real places, there is little chance that the loss of environments and the practice of unsustainable patterns of consumption and resource exploitation will be reversed."[44] Adaptive regenerative landscapes can surely be nurtured to develop into real places. The "history and heritage of a [landscape] can and should be a major starting point in creating places."[45]

Localism, with its emphasis on the perpetuation of local values and traditions, has long been proposed as a way to counteract the homogenization of landscapes. It was clearly evident in the writings of visionary Ralph Waldo Emerson and sociologist John Dewey.[46] Today, it is embedded in Peter Berg and Robert Thayer's ideas on *bioregionalism*.[47] A bioregion is "a unique region definable by natural (rather than political) boundaries with a geographic, climatic, hydrological, and ecological character capable of supporting unique human and nonhuman living communities."[48] These areas can be defined based on the geography of the watersheds, related flora and fauna, and identifiable physiographic features (e.g., coastal plains, unique mountain ranges) and cultural attributes that emerge from the natural potentials or limitations of the region.

We can learn ideas from the bioregional approach to create adaptive regenerative places because it suggests a "means of living by deep understanding of, respect for, and ultimately, care of naturally bounded region or territory."[49] *Particularness* is a related concept associated with Randolph Hester, a University of California landscape architect professor emeritus. It focuses on the unique, cultural adaptations people have made to fit well into the distinctive natural ecosystems of which that habitat is a part.[50] Conveying visually and through other means, the expressive elements of cultural adaptation within the landscape is a promising way to enrich the meaning people make of these places.

The ideas for rebuilding places are numerous and well documented.[51] They include integrating and expressing the particulars of a place (context)—topography, climate, light, building technology, and materiality in the design of landscapes;[52] preserving, strengthening, and making visible a community's historic heritage through buildings and landscapes;[53] and searching for regional and local identity by exploring the natural history, regional and local ecosystems, native flora, and social values people hold.[54] Each idea should be evaluated for its relevance, merit, utility, appropriateness, and timeliness in achieving the desired purpose, including creating adaptive regenerative places. I caution, as many others have done, that creating such places will not be an easy task, given the contemporary forces of change that give rise to social, cultural, and economic impediments. But we can build on demonstrated successes, many of which have been documented.[55]

Regional Thinking and Action

A substantial body of evidence indicates that the most appropriate spatial scale for creating adaptive regenerative places is the region.[56] The intellectual tradition of regionalism was articulated in the early twentieth century by Scottish biologist and planner Patrick Geddes, urban historian and critic Lewis Mumford, and forester and planner Benton MacKaye. These visionaries viewed the region as the appropriate spatial unit for understanding and managing rapidly expanding metropolitan areas in the United States and the United Kingdom in the early to mid-twentieth century. Ian McHarg and his colleagues expanded and significantly reformulated these regionalist ideas in the 1960s and 1970s (figure 8-5).[57]

The term *region* has different meanings, depending on one's field of expertise. For geographers, it is "an uninterrupted area possessing some kind of homogeneity in its core, but lacking clearly defined limits."[58] Environmental scientists view regions in regard to parts of the landscape, such as physiographic provinces, drainage basins, and climate zones.[59] The region is also considered an interacting biophysical and cultural entity, which can be understood by examining each of its components.[60] In addition, we have eco-geographical,

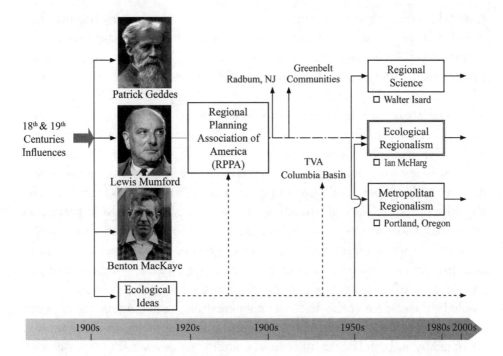

Figure 8-5 Conceptual framework for sustainable regionalism (Ndubisi, 2008, Reproduced with permission of University of Wisconsin Press, Redrawn by Yuan Ren, 2014).

ecological, political, administrative, cultural, and metropolitan regions.[61] I use *region* to refer to a geographic location that is larger than a local area in spatial extent, distinguished by common or unifying attributes, and composed of interacting physical, biological, and cultural phenomena that establish its natural and cultural character over time.[62]

Support for employing the region as the spatial framework for balancing human use with environmental concerns and, by extension, creating and maintaining adaptive resilient places, comes from different perspectives. Out of regional planning came regionalism, which was promoted by Geddes, Mumford, and MacKaye and solidified by the Regional Planning Association of America (1922–1932). It was later reconceptualized by Ian McHarg. Geddes called for regional surveys aimed at identifying the area's opportunities and constraints. Building on Geddes's and Mumford's ideas, McHarg advocated exploring the components of the ecological region as an entity that can be understood.

Landscape ecologists view the interactions of ecosystems across the landscape mosaic as being conditioned by the larger system in which they are nested—the region.[63] Ecologist Richard Forman pointed out explicitly that the regional level is the most appropriate spatial scale to engage in sustainability due to its larger spatial extent and slower rate at which ecological processes occur compared to the local level.[64] Crawford S. Holling argued that a management approach based on resilience "would need to view events in a regional rather than a local context."[65] Place theorists call for a regional approach within which local or "home areas" are an integral part. For instance, Robert Thayer advanced bioregional thinking and offered a "life place" approach.[66] In short, a regional perspective is clearly evident in many of the articles examined in this book.

Embracing a regional approach to creating adaptive regenerative places will involve thinking about and responding to urban and rural issues from a regionally based perspective; understanding that regions are composed of hierarchical, nested places that serve as the context for understanding the communities within them; when appropriate, formulating a regional framework or visioning plan that lays out its basic structure by revealing land uses and the linkages among them (the framework plan provides directions rather than specifics, as would be the case for traditional regional plans); and searching for the regional essence of a locality, interpreting it, and translating it into design and planning. As noted by Robert Thayer, all regions contain "an essence that must be discovered or preserved and which expresses the uniqueness of place."[67]

Any discussion of a regional outlook urgently necessitates the establishment or reestablishment of clear and unimpeded connectors for goods, services, information, and energy to circulate within the region.[68] Connectors may be natural, such as environmental corridors consisting of ecological networks, drainage corridors, or habitat corridors, or based on infrastructure, such as roads, transit systems, bikeways, water supply and utility lines, or communication linkages, such as cell phones.

I recommend that environmental corridors should receive the highest priority as pathways for connectivity. They help to establish the natural character of the region, especially in built-up areas where the corridors may have eroded due to land alteration.[69] Moreover, "establishing and maintaining a continuous network of natural corridors throughout the region—block level, neighborhoods, villages, and cities—minimizes the loss of biodiversity and provides spaces for people to interact and recreate."[70] Natural corridors are also unique to their region in contrast to other types of corridors, such as transportation infrastructure, which tend to be uniform throughout the extent of whole continents where they are employed.

However, creating and establishing adaptive resilient places that perform an important role for the region will not be easy, especially in the United States, although we have had successes. Anthony Downs informed us that design and planning frameworks calling for a vital role for the region are *unlikely* to be implemented because they require a shift in power and authority from the local to the regional level of governance.[71] Local governments typically tend to be opposed to such shifts. Some regions have legislative mandates for regional governance, such as in Portland, Oregon (METRO), and Minneapolis-St. Paul, Minnesota (MET Council). Others are mandated as a part of state planning legislation, such as in Georgia. There are also those organized as a "loose" network of councils of governments, as in Texas. Affected parties will occasionally come together to develop regional visioning plans, such as those undertaken by the Envision Utah and Envision Central Texas coalitions.[72] We can learn from these successful efforts. At the same time, we can engage in new research focused on ways to creatively implement regional thinking and action plans, including building more political support for a regional approach. A regional perspective is critical to successfully creating and maintaining adaptive regenerative places.

Coupled Design-Management Imperative

The intentional integration of design and management as a unified activity is an important vehicle for creating and maintaining adaptive regenerative places. Management involves organizing and coordinating activities so as to accomplish a desired goal or defined objectives. The outcome of any design or plan is probabilistic in that we anticipate and implement actions to ensure that the design intensions are realized.[73] In this context, management involves observing, monitoring, and taking corrective action as needed to ensure that the resulting landscape will reflect the intended design or planning goals over time. Following this line of thinking, "management assumes a more creative role than has usually been expected. ... [This] interlocking relationship between design and management is a *particularly* important feature of any ecosystematic design process."[74] This relationship is even more important in creating and maintaining adaptive regenerative places. I term this relationship a *coupled design-management imperative* that serves as a foundational element for creating these places.

Ongoing monitoring and consistent, timely feedback are crucial to the success of adaptive systems.[75] It is through establishing, tightening, and maintaining the strength of these feedback loops that tensions or stresses in ecosystems and landscapes can be detected for corrective measures in a timely manner, in advance of minor and major perturbations or disturbances.[76] Creative opportunities can be detected through focused, consistent, and timely monitoring prior to and after such disturbances. Necessary actions may be devised and implemented to transition the disturbed ecosystems more effectively into the adaptation phase of *renewal and reorganization*. This proposition for permanently *coupling design and management* also recognizes that natural processes have tolerance limits for absorbing change. Intentional monitoring and feedback of the performance of designed landscapes may necessitate implementing corrective actions, which may include regeneration. Coupling may require developing and implementing tight monitoring protocols and detailed management plans.[77] These actions are likely to increase the overall tolerance limit and carrying capacity of the ecosystems by augmenting those in the natural systems. John Tillman Lyle added emphatically, "[An] intentionally designed and managed ecosystem represents a symbiosis of urban and natural processes."[78]

Permanently coupling design and management activities has profound ramifications for how we engage in ecological design and planning. It requires that a linked design-management framework be regarded as both a goal and a process for engaging in ecological design and planning. It involves establishing integrated design, planning, and management contracts and protocols, which will require designers, planners, managers, and others who are relevant to the process to work together as members of multidisciplinary or interdisciplinary teams. Resources are more likely to be committed to project implementation, especially enduring management and monitoring activities. Unfortunately, they are rarely committed to post-occupancy monitoring and feedbacks. What remains is to provide the specifics for how this can be effectively achieved, which is another domain in which new research and purposeful reflective practice is needed.[79]

Performance-Based Thinking and Practices

Landscape performance is "a measure of the efficiency and [effectiveness] with which landscape solutions fulfill their intended purpose and contribute toward sustainability."[80] Integrating performance measures into interventions for creating and maintaining adaptive regenerative places is likely to dramatically increase the reliability, validity, and quality of feedback generated during the monitoring phase of the intervention process and, as a result, may significantly improve the overall quality of the resultant corrective actions. Permanently coupling design and management activities increases the probability that performance measures are employed in a consistent fashion throughout a project's life span, thereby increasing the likelihood of the creation of high-performing places.

Planning and design professionals employ benchmarks to establish performance expectations for designed and planned landscapes. The U.S. Green Building Council (USGBC) developed a voluntary, performance-based green rating system for design, construction, maintenance, and operation of buildings and sites known as Leadership in Energy and Environmental Design (LEED).

The intent of LEED, established for the building level in 1988, is to help users, building owners, and property managers to use resources wisely and to minimize waste. Today, specialized LEED systems exist, such as LEED for Neighborhood Development. Developed in 2009 in partnership with the Congress for New Urbanism, the Natural Resources Defense Council (NRDC), and the USGBC, LEED for Neighborhood Development integrates the principles of smart growth, urbanism, and green building into a rating system that extends beyond the building to the site, whole neighborhoods, and multiple neighborhoods. According to USGBC, it "emphasizes elements that bring buildings and infrastructure together and relates the neighborhood to its local and regional landscape."[81]

LEED provided the context for the development of the Sustainable Sites Initiative (SITES), a related ecological accounting and measurement system for ascertaining landscape performance. SITES is a joint endeavor by the Lady Bird Johnson Wildflower Center at the University of Texas at Austin, the American Society of Landscape Architects, and the U.S. Botanic Garden to create a voluntary set of national guidelines and performance benchmarks for landscape design, construction, and management practices. Portions of SITES have been incorporated into the LEED rating system.

A complementary performance system is currently being developed by the Landscape Architecture Foundation (LAF), a nonprofit organization devoted to the improvement and enhancement of the environment. LAF established a Landscape Performance Series in 2010 containing tools for bringing together state-of-the-art online information on landscape performance. Unlike SITES, which is a rating tool, LAF's landscape performance case study initiative evaluates the performance of designed landscapes (after construction and post occupancy).[82]

The Living Building Challenge is another complementary international sustainable building certification program that promotes the measurement of sustainability in the built environment.[83] Developed by the Cascadia Green Building Council (whose parent organization is the International Living Building Institute and is a chapter of both the United States and Canadian Green Building Councils) in 2006, the certification program can be applied to development at all spatial scales: buildings, new and revitalization projects, infrastructure, sites, and neighborhoods. The proponents of the program claim that it is more rigorous than green certification schemes such as LEED.

Integrating performance measures in creating and maintaining adaptive regenerative places promises to elevate the quality of designed and planned landscapes, including the preservation of ecosystem services. As we continue to know more about ecological accounting involving landscape performance, it may be feasible to set concise expectations for design and planning interventions. That is, we may adopt an outcome-based performance approach in which the designer or planner formulates viable strategies for reaching desired expectations, similar to the way performance expectations have been used in zoning.

Unlike estimating performance in buildings that are closed systems, landscapes are interacting, open-ended, complex ecosystems across whose boundaries materials, energy, and species flow freely. These flows are dynamic and linked to time. As such, estimating accurate and valid performance measurements occurs over a longer time horizon than that required for designing and planning many projects. Moreover, it is difficult to estimate landscape performance when the baseline data are incomplete, unreliable, and in many cases, nonexistent. Regrettably, monitoring and feedback are rarely included in the budgets of most projects. Designers', engineers', planners', and conservation biologists' experience and knowledge of the methods for quantifying landscape performance are slim; however, success stories are emerging and growing.[84] These gaps suggest additional exciting areas of research, scholarship, and reflective practice in ecological design and planning directed at solidifying the theoretical foundation and developing reliable metrics for measuring the social, economic, and environmental phenomena needed for estimating landscape performance.

Collaborative and Interdisciplinary Teams

Articulating the precise nature of the problems and formulating effective solutions require the intimate and sustained involvement of individuals with the relevant technical expertise, knowledge, and skills, as well as experiential and intimate understanding of the pertinent issues and access to power and resources. As complex systems, the secret to understanding the behavior of adaptive regenerative places involves searching for insights from diverse perspectives as to how their interacting physical, social, cultural, and economic components perform and adapt to landscape change.[85]

The complexity of ecological design and planning problems and solutions suggests that multidisciplinary and interdisciplinary teams are much better suited than individuals to support the design, planning, and ongoing management. Teams will vary depending on projects and factors such as whether or not the project is located in a private or public domain. A key to accomplishing successful interventions is to establish and maintain effective productive teams. I suggest that, in doing so, teams may employ the principles I have provided here to frame their debates in their search for solutions to these ecological problems.

There is a rich body of documented work on how to establish productive teams, and there are a number of ways to manage them.[86] I find that collaborative group processes have proven to be useful in managing productive and effective teams. They are designed to build consensus among competing interests through "processes that engage individuals in idea generation, critical reflection, and analysis of options and selection of the action plan."[87] In the context of creating and maintaining adaptive regenerative places, evidence-based and empirically validated knowledge as drawn from research and reflective professional practice is likely to elevate the quality of input during the deliberations and, by extension, increase the likelihood of quality outputs and solutions.

Learning is an important dimension of collaborative group processes. It occurs as individuals within groups clarify each other's values and ideas through dialogue.[88] Combined with conflict mediation, scenario discovery, and visualization techniques, collaborative group processes can become a powerful way for managing teams to create and maintain adaptive regenerative places. Adaptive organizations require learning; collaborative group processes embrace learning as a fundamental organizing principle and provide breadth in the establishment of metrics with which to evaluate landscape performance.

Looking Forward and Future Practices

We need new ways of thinking about how to effectively and permanently balance human use with ecological concerns (figure 8-6). Many promising solutions have been proposed, but the concerns are increasingly challenging to address. Our inability to balance them effectively is clearly visible in the landscapes where we live today. I have offered principles that would frame discussions about deeper understandings of the problems and guide the search for their resolutions. These principles are built on the rich foundations laid by others and, as such, are intended to be complementary to them.

One noteworthy observation is that the implementation of these principles is likely to generate powerful synergistic outcomes. For instance, an ethical foundation is needed to guide the choices we make about how we relate to the landscape. Adopting an evolutionary ethical position brings to light the consequences of the choices we make about how the landscape may be used when we pursue one course of action over another. The need to preserve and conserve entire valued ecosystems is an outcome of embracing this position. Appreciating the beauty of these ecosystems "touches on the broader realm of human values, perceptions, and experiences, which many have argued, are crucial in creating socially responsible, ecologically sound landscape configurations."[89] Experiencing them is essential in sustaining one's aesthetic appreciation of natural systems and processes, including those that provide ecosystem services. Creating and maintaining adaptive regenerative places embrace, as a

Figure 8-6 Red Ribbon Park, Qinhuangdao, Hebei Province, China (2007, Reproduced with permission of Kongjian Yu).

goal, the preservation and conservation of ecosystems that provide a variety of ecosystem *benefits* and *services*.

My proposition to create and maintain adaptive places necessitates establishing ongoing feedback mechanisms essential to monitoring the health, integrity, and behavior of place-based ecosystems as they respond to change. Corrective measures may be devised accordingly, targeting the precise nature of restoration to be affected. Establishing performance measures and employing validated evidence from research and reflective practice enriches the quality of deliberations among multidisciplinary and interdisciplinary teams. In addition, aside from curtailing the homogeneity of landscapes, seeking ways to transform them into recognizable and valued places is a promising way to make adaptive regenerative landscapes more livable and healthy for their inhabitants. Preserving and strengthening the history and heritage of a landscape is a place-making strategy that has been proven to reduce ecological impacts, stimulate economic development, and advance the goals of sustainability.[90] Future research and new knowledge drawn from reflective practice can enrich our understanding of the challenges of implementation and management and enable us to be more effective in creating and maintaining viable adaptive and regenerative places.

Notes

1. J. Baird Callicott, "Whither Conservation Ethics?" in *Beyond the Land Ethic: More Essays in Environmental Philosophy* (New York: SUNY Press, 1999), 327.
2. Ibid., 326.
3. Timothy Beatley, "Ethical Duties to the Environment," in *Ethical Land Use: Principles of Policy and Planning* (Baltimore, MD: Johns Hopkins University Press, 1994).
4. Ibid.
5. E. O. Wilson (2002) made this proposition. Edward O. Wilson, *The Future of Life* (New York: Knopf, 2002). However, the prioritizing of species for protection may speak against the view of ecosystems as being wholes in which all components have value without which the system as a whole collapses and as an implied rationale for letting those "at the bottom of the list" go to protect those at the top. For example, people would have difficulty surviving without bees (Dr. Michael Murphy, pers. comm., 2013). Yet we have to make choices that include economic considerations about the competing uses of the landscapes.
6. Aldo Leopold, "The Land Ethic," in *A Sand County Almanac, and Sketches Here and There* (New York: Oxford University Press, 1949).
7. To illustrate, Texas A&M University at College Station received a gift in 2010 to establish a nature preserve on a seven-acre site within an established neighborhood close to the university campus. We, the departments of landscape architecture and urban planning and park, recreation, and tourism sciences, collaborated to develop a master plan that includes implementing a successional sequence for restoring and reclaiming the site's native landscape using native grasses and other locally adapted ground covers and shrubs. The foundational planting is not yet established, and the neighbors are already complaining that the site looks "weedy" and lacks aesthetic appeal. We are currently embarking in an intervention program with the neighborhood residents to educate them about the aesthetic appeal and value of native landscapes.
8. Elizabeth Meyer, "Sustaining Beauty. The Performance of Appearance: A Manifesto in Three Parts." *Journal of Landscape Architecture* 3, no. 1 (2008): 6–23; Michael Rosenzweig, *Win-Win Ecology: How the Earth's Species Can Survive in the Midst of Human Enterprise* (Oxford: Oxford University Press, 2003); James Miller, "Biodiversity Conservation and the Extinction of Experience," *Trends in Ecology & Evolution* 20, no. 8 (2005): 430–34; Joan Nassauer, ed., *Placing Nature: Culture and Landscape Ecology* (Washington, DC: Island Press, 1997). Cited in Laura Musacchio, "The Scientific Basis for the Design of Landscape Sustainability: A Conceptual Framework for Translational Landscape Research and Practice of Designed Landscapes and the Six Es of Landscape Sustainability," *Landscape Ecology* 24, no. 8 (2009): 993–1013. Musacchio argued for the need to reconcile people's experiences and ethics about nature and for designing places that inspire people to experience nature. She introduced the notion of *landscape sustainability*, traced its evolution and proposed an expanded definition that comprises the traditional components of sustainability debates (3 Es)—*environment, equity, economics*—and embraces new ones—*aesthetics, experience, and ethics*. These constitute the 6 Es that become the key drivers in establishing landscape suitability.
9. Ibid.
10. J. Baird Callicott, "Whither Conservation Ethics?"
11. David Nowak, Daniel Crane, and John Dwyer, "Compensatory Value of Urban Trees in the United States," *Journal of Arboriculture* 4, no. 28 (2004), 194–99; Sustainable Sites Initiative, "The Sustainable Sites Initiative: Guidelines and Performance Benchmarks 2009," accessed November 29, 2013, www.sustainablesites.org/report.
12. Ecosystem *processes* are defined as the fundamental maintenance activities (e.g., water cycle, mineral cycles, energy flows, and community dynamics) required to keep the ecosystem in good health and working order. Ecosystem *goods* are things with value to the community (e.g., clean air, fresh water, and pollinators of crops) that are extracted from the

environment and exchanged for economic return. Ecosystem *services* are the processes that have value (e.g., purifying water and air, decomposing waste and generating soil) but are rarely exchanged for monetary benefit. Jane Lubchenco, Annette Olson, Linda Brubaker, Stephen Carpenter, Marjorie Holland, Stephen Hubbell, Simon Levin et al. "The Sustainable Biosphere Initiative: An Ecological Research Agenda: A Report from the Ecological Society of America," *Ecology* 72, no. 2 (1991): 371–412; Gretchen Daily (ed.), *Nature's Services: Societal Dependence on Natural Ecosystems* (Washington, DC: Island Press, 1997).

13. Millennium Ecosystem Assessment, "The Millennium Ecosystem Assessment" (2005), http://www.scribd.com/doc/5250322/MILLENNIUM-EC, accessed October 10, 2013.

14. Forster Ndubisi, Terry DeMeo, and Niels Ditto, "Environmentally Sensitive Area: A Template for Developing Greenway Corridors," *Landscape and Urban Planning* 33 (1995), 159–77.

15. Jamie Bastedo, Gordon Nelson, and John Theberge, "Ecological Approach to Resource Survey and Planning for Environmentally Significant Areas; The ABC Method," *Environmental Management* 8, no 2 (1984), 125–34.

16. Ecologist Eugene Odum argued forcefully for the preservation of ecosystems that serve as "life support systems" for humans. Eugene Odum, *Ecology and Our Endangered Life-Support Systems* (Stamford, CT: Sinauer, 1989). Sustainable Sites Initiative (SITES), a project of the University of Texas Lady Bird Johnson Wildflower Center, the American Society of Landscape Architects, and the U.S. Botanic Garden, was established to develop a measurement system for evaluating landscape performance. SITES's 2009 report, *Guidelines and Performance Benchmarks,* clearly advocated employing ecosystem services as a basis for design and planning. This theme formed the basis for the *Sustainable Sites Handbook* (Meg Calkins, New York: John Wiley & Sons, Inc., 2012), which was written in response to the SITES report. Laura Mussachio (2009) viewed ecosystem services as a major consideration in determining landscape sustainability. Frederick Steiner (2011) suggested a design and planning framework, *Landscape Ecological Urbanism,* with a goal of designing cities to increase rather than decrease ecosystem services.

17. Calkins, *The Sustainable Sites Handbook*, 1.

18. One of the first published references to explicitly suggest a shift in design attention from the creation of static to dynamic forms in the landscape appeared in Michael Murphy's book, *Landscape Architecture Theory: An Evolving Body of Thought* (Waveland Press, 2005), 150–151.

19. Ibid.

20. Carl Steinitz, *Alternative Futures for Changing Landscapes: The Upper San Pedro River Basin in Arizona and Sonora* (Washington, DC: Island Press, 2003); Sustainable Sites Initiative, "The Sustainable Sites Initiative"; Landscape Architecture Foundation, 2010; Calkins, *The Sustainable Sites Handbook*.

21. Bo Yang, Ming-Han Li, and Shujuan Li, "Design-with-Nature for Multifunctional Landscapes: Environmental Benefits and Social Barriers in Community Development," *International Journal of Environmental Research and Public Health* 10 (2013), 5433–58.

22. Crawford Holling, "Resilience and Stability of Ecological Systems," *Annual Review of Ecology and Systematics* 4 (1973), 1–23; Crawford Holling, "Understanding the Complexity of Economic, Ecological, and Social Systems," *Ecosystems* 4 (2001), 390–405; Frederick Steiner, *Design for a Vulnerable Planet* (Austin, Texas: University of Texas Press, 2011); Calkins, *The Sustainable Sites Handbook*; Jianguo Wu and Tong Wu, "Ecological Resilience as a Foundation for Urban Design and Sustainability," in *Resilience in Ecology and Urban Design* (Springer Netherlands, 2013). Also, I find that Calkins' edited book, *The Sustainable Sites Handbook* (2012), is an important foundation in designing with ecosystem services in mind.

23. Steward Pickett, Mary Cadenasso, and Morgan Groove, "Resilient Cities: Meaning, Models, and Metaphors for Integrating the Ecological, Socio-Economic, and Planning Realms," *Landscape and Urban Planning* 69 (2004), 369–84; Brian Walker and David Salt, *Resilience*

Thinking: Sustaining Ecosystems and People in a Changing World (Washington, DC: Island Press, 2006); Wu and Wu, "Ecological Resilience as a Foundation for Urban Design and Sustainability."

24. Lance Gunderson, Craig Allen, and Crawford Holling, *Foundations of Ecological Resilience* (Washington, DC: Island Press, 2010).

25. Kevin Lynch, *Good City Form* (Cambridge, MA: MIT Press, 1981).

26. Spirn, "Ecological Urbanism: A Framework for the Design of Resilient Cities." Initially to be published in Pickett, Cadenasso, and McGrath (eds.), *Resiliency in Ecology and Urban Design* (2013).

27. Wu and Wu, "Ecological Resilience as a Foundation for Urban Design and Sustainability."

28. Gunderson, Allen, and Holling, *Foundations of Ecological Resilience*; Steiner, *Design for a Vulnerable Planet*; Spirn, "Ecological Urbanism: A Framework for the Design of Resilient Cities"; and Wu and Wu, "Ecological Resilience as a Foundation for Urban Design and Sustainability."

29. Calkins, *The Sustainable Sites Handbook*.

30. Merriam-Webster Dictionary Online, http://www.merriam-webster.com/, accessed November 30, 2013.

31. William McDonough, *Cradle to Cradle: Remaking the Way We Make Things* (New York: North Point Press, 2002); Bob Rodale—Rodale Institute of Regenerative Agriculture. Architect and landscape architect Pliny Fisk III is one of the pioneers of regenerative design. He is the cofounder of the Center for Maximum Potential Building Systems in Austin, Texas. He was instrumental in developing one of the first input/output life cycle assessment models for material flows in the United States. He employed geographic information systems to demonstrate how human activities can be embedded in the context of national systems on a national scale. He is a pioneer of numerous innovative ideas and approaches, including *Eco balance*, a sustainable land use planning and design method that uses life cycle principles as a framework for sustaining basic life support systems.

32. John Tillman Lyle, *Regenerative Design for Sustainable Development* (New York: John Wiley, 1994).

33. Crawford Holling, "The Resilience of Terrestrial Ecosystems," in P. Schulze, ed., *Engineering within Ecological Constraints* (Washington, DC: National Academy Press, 1986).

34. Holling, "The Resilience of Terrestrial Ecosystems"; Wu and Wu, "Ecological Resilience as a Foundation for Urban Design and Sustainability."

35. I rely on the succinct explanation of the adaptation process as documented by Wu and Wu, "Ecological Resilience as a Foundation for Urban Design and Sustainability," 216–19.

36. Forster Ndubisi, *Ecological Planning: A Historical and Comparative Synthesis* (Baltimore, MD: Johns Hopkins University Press, 2002), 112.

37. Edward Relph, *Place and Placelessness* (London: Pion, 1976); Edward Relph, *The Modern Urban Landscape* (Kent, England: Croom Helm, 1987); David Hummon, "Community Attachment: Local Sentiment: Local Attachment and Sense of Place," in I. Altman and S. Low (eds.), *Place Attachment* (New York, NY: Plenum Press, 1992).

38. Timothy Beatley, *Native to Nowhere: Sustaining Home and Community in a Global Age* (Washington, DC: Island Press, 2005), 26.

39 Yi-Fu Tuan, *Space and Place: The Perspective of Experience* (Minneapolis, MN: University of Minnesota Press, 1977).

40. David Canter, *The Psychology of Place* (London: Architecture Press, 1977); Michael Hough, *Out of Place: Restoring Identity to the Regional Landscape* (New Haven: Yale University Press, 1990).

41. David Canter, *The Psychology of Place*; Stephen Kaplan, "The Restorative Benefits of Nature," *Journal of Environmental Psychology* 15 (1995), 169–82; Edward O. Wilson, *Biophilia: The Human Bond with Other Species* (Cambridge, MA: Harvard University Press, 1984).

42. Ndubisi, *Ecological Planning: A Historical and Comparative Synthesis*, 112–13.

43   Beatley, *Native to Nowhere*, 20.
44. Ibid., 3.
45. Ibid., 55.
46. Ralph Waldo Emerson, "Nature," *The Oxford Companion of American Literature*, E. James, D. Hart, and P. Leininger (Oxford University Press, 1995); John Dewey, *Experience and Nature*, reprint (New York: Dover, 1929).
47. Peter Berg, *Bioregionalism* (2005), http://www.diggers.org/freecitynews/_1/00000017.htm, accessed November 15, 2013; Peter Berg, *Discovering Your Life-Place: A First Bioregional Workbook* (San Francisco: Planet Drum Foundation, 1995); Robert Thayer, *Life Place: Bioregional Thought and Practice* (Los Angeles: University of California Press, 2003); Wes Jackson, *Becoming Native to This Place* (Lexington: University of Kentucky, 1995).
48. Thayer, *Life Place: Bioregional Thought and Practice*, 3.
49. Ibid., 4.
50. Randy Hester, *Design for Ecological Democracy* (Cambridge, MA: MIT Press, 2006), 145.
51. For instance, see Wes Jackson, *Consulting the Genius of Place* (Berkeley, CA: Counter Point, 2011) or Tim Beatley, *Native to Nowhere* (Washington, DC: Island Press, 2005).
52. Kenneth Frampton, "Toward a Critical Regionalism: 6 Points for Architecture of Revolution," in H. Foster (ed.), *The Anti-Aesthetic: Essays on Post Modern Culture* (Port Townsend, WA: Bay Press, 1983), 16–30; David Miller, *Toward a New Regionalism: Environmental Architecture in the Pacific Northwest* (Seattle, WA: University of Washington Press, 2005).
53. Beatley, *Native to Nowhere*.
54. Hough, *Out of Place*.
55. Beatley, *Native to Nowhere*; Hough, *Out of Place*.
56. Patrick Geddes, *Cities in Evolution: An Introduction to the Town Planning Movement and the Study of Cities* (London: Williams and Norgate, 1915); Benton MacKaye, *The New Exploration* (New York: Harcourt Brace, 1928); Lewis Mumford, *The Culture of Cities* (London: Secker & Warbug, 1938); Ian McHarg, *Design with Nature* (Garden City, New York: Natural History/Doubleday, 1969).
57. McHarg, *Design with Nature*; Ian McHarg, *A Quest For Life* (New York: John Wiley & Sons, 1996); Mark Luccaleri, *Lewis Mumford and the Ecological Region* (New York: The Guilford Press, 1995).
58. Frederick Steiner, *Human Ecology: Following Nature's Lead* (Washington, DC: Island Press, 2002), 95.
59. McHarg, *Design with Nature*.
60. Ibid.
61. Robert Bailey, *Ecoregions: The Ecosystem Geography of the Oceans and Continents* (New York: Springer-Verlag, 1998).
62. Forster Ndubisi, "Sustainable Regionalism: Evolutionary Framework and Prospects for Managing Metropolitan Landscape," *Landscape Journal* 21 (2008), 51–68; Steiner, *Human Ecology*.
63. Richard Forman and Michel Godron, *Landscape Ecology* (New York: John Wiley, 1986).
64. Richard Forman, *Land Mosaics: The Ecology of Landscapes and Regions* (Cambridge University Press, 1995).
65. Holling, "Resilience and Stability of Ecological Systems," 46.
66. Thayer, *Life Place: Bioregional Thought and Practice*.
67. Ibid., 4.
68. Michael Newman, "Regional Design: Recovering a Great Landscape Architecture and Urban Planning Tradition," *Landscape and Urban Planning* 47, 3–4 (2000), 115–128.
69. Ndubisi, "Sustainable Regionalism: Evolutionary Framework and Prospects for Managing Metropolitan Landscape," 58–62.
70. Ibid., 60.
71. Anthony Downs, "Smart Growth: Why We Discuss It More than We Do It," *Journal of the American Planning Association* 71, no. 4 (2005): 374–76.

72. Envision Utah, http://envisionutah.org, accessed October 2010; Envision Central Texas, http://envisioncentraltexas.org, accessed February 6, 2013.

73. John Tillman Lyle, *Design for Human Ecosystems* (New York: Van Nostrand Reinhold, 1985), 18.

74. Ibid.

75. Holling, "The Resilience of Terrestrial Ecosystems"; Lance Gunderson, "Ecological Resilience in Theory and Practice," *Annual Review of Ecology and Systematics* 31 (2000), 425–39; Pickett, Cadenasso, and McGrath, "Resilient Cities: Meaning, Models, and Metaphors for Integrating the Ecological, Socio-Economic, and Planning Realms." *Landscape and Urban Planning* 69 (2004), 369–84.

76. Wu and Wu, "Ecological Resilience as a Foundation for Urban Design and Sustainability," 225.

77. Calkins, *The Sustainable Sites Handbook,* 20.

78. Lyle, *Design for Human Ecosystems,* 21.

79. In his review of this manuscript (January 28, 2014), Michael Murphy pointed out that one of the main reasons that design and management are decoupled today is our narrow (perhaps, American) focus on and value of immediate action (design and implementation) as opposed to the low esteem for the mundane work of "maintenance." Also, there is a disincentive to learn anything that might be less than perfect (and its potentially negative effect on reputation and, thus, financial reward) compared to the more glamorous "creative" work of "Design" among design professionals. This, along with value for ecosystems and aesthetics, will require reeducation to build long-term, entrenched understanding and support—i.e., a radical paradigm change.

80. Landscape Architecture Foundation, http://lafoundation.org, accessed September 10, 2011, December 4, 2013. The words in brackets are mine. LAF, a nonprofit organization devoted to the improvement and enhancement of the environment, established a Landscape Performance Series in 2010 composed of an online set of resources to display, demonstrate, and provide tools for designers, allied landscape architecture professionals, agencies, and advocates to evaluate performance and establish a case for sustainable landscape solutions. I have served as LAF vice president for research and information since 2008 and currently chair the research committee that has responsibility for overseeing the development of landscape performance.

81. Leadership in Energy and Environmental Design, accessed January 24, 2014, http:\\www.usgbc.org. According to the USGBC, over 57,000 commercial and institutional projects comprising 10.5 billion square feet of construction space are currently participating in LEED. These projects span over 147 countries, which is an indication of the popularity of the rating system.

82. Landscape Architecture Foundation, http://lafoundation.org, accessed September 7, 2013.

83. Living Building Challenge, http://living-future.org/lbc, accessed November 13, 2014. The certification program has seven performance areas, namely site, water, energy, health, materials, equity, and beauty. In turn, these are subdivided into a total of twenty imperatives, with each focusing on a specific domain of influence.

84. Ming Han Li, Bruce Dvorak, Luo Yi, and M. Baumgarten, "Landscape Performance: Quantified Benefits and Lessons Learned from a Treatment Wetland System and Naturalized Landscapes," *Landscape Architecture Frontiers* 1 (4) (2013): 56–68.

85. See Michael Murphy, *Landscape Architecture Theory: An Evolving Body of Thought* (Waveland Press, 2005), 189–211.

86. John Adair, *Effective Teambuilding* (London: Pan Books, 1986); Harvey J. Bertcher and Frank F. Maple, *Creating Groups,* 2nd ed. (Thousand Oaks, CA: Sage Publications, 1996); William W. Caudill, *Architecture by Team* (New York: Van Nostrand Reinhold, 1971); Donelson R. Forsyth, *Group Dynamics,* 2nd ed. (Pacific Grove, CA: Brooks/Cole, 1990); Jon R. Katzenbach and Douglas K. Smith, "The Discipline of Teams," *Harvard Business Review* (Mar.–Apr., 1993); Lisa R. Lattuca, *Creating Interdisciplinarity: Interdisciplinary Research and Teaching*

Among College and University Faculty (Nashville: Vanderbilt University Press, 2001); Chris Mulder, "*Sustainable Development through Collaborative Design: Thesen Island—A Case Study*" (College of Architecture Lecture Series, Texas A&M University, College Station, Texas, April 7, 2010); Michael Murphy, "Design Collaboration," in *Landscape Architecture Theory: An Evolving Body of Thought* (Long Grove, IL: Waveland Press, 2005); Glenn M. Parker, *Cross Functional Teams: Working with Allies, Enemies, and Other Strangers* (San Francisco: Jossey-Bass Publishers, 1994); Peter M. Senge, *The Fifth Discipline: The Art and Practice of the Learning Organization* (New York: Doubleday, 1990); Gunther Tress, Arnold van der Valk, and Gary Fry (eds.), *Interdisciplinary and Transdisciplinary Landscape Studies: Potential and Limitations* (Wageningen: Delta Series 2, 2003); Margaret J. Wheatley, *Leadership and the New Science: Learning about Organization from an Orderly Universe* (San Francisco: Berrett-Koehler, 1992).

87. Allen Moore and James A. Feldt, *Facilitating Community and Decision-Making Groups* (Malabar, FL: Krieger Publishing Company, 1993), xvii; Ndubisi, "Sustainable Regionalism: Evolutionary Framework and Prospects for Managing Metropolitan Landscape."

88. Ndubisi, "Sustainable Regionalism: Evolutionary Framework and Prospects for Managing Metropolitan Landscape."

89. Ndubisi, *Ecological Planning: A Historical and Comparative Synthesis*, 239.

90. Beatley, *Native to Nowhere*, 54.

Copyright Information